www.ingramcontent.com/pod-product-compliance
Lightning Source LLC
Chambersburg PA
CBHW070233230426
43664CB00014B/2281

THE

MASSORETH HA-MASSORETH

OF

ELIAS LEVITA,

BEING AN EXPOSITION OF THE MASSORETIC NOTES
ON THE HEBREW BIBLE,

OR

THE ANCIENT CRITICAL APPARATUS OF THE OLD TESTAMENT

IN HEBREW, WITH AN ENGLISH TRANSLATION,

AND

CRITICAL AND EXPLANATORY NOTES,

BY

CHRISTIAN D. GINSBURG, LL. D.

WIPF & STOCK · Eugene, Oregon

Wipf and Stock Publishers
199 W 8th Ave, Suite 3
Eugene, OR 97401

The Massoreth Ha-Massoreth of Elias Levita
Being an Exposition of the Massoretic Notes on the Hebrew Bible,
or the Ancient Critical Apparatus of the Old Testament in Hebrew,
with an English Translation, and Critical and Explanatory Notes
By Ginsburg, Christian D.
ISBN 13: 978-1-60608-444-1
Publication date 9/29/2010
Previously published by KTAV, 1867

PREFACE.

THE work now submitted to the public in the original Hebrew, with an English translation, is an explanation of the origin and import of the Massorah. Those who are acquainted with the fact that our Hebrew Bibles abound with marginal and textual glosses,—to which even the Bibles issued by the Bible Society, which boasts that it circulates the pure word of God without note or comment, form no exception,—and who know that there is no guide in our language, or in any modern language, to these enigmatical notes, will welcome this Treatise, written by the first, and almost the only, Massoretic expositor. For be it remembered that BUXTORF's Latin Dissertation, entitled, *Clavis Masoreticus*, published in 1620 and 1665, is to a great extent made up of LEVITA's work, interspersed with notions utterly at variance with those of LEVITA, and without giving his explanation of the plan of the Massorah.

For an account of LEVITA himself, and the extraordinary controversy to which this Treatise gave rise almost all over Europe during the time of the Reformation, we must refer to the Life prefixed to this volume.

The text of the Work is that of the *editio princeps*, 1538, carefully collated with the only two other editions of it, Basel, 1539, and Sulzbach, 1771. The results of the collation have been duly given in the notes.

All that I have ventured to do with the text has been to divide it into paragraphs, and to print in larger type, or to point, those words only which are the subject of Massoretic annotation, so as to enable the student to see which word is selected for discussion; since in the original, where chapter and verse are not specified, several words of a passage had to be quoted to indicate the section from which it was taken.

By comparing every allusion to the Massoretic registers with the Massorah itself, and by giving every such rubric in full, I have not only been enabled to correct many errors in the text of the Treatise, which had arisen either from a slip of the pen on the part of the author, or through misprints, but have supplied the student with the most important part of the Massorah, as will be seen from the extensive Index of the Massoretically annotated passages and the Index of parallels between the Massoretic lists and the *Ochla Ve-Ochla* appended to the work.

The order of the passages of Scripture, in any of the rubrics quoted in the notes, is that of the Massorah, and it is to be hoped that the trouble and labour which I have expended in appending book, chapter, and verse to every expression, in every list, will help the Biblical student to prosecute his Massoretic studies. The edition of the Massorah referred to throughout the work is that contained in FRANKFURTER'S Great Rabbinic Bible, Amsterdam, 1724-27.

I take this opportunity to express my hearty thanks to the learned Dr. STEINSCHNEIDER and the Abate PIETRO PERREAU, Librarian of the Bibliotheque at Parma, for information duly acknowledged in the proper place.

BROOKLEA, AIGBURTH ROAD,
LIVERPOOL, *December*, 1866.

LIFE OF ELIAS LEVITA.

THE perpetual expulsions and wanderings to which the Jews have been subjected, ever since their dispersion, have not been favourable to the writing of Biographical Dictionaries. Though they may have had enterprising compilers, who were ready to issue "The Men of the Time," the fact that the children of the same parents were often born and brought up in different countries, wasting their youth in journeys often, in perils of waters, in perils of robbers, in perils by their own countrymen, in perils by the Christians, would have almost precluded the possibility of such an undertaking. Hence it is that the very names, as well as the mere dates and birth-places, of some of the most distinguished Jewish *literati*, are matters of dispute, and that next to nothing is known of their private history and domestic life. But for the Oriental custom of giving some scraps of autobiography in the Introductions and Appendices, in the Prologues and Epilogues, of their works, many of the Jewish authors, to whom political economy, medicine, astronomy, philosophy, philology, exegesis, and poetry owe an immense debt of gratitude, would have been, to the honest historian and grateful student, like Melchisedec, without father, without mother, without descent, having neither beginning of days nor end of life.

The history of the author of the famous *Massoreth Ha-Massoreth*, now published with an English translation, and of many other works, fully illustrates these remarks. The year of his birth, his proper name, and the incidents of his life are only to be gathered by piecing together the autobiographical fragments scattered through his different works. Inattention to this fact has caused the greatest divergence of opinion among scholars on almost every point of his life.

His name among Christians is Elias Levita. Elias, or more correctly Elijahu (אליהו), was the name given to him by his parents on the eighth day of his birth, when he was dedicated to the Lord and made a member of the Jewish community by the sign of the covenant enjoined in Gen. xvii. 10-14; whilst Levita = Ha-Levi (הלוי) simply denotes that he belonged to the tribe of Levi. His name among the Jews, which is given by himself in sundry places of his writings, is

B

Elijahu Bachur, the German (אליהו בחור אשכנזי). Now Landau,[1] Steinschneider,[2] Dr. Holmes,[3] and others, maintain that he obtained the appellation *Bachur* from his Hebrew Grammar, which he designated by this title. But Levita himself tells us the very reverse, that he called the work in question by his own surname, which he had from his youth. Thus, in the Introduction to the *Book Bachur*, he says, "Behold, I have called this book Bachur, for three reasons:—i. Because the book itself is choice and excellent [in allusion to Is. vii. 15, 16], being entirely pure meal without any chaff. ii. Because it has been compiled for every young man to study therein in the days of his youth, so that his heart might be improved in his later days; and, iii. Because it is my surname I have founded it upon the name Bachur."[4] To the same effect is his remark at the end of the book: "To those who ask thee, whose book art thou? say Elijahu's, whose surname is Bachur;"[5] as well as the poem to the second edition: "Because it is useful for the young, as well as excellent, and my own name is Bachur, I called it Bachur."[6] This is moreover corroborated by the fact, that he calls himself Bachur in the Fiction entitled *Baba-Buch*, which he wrote *eleven years before* he published the Grammar in question, (*vide infra.* p. 14).

He was born in 1468, as is evident from the poem which he appended to his edition of R. Isaac Duren's[7] work on the Ceremonial Law, published at Venice, 1548, and which is as follows:—

[1] In his edition of R. Nathan b. Jechiel's *Aramaic Lexicon*, called הערוך, vol. i., p. 38. German Introduction. Prague 1819. For an account of the life of R. Nathan and his celebrated Lexicon, we must refer to Kitto's *Cyclopædia of Biblical Literature*, Alexander's edition, *s. v.* NATHAN.

[2] *Catalogues, Libr. Hebr., in Bibliotheca Bodleiana*, col. 934.

[3] Kitto's *Cyclopædia of Biblical Literature, s. v.* ELIAS.

[4] והנה קראתי שם הספר הזה הספר הבחור. זה הספר לשלש סבות. האחת בהיות הספר הזה בחור ושוב. וכלו סלת אין בו מסולת. השנית בעבור היותו מחובר אל כל בחור ללמוד בו בימי בחרותו וייטיב לבו באחריתו. השלישית בעבור היות כנוי משונה. ובשם בחור אכונה.

[5] לשואלי ספרי למי ארחה, יאמר לאליהו כנוי שמו בחור.

[6] יען לכל בחור הוא טוב וגם בחור ואני שמי בחור קראתיהו.

[7] R. Isaac b. Meier flourished A.D. 1320–1330, at Düren on the Röer, where he was Rabbi of the Jewish community, and whence he derived his surname. His work on the Ceremonial Law he entitled שערים *Gates*, because it discusses the laws of legal and illegal meats (הלכות איסור והיתר) in ninety-six gates or sections. It is, however, commonly called (שערי דורא) *the Gates* of or by *Duren*, which some have erroneously translated *porta habitationis*. It was first published at Cracow, 1534. The edition to which Elias Levita wrote the poems is either the second or third. Comp. Fürst, *Bibliotheca Judaica*, i., 213; Steinschneider, *Catalogus Libr. Hebr. in Bibliotheca Bodleiana*, col. 1104–8.

"An excellent work is the 'Gates of Duren,' by Isaac Rabbi of Duren.
Therein are described all proscribed meats; there is nothing like it in propounding the laws.
Therein, too, are exhibited the laws of purification, with most of the opinions of the learned in the law.
Published *Shebat* 3, 308 [= Decemb. 13, 1548], of the short era of the creation.
The writer of this poem is Elijahu Bachur, aged four-score years by reason of strength."[8]

To understand the dates of this epilogue, it is necessary to remark that the Israelites reckon from the creation of the world, and that their chronology is 230 years shorter than ours. Thus, for instance, whilst this year, *i.e.* 1866 A.D., is with us 5856 A.M., it is with the Jews 5626 A.M. Moreover, it is to be noted that in Hebrew MSS., as well as in printed books, two modes are adopted of expressing the date. The one is by writing the full numbering: that is, 5626 A.M. = 1866 A.D., which is called *the Great* or *Full era* (פרט גדול); and the other is by omitting the thousands, and leaving them to be understood as 626, instead of 5626, which is called *the Short era* (פרט קטן) abbreviated (לפ״ק), and which is more generally used for the sake of brevity. Accordingly, 308 stands for 5308 = 1548, and if Elias Levita, as he tells us himself, was eighty years old in 1548, he must have been born in 1468.[9]

[8] ספר נעים ,שערי דורא ,אלאטם יצחק רב מדורא:
בו אסור כל דברי מאכל ,אין כמוהו ,דינים הורה,
בו נצמדה הלכות נדה ,עם רוב דיעות ,לומדי חודה,
נדפס לפרט נימ״ל משב״ח ,כן מספר קמן של היצירה
המשורר הוא אליהו בחור וקן פ' לגבורה —

[9] With Elias Levita's own statement before us, the reader will be surprised at the following difference of opinion about the date of our author's birth:—

Dr. Holmes (*Kitto's Cyclopædia*, new ed. s. v. ELIAS) . . . A.D.	1470.
Fürst (*Bibliotheca Judaica*, i., 239) . . . . ,,	1471.
Kalisch (*Hebrew Grammar*, ii., 33) . . . . ,,	1474.
Ganz (*Zemach David*, i., Anno. 277), Jechiel (*Seder Ha-Doroth* i. 95a, ed. Lemberg 1858), &c., &c. . . . . ,,	1477.
Landau (*Nathan's Aruch*. i., 38, German Introd. Prague, 1819) ,,	1509.

We are surprised at Dr. Kalisch's error, since this learned scholar quotes in the foot note on p. 34 of his Hebrew Grammar, the life of Levita, by Buber, in which it is proved to demonstration that Levita was born in 1468, and since Jost, who was also formerly in error upon this subject, has corrected his mistake in his *Geschichte des Judenthums*, (iii., 119, Leipzig 1859,) four years before the appearance of the Hebrew Grammar. (Longman, 1863). Comp. also Graetz, *Geschichte der Juden*, ix., 284, Leipzig 1866.

Exceedingly little is known of Elias Levita's family. From his own signature we learn that his father's name was Asher, and that he was born in Germany. The celebrated Sebastian Münster, in whose house Levita lived for some time, who translated many of his books into Latin, and who ought therefore to be regarded as the highest authority on this subject, distinctly tells us that the place where his parents resided, and where he was born, is Neustadt, on the Aisch, near Nurmburg.[10] Münster's statement is fully borne out by Levita's own remarks in his different works, in which he always includes himself when speaking of the Germans. Thus, in his Exposition of 712 words from Jewish literature, he says, on the expression משקים "it denotes small writing; that is, when the writing is not in square characters it is משקים. It is now many years ago that I was told that it is an Arabic expression, signifying *thin, attenuated*; but I afterwards got to know that it is not Arabic at all. I have asked many Jews from Italy, France, Spain, Greece, and Arabia, all of whom pronounce it in this way, but none of them knew its derivation. *We Germans*, however, pronounce it מעשׂים, and we too do not know whence it is derived."[11] To the same effect is Levita's remark in the Introduction to his Massoretical work, entitled *the Book of Remembrance*: "I shall put down in the explanation of each word its signification in German, *which is the language of my countrymen.*"[12] From the words, "to those who ask thee who made thee, say the hands of Elias made

[10] Comp. Wolf, *Bibliotheca Hebræa,* i. 153; iii. 97.

[11] משקים קורין לכתיבה דקה רוצה לומר שאינה כתיבה מרובעת משקים: וזה ימים רבים שהוגד לי שהוא לשון ערבי פרוש רזה וכחושה, ואחר כך נודע לי שאינו לשון ערבי כלל: ושאלתי ליהודים רבים לרומים וצרפתים וספרדים ויונים וערביים וכולם קורין לה כן ולא ידעו לטרו מה הוא   ואנחנו האשכנזים קורין להם מעשׂים ולא ידענו מה הוא.

See also *the Tishbi* under the expression פתח קרבץ רב תקן and other places, in all of which he classes himself with the Germans, saying אנחנו האשכנזים *we Germans*. The passage quoted from Levita's Epilogue to his מתורגמן, where he says, אלך לי אל ארצי אשר יצאתי משם. היא מדינת ויניציאא ואמות בעיר עם אשתי הזקנה, *I shall now return to my country, which I have left*, namely, to the city of *Venice, and die in my town with my aged wife*, to prove that he was born at Venice, is both at variance with his other remarks and inconclusive. For it will be seen that he does not call Venice his native place (עיר מולדתי), which he would undoubtedly have done had he been born in it, but simply styles it "*my town*" (עירי), "*the town which I left*" (אשר יצאתי משם), which any one would do who had lived in a town many years, and left there his wife and family.

[12] See. גם אכתוב אצל כל ביאור כל מלה ומלה פתרונה בלשון אשכנז שהיא לשון בני עמי Frankel's *Monatschrift fur Geschichte und Wissenschaft des Judenthums*, xii. 96—108. Breslau, 1863, where the learned Frensdorff has printed the Introduction to this unpublished work.

me, the son of a man who is called Asher Levi, a German, a man of valour and distinction," in the Epilogue to the book now edited with an English translation, the erudite Frensdorff ingeniously conjectures that R. Asher, Levita's father, was a military man, perhaps holding the office of a commissary in the German army, since the phrase איש חיל *men of valour* also denotes a military man, and the expression אפרתי is used in later Hebrew for *rank*. Frensdorff moreover submits that this will explain the origin of Levita's surname, Bachur, inasmuch as, the son of a military man, he could legitimately substitute for איש חיל *military man*, and אפרתי *officer*, the word בחור in allusion to Exod. xiv. 7; Judg. x. 15; 1 Sam. xxiv. 8; Jerem. xlix. 19; &c., &c.[13]

From the day of his birth to his thirty-sixth year (1468-1504) we hear nothing either of him or his family. The state of the Jews in Germany was too deplorable to admit of any record being kept about the personal circumstances and doings of private individuals. Indeed, it may well be questioned whether, since the advent of Christ, the destruction of Jerusalem, and the dispersion of the Jews, there was a period in the history of the world pregnant with greater events for the Christian nations, and fraught with more terrible results for the Jewish people, than that in which Levita spent his youth. When he was two years of age, all his brethren were expelled from Mayence and the Rheingau by Adolph of Nassau (October 29, 1470), after being recognised Archbishop of electoral Mayence by the Pope, on the deposition of Diether of Isenburg, the rival Archbishop, who converted the ancient synagogue into a church. When he was seven years of age, his youthful heart was afflicted with the horrible tidings that Bishop Hinderbach had the whole Jewish community at Trent burned (1475), in consequence of a base calumny that they had killed for their Passover a Christian boy named Simon. The infamous calumny about the murder of this boy rapidly spread through Christendom, and everywhere kindled the fires of persecution, so much so that, notwithstanding the prohibition of Pope Sixtus IV. (October 10, 1475) to worship Simon of Trent as saint till the charge had been properly investigated, the Jews in Germany were massacred whenever they quitted their quarters. The Bishop of Nassau nearly exterminated all the Jews under his jurisdiction; and the magnates of Ratisbon, in the very neighbourhood of Levita's birth-place, expelled all the Jewish popula-

[13] In Frankel's *Monatschrift*, xiii. p. 99.

tion from their dominions (1477-1480) when he was about twelve years of age.

The awful sufferings which the Jews had to endure in Germany, from those whose Saviour was a Jew, and whose Apostles and Prophets were Jews, strangely contrasted with the kind treatment which they experienced in Turkey, from the infidels, the followers of the false prophet, and must have produced an extraordinary and indelible impression upon so shrewd a mind as that of Levita. When he was about fifteen years of age, Isaac Zarphati (1475-1485), one of the numerous Jews who fled from the fiery persecutions under the Cross to seek safety under the Crescent, addressed the following epistle to his brethren in Germany:—"I have been informed of the calamities, more bitter than death, which have befallen our brethren in Germany; of the tyrannical laws, the compulsory baptisms, and the banishments which take place daily. And if they fly from one place, greater misfortunes befall them in another place. I hear an impudent nation lifting up its raging voice against the faithful, and see its hand swinging over them. There are woes within and woes without; daily edicts and taskmasters to extort money. The spiritual guides and the monks, the false priests, rise up against the unhappy people, and say, 'We will persecute them to destruction, the name of Israel shall no more be remembered.' They imagine that their religion is in danger, because the Jews in Jerusalem may, peradventure, purchase the church of the sepulchre. For this reason, they have issued a decree that every Jew who is found on a Christian ship sailing for the East is to be thrown into the sea. How are the holy German community treated; how are their energies weakened! The Christians not only drive them from place to place, but lurk after their lives, brandish over them the sharpened sword, cast them into the flaming fire, into surging waters, or into stinking swamps. My brethren and teachers, friends and acquaintances, I, Isaac Zarphati, who come from France, was born in Germany, and there sat at the feet of masters, proclaim to you, that Turkey is a land in which nothing is wanted. If ye are willing, it will be well with you. You will be able safely to go from Turkey to the Holy Land. Is it not better to live among Mahommedans than among Christians? Here, we are allowed to dress in the finest materials; here, every one sits under his own fig-tree and vines; whilst in Christian countries, you are not even permitted to dress your children in red or blue without exposing them to be beaten red or blue. Hence you are obliged to walk about like beggars and in rags! All your days are gloomy, even your Sabbaths and festivals; strangers enjoy your possessions, and what use are treasures to a wealthy Jew? He only keeps them to his own misfortune, and they are all lost in one day. You call them yours; no! they are theirs. They invent lying accusations against you; they regard neither age nor knowledge. And when they give you a promise, though sealed with sixty seals, they break it. They always inflict upon you double punishment, the most cruel death, and plunder. They prohibit the instruction in our schools, disturb our prayers forbid the Jews to work on Christian festivals, or to carry on business. And now, O Israel! why sleepest thou? Arise, and quit this cursed land!"[14]

Such lessons of Christian persecution and Mahommedan protection did Levita learn when he was about fifteen years of age; and there can be but little doubt that it was in consequence of the terrible sufferings which the Jews had to endure in Germany, and Isaac Zarphati's thrilling summons to his brethren to quit this hot-bed of suffering, that Levita's family, and as many other Jews as could afford it, emigrated, and sought an asylum wherever it could be found. The fact that Levita had already acquired a very high reputation, and delivered lectures on Grammar, at Padua, in the thirty-sixth year of his age, shews that his family must have settled in this town some years before, to allow sufficient time for the acquisition of his learning and influence in a place which was then the chief seat of Jewish learning in Italy. His flight into Venetia, however, did not place him beyond the reach of the agonising cry of his suffering brethren. Whilst diligently engaged in the study of Grammar and the Massorah, at the age of twenty-four (1492), Levita heard of the harrowing scenes enacted in Spain, where the whole Jewish population, about 300,000 in number, were expelled,—a calamity which, in Jewish history, is only equalled in magnitude by the destruction of the Temple and the dispersion of the Israelites by Titus. Many of these brokenhearted wanderers who sought refuge in Italy, Levita must have seen. But the cup of bitterness was not yet full. In his twenty-eighth year,

[14] This interesting Address to the Jews of Germany by Isaac Zarphati, which is to be found in the Imperial Library of Paris, (*ancien fonds* No. 291), has been published by Dr. Jellinek, in his work entitled קונטרס גזרות תתנ"ו *Contribution to the History of the Crusades*, p. 14, &c. Leipzig, 1854. For a thorough and most masterly critique on the Epistle, we must refer to Graetz, (*Geschichte der Juden*, viii., pp. 288 and 446, &c. Leipzig, 1864,) whose translation we have followed.

he heard of the edict issued (December 20, 1496) by Emanuel, King of Portugal, that all the Jews and Moors of his dominions should submit to Christian baptism, or quit the country by October next (1497) on pain of death. He, moreover, heard that the king, disappointed at so few Jews embracing Christianity, issued a secret command from Estremo Castle (February 4, 1497), forcibly to take all Jewish children of his dominion, both boys and girls, up to fourteen years of age, from their parents, and to baptise them on Easter Sunday; the heart-rending effects of which are described by an eye-witness to the scene in the following terms:—"I have seen," relates Bishop Ferdinando Couthin, of Algarve, who protested against this compulsory baptism, "how multitudes were dragged by the hair to the baptismal font, and how the afflicted fathers, with their veiled heads, and agonising cries, followed their children, and protested at the altar against this inhuman compulsory baptism. I have also seen other inexpressible barbarities which were heaped upon them."[15] And when at last the period fixed for their departure had arrived, and about 20,000 Jews were again driven from their homes into the wide, wide world, to seek a resting-place, Levita again saw many of his wandering brethren, who filled his heart with their afflictions, more bitter than death. We shall hereafter see that it is necessary to bear these things in mind, in order to understand the charges against which Levita defends himself in the second introduction to this work.

These sufferings and repeated expulsions of the Jews, however, were overruled by Him who makes the wrath of man to praise Him, for the advancement of Hebrew literature, for the extension of Biblical knowledge, and for kindling the light of the Reformation, in which Elias Levita played an important part. Though the bulk of the Jewish population in Germany, 300,000 in Spain, and 20,000 in Portugal preferred to quit their homes and everything dear and near unto them; and though many of them submitted to the most cruel deaths rather than embrace the Christianity in the name of which these barbarities were perpetrated; yet an immense number of them, not having a martyr's courage, or being reluctant to lose their children, who were snatched from them, embraced the Christian faith. Many of these Neophytes secretly remained Jews, whilst others sincerely believed the religion which they were at first forced to embrace. Among them were men of most distinguished attainments and extraordinary know-

[15] Graetz, *Geschichte der Juden*, viii., 390, &c. Leipzig, 1864.

ledge of Hebrew and Biblical literature. These soon began to spread the knowledge of the sacred language among Christians, by the aid of the newly invented art of printing. And as many of the Jewish converts were Kabbalists, they also initiated their Gentile disciples into its mysteries, and made almost as large a number of converts among Christians to this esoteric doctrine as Christianity had gained among the Jews.

Foremost in the ranks of Jewish converts who laboured in the department of Biblical literature were Alphonso de Alcala, Paul Coronel, and Alphonso de Zamora, who were employed in editing the celebrated Complutensian Polyglott, the sixth volume of which is almost entirely the work of Zamora. To these are to be added Felix Pratensis, the famous editor of the *editio princeps* of Bomberg's Rabbinic Bible, and Jacob b. Chajim, the editor of the second edition of Bomberg's Rabbinic Bible, who immortalised his name by his elaborate Introduction to this Bible, and by compiling and editing for the first time the critical apparatus of the Old Testament, called the Massorah. As propounders of the Kabbalah, among the Jewish converts, are to be mentioned Paul de Heredia, the author and translator of sundry Kabbalistic works, which he dedicated to Pope Innocent VIII.; Paul Ricio, professor at Pavia, physician to the Emperor Maximilian I., who translated a large portion of Joseph Gikatilla's Kabbalistic work, entitled "The Gates of Light," which he dedicated to Maximilian, and which Reuchlin used very largely; Vidal de Saragossa de Arragon, Davila, &c.[16]

The Jews themselves had a still greater phalanx of literary and scientific men who laboured in the departments of Biblical exegesis, the traditional law, the Kabbalah, philosophy, astronomy, &c. These literati supplied those Christians who impugned the infallible decisions of the Pope and his conclave respecting matters of doctrine, and who appealed to the Word of God as their sole guide, with the means of understanding the original language in which the greater part of the Bible is written. At the head of those who were thus enriching Biblical literature were Don Isaac b. Jehudah Abravanel (1437–1509), the

---

[16] According to a statement by Abraham Farissol, in his MS. work entitled *the Shield of Abraham* (מגן אברהם), twelve distinguished converted Jews formed themselves into a literary society, and conjointly issued works to prove the truth of Christianity from the *Sohar* and other Kabbalistic writings. The passage from Farissol's MS. work, giving this account, has been printed by Graetz, *Geschichte der Juden*, ix. 195.

famous statesman, philosopher, theologian, and commentator, who wrote copious commentaries on nearly the whole of the Hebrew Scriptures; Messer Leon, or Jehudah b. Jechiel, as he is called in Hebrew (1480-1505), Rabbi and physician at Mantua, who wrote a very elaborate Hebrew Grammar, a masterly Treatise on Hebrew Rhetoric, after the manner of Aristotle, Cicero, and Quintilian, and a Treatise on Hebrew Logic, and who was called the Hebrew Cicero; the two Aramas, Isaac, the father (1430-1494), and Meier, the son (1470-1556), both of whom wrote extensive expositions of sundry books of the Scriptures; Abraham Saccuto (1450-1520), the famous historian and lexicographer; Saadia Ibn Danan (1450-1502), poet, lexicographer, and commentator; Abraham de Balmes (1450-1521), physician, philosopher, and grammarian; Jacob Mantino, a distinguished Hebraist and physician; Abraham Farissol (1451-1525), the famous cosmographer and commentator; Levi b. Chabib, Isaac b. Joseph Caro, Jacob Berab Obediah Seforno, Jacob b. Jechiel Loanz, Joseph Ibn Jachja, &c., &c., all of whom contributed materially to the diffusion of Biblical knowledge in its sundry departments. None of these Hebraists, however, who were the contemporaries of Elias Levita, and with many of whom he had personal intercourse, surpassed, or even equalled, our author in his successful efforts, either in mastering the grammatical structure of the Hebrew language,' or in diffusing the knowledge of this sacred tongue among Jews, but more especially among Christians, than Levita. And it is not too much to say, that the revival of Hebrew learning and Biblical knowledge in Europe, towards the close of the fifteenth and the commencement of the sixteenth centuries, resulting in the Reformation, which was effected by the immortal Reuchlin, was the result of the tuition which this father of the Reformation received from Jacob b. Jechiel Loanz, physician to the Emperor Frederick III., Obadiah Seforno, and from Levita.

It was not, however, the wish to become more thoroughly acquainted with the import of the Scriptures which kindled the desire in Reuchlin, and in a number of other eminent Christians, to learn Hebrew, which made them seek the tuition of Loanz, Levita, Seforno, and a host of other Hebraists, and which was the means of calling forth the energies and works of Levita. The Kabbalah was the primary cause of the rage among the Christian literati of those days to study Shemitic languages. This esoteric doctrine, which was declared by the celebrated scholastic metaphysician, Raymond Lully (1236-1315), to be a divine science, and a genuine revelation whose light is revealed to a rational soul, captivated the mind of John Pico della Mirandola (1463-1494). Mirandola, the marvellously gifted son of the sovereign of the small principality of Mirandola, in Italy, received his first lessons in Hebrew, as well as in Aristotelian Arabic philosophy, from Elias del Medigo, or Elias Cretensis, as he is sometimes called, who was born of Jewish parents in the same year as his distinguished pupil and faithful friend. But as Elias del Medigo was hostile to the Kabbalah, and could not, therefore, initiate Mirandola into its mysteries, the Count, who was the wonder of his days, had to put himself under the tuition of Jochanon Allemano, a Rabbi from Constantinople, who had settled down in Italy, and who was very profound in this theosophy. With his marvellous retentive faculties, extraordinary intellectual powers, and almost boundless knowledge, Mirandola soon overcame the difficulties and unravelled the secrets of the Kabbalah. To his amazement, he found that there is more Christianity than Judaism in the Kabbalah. For, according to his showing, he discovered therein proofs of the doctrine of the Trinity, the Incarnation, the divinity of Christ, original sin, the expiation thereof by Christ, the heavenly Jerusalem, the fall of the angels, the order of the angels, purgatory, and hell-fire; in fact, the same Gospel which we find in St. Paul, Dionysius, St. Jerome, and St. Augustine.

As the result of his Kabbalistic studies, he published in 1486, when only twenty-four years of age, *nine hundred theses*, which were placarded in Rome, and among which was the following: "*No science yields greater proof of the divinity of Christ than magic and the Kabbalah.*" So delighted was Pope Sixtus IV. with the discovery, that he wished to have Kabbalistic writings translated into Latin, for the use of divinity students; and Mirandola, with the aid of his Jewish teacher, did not delay to gratify the wish of the supreme Pontiff.[17]

The Kabbalah and Hebrew, as well as Aramaic, the clue to this esoteric doctrine, now became the favourite studies, to the neglect of the classics. Popes, cardinals, princes, statesmen, warriors, high and low, old and young, were in search for Jewish teachers. Whilst this Kabbalistic epidemic was raging in Italy, Reuchlin (1455-1521), the reviver of literature in Germany, arrived at Rome with Eberhard the

[17] For an account of the import and history of this esoteric doctrine, see *The Kabbalah*, &c., by Ginsburg, Longmans, 1865.

Bearded (1482), in the capacity of private secretary and privy councillor to this prince. From the eternal city he accompanied him to Florence, where he became acquainted with Mirandola, and caught the infection of the esoteric doctrine. The infection, however, proved innocuous for a little time, since, on his return to Germany (1484), he was appointed licentiate and assessor of the supreme court in Stutgard; and, as the Dominicans elected him proctor of their order in the whole of Germany, it precluded the possibility of his entering at once upon the study of Hebrew and Aramaic. But the disease fully developed itself when he returned from his second journey to Rome and Florence (1490), after having come into contact a second time with Mirandola, who told him of the wonderful mysteries concealed in the Kabbalah.

The great influence of Reuchlin soon spread the desire for studying Hebrew and the Kabbalah among Christians in Germany. Every one who had any claim to literary attainments was now in search of a Jewish teacher. Reuchlin put himself under the tuition of R. Jacob b. Jechiel Loanz, physician to Frederick III., and made such extraordinary progress, that, within four years of beginning to study Hebrew, he published his first Kabbalistic Treatise, entitled, *" Concerning the Wonderful Word,"* which he dedicated to Dalberg, Bishop of Worms. It was this intense love for Hebrew and Hebrew literature which made Reuchlin espouse the cause of the Jews, and defend them and their writings against the misguided and malicious assaults of the fanatical Pfefferkorn on his former co-religionists, and which kindled the fire of the Reformation.

In Italy the Kabbalah and Hebrew were studied to a still greater extent. Here Abraham Saba, Jehudah b. Jacob Chajath, Joseph Shraga, Kana or Elkana, Jehudah Ibn Verga were the teachers of this theosophy among the Jews; whilst among the Christians the chief Jewish teachers were R. Jachanon Alleman, who initiated Mirandola into its mysteries, and Samuel Abravanel, in whose house Baruch of Benevent delivered lectures on the Kabbalah to most distinguished Christians. Baruch of Benevent also instructed Egidio de Viterbo (afterwards cardinal) in this esoteric doctrine, and translated the Sohar into Latin for him. It was this Egidio, as we shall see hereafter, who, in consequence of his being seized with the general desire to study the Kabbalah, was the means of calling forth Elias Levita, and of encouraging our author to write most of his works, thus constituting him the chief teacher of Hebrew among Christians.

We have already seen that, up to his thirty-sixth year (1504), Levita delivered lectures on Hebrew grammar in the great Jewish academy at Padua to a large number of Jewish students, who came to be taught by him from far and wide. As the text-book for these lectures he took R. Moses Kimchi's Outlines of Hebrew Grammar, entitled "Journey on the Paths of Knowledge,"[18] which most probably commended itself to him because of its conciseness, and because its author was the first who employed therein, as a paradigm of the regular verbs, the word פָּקַד, instead of the less appropriate verb *mediæ gutteralis* פָּעַל, which, in imitation of the Arabic grammarians, had been used in all other grammars. Though Moses Kimchi flourished about 1160–1170, and must have written this short grammar three hundred and fifty years before it was annotated by Levita, yet the manual was still in MS., and the copy which Levita used as the basis for his lectures must have been made by himself. His explanations were so acceptable, that he was requested by his pupils to publish them, together with the text book (1504).

Unhappily, however, the plague broke out at Padua, and as Christians usually believed that the Jews were the cause of every epidemic and calamity, the Jewish quarter was blocked up, and the entrance to the street in which Levita resided was closed. When thus shut up in the house, his amanuensis escaped with the MS. to Pesaro, where he had the work printed without Levita's name, but with an Introduction by Benjamin of Rome, who was, consequently, taken by every body to be the author of the Commentaries to M. Kimchi's Grammar. The plagiarist also interpolated the annotations with excerpts from another work, and in this form Levita's maiden production was most incorrectly printed in another name at Pesaro (1508). In this mutilated form, and under the surreptitious name, M. Kimchi's "*Journey on the Paths of Knowledge*," with Levita's Commentary, became the manual for students of the Hebrew language, both among Jews and Christians. It was speedily reprinted several times at Pesaro (1509–18, 1518–1519); it made its way to Germany and France, where it was reprinted (Hagenau, 1519; Paris, 1520); and became the text book of the early Reformers, who were

---

[18] The full Hebrew title of this concise Grammar is מהלך שבילי הדעת קרבת מליצה חכמה יתרון, the initials of which yield the author's name, משה קמחי. Sometimes it is simply called המהלך or מפר דקדוק. For an account of the life and writings of Kimchi, we must refer to Kitto's *Cyclopædia of Biblical Literature*, new ed. *s. v.* MOSES KIMCHI.

studying Hebrew to translate the Scriptures; and was translated into Latin by Sebastian Münster (Basle, 1531; ibid, 1536). We shall have to recur to this production when we come to the period of Levita's life when he thought it his duty to claim the paternity of the annotations.

The dry studies of grammar and philology did not deprive him of his humour, for, three years after the publication of the annotations to M. Kimchi's work, Levita amused himself by writing, in German, a fiction, entitled *Baba-Buch* (בבא בוך), purporting to be a history of the Prince of Baba. It was evidently intended to be a song, since he remarks in the rhythmical Preface—"*Aber der* ניגון (= Melody) *der darauf wird gehen, Den kenn ich nit geben zu verstehen, Denn einer kennt musiga oder* (טולפה). *So wollt ich ihm wohl haben geholfen, Aber ich sing' es mit einem welschen Gesang, Kann er drauf machen ein bessern so hab er Dank.*" That he composed it in 1507, he most distinctly declares at the end of the book in the following words—"*Damit hat das Buch ein Enden. Doch will ich nennen vor . . Elia Bachur nennt er sich zwar, Ein ganz Jahr hat er drüber verschrieben, Und hat es gemacht das selbig Jar, Das man zählt* 267 [=1507], *Er hot* [lot = lost?] *es aus in Nisan und hob es an in Ijjar . . . soll uns führen ken Jerusalem hinein, Oder irgend ein Dörfel daneben* חסלת אסטוריא של בבא דאנטונא. Here endeth the history of Baba de Antona." This book was first printed in 1508.[19]

But Levita was not destined long to enjoy his peaceful studies and innocent recreations. Five years after the outbreak of the epidemic, and only twelve months after the publication of this fiction, the army of the league of Cambray took Padua (1509) and sacked it, when Levita lost every thing he possessed, and in a most destitute condition had to leave the place in which he had successfully taught for some years, and where he was held in high estimation, to seek a livelihood in the wide wide world. As the Kabbalah was a classical study at Rome, where the popes and cardinals looked upon it as an important auxiliary to Christianity, Hebrew teachers were in great requisition in the Eternal City. Knowing this, Levita at once betook himself to the capital. It was here that he heard of the scholarly and liberal minded Egidio de Viterbo, general of the Augustine order, and

---

[19] The above extract is made from Steinschneider's *Catalogus Libr. Hebr. in Bibliotheca Bodleiana*, col. 935, where an account is also given of the different editions of the Fiction in question, and the errors of biographers are corrected.

afterwards cardinal, who was engaged in studying Hebrew, and of course the esoteric doctrine. He therefore determined to call upon him.

The first interview between the eminent Christian scholar and the famous Hebrew grammarian is thus described by the latter. "When I heard of his fame, I waited upon him at his palace. On seeing me he enquired after my business; and when I told him that I am the grammarian from Germany, and that I devote my whole life to the study of Hebrew philology and the Scriptures, . . . he at once rose from his seat, came towards me, and embraced me, saying, 'Are you forsooth Elijahu, whose fame has travelled over countries, and whose books are circulated everywhere? Blessed be the Lord of the Universe for bringing you here, and for our meeting. You must now remain with me; you shall be my teacher, and I will be a father to you. I will maintain you and your family,'" &c.[20]

Such a cordial reception could not fail in its effect, and Levita at once accepted the offer of the generous Egidio. As Egidio's chief object in learning Hebrew was to be able to fathom the mysteries of the Kabbalah, Levita had not only to instruct his pupil in the sacred tongue, but to aid him in his endeavours to acquire a knowledge of the esoteric doctrine. Hence we find that as early as 1516—that is before Egidio was elevated to the dignity of Cardinal—Levita copied for him three Kabbalistic works, viz., i. *A Commentary on the Book Jetzira* (פירוש ספר יצירה); ii. *The Mystery of the Angel Raziel* (סוד רזיאל); and iii. *The Book on the Wisdom of the Soul* (ספר חכמת הנפש). It is also supposed that Levita supplied at this time the passages from the Sohar to the work entitled, "*On the Mysteries of the Catholic Truth*," by Petrus Galatinus, which was finished in September, 1516, and published in 1518, since its Gentile authors could not possibly, without the aid of a Jew, have dived into the Sohar. We do not, however, lay much stress on this, though the supposition proceeds from no less an authority than the celebrated historian, Dr. Graetz.[21] We have seen that there were plenty of converted Jews, Kabbalists, to aid Galatinus in a work, the express design of which was to convince the Jews of the truth of the Catholic religion, without being obliged to appeal to Levita for

---

[20] See below, in the Second Introduction, where the whole of the interview is narrated.

[21] *Geschichte der Juden*, ix. 99.

help in such an undertaking, which must have been repugnant to his Jewish feelings.

The intimacy of Levita with Egidio, however, was the means of producing works of far greater importance, and of more permanent utility to Biblical literature, than the *De Arcanis Catholicæ Veritatis* of Galatinus. The very year in which this assault on the Jews and Judaism appeared, Levita published his grammar (1518), entitled, *The Book Bachur* (ספר הבחור). This grammar he wrote at the suggestion, and for the use, of Cardinal Egidio, to whom he dedicated it, as may be seen from the following words in the Introduction to the work in question: "In the year 5277 A.M. [= 1517 A.D.] the Lord stirred up the spirit of a wise man, conversant with all sciences, and of high dignity, Cardinal Egidio — may his glory be exalted! He was anxious to find out the excellent words and the beautiful writing in the books of our sacred language. For this reason he called on me, his servant, Elijahu Levita, the German, the least of the grammarians, and said to me, What art thou doing, Elijahu? Arise now, and make a book which shall pleasantly set forth the grammar of the Hebrew language, since all the Hebrew grammars which I have seen do not satisfy me, nor do they quench my desire for grammar; as some of them are too lengthy, multiplying useless rules, and some are too short in stating what is necessary. Gird up thy loins, therefore, like a man, and adopt the medium between the two extremes, propound the science of grammar in rules not hitherto laid down, but necessary to be exhibited; make them into a book for the benefit of the multitude, so that it may be an ensign for the people, whereunto the Gentiles shall come, and find rest for their souls. When I heard his encouraging words, I at once determined to accede to his request, and compiled this little work on grammar."

Levita, as we have seen, called this grammar *Bachur* (בחור), for three reasons, which are based upon the threefold meaning of the expression, as well as upon the design of the work. As the word בחור denotes both *youth* and *excellent*, and is also his surname, he called it by this name, because, he naïvely tells us, it is designed for the young, it is excellent, and it is his proper name. The treatise is divided into four parts, each one of which is subdivided into thirteen sections, answering to the Thirteen Articles of the Jewish Creed, whilst the total number of all sections, being fifty-two, represents the numerical value of the name אליהו. The first part discusses the nature of the

Hebrew verbs; the second the changes in the vowel-points of the different conjugations; the third the regular nouns; and the fourth the irregular nouns. The simple and beautiful Hebrew in which it is written, as well as the clearness and perspicuity with which it sets forth the structure of the sacred language, at once made the treatise a universal favourite with Hebrew students, both Jewish and Gentile. Not even the very elaborate and masterly Grammar of Abraham de Balmes, which was published five years later (1523), could supersede it. The *Baćhur* was the Gesenius of the time, whilst the *Mikne Abraham* (מקנה אברהם), which is the name of De Balmes' Grammar, was the Ewald among Hebrew students. Münster published it, with a Latin translation, for the use of Christians in Germany and elsewhere (1525). The revision of it will be discussed when we arrive at that part of Levita's life when he engaged in it.

In the same year in which Levita carried through the press in Rome (1518) his excellent Grammar, he also published "*Tables of Paradigms,*" (לוח בדקדוק הפעלים והבנינים), exhibiting in an elementary form the Hebrew conjugations. The design of these Paradigms, which he compiled from two different sections of the *Bachur*,[22] is to give to the tyro some notion of Hebrew Grammar. These Paradigms are of such extreme rarity, that no Hebrew copy of them has as yet been discovered, and they are only known from Münster's translation. He moreover completed and printed a treatise on the Irregular Words in the Bible, the discussion of which he designedly excluded from his Grammar. This dissertation is entitled "*The Book on Compounds*" (ספר ההרכבה), because it treats on words composed of different words and conjugations. It consists of two hundred and twelve articles, answering to the numerical value of Levita's surname בחור *Bachur*; so that the two numbers together, viz., of the sections in the grammar, and of the articles in this treatise, represent the complete name אליהו בחור *Elijahu Bachur*. The 216 words in this dissertation are not arranged according to their roots, because there is a great difference of opinion among grammarians and lexicographers respecting the etymology of some of them, but they are put down in alphabetical order. The manner in which he treated them

[22] אני אליהו הלוי חברתי הלוח הזה לתת לנער דעת בדקדוק - - ויוסף לקח משני המאמרים משונים של ספר הבחור. Comp. Steinschneider, *Catalogus Libr. Hebr. in Bibliotheca Bodleiana*, col. 2012, &c., and by the same Author, *Bibliographisches Handbuch*, p. 81, No. 1162.

will be best seen from his own description of the plan of the work: "As my design in this treatise," he says in the Introduction, "is to explain those words only which are anomalous in their grammatical structure, and since the principal grammarians advance different opinions about them, I have stated all their various opinions, and sometimes also contributed my share, according to my limited understanding." This work, too, was translated into Latin by Münster, and published at Basle, 1525. It had such a wide circulation among Christian students, and especially among the early Reformers, that it was reprinted in the Latin version, Basle, 1536, and underwent several editions in the original Hebrew.

His desire to explain every intricacy and anomaly in the Hebrew language, and yet the fear lest hampering his Grammar with too many digressions might preclude it from becoming a manual for the people at large, produced in him the conviction that those points which required lengthy and elaborate explanations would be more acceptable if appended to the book in the form of Dissertations. He therefore promised, in sundry parts of the *Bachur*, to discuss these subjects at the end of the Grammar. But, as is often the case, when he had finished the book, he found that untoward circumstances rendered it impossible for him to compile the promised Appendices, and had to publish it without them. This he tells us is the reason why he was obliged to publish the dissertations separately. As soon as he had carried through the press his "*Treatise on the Compounds*," he betook himself to the work of these dissertations, and succeeded in publishing them two years after the appearance of the preceding treatise (1520). As the Grammar was the centre around which the sundry treatises clustered, he constituted it the model after which he formed these dissertations. Hence, like the Grammar, he divided them into four parts, consisting respectively of thirteen sections, according to the thirteen articles of the Jewish creed, whilst the sum total of the sections, namely, fifty-two, like that of the Grammar, represents the numerical value of the author's name (אליהו). The first section, or dissertation, which is preceded by a separate Introduction and Table of Contents, discusses, in thirteen stanzas or poems, the laws of the letters, the vowel points, and the accents; and in consequence of its being written in separate poems or stanzas it is denominated "*The Poetical Section or Dissertation*" (פרק שירה). The second section, which is also preceded by a separate Introduction and Table of Contents, discusses, in thirteen chapters, written in prose, the different parts of speech, and hence is called "*The Section on the Different Kinds of Words*" (פרק המינים). The third section, which is preceded by an Introduction only, treats on the numbers and genders of the several parts of speech, seeing that some of them only occur as masculine, some only as feminine, some only in the singular, some only in the plural, some only in the singular and plural feminine, some only in the singular and plural masculine, and some as common genders. These words are here classified according to rules; hence it is styled "*The Section of Rules*" (פרק המדרות). The fourth section treats on the seven servile letters (מש״ה וכל״ב), and hence is denominated "*the Section on the Serviles*" (פרק השמושים). The four dissertations were first published at Pesaro (1520), under the general title "*the Sections of Elijahu*" (פרקי אליהו). They also soon found their way into Germany, where they were re-published, with a Latin translation by Münster, Basle, 1527.

The four grammatical treatises which he composed at Rome, and his residence for thirteen years at the palace of Cardinal Egidio, where he constantly came into contact with the chief literary men of the day, extended Levita's fame over Europe, and he was appealed to from far and wide for his opinion on matters of Hebrew literature. No allurements of society, however—no worldly pleasures or gain—could tempt him from his work. Whilst in the house of his friend the Cardinal, he not only devoted his time to the instruction of his eminent pupil, and writing the valuable grammatical treatises, but took lessons from Egidio in Greek, and made such rapid progress, that he could read with fluency the Septuagint and the Greek classics.

There can be but little doubt that Levita's writings were intimately connected with the studies of his most distinguished and accomplished pupils. Their rapid progress in Hebrew, their desire to master those portions of the Scriptures which are written in Chaldee, as well as to read the paraphrases, and their diving into Kabbalistic works, necessarily involved more extensive instruction, both in the higher branches of Biblical literature and in the special dialects in which the important documents of the esoteric doctrine are written. Hence it is that we now find him (1520) most industriously engaged upon two particular works: one a most gigantic work on the Massorah, to which we shall have to recur when we arrive at the period of its completion; and the other an Aramaic Grammar. After labouring nine years on a Concordance to the Massorah, and making considerable progress in the Aramaic Grammar, he was again driven from his peaceful studies at the sacking of Rome by the Imperialists under Charles V. (May 6, 1527), when the greater part of his MSS. and property were destroyed.

The plan which he adopted in compiling the Aramaic Grammar will best be gathered from his own words: "Since the time when the Chaldee Paraphrases were made," Levita says, in the Introduction to his Lexicon on the Targumim, "there has not been a wise and intelligent man in Israel who could make a Grammar to them, such as was made by Jehudah, who was the first Hebrew grammarian of blessed memory, and before whom there was no Grammar at all to the sacred language. Having found the twenty-four sacred books pointed, accented, and annotated by the Massorites, he set about to aid the Israelites, and to enlighten the eyes of the exiles in the grammar thereof. After him came R. Jonah, after him R. Saadia Gaon of blessed memory,[23] and after them again grammarians without number. But there was no one engaged in the grammatical study of the Targum to correct its blunders; every one turned his back to it. Hence came to pass the general confusion. I, therefore, submitted that there is a proper way for making a Grammar to the language of the Targum; that the Targum of Daniel and Ezra should be made the basis, and the conjugations should be founded upon it alone, and not upon the Targumim generally; and that the rules of grammar should be deduced therefrom, though they may not all be obtained from such scanty materials. Now, when I was at Rome, my heart was filled

[23] The above piece of literary history fully illustrates our remark on page 1 about the ignorance which prevails respecting even the dates of the most distinguished Jewish literati. Even Levita, with all his learning, describes Jehudah Chajug as the oldest, Jonah Ibn Ganach as the next in age, and Saadia as the third in chronological order. Whereas Saadia was born A.D. 892, Ibn Ganach about 995, and Jehudah Chajug about 1020–1040. For notices of the lives and works of these eminent Hebraists we must refer to Kitto's *Cyclopædia of Biblical Literature*, new ed., and only add here, as supplementary to the article JEHUDAH CHAJUG in the Cyclopædia, that he also wrote a Commentary on the Song of Songs, which is referred to Ibn Aknin, as will be seen under the article IBN AKNIN in the Cyclopædia. He has, moreover, written Commentaries on *the Pentateuch* (quoted by Ibn Ezra on Gen. xli. 48; Exod vii. 5; x. 8; xxi. 8; Numb. x. 36; xxiii. 13; Deut. xxix. 29): on *Isaiah* (quoted by Ibn Ezra on Is. xiv. 20, xxvi. 20, xlix. 8, lxi. 10): on *Habbakuk* (quoted by Ibn Ezra on Habak. ii. 19, iii. 2): on *the Psalms* (quoted by Ibn Ezra on Ps. lxviii. 14, lxxxiv. 7, cii. 28, cxxxvii. 2, cl. 6): on *Job* (quoted by Ibn Ezra on Job xxxviii. 5): on *Ruth* (comp. Ibn Ezra on Ruth i. 20): and on *Ecclesiastes* (comp. Ibn Ezra on Eccl. ix. 12, xii. 5).

with the desire to undertake this work, and I actually finished one part. But the evil days came, and the city was captured, when this portion was either destroyed or taken away, since no one knows what has become of it."

Deprived of his MSS., despoiled of his property, driven from his peaceful studies and from an influential circle of literary friends at Rome, Levita betook himself to Venice in a most destitute and deplorable condition, in 1527. Venice was then the chief seat of Hebrew learning, and had the chief printing establishment for Hebrew books. Here Daniel Bomberg, of Antwerp, established his celebrated printing office in 1516, which created a new epoch in Jewish typography. Within the ten years which intervened between its establishment and the arrival of Levita at Venice (1516-1527), the indefatigable and enterprising Bomberg had already issued from his press the first two editions of the celebrated Rabbinic Bible, the one edited by Felix Pratensis (1516–17), a converted Jew, and the other by Jacob b. Chajim (1524–25), who also embraced christianity; two beautiful editions of the Hebrew Scriptures without the Rabbinic commentaries (1518, 1521); the first complete edition of the Babylon Talmud, which is the model of all succeeding editions; the *editio princeps* of the Jerusalem Talmud (1523); the *editio princeps* of the first Hebrew concordance to the Scriptures, by Isaac Nathan b. Kalonymos (1523); the elaborate Hebrew grammar by De Balmes (1523); and a host of other very important Biblical and Rabbinic works. It was this honourable distinction which Venice obtained as the seat of Hebrew literature, which made Levita decide to make it his future abiding place.

Destitute and deplorable as his condition was on arriving with his wife and children at Venice in 1527, it was not as calamitous as his plight after the sacking of Padua in 1509, when he arrived at Rome. His four works on the grammar and structure of the Old Testament Hebrew, had now obtained for him a world-wide reputation. They had been reprinted, translated into Latin, circulated all over Europe, studied by the most distinguished scholars of Christendom, and were constantly appealed to as the highest authority. Levita himself in the truly Oriental manner, which was also the fashion among Occidental scholars at that time, naïvely recounts the glory of his own productions and success in the following words : "The four works of mine, owing to their wisdom and knowledge, have been published several times,

translated into languages of the Christians, and are studied both by
Jews and Christians, as their fame has travelled far and their excellence is known all over the world; they send forth an odour like
precious ointment, on which account I congratulate myself. Now I
speak the truth when I say that there is no author whom God has
permitted to see in his lifetime, his works so much referred to and
studied, and so many times reprinted as He has permitted me during
my lifetime." This Eastern self-laudation is, according to the modern
interpretation of some great and good men who have resorted to it in
our days, simply giving the opinion of others about ourselves.

With such a world-wide reputation, Levita had no difficulty in
finding occupation at Venice. Indeed Bomberg, who was the great
centre of Hebrew literature in this city, knew Levita personally, and
published a poem of his in the second edition of the Rabbinic Bible
(1525), two years before his arrival at Venice. He therefore at once
employed him as corrector of the Hebrew Press, and editor of sundry
Hebrew works. As the first instalment of his labours in connection
with Bomberg's printing office, is to be mentioned the new edition of
David Kimchi's (1160–1285) Hebrew Lexicon, commonly called "*The
Book of Roots*" (ספר השרשים), which, though corrected by Isaiah b.
Eleazar Parnas, was revised by Levita, who also wrote a laudatory
poem to it by way of Epilogue (1529). Besides revising the works
published by Bomberg, he devoted all his spare time to the elucidation
of the Massorah, which, as we have seen, he had already begun when
at Rome. The means for supporting his family he chiefly derived from
tuition, as the salary which he got from Bomberg must have been
exceedingly small.

To the furtherance of Biblical literature, it happened that the
erudite and liberally-minded George de Selve, afterwards bishop of
Lavour, was then the French Ambassador of Francis I., at Venice.
Though occupying a most distinguished position among the statesmen
and scholars of the sixteenth century, he placed himself under the
tuition of Levita, and made such marvellous progress in Hebrew, that
he could express himself with the same facility in it as in Latin and
Greek, which constituted the three literary languages of the day. The
intimacy which arose between the distinguished pupil and the renowned
teacher was the means both of enriching Biblical literature and of
promoting the study thereof in France, for De Selve most generously put him in a position to complete his stupendous Massoretic

Concordance. With such princely aid, Levita could devote himself more than ever to his darling work; and after labouring over it more than twenty years, and getting all the help he could obtain in the investigation of MSS., collating, copying, &c., &c., he completed his gigantic "*Book of Remembrance*," as he called it, in 1536, and dedicated it to his friend and liberal patron, George de Selve, Bishop of Lavour. As this important work has never been printed, and moreover as its history and De Selve's connection with it can only be seen from Levita's most simple and most beautiful Hebrew Dedication, we subjoin the following translation of it:[24]

"To his most exalted Eminence, my lord, George de Selve, Bishop of Lavour, peace be multiplied! It is now some years since I began a work which appeared to me important and very useful to those who study the structure of the sacred language. The devastation of Rome, however, which took place shortly after it, was the cause of my not finishing it at that time and leaving it incomplete. And even the incomplete part was taken from me, and became a prey of spoil; it was torn and shattered so that nothing but a small portion was left to me, which I brought with me here to Venice, and I gave up all thought of finishing the work any more. But God, who willed that I should complete it, and that the book should be published, stirred up your spirit, and put it into your heart, to study the sacred language under me, which you learned from me with great ease and in a very short time; so that you are famed for your knowledge of the three classical languages—the sacred Hebrew, the rich Greek, and the elegant Latin tongues; you have now acquired all accomplishments,

[24] The only portions of this gigantic work which have been published are the Dedication and the Introduction. These the learned Frensdorff printed in Frankel's *Monatschrift für Geschichte und Wissenschaft des Judenthums*, vol. xii., pp. 96–108; Breslau, 1863. Our translation is made from the Hebrew text, which, with a few manifest errors, we also reprint below, as the periodical in which they are published is not possessed by every reader who might wish to be acquainted with Levita's text.

אל רום מעלת השר המאושר אדוני וור'זו דסאל'וא הגמון דלאב'ור שלום רב בהיות כי בשנים
שעברו התחלתי במלאכה אחת הנראה בעיני היותה נוגחה ומעלה מועילה מאד לכל הבאים ללמוד
להבין דרכי לשון הקודש הזה אכן החורבן של רומי הבא סמוך אחרי זאת היה סבה שלא השלמתיה
בעת ההיא סבתיה הסרה . ואף אותו חלק הבלתי שלם לוקח ממני והיה לשלל לבזה מקורע ומטושטש
לא נשארו בידי רק מעט מהבאתיו עמי הנה בעיר ויניס'יאה, ולא היתה מחשבתי להשלים הספר הזה
עוד . אכן ברצות ה' שהמלאכה הזאת תהיה נגמרת והספסר הזה יצא לאורה היעיר ה' את רוח אדוני
וישם בלבבו ללמוד עמי בלשון הקודש הזה ולמדתהו ממני בקלות ובוזמן קצר מאד , והרי לך שם
בשלושה . לשון עברי הקדושה . ולשון יון הדשנה , ולשון לאמי'ני הצחה . כדי שתהיה שלם בכל השלמיות.

and you, my lord, are among the wise like the sun among the stars.
You know, my lord, that we one day happened to converse about
this work, and that you asked me to show you the disordered portion
of it which was still left to me. When you read it you were pleased
to think highly of it, and of the advantage which it would be to those
who study the Hebrew language. You urged me with all your might
to undertake the labour of completing it, and you promised to pay
the expenses of the amanuensis, punctuators, and all the rest of them,
to bring it to completion, and did it. All this devolved upon you.
Thus was I encouraged to undertake this great labour, as well as
great honour. I rested neither day nor night till, by the help of God,
and by the munificence of you, my lord, I have been permitted to
complete it.

"Now, since it is the general custom of the country for everyone
who has written a book to dedicate it to one of the great princes of the
earth, it is my bounden duty to inscribe this work to no one else but
to you. I am, however, far from doing this simply because of the
highly exalted position which you occupy, but because of your liberal
hand and generous heart, since you, my lord, are the cause of my
having completed it, and it is through you that we hope soon to see it
printed, published, and fill the earth with its glory. Accept therefore,
my lord, this work with the same benign countenance which you have
always shown to me; not as if it were mine, sent as a present from me
to you, but as from a servant who has laboured for his master, and
whose earnings are the earnings of the master. When you read it,
you will gather therein some of the fruits of your generosity, and of
the silver and gold you have spent on it, which exceeds all the labour
and trouble I have spent on it. I cannot sufficiently commend, extol,

ודרי אדוני בין החכמים. כמו השמש בין הכוכבים. והנה ידעת אדוני כי יום אחד נפל בינינו הדבור.
ודברנו מזה החבור. ובקשת ממני אדוני להראותך הקונטרסים הנשברים. אשר בידי נשארים. ובקראך
בו. וכרת רב טובו ותועלתו המגיע כמונו לתלמידי הלשון הזה ובקשת ממני בכל עז שאקבל עלי הטורח
להשלימו. והבטחת וקיימת לתת שכר הסופרים והנקדנים וכל אשר יצא עליו לחזק את בדקו ולגדור את
פרצו עליך היו כלנה. ובכן התעוררתי וגכנסתי במורח הגדול וטל הכבד הזה. וביום ובלילה לא שכב
לבי עד כי זכיתי להשלימו בעזרת ה׳. ובעזרות נדבת יד אדוני המטובה עלי. והנה בהיות הכמנהג הנדהוג
בארץ שכל מי שיחבר ספר חדש להדפיסו ליחסו לשם אחד מהשרים הגדולים אשר בארץ המדה. היה
מן העול החחכם ליחס את הספר הזה כי אם אליך השר. וחלילה לי מעשות כדבר הזה לא בלבד בעבור
כבוד מעלתך ויקר תפארת גדולתך כי רבה היא. כי גם בעבור נדבות ידך ורחב לבבך באשר אתה אדוני
היית סבה להשלימו ולהקימו על רגליו ועל ידך נוכה כלנו במהרה לאורה ולחדפיסו. ותמלא כל הארץ
כבודו. על כן תקבל נא אדוני את הספר הזה בסבר פנים יפות כמו שחראית לי תמיד. ולא כאלו הוא של
ודורון שלוח לך ממני. כי אם כעבד המשועבד לרבו. וכל מה שקונה עבד קונה רבו. ובקראך בו תלקט קצת
פרי נדבתך אשר התנדבת וכספך וזהבך אשר הוצאת על ככה. והוא שקול כנגד כל הטורח והעמל אשר
אנכי טורחתי ועמלתי ויותר. והנה לא אוכל לשבח ולהלל ולפאר את מלאכת הספר הזה כראוי לו אך יהללהו

and magnify the book, but its labour will praise it in the gates; and I trust to God that every scholar like you, who reads it, and sees its excellence and usefulness, will be delighted with it, find in it what he wants, praise it, and put it as a crown on his head. Now you, my lord, will be praised in the mouths of all far more than the book and I. To you the highest praise is due, for the virtues which you have displayed in the faithful discharge of your duty, both towards God and man. Every one who sees you reveres you, and every one who hears of you speaks highly of you. Happy the sovereigns who have such learned and wise ambassadors and ministers as you are, and happy the learned and wise who have such masters and princes as you have," &c., &c.

As to the plan, contents, and design of this Massoretic Concordance, these will be gathered from the following translation of the Introduction[25] to it:—

"Thus says Elias Levita. Having determined to compile this great and stupendous work, to put down therein some of the Massoretic annotations wherever required, and to arrange it grammatically, I must acquaint you with what I have done in this my book, and also explain to you the method which I followed, the good hand of the Lord helping me. Notice, in the first place, that this book is arranged according to the order of '*The Book of Roots*,' by David Kimchi of blessed memory; but with this difference, that whilst he only adduces under every root one or two examples of each conjugation and tense, or two examples of each of the different nouns, I give under every root all

בשׂתּים מעשׂיו · ואקוה לאל שׂכל חכם לב כמוך היום אשׂר יקרא בו ויראה את טובו ותועלתו יענּנג בו ויטצא מרגוע לנפשו וישׂבחנו · וכתר לראשׂו יעבדנו · ואתה אדוני חשׂובח בטי כל יותר מהטׂבר וממני כי לך נאה להודות באשׂר נחרשׂת ונכרתת זה שׂנתים בקרב הארץ ובמקום הזה אשׂר עמדת מה שׂליח שׂלחת ומאת אדונך המלך הגדול מלך צרפת יר׳ה אל יקר תפארת גדולת השׂרחה יר׳ה אשׂר בוויני"סיא · ועשׂית הטוב החשׂר בעיני אלהים ואדם כל הימים · וכל עין ראתה אורך תעידך ואזן שׂמעה ותאשׂרך · ואשׂרי למלכים אם היו להם משׂרתים שׂרים חכמים ונבונים כמוך · ואשׂרי לחכמים ונבונים · אם היו להם אדונים ושׂרים כמוך · ובזה הנני אשׂתחוה לאדוני אפס ארצה · ושׂר רגלי אלחך · ואחיה עבד נרצע לאהבתך · תמיד מוכן לשׂירותך · ואשׂתיר לאל בעד הצלחתך · ובהתמדת בריאותך · כרצון נפשׂך וכבקשׂת ובקשׂת מזה'ות אחד מעבדי אדוני הקטנים · רך בחכמה ואב בשׂנים ·

אליה הלוי אשׂכנזי·

[26] אמר אליהו הלוי אחרי אשׂר חשׂכתני לחבר את הספר הזה חבור גדול והפלא ולשׂים בו קצת ענינים מדברי המסורת במקום הצורך ולסדרהו על פי הדקדוק אודיע נא אתכם את אשׂר אני עושׂה לספרי זה, ואורה אתכם את הדרך אשׂר אלך בה כיד ה' הטובה עלי . ראשׂונה דעו נא לכם כי הספר הזה יהי' מכוודר על סדר ס' השׂרשׂים שׂל הר״דק ז"ל, אבל הוא לא הביא בכל שׂרשׂ רק ב' או נ' פטוקים מכל בנין ופעולה או ב' מכל מין ממיני השׂמות הנמצאים בשׂרשׂ חהוא אמנם אני אביא בכל שׂרשׂ כל הפעלים והשׂמות וחמלות אשׂר נמצאו

E

the verbs, nouns, and expressions which are to be found from this root in all the Hebrew Scriptures, and arrange them according to the order of the seven conjugations as classified in the paradigm of the grammar. Thus, for instance, I first give the *Kal*, then *Niphal*, then *Piel*, *Pual*, *Hiphil*, *Hophal*, and *Hithpael*, having already proved in the *Book Bachur* that the quadriliteral conjugation has no real existence. I have then divided each conjugation into its six tenses, viz., Præterite, Participle present, Past participle, Infinitive, Imperative, and Future.

"Having enumerated all the conjugations in this manner, I give the nouns which occur from this root. I give first nouns-adjective, which are again subdivided according to their order; that is, the singular masculine is separate, the plural masculine, the singular and plural feminine, as well as each construct and absolute state, are given separately. I also give separately each word which begins with one of the seven servile letters (משׁ״ה וכ״לב), always giving first the *Vav*, which is the most frequent prefix, and then stating those with prefix *Beth*, and the rest in their alphabetical order. The same plan I pursue with the other nouns, always giving first those which have no formative additions from the letters האמנ״תי, as well as with the sundry proper names, *ex. gr.* names of men, countries, cities, deserts, pools, rivers, and seas. Of these I only adduce those which are found in the Massorah, and they are very numerous. Last of all follow the conjunctions. Of these, too, I only give those which occur in the Massorah, and which are very numerous.

"Now let that which I have written on the root אכל serve as an illustration. I have put together—i., All the passages of the Scrip-

בשרשׁ ההוא בכל עשׂרים וארבעה ספרים, ואסדרם על סדר שׁבעה הבנינים כמו שׁהם מסחדרים בלוח הדקדוק. דהיינו אתחיל בבנין חקל ואח״כ נפעל ופעל הדנוש ופעל והפעיל והפעל והתפעל, וכבר הוכחתי בספר הבחור כי הבנין המדובע במל מעיקרו ואין בו ממש, ואחלק כל בנין לשׁשׁ פעולותיו, דהיינו עבר ובינוני ופעול ומקור וציווי ועתיד, ואחר שהשׁלמתי כל הבנינים בזה האופן אתחיל בשׁמות הנמצאים באותו חשרשׁ. ובראשׁונה יסעו שמות התארים ואחלקם נ״כ לפי חסדר דהיינו יחידים לבד והרבים לבד וכן היחידות וחרבות, וחמוכרחים שׁל כל אחד לבד והסמוכים לבד ועם שׁבע אותיות המשׁמשׁות בראשׁם סימנם משׁ״ה וכ״לב, ואתחיל תמיד באות הו״יו כי היא חשמשׁ יותר מכולן, ואח״כ אסדר אותם שעם בי״ת השׁמושׁ והשׁאר אסדר לפי סדר הא״לף בי״ת. וכן אעשׂה בשׁאר מיני השׁמות, ובתחלה אשׂים אותם שׁחם בלי תוספת אוחיות האמנ״תי, ואף שׁמות העצמים הפרמים כמו שמות בני אדם ושׁמות ארצות ועיירות ומדברות ונחרות ואנמים וימים, אמנם לא אביא מחם דק שׁנמצא ומחם במסורה והם רבים מאד, ואחרונה יסעו מלח הטעם ונם מהם אקח כל מה שנמצא ומהם במסורה ונם הם רבו למעלה ראש, והמשׁל מכל מה שׁאמרתי מן שׁרש אכל אכתוב כל אכל הנמצאים בכל כ״ד ספרים יחד ואח״כ כל ואכל ואח״כ כל אכלת ואח״כ כל

tures in which אָכַל Kal pret. 3rd pers. sing. mas. occurs; then all of וְאָכַל Kal pret. 3rd pers. sing. mas. with the conjunct.; then all of אָכַלְתָּ Kal pret. 2nd pers. sing. mas.; then all of וְאָכַלְתָּ Kal pret. 2nd pers. sing. mas. with the conjunct.; and so the whole of the praeterite. Then, ii., The present participle, beginning with אוֹכֵל of which I say there are ten instances of plene, and give them all. I then state all the defectives, then follow all the instances of בְּאָכֵל וְאָכֵל הָאֹכֵל, &c., &c. The same method I pursue with all the conjugations, that is, giving all the passages of the Niphal, and of all the other conjugations. Then, iii., I give the nouns, beginning with those instances of אֹכֶל which are *Milel*; then follow those with the formative prefix *Mem*, *ex. gr.* מַאֲכָל, which occurs four times with *Pattach* under the *Caph*, all the others having *Kametz*; then follow all the instances of the forms מַאֲכֹלֶת. מַאֲכֶלֶת and in this manner all the words which are alike in spelling and pronunciation are put together, and the whole of such a class is called a camp or rubric. And if there happens to be any word with Massoretic annotations, I divide the camp into two camps, as I have remarked above under the rubric אוֹכֵל, where I put the ten instances of plene as one class, and the defectives into another, thus making two camps. You are moreover to observe that I give after every class the verbs with the suffixes of the same rubric. Thus, for instance, after the verb אָכַל I give all the instances in which it occurs with the suffix, as אֲכָלוֹ Kal pret. 3rd pers. sing. mas., with suff. 3rd pers. sing. mas., אֲכָלַנִי pret. 3rd pers. sing. mas., suff. 1st. pers. sing.; so also וַאֲכָלָם, and after every rubric. The same is the case with nouns; after אֹכֶל I give all the instances of it with the pronominal suffixes, as אָכְלְךָ, אָכְלָם and so all the ten pro-

ואכלת וכן כל העבר ואח"כ אתחיל בבינוני ואתחיל אוכל י' מלאים ואביא את כלם ואח"כ אביא כל החסרים, ואח"כ ואכל ואח"כ באכל ואח"כ האכל וכן כלם וכן כל הבנין. ואתחיל בבנין נפעל נאכל וכל מה שנמצא ממנו בבנין נפעל וכן בשאר הבנינים אכתוב כל מה שנמצא ממנו. ואח"כ אתחיל בשמות ואתחיל אכל אותם שהם מלעיל ואח"כ בתוספת מ"ם האמנ"תי. מאכל ד' פתחין וחשאר קמוצין ואח"כ משקל אחד מאכלת ואח"כ משקל אחר מאכלת ובזה האופן יחיו כל המלות השוות במכתב ובמבטא מקובצים יחד ואקרא לכל קבוץ מלות באלה מחנה אחת, ואם יהיה במחנה אחת איזה דבר של מסורת אחוץ את המחנה ההיא לשתי מחנות כמו שכתבתי לעיל במחנה אוכל י' ומלאים הרי מחנה אחת והחסרים יהיו למחנה אחרת הרי ב' מחנות. ועוד תדע כי אחר כל מחנה ומחנה אכתוב הכנויים הנמצאים במלות של המחנה ההיא, והמשל אחר מחנה אכל מחנה אכל כנוייו כל כנוייו כמו הראשון אכלו. אכלני הדב וכן וכאלם. וכן אחר כל מחנה וכן בשמות אחר מחנה אכל אכתוב כנוייו את כל אכלם, לא תתן את אכלך. וכן כל עשרה חכנויים על הכדר נסתר נוכח מדבר בעדו וכן הרבים וכן

nominal suffixes in the order of third person, second person, and first person, as well as the plural and feminine.

"Not to increase, however, the size of the book beyond what is necessary, I have taken care to give each noun and verb in one place only, and not to repeat it in two or three different places, as the author of the Concordance[26] has uselessly done. Hence, where two verbs occur in several places, joined together, as לאכול ולשתות, *to eat and to drink*, I cite all the instances under the root אכל, *to eat*, in the section comprising the Infinitive; and when I come to the root שתה, *to drink*, in the section containing the Infinitive, I state 'See the root אכל, *to eat*, under the Infinitive.' The same is the case with the combined words לשמור ולעשות, *to observe and to do*, I give all the passages under the root שמר, *to observe*, and state, under the root עשה, *to do*, 'See under the root שמר, *to observe*;' as well as with nouns joined to verbs, or with verbs joined to nouns, I always adduce them under the root of the verbs, and do not give them again under the root of the nouns, provided the Massoretic annotations do not necessitate their being given a second time under the root of the nouns.

"Before, however, I illustrate this by an example, you must notice that each book of the Hebrew Scriptures is divided into small sections, which the Christians call chapters. The same is the case with the Pentateuch, each book of which has been divided by the Massorites into sections. Thus, for instance, the book of Genesis, they divided into twelve sections, Exodus into eleven sections,

הנקבה, והנה כדי שלא להרבות כמות הספר יותר מדי הסכמתי לחיות נזהר בכל עוז שלא
לכתוב שם או פעל אחד רק במקום אחד ולא בשנים או בשלושה מקומות כמו שעשה בעל
הספר הקונקרדנצייה [20]ללא תועלת ולכן הסכמתי כשיבאו שני פעלים הנמצאים בהרבה מקומות
סמוכים יחד כמו לאכול ולשתות אכתוב את כלם בשרש אכל במהנה לאכול וכשאגיע לשרש
שתה במהנה לשתות אכתוב עיין בשרש אכל במהנה לאכול, וכן לשמור ולעשות אכתוב כלם
בשרש שמר ובשרש עשה אכתוב עיין בשרש שמר, וכן השמות הסמוכים אל הפעלים או
שהפעלים סמוכים אליהם אכתוב אותם תמיד בשרשי הפעלים ולא אכתבם פעם אחרת בשרשי
השמות אם לא תכריחני המסורת לכתוב אותם פעם שני בשרש השמות, ומרם אבאר זה לך
במשל צריך שתדע כי כל ספר של העשרים והארבעה נחלק לפרשיות קטנות קראו להם
הגוים קאפימולי וכן בה' חומשי תורה כמו שחכמי המסורת חלקו כל ספר לפרשיות כגון ספר
בראשית פרשיותיו י"ב ס' שמות פרשיותיו י"א וכן כלן, הנה הם חלקו ס' בראשית לנ'

---

[26] The author of the above-named first Hebrew Concordance is R. Isaac Nathan b. Kalonymos. He lived at Avignon, Montpellier, in the time of Peter de Luna, or the anti-pope Benedict XIII. R. Nathan devoted eight years of his life (1487-1445) to this Concordance, which was first printed by Bomberg, Venice, 1523. Comp. *Kitto's Cyclopædia of Biblical Literature*, new ed. *s. v.* NATHAN.

&c., &c., whereas the Christians divided Genesis into fifty chapters, Exodus into forty chapters, and so all the books of the Bible, as Joshua into twenty-four chapters, Judges into twenty-one chapters, &c., &c., making many chapters in the large books, and few chapters in the smaller ones. You are, moreover, to observe, that the Christians also divided Samuel and Kings into two books respectively; the second book of Samuel beginning with 'And it came to pass after the death of Saul,' and the second part of Kings with 'Then Moab rebelled.' Hence, wherever you find Samuel or Kings with two over it, it denotes 2 Sam. or 2 Kings. They also divided Chronicles into two books, the first book extending to the words 'And Soloman was strengthened,' whilst from these words onward is the second book. Hence, whenever you find Chronicles with two over it it denotes 2 Chronicles.

"And now for the illustration of what I have written above. The words ויכלו השמים and *the heavens were finished* (Gen. ii. 1), I give under the root כלה *to finish;* האזינו השמים *Give ear, O ye heavens!* (Deut. xxxii. 1,) I give under the root אזן *to be acute.* The same is the case with מוסדות השמים *the foundations of the heavens* (2 Sam. xxii. 8); בסערה השמים *by a whirlwind to the heavens* (2 Kings ii. 1); נפתחו השמים *the heavens were opened* (Ezek. i. 1); ישמחו השמים, *let the heavens rejoice* (Ps. xcvi. 2); ויצעקו השמים *and they cried to the heavens* (2 Chron. xxxii. 20), &c., &c.; which I give under the roots of the respective verbs; and when I come to the root שם, section השמים *the heavens,* I put down all the above phrases

קאפימולי וס' שמות לם' קאפיטולי וכן כל שאר ספרי המקרא כגון יהושע כ"ד קאפיטולי
שופטים כ"א וכן כלם הגדול לפי נדלו והקטן לפי קטנו . וצריך שתדע עוד כי הם חלקו ס'
שמואל לב' חלקים וס' מלכים לב' חלקים, החלק השני משמואל מתחיל ויהי אחרי מות
שאול, והספר השני ממלכים מתחיל ויפשע מואב ולכן בכל מקום שתמצא שמואל עם בי"ת
למעלה ר"ל מן ויהי אחרי מות שאול והלאה וכן כשתמצא מלכים עם בי"ת למעלה ר"ל מן
ויפשע מואב והלאה, וכן חלקו דברי הימים לב' ספרים הספר הראשון עד ויתחזק שלמה
ומשם והאלה נקרא ספר שני ולכן בכל מקום כשתמצא ד"ה עם בי"ת למעלה ר"ל דברי
הימים שני . והנה המשל על מה שכתבתי לעיל אכתוב ויכלו השמים (ראשית ב') בשרש
כלה, האזינו השמים (דברים ל"ב) בשרש און, מוסדות השמים (שמואל כ"ב), בסערה השמים
(מלכים ב'), נפתחו השמים (ביחזקאל א') ישמחו השמים (תלים צ"ו), ויצעקו השמים
(ד"ה ל"ב) ודומיהם, והנה כשאניע לשרש שם במחנה השמים אכתוב את כלם יחד בלי
מראה מקום כגון ויכלו השמים, האזינו השמים, מוסדות השמים, בסערה השמים, נפתחו
השמים, ישמחו השמים, ויצעקו השמים ודומיהם כל חד בשרשי המלות שלפניהם ואקרא

have not omitted a single one. But the words of which the Massorites have not given the number, I have not had the heart to enumerate, for fear I should give the wrong number. As a rule, whatever I could put into a separate section I did put. Now I called this book the 'Book of Remembrance,' because therein are mentioned all the subjects which are advantageous to the study of the Scriptures, and therein all the words are examined. The use of this work is tenfold.

"i. It is like a Lexicon, explaining all the words which occur in the Hebrew Scriptures, as I give under each root an explanation of all the words in succession which occur in this root. For it sometimes happens that one root has two, three, four, and as many as ten different significations. I moreover give with the explanation of every word its meaning in German, which is the language of my countrymen. ii. It is as a Grammar, because therein is explained the grammatical structure of all the words under their respective roots, so that the things explain themselves. Thus, if one has any difficulty about the grammar of a word, he need only look at the section, and under the part of speech into which I have put it, *ex. gr.* וָאֶהָבָה you will know that its root is חבא, and you will see that I put it under the *Niphal*, future, first pers. The same is the case if it is a noun, you will recognise whether it is a noun-adjective or substantive, or to what form it belongs, from the sections into which it is placed. iii. It is a model for the Codices of the Law, for thereby may be corrected all the Hebrew Scriptures with regard to plene and defective, Milra, Keri

כ״ד, מראש י״ד, ראשון ה' הראשון ס״נ ודומיהון וכן וראיתי י״ב, ויאמר צ״א פתחין לא אניח אף אחד מהם, אבל המלות שלא כתבו הם מינם לא ימלאני לבי לכתוב מספרם מידאתי פן שניתי במספרם, והכלל כל מה שאוכל לעשות מהם האספסוף אעשה.
והנה קראתי שם הספר הזה ספר הזכרונות כי זכר כל המעשים המועילים למקרא בתוכו בא וחוא דורש את עניני המלות כלם. והנה התועליות חמניעות מזה הספר הם עשרה:
התועלת הא' הוא שיחי' הספר חזה כדמות ספר השרשים מבאר כל המלות חנמצאים בכ״ד ספרים, ואכתוב בכל שרש ביאורי כל המלות הנמצאות בשרש החוא זו אחר זו כי לפעמים יהיו בשרש אחד ב' או ג' או ד' וכו' עד י' ענינים גם אכתוב אצל כל ביאור מלה ומלה פתרונה בלשון אשכנז שהיא לשון בני עמי.
התועלת הב' שיהיה הספר הזה כדמות ספר דקדוק, וזה כי יבוארו בו דקדוק של כל המלות הנמצאות בשרש החוא זה כי יבוארו מצד עצמם כי כאשר יקשה לאדם דקדוק של מלה אחת הלא יראה המחנה אשר שמתיה בו באיזח מין ונפעולה ודבור, והמשל כי עדום אנכי **ואחבא** ידעת ששרשו חב״א ותראה כי שמתיה בבנין נפעל בעתיד במחנה המדבר בעדו וכן אם הוא שם יכיד שם הוא תאר או שם דבר או איזה משקל הוא לפי המחנה אשר יחנה שם.
התועלת הג' הוא שיהיה הספר הזה כדמות תקון ספר תורה כי בו יניח אדם כל כ״ד ספרים

and Kethiv, Tikkun Sopherim, the large and small letters, and as I have stated above in the Introduction. iv. It explains the great and small Massorah, and I am persuaded that whoso consults this book will understand most of the Massoretic remarks and signs which were unknown to him before. v. It serves as a concordance for those who read the Bible, the Mishna, the Talmud, the Kabbalah, Grammar, or Commentaries, and who meet in these works passages of Scripture adduced as evidence which they cannot find in the Bible. Now this book will enable them easily to find the place, and show them the book and chapter in which these passages occur, as I have mentioned in the Introduction above. vi. It will be of use to preachers who, in composing sermons, want to find passages illustrative of their text. Thus, for instance, if one has to preach about *righteousness*, he needs only look into the root צדק, section צדקה, and he will not require to search through all the sections of this root, comprising either verbs or nouns, but simply section צרקה and section לצדקה, הצדקה, בצדקה. So also if he has to preach about *peace* or *joy*, he only needs to look into the roots שלם and שמח. vii. To those who wish to write Hebrew letters, adopting the style of the Bible, they will easily find the passages, as I have illustrated it, with respect to preachers. Thus, for instance, if anyone wishes to write a letter to his friend to buy or to make him some garments, he need only look into the root לבש, and if he does not find under it what he wants, he is to look into the root בגד or

במלוי וחסרון ובמלרע בקריין וכתיבן בתיקין סופרים באותיות גדולות וקטנות כאשר כתבתי לעיל בהקדמה.

התועלת הד' הוא שיהי' הספר הזה כדמות באור למסדה גדולה וקטנה, ומבטיח אני כל המעיין בספר הזה יעכיל ויבין רוב דברי בעלי המסרה וסימניהם אשר לפניו לא ידעם.

התועלת ההח' הוא שיהי' הספר הזה כדמות מראה מקום לכל מי שיקרא באחד מהספרים מקרא משנה גמרא קבלה ודקדוק ופידושי' וימצא שם ראיית פסוק ולא ידע מקומו איו הלא בזה הספר קל מהרה יבין דרכו וידע את מקומו וימצאהו באיזה ספר ובאיזה פרשה ר״ל קאפיטולו הוא כאשר הראיתיך בהקדמה לעיל.

התעלת הו' הוא שיהי' חספר הזה מבחד ומוב לכל הבא לעשות איזה דרשה וירצה לחביא ראייות מהפסוקים לדדוש ההוא, והמשל הדוצה לדדוש בעניני הצדקה חלא יעיין בשרש צדק במחנה צדקה ולא יצמרך לבקש בכל מחנות השרש לא בפעלים ולא בשמות דק במחנה צדקה ובמתנה בצדקה הצדקה לצדקה, וכן אם ידרוש בענין שלום או בעניו שמחה יבקש בשרש שלם ושמח.

התועלת הז' מי שירצה לכתוב כתבים בלשון עברי על פי פסוק הלא ימצא הפסוקים כפי הדרוש אשר יחפוץ, לפי המשל שנתתי למעלה בענין הדורש, והמשל אם רוצה לכתוב כתב לחבידו מענין מלבושים שיקנה לו או יעשה לו יעיין בשרש לבש ואם לא ימצא בו מבוקשו יעיין בשרש בגד או בשרש כסה בענין או בשרש חליץ בענין מחלצות.

F

כסה under כסות, or into the root חלץ under מחלצות. viii. To those
who want to write poetry, they will find under every root the words
which rhyme. Thus, for instance, if one wants to write a poem,
each line of which is to terminate in בָרִים, and he requires אֲבָרִים,
שְׁבָדִים. עֲבָרִים. גְבָרִים. חֲבָרִים. דְּבָרִים. גְּבָרִים, he is only to look under
the roots of these words, and he will find verses containing all these,
and will be able to select the most appropriate ones. ix. The book
will be of use to those who study the Kabbalah, for they will find in it
all the sacred names. Thus, for instance, the Kabbalistic student who
wants to know the virtue of the divine names representing judgment
or mercy, or what other powers or attributes they have, he will find
the divine names divided into classes, as the name אדני occurs 184
times, exclusive of those passages in which it is joined to יהוה, &c.,
&c. x. It will be useful as a defence of our faith against those who
attack our religion; and in two respects. In the first place, those
who dispute with us are in the habit of adducing passages according to
the signs which the Christians made in the Bible, and which they call
chapters, saying, Is it not written in such and such a book, and in
such and such a chapter? Now he who uses this book will also be
able to do the same thing. Secondly, it is well known that most of
the controversies which take place between us and them are about
the Messiah — whether he has already come, or whether he is

התועלת חח' הרוצה לעשות חדוז או שיר שקול הלא ימצא בכל שרש חמלות הדומות
במבטא בסוף התיבה והמשל הרוצה לעשות שיר משובח שיח' סוף כל חרחתו ברים וצריך
לעשות אברים גברים דברים חברים נברים עברים שברים הלא יעיין בשרשי המלות
האלה וימצא פסוקים מכל אלה ויבחר מהם הנאותים למבוקשו, ודוק.
התועלת הט' הוא שיחי' הספר הזה טוב לענין הקבלה כי ימצאו בו כל השמות הקדושים,
והמשל המקובל חדוש לדעת כח השמות של מדת הדין או של מדת הרחמים או שאר הכחות
או המדות שיש לחם חלא ימצא בו השמות נחלקים למיניהם כגון הסם של אדנות הנכתב
א"לף ד"לת נו"ן יו"ד שהוא אדני הס קל"ד זולת אותם שהם סמוכים לשם י' ה' ו' ה' כמו כה
אמר אדני יהוה שהם רבים מאד מאד, וכן אדני אלהים, אלהים אדני, ואלה שהם מלעיל
ואלוה שהם הסרים ואלוהים שהוא מלא אשר לכלם מדות וכחות מיוחדות הנורעות לבעלי
הקבלה חלא ימצא כלם בזה הספר איש בשרשו ובמחנהו.
התועלת העשירי הוא שיחי' הספר חזה טוב לספר נצחון ויועיל מאד לחתווכה עם
המתנגדים אלינו באמונתנו, וזה בשני אופנים, האחד שהם דגילים לחתווכה עמנו ומביאים
ראי' מן חפסוקים על פי הסימנים שעשו בכל העשרים וארבע וקראו לחם בלשונם קאפיטולי
ואומרים הלא כתוב בספר פלוני בכך וכך קאפימולי, ומי שירגיל את עצמו בספר הזה ידע
ייבין לעשות כן כמו הוא, והאופן חשני ידוע הוא כי רוב הוויכוח אשר בינגו ובינם הוא בענין
חמשיח אם כבר בא או עתיד לבוא, ועל אריכות הגלות ועל הגאולה ועל הגן עדן וחגיהנם,

yet to come; about the duration of our dispersion, about our restoration, about Paradise and Hell. Now, he who wants to enquire into these matters, let him look into the roots משח, *to anoint;* גלה, *to take captive;* גאל *to redeem,* &c., and he will find all the passages treating thereon. Also, as to their opinion about the word שאול, explaining, 'I will go down into *Sheol* unto my son' (Gen. xxxvii. 35) to mean *hell,* if you look under the root שאל you will there find proof that, in most cases, it denotes *the grave,* and not *hell.* The Holy One, blessed be He, save us from its power. Blessed be His glorious name!"

It is greatly to be regretted that this stupendous work has not been published. Levita himself often refers to it as his *chef-d'œuvre*: he laboured over it more than twenty years (1514–1536). Through the intervention of his pupil, patron, and friend, De Selve, he sent the MS. to Paris, to be printed, and in 1538, when Levita wrote the third Introduction to his *Massoreth Ha-Massoreth,* he fully believed that it was actually in the press. "I hope to God, blessed be His name," says he, in this Introduction, "that it will soon see the light, having given it to be printed in the great city of Paris, in the kingdom of France;" and even three years later, he still says, in the Introduction to his Explanation of the 712 words, "*The Book of Remembrance* I am now printing." From some unknown cause, however, the work was not printed, and the MS., consisting of two immense folios, is in the Imperial Library at Paris. The copy is the identical one which Levita sent there to be printed. It has his autograph subscription, and the only defect in it is supposed to be in the absence of an Introduction, to which Levita refers. This Introduction, however, could not have been lost, since the present binding of the MS. is that in which it was put under Henry II., as has been pointed out to Frensdorff by the learned librarian, M. Breal.[27]

Whatever might have been the cause of the non-publication of *The Massoretic Concordance,* and however great his disappointment, Levita, in other respects, had to congratulate himself on the good

ומי שבא להתווכה על זה יעיין בשרש משח ובשרש גלה ובשרש נאל וימצא כל הפסוקים שמדברים מזה, וגם מה שהם מחזיקים דתם עם מלת שאול ומפרשים ארד אל בני אבל שאולה ניהנם והנה המעיין בשרש שאל ימצא שם ראיות שרובם נאמרים על הקבר ולא על הניהנם — הק״בה יצילנו מידו, ברוך שם כבודו :

[27] Comp. Fraukel's *Monatschrift fur Geschichte und Wissenschaft des Judenthums,* vol. xii., p. 101.

effect which his MS., accompanied by the warm and laudatory recommendations of his friend the Bishop of Lavoure, produced at Paris. Paris, for more than a century, had not a single Jewish inhabitant. Ever since the expulsion of the Jews from France, in 1395, in consequence of the decree passed by Charles VI., September 17, 1394; "commanding it, as an unalterable law, that, in future, no Jew is to live, or even temporarily to abide, in any part of France, whether in Languedoil or in Languedoc:" the sovereigns of that country—Charles VII., Louis XI., Charles VIII., Louis XII., and even Francis I. in the earlier part of his reign—would not tolerate any Jews in their dominions. The Kabbalistic epidemic, however, from which the Pope himself was suffering, the rage for studying Hebrew amongst the highest of the land, and the great demand for Jewish teachers, had now changed the aspect of affairs. So marvellous was the change, that Guillaume Haquinet Petit, father-confessor of Louis XII., the very man who, in 1514, effected the condemnation, by the Paris University, of Reuchlin's work, as heretical, because it defended the Jews and the Jewish writings against the infatuated assaults of Pfefferkorn, now appeared as the promoter of Hebrew literature. It was upon his advice that Francis I. invited Augustin Justiniani, bishop of Corsica, to Paris, to become professor of Hebrew in the University. Justiniani, who learned his Hebrew from the celebrated Jewish physician, Jacob Mantin, also conducted the Hebrew studies at the University of Rheims. As a text-book for teaching the Grammar, he reprinted the vitiated edition of Moses Kimchi's *Outlines of Hebrew Grammar*, with Levita's annotations (Paris, 1520).[28] To shew the French Christians at large the value of Hebrew literature, and to point out the great advantage to be derived from studying it, this Dominican, Justiniani, also published in the same year (1520) a Latin translation, from the Hebrew, of Maimonides' clebrated religio-philosophical work, entitled *The Guide of the Perplexed*,[29] the very book which, three centuries ago, the hyper-orthodox Jews, with the

[28] A description of this Grammar has already been given, *vide supra*, p. 13.
[29] Maimonides was born at Cordova, March 30, 1135, and died December 13, 1204. A biographical sketch of this most distinguished Jewish philosopher, as well as an analysis of his remarkable works, will be found in Kitto's *Cyclopædia of Biblical Litarature*. We have only here to add that Justiniani, who was aided by his teacher, Jacob Mantin, in the translation of *The Guide of the Perplexed*, entirely omitted to acknowledge the important help he obtained from this Jewish physician. Comp. Wolf, *Bibliotheca Hebræa*, iii. 780, &c.

assistance of the Dominicans, publicly committed to the flames, as a most heretical and pernicious production.

Great as was the change which had now taken place in France with regard to Hebrew literature (1520), it had not as yet reached its culminating point. It was only on the arrival of Levita's MS. of *The Massoretic Concordance* at Paris, whither De Selve had sent it to be printed at his own expense, that we actually see how love for Hebrew overcame hatred of the Hebrews. Attracted by his fame, and highly recommended by his pupil, the bishop of Lavour, Levita received an invitation from Francis I. to come to France, and accept the chair of Hebrew at the University; the very country which, for a hundred and thirty years, had been shut against the Jews, and where, at the time when he received this invitation, not a single Jew was to be found! But Levita declined the honourable position. Much as he loved to be the first Hebraist in Europe, he did not like to be a unique Hebrew in France. He therefore preferred to remain at Venice, in the midst of his friends and disciples.

He also declined invitations from several cardinals, bishops, and princes, to become Hebrew professor in Christian Colleges.[80] Though he cheerfully gave Hebrew instruction to single Christian pupils, such as cardinal Egidio, Reuchlin, De Selve, and other eminent men, yet his motives for declining to separate himself from his Jewish disciples altogether, and to become entirely a teacher of the Gentiles, may easily be understood. Notwithstanding the express avowal of these eminent Christians, that they learned Hebrew in order to study the Kabbalah, and to convince the Jews from this esoteric doctrine of the truth of Christianity, they imbibed an interest in and love for the Jews with their attachment to the Hebrew language. Reuchlin most nobly pleaded the cause of the Israelites in Germany against the calumnies of Pfefferkorn[81] and the Dominicans.

[80] Comp. כי כמה פעמים נקרא נקראתי מקראתי משרים רבים ונכברים גם מקרדינאלי גם מהגמונים גם מעיר פרי'ז אשר בצרפת בצואת המלך יר ה ולא הטיתי אזן in the second Introduction to his explanation of the 712 words in Hebrew literature, entitled *Tishbi*.

[81] The fanatical and misguided Joseph Pfefferkorn was born at Moravia, 1469, only twelve months after the birth of Elias Levita; he embraced Christianity, and was publicly baptised at Cologne, 1505, when thirty-six years old. His works against his former co-religionists and Reuchlin, which obtained such unenviable notoriety, and which were the means of calling forth the Reformation, are—i. *Der Judenspiegel*, Nurmberg, 1507; ii. *Die Judenbeichte*, Cologne, 1508; iii. *Das Osternbuch*, Cologne and Augsburg, 1509; iv. *Der Judenfeind*, *ibid*, 1509; v. *In Lob und Ehren dem Kaiser Maxi-*

Egidio befriended them at Rome, whilst De Selve, bishop of Lavour, effected such a change in France in favour of the Jews, that Levita, as we have seen, was invited by the king to the professorial chair at the University. Luther too, as long as Reuchlin was living, entertained the highest opinion of the Jews. In his treatise, entitled, "*That Jesus Christ is born a Jew*" (1523), which he published two years after Reuchlin's death, he still exclaimed, "Our fools, the popes, bishops, sophists, and monks, those coarse asses'-heads, have hitherto proceeded with the Jews in such a fashion, that he who was a good Christian might well have desired to become a Jew. And if I had been a Jew, and had seen the Christian faith governed and taught by such blockheads and dolts, I should sooner have become a hog than a Christian; for they have treated the Jews as though they were dogs and not men."[32]

There were, however, circumstances aggravating both to the Jews and Christians. The Jews were exceedingly vexed by the avowal that the object of the Christians in studying Hebrew was to proselytise them ; that many eminent Jews had been gained over to the Church; and that at this very period of Levita's life, no less a man than the pious and learned Jacob b. Chajim, to whom the world is indebted for the celebrated Rabbinic Bible, and for editing the Critical Apparatus of the Old Testament, had now also embraced Christianity (1536).[33]

milian, Cologne, 1510; vi. *Ein Brief an Geistliche und Weltliche in Betreff des kaiserlichen Mandats die judischen Schriften zu vertiligen*, given by Graetz, note 2, p. xiii. ; vii. *Der Handspiegel*, Mayence, 1511 ; viii. *Der Brandspiegel*, 1513 ; ix. *Die Sturmglock*, Cologne, 1414 ; x. *Streitbüchlein uider Reuchlin und seine Jünger*, Cologne, 1516 ; xi. *Eine mitleidige Clag' gegen den unglaubigen Reuchlin*, 1521 ; comp. Graetz, *Geschichte der Juden*, vol. ix. Supplementary Notes, p. x. &c., Leipzig; 1866.

[32] Hengstenberg, Commentary on Ecclesiastes, with other treatises. Clark's Translation, p. 415, Edinburgh, 1860.

[33] This celebrated Hebraist and Massorite was born about 1470, at Tunis, whence he is also sometimes called *Tunisi*. Besides editing the stupendous Rabbinic Bible (1524-5), and publishing the *editio princeps* of the *Jerusalem Talmud* (1523), Biblical literature is indebted to him for a *Dissertation on the Targum*, which is prefixed to the edition of the Pentateuch with the Targum and the Five Megilloth (Bomberg, 1527, 1543-4). His elaborate Introduction to the Rabbinic Bible has recently been re-published, with an English Translation and Notes by Ginsburg (Longmans, 1865). Fürst's assertion, (*Bibli theca Judaica*, iii., 452) that this Introduction had been translated into English by Kennicott, in his work entitled *The state of the printed Hebrew text of the Old Testament*, Oxford, 1758, is incorrect. Kennicott simply published an abridged and incorrect *Latin* version, from a MS. which he found in the Bodleian Library. From the remark of Levita in the second Introduction to the *Massoreth Ha-Massoreth* (comp. *infra*), it would seem that Jacob b. Chajim was already dead in 1538. That he had then

Impatient Christians, again, though now ranged in battle array against each other as Catholics and Protestants, and consigning one another to eternal damnation as heretics, were extremely angry with the Jews for not at once relinquishing their religion and embracing Christianity, which was then torn in pieces and weltering in blood. So wroth were the Christians of that day with the Jews for not filling up with converts from Judaism the ranks in the Church, which the professed followers of the Prince of Peace had decimated in the religious wars, that even Luther, forgetful of his former kindly feelings, and with strange inconsistency, admonished his protestant followers to "burn their synagogues, force them to work, and treat them with all unmercifulness!"[84] Such love and hatred alternately displayed, for the express purpose of gaining converts, had its effect upon the Jews. The orthodox portion of the Hebrew community began to realise that in teaching Christians Hebrew, and in initiating them into the mysteries of the Kabbalah, they were furnishing them with weapons against the Jews. They, therefore, became exceedingly displeased with those members of the synagogue who were engaged in tuition among Christians; and as Levita was the most distinguished teacher of the Christians, the cry of the Jews was loudest against him. His manly, straightforward, and noble defence of himself is contained in the second Introduction of his *Massoreth Ha-Massoreth*, and may be seen below, for which reason we do not reproduce it here.

been a Christian, is not only evident from Levita's vituperations in question, but also from the statement of the editor of the *Mishna*, with Maimonides' commentary, published at Venice, 1546. At the end of Tractate *Taharoth*, the editor remarks אלה הם דברי המניה הראשון שהיה שמו לפנים בישראל יעקוב בר חיים שהניה סדר מהדורות עם פירוש רבינו שמשון ז"ל ולמי שאמר החכם קבל האמת מטי שאמרו ראינו להדפים דבריו פה: "these are the words of the first editor, whose name was formerly among the Jews, Jacob b. Chajim, and who revised the Tractate *Taharoth*, with the commentary of R. Shimshon of blessed memory. Now since the sage said, 'Receive the truth by whomsoever it is propounded,' we deemed it proper to print his remarks here." This apology from the second editor for printing, in a work intended for the Jews, opinions propounded by one who had ceased to be a member of the community, puts the question beyond the shadow of a doubt. The learned Frensdorff was so much struck with the remark of Levita upon this subject, and was so unwilling to believe it, that he wrote to Professor Luzzatto for more information about it; and Luzzatto again, who communicates the above extract from the editor of the Mishna, was so afflicted by finding it to be true, that he delayed replying to Frensdorff's letter, because he was unwilling to make it known that so learned a man had embraced Christianity. Comp. *the Hebrew Essays and Reviews*, entitled *Ozar Nechmad*, vol. iii., p. 112, &c., Vienna, 1860.

[84] Hengstenberg, Commentary on Ecclesiastes, with other treatises. Clark's Translation, p. 418, Edinburgh, 1860.

By the extraordinary amount of labour, research, and study which he bestowed, for more than twenty years, on collating and elaborating the materials for the Massoretic Concordance, Levita became one of the most accomplished scholars in this singular department of recondite Biblical learning. His pupils, to whom he had often explained the import of the enigmatical phrases and peculiar signs whereby the Massorites indicate the correct readings, orthography, and exegesis of the Hebrew text, and who were delighted to see the meaning of the Massoretic signs surrounding the margins of Hebrew bibles, at last urged him to write them a Commentary on the Massorah, which they might use as a manual. To this earnest and flattering request of his disciples he could all the more cheerfully accede, since he himself had been contemplating writing such a treatise for twenty years, and was only prevented from carrying out his design by untoward circumstances. Now that he had finished the Massoretic Concordance, and had the leisure, he at once betook himself to the work of supplying his disciples with the desired text-book, and two years after the completion of the gigantic Concordance he published at Venice (1538), by the aid of his friend Bomberg, the celebrated *Massoreth Ha-Massoreth* (מסורת המסורת).

Before entering into the history of this book and the extraordinary controversy it called forth, it will be necessary to give a succinct analysis of its contents. The *Massoreth Ha-Massoreth* consists of three parts, preceded by a Notice to the Reader, a Preface, and three Introductions. The Notice to the Reader explains the references in this book to the then newly introduced division of the Hebrew Scriptures into chapters, and the books of Samuel, Kings, and Chronicles, respectively, into two books, and shews how any original ideas propounded by the author are indicated. The Preface sets forth the plan and contents of the book. The first Introduction consists of a Song of Praise to the Creator, who guided his people in former days, and who vouchsafed wisdom to the Massorites in their work, as well as to the author, in order to explain the Massorah. The second Introduction begins with a piece of autobiography; then states how the author came to compile this book; describes his researches in the Massorah, the state of the Massoretic MSS., the importance of the Massorah, his connection with Cardinal Egidio, and his defence for teaching him Hebrew. The third Introduction explains the meaning of the word *Massorah*; discusses different opinions about the origin of the Massorah, the vowel points, the accents, &c., &c. Then follow the three parts which, according to the Jewish custom of naming things after national events, are respectively denominated the *First Tables*, the *Second Tables*, and the *Broken Tables*, after the events recorded in Exodus xxiv. 12, xxxi. 18, xxxii. 19, xxxiv. 1–4. In harmony with its appellation, the *First Tables*, or the first part, he divided it into ten sections, denominated commandments (עשרת הדברים), answering to the Decalogue on the tables; whilst each of these sections actually begins with the very words which commence the respective commandments of the Decalogue. These ten sections are occupied with the discussion of *plene* and *defective*. The *Second Tables*, or part, also consists of ten commandments, or sections, which discuss respectively the important Massoretic points of—i. The *Keri* and *Kethiv*; ii. *Kametz* and *Pattach*; iii. *Dagesh, Raphe, Mappick*, and *Sheva*; iv. The accents on the tone-syllable, and *Psick*: v. Registers, groups, parallels, and analogous forms; vi. Peculiar conjunctions, disjunctions, and resemblances; vii. Words with prefixes, serviles, and solitary; viii. Conjectural readings, errors, and variations; ix. The terms for letters, written and oral words, small letters, accents, certainties, and transpositions; and, x. The Massoretic expressions for Scriptures, a single Book of the Scriptures, form, dividing spaces, &c. The *Broken Tables*, or the third part, discusses the abbreviations, or broken words, used by the Massorites, whence the part obtained its name. It also describes some of the principal men who have written on the Massorah, as well as some ancient Codices.

This remarkable book was first printed by his friend, M. Bomberg, at Venice, 1538, the text not being pointed. Levita appended to this edition the poem of Saadia, giving the number of times which each letter of the alphabet occurs throughout the Hebrew Scriptures, as well as an explanation of this poem. In less than twelve months it was re-published at Basle, 1539, the text pointed. In this edition Münster translated into Latin the three Introductions, the first and second being in an abridged form, and gives a brief summary of the contents of the three parts. He, however, omitted Saadia's poem, with Levita's explanations. It is very strange that Münster does not mention on the title-page that the book had already appeared at Venice, and that his edition was a reprint.

The third part, or the *Broken Tables* as it is called, was republished separately, in Rabbinical characters, at Venice (שכ״ו = 826 =) 1566, some copies being dated (ש״ו = 306 =) 1546, under the title, *A Commentary on the Massorah, called the Gate of the Broken Tables* (פירוש המסורת וקרא שמו שער שברי לוחות). This part of the book was also re-published with additions by Samuel b. Chajim, Prague, 1610. The three introductions were also translated into Latin by Jo. Lud. Mich. Nagel (Altdorf, 1758–71). The third and last edition of the entire Hebrew text was published at Sulzbach, 1771, in Rabbinical characters. This edition is exceedingly defective, whole passages being omitted, as will be seen in the notes to our edition. The editor, Kalmen Dishbek, misled by Münster's silence about the Venice edition, describes the Basle edition (1539) as the *editio princeps*, and hence, necessarily, also omitted Saadia's poem and Levita's explanation of it. Fürst, indeed (*Bibliotheca Judaica*, ii. 240), and others, say that there was also an edition of it at Sulzbach, 1769, two years before the one we have specified. But this must be a mistake, since the editor of the 1771 edition distinctly describes it as *the second*, and the Basle as *the first*.[35]

The only translation extant of this book is the German, which was published at Halle, 1772,[36] and which is generally, but incorrectly, ascribed to the celebrated Joh. Salomo Semler. That Semler himself was not the translator, but that he simply superintended the translation, and made notes to it, is stated on the very title-page of the book.[37] The preface, however, which was written by this scholar, puts the whole question beyond the shadow of a doubt; and the erroneous opinion of bibliographers on this subject can only be accounted for on the supposition that they have either not perused the preface or

---

[35] Thus the editor distinctly says on the title-page נדפס מקדמת דנא בעיר באזיל בשנת רצ״ט לפ״ק: והובא שנה שניה לבית הדפום ע״י הנעלה כמהורר קלמן דישבעק

[36] From a passage quoted by Semler, in his Preface to Meyer's German Translation (p. 9), it indeed appears that the celebrated Reformer, Conrad Pellican (1487-1556), translated the whole book into Latin shortly after the publication of the Hebrew. The passage in question, which is quoted from *the Life of Pellican*, prefixed to the first volume of his *Commentaries*, is as follows: "Adhæc tota biblia *transtuli* e chaldaico in latinum . . . . et utrumque Targum libri Esther, de quo sibi Judæi mire placent. Quin et Targum Hierosolymitanum in quinque libros Mosis. Præter hæc *transtuli* quædam Talmudica opuscula: *librum Massoreth*, quem Hebraicum edidit *Elias* grammaticus." But this Latin version has never been published.

[37] Uebersetzung des Buches Massoreth Hammassoreth. Unter Aufsicht und mit Anmerkungen D. Joh. Salomo Semlers.

not seen the book. In this preface Semler gives the following history of the translation. A respectable young man, named Christian Gottlob Meyer, who had an excellent opportunity, at Berlin, to acquire, under the guidance of an expert teacher, a greater knowledge of Jewish learning than ordinary Jewish youths, became convinced of the truth of Christianity. He therefore left Judaism, and was publicly admitted into the church at Halle. Here, whilst prosecuting his study, Semler became acquainted with him. Convinced of the sincerity of the young man, and being anxious that he should not neglect his Hebrew learning, Semler asked him to translate the *Massoreth Ha-Massoreth* after his college hours, omitting, however, the poetical Introductions, which are somewhat more difficult. The translation thus made by Meyer, Semler sometimes read with the translator, and endeavoured to arrange the German in such a manner as to make it more intelligible. He also did the same with the German translation of the poetical Introductions, which was made by another Jew, named Aaronssohn, a clever *Candidatus Medicinæ* at the University. Semler, moreover, made sundry notes to this German translation.[88] With this plain statement of Semler before us, we

---

[88] Die Gelegenheit zu dieser deutschen Uebersetzung ist diese. Ein artiger junger Mensch, Christian Gotlob Meyer, der in Berlin ehedem die gute Gelegenheit, in jüdischer Gelersamkeit unter Anführung eines geschickten Lehrers weiter als andere Judenknaben zu kommen, sehr gut genutzt hatte, ist nach und nach, zumal durch den Gebrauch deutscher moralischer Schriften, in gebundener und ungebundener Rede, zu eignem Nachdenken gekommen, und hat über den Grund und die Art seiner bisherigen jüdischen Religion so lange ernstliche Betrachtungen fortgesetzt, daß er endlich sich entschlossen, von den Grundsätzen der christlichen Religion eine nähere Erkentnis zu suchen. Er kam endlich nach Halle, wo er unter der Anleitung des Magister und Oberdiaconus an der Ulrichskirche, Hrn. Schultze, sehr bald in der Einsicht so weit gekommen, daß er sich von selbst entschlossen, öffentlich zu der christlichen Religion überzutreten.—

Da ich nun gerne auch dazu helfen wolte, daß er seinen guten Anfang hebräischer oder rabbinischer Lectüre nicht etwa wieder vernachläßigen solte; so habe ich'ihm dieses Büchelchen gegeben, nach und nach, ohne seinen Schulstudien Eintrag zu thun, eine Uebersetzung davon vorzunemen; doch mit Auslassung der poetischen Vorreden, welche etwas schwerer seien.—

Diese Uebersetzung habe ich zuweilen mit dem Uebersetzer wieder durchgegangen, und habe die deutsche Schreibart etwas verständlicher einzurichten gesucht, obgleich der Charakter eines jüdischen Aufsaßes nicht ganz zu verändern war. Hie und da bemerke ich aber doch einige Stellen, die noch deutlicher hätten ausgedruckt werden können; so auch hie und da von der Uebersetzung der poetischen Vorreden gilt, welche Hr. Aronssohn,

hope that the question as to the authorship of the German version will in future be regarded as settled.

As to the merit of it, considering that it was made by a young man, and the great difficulties he had to encounter, the translation must be pronounced pretty fair. For critical purposes, however, the utility of it is greatly impaired, for the following reasons. Passages are frequently altogether omitted. The elaborate and most difficult second Introduction has not been translated into German at all. And, lastly, young Meyer, remarkable as was his knowledge of Hebrew considering his age, was not familiar with the Massoretic language, which requires special study. Hence it is that many of the passages, though literally translated, are less intelligible in the German than they are in the Hebrew. Hence, too, the many serious blunders and mistranslations which are dispersed throughout the work.

The storm which the original publication of this work raised (1538) was truly marvellous, and, after raging for more than three centuries, cannot be said to have as yet fully subsided. The cause of this storm was the array of most powerful arguments which Levita made in the third introduction, to prove that the vowel-points now to be found in the Hebrew Bibles are not of the same antiquity with the text, but that they were invented and put there by the Massorites about five hundred years after Christ. The authority of the vowel-points had indeed been questioned by some Jewish authorities long before Levita's time. As early as the ninth century, Natronai ii. b. Hilai, who was Gaon or spiritual head of the College in Sora (859– 869), in reply to the question whether it is lawful to put the points to the Synagogal Scrolls of the Pentateuch, distinctly declared that " since the Law, as given to Moses on Sinai, had no points, and the points are not Sinaitic [*i. e.* sacred], having been invented by the sages, and put down as signs for the reader; and moreover since it is prohibited to us to make any additions from our own cogitations, lest we transgress the command ' Ye shall not add,' &c. (Deut. iv. 2); hence we must not put the points to the Scrolls of the Law."[89] Three

ein geschickter Candidatus Medicinæ auf hiesiger Universität, gemacht hat. Ich habe hie und da einige Anmerkungen dazu gesetzt, welche theils das Nachdenken befördern, theils auf einige andere Bücher weisen; habe aber freilich nicht viel Zeit darauf wenden können.—Seite 12—15.

[89] This fact, which is cited in *the Vitry Machsor*, from the Theological decisions, (תשובת הגאונים) is communicated by Luzzatto in *the Hebrew Essays and Reviews*,

centuries later, no less a scholar than the celebrated Ibn Ezra, in speaking of the two dots over the letter ש, the one on the right indicating that it is *Shin* and the one to the left shewing that it is *Sin*, remarked that "it was the custom of the sages of Tiberias to put down these points to mark the double pronunciation, and that they were the chief authorities, since from them proceeded the Massorites, from whom we obtained the whole system of punctuation."[40]

From Ibn Ezra this opinion was also espoused by some Christian scholars in the middle ages, who, hating the Jews, wished to base upon the late origin of the points the charge against them of having introduced innovations and corruptions into the text of the Bible. Thus, the celebrated Dominican, Raymond Martin, who studied Hebrew, Chaldee, and Arabic, to convert the Jews and the Mahommedans to Christianity, and who had acquired such a knowledge of Rabbinical Literature that he even excelled St. Jerome, boldly, but most incorrectly, asserted that the vowel-points in the text of the Old Testament were put there by Ben Naphtali and Ben Asher, *circa* 900–960, and that the *Emendations of the Scribes* (תקון סופרים) are simply a few of the many wilful corruptions and perversions introduced by the Jews into the sacred text, to obliterate the prophecies about

---

called *Kerem Chemed* (vol. iii., p. 200, Prague, 1838). The *Vitry Machsor*, or Ritual of the Synagogue, of Vitry, in France, was compiled, *circa* 1100, by R. Simcha of Vitry, a disciple of Rashi, and obtained its name from the place in which the compiler lived. It not only comprises the whole *Cycle of the Daily and Festival Services*, but various legal and ritual laws from ancient documents. The passage in question is as follows in the original וששאלתם אם אסור לנקוד ספר תורה· ספר תורה שניתן למשה בסיני לא שטמענו בו ניקוד· לא ניתן ניקוד בסיני· כי החכמים צייגוהו לסימן· ואסור לנו להוסיף מדעתנו סן נעבור בבל תוסיף· לפיכך אין נוקדין ספר תורה. It is also to be remarked that the MS. of this *Machsor*, which is one of the only two copies which have survived the ravages of time, and a description of which was published by Luzzatto in 1838, in the above-named Essays, was formerly the property of the celebrated antiquarian Guiseppe Almanzi, of Padua, and is now in the British Museum (Add. 27200-201). Dr. William Wright has given an account of it in the *Journal of Sacred Literature*, July, 1866, p. 356, &c. See also Fürst, *Geschichte des Karäerthums*, vol. i., pp. 114 and 179, Leipzig, 1862.

[40] Abraham b. Meier Ibn Ezra, was born in Toledo, 1088-9, and died 1176. He was a most distinguished mathematician, astronomer, philosopher, poet, physician, theologian, grammarian, and commentator. A sketch of his life, with a description of his works, will be found in Kitto's *Cyclopædia of Biblical Literature*, new ed. *s. v.* IBN EZRA. The above quotation is from his Hebrew Grammar, entitled *On the Purity of the Hebrew style*, (צחות) which he wrote at Mantua in 1145. It is as follows in the original כן סמהו חכמי טבריא· והם היקר· כי מהם היו אנשי המסורה ואנחנו מהם קבלנו כל הנקוד Comp. p. 7, *a*, editio Lippmann, Fürth, 1827.

the incarnation of the Deity.[41] As Raymond Martin was the great Rabbinical oracle of the Christians in the middle ages, and moreover as his opinion was confirmed by no less an authority than the celebrated Nicolas de Lyra,[42] it was regarded as paramount by all succeeding Catholic writers.

[41] This remarkable Spanish Dominican was born about 1220, and died about 1287. He was greatly aided in his Hebrew and Chaldee studies by Pablo Christiani, a celebrated converted Jew, who was also a Dominican, and who held at Barcelona the famous discussion with the learned Nachmanides, about the questions at issue between Judaism and Christianity (July 20, 24, 1263), an account of which is given in Kitto's *Cyclopædia of Biblical Literature*, new ed. *s. v.* NACHMANIDES. Raymond Martin, himself, sat with Pablo Christiani, Arnold de Singarra, and Peter de Janua, in the commission appointed by the Bull of Clement iv. (1264), to examine the charges which Pablo Christiani brought against the Talmud, that it blasphemes Christ and the Virgin Mary. The work which has immortalised Raymond Martin's name is entitled *the Dagger of Faith* (FUGIO FIDEI). He completed it in 1278. He quotes in it extracts from the Talmud, Rashi, Ibn Ezra, Maimonides, Kimchi, and the writings of other Jews, with the greatest ease; showing from them that Jesus is not only foretold in the Hebrew Scriptures as the Messiah, but also in the Rabbinical writings. From its immense erudition, this work became the grand storehouse from which Christians in the middle ages and in modern days derived their Jewish learning, and weapons against the Jews. It was first edited with very elaborate annotations by Jos. de Voisin, Paris, 1651, and then again, with an introduction and the treatise by Hermann, a converted Jew, by Joh. B. Carpzow, Leipzig, 1687. It is to the second edition that our references are made. The passage in question bearing on the vowel-points contains properly his criticism on Hos. ix. 12, and is as follows:—
"Cæterum sciendum, quod nec Moyses punctavit legem, unde Judæi non habent eam cum punctis, *i. e.* cum vocalibus scriptam in rotulis suis; nec aliquis ex prophetis punctavit librum suum; sed duo Judæi, quorum unus dictus est *Nepthali*, alter vero *Ben Ascher*, totum vetus Testamentum punctasse leguntur; quæ quidem puncta cum quibusdam virgulis sunt loco vocalium apud eos: cumquæ venissent ad locum istum, et secundum orthographiam debuissent punctare בְּשׂוּרִי *incarnatione mea*, punctaverunt בְּסוּרִי *in recessu meo*, ut opus incarnationis removerent a Deo." (*Pars* iii., *Dist.* iii. cap. xxi., p. 895.)

[42] Nicolas de Lyra was born of Jewish parents about 1270, at Lyre, a small town in the diocese of Eurecca, whence he obtained his name *Lyra*. Having embraced Christianity when young, he entered the Church in 1291, and became such an accomplished scholar and lecturer on the Bible that he was styled *the most distinguished doctor*. He died at Paris, October 23, 1340. The work which has immortalised his name is a commentary on the Bible, entitled "*Postillæ perpetuæ in universa Biblia*," in which he advanced the most enlightened views to such an extent that he is justly regarded as the forerunner of the Reformation. The extent to which Luther is indebted to him for his sentiments may be gathered from the couplet of the Reformer's enemies,

Si Lyra non lyrasset,
Lutherus non saltasset.
If Lyra had not harped profanation,
Luther would never have danced the Reformation.

As to the passage bearing on the origin of the vowel-points, after quoting with approval Raymond Martin on Hos. ix. 12 (see the preceding note), he remarks, "Puncta

To invest it with an air of originality, Jacob Perez de Valencia gives the following amusing account of the origin of the vowel-points—" After the conversion of Constantine the Great, the Rabbins perceived that great multitudes of Gentiles embraced Christianity with the greatest devotion all over the globe; that the Church prospered very favourably; and that also of the Jews an immense number became convinced of the truth by experience and miracles, whereby their gains and revenues were lessened. Roused by this wickedness, they assembled in great multitudes at the Babylon of Egypt, which is called Cairo, where they, with as much secresy as possible, falsified and corrupted the Scriptures, and concocted about five or seven points to serve as vowels, these points having been invented by Ravina and Ravashe, two of their doctors. The same Rabbins also concocted the Talmud.[43] Hence De Valencia maintains "that no faith is to be placed in the Holy Scriptures, as the Jews now interpret and punctuate them."[44]

Jewish commentators and grammarians, however, as a rule, when they had not to dispute with the Karaites for rejecting the traditions of the Fathers, maintained that the vowel-points were either given to Adam in Paradise, or communicated to Moses on Sinai, or were fixed by Ezra and the Great Synagogue. This view was deemed all the more

non sunt de substantia littere, nec a principio scripturere fuerunt, unde et rotuli qui in synagogis eorum legentur sunt sine punctis, sed permagnam tempus postea inventa sunt hujus modi punctu ad facilius legundum." *Comment. on Hos.* ix. 12. For a sketch of his life and writings, see Kitto, *Cyclop. of Bib. Lit.*, new ed., *s. v.* LYRA.

[43] Jacob Perez de Valencia, commonly called Bishop of Christopolitanus, was born about 1420, at Valencia, whence he derived his name. He became a hermit of the order of Augustin, and died in 1491. He was a voluminous writer, and the above extract which is from his commentary on the Psalms, is as follows in the original. "Post conversionem Constantini M. videntes Rabbinos omnes gentiles cum tanta devotione ad fidem Christi converti per totum orbem, et Ecclesiam tanto favore prosperari et etiam quod infinita multitudo Judæorum videntes manifestam veritatem per experientiam et miracula, pariter convertebantur, et sic deficiebant quaestus, et reditus, et tributa Rabbinorum, hac iniquitate comm tos magna multitudine congregatos fuisse apud Babyloniam Ægypti, quae dicitur Cayre: ibique quanto magis caute potuerunt, conatos fuisse falsifiâcre et pervertere Scripturas a vero sensu e significatione. Inde confinxisse supra 5, vel. 7, puncta loco vocalium. Quorum punctorum inventores fuisse Ravina Ravasse, duos Doctores eorum. Addit, istos Rabbinos confinxisse libros Talmud." *Prolog. in Psalmos Tract. vi.*, Comp. Hody *De Bibliorum Textibus Originalibus*, lib. iii., p. ii., p. 442. Oxford, 1705.

[44] "Ideo nulla fides adhibenda est scripturæ s.; sicut hodie habent (Judæi) sic interpretatam et punctuatam." *Ibid.* Tract. ii.. fol. xxiii.

orthodox, since the famous *Sohar*,[45] the sacred code of the Kabbalists, which was believed to be a revelation from God, communicated through R. Simon b. Jochai (*circa* A.D. 70–110), declared that "the letters are the body and the vowel-points the soul, they move with the motion and stand still with the resting of the vowel-points, just as an army moves after its sovereign"[46] (*Sohar* i., 15, *b.*); that "the vowel-points proceeded from the same Holy Spirit which indited the sacred Scriptures, and that far be the thought to say that the scribes made the points, since even if all the prophets had been as great as Moses, who received the law direct from Sinai, they could not have had the authority to alter the smallest point in a single letter, though it be the most insignificant in the whole Bible"[47] (*Sohar on the Song of Solomon*, 57 *b*, ed. Amsterdam, 1701). As the Kabbalah was believed to be a genuine revelation from God, its opinion about the antiquity and divinity of the vowel-points was adopted as final. Great therefore was the consternation which the appearance of the *Massoreth Ha-Massoreth* created. For the chief teacher of the age to deny the divine origin and the antiquity of the vowel-points, and more especially to defend his heterodoxy by unassailable arguments, was a most unpardonable sin.

As Levita's arguments became known to the Christian world, through Münster's Latin translation of the Introductions, as well as through Pellican's unpublished version of the entire Book, within twelve months after the publication of the original work, divided Christendom, though differing on almost all other points, at once agreed to welcome the great grammarian's results, from diametrically opposite motives. The unwary Protestant leaders who were already prepossessed with the notion of the late origin of the vowel-points, from the assertions of Raymond Martin, Nicolas de Lyra, Jacob Perez de Valencia, John Pico della Mirandola, and Reuchlin, rejoiced that their predilections were now confirmed by arguments. Hence Luther, Calvin, Zwingle,

---

[45] For an analysis of the *Sohar*, see Ginsburg, *The Kabbalah*, &c., p. 78, &c. Longmans, 1865.

[46] והכמשכילים יזהירו כנונא דתנועי (נ"ע דטעמי) דמנגני ובננוני דילהון אזלין אבתרייהו אתון ונקודי ומתנענען אבתרייהו כדילין בתר מלכיהון גופא אתון ורוחי נקודי כלהו נטלי במטלנון בתר תנועי (ונ"ע טעמי) וקיימי בקיומייהו כד ננונא דטעמי נטיל דאשתי אתון ונקודי אבתרייהו כד אידו פסיק אינון לא נטלין וקיימי בקיומייהו : וזהר חלק א' דף ט"ו ב'.

[47] נקודין אינון נטקין מרחא דמודחא לקיימא אתון על תיקונייהו ובנקודה חדא אשתני תיבה ואעבר להדיא תיבה מקיומא כנונא אחרא : בוצינא דקרדינות' כד במא ההוא אוריא דכיא במורחא בטש ולא בטש מטא לנביה דההוא מודחא ואסתליק מניה כימא ולא מטא כדן ההוא בטישו נטיק לנביה אתון כנו מודחא דאתון אתנקדו אם תאמר נקודי תקן טופרים הוא חס ושלום דאסלו כל נביאי דעלמא יהון כמשה דקביל אורייתא מטוורא דסיני לית לון רשו להדתא אסילו חדא נקודא וציוא באת חד אסילו את זעירא דאורייתא : וזהר שיר השירים דף נ'ז ב'.

Mercer,[48] &c., boldly disclaimed the antiquity, divine origin, and authority of the points. Their conviction undoubtedly was, that by liberating themselves from the traditional vowel-point of the Synagogue, after having discarded the traditions of the Church of Rome, they could more easily and independently prosecute their Biblical studies without any trammels whatsoever. Besides having rejected the traditions of the Fathers, the Reformers could not, without exposing themselves to the charge of inconsistency from their antagonists, adhere to the traditions of the Rabbins.

To the Church of Rome, again, which was embittered by the cry of the newly risen protestant leaders, that the Bible, and the Bible alone, without gloss and without tradition, is the rule of faith and practice, Levita's work was like a God-send from another point of view. She eagerly laid hold of the admission made by this great teacher of the age, that the vowel-signs are an uninspired invention of the Jews, made centuries after Christ, in order to confute thereby the claims of her opponents. From the novelty of the points she deduced,

---

[48] Dr. Kalisch (*Hebrew Grammar*, Part ii., p. 65, note *d*. Longman, 1863,) is surely incorrect in his statement, that "the Reformers, as Luther and Calvin, were of opinion that the vowel-points were at least fixed by Ezra, or the Great Synagogue." Nothing can be more explicit than Luther's remark on Gen. xlvii. 31 : "At the time of St. Jerome, the points did not as yet exist, and the whole Bible was read without them. I submit that it is the modern Hebrews who affixed them, in order to give a proper sense and meaning to the Hebrew language. However, since they are not friends but enemies of Holy Writ, I often utter words which strongly oppose these points." In his Comment. on Is. ix. 6, he says " that most dangerous people, the Jews, falsify the words of the prophets with the points and distinctions; and their points, which are nothing but a modern invention, most assuredly are not to be preferred to the simple, correct, and grammatical sense." And again, in his Treatise entitled Schem Hamphoras (1543), he says, mit biefer Weife fönnte man ber Jüben Verftanb in ber Bibel fein fchwächen, unb ift bas Vortheil ba, baß Mofe unb bie Propheten nicht haben mit Puncten gefchrieben; welches ein neu Menfchenfünblein, nach ihrer Zeit aufbracht; barum nicht Noth ift biefelben fo fteif zu halten, als bie Jüben gerne wolten, fonberlich wo fie bem neuen Teftament zuwiber gebraucht werben. Eben fo foll man auch mit ber æquivocatio unb distinctio thun, wo fie wiber bas neue Teftament bienen. Die Jüben haben boch Luft, alle ihr Ding zweifelhaftig unb nichts gewiffes zu machen.

Equally explicit is the remark of Calvin, in his commentary on Zechariah xi. 7. " Scio, quanta industria veteres scribæ puncta excogitarint, cum jam linguæ non esset tam communis et familiaris usus : qui ergo puncta negligunt, vel prorsus rejiciunt, certe carent omni judicio et ratione : sed tamen habendus est aliquis delectus. Si enim legamus hic, proditores, nullus est sensus : si legamus, funiculos, nulla littera mutatur; interea mutantur duo puncta. Cum ergo id necessario postulet res ipsa, miror cur interpretes ita serviliter passi fuerint se regi, ut non spectarent Prophetæ sensum."

i. That the Bible could only be read in ancient days by the few authorised spiritual teachers, and, ii., That the Scriptures without these points cannot possibly be understood, apart from the traditional interpretation transmitted by the Church of Rome. This opinion soon found its way into England, and when the controversy between the Roman Catholics and Protestants had fairly began, we find Dr. Thomas Harding (1512–1572), who was Professor of Hebrew at Oxford, in the reign of Henry VIII., a staunch Protestant in the reign of Edward VI., who became a zealous papist at the accession of Queen Mary to the throne, and the celebrated antagonist of Bishop Jewel, arguing as follows : — " Among the people of Israel, the seventy elders only could read and understand the mysteries of the holy books, that we call the Bible. For, whereas the letters of the Hebrew tongue have no vocals, they only had the skill to read the Scripture by the consonants ; and thereby the vulgar people were kept from reading of it, by special providence of God, as it is thought, that precious stones should not be cast before swine, that is to say, such as be not called thereto, as being, for their unreverend curiosity and impure life, unworthy."[49]

Similar was the language which the Romanists used on the Continent against the Protestants, who appealed to the Scriptures in matters affecting their faith and practice. John Morinus (1591–1659), the distinguished Orientalist, who renounced Protestantism, and entered the congregation of the Oratory in 1618, solemnly declares, in his learned " *Biblical Exercitations on the Hebrew and Greek Texts*," that " the reason why God ordained the Scriptures to be written in this ambiguous manner (*i. e.* without points), is because it was His will that every man should be subject to the *Judgment of the Church*, and not interpret the Bible in his own way. For seeing that the reading of the Bible is so difficult, and so liable to various ambiguities, from the very nature of the thing, it is plain that it is not the will of God that every one should rashly and irreverently take upon himself to explain it ; nor to suffer the common people to expound it at their pleasure ; but that in those things, as in other matters respecting religion, it is His will that the people should depend upon the priests."[50]

[49] The works of John Jewel, Bishop of Salisbury, vol. ii. p. 678. The Parker Society edition.

[50] Comp. Morinus, Exercitationes Biblicæ de Hebraici Græcique textus Sinceritate. Exercitat. iv. cap. ii., s. 8, p. 198. &c. Paris, 1633.

Alarmed at the use made by Catholic controversialists of the avowal that the points are a late human invention, and bitterly smarting under the arguments deduced therefrom, the defenders of Protestantism commenced beating a retreat. Forgetting that the very originators and leaders of the Reformation, partly from a desire to throw off every thing traditional, and partly from undisguised hatred of the Jews, had decried the vowel-points as lustily as the Catholics, Protestant champions changed their tactics, and began to declare that the points were put to the text by the Prophets themselves, and that to say otherwise is nothing more nor less than *heathenism* and popery. Thus, the charge of Gregory Martin (*circa* 1584–1582), in his work, entitled "*A Discovery of the Manifold Corruptions of the Holy Scriptures by the Heretics*" (1582), that Protestants in their versions follow the Hebrew vowels, which are not only a late invention of, but have been wilfully corrupted by, the Jews, was rebutted by the celebrated Fulke, the great champion of Protestantism, with the declaration, that, "seeing our Saviour hath promised that never a prick [= a vowel-point] of the law shall perish, we may understand the same also of the Prophets, who have not received the vowels of the later Jews; but even of the Prophets themselves, however, that heathenish opinion pleaseth you and other papists."[51] Among those who beat a retreat, are also to be found the very eccentric but very distinguished Hebraist, Hugh Broughton (1549–1626), who likewise deduced the antiquity and authority of the points from Matt. v. 18;[52] and the celebrated John Piscator (1546–1626), who remarks, in his Commentary on the passage in question, that "it appears from this that the Holy Bible in the time of Christ had the points, and that the punctuation was approved by our Saviour."

Both Catholics and Protestants, however, chiefly relied upon abusing each other, and upon their common hatred of the Jews, to make good their assertions. To examine Levita's arguments, to test his appeal to the Talmud and other Jewish writings of antiquity, and to corroborate or refute his statements—for this there was not

[51] A defence of the sincere and true translations of the Holy Scriptures into the English tongue, against the manifold cavils, frivolous quarrels, and impudent slanders of Gregory Martin, one of the readers of Popish divinity, in the traitorous seminary of Rheims, by William Fulke, D.D. (1583). Parker Society edition, p. 578, with p. 55.

[52] Broughton's opinion on the vowel-points is to be found in his Commentary on Daniel, chap. ix. 26, published under the title Daniel: his Chaldee visions and his Hebrew; both translated after the original and expounded, &c. London, 1597.

sufficient Talmudical learning and critical tact, either in the Church of Rome or among Protestants. Their Oriental studies were chiefly intended to fathom the mysteries of the Kabbalah and to convert the Jews. The first attempt to meet Levita's book with arguments, derived from ancient Jewish documents, as far as we know, was made by the learned Azzariah de Rossi,[58] in 1574-5, nearly forty years after the appearance of the *Massoreth Ha-Massoreth*. In his celebrated work entitled *The Light of the Eyes* (מאור עינים), De Rossi devotes the fifty-ninth chapter of Part iii. to an examination of the arguments advanced by Levita against the antiquity of the points, and maintains therein that—i. The existence of the vowel-points seems to be indicated in the Talmud *(Nedarim*, 87, 6; the corresponding passage in the *Jerusalem Gemara* and the *Midrash Bereshith Rabba*, cap. xxxvi.) ii. The *Bahir* and *Sohar*, which according to De Rossi were respectively compiled by R. Nechunja b. Cahana and R. Simon b. Jochai, before ever the Mishna was edited, specify the vowel-points by name, and describe them as having a divine origin. iii. The analogy of other languages, and especially the Eastern and cognate tongues, such as the Syriac, Chaldee, Arabic, and Persian, all of which have vowel-signs, shows beyond doubt that the Hebrew too had points from the remotest antiquity. iv. The nature and genius of the Hebrew language absolutely pre-supposes the permanent existence of points, since, in the case of certain expressions, it cannot be told, without these signs, whether they are nouns, verbs, or particles. Thus, for example; without points it is impossible to say what the word שלמה is; whether it is שְׁלֹמֹה *Solomon*, שַׁלְמָה *retribution*, שְׁלֵמָה *whole*, or שָׁלְמָה *wherefore*. v. The command (Deut. xxvii. 8) to write *very plain and intelligibly* (בָּאֵר הֵיטֵב) unquestionably premises that, under certain circumstances, though not generally, the Law was written with vowel-signs, else it would not have been "very plain and intelligible;" and, vi. He appeals to St. Jerome's

---

[58] De Rossi, also called among the Jews *Azzariah Min Ha-Adomim*, was born at Mantua in 1513, and died in 1577. He was the first and most distinguished Biblical critic among the Jews of the sixteenth century; and his celebrated work, entitled *the Light of the Eyes* (מאור עינים), which consists of three parts, may almost be designated a Cyclopædia of Biblical Literature. It was first printed at Mantua 1574-5, in square characters; a second edition of it was published at Vienna, 1829, in Rabbinical characters. The chapter treating on the vowel-points is p. 178 *b*—181 *a*, ed. Mantua. and, p. 286 *b*—292 *a*, ed. Vienna. For a sketch of De Rossi's life, and an analysis of his works, see Kitto's *Cyclopædia of Biblical Literature*, new ed., *s. v.* Rossi.

statement in his epistle to Evagrius, where, in speaking of Enon near Salim, he remarks "it matters not whether it be called *Salem* or *Salim*, since the Hebrews very seldom use the vowel letters in the middle: and the same words are pronounced with different sounds and accents, according to the pleasure of readers and the variety of country;"[54] whence De Rossi deduces that *perraro* implies their existence and occasional use.

As to the origin and development of the vowels, he submits that their force and virtue were invented by, or communicated to, Adam, in Paradise; transmitted to and by Moses; that they had been partially forgotten, and their pronunciation vitiated during the Babylonian captivity; that they had been restored by Ezra, but that they had been forgotten again in the wars and struggles during, and after, the destruction of the Second Temple; and that the Massorites, after the close of the Talmud, revised the system, and permanently fixed the pronunciation by the contrivance of the present signs. This accounts for the fact that the present vowel-points are not mentioned in the Talmud. The reason why Moses did not punctuate the copy of the Law, which he wrote, is that its import should not be understood without oral tradition. Besides, as the Law has seventy different meanings, the writing of it, without points, greatly aids to obtain these various interpretations; whereas the affixing of the vowel-signs would preclude all permutations and transpositions, and greatly restrict the sense, by fixing the pronunciation. This is an epitome of the arguments used by De Rossi against Levita.

Being thus supplied with weapons from the Sohar and the Talmud, the hard-pressed Protestants, who were smarting from the onslaughts of the Catholics, and had beaten a retreat, now opened a new campaign. Under the leadership of Buxtorf, the father, they began defending, with a display of Rabbinical bayonets, the antiquity and divinity of the vowel-signs which they had formerly abandoned. Undaunted by the fact that the Catholics had been the undisputed masters of the field for three centuries, and that they had been strengthened in their position by the leaders of the Reformation, yet, to oust their common enemy, the Jews, the Protestant champion,

---

[54] The passage in question is as follows in the original, "Nec refert, utrum *Salem* [שלם], an *Salim* [שלים] nominetur; cum vocalibus in medio litteris perraro utantur Hebræi; et pro voluntate lectorum, atque varietate regionum, eadem verba diversis sonis atque accentibus proferantur." *Ad Evagrium Epist.* cxxvi., Opp. vol. i., p. 1062, ed. Paris.

Buxtorf, made his first appearance on the field in 1620. As the Christian opponents of the vowel-points, whether Catholics or their allies the Protestants, used no arguments, but contented themselves with mere assertions, and as, moreover, Levita was the first who defended his position with appeals to ancient documents, Buxtorf's attack was entirely directed against the renowned teacher of Hebrew, who was the leader of the opinions on this point of the allied Catholic and Protestant armies.

The arguments which were to discomfit Levita, Buxtorf published in his *Commentary on the Massorah*.[55] The ninth chapter of this work, which contains the defence of the antiquity and divine authority of the points against Levita, is chiefly made up of De Rossi's arguments and quotations from Jewish writings, whilst the rest of the book, which is an explanation of the Massorah, is, to a great extent, an elaboration of Levita's *Massoreth Ha-Massoreth*, the very treatise which had caused this controversy. Feeble as the arguments are, they appeared, nevertheless, very plausible and very learned; so that those who earnestly wished the points to be of divine origin at once ranged themselves under the leadership of the justly-renowned Buxtorf.

But Buxtorf was not destined to carry every thing before him in this first battle against Levita. His alliance with the learned De Rossi only produced a counter alliance and a masterly defence, under the leadership of Lewis Cappellus, who elaborated, expanded, and supplemented Levita's arguments against the points with far greater skill than that displayed by Buxtorf in his elaboration of De Rossi's arguments for the points. The treatise thus produced Cappellus sent in MS. to be examined by his opponent Buxtorf, who returned it with the request that it might not be printed. He then sent it to Erpenius, Professor of Oriental languages at Leyden, who was so convinced by its arguments and learning that, with the sanction of the author, he printed it at Leyden, under the title, "*The Mystery of the Points Unveiled.*"[56]

Its immense erudition, conclusive reasoning, and overpowering arguments soon convinced the most learned Biblical scholars that

---

[55] Tiberias sive Commentarius Masorethicus. Basle, 1620.

[56] The *Arcanum punctationis revelatum* was first published anonymously at Leyden, 1624, 4to. It was afterwards republished, with the *Vindiciæ Arcani punctationis* and Cappellus' other works, by his son; Amsterdam, 1689, fol. It is to this edition of the collected works that our references are made.

the vowel-points were centuries later than the Christian era; and Protestants, instead of combating the Roman Catholics on this point, were now fairly divided into two hostile camps, under the respective leadership of Cappellus and Buxtorf. The followers of Buxtorf were for a considerable time doomed to almost fatal inaction. For though Cappellus' work, as we have seen, appeared in 1624, and though Buxtorf had carefully perused it in MS. before this date, yet he made no reply to it for several years, and died (Sept. 13, 1629) without answering it. It was during this time of anxious suspense that Father Morinus published his merciless attack on the vowel-points, already alluded to (*vide supra*, p. 50), in which he compared the Scriptures to a mere nose of wax, to be turned any way, to prove thereby the necessity of one infallible interpretation.

At last, however, after a silence of four and twenty years, Buxtorf, the son, who succeeded his father in the Hebrew chair at Basle, published, in 1648, a reply to Cappellus' work, entitled, "*A Treatise on the Origin, Antiquity, and Authority of the Vowel Points and Accents in the Hebrew Scriptures of the Old Testament, against Lewis Cappellus' Mystery of the Points Unveiled;*" thus assuming the leadership of the vowelist party, whom death had deprived of their great champion. But, though the work occupies upwards of 450 small quarto pages, it contains very little more than an expansion of the arguments used by Buxtorf senior, in his *Tiberius*, with an increased number of quotations from Jewish writings. It was not to be expected that Cappellus would be silenced by this reply, and he at once wrote a rejoinder to it, entitled, "*A Vindication of the Mystery of the Vowels Unveiled;*" but he died (June 18, 1658) before the publication of it, and his son, Jacques Cappellus, to whom the MS. was left, did not publish it till 1689, five and twenty years after the death of Buxtorf junior.

An important point is to be noticed in this controversy, in which Cappellus entirely deviates from the opinion of his master, Elias Levita. Levita, though maintaining the novelty of the vowel-points, firmly believed that the very same pronunciation and sounds, which are now denoted by the vowels and accents, were perfectly known and used by the Jews from the remotest antiquity, long before these arbitrary signs were invented, and that they represent the true and genuine reading as it came from the inspired writers of the respective books; and, consequently, the reading which these points have fixed is as much of divine authority as the letters, the difference between them being, that the letters were written, whilst the points were transmitted by oral tradition. At first Cappellus seems also to have endorsed this view of Levita in a somewhat modified form. Thus he distinctly declares that, "when I say that the points were invented and added to the consonants by the Massorites of Tiberias, I do not mean, as I have stated before, that the reading of the sacred text was invented by them out of their own brain, and that they fixed, according to their own will and fancy, what these points denote and express; but what I mean is, that they express by these marks of their own invention the reading of the sacred text which obtained everywhere among the Jews, which they themselves had been taught by their masters in the scholastic institutions, which they had received by oral tradition from the Fathers, and which reading the Jews believed to be the same ancient and authentic reading of Moses and the prophets. Since, therefore, these Tiberian masters did nothing more than express, with all possible accuracy, the reading which they had been taught, which they had received from their ancestors, by tradition from the Fathers, and which all the Jews believed to be the very ancient and authentic reading of Moses and the prophets, by signs of vowels and accents of their own invention, there is no reason why this reading should not be accepted by all the Jews."[57]

Later on, however, Cappellus changed his mind, or, perhaps, more boldly avowed, what he had hitherto kept back, that, with the changing of the ancient letters in which the Hebrew was originally written, and in adding the points, the *matres lectiones* were eliminated and the Hebrew text was greatly corrupted. His assault on the inte-

---

[57] "Cum dico a Masorethis Tiberiensibus excogitata esse puncta et consonis addita, non hoc volo, uti jam monui, ab iis excogitatam, atque de proprio cerebro pro eorum libitu et arbitrio confictam esse lectionem sacri textus, quam punctis illis signarunt, atque expresserunt; sed hoc duntaxat volo, expressam esse ab iis, notulis a se excogitatis, lectionem sacri textus, quae tum ubique inter Judæos obtinebat, quamque ipsi edocti fuerant a suis magistris scholastica institutione, atque orali, et πατροπαραδότῳ traditione ab iis acceperant, quam lectionem credebant Judæi antiquæ Mosaicæ et Propheticæ authenticæ conformem esse. Cum itaque magistri illi Tiberienses nihil aliud praestiterint, quam ut lectionem quam edocti erant, et a majoribus suis traditione πατροπαραδότῳ acceperant, quamque omnes Judæi propterea eandem esse cum antiqua Mosaica et authentica Prophetica existimabant, vocalium et accentuum figuris a se excogitatis exprimerent quam poterant accuratissime, nihil est quod quis putet, non potuisse illam lectionem omnibus Judæis probari." *Arcanum punctationis revelatum*, lib. ii., cap. xvii. 5 & 6, Opp. p. 775, ed. Amsterdam, 1689.

grity of the Massoretic text he published at Paris, 1650, under the title of *Critica Sacra*. To this work Buxtorf junior replied within three years of its publication, in a volume containing no less than 1040 quarto pages.[58] But though both these works repeatedly touch the question about the origin of the vowel-points, and though the controversy about the integrity of the text has arisen from, and is in some measure connected with, the dispute about the points, yet the two controversies are totally distinct, and ought not to have been confounded with each other.

The "*Mystery of the Points Unveiled*" created quite as great a revolution among scholars in the seventeenth century as the *Massoreth Ha-Massoreth*, of which it was an exposition. Its author's fame as a critic soon spread over Europe, and his work, as well as the rejoinder to it by Buxtorf junior, divided Protestant Christendom everywhere into two hostile camps — vowelists and anti-vowelists. The controversy was soon transplanted into England, where Cappellus was known, having studied two years at Oxford, and where Biblical and Talmudical studies were at that time zealously prosecuted, under the guidance of Brian Walton, and Lightfoot. In the Prolegomena to the London Polyglott, Levita's original opinion is more strictly followed than that of Cappellus. It is there maintained that the vowel-points were invented by the Massorites about A.D. 500; that these points were not arbitrary inventions of the Massorites, but express the traditional and true reading of the text and the sense of the Holy Ghost; that it is not lawful for any one to reject the Massoretic reading at pleasure; that all Christians are tied to it, unless some error or better reading can be clearly proved; and that the controversy, therefore, "is only about the present points, in regard of their forms, not of their force and signification."[59]

Whilst Levita and Cappellus were represented in England by Walton, De Rossi and Buxtorf had their chief representative here in Lightfoot. This learned Hebraist thought that his dicta would be quite sufficient to silence his opponents, and therefore deigned no more than to deliver himself as follows, after the masterly recapitulation of the arguments against the antiquity of the vowel-points given

[58] Anticritica, seu vindiciæ veritatis Hebraicæ; adversus Ludovici Cappelli Criticam quam vocat sacram. l'asle, 1653.

[59] Comp. Prolegom. iii., sect. 38 — 56, with Walton's *Considerator Considered*, ed. Todd, p. 210, &c. London, 1821.

in Walton's Prolegomena: "There are some who believe the Holy Bible was pointed by wise men of Tiberias. I do not wonder at the impudence of the Jews who invented the story, but I wonder at the credulity of Christians who applaud it. Recollect, I beseech you, the names of the Rabbins of Tiberias, from the first situation of the University there to the time that it expired; and what at length do you find, but a kind of men mad with Pharisaism, bewitching with traditions and bewitched, blind, guileful, doting, they must pardon me if I say, magical and monstrous! Men, how unfit, how unable, how foolish, for the undertaking so divine a work! Read over the Jerusalem Talmud, and see there how R. Judah, R. Chaninah, R. Judan, R. Hoshaia, R. Chija Rabba, R. Chija bar Ba, R. Jochanan, R. Jonathan, and the rest of the grand doctors among the Rabbins of Tiberias, behave themselves, how earnestly they do nothing, how childishly they handle serious disputes! And if you can believe the Bible was pointed in such a school, believe also all that the Talmudists wrote. The pointing of the Bible savours of the work of the Holy Spirit, not the work of lost, blinded, besotted men."[60]

It was this dogmatic and abusive assertion, of one who was deemed the highest authority in matters of Hebrew learning in England, as well as the conviction that those who defend the novelty of the points "not only make doubtful the authority of the Scriptures, but wholly pluck it up by the roots," which stimulated the celebrated Dr. Owen to issue his attack on Walton's Polyglott and the anti-vowelists.[61] With the exception of the endorsement and elaboration of Lightfoot's diatribe, Dr. Owen's work in defence of the vowel-points is simply made up of the De Rossi-Buxtorf arguments greatly diluted. The high esteem, however, in which Dr. Owen was held made it necessary that his book,—in which he declared that he "had rather that this work of the *Biblia Polyglotta*, and all works of the kind, were out of the world, than that this one opinion should be received with the consequences that unavoidably attend it,"—should not be left unnoticed. Within twelve months therefore of the appear-

[60] A Chorographical Century, searching out some more memorable places of the Holy Land of Israel, chiefly by the light of the Talmud. Chap. lxxxi., works, vol. ii., p. 73, &c., ed. 1684.

[61] Of the Integrity and Purity of the Hebrew and Greek Text of the Scriptures; with considerations on the Prolegomena and Appendix to the late Biblia Polyglotta. London, 1659, vol. iv., p. 447, &c., of his collected works, London, 1823, to which the references are made.

ance of the attack, Walton published a reply, which, though greatly defaced by bitter invective and inexcusable abuse, contains additional and valuable contributions to the literature of this controversy.[62]

Although the antiquity of the vowel-points still found advocates in Joseph Cooper,[63] Samuel Clark,[64] Whitfield,[65] and Dr. Gill,[66] who published learned dissertations in defence of Dr. Owen and against Bishop Walton; yet it must be admitted that the *Prolegomena* and "The Considerator Considered" decided the battle in England in favour of the anti-vowelists. Henceforth all Biblical critics, with very few exceptions, regarded the points as modern, useless, and of no authority, though Walton himself, as we have seen, maintained that they, as a rule, represented the ancient and genuine reading. The utter rejection of the points, and the espousal of Cappellus' notions propounded in his *Critica Sacra*, produced lamentable effects in England as far as the criticism of the Old Testament was concerned, from which we are only now recovering. Two different schools of interpreters were erected here upon the ruins of the antiquity of the vowel-points.

The characteristic dogmas of the first school are, that "the Massoretic punctuation is an interpretation of the text made by the Jews, probably not earlier than the eighth century, and that, accordingly, our public translations in modern tongues, for the use of the Church among Protestants, and so likewise the modern Latin translations, are, for the most part, close copies of the Hebrew pointed text, and are in reality only versions at second hand, translations of the Jews' interpretation of the Old Testament;"[67] that the Hebrew text "is

[62] The Considerator Considered, &c. London, 1659. Todd has reprinted this rare book in the second volume of his Memoirs of the life and writings of Bishop Walton. London, 1821.

[63] His Dissertation is entitled Domus Mosaicæ Clavis, sive Legis Septimentum; in quo punctorum Hebraicorum adstruitur antiquitas; eaque omnia, cum accentualia tum vocalia ipsis, literis fuisse coæva, argumentis, undiquie petitis demonstratur. Quæ vero in contrarum ab Elia Levita primipilo, Ludovico Cappello, D. Doctore Waltono, &c., adducuntur, multa cum fidelitate examini subjiciuntur et diluntur, &c. London, 1673.

[64] An Exercitation concerning the original of the chapters and verses in the Bible; wherein the divine authority of the points in the Hebrew text is clearly proved by new and intrinsic arguments. London, 1698.

[65] A Dissertation on the Hebrew vowel-points, showing that they are an original and essential part of the Language. Liverpool, 1748.

[66] A Dissertation concerning the antiquity of the Hebrew language, letters, vowel-points, and accents. London, 1767.

[67] Preliminary Dissertation to his translation of Isaiah, new ed., p. xxxviii. London, 1836.

considerably injured, and stands in need of frequent emendation." Hence the disciples of this school resorted to amend the text by the aid of the ancient versions, and had recourse to the most unwarrantable conjectures, thus unsettling the original text and impugning its integrity. The principal disciples of this school are Archbishop Secker, Drs. Durell, Judd, Lowth, Blayney, Newcome, Wintle, Horsley, Good, Boothroyd, and others.

The second school, which is less accomplished, but more lamentable, is the one known by the name Hutchinsonian, after its founder, John Hutchinson (1674–1737). Believing that "Holy Scripture has a language of its own, which does not consist of words, but of signs or figures taken from visible things; so that the world which we now see is a sort of commentary on the mind of God, and explains the world in which we live;" this peculiar philosopher, like his Kabbalistic prototypes, was obliged to discard the vowel-points, and everything else which determined the pronunciation of the words and fixed their meaning. Hutchinson endorsed and reproduced all the base calumnies brought together by Raymond Lully, Wagenseil, &c., against the Jews, whom he always styles *the apostates*, and maintains that the sacred text was designedly corrupted by these apostates through the insertion of the points and letters, which was "their last shift to change their evasions of the truth;" that thereby "they make the words different from what they were, or of another root, or of another signification, than the words would have been without pointing in that context."[68] To this wild school belonged the eminently orthodox and pious Romaine, Bishop Horne, the lexicographer Parkhurst, and others.

It was this unwarrantable liberty taken with the text, first started by Cappellus' *Critica Sacra*, and the resort to all sorts of conjectural

[68] The system and the plan of the work may be gathered from its lengthy title; "The Covenant in the Cherubim, so the Hebrew writings perfect. Alterations by Rabbies forged. Shewing the evidence for the Scriptures; that Christianity was exhibited to Adam, invisibles by visibles; past and to come by types; by Cherubim, Urim, Thumim, Sacrifice, Cloud, &c.; that the Jews and Gentiles understood them; that tradition was of the things typified. That though they understood the tradition even of the covenant before the world, they had perverted the intent of it. That the alterations and stories of the Jews, after they had lost their types and Hebrew, are not traditions, but studied evasions to expositions of inspired Christians, &c., and to support their apostacy. That the grammatical formation of the Hebrew, which is descriptive, so gives proper names, cannot admit vowel-pointing, nor Mr. Masclef's method. By J. H." Collected Works, vol. vi., p. 153. London, 1749.

emendations, in order to deduce from the Scriptures the peculiar and preconceived fancies of the different schools, which converted the controversy about the vowel-points into an article of faith in the Reformed Churches of Switzerland. In Switzerland, where the two Buxtorfs successively occupied the professorial chair of Oriental literature, and where their opinions, in matters of Hebrew and Talmudic lore, was regarded as paramount, the theologians enacted a law in 1678, that no person should be licensed to preach the gospel in their churches unless he publicly declared that he believes in the integrity of the Hebrew text and in the divinity of the vowel-points and accents.[69]

After a controversy raging vehemently for more than three centuries, and notwithstanding that the antiquity of the points had been raised to the sanctity of a dogma, modern research and criticism have confirmed the arguments urged by Levita against the antiquity of the present vowel-signs. It is now established beyond the shadow of a doubt, from the discovery of ancient MSS., that there were two systems of vocalisation contrived almost simultaneously, and that the system hitherto regarded by the vowelists as of divine origin is simply one of the two. Indeed the present system, around which the whole controversy clusters, and which has been canonised, is actually the later of the two in point of age.

The earlier, or first system, was developed by Acha or Achai of Irak (Babylon), about 550, from the few simple signs which represented the traditional pronunciation of the text in the East. The peculiarity of this system consists in having signs of a different shape to represent the vowels, and that these are almost uniformly placed *above* the letters. It is therefore designated *the Superlineary system* (מנוקד למעלה). From the fact that its contriver lived in Babylon, it is also called *the Babylon*, or *the Assyrian system*, (נקוד אשורי, נקוד הבבלי) and *the Eastern system*. It has been preserved in the following MSS., i. A MS. of the Pentateuch, embracing only fifteen fragments of Deuteronomy, with Targum Onkelos after each verse, the Massorah marginalis, and the Haphtaroth with the Massorah; the whole consists of seventy-seven leaves, and was most probably written in

---

[69] "Codicem Hebr. V. T. tum quoad consonas tum quoad vocalia sive puncta ipsa sive punctorum saltem potestatem θεόπνευστον esse." *Formula Consensus*, art. iv., comp. Keil's edition of Hävernick's *Allgemeine Einleitung in das Alte Testament*, vol. i., p. 315.

Persia. ii. An equally ancient MS. of the Haphtaroth, consisting of twelve fragments, and containing the Haphtaroth to Exod., Levit., and Numb., which are wanting in the preceding MS., as well as the Haphtaroth of New Year, the Day of Atonement, and the feasts of Tabernacles and Pentecost, the Targum, and the Massorah. iii. A MS. of the major and minor Prophets, consisting of two hundred and twenty-five parchment leaves, and written about A.D. 916.[70]

The later, or second system, is the one which has been for centuries commonly adopted both by Jews and Christians in the pointed editions of the Hebrew Bibles. It was contrived by Mocha, of Tiberias, about A.D. 570, to denote the traditional pronunciation of the text in the West. Hence it is called *the Tiberian system* (נקוד טברני), and *the Palestinian* or *Western system* (נקוד ארץ ישראל). It is far more complete and extensive, and exhibits more sharply the niceties of the traditional pronunciation and intonation of the text, than the Babylonian system, with which it competed.

As the Babylonian system, with all its imperfections, was the first promulgated, and moreover as it obtained prior to the separation of the Karaites from the Rabbinic Jews, it was staunchly followed by the Jews in Babylon, and more especially by the Karaites. The Rabbinic Jews, however, soon discarded the Babylonian system, when they found that the Tiberian or present system of vocalisation was more perfect, and represented more adequately the traditional pronunciation, whilst the Karaite Jews clung to the first or Babylonian system. It was not till the year 957, when the Jews of Palestine sent Missionaries to the Crimea to reclaim the Karaites to Rabbinism, and when these Missionaries succeeded in converting many of the distinguished families, that the said Missionaries, Ephraim, Elisha, and Chanuka, punctuated the Bible MSS. according to the Tiberian or present system, and induced the Karaites to substitute it for the one

---

[70] For a further account of this system, and of the MSS. which exhibit it, we must refer to Pinner, *Prospectus der der Odessaer Gesellschaft für Geschichte und Alterthümer gehörenden ältesten hebräischen und rabbinischen Manuscripten.* Odessa, 1845; Luzzatto's treatise in Pollak's Dissertations, entitled,, *Halichoth Kedem*, p. 23—231. Amsterdam, 1846; Ewald, *Jahrbücher der biblichen Wissenschaft*, vol. i., p. 160—172, Gottingen, 1849; Geiger, *Urschrift und Uebersetzungen der Bibel*, p. 167—170. Breslau, 1857; Fürst, *Geschichte des Karäerthums*, vol. i., pp. 19, &c., 134, &c. Leipzig, 1862; Kallisch, *Hebrew Grammar*, vol. ii., p. 63, &c. London, 1863; Pinsker, *Einleitung in das Babylonisch-Hebräische Punktationssystem*, Vienna, 1863; Fürst, in the *Zeitschrift der deutschen morgenländischen Gesellschaft*, vol. xviii., p. 314—323. Leipzig, 1864.

which was previously in vogue, and which has only survived in the most ancient MSS. This discovery of modern research, therefore, fully confirms Levita's arguments against the antiquity of the present vocalisation, and must for ever settle the long and vehement controversy.

Within twelve months of the appearance of the *Massoreth Ha-Massoreth*, which caused this protracted and vehement controversy, Levita published (1538) a treatise on the laws of the accents. The rapid succession of these two works is easily accounted for. The vowel-points and accents are most intimately connected with each other, and proceeded from the same authors. Both R. Acha, and R. Mocha, the compilers of the Babylonian and Tiberian systems of vocalisation, included the accents in their respective systems. Indeed the accents determine the sense of a passage quite as much as the vowel-points. If the points fix the pronunciation and meaning of words, the accents indicate the logical relation of each word to the whole sentence and the close of sentences. Hence those who contrived the vowel-signs, to denote the traditional pronunciation of the words, were also obliged to invent the accents, to represent the traditional construction of the sentences. This accounts for the frequent remark of the celebrated commentator Rashi, in his exposition of the Scriptures—"but for the accents on this verse, I could not have made out its meaning;" and the warning of the famous Ibn Ezra—"an interpretation which is not according to the accents is neither to be received nor listened to, for the author of the accents knew the import much better."

It is this importance of the accents which has invested them with a divine halo, and which has made the defenders of the antiquity and divinity of the vowel-points also maintain their antiquity and divinity. Consistently with his arguments against the points, Levita rejects the divine origin of the accents, maintaining that they proceed from the same Tiberian Massorites who contrived the system of vocalisation. As his arguments against the points are also directed against the accents, he refrains from repeating them, and simply refers the reader to the *Massoreth Ha-Massoreth*.

In harmony with its import, he denominated this treatise *The Book of Good Sense* (ספר טוב טעם), since the accent on each word is called in Hebrew טעם *reason, principle*, because it furnishes principles and rules to deduce the import of each verse. The whole treatise consists of eight sections, and discusses the following points. Section i. discusses the number and names of the accents, and their proper division into three classes, viz., 14 *Kings*, so called, because, like monarchs who restrain their subjects, these accents respectively stand between sentences, keeping them within proper bounds. ii. *Servants*, so called, because they act as servants of the monarch, bringing the sentence without pause to the resting place of the kings; and 5 who are neither kings nor servants, thus making 30 in all. Section ii. explains the names of the accents, their laws, the position of the serviles, &c. Section iii. explains how it is that half the number of royal accents follow each other, and the other half does not follow; that most of the regal accents are placed above the letters, whilst most of the servile accents are placed under the letters; as well as the reason why some serviles are above the letters. Section iv. explains the distentives, shewing the smaller kings, which cause a longer pause than the greater kings; that kings have servants, and how many, and which have no servants, and which servants only serve one or two or more kings. Section v. describes the form and names of all the thirty accents. Section vi. treats on the laws of those words which have the accents on the ultima and penultima. Section vii. discusses the laws of the *Metheg* and *Gaja*; and Section viii. the *Makkeph*.

This Treatise, which is a very valuable contribution to Biblical exegesis, was first published by his friend Bomberg, Venice, 1538. Levita appended to this edition a list of printers' mistakes which have crept into the *Massoreth Ha-Massoreth*, as well as into this book. Within twelve months of its appearance, Münster re-published it, with a Latin summary of its contents (Basle, 1539). It is generally bound up with the *Massoreth Ha-Massoreth*, as these two works were re-published in the same year. Münster's edition is not as correct as the *editio princeps*. Although it is acknowledged, by grammarians and expositors of the highest authority, that the accents are not only marks to indicate the tone-syllable, but to show the logical relation of each word to the whole sentence, thus serving as signs of interpretation, yet this branch of ancient exegesis has been greatly neglected. The grammars, while devoting ample space to the discussion of the vowel-points, rarely ever give more than a paragraph or two to the explanation of the laws of the accents, which are of equal importance to the interpretation of the Old Testament. Hence it is, that, whilst Levita's works on the other departments of Biblical literature and exegesis have been reprinted several times, and elaborated and superseded by succeeding researches, the treatise on the accents has never been published again since 1539, and the system of accentuation in the Old Testament is less understood by the generality of Hebrew students in the present day than it was in the days when Elias Levita's treatise first appeared.[71]

Levita's consummate mastery of Hebrew literature in all its different branches was only equalled by his indefatigable zeal and untiring labours to simplify and promote its study. Though he was now seventy years of age, his energies had not abated. No sooner had he finished the *Treatise on the Accents*, than he commenced a Lexicon, explaining those words in the Talmud, Midrashim, and other works in the Rabbinical literature, which were either entirely omitted in the standard Lexicons of R. Nathan b. Jechiel and R. David Kimchi, or had not been treated in all their sundry meanings. He was all the more induced to undertake this work by the rapid progress of his pupils in Biblical Hebrew, and through the great demand, especially on the part of Christians, for keys to the Kabbalistic and Rabbinical writings. In his entire absorption in this Lexicon, and another which we shall soon mention, he forgot the altered circumstances in which he was then placed, and it was not till he had nearly completed the work, after labouring three years over it, that he began to think of the difficulties of finding a publisher, as his friend and patron, "the great printer, D. Bomberg," he tells us, "had given up his printing-office some time since."

But at the very time when he was in this perplexity, and when

[71] The above remark does not imply that no superior Treatise has appeared since the publication of Levita's *Dissertation on the Accents*. The learned Heidenheim published an Essay, entitled *The Laws of the Accents*, (ספר משפטי הטעמים) Rödelheim, 1808; chiefly compiled from the ancients, the Massorites, Ben-Asher, Ibn Balaam, Chajug, &c., which is of superior excellence, and in which he corrects some of Levita's mistakes. But Heidenheim's Essay is very rare; being written in Hebrew, it has therefore little advanced the general knowledge of the accents. Separate Treatises have also been published by J. D. Michaelis, *Anfangs-Gründe der Hebräischen Accentuation*, with an Introduction by C. B. Michaelis, 2nd edition, Halle, 1753; Stern, עין הקורא *Lescauge*, illustrated with 900 examples, Frankfort on the Maine, 1840; and recently by A. B. Davidson, *Outlines of Hebrew Accentuation, Prose and Poetical*, London, 1861; in which the part treating on the prose accents is exceedingly defective, as Mr. Davidson could not avail himself of so able a guide in this department as he had in Baer's masterly Treatise on the Poetical Accents, entitled *Torath Emeth*. Mr. Davidson, moreover, whilst he mentions men who have not written separate Treatises on this subject, does not even allude to Levita's excellent *Dissertation on the Accents*.

K

his plan for sending the Lexicon to Bologna was defeated by the information that the Hebrew press had stopped there, Levita received a letter from Paul Fagius, inviting him to go to Germany, to undertake the supervision of the Hebrew press and the editorship of sundry Biblical works. To us, in whose country the remains of Fagius were ignominiously exhumed and burned, by the command of Mary, in 1556, and the ashes collected again, and honourably interred, by the order of Elizabeth, July 30, 1560, the connection of this learned Hebraist and eminent Reformer with Levita is of special interest. Fagius, who was born at Rheinzabern, in 1504, received his first instruction in Hebrew from Wolfgang Fabricius Capito (1478-1541), who acquired his Hebrew knowledge from two converted Jews, one unnamed, and the other named Matthew Adrian, the well-known author, or compiler, of the *Libellus Hora*, in Hebrew and Latin (1518), now one of the rarest books in existence.[72] Though Capito himself was no profound Hebrew scholar, as may be seen from his writings,[73] yet he imbued Fagius with an intense love for the language.

When Fagius was appointed Protestant pastor of Isny, in Allgau, in 1537, where he had formerly been rector of the Grammar School, he more than ever devoted himself to his Hebrew studies. He was also exceedingly anxious to diffuse the knowledge of the sacred language by means of good elementary books, which were much wanted at that time. To effect this he not only compiled the required manuals himself, but, with the aid of his friend and patron, counsellor Peter Buffler, he established a Hebrew press in the town of his pastoral labours. Feeling, however, his own inefficiency to conduct the printing of books in a language which, with all his love for it, he had not as yet properly mastered, he at once invited Levita to accept the office of supervisor, and offered also to print at Isny his own books, which were then ready for the press, as well

[72] For a description of this literary curiosity, see Steinschneider, *Bibliographisches Handbuch*, p. 2, *s. v.* ADRIANUS. Leipzig, 1859.

[73] Capito's works on Hebrew literature are, i. *Institutiuncula in Hebr. ling.* together with the Psalms in Hebrew, and an introduction by Pellican, Basel, 1516; Luther's own copy of this work, with his marginal annotations in MS., from the library of De Rossi, is to be found at Parma. This is exceedingly interesting to the student of the history of the early translations of the Bible, inasmuch as it shows the Manual which the great Reformer used to acquire his Hebrew knowledge. ii. *Institutiones Hebraicæ*, libr. ii., Basel, 1518, 1525; and iii. *Enarrationes in Habacuc et Hoseam*, 1537.

as those which had already been published. Levita regarded this invitation as providential, and though he tells us he had refused before "sundry calls from princes, cardinals, and bishops, as well as from the king of France," to professorial chairs, the septuagenarian felt that it was the voice of God, and that he must not disobey it.

In the year 1540, therefore, the aged Levita left his wife, children, and numerous friends in Venice, and departed for Isny, carrying with him the MSS. of his two Lexicons, and of the second edition of the Grammar called the *Bachur*, which were then nearly finished, and which Fagius had promised to publish. When the extreme difficulty and discomfort connected with travelling three centuries ago is borne in mind, we shall be able to appreciate the unquenchable zeal of this veteran, who, at the age of seventy, when men generally cling to their homes most tenaciously, left everything near and dear to him, and willingly braved all fatigue and difficulties, to promote the knowledge of the sacred language. Indeed, in the Epilogue to the *Tishbi*, which was the first book printed by Fagius, Levita tells us that he had to finish it on the road. "When I was on my journey," he says, "travelling over a land of mountains and valleys, exposed to the rain of heaven and to the snow which covered the ground, I often stood still, thought over in my mind sundry of the articles, wrote them down upon the tablet of my heart, and when I reached the inn I opened my bag, took out the MS., and put down the things which God put into my heart."[74]

Such was the journey which Levita made to come to Fagius. Let us now hear from the learned Jew what impression he received of the Christian scholar, when the two met together. "When I arrived here," says Levita, "I tasted his pitcher, and found it full of old wine. Indeed, I had not been told half of his wisdom and knowledge. Many draw from the fountain of his learning; he is a great oracle for his people, a beautiful preacher, and an excellent expositor. He is truly worthy that his people should describe him as we describe our Rabbin Moses Maimonides. For just as we say, 'From Moses the law-giver to Moses [Maimonides] none has arisen like Moses;' so they should say, 'From Paul [the Apostle] to Paul [Fagius] none

---

[74] כי בצאתי מביתי לא היה הספר הזה נשלם ובאמת בהיותי בדרך הולך למסעי ארץ הרים וגבעות למטר השמים ולשלג אשר הוא ארץ עמדתי מועיד עיינתי דברים בשכלי וכתבתים על לוח לבי ובבואי אל הסלון טחזרתי פי אמתחתי והוצאתי פנקסי ורשמתי בו את הדברים אשר נתן אלהים בלבי. *Tishbi*, p. 271.

has arisen like Paul.' "[75] This cordiality Fagius fully reciprocated, as may be seen from his Latin Address to the Reader prefixed to the *Tishbi*. Entertaining the same ardent love for Hebrew, agreed upon making united efforts to diffuse the knowledge of it, and thoroughly appreciating each other's character, Levita and Fagius soon became ardent friends, and conjointly produced works which, at that time, were an honour to their authors, and formed important contributions to Biblical literature.

The first work issued from this newly established Hebrew press was Levita's Lexicon, comprising seven hundred and twelve words used in the ancient Jewish literature. He called it *Tishbi*, for three reasons: i. In allusion to the gentile name of his namesake the prophet (i. Kings xvii. 1), whose appellation Levita assumed in accordance with an ancient conceit; ii. Because the last word in this Lexicon is *Tishbi;* and iii. Because the numerical value of the word *Tishbi* (viz. י $10 +$ ב $2 +$ ש $300 +$ ה $400 = 712$) represents the total number of sections in this Lexicon. To perfect himself in Rabbinical Hebrew, under the guidance of so excellent a master, as well as to enable Christian students at large to use it as a guide, Fagius, assisted by Levita, translated the whole *Tishbi* into Latin, with the exception of the poetical and rhythmical introductions, which were translated by James Velocian. The third Introduction, which is in prose, is not translated at all; most probably because, as it contains so flattering an account of Fagius, his sincere humility would not tolerate its being translated into a language commonly understood among Christian scholars. Thus, the Hebrew of Levita on the right page and the Latin of Fagius on the left, the Jew and the Christian published their conjoint work, under the same cover, at Isny, 1541. The *Tishbi* was reprinted with the Latin translation by Fagius at Basel, 1557, and without the Latin, *ibid.* 1601; Grodno, 1805, and Chernowitz, 1856.

In the same year in which the *Tishbi* appeared, Levita also carried through the press another Lexicon, comprising all the words which occur in the Chaldee paraphrases of the Old Testament. The diffi-

---

[75] Compare מחכמתו: החצי לי הונד ולא ישן מלא ומצאתיו בקנקנתו תחזתי המה ובבאי הוא ראוי ובאמת מטרש ונאה דורש נאה לעמו ורורש תורתו מי שואבים ורבים ידיעתו כך במשה קם לא משה עד ממשה מיימון בן משה קוראין שאנו כמו עליו יקראו עמו שבני כשאולש קם לא מאולש עד מסאולש עליו יאמרו Introduction iii., to the *Tishbi*, or the Introduction in prose, as it is called, towards the end.

culties which he had to encounter to reduce the language of the Chaldee paraphrases to grammatical and lexical form were enormous. The only Aramaic Lexicon extant was the *Aruch*, by R. Nathan b. Jechiel (*circa* 1030–1106), which was completed A.D. 1101, and of which three different editions appeared before the publication of the Lexicon on the *Targumim*. One of these three editions, *i.e.* the *editio princeps*, was published before 1480; the second appeared at Pesaro, 1517; and the third was edited by Levita himself, and published by his friend Bomberg, Venice, 1531. But, marvellous as is the *Aruch*, and though it is still the only clue to the ancient Jewish writings, it is not designed for students of the Chaldee paraphrases. It does not separate the dialects of the Mishna, Gemara, Midrashim, and Targumim, but mixes them up all in one treatise. In addition to the want of forerunners in the lexicography of the Targumim, there was the great difficulty arising from the confused condition of the texts of these paraphrases. But here we cannot do better than give Levita's own words upon the subject, which are as follows:

"I have been asked whether it is possible to make a grammar on the Targum, to which I replied that, in my opinion, the possibility is very remote, owing to the great variations in the Codices with regard to the words and letters, and more especially the vowel-points, which differ exceedingly. This arises from the fact that the Targumists most unquestionably wrote their paraphrases without points, which had not then been invented, as I have previously shown in the Introduction to the *Massoreth Ha-Massoreth*. In confirmation of this, it is also to be adduced that the most ancient Codices are all without the points; for the Massorites, who pointed the Hebrew Scriptures, did not point the Chaldee paraphrases. These were pointed much later, by one or more individuals, men without a name, who exercised an arbitrary independence of each other. Hence it is that their rules are contradictory, and that no examples can be adduced from them to found thereupon a grammar. Hence, too, the fact that, since the Targum was made, there has not been a wise and intelligent man in Israel who could make a grammar to it.

"Not only, however, has no grammar been written, but no one has compiled a lexicon to explain the words, except, indeed, R. Nathan of Rome, in his *Aruch*, which he made in explanation of the Talmud, and in which he adduces some words from the Targumim. But these are chiefly Greek and Latin expressions, occuring for the most part in the Jerusalem Targum, and even many of these he quotes without explaining them, about which I have already had occasion to complain in the *Massoreth Ha-Massoreth*. After him, however, there has been no one who had the courage to handle either the grammar or the lexicography of the Targumim. Now I have been inclined to think that the reason of it is, because that, in years bygone, *i.e.* before the invention of printing, not one copy of the Targum on the Prophets and Hagiographa was to be found in a town, or two in a province. Hence nobody could be found to study them. The Targum Onkelos, which was always to be found plentifully, because we are obliged to read every week the hebdomadal lesson from the law, twice in Hebrew and once in Chaldee, there have indeed been some who studied it; they have also written something on it, but I have not found it of much use; they have likewise made a *Massorah* to it, which, however, I have not yet succeeded in seeing. But with regard to the Targum on the Prophets and Hagiographa, they have not opened their mouth, nor uttered a syllable about it; being neither studied nor asked for, they say, Let it tarry till Elisha cometh." [76]

It was this neglect of the Chaldee paraphrases, and his determination to supply the desideratum, which induced Levita, in spite of all the difficulties to be encountered, to undertake the compilation of a Chaldee Lexicon. He called it *Methurgeman* (מתורגמן), or *the Interpreter*, "because it interprets the Hebrew in Aramaic, and the Aramaic in Hebrew." It was published by his friend, Paul Fagius, at

[76] והנה רבים שאלוני האם אשר לעשות דקדוק על התרגומים האלה· אמרתי לפי דעתי כי אפשרי רחוק הוא· וזה מפני השתנות הנוסחאות במלות ובאותיות ועל כלם בנקדות הם מתחלפות מאד· וזה לפי שבלי ספק המתרגמים כתבו תרגומם בלי נקוד כי לא היו נמצאות· כמו שהוכחתי היטב בהקדמת ספר מסורת המסורת, והראיה עוד כי הנוסחאות הישנות מאד כלם בלתי נקוד· כי לא נקדום בעלי המסורת· כמו שנקדו כל כ"ד הספרים· אלא אחר כך זמן רב נקדו על יד יחיד· או רבים אנשים בלי שם כל אחד כרצונו על כן יצא משפטן מעוקל· ואין להביא מזהן ראיה לפשוט עליהם דקדוק· ולולי כן התחשוב שמיום שנעשו התרגומים לא היה איש חכם ונבון בישראל שהיה יודע לעשות עליהם הדקדוק · · · ·

ואומר כי לא רי שלא היה איש שעשה הדקדוק כי אפילו לעשות חבור לפרש המלות לא היה איש חוץ מהרב רבי נתן איש רומי בספרו הערוך שחבר על מלות התלמוד ואגב גררא הביא קצת מלות מהתרגומים ורובם מלות של יון או רומי הנמצאים לרוב בתרגום ירושלמי וככמה מהם הביא ולא בארם וזאת היתה תלונתי עליו בספר מסורת המסורת ואחריו לא קם איש שהתעורר להחזיק בו לא בדקדוק ולא בביאור המלות וחשבתי שההסבה בזה לפי שבשנים שעברו רצה לומר קודם שנמצאה מלאכת הדפוס לא היו נמצאים תרגום נביאים וכתובים כי אם אחד במדינה ושנים באיקלים לכן לא היה מי שהשגיח בהם אבל תרגום אונקלוס תמיד נמצא לרוב וזה מפני שחייבים אנחנו לקרא בכל שבוע הפרשה שנים מקרא ואחד תרגום נמצאים קצת אנשים שהשגיחו בו וכתבו עליו דבר מה ולא מצאתי בהם תועלת רב גם נעשה עליו מסורה ולא ראיתים עד הנה· אבל על נביאים וכתובים לא היה פוצה פה ומצפצף· ואין דורש ואין מבקש אלא אמרו יהי מונח עד שיבא אליהו Introduction to the *Methurgeman*.

Isny, in the month of August, 1541. At the end of the volume is Fagius's Colophon, which consists of a book with a tree on it, as Fagius properly denotes *book*; on the right of it is the letter פ, initial of Paul; 'on the left of it is the letter ב, the initial of *book* = Fagius; whilst underneath it is the Hebrew inscription כל אילן טוב נושא פרי טוב, *Every good tree bringeth forth good fruit*. The Colophon of the *Tishbi*, which as we have seen contains the Latin translation of Fagius, is different. Instead of the letters פ and ב there are on the right and left hand the Latin and the Hebrew of the inscription, and underneath are the Hebrew words תקותי במשיח הנשלח שהיא עתיד לדין חיים ומתים, *My hope is in the Messiah who has come, and who will judge the quick and the dead*. This difference is undoubtedly owing to the fact that Fagius, as the joint editor, claimed to have the expression of his faith on the *Tishbi*; whilst the *Methurgeman*, which is the sole work of Levita, has simply the Hebrew date, and no reference to Christ.

In the Epilogue to the *Methurgeman*, Levita tells us that he laboured over it nearly four years; which is fully confirmed by the fact that he already alludes to his being engaged on it in the third Introduction to the *Massoreth Ha-Massoreth* (1538), whilst in the third Introduction to the *Tishbi*, which was written after he had only been three years at work over it, he says, "I know that many will be astonished at the multitude of words from the Targum which I quote, saying, in different places, this expression does not occur again in the Targum, or this expression only occurs once or twice, or it is thus rendered throughout the Chaldee version, except in Job, Psalms, and Proverbs, &c., &c., and will scarcely be inclined to believe all the remarks which I made therein. But if they only knew the great labour which I spent over the *Methurgeman*, they would not be surprised at it. Forsooth, I have been three years writing it, and during this time I have read through all the Chaldee paraphrases over and over again, as the references will show to anyone who consults it. Others, again, may be astonished at my quoting Greek in many places, knowing that I was not learned in this language. But the fact is, that these people do not know that I have learned it from Cardinal Egidio, with whom I resided thirteen years, and who was exceedingly expert in Greek." [77]

[77] וידעתי כי רבים תמהו על רוב מלות התרגו׳ שהבאתי באמרי בהרבה מקומות זה הלשון לא נמצא עוד בתרגום או לא נמצא רק במקום אחד או שנים או כך הוא מתורגם בכל המקרא חוץ מן איוב משלי ותלים וכנו אלה רבום ולא יאמינו לי בכל האותות אשר עשיתי בקרבם. אמנם אם ידעו המורח

But though Levita spent such extraordinary labour over this Lexicon, and though the *Methurgeman* is still the only work in which the whole language of the Chaldee paraphrases is treated separately, it has never been republished. The introduction, was translated into Latin by his friend Paul Fagius, Isny, 1542. The single article comprising the root משח which discusses the question of the Messiah in the Chaldee paraphrases, has also been translated into Latin by Gilb. Genebrard, Paris, 1572.[78] Buxtorf has incorporated most of it in his Rabbinical and Talmudical Lexicon, which, however, is not as convenient for the use of students as Levita's work, inasmuch as it mixes up the dialects of the Talmud and Midrashim with the language of the Chaldee paraphrases. The only Lexicon which will supersede it is the one now in course of publication by Dr. Levy.

With the completion of the Chaldee Lexicon, Levita thought he had finished his active life, having now reached his seventy-fourth year. In most affecting language, therefore, he says in the Epilogue to the work in question, that the time has now arrived when he must relinquish his literary labours, since his advanced age and failing health compel him to retire from the battle field. "Seeing that age has overtaken me, that I am very old, that my eyesight grows dimmer every day, and that my strength is fast leaving me, I must retire from the ranks and serve no more. I shall now return to my country which I left, namely, Venice, and die in my town with my aged wife, and no more move my foot from her. She shall close my eyes, and death alone shall henceforth separate me from her. I shall abide there the remaining days of my life, finish the books which I have begun, and then say to the God who created me, Take now my life, for it is better that I should die."

But, notwithstanding this resolution to return to Venice, his unquenchable love for the work, coupled with the fact that he had still some treatises ready for press, and that his friend Fagius too was actually printing sundry books which required his help, induced the

הגדול שטרחתי בחבור ספר המתורגמן גם בעיניהם לא יפלא כי באמת שלש שנים עמדתי בחבורו ואנו
יגרתי על כל התרגמים כמה ובכמה והנסיון יוכיח למי שייגע בו גם יתמהו על לשון יין שהבאתי
בחרבה מקומות בידעם שאינני מכיר הלשון ההוא אבל לא ידעו שמן הקארדינאל אשר עמדתי עמו
שלש עשרה שנה קבלתי כל אלה בי הוא היה בקי מאד מלשון יון Introduction iii. to the *Tishbi*.

[78] Dr. Kalisch (*Hebrew Grammar*, ii., p. 34, note d.) is surely mistaken in his remark that Fagius likewise translated this valuable Chaldee Dictionary in 1542. Fagius translated the Introduction only.

aged Levita to remain a little longer at Isny. With impaired eyesight and failing health, but with an enthusiasm for Biblical literature, and an industry which defied and vanquished bodily infirmities, he not only most vigorously continued his own works, but largely aided Fagius in writing and carrying through the press his productions. Some idea may be formed of the amount of mental and physical labour which Levita was still able to perform, though now seventy-four years of age, from the fact that, within twelve months of the appearance of the stupendous Lexicon on the Chaldee paraphrases, he wrote and carried through the press an *Alphabetical List of the Technical Hebrew Words* or *Nomenclature* (שמות דברים), in four columns. Column i. gives these words in Judaio-German, with Hebrew characters. Column ii., in Hebrew. Column iii., in Latin, by Fagius; and column iv. gives them in German, with German characters, Isny, 1542. It was afterwards republished, with an additional column, by Drusius the son, containing the corresponding Greek words, and enriched with explanations by Drusius the father, Francker, 1652, and *ibid.*, 1581.

Besides the *Nomenclature*, Levita also carried through the press this year (1542), a new and thoroughly revised edition of his Grammar, entitled *Bachur*, which as we have seen he published twenty-four years before (1518), at the suggestion and for the use of his pupil Cardinal Egidio. Münster had already republished it, with a Latin translation (1525), seven years after the appearance of the original work, but Levita had nothing to do with it, and made no alterations in it. As it is the new preface added by Levita to this edition which gave rise to the great divergency of opinion about the date of his birth, we shall give it entire. By so doing, the origin of the errors will best be understood. But before doing this, it is necessary to remark that Levita completed the second edition in 1540, when still at Venice, and that it was one of the three MSS. which he took with him to Isny, the other two being the *Tishbi* and the *Methurgeman*. This is evident, from his remark in the Epilogue to the second edition of the *Bachur*, where he distinctly says, " Whoso wishes to know its date, let him take 22 (בידו) from 822 (ערב״ים),"[79] thus leaving 800=1540, the very year in which he received the invitation

---

[79] והרוצה לדעת עת פרסומ
הלא יקח בידו מן ערב״ים

Bachur, p. 103, 2nd edition, Isny, 1542.

from Fagius, and in which he started for Isny. It was very natural that he should print the three new works (namely, the two Lexicons and the Nomenclature) first, and then the second edition of an old work.

Now, in the Introduction to the *Bachur* in question, which he completed in 1540, but which was not printed till 1542, he gives the following piece of autobiography, which caused the errors already alluded to. "Thus sayeth Elias Levita, the German,[80] I was about forty years of age when fate sent me from Venice, and I came to Rome. Here I was requested to compile this book, and I put down its import according to my knowledge. Now the Lord has spared me thirty years longer, and I am now about seventy years old, and am as able now as I was then to engage in the discussion on matters of Grammar, the Bible, and the Massorah. Yea since then I have acquired different ideas, and formed opinions which I did not know before. Moreover, I have since found that I have omitted some things which ought to have been put down, and that I have stated things which ought not to have been written. I regret that I have done it. Still it is not to be wondered at, since we find that even our Rabbins of blessed memory said things in their youth, which they recalled in their old age. Thus we find, 'Raba changed from this;' 'R. Ashi changed from what he said in the former statement, and the law is according to his second statement,' (comp. *Baba Bathra* 157, *b*.) Now as were their thoughts so are mine, and I am not to be better than my fathers. For this reason I have resolved to publish a second edition of this work, with such additions and diminutions as shall make the last edition better than the first. I shall thus prevent students studying erroneous introductions, inconclusive arguments, and incorrect rules, and those

[80] אמר אליהו הלוי האשכנזי בן ארבעים שנה אנכי בשלוח הזמן אותי מוויניסיה ובאתי לרומא ושם נדרשתי לאסר שאלוני בחבור הספר הזה ואשיב בו דבר כאשר עם לבבי והנה הזיה י״ל אותי מאז זה שלשים שנה וחרי אני כבן שבעים שנה ועדיני היום חזק במה אז וכבחד עתה לצאת ולבא למלחמת הדקדוק והמסרת והמסורת כי מאז נתחדשו בי דעות אחרות וסברות חדשות אשר לפנים לא ידעתים מצורף לזה כי מאותו היום והלאה מצאתי שהנחתי קצת דברים שהיו ראויים להכתב ולא כתבתים גם כתבתי דברים הלואי ולא כתבתים נחמתי כי עשיתים ואין לתמוה על ככה כי כן נמצא לרבותינו זכרונם לברכה שאמרו דבר בילדותם וחזרו בו בזקנותם כמו שמצינו הדר ביה רבא מההיא וכן רב אשי חזר ממה שאמר במהדורא קמא ותלכה כמהדורא בתרא כדאיתא בסוף פרק מי שמתו ׃ והנה כמחשבותם מחשבותי לא טוב אנכי מאבותי לכן הסכמתי עם לבבי להדפיס הספר הזה שנית ולהוסיף עליו לגרוע ממנו ובה איטיב חסרי האחרון מן הראשון לבלתי לה אחרי הבחורים ללמדם הקדמות כוזבות וראיות בלתי צודקות וחקים לא טובים וילמדום החל התלמידים הבאים אחרי ונמצא שם שמים מתחלל חם ושלום לכן בהשחקה הזאת אתקן המטוות הדורים אשר והמקלקל אכשר חרים מכשול מדרך עמי ונזה יהיה אדהים עמי

that follow, learning blunders, and thereby peradventure profaning the divine name. For this reason, I correct in this edition that which is erroneous, rectify the mistakes, and remove the stumbling block from the way of my people. To this end may the Lord be with me."

It was David Gans,[61] the eminent historian, who first took Levita's remark—"I was about forty years of age when fate sent me from Venice, and I came to Rome," &c.—also to refer to Levita's period of life when he published the Grammar in question. Accordingly, as the first edition of the *Bachur* was published, Rome, 1518, Gans concluded that Levita was born in 1477, and that the second edition appeared in 1547, since Levita himself states that he compiled it forty years later, when he was seventy years of age. This statement of Gans was adopted by Jechiel,[62] in his historical work, by Semler, and others.

[61] David Gans was born in 1541, at Lippstadt, in Westphalia, and died 25th August, 1613, at Prague. He was the first German Jew of his age who was distinguished as a historian, geographer, and astronomer; he was acquainted with John Müller, Kepler, and Tycho de Brahe, with whom he carried on a literary correspondence; for the latter he translated into German, extracts from a Hebrew translation of the Tables of Alphonso, composed in 1260. The works which have immortalised his name are as follows: i. A Compendium of History, from the Creation to A.D. 1592, in the form of annals, entitled *The Sprout of David* (צמח דוד), first published at Prague, 1592, then with a continuation to A.D. 1692, by Reindorf, Frankfort on the Maine and Amsterdam, 1692, Furth 1785, and part iii. improved by Mohr, Lemberg, 1847. This chronicle was translated into Latin by Vorst, Leyden, 1644, the second part being abbreviated; and into Judaio-German, by Hena, Frankfort on the Maine, 1698; and ii. An Introduction to Astronomy, the Calendar, and Mathematical Geography, entitled, *A Pleasant and Agreeable Work* (סמר נחמד ונעים), in twelve parts, subdivided into three hundred and five sections. It was finished by the author in 1613, and continued by Joel b. Jekuthiel, Jesnëtz, 1743. The passage in question, which has been the source of the perpetual error respecting the date of Levita's birth, is as follows in the original: רעז : אליהו המדקדק חבר ספר הבחור Anno 277 [= 1518]; ברומי בשנת רע'ז ובן ארבעים שנה וכמהדורתו בשנת ש'ז היה בן שבעים שנה *Elias, the German, composed the Book Bachur, at Rome, in the year 277* [=1518], *when he was forty years old; and when he published the second edition, in the year 307* [= 1547], *he was seventy years of age*. Comp. part i., p. 43, *b*, ed. Frankfort, 1692. In Vorst's Latin translation of this work, the whole passage is thus erroneously rendered, "Elias Grammaticus composuit librum *Bachur* Romae anno 277; et ista aetate sua anno 307, erat filius 70 annorum." Comp. p. 151.

[62] Jechiel Heilprin, the author of the chronicle of Jewish history and literati, entitled, *The Order of Generations* (סדר הדורות), was Rabbi at Minsk, where he died about 1731. His Chronicle was first published at Carlsruhe, 1769 A new and improved edition, edited by H. Sperling and B. Lorje, appeared in Lemberg, 1858. The passage relating to Levita, which the author transferred into this work from the chronicle of Gans, is erroneously copied. It is here as follows: ס' הבחור ברומי רע'ז [read חבר] חסר, בן מ' שנה ומסורות המסורות חבר רצ'ה ובמהדורתו הי' בן ע' שנת ש'ז *He composed the Book Bachur, at Rome, in 277* [= 1518]. *when forty years of age, and the Massoreth*

Levita's remark, however, that he was forty years of age, does not refer to the publication of the first edition of the Bachur, but to his leaving Venice and arriving at Rome in 1509, as is evident from the following facts: i. The second edition of the *Bachur* was not published in 807 [= 1547], as stated by Gans and those who follow him, but in 1542.[68] ii. This revised edition, according to his own explicit statement (*vide supra*, p. 78), he finished in 1540. iii. He tells us himself that he was not then seventy years old, but *about* seventy years of age (והרי אני כבן שבעים שנה), that is a little more than seventy, or seventy-two. iv. As this second edition was published two years after its completion, *i. e.*, in 1542, when he was seventy-four years of age, he most unquestionably was born in 1468; and v. This date of his birth is confirmed by Levita himself, for he tells us distinctly (*vide supra*, p. 3), that he was eighty years old in 1548.

In addition to his own two productions, which he published in 1542, the aged Levita carried through the press, in the same year, no fewer than four works published by his friend Fagius. They are as follows: i. The Book of Tobit, in Hebrew, with a Latin translation by Fagius on the opposite page, Isny, 1542, which has been incorporated in the London Polyglott by Walton. ii. The so-called Alphabet of Ben Sirah, in Chaldee, with a Commentary, and a Latin translation by Fagius, Isny, 1542. iii. Gen. cap. i.—iv., with a Latin translation, as well as with an explanation of every word, and a Latin translation of

---

Ha-Massoreth he wrote in 298 [= 1538], *and at the second edition he was seventy years old, which was in* 307 [= 1547]. Comp. vol. i., p. 95, a, ed. Lemberg. It will be seen that the words, "and at the second edition he was seventy years of age, which was in 307," have been incorrectly put after the *Massoreth Ha-Massoreth*.

[68] The second edition is now before us, and the complete title and date are thus given by Levita himself:

דקדוק אליהו הלוי
האשכנזי אשר שמו

ספר בחור הוסד שנית   טוב מהדתקה ראשונית
עשהו האריך בו דעניח   ולמליא שנת תבנית
ודברים טובים הוסיף בה   שם בו הגה העיונית
בראשרי היתה בו קצנית   עתה כלו חמי מנית׳
נדפס באיזנא הביהה בשנת
מבריאת עלם ש׳ב לפר׳ט
קמון בחדש סיוי
תהלה לשם
עליוי

ב   פ

Onkelos' paraphrases of the same chapters, Isny, 1542; and iv. An Ethical Treatise in Judaio-German, Isny, 1542. This book, which was afterwards translated into Hebrew, and published under the title, *The Paths of the Righteous* (אורחות צדיקים), Prague, 1581, no less an authority than Jost asserts was written by Levita.[84] Steinschneider and Cassel, however, who are authorities of equal weight, will have it that Levita simply edited it.[85]

Levita's departure from Isny was at last accelerated by the impending change in the position of his friend Fagius. Capito, who, as we have seen, was Fagius's first Hebrew teacher, and who occupied both the office of evangelical pastor and the professorial chair at Strasburg, died of the plague in December, 1541. The choice of a successor was soon made. The name of Fagius at once suggested itself to the managers of the Protestant interests at Strasburg, and accordingly this pious, amiable, and learned clergyman was asked to succeed Capito in the pastorate and professorship. Fagius, in accepting this invitation, stipulated that he should be allowed to go first to Constance, for two years, to organise and consolidate the Protestant interests, in the place where the celebrated council condemned Huss and Jerome of Prague. But, in going to Constance for this short period, he was determined to infuse into the minds and hearts of the Protestants there, a conviction of the importance, and a love for the study, of the Hebrew language, knowing that the most effectual way to strengthen the cause of Protestantism was to advance the cause of Biblical literature.

In going therefore to Constance in 1542, Fagius felt that he could not as yet dispense with the help of Levita. Levita was too sincerely attached to his friend, and had too great a love for Hebrew, not to comply with the appeal of Fagius in behalf of the cause of Oriental learning in his self-imposed sphere of labour; and accordingly the aged Jew accompanied the Christian pastor to Constance. As Fagius's stay here was very limited, and as Levita was very anxious to get back to his wife and children at Venice, they at once set to work. Their efforts were directed to supply students with appropriate elementary books. The first book, therefore, which Fagius published consisted of Gen. i.—iv. in Hebrew, with a German translation, and an appendix

[4] Comp. the article *Judenteutsch*, in Ersch and Gruber's *Encyklopädie*, sect. ii., vol. xxvii., p. 323, note i.
[85] Comp. Ersch and Gruber's *Encyklopädie*, article *Jüdische Typographie*, p. 33.

of such notes as should help the tyro in Hebrew to acquire the language, Constance, 1543.[86] Having supplied them with an elementary book for the study of Biblical Hebrew, Fagius was also anxious to furnish the students with a guide to Rabbinical Hebrew, and hence published within twelve months Psalms i.—x. in Hebrew, accompanied by David Kimchi's Rabbinical commentary, with a Latin translation, Constance, 1544.

Whilst Fagius thus manifested his anxiety to supply, with the aid of his Jewish friend, the Protestant Christians at Constance with manuals, Levita was equally anxious to benefit his Jewish brethren, with the help of his Christian friend. As Protestants and Romanists were now vying with each other to furnish their respective communities in Germany with translations of the Scriptures in the vernacular of the people, Levita saw the importance of supplying the German speaking Jews with a Judaio-German version of that portion of the Bible which is hebdomadally read, both publicly and privately. He accordingly translated the Pentateuch, the Five Megilloth, and the Haphtaroth, or lessons from the Prophets, into that dialect. This translation he got Fagius to publish, and it appeared at Constance, 1544.[87]

It was not till the autumn of 1544, when Fagius's two years' term at Constance had expired, and he went to Strasburg to enter upon his duties there, that Levita arrived at Venice, after an absence of nearly four years. Though he was now seventy-six years of age, his intellect was still very active, and the tenderness of his heart was intense. His delight in meeting again those who were dear and near to him, and from whom a literary mission had temporarily separated him, may be surmised from the following touching prayer in poetry, which he offered up for his wife, at the conclusion of his Chaldee Lexicon: "O Lord, I beseech thee, grant to me and my wife this mercy, that she should not be a widow, and that I should not be a widower! Let

---

[86] Comp. Wolf, *Bibliotheca Hebraea*, ii., 396, 456; iv., 135.

[87] Some bibliographers question whether Levita is the author of this Judaio-German version. Steinschneider (*Catalogus Libr. Hebr. in Bibliotheca Bodleiana*, col. 942), puts it among the *opera supposititia*, whilst Graetz (*Geschichte der Juden*, ix., 229, Leipzig, 1866), the latest historian of the highest authority, positively states that Levita made this translation at Constance, when on his way from Isny to Venice. A specimen of this curious version, comprising the first chapter of Genesis, is given by Wolf, *Bibliotheca Hebraea*, iv., 194—198. Comp. also Buber, *Life of Elias Levita*, in Hebrew, p. 31, note 49, Leipzig, 1856.

us both die together; let me sleep in her bosom till the appointed time, when the end shall be ushered in, and we shall rise again, and together be destined for everlasting life."[88]

No sooner had he arrived at Venice, than he began publishing again. He re-commenced his literary work in his old sphere of labour, by editing a *Rhythmical Exposition of the Book of Job* (פירוש איוב), Venice, 1544. Some indeed will have it that Levita is the author of this production, and appeal to Steinschneider in corroboration of this assertion; but this learned bibliographer has shown that it was written by Sarek Barfat, who flourished in the middle of the fourteenth century.[89] When he had, however, fairly settled down, he continued the translation of the Scriptures which he began at Isny; and in 1545, he published a German version of the Book of Psalms, which, like the portion of his former selection, constitutes an essential part of the Jewish Ritual. This version was afterwards re-published at Zurich, 1558, and in other places.[90] In the same year, he also edited a new edition of the first part of Kimchi's celebrated grammar and Lexicon, entitled, *Perfection* (מכלול). This part, which contains the grammar, and ought properly to be called *the grammatical part* (חלק הדקדוק), but which usually bears the general title of the whole work, namely, *Michlol*, had indeed been published three times before, twice in Constantinople, 1532, 1534, and once with a Latin translation by Guidacerus, Paris, 1540. But as a new edition was called for, the publisher entrusted it to the aged Grammarian and Lexicographer, who enriched it with valuable annotations (נימוקים), Venice, 1545.

How powerless age was, in either quenching his zeal or diminishing his labour, may be seen from the fact that when he was seventy-nine

[88] אנא אלי לי תלאשתי   החסד גם האמת מן
שדיא לא תהיה אלממה   ואני לא אהיה אלמן
יחד נמות ובגן עדנות   תוך דיקה אישן על לומן
יבא הקץ ואני נקיץ   ולהי עד יחד נודמן.

Epilogue to the *Methurgeman*.

[89] Thus Dr. Holmes, in *Kitto's Cyclopædia of Biblical Literature*, new ed., *s. v.* ELIAS, says, "that E. Levita was its author, and not editor only (as Wolf, *Bibl.* iii., would have it), is demonstrated by Steinschneider (*Catal*, 939, 940)." Now, on referring to Steinschneider, at the column in question, the reader will see that this bibliographer heads this section, *i. e.*, No. 33, as follows: "פירוש איוב, *Expositio libri Job*, rhythmica [auctore Sarek Barfat], (ff. 17)." If any more evidence should be required, we refer to the same *Catalogue*, col. 2500, where Steinschneider has a separate section for Sarek, and the only published work of his there specified is "Historia Jobi Carmine; *anon.* ed. ab Elia Levita, q. v. op. 33–4."

[90] Comp. Steinschneider, *Catalogus Libr. Hebr. in Bibliotheca Bodleiana*, col. 188.

years old (1546), he carried through the press, with the utmost care, no less than seven different works. The first of these was the stupendous Hebrew Lexicon, by Kimchi, which is commonly called *the Book of Roots* (ספר השרשים), but the more proper name of which is *the Lexicon part* (חלק הענין), being the second part of the general work, entitled, *Michlol*. Of this famous Lexicon, seven editions had been published before this date, namely, before 1480; Naples, 1490; *ibid.* 1491; Constantinople, 1513; Venice, 1529; Soncino, 1532–3; and Venice, 1546: and Levita himself, as we have already seen (*vide supra*, p. 22), took part in the fifth edition, immediately after he was employed by his friend Bomberg as corrector of the press. To the edition, however, which now appeared, as also to that of the first part of this great work published in the preceding year, Levita added valuable annotations (נימוקים). His second and third publications, this year, were, new and thoroughly revised editions of his *Treatise on the Compounds* (ספר הרכבה), with the text pointed, and *the Poetical Dissertations* on various parts of Hebrew Grammar, entitled, *the Sections of Elijahu* (פרקי אליהו); whilst his fourth work was a greatly improved edition of his maiden production, which consists of the commentary on M. Kimchi's *Journey on the Paths of Knowledge*.

The curious history of the last mentioned production deserves to be noticed at greater length. We have already seen that Levita's first literary production was published surreptitiously (*vide supra, p.* 13). As he soon after was occupied with more important literary works, which secured for him a world-wide renown, he did not much care to claim the book, which was most negligently printed, and swarmed with blunders. But his friends, who knew that he was its author, were very anxious that he should not depart this life without claiming and correcting it. With this wish he now complied; and, as the work had so long passed in another person's name, Levita felt obliged to give the following account of it, which is written in poetry, and is appended to the edition revised by him:—

אנכי אליהו הלוי דל באלפי
כאשר הייתי בימי חרפי:
בק״ק פאדואה הבירה שנת סד״ר ליצירה:

When I, Elias Levita, the least in my family,
Was, in the days of my manhood,
In the city of Padua, A.M. 264 [= A.D. 1504],

כאשר מתלמידי נתבקשתי :	זה הספר פירשתי
החל הנגף בעם	ויהי באותו הפעם
ברחוב אשר אנכי בקרבו :	וסוגר כל בית ומבוא
ואז עבדי רמני :	ונסגרתי גם אני
והוא הרחיקהו מעל גבולי :	כי נתתי לו הספר להעתיק לי
ולהדפיסו לו ממון פזר :	והוליכו עמו לעיר פיזור
היתה בעיניו נקלה :	והנה זאת הנבלה
ושמי על הספר לא זכר :	ואת כבודי עכר
מר בנימין מעיר רומא : [91]	אך שם בראשו הקדמה
שהוא הפירוש הזה חיבר :	שכל הרואה אותו סובר
קצת עניינים מדעתו :	גם הוסיף בו לפי שעתו
עקודים נקודים וברודים :	גם לקט מלשון למודים [92]

I composed this book according to the request of my disciples.
It came to pass, that the plague broke out among the people,
Whereupon every entrance was blocked up in the street where I lived,
So that I too was closed in; then my messenger deceived me.
For I gave him the book to print it for me, and he took it away;
He took it to Pesaro, and spent money in printing it for himself.
This shameful deed appeared a small thing in his eyes.
Most insultingly, he did not mention my name in the book,
But put at the beginning of the Introduction ' R. Benjamin's of Rome,'[91]
That all who use it may think he was the author of this Exposition.
He also erroneously added some things from his own cogitations,
And inserted from the 'Language of the Learned,'[92] diverse fragments,

[91] It is now established almost to a certainty, that this Benjamin of Rome, the author of the propædeutical treatise prefixed to Levita's commentary on the *Journey on the Paths of Knowledge*, is Benjamin b. Jehudah, called הרב"א, who flourished A.D. 1330, and is the well known author of commentaries on the books of Chronicles, Proverbs, and other portions of the Old Testament; and that Levita headed his commentary in question by this treatise, because, like his own commentary, it was designed to simplify the study of Hebrew Grammar. The messenger, whose name Levita does not condescend to give in this poetical description, by putting the name 'R. Benjamin of Rome' at the head of it, and withholding Levita's name altogether, led people to believe that this Benjamin was the author of the commentary itself, as well as of the propædeutics. This is the cause of Levita's complaint. Comp. Wolf, *Bibliotheca Hebraea*, iii., p. 152, No. cccxciii.; Steinschneider, *Catalogus Libr. Hebr. in Bibliotheca Bodleiana*, pp. 790, 1840, 2769; by the same author, *Jewish Literature*, pp. 146, 376, London, 1857; and *Bibliographisches Handbuch*, p. 21, No. 206. Leipzig, 1859.

[92] "*The Language of the Learned*," (לשון לימודים) is an extensive Hebrew Grammar, to which is appended a treatise on Hebrew Poetry and Metre (מאמר קצר במלאכת השיר), entitled, *The Holy Shekel* (שקל הקדש). The author of this Hebrew Grammar is David Ibn Jachja, of the celebrated ancient family, Jachja, who also wrote a commentary on Proverbs, entitled, *Select and Pure* (קב ונקי), which was first printed at Lisbon, 1492; and has since been incorporated in the Rabbinical Bibles published at Venice, 1516-7, and

M

וכל זה עשה בלי ידעיתי | והשאיר בו מה ששניתי :
מצורף לזה למען תדע אתה | כי לא היחה כחי אז ככחי עתה :
ועם כל זה נדפס כמה פעמים | על ידי יהודים ועממים :
ונמכרים עם כל השניאות | עד שלא נשאר מהם במציאות :
ובאמת על הראשונים אנכי מצטער | שהיה להם הקוצים לבער :
ולא די שהניחום כמו שהם | אך שהוסיפו טעיות עליהם :
ונם אנכי לב עליהם לא שמתי | אך כי עשיתים נחמתי :
אבל ספרים אחרים חברתי | והטיבותי את אשר דברתי :
ועתה אחרי אשר ימי פני לערב | הפצירו בי אנשים לרוב :
מהם מולים מהם ערלים | אשר בדקדוק לשונינו עמלים :
שאקימהו על מכונו | ואמלא את חסרונו :
ואאיר את חשכו | והאמת יעשה דרכו :
אע״פ שהקטן הוא זה החבור | יש בו צרכי צבור :
וכל העוסקים בו באמונה | תהיה המלאכה בידם נכונה :
כי הוא מסודר בסדר יפה | ללמוד כל הדקדוק על פה :
ובזה אין לי ספק | כי כל איש ממנו יסתפק :
ואף אם הספר כבר בידו המציא | ישן מפני חדש יוציא :

All this he did without my knowledge, and left in it my errors;
For you must know, that I was not so expert then as I am now.
It was thus re-published several times, both by Jews and Christians,
Sold with all its blunders, and nothing is left of the editions.
I greatly regret my first blunders, which ought to have been corrected;
And which have not only been left, but increased by fresh blunders.
I did not notice it, but simply regretted that I had made blunders,
And wrote other books wherein I corrected my former mistakes.
Now that my life is drawing near to its evening, many of my friends,
Both Jews and Christians, who studied the grammar of our language,
Have urged me to place it in its right position, supply its deficiencies,
Enlighten its darkness, and make straight its path.
For, although the book is but small, it is much wanted;
And those who study it properly derive advantage from it,
Since it is so arranged that the rules may easily be learned by heart.
I have no doubt that every student will benefit from it,
And even if he has the former edition, he'll prefer the new to the old;

Amsterdam, 1724-7; he died about A.D. 1504. The Grammar was published in Constantinople, 1506, 1519, and an improved edition, *ibid.* 1542. The treatise on Hebrew Poetry is from the pen of an anonymous writer. It consists of seventeen chapters, of which cap. i.—xiv., appended to Ibn Jachja's Grammar, treats on the grammatical points necessary for writing poetry, whilst cap. xv.—xvii., which treats on the construction and metre of the Hebrew poetry, was appended to Levita's commentary on Kimchi's *Journey on the Paths of Knowledge*, by the person who published it surreptitiously. It is to these excerpts that the words עקודים נקודים refer. Comp. Steinschneider's *Catalogus Hebr.*, p. 864, &c., and *Bibliographisches Handbuch*, p. 9, No. 78.

כי יראה בזה סימן ברכה   ואשרי האיש שלו ככה:
ובכן אשלם המלאכה   ואסיר כל טעות וטבוכה:
כדין וכהלהכ   בשם היחיד במלוכה:

For he will find therein an advantage, and hail the man who follows it.
Herewith I finish the work, having corrected in it all mistakes,
As it is meet and proper, in the name of Him who alone is Sovereign.

The other three works which Levita published in 1546 are bound up with the Exposition of the *Journey of the Paths of Knowledge*, and are as follows:—i. A concise Hebrew Grammar, entitled, *The Beginning of my Words* (פתח דברי), from an anonymous pen, "written many years ago in Spain, and exceedingly adapted to learn briefly the sacred language," first published at Naples, 1492, then at Constantinople, 1515, and now "carefully revised by Elias Levita, the Grammarian." ii. The well-known grammar of Ibn Ezra, entitled *On the Purity of the Hebrew Style* (צחות); and, iii., another grammatical treatise by Ibn Ezra, called *The Balance of the Sacred Language* (ספר מאזני לשון הקדש). The pagination of these four treatises is continuous: the first extends over leaf 1—51, the second over 52—132, the third over 133—194, The fourth over 195—286. Levita published these treatises under the general title of *Grammars* (דקדוקים).

Extraordinary as was his prowess to battle against the infirmities of old age, and determined as he was not to relinquish his literary labours till his arms were paralysed and his eyesight completely extinguished, Levita was at last compelled, by the irresistible and overpowering effects of the seventy-nine years which had now passed since he had seen the light, to confine himself to editing valuable works written by others. We cannot ascertain the number of works which he published this year, but we have before us Ralbag's Commentary on the Pentateuch, which Levita edited in 1547. Some idea may be formed of the labour required to carry it through the press, when it is stated that it consists of four hundred and ninety-six folio pages, closely printed, in square Hebrew characters. Levita appended to it a short poem in Hebrew. Twelve months later, he edited R. Isaac Duren's work on the Ceremonial Law, published at Venice, 1548, and appended to it a poem, which we have already mentioned, stating that he was then eighty years of age (*vide supra*, p. 2). This, as far as we know, is the last effort of the great teacher of cardinals and bishops of the Romish Church, and of the originators and leaders of the reformation, and who may justly be regarded as the reviver of Hebrew learning among Christians at the commencement of the sixteenth century, and as one of the most distinguished promoters of Biblical literature. He died, as he prayed to die, at Venice, aged eighty-one. The following simple epitaph indicated, to those who looked at the tomb-stones of the Jewish cemetery, the grave in which were deposited the remains of Elias Levita:—

הלא אבן מקיר תזעק
ותהמה לכל עובר
עלי זאת הקבורה
עלי רבן אשר נלקח
ועלה בשמים
אל–יה י׳ בסערה
הלא הוא זה אשר האיר
בדקדוק אפלתו
ושם אותו לאורה
שנת ש״ט שבט עלה
בסופו ונפשו בצרור החיים צרורה.

The stone cries from the wall,
And mourns before every passer by
Over this grave—
Over our Rabbi who has departed,
And ascended into heaven.
Elias is gone to the Lord in a whirlwind!
He who has shed light
On the darkness of grammar,
And turned it into light.
He ascended Shebat towards the end,
In the year 309 [=1549],
And his soul is bound up in the bundle of life.

INFORMATION FOR THE READER.[1]

THIS is for the information of every reader of this book. The celebrated printer, M. Daniel Bomberg, a Christian,[2] having resolved to issue the 24 sacred books, both in large and small sizes, is now printing them with the divisions, which are called in their language chapters, according to the order of the Christian books. And as there is a great advantage in it, which I have shown long ago in the introduction to the *Book Bachur*,[3] and as he who made the divisions of chapters also divided the books of Samuel, Kings, and Chronicles, respectively, into two books, I too was obliged to follow this method. You are, therefore, to observe, that wherever you will find the word Samuel with the letter *Beth* above it,[4] *e.g.* שְׁמוּאֵל, it means 2 *Samuel*, which begins with, "And it come to pass after the death of Saul," &c. The word Kings, too, with *Beth* above it,[4] *e.g.* מְלָכִים, means 2 *Kings*, and begins with, "Then Moab rebelled," &c.; and also the word Chronicles, or its initials ד״ה, with *Beth* above it,[4] *e.g.* ד״ה, means 2 *Chronicles*, and begins with, "And Solomon, the son of David, was strengthened," &c.

I must moreover inform you, that wherever I have propounded something new[5] in this book, or any important rule in which I have

---

[1] The words אזהרה למעיין, *Information for the Reader*, are omitted in the Sulzbach edition.
[2] The word הנוצרי, *a Christian*, is omitted in the Sulzbach edition.
[3] For a description of the Book Bachur, see above, page 16, &c.
[4] The word למעלה, *above it*, is omitted in all the three instances in the Sulzbach edition.
[5] The Sulzbach edition erroneously has the word דבר, *string*, after שאחדש, *I propound new*, as well as before אזה, *something*.

not been anticipated by any one, you will find the form of a hand in the margin against the remark in question, pointing with its finger ☞ and saying, as it were, 'see, something new is here told you, and this is to indicate it to you!' Let me now begin the Preface, in the name of the Lord of Hosts.

שפתו בנליון מראה באצבע לאמור כוח ראה
☞ וחדש יחדש לך דבר זה לך האות ובכן אתחיל בשם ה' צבאות:

PREFACE.

THUS says Elias, son of Asher the Levite, the German, behold, before I begin to speak, and compose an explanation of the plans of the Massorah, I must tell you what I am going to do in this book. I shall first divide the chief contents of the book into two parts, after the manner[6] of the two tables of stone, and write upon the first tables ten commandments [*i.e.* chapters.] In each one of these commandments I shall give useful rules respecting *defectives* and *plenes*.[7] The second tables will contain ten other injunctions [*i.e.* chapters.] In these I shall explain all the matters wherein all those who have laboured in this department are agreed; *i.e.*, show what the Massorites say about *the Keri* and *the Kethiv, the Kethivs*, which are disregarded, *the Kametz, Patach, Makeph, Sakeph, Chateph, Transpositions*, &c., &c. I shall then make an ark, open the door thereof, and put therein the broken tables, which are the work wherewith the authors of the *Massorah-porva* have occupied themselves, as I shall explain in the Introduction thereunto: and before it is yet born its name shall be called "the gate [*i.e.* the section] of the Broken Tables." This will form the last part of this book, and the sign thereof is, "the broken tables laid down in the ark."

הקדמה.

אמר אליהו ב"ר אשר הלוי האשכנזי, הגה אנכי טרם אחל לדבר, וביאור דרכי המסורת לחבר, אודיע נא אתכם את אשר אני עושה לספרי זה, ראשונה אחלק עקר הספר הזה לשני חלקים כדמות[6] שני לוחות אבנים, וכתבתי על הלוחות הראשונים, את עשרת הדברים, ובכל דבור ודבור אתן כללים מועילים, בעניני החסרים והמלאים:[7] וחלחות השניות, יהיו בעשרה מאמרים שנויות, ובהם אבאר כל הדברים, אשר הסכימו עליהם אנשי זאת המלאכה, ר"ל בעלי חמסורת לדבר בם, כגון קריין וכתיבין, וכתיבין ולא חשיבין, וקמצין ופתחין, ומקפין וזקפין וחטפין ומוקדמין ומאוחרין, וחרומים לאלה רבים, ואח"כ אעש ארון אחד ואפתח בו שער, ואשים בו שברי לוחות, הן הם חמלות אשר נתנו בהן בעלי המסורה הקטנה כאשר יתבאר בהקדמתו, וטרם חולדו נקרא שמו שער שברי לוחות, והוא יהיה חחלק האחרון מן חספר, וסמנך שברי לוחות מונחים בארון.

[6] The Sulzbach edition erroneously has כשמות, *according to the names of*, instead of כדמות, *after the manner of*.

[7] The Sulzbach edition incorrectly puts המלאים, *plene*, before החסרים, *defective*.

But since I have seen that it is not good for this book to be alone, I shall make for it a help-mate, in the form of an Introduction, of such things which have not hitherto been propounded. Therein shall I dispel questions, explain difficulties, and remove doubts which fall under this investigation, and which are to be found in the treatises of our Rabbins of blessed memory, the men of the Great Synagogue and of the Massorah. And the eyes of those who will see shall behold that which is upright, for they perceive the truth. Moreover, things and remarks occur in this book which will be difficult of understanding to the students thereof, unless they read first the introductions which I have prefixed, and which are three in number. The first is in poetry (שיר), the second in rhyme (בחרוזה), and the third in ordinary prose.

And if I had the power to exact an oath from an Israelite, I would make every one who is about to study this book swear that he will not peruse it till he has read these introductions. However, I beseech and pray you to take my advice about it, and those who will do it will derive the benefit. Now, I am persuaded that no man[8] will regret the time spent in perusing them, but that it will be a pleasant task to those who read them; for they will find therein things, both new and old, which they did not know and never heard before, not only connected with the Massorah, but with grammar, vowel points, &c., which are not mentioned in the works of ancient or modern writers. I will, also, relate ordinary conversations, the talk of the world, what has befallen me, and what I have seen, as well as my defence against many people who have risen against me, and abused me for teaching the law to disciples that are unworthy thereof.[9] All these things are desirable to make us wise, and are pleasant to the imagination. For, verily, my words are not false; whoso is on the Lord's side let him come to me.

---

8 & 9 The word איש, *man*, as well as the passage beginning with ונם דבר מתנצלותי, *and also my defence*, and ending with הגונים, *worthy*, is wanting in the Sulzbach edition.

שירת משובחה פשוטה ומרובעת [10]

אֶתֵּן שֶׁבַח גַּם תִּפְאָרֶת, לָאֵל תִּקֵּן רוּם בְּזֶרֶת;
לֹא לְהֶבֶל בָּרָא תֵבֵל, לְשֶׁבֶת הָיְתָה נִגְמֶרֶת;
יָסַד אֶרֶץ עַל רְחָמִים, פָּשַׁט אוֹתָהּ כְּאִגֶּרֶת;
הִבִּיט וְיֶתֶר הַגּוֹיִם, לָקַח לוֹ אוּמָּה נִבְחֶרֶת;
וַיּוֹצִיאֵם מֵאֶרֶץ כּוּשׁ, מָהוֹן וּרְכוּשׁ נוּף נִנְעֶרֶת;
הֵנִיף בַּעִים יָדוֹ עַל יָם, צָרִים צָלְלוּ כְּעוֹפֶרֶת;
לֵמוֹ אֵשׁ דָּת נָתַן מַתַּת, צוּם לִהְיוֹתָהּ נִשְׁמֶרֶת;
וַיַּנְחִילֵם אֶרֶץ חֶמְדָּה, וּרְחָבָה עַד יָם כִּנֶּרֶת;
יַחַד שָׁמְנוּ וַיִּבְעָטוּ, הָיוּ כְּפָרָה סוֹרֶרֶת;
אָוֶן חָמְדוּ וַיִּצְמְדוּ, אֶל הַבַּעַל וּלְעַשְׁתֹּרֶת;
שָׁמַע דָּאֵל וַיִּתְעַבָּר, וַיִּשְׁלַח בָּם הַמְּנַעֶרֶת;
כֻּלָּם בַּדֶּבֶר וּבַחֶרֶב, גַּם בָּרָעָב שֶׁל בַּצֹּרֶת;
נָטַשׁ הָעִיר סֵתֶר רוּדִיר, הָיְתָה הַצֹּאן צָאן נִפְזֶרֶת;
זָרַם מֵעֶבֶר לִנְהַר־ור, כְּיוֹם אֶל אֶרֶץ אַחֶרֶת;
יוֹרְדֵי שֶׁנְעָר עָמְדוּ מִצֵּעָר, לְמַלֵּא עֵת הַנִּגְזֶרֶת;
שִׁבְעִים שָׁנָה אָבֵן שָׁמָּה, הָיְתָה הַתּוֹרָה נֶעְדֶּרֶת;
וּשְׁמוֹתָם שָׁנוּ וּלְשׁוֹנָם, לָבְשׁוּ כֵּנִים אַדֶּרֶת;
אָדָם הָיָה נוֹשֵׂא גּוֹיָה, אוֹ נָכְרִיָּה אוֹ מַמְזֶרֶת;
וּבְנֵיהֶם לֹא הִכִּירוּ רַק, לָשׁוֹן שֶׁאִמָּם דּוֹבֶרֶת;
וּבָעֵת רָקַע רוּחַ כּוֹרֶשׁ, מֶלֶךְ פָּרַס מְעוֹרֶרֶת;
אָמַר לָאֲסִירִים תֵּצֵאוּ, וּבְנוּ הָעִיר הַמְעוֹטֶרֶת;
עָלָה עֶזְרָא הוּא מַלְאָכִי, דוֹמֶה אֶל מַלְאָךְ הַשָּׁרֵת;
כֹּהֵן וְרַב וְלַסּוֹפְרִים אָב, אֵם לַמִּקְרָא וְלַמָּסּוֹרֶת;
עָשָׂה אָז בַּכֹּל כִּמְצוּלָה, שֶׁאֵין בָּהּ דָּגָה נִשְׁאֶרֶת;
שׁוּם שֵׂכֶל הֵבִין בַּמִּקְרָא, בִּכְתִיבָה זוֹ הַמְאֻשֶּׁרֶת;
קוֹצִים בְּלֹה מִכָּל מִלָּה, הֶחֱזִיר אֶל יוֹשְׁנָהּ הָעֲטֶרֶת;
אַחֲרָיו לַאֲלָפִים וּרְבָבוֹת, עָשׂוּ מִשְׁמָר אֶל מִשְׁמֶרֶת;
רוֹב כַּת אַנְשֵׁי זֶה הַמַּעֲשֶׂה, אָז בְּטִבֶּרְיָא מִתְגּוֹרֶרֶת;
יָדָם הָיְתָה בָּרִאשׁוֹנָה, בַּחָכְמָה זוֹ הַמְפֹאָרֶת;
גַּם הִמְצִיאוּ דָּת הַנִּקּוּד, מֵהֶם הִיא לָנוּ נִמְסֶרֶת;
גַּם הַטְּעָמִים הָיוּ שָׁמַיִם, לִחְיוֹת בָּם תּוֹרָה נִפְתֶּרֶת;

[10] It will be seen that the commencing letters of the first fifteen lines, are the acrostic of אליהו הלוי אשכנזי, *Elijahu Ha-Levi, the German*. In Münster's edition (1539), this acrostic is entirely obliterated by the peculiar mode in which the editor arranged the lines.

INTRODUCTION I.

A SONG OF PRAISE, SIMPLE, AND OF FOUR FEET.

I render praise and glory[10] to the Lord, who made the heaven with His span.
Not in vain did He create the world; for a habitation has He made it.
He founded the earth upon the waters; He unrolled it like a scroll.
He looked and rejected the Gentiles; He took to Himself His chosen people.
He brought them out of Egypt, which was spoiled of its treasure and wealth.
He stretched his mighty hand upon the sea, and the enemy sunk down like lead.
To His people He gave the fiery law as a gift; commanding them to observe it.
He caused them to inherit a goodly land; extending to the sea of Gennesareth.
But they grew fat and kicked; they became like a refractory heifer.
They lusted after vanity, and joined themselves to Baal and Ashtoreth.
The Lord heard it, and was angry, and sent a curse among them.
He destroyed them by pestilence, and by sword, and by famine.
He abandoned the city, destroyed the sheepfold, and scattered the sheep.
He drove them beyond the sea, as at this day; into a foreign land.
They abode in Shinar a little while, according to the time appointed.
Seventy years the temple laid waste; the law was forgotten.
The people changed their names and tongue; they dressed like the Gentiles.
The Jew married a Gentile wife, or a stranger, or a bastard;
And the children knew nothing, except the language which their mother spoke.
At the appointed time, the spirit of Cyrus, the king of Persia, was stirred up.
He said to the Captains, Go forth, and build the glorious city.
Ezra then went, who is the messenger, like a ministering angel;
The priest, the prince, and the father of scribes, the nursing mother of the Scripture and Massorah.
By his departure, Babylon remained like a pond, wherein no fish are left.
He applied wisdom to understand the Scripture, in its present superior characters.
He cut off thorns from every word; he restored the crown to its pristine splendour.
After him, thousands and myriads added fence unto fence.
Most of these indefatigable workers sojourned then in Tiberias;
They were the first in this wonderful science;
They invented the system of punctuation, and transmitted it to us.
They, too, added the accents, whereby the law might be explained;

כי לולי טעמי דהפסוק, הבנתו לא נכרת;
כי הם ידעו באור המקרא, מכל נולה הנשארת;
לכן פירוש נגד טעמו, נחשב כסיג או כנעורת;
הורו תיבות איך נכתבות, המלאה או המחוסרת;
גם אם מלה טעמה מעלה, או מקצה בחוברת;
לכללים עשו סימנים, להיות על לב למזכרת;
אך שמו אותותם אותות, חידות עם לשון ברברת;
הרבים לא יחכמו בה, אין מבין מה היא אומרת;
עד כי בא יום אמרו אלי, חברת רעי המהודרת;
נא מה לך פה אליהו, קום ועשה לך שם הפארת;
ולמסרה תאיר אורה, ופתח נא בה המסגרת;
ידענו בך כי זאת עמך, בהיד שכלך היא נוברת;
אז אמרתי שמעי נפשי, למה זה את מתנכרת;
קומי ועשי עת לד׳׳י, פן תהיה תורה מופרת;
מקום הניחו לך אבות, להיותך בו מתנדרת;
אז אמרה לי נפשי האח, בזה אנכי בוחרת;
ובכן קמתי לא דוממתי, גם קדמו עיני אשמורת;
עד אוציא לאור תעלומה, היתה עד הנה נסתרת;
אל כל אדם אמתיק סודם, אפקח כל עין עורת;
קצור מלים המועילים, בשני לוחות אהיה תורת;
אתן הלוחות בפומבי, ודלא כמלתא נטמרת;
לעד בנייר יחצבון, עם עט ברזל ובעופרת;
הלוקח לא יחשב, גנב נמצא במחתרת;
לכן אל כל כשופר קול, ארים על נבי רום קרת;
הזריז יקדים למצוה, כי מצוה מצוה גוררת;
לסחורה זאת זרוז יאות, פן תהיה כלה נמכרת;
כי טוב סחרה מכל מסחר, מה לך אל דר או סוחרת;
הא לך אורח למסרה, כי לתורה היא עקרת;
על כן אקרא שם הספר, זה מסורת המסורת;
השיר נשלם אל אל עולם, אתן שבח גם תפארת;

But for the accents, the sense could not be discerned.
They knew the interpretation of the Scriptures better than all the rest of the captivity ;
Therefore, an interpretation contrary to the accents must be regarded as dross or as chaff.
They taught how the words should be written, whether plene or defective ;
Whether a word is to be connected with the preceding, or the following sentence.
They made signs, to serve as rules to aid the memory.
The signs, however, are problems ; riddles taken from foreign languages ;
Many could not understand them ; and did not know what they mean ;
Till the day when it was said to me, by my estimable friends,
" Now, what dost thou here, Elias ? Arise, and make thyself a great name.
Throw light on the Massorah ; and open that which is locked up therein :
We know that this is within thy power ; that thou possessest the mastery over it."
Then said I to myself, 'Hearken, my soul ; Why art thou disquieted?
Arise, it is time to work for the Lord, lest the law become void :
Thy fathers have left a place wherein thou mayest fortify thyself.'
My soul then responded, 'Ah ! This I gladly choose.'
I therefore bestirred myself, and did not rest ; yea, my eyes prevented the night watches,
Till I brought to light the hidden things, which have hitherto been concealed.
Their counsel will be sweet to every man, and the eyes of the blind will be opened.
An abridgment of useful words I will propound, on two tables ;
I will put these tables openly, and not as secret words.
For a witness, they shall be printed on paper with an iron and leaden pen.
The buyer shall not be accountable, if a thief is found breaking in.
Therefore, to all, as with a trumpet, I raise my voice upon the heights of the city.
Let the quick hasten to the good work ; for one good work leads to another.
For such merchandise, quickness is becoming, lest it be all sold ;
As its merchandise is better than all traffic. What are precious stones to thee ?
Behold here an explanation of the Massorah, which is the basis of the law.
Therefore, I call the name of this book, *Massoreth Ha-Massoreth*.
The song is finished, to the God of the universe, I give praise and glory.

INTRODUCTION II.

| THE RYTHMICAL INTRODUCTION, ACCORDING TO GERMAN RHYME. | וזאת ההקדמה החרוזית, על דרך חרוזה אשכנזית: |

Thus saith Elias Levita, who gathered together counsels afar off from innumerable works to compile Treatises on grammar in as few words as possible, and to make a path to the various voices, both small and great. These are my four small productions, all treating on the science of our language. The first volume which I composed is my explanation of the *Journey on the Path of Knowledge;* its utility is known to all. The second is the *Book Bachur*, which animadverts on Grammarians.[11] The third is the *Book on Compounds*, in which all irregular words are explained. The fourth is a *Poetical Section*, together with other Sections appended thereunto. These four productions of mine, owing to their wisdom and knowledge, have been published several times, translated into the languages of the Christians, and are studied both by Jew and Gentile, as their fame has travelled far and their excellence is known all over the world. They send forth an odour like precious ointment, on which account I congratulate myself. Now I speak the truth when I say, that there has been no author, whose works God has permitted him in his lifetime to see so much referred to and studied, and so many times reprinted, as he has permitted me during my lifetime. My hand is still ready to give more help, and to benefit the public. My worthy disciples are around me now, as well as all my old friends; they earnestly entreat me, saying, for God's sake, and for the glory of Holy Writ, explain to us the Massorah; for we know that it is in thy power, as we have heard that thy hand is strong in all Massoretic matters, above all our contemporaries, as well as above all of whom we have heard.

נאם אליהו הלוי. חמוציא והמביא, עצות
מרחוק, לשום לדקדוק חוק, ודרך לחיי
קולות, קמנת עם גדולות, במיעוט דברים,
בחבור ספרים, פרצו עליהם פרץ, ארבעה הם
קמני ארץ, כלם בחכמת הלשון, והספר
הראשון, אשר בהם חברתי, הוא אשר בארתי,
מהלך שבילי הדרך. רתועלתו לכל
מודעת, ואחריו ספר הבחור, משיב
מדקדקים אחד,[11] ואחריו ספר ההרכבה
כל מלה זרה בו נכתבה, ואחריו פרק שירה
עם שאר פרקים עד נמידה, וחילדים אלה
ארבעתם, לחכמתם ולדעתם, כמה פעמים
נחקקים, וללשון הנים מועתקים, ובהם
עמלים, מולים וערלים, ומרחוק נשמע קולם,
וכבורם מלא עולם, וכשמן המוב נותנים ריח,
ובוה את עצמי אשבח, וחיוטר אדבר, כי לא
היה מחבר, שזכה אלהים אותו, שראה לפני
מותו, ספריו נזכרים ונעשים, וכמה פעמים
נדפסים, כמו שזכה אותי, בעוד בחיים היותי,
ועוד ידי נטויה, להגדיל תושיה, ולזכות את
הרבים, ועתה אותי מסבים, תלמידי החגונים,
וכל יודעי לפנים, ומבקשים את פני, לאמר
למען י"י, ולכבוד קדושת התורה, תבאר לנו
המסרה, כי ידענו כי זאת עמך, כי שמענו
ממך, כי ידך גוברת, בכל דברי המסורת, מכל
אנשי דורנו, ומאשר שמענו באזנינו.

---

[11] The words ואחריו ספר הבחור משיב מדקדקים אחור, *the second is the Book Bachur, which animadverts on Grammarians*, without which Levita's statement is unintelligible, are omitted in the Sulzbach edition.

When I heard their flattering words, I inclined my ear to them and answered, I accede to your entreaty. And indeed their wish fully harmonised with my intention. Now I swear, by the Lord, that this very thing was in my mind before, when I was still in Rome, where I temporarily resided, and composed the above-named works, only that I had not sufficient time, as the evil days came and the city was captured,[12] and I, insignificant one, was compelled by fate to relinquish the contemplated Treatise. Now, after the lapse of years, God having permitted me to settle in this beautiful place, the celebrated Venice, the great city, I comply with their wish, and will perform a work in Israel that whosoever sees it may tell its wonders. I have, therefore, compiled this Treatise on all Massoretic matters, connected with both the Massora *magna* and *parva*, as it is now twenty years that I have been in the way to find out its value, to unfold its import and its laconic style, which is often as obscure as the words of a sealed book.

How I laboured therein, neither resting nor being satisfied, and searched in the correct and excellent books, giving my mind hereunto! Now I swear, by truth and justice, and may God give me riches, that more than once or twice I performed a day or two day's journey to a place, which I either knew myself or of which I had been informed, that there is to be found therein a reliable index of the Massorah. When I examined it, and found it correct, I selected from it the choice and correct articles, as roses from among thorns. Indeed, most of the correct Codices I found to be Spanish, and it is upon these that I relied, and it is their method that I followed. Still, my soul was not as yet satisfied, until I found the *Book Ochla Ve-Ochla*.[13] I got much out of it, and adopted its rules; and, though

ובשמעי דבריהם כי נעמו, המיתי את
אזני אליטו, ואמרתי את קולכם שמעתי,
ובאמת כוונתם דעתי, והנני נשבע בי"י, כך
עלתה במחשבה לפני, בעוד היותי ברומי,
אשר שם היה מקומי, וחברתי שם הספרים,
אשר למעלה נזכרים, ולא הספיקה לי השעה,
כי באו ימי הרעה, ונלכדה העיר,[12] ואנכי
הצעיר, הייתי אנוס על פי הדבור, ולא עשיתי
החבור, ועתה אחרי בלותי, שזכה אלהים אותי,
ובאתי לכלל ישוב, בזה המקום החשוב,
וניזיי"א המהוללה, היא העיר הגדולה, הנני
לבקשחכם אואל, ואעשה דבר בישראל, אשר
כל רואיו, יספרו פלאיו, ואחבד זאת המחברת,
בכל דברי המסורת, גדולה וקטנה, כי זה לי
עשרים שנה, אנכי בדרך, למצא לה ערך,
לבאר ענינה, וקצור לשונה, אשר הוא סתום,
כדברי הספר החתום.

וכמה בזה טרחתי, ולא שקטתי ולא נחתי,
ועיינתי בספרים, מדויקים וישרים, ונתתי
עליהם דעתי, והנני נשבעתי, בחי האמת
והיושר, וכח יתן לי אלהים עושר, כי לא אחת
ולא שתים, הלכתי דרך יום או יומים, למקום
שידעתי, ומפי השמועה שמעתי, ששם מצויה,
מסרת הראויה, לסמוך עליה, וכאשר קרבתי
אליה, ולא מצאתי לה פסולים, חקחקתי ממנה
מלים, הטובים והנכוחים, כשושנה בין
החוחים, ובאמת רוב הנוכחאות, המונחות
הנמצאות, הם ספרים אחרים, מספרי הספרדים,
ועליהם נסמכתי, ובנתיבותיהם דרכתי, ועם
כל זאת, צמאי לרוות, נפשי לא יכלה, כי אם
מספר אכלה ואכלה,[13] והרבה ממנו לקמתי,

---

[12] The capture and sacking of Padua took place in 1509, as described above, *vide supra*, p. 14.

[13] This long lost and most valuable Massoretic work has now been published, with

it is a book of small dimensions, there is nothing like it in the department of the Massorah. It treats upon important matters, and there is no other book which so thoroughly treats on the Massoretic rules, excepting the scattered glosses around the margin in the Codices, which, however, contain numberless errors. For the Scribes have perverted them, as they did not care for the Massorah, but only thought to ornament their writing, and to make even lines so as not to alter the appearance, in order that all the pages should be alike. Moreover, they ornamented them with illuminations of divers kinds of buds, flowers, &c. Hence they were obliged sometimes to narrow and sometimes to widen the margins round the illustrations with words already stated, although they were superfluous and out of place, whilst the Massoretic signs were entirely omitted in their proper place because the space did not suffice; and hence they had to break off in the middle of a sentence,[14] thus leaving the whole edifice incomplete and greatly defective.[15]

As to the Massorah, in the twenty-four sacred books printed here, I have not seen anything like it, among all the ancient books, for arrangement and correctness, for beauty and excellence, and for good order. They were edited by one of the learned, whose name was formerly Jacob (let his soul be bound up in a bag with holes).[16] But although his edition is exceedingly beautiful, he committed many

וכלליו בידי נקמתי, והוא ספר קמן הכמות,
ובמסורת אין לו חרמות, ונכבדות בו מדובר,
ולא נמצא ספר מחובר, המדבר מהמסודה
וכללם, רק הוא לבדו בעולם, חוץ ממה שנרשם
זעיר שם זעיר שם, סביב הספרים בגליונות,
ובהם חסרון לא יוכל להמנות, כי הסופרים
הזידו, ועל המסורת לא הקפידו, רק עיקר
חשיבותם, ליפות את כתיבתם, ולכוון את
השורות, שלא ישנו את הצורות, וחתינה שוה
בכל הדפין, ועוד אותן מיפין, בתמונות
וציורים, בסכסוכים ובקישורים, ובציצים
ובפרחים, ועל כן הם מוכרחים, לפעמים לקצר,
ולפעמים לבצד, חומות הציורים, בדברים
האמורים, במקומות אחרים, והם פה יתרים,
ואין כאן מקומם, ולפעמים רשומם, במקום
הראוי לא נכר, ולא זכרום כלל ועקר, כי
המקום לא הספיק, והוצרכו להפסיק, באמצע
הענין, ולא נשלם הבנין,[14] וחסורי מחסרים.[15]

אכן המסורת מהארבע ועשרים, הגדפסות
הנה, לא ראיתי כהנה, בכל ספרי הקדמונים,
מסודרים ומתוקנים, ביופי ובהדור, ובמוב
חסדור, סדרם אחד מהגבונים, היה שמו לפנים,
בישראל נקרא יעקב,[16] תהי נשמתו צרורה
בצרוד נקוב, ואף שחבורו במאוד נאה, הרבה

---

learned annotations, by Frensdorff, Hanover, 1844. The reader will find all Levita's references to the *Massorah*, contained in the *Massoreth Ha-Massoreth*, compared with the statements in the *Ochla Ve-Ochla*.

[14] The above description of the condition of the Massorah, and of the manner in which it has been treated by the copyists, is almost literally the same as that given by Jacob b. Chajim, the first editor of the Massorah. Comp. Jacob b. Chajim's *Introduction to the Rabbinic Bible*, p. 12 in the Hebrew, and 35 in the English translation, ed. Ginsburg, Longmans, 1865.

[15] The words וחסורי מחסרים are omitted in the Sulzbach edition.

[16] For this celebrated Massorite, and the Bible here alluded to, see above, p. 38. From Levita's vituperation, it is evident that Jacob b. Chajim was now dead, inasmuch as the phrase, "let his soul be bound up in a bag of holes," is a spiteful and unworthy perversion of the beautiful, charitable, and reverential prayer, which the Jews use when speaking of or writing about any one of their brethren who has departed this life, in allusion to 1 Sam. xxv. 29, because he had embraced Christianity.

mistakes, and bore false testimony in many places. This, however, is not to be wondered at, for the work was new, and every beginning is difficult. With great diligence, therefore, with little sloth, and with immense toil, I laboured to separate that which is clear from that which is obscure,—brought the Massoretic materials into order, and put a proper space between each section and every article. You may believe that I have laboured and found what none else has discovered, and discharged my duty in such things in which nobody has preceded me, knowing that the words of the Massorah are completely hidden from our contemporaries. Indeed very few understand the language thereof, which is to them as a dream without an interpretation, and from which they have no advantage; they neither know nor understand, for they dwell in darkness. Yet the Massorah is the fence of the law, and from it are deduced many essential *Halachoth*, reasons and explanations, literal and homiletical meanings, whilst from the defective and plene many laws are deduced; *ex. gr.*, from רב [Exod. xxiii. 2] which is defective;[17] from the first מזוזת [Deut. vi. 9][18] which wants the second *Vav*, and many other similar instances from which laws are deduced. It is for this reason that I purpose to explain its import, laws, and rules in this little volume in brevity, and without tediousness, yet in words of great might; propound new things recently brought to light which did not exist before, and they shall be as luminaries in the firmament of the Massorah, so that the wise will understand and prepare their hearts to be wise in the Scriptures; and the name thereof shall be known in

שנה ברואה, ובמקומות אין חקר, העיד עדות שקר, ואין לתמוה על ככה, כי בזאת המלאכה, היה חנור חדשה, וכל התחלה קשה, ואני ברוב השתדלותי, ובמטום עצלותי, ובעמל שעמלתי, בין אור לחשך הבדלתי, ונתתי לביאורם סדר, והיה שמתי בין עדר ובין עדר, ובין כל מין ומין, ינעתי ומצאתי תאמין, מה שלא מצא זולתי, ודי חובתי יצאתי, בדברים אשר לא קדם, אותי בהם אדם, בידעי כי דברי המסורות, מאנשי אלה הדורות, נכחדו ונעלמו, ולא רבים יחכמו, להבין את דבריהם, וחסח בעיניהם, כחלום בלא פתרון, ואין בהם יתרון, ולא ידעו ולא יבינו, כי בחשיכה ילינו, והלא חמסרה, היא סיג לתורה, וממנה נמשכות, כמה גופי הלכות, ומעמים ופירושים, ופשטים ומדרשים, ומן החסרים והמלאים, כמה דינים מוציאים, כגון ולא תענה על ריב,[17] הוא חסר כתיב, וכן על מזוזת[18] ביתך קדמאה דענינא, חסר וי"ו תנינא, וכן כמה מינים, שיוצאין מהם דינים, ולזאת הכבה, אבאר מה מבח, ודינן ומשפטן, בזה החבור הקמן, בקיצור ולא באריכות, בדברים רב האיכות, חדשים מקרוב באו, ולא מאז נבראו, והיו למאורות, ברקיע המסורות, והמשכילים יבינו, ולבם יבינו, להשכיל במקרא, ויחיח שמו נקרא, בפי

[17] Hence it is taken for רב, *chief*, and it is deduced that no one is to speak against its chief, i.e., the King or High Priest, comp. *Sanhedrin* 18, *b.*, and Rashi on Exod. xxiii. 2.

[18] מזוזה, with the Jews, denotes the piece of parchment whereon are written the passages in Deut. vi. 4-9, xi. 13-21, which they regard as containing the injunction to inscribe on the door-posts the words of the Law. The slip of vellum thus written upon is enclosed in a cylindrical tube of lead, cane, or wood, and to the present day is nailed to the right door-post of every door. For a detached description of this institution, we must refer to Kitto's *Cyclopædia of Biblical Literature*, new ed., *s. v.*, *Mezuzah*; and for the law deduced from the word מזוה, being written definitely in Deut. vi. 9, to which Levita alludes, we must refer to Jacob b. Chajim's *Introduction to the Rabbinic Bible*, p. 9 Hebrew, and p. 21 English translation, ed. Ginsburg.

the mouth of all students, both Jews and Christians,[19] who delight in our Law and profit therefrom.

Now I swear, by my Creator, that a certain Christian encouraged it, and brought me thus far. He was my pupil ten years uninterruptedly,[20] I resided at his house and instructed him, for which there was a great outcry against me, and it was not considered right of me. And several of the Rabbins would not countenance me, and pronounced woe to my soul because I taught the law to a Christian,[21] owing to the interpretation assigned to the words, "And as for my judgments they [*i.e.* the Gentiles] are not to know them; praise the Lord for it." [Ps. cxlvii. 20). Now my tardiness will not prevent me from making a defence. I shall, therefore, state all that took place. In the year 269 [= 1509], violence rose up into a rod of wickedness, and the arrow was desperate without any fault; for it came to pass, when I was in Padua, that the celebrated city was captured, and sacked, and devastated; the enemies then destroyed my dwelling, together with that of other Jews, and all that I had became a prey, and was like the leaving when the dung is cleared away. Then it fell into my lines to be a roamer at the head of the exiles. I left my place and went to Rome, where resided a very distinguished nobleman, a prince of great dignity, and wise as Solomon, and his name was Cardinal Egidio. When I heard his fame, I paid him a visit.

When he saw me, he asked me about my affairs. I said, Know, my lord, that I am the German grammarian, who possess the sundry secrets connected with the grammar and Scripture, for I have always been

---

[19] The Sulzbach edition substitutes כנכרים, *strangers*, for נרים, *Christians*.

[20] The apparent contradiction between the above statements, that he lived in Egidio's house about *ten* years, and the remark in the Introduction to the *Tishbi*, that he had learned from Cardinal Egidio, with whom he was *thirteen* years (הקרדינאל אשר עמדתי עמו שלש עשרה שנה קבלתי כל אלה), is to be accounted for thus: in the *Massoreth Ha-Massoreth*, Levita gives the *round* number, i. e., *about* ten (וכמשר) years; Graetz (*Geschichte der Juden*, ix. 224), explains it, that as Cardinal Egidio was about several years from Rome (comp. Reuchlin's Letters in Friedländer's *Beiträge zur Reformations Geschichte*, pp. 89, 99), Levita was ten years in his house at Rome, and three years with him away from the Eternal city.

[21] The words ואמרים לנפשי אוי על שלמדתי תורה לנוי, *and they say, Woe to my soul, because I taught a Christian the Law*, are omitted in the Sulzbach edition.

occupied with this work, therefore is no man to be found who is more conversant therewith than I am; as a poet said, that he was never conquered except by a man of one idea. Moreover, I have learned wisdom from my disciples, and they aided me in this knowledge; as a certain Talmudist said, I have learned much from my teachers, more from my fellow students, and most from my learned disciples.[22]

When the prince heard my statement, he came to me and kissed me with the kisses of his mouth, saying, Art thou, my lord, Elias, whose fame has travelled over all countries, and whose books are to be found in every corner?[23] Blessed be the God of the Universe, who brought thee hither, and bade thee come to meet me. Now abide with me and be my teacher, and I shall be to thee as a father, and shall support thee and thy house, and give thee thy corn, thy wine, and thy olives, and fill thy purse, and bear all thy wants. Thus we took sweet counsel together, iron sharpening iron. I imparted my spirit to him, and learned from him excellent and valuable things, which are in accordance with truth. I followed the advice of the sage, who says, "Learn truth, from whomsoever it is propounded."

In conclusion, I fully acknowledge it, as one confesses before a solemn tribunal, and shall not withdraw it, that I have been a teacher to Christians;[24] yea, I have assuredly been; but nevertheless, know that I am a Hebrew, praise the Lord, and revere the Lord, who made heaven and earth; I have not sinned, and am innocent and guiltless. For

---

[22] The above quoted saying is recorded in the Talmud (*Taanith* 7 a), as having been uttered by R. Chanina, and is literally as follows: הרבה למדתי מרבותי ומחברי יותר מהם, ומתלמידי יותר מכלן, *much have I learned from my teachers, more from my associates, but most from my disciples*. Levita varied it a little to adapt it to his rhyme. In the *Midrash Jalkut* on Ecclesiastes v. 7, where the same saying is quoted, it is ascribed to R. Berachja. Comp. sect. 973, vol. ii., p. 185 *a*, ed. Frankfort on the Maine, 1687.

[23] This remark is certainly proleptical, since, at the time when Levita had his first interview with Cardinal Egidio, (*circa* 1510), he had not as yet published any books of his own, and even his small maiden production, which appeared in 1508, was published surreptitiously, *vidé supra*, pp. 13, 80, &c.

[24] In the Sulzbach edition, נכרים, *foreigners*, is substituted for גוים, *Christians*.

o

the sages only prohibit[25] the communication to a Gentile of the import of the Law,[26] but do not forbid teaching. Their interdict only refers to subjects which contain esoteric doctrines, as the Creation, the Vision of Ezekiel, and the Book Jetzira,[27] which must only be disclosed to the pious, to men of wisdom and intelligence who are of the children of Israel. Thus, also, the passage, "Like a bag of gems in a heap of stones" [Prov. xxvi. 8], which they interpret of an unworthy disciple, whom they liken to one who cast stones at the statue of Mercurius,[28] saying, Whoso teaches the law to an unworthy disciple shall descend

כי חכמים אינם אומרין,[25] רק שדברי תורה לגוי אין מוסרין,[26] ולא אמרו אין מלמדין, רק עקרי דבריהם עומדין, על דברין ששייך בחן מסירה, כגון [27]מעשה בראשית ומעשה מרכבה וספר יצירה, שאין מנלין אלא לצנועים, אנשים חכמים וידועים, אשר מבני ישראל המה, וכן כצדור אבן במדינה, אשר על תלמיד שאינו חנון דרשוחו, ולזורק אבן למרקוליס[28] דמוחו, ואמרו כל חלומד תורה לתלמיד

[25] The Sulzbach edition has substituted במה שאמרו, in what they say, for רק ש, but what, in consequence of the omission presently to be noticed.

[26] From ולא אמרו, but they did not say, to כל הלומד, whoso teaches, is omitted in the Sulzbach edition, and the editor substituted, from his own cogitations, the following: אלא בזמנם· שהגוים החמה בנואה אינם מאמינים· אבל בזמנו זה· לא יעשה כזה· כי אין להם דין גוים הנוכרים בגמרא· מה שטומו בפוסקים ובסברא· וכיה ש—, it only refers to their time when the Heathen did not believe in the Creator, but in our time, this is not applicable, since they are not like the Gentiles mentioned in the Talmud, as is evident both from the later legislators, and common sense, and what—. The omission of the lengthy paragraph from the text, as well as the insertion of the concocted passage in question, which was dictated by the censorship of the press, has given rise to the alteration mentioned in the preceding note.

[27] The work of the Hexahemeron is technically called, in the Jewish literature, מעשה בראשית, because the first book of Moses, or more especially the history of the cosmogony, begins with the word בראשית, (comp. Mishna Taanith iv. 2, Megilla iii. 6; Chullin v. 5.) The Vision of Ezekiel, again, is denominated the Chariot (מרכבה), or the Work of the Chariot (מעשה מרכבה), in conformity to the former phrase, with which it is generally associated, and comprises Ezekiel, chapters i. and x., which treat on the Divine Throne, resting on wheels, and carried by sacred animals. The Jews, from time immemorial, have attached great mysteries to these sections of the Hebrew Scriptures, which discourse on the cosmogony and theosophy of the Old Testament, and have invested them with the halo of peculiar sanctity. Special directions are given to those who study these biblical questions. Thus the Mishna declares that "the work of the Hexahemeron (מעשה בראשית) must not be expounded in the presence of two persons, and the Chariot (מרכבה), not even in the presence of one person, unless he is a sage, and understands it already from his own cogitations" (Chagiga iii. 1). It is to this enactment that Levita evidently refers, since he uses almost the very words of the Mishna.

As to the Book Jetzira (ספר יצירה), or the Book of Creation, to which reference is made in the text, it purports to be a monologue of the patriarch Abraham, giving the contemplations which led the father of the Hebrews to abandon the worship of the stars, and to embrace the faith of the true God. Its design is to exhibit a system, whereby the universe may be viewed methodically, in connection with the truths given in the Bible, by means of the double value of the twenty-two letters of the Hebrew alphabet, as well as by the ten digits. For an analysis of this famous document, see Ginsburg, the Kabbalah, pp. 65–77, Longmans, 1865.

[28] Levita alludes to the ancient mode of worship offered to the heathen deity Hermes, which consisted in mere heaps of stone, called Ἑρμαῖοι λόφοι, ἑρμαῖα or ἕρμακες, being the symbol of Phallus, and thus giving rise to the ithyphalic arrow-form of Hermes. These heaps of stones were more especially collected on the road-sides, and each traveller paid his homage to the deity by throwing a stone to the heap as he passed by, or anointed the heap of stones in which a Hermes was frequently set up, or offered up the firstlings. Comp. Gen. xxviii. 10–22, xxxi. 45–48; Sanhedrin 61 a–64 a; Midrash on Prov. 26 a, כל מי שחולק כבוד לכסל כזורק אבן למרקולים, being the law referred to by Levita. Pauly, Real Encyclopädie der classischen Alterthumswissenschaft, s. v. MERCURIUS.

into the grave with sorrow, and his spirit and soul shall be destroyed; as it is written, "a fire not blown shall consume him" [Job xx. 26]; this only refers to an Israelite, but not to a Christian or Mahommedan.

Again,[29] when the Talmud says that the secrets of the law are not to be disclosed except to one who has the five qualifications, viz., advanced age, respectability, and all the rest as they are found in Isaiah," we have sufficient argument in this, that the sages have not enacted a decree that whosoever teaches a Gentile commits a sin. For even according to their words it is permitted to teach Gentiles the Seven Noahic Commandments.[30] Now this argues most powerfully for me. For how can they possibly know these, and fully comprehend the import of the seven precepts, unless they first know the Hebrew language?

שאינו הגון, ידד שאולח בינון, ורוחו ונשמתו תפח, שנאמד תאכלחו אש לא נפח, לא דברו אלא בישראלי, ולא באדומי או ישמעאלי.

ועוד מה[29] שאמרו בנמרה, אין מוסרין סתרי תורה, אלא מי שיש בו חמישה ענינים, זקן ונשוא פנים, וכולי כדאיתא בישעיה, ודי לני בזו ראיה, שחכמים לא גזרו גזרה, שהלמוד לנוי יחיח עבדה, כי אפילו לפי דבריהם, מותר ללמור עמהם, שבע מצוח בני נח,[30] וזה לי ליפוי כח, כי איך אפשר זח לחתריעם, ודין ז' מצות לחשמיעם, אם לא ידעו בראשון, להבין את חלשון, וגם יש לי לחחלות, ברחבה אילנות גדולות, אנשים שחיו לפני, אשר קמנם עבח ממחני, ולוכד בשמם ראוי אינני, ולמדו נוים יותר ממני, מהם שהם חיים עדן, ומחם נשמתם בגן עדן, מהם לומדים ודבנים, מהם זקנים ונשואי פנים, מחם חכמים ורופאים, מהם עשירים שעל שמריהם קופאים:[31]

ומה גם אני, הנלכד בחבלי עוני, איש שפל ומשופל, בבנים ובבנות ממופל, ומאומה אין בידי, ונסתחפה שדי, ואין בה חמח ושעורה, רק חחה וסערה,[32] נורעו בה כלאים,

Moreover, I should have to hang on many lofty trees men who preceded me, whose little finger is thicker than my thighs, whose name I am not worthy to mention, and who have taught Christians more than I. Of these, some are still living, some are resting in Paradise, some are teachers and Rabbins, some are elders and men of reputation, some are sages and physicians, and some are rich and settled on their lees.[31]

Now what am I that I should be caught in the snares of my sin, poor and low, burdened with sons and daughters, and having nothing in my possession. My field has been so inundated that there is in it neither wheat nor barley, but terror and storm,[32] and they have

---

[29] The whole passage from ועוד מה שאמרו, *again what they say*, to הנני אמות, *behold am I to die*, consisting of fifty-four lines in the Hebrew, is entirely omitted in the Sulzbach edition.

[30] According to ancient tradition (comp. *Sanhedrin*, 59 a), God enjoined the following seven commandments on Noah, which both he and all his descendants, that is all mankind, were to observe. To abstain, i. from idolatry; ii. from blasphemy; iii. from murder; iv. from incest; v. from plunder; vi. from disobedience to the powers that be; and vii. from eating flesh cut off from a living beast (אבר מן החי). These seven commandments were imposed upon every heathen who wished to settle down among the Jews in Palestine. The foreigners who accepted and submitted to these conditions were denominated *Proselytes of the Gate* (גרי שער). Comp. also *Sanhedrin*, 56 a; Rashi on *Aboda Sara*, 51 a; Maimonides, *Jad Ha-Chezaka, Hilchoth Melachim* ix. 1.

[31] For the cause of this phalanx of Jewish teachers among Christians, as well as for the outcry of the orthodox Jews against Levita, see above, pp. 9, &c., 38, &c.

[32] The words חמה ושעורה, *wheat and barley*, and חתה וסערה, *terror and storm*, are designedly selected by Levita to form a paronomasia, and though they sound somewhat strangely in the translation, they are very beautiful in the original.

sown therein heterogeneous things. Twice has misfortune laid hold of me. In Padua it took away my money [1509], and then it set its evil eye upon my precious things, which it delivered over into the hands of the rebels. This happened in the year 287 (= 1527), when Rome was destined to destruction and desolation like a plain. Not a single farthing was then left to me; and it was a time of great distress, for there was no covering in the frost, no bread or fuel in the house, my wife was nursing her young ones and was about to be confined, while my daughters had reached puberty, and were ripe for marriage according to custom. Now what can a man do who has thus been overtaken by misfortune, and not to offend in such a burning snare? This ye ought to consider, that the law of nature teaches me that nothing is to be allowed to stand in the way of saving life.

ויעקבני חזמן פעמים, בפדואה ממוני לקח, ועתה עיניו פקח, על כל מחמדי המובים, ונתנם ביד שובים, וזה היה בשנת פז״ד, כאשר על רומי נגזר, חורבן ובליח כפשומה, לא נשארח בידי פרומה, והיתה עת צרה, כי אין כסות בקרה, ובבתי אין לחם ואין עצים, וחאם רובצת על האפרוחים או על הבצים, וחבנות עומדות על פרקן, ראויות לבעל כדרכן, ותנה איש שזה עליו כלא ממא, מה יעשה ולא יחמא, במכשלה נקלח כזאת, וזה לכם חאות, חדין הפשום אותי לומר, שאין דבר בפני פקוח נפש עומד.

ועוד לכם אודיע, רב מוב אשר מזה חניע, כי חנני נשבעתי, כי כל חנוים שידעתי, אשר למדתי אני ואחדים, כלם אנשים מובים וכשרים, ובכל מה שהיה ידם לאל, המיבו לישראל, חרי לשונינו שהיא לנוים ידועה, גם היא לנו לישועה, וזה פתחון פה אלי, לחחריק תלונה מעלי, ועוד כי עקר לימודי, עם נוי כיהודי, אינו אלא בדקדוק לשון חקרש, וכללים אשר לחם אחדש,[33] ואם בזה לפני נקרא, פסוק אחד במקרא, למה לא אבארחו, ומה עשיתי חלא דבר הוא.

ועוד אם לא אבאריו אנכי, הלא יבינחו בלאו הכי, מחבודי אשר תחת ידם, שיבינם

Furthermore, I must inform you, that much good has resulted therefrom; for I solemnly declare that all the Christians whom I know, and whom I or others have instructed, are all of them good and upright men, and with all their power have acted kindly towards Israel; so that the very knowledge of our language among Christians has actually been to our advantage. Surely this speaks greatly for me, and must remove the reproach from me. Moreover, the import of my teaching, whether to Christian or Jew, is simply the grammar of the sacred language, as I only explain to them the rules thereof.[33] If, with this view, they read to me a verse in the Scriptures, why should I not explain it? What impropriety then have I committed?

Besides, if I were not to explain it, will they not learn it from my works which they possess, which everyone can understand, and in which they will find help and satisfaction? Even now I have, day

---

[33] That Levita did not exactly confine himself to teaching Christians Hebrew, but that he also aided them to fathom the mysteries of the Kabbalah, for which there was such a rage in Europe at that time, is evident, from the fact that he copied *the Book Jetzira*, and two other theosophic treatises, for Cardinal Egidio (*vide supra*, p. 15). These three documents, which were formerly in the possession of Almanzi, of Padua, are now in the British Museum, Add. 27,199. Comp. Dr. William Wright, in the *Journal of Sacred Literature*, July, 1866, p. 356, note.

after day, Christians coming to me asking instruction in Hebrew, and I respond to everyone who wants me. And why should I be condemned for it, and a reproach be fastened upon me? I speak this in defence of myself. Again, if I also have received, and opened my mouth, and tasted excellent instruction and learning [from Christians],—a honeycomb, and delightful words, which distilled from their mouths drop by drop,—and have eaten the inside and thrown away the shell, but have not eaten the insipid and the white of the egg, if I have tasted a little of this honey, am I to die for it?[84]

כל אדם, ובהם ימצאו מדנוע ופריום, ועדין מדי יום יום, אלי גוים ידרשון, וקרבת חלשון יבקשון, ונדרשתי לאשר שאלוני, ולמה בעבור זה האשימוני, ותחזיקוני לנבזה, וכי בנפשי דברתי את הדבר הזה, וכן גם אני קבלתי, ופתחתי את פי ואכלתי, טוב דעת וטעם, צוף דבש אמרי נעם, אשר נטף מפיהם מפות מפות, ואכלתי התוך ודקתי הקליפות, ולא אכלתי התפל וריד חלמות, וטעמתי מעט דבש הזה הנני אמות.[84]

לבן קבלו נא חכמים מלי, וחבל חלתוחכם מעלי, כי עיניכם הרואות, כי בתום לבבי עשיתי זאת, וחלילה לי להחיר האסור, והדבר הזה ללב מסור, ורחמנא לבא בעי, והנה כדקאי קאי:

Receive, therefore, ye sages, my apology, and let your complaint cease, for your eyes behold that I have done it in the integrity of my heart, not intending to convert wrong into right. I had a clear conscience in this matter, as is known to the Merciful One who searches the heart. Behold, the matter must remain as it stands.

---

[84] Levita refers to the instruction in the Greek language, which he received from Cardinal Egidio (*vide supra*, p. 71, &c.), and to his knowledge of various departments of secular literature, which he acquired with the aid of his Christian pupils.

INTRODUCTION III.

I SHALL NOW TURN MY FACE TO THE THIRD INTRODUCTION.

ועתה פני אשית‚
אל החקדמה השלישית:

After those truthful words, let me discourse more largely on our subject in general. But, first of all, I must explain what is meant by מסרת, and what is its etymology. Indeed this word does not occur more than twice in the whole Scriptures, viz., למסר [Numb. xxxi. 5], and ימסרו [ibid. xxxi. 6], and Kimchi explains it to mean *a gift made with the whole heart, and put into the possession of another*. Thus, also, the Targum renders ויתנהו, *and he gave him up* [Deut. ii. 33], by ומסריה (*see the root* מסר.)

It is, however, necessary to remark that the word נתן is never rendered by מסר, unless it is construed with the word ביד, *into the hand, ex. gr.* ויתנהו יהוה אלהנו בידינו or אתן בירך [Exod. xxiii. 31; 2 Sam. v. 19; Jerem. xx. 4, 5], &c., &c.[35]

אחר הדברים והאמת האלה ארחיב הדבור בחלצה‚ ללמד על הכלל כלו יצא, וקודם כל אבאר מהו ענין מסורת, ומאיזה לשון הוא, ואמת כי הלשון הזה לא נמצא בכל המקרא רק בפרשת מטות שתי פעמים וַיַּמְסְרוּ · לִמְסֹר: ופרש בו חרד"ק שהוא ענין נתינה בכל לב והרתשומה ברשות אחד וכו', עד ותרגומם ויתנחו ה' אלהינו ומסריה וכו' עין בשורש מסר:

ואומר אני כי לשון נתינה אינו מתורגם בלשון מסידרה רק כשהוא סמוך אצל לשון יד, כמו ויתנהו ה" אלהנו בידינו, אתן בירך ודומיהם[35] והכלל כ' לשון מפידה נופל על דבר שיתן או יפקיד אדם ביד אחר, שיחזיקנו ברשותו, כרצונו כאלו הוא שלו ; וכן בענין הלמוד והחגדה שילמד אדם או יגיד לחבורו איזה סוד או ענין שקודם זה לא ידעהו, נופל בו לשון מסירה, כמו שאמרו במשנה משה קבל תורה מסיני ומסרה ליהושע וכו' ; וכן ענין המסורת הזאת לפי שנמפדה

We thus obtain the rule that the word מסר denotes *to give*, or *entrust, something into the hands of another person, that he might retain it in his possession according to his pleasure, as if it were his own.* The same is the case with the doctrines and Hagadah; if one teaches or propounds to another any mysteries, or anything which he did not know before, it is described by the word מסר. Thus it is said in the Mishna, *Moses received the Law from Sinai* (ומסרה), *and delivered it to Joshua, &c.* [*Mishna, Aboth,* i. 1]; and this is the meaning of the word מסר in question; since it was transmitted to sages, from mouth to mouth, till

---

[35] That נתן, followed by ביד, is not always rendered in the Chaldee by מסר, is evident from Is. xxii. 21. Indeed Levita's whole stricture on Kimchi's explanation is incorrect, inasmuch as in the passage adduced by Kimchi, namely, Deut. ii. 33, ויתנהו is not followed by ביד, but by לפנינו, and yet the Chaldee paraphrases translate it ומסרה and ומסר, and there is no other instance in the whole Hebrew Scriptures, where ויתנהו,—Kal future, third person singular masculine, suffix third person singular masculine, with Vav conversive, of which the subject is יהוה אלהינו,—is followed by ביד. The only instance which *approaches* the one in question, is the phrase ויתנהו יהוה אלהיו ביד 2 Chron. xxviii. 5, where indeed the Targum translates it ומסריה; but here it is אלהיו, with suffix third person singular masculine, and not אלהינו, suffix first person plural. Besides, the Chaldee paraphrase of Chronicles was not known till the middle of the seventeenth century, and was published for the first time at Augsburg, 1680-3, more than a hundred and thirty years after the death of Elias Levita.

the time of Ezra and his associates, and by them again to the sages of Tiberias, who wrote it down, and called it *Massorah*.

Now, since in this book I impart some rules to decipher the sage remarks, couched in the enigmatical expressions which occur in both the major and minor Massorah, therefore I deemed it proper to call this book *Massoreth Ha-Massoreth*, as this name is suitable for the book, and the book suitable for the name. I shall now proceed to explain the nature, quality, and object of the Massorah; who compiled it, whether one or many; who invented the vowel-points and accents, and when they were attached to the letters; and shall state the opinion of both the ancients and moderns, as well as give my own, upon this subject. I shall then point out to you, according to the good hand of the Lord upon me, the method which the Massorites adopted, and the work which they have done; what their chief aim was; what they wished, and what they did not wish, to say.

לחכמים איש מפי איש עד עזרא וסיעתו, ומהם לחכמי מבריא אשר כתבוה וקראו לה מסרה:

ונם אני בזה הספר אמסור כללים להבין אמרי בינה, בדברים הסתומים במסרה גדולה וקטנה, לכן ראיתי לקרא לו ספר מסורת המסורת, ושם זה נאה לו, והוא נאה לשמו: ועתה אבאר כמותה ואיכותה ותועלתה, ומי שחבר אותה יחיד או רבים, ומי שהמציא הנקודות והטעמים, ומתי חוברו עם האותיות, ואכתוב דעת הראשונים והאחרונים, ואחוה דעי אף אני, ואחרי כן אודה אתכם כיד ה' הטובה עלי, את הדרך אשר הלכו בעלי המסורת, ואת המעשה אשר עשו, ומה היתה עקר כונתם, ועל מה דברו, ועל מה לא הקפידו לדבר:

ואתחיל ואומר, הנה דעת רוב האנשים שעזרא הסופר וסיעתו, שהם אנשי כנסת הגדולה, עשו המסורת והנקוד והטעמים על כל המקרא, ומביאים ראיה שדרשו רז"ל בנדרים ויקראו בספר בתורת אלהים (נחמיה ח') זה מקרא, מפרש זה תרגום, ושום שכל אלו הפסקים, ויבינו במקרא זה פיסוק טעמים, ואמרי ליה אלו מסורת עכ"ל[86] והנה לפי פשוטו של מקרא אין הפסוק

In the first place, let me remark, that, according to the opinion of most men, Ezra the Scribe, and his associates, who were the men of the Great Synagogue, made the Massorah, the vowel-points, and the accents through all the Scriptures. In support of this, they insist that the explanation (in *Nedarim* [37 *b*,]) which our Rabbins of blessed memory give of Nehem. viii. 8, viz., "And they read in the book, in the Law of God," means *the original text;* "explaining it," means *the Chaldee paraphrase;* "and gave the same," means *the division of the verses;* "and caused them to understand the Scripture," means *the dividing accents;* or, according to others, it signifies *the Massorah.* Thus far are their words.[86] Now, according to the natural meaning of

---

[86] The passage quoted by Levita is from the *Babylonian Talmud, Nedarim* 37 *b*, *Megilla* 3 *a*. It also occurs with the following variations in the *Jerusalem Talmud*, רבי ושרה בשם רב חננאל ויקראו בספר תורה ה' זה המקרא· מפורש זה תרגום· ושום שכל אלו הפעמים· ורבינו במקרא זה המסורה· ויש אומרים אלו ההכריעים· ויש אומרים אלו ראשי הפסוקים: פרק ד' הלמה א'. R. Seurah propounded, in the name of Hananeel, "they read in the book, in the Law of God," means *the original text;* "explaining it," means *the Chaldee paraphrase;* "and gave the sense," means *the division according to the sense;* "and caused them to understand the Scripture," signifies *the Massoreth.* Some,

the context, this verse does not at all speak of Ezra, but refers to the statement in the preceding verse: "Also Joshua, and Boni, and Sherebiah,[87] and the Levites caused the people to understand the Law," and it is of them them that he says, "And they read in the book of the Law," &c., and not of Ezra.

This Midrashic explanation, however, can be consistent with the natural meaning of the text, in the following manner: "And they read in the book, in the Law of God" means *the original text*, that is to say, these men first read the text in Hebrew; then "explained it" in *the Chaldee paraphrase;* that is to say, they translated the verse to themselves into Aramaic, because everybody understood that language; "and gave the sense" means *the verses*, that is to say, they made pauses between every verse, in accordance with the tradition which they possessed from our teacher Moses, of blessed memory, as our Rabbins of blessed memory tell us in *Megilla* [3, a], and these are the words: "A verse which was not divided by Moses must not be divided by us." Those who refer the verse in question to Ezra, regard וְשׂוֹם as singular, but they do not know that it is *the infinitive*, and is tantamount to וַיָּשִׂימוּ because of ☞ the word וַיִּקְרְאוּ by which it is preceded, and the word וַיָּבִינוּ by which it is followed; since the *infinitive* is everywhere rendered in the singular or plural, in the second person or in the third, masculine or feminine, in agreement with the verbs with which it is connected, and which may either precede or follow it. But this is not the place to expatiate upon this subject.

Now, as to the remark, "'and caused them to understand the Scripture,' denotes *the division of the accents;*" this means, that when reading to the people, they [Ezra and his associates] made[38] pauses

however, say it denotes the *pauses*, and others *heads of verses* (*Jerusalem Megilla* iv. 1, 67 b, ed. Krotoschin). It is necessary to remark, that in all these passages, the expression בְּמָסוֹרֶת, denotes *the traditional pronunciation of the text*, and that it is not to be confounded with the technical meaning "*critical apparatus*," which it was made to signify in after times.

[87] The word עַד, *till*, is omitted in the Sulzbach edition.

[88] The Sulzbach edition erroneously repeats לְהוּ, *to themselves*, after עָשׂוּ, *they made*.

in the middle of the verse, according to the sense of the context, in the same manner as our teacher Moses, of blessed memory, read to the elders. Thus, for example, when he [Ezra] read to them "are they not on the other side Jordan, beyond?" he paused a little at the word "beyond," and then read "the way where the sun goeth down" (Deut. xi. 30), as Rashi explains it on this passage *(vide in loco)*.[39] It is this which our Rabbins, of blessed memory, call *pause* or *division according to the sense*, because the pause makes the verse intelligible and perspicuous; not that they had the accents which we now possess, for they had not as yet been invented, as I shall show in the sequel. And as to the other remark, that "and they caused them to understand the Scriptures," means *the Massorah;* the explanation of this is, that they read every word as it was transmitted to them from our teacher Moses, of blessed memory, ex. gr. the *Keris*, and the *Kethivs*, as I shall explain afterwards. It must not, however, be supposed that they [Ezra and his associates] read to them [the people] the Massorah from tradition, or that they wrote the Massorah on the Pentateuch, much less on the whole[40] Bible, as we now have it; for there is no doubt that Ezra did not write anything except in the Law of Moses, as it is written, "This Ezra went up from Babylon, and he was a ready scribe in the Law of Moses, which was given by Jehovah, the God of Israel" (Ezra vii. 6), and again [*ibid.* ver. 11], "Ezra, the priest, the scribe of the words of Jehovah's commandments and of His statutes." He is also called in Aramaic, *the scribe of the Law of the Lord of heaven.*

באמצע הפסוק לפי כוונת הענין, כמו שהיה קרא מרע"ה לזקנים; וחמשל כשהיה קרא לחם הלא המה בעבר הירדין אחרי (דברים י"א), חיה מפסיק מעט במלת אחרי, ואחרי כן קרא דרך מבא השמש כמו שפירש רש"י ע"ש:[39] ורז"ל קראו לזה פיסוק פעמים, לפי שהחפסק נותן טוב מעם ודעת להבנת הפסוק, לא שהיו להם הפעמים אשר בידינו היום, כי עדיין לא נעשו כמו שאוכיח אח"כ, ולמאן דאמר אלו המסורת, פי' שהיו קוראים לחם כל המלות כמו שחיתה מסורח בידם ממר"עה, כגון קריין וכתבן, כמו שהבאר אח"כ, ואין להבין כלל שחיו קוראים לחם חמסורח על פה, או שחם כתבו חמסורת על החורה, כ"ש על כל[40] המקרא כמו שהיא בידינו היום, כי בלי ספק עזרא לא כתב דבר רק בתורת משה לבד, כי כן כתיב הוא עזרא סופר מהיר בתורת משה אשר נתן יהוה אלהי ישראל (עזרא ז') ופסוק אחד אומר עזרא הכהן הסופר דברי מצות יהוה וחקיו, וכן נקרא בלשון ארמי ספר דתא די אלה שמיא:

---

[39] *Rashi*, רש"י, is the acrostic of רבי שלמה יצחקי, *Rabbi Solomon Isaki* or *Itzchaki* = R. Solomon ben Isaac, the renowned Jewish commentator, who was born A.D. 1040, at Troyes, in Champagne, and died 26th July, 1105. For a sketch of his life, see Kitto's *Cyclopædia of Bibl. Literature*, s. v. RASHI. His explanation of אחרי דרך, Deut. xi. 30, to which Levita refers, is as follows: ומעם המקרא מוכיח שהם שני דבורים שנקדו בשני פעמים אחרי נקוד בפשטא ודרך נקוד במשפל והוא דגש אם היה דבור אחד היה נקוד אחרי במשרת בשופר הפוך [מרכא] ודרך בפשטא ורפי, *the accents plainly show that they are two separate statements, inasmuch as they are pointed with two separate accents,* אחרי, *being pointed with the distinctive accent Pashta, and* דרך, *with Jethiv, and having Dagesh. Now if they had been joined together,* אחרי *would have been pointed with the conjunctive accent Mercha, and* דרך *with Pashta, and would have been without Dagesh in the Daleth. According to this interpretation, therefore, the verse ought to be translated "these [mountains] are situate on the other side Jordan, far beyond it, towards the way where the sun goeth down."*

[40] The word כל, *all*, is omitted in the Sulzbach edition.

P

Accordingly, I find it very difficult to make out what it was that Ezra wrote in the Law. For there are only two alternatives. Either that he possessed a scroll of the Law, and made another copy from it, without adding to it or taking from it anything, in which case he would be nothing more than any other scribe who copies one book from another; but, from this, no distinction could have accrued to him, since any one of the ordinary writers might have done the same thing, as it is difficult to believe that there were no other writers in all Israel except he. Or it may be said that the scroll of the Law which he had before him was not correctly written as regards *plenes* and *defectives*, *open* and *closed sections*, *large* and *small letters*, &c., &c.,[41] and he wrote them correctly. Here, again,[42] it is difficult to believe that there was not a single correct copy of the Law to be found among all the people of Israel. Forsooth this difficulty puzzled me so much for many years, that I mentioned it to the learned, but they could not give me any explanation of it.

ולפי זה קשה לי מאד מהו שכתב עזרא בתורה, כי לא ימנע מחלוקה אם נמצאה בידו ס"ת והוא כתב כן אחוה ולא הוסיף ולא גרע, א"כ לא היה אלא כסופר המעתיק ספר מספר אחר, ומה מעלה היתה זאת לו, והלא כל סופר חדיום יכול לעשות כן, ואין להאמין שלא היה בכל ישראל סופר אחר כי אם הוא לבדו: ואם נאמר שהס"ת שהיתה לפניו לא היתה כתובה כתקונה, במלאים וחסרים, ובפרשיות פתוחות וסתומות, ואותיות גדולות וקטנות וכדומה לזה[41] והוא כתב אחת כתקונת, גם זה[42] קשה להאמין שלא נמצאה ס"ת כשרה בכל ישראל, ובאמת כמה שנים הוקשה לי זה ואומר אל החכמים ואין מגיד לי:

I have, also, felt a great difficulty about the import of the *Keri* and the *Kethiv*. Now, according to the opinions of many modern [grammarians], the *Keri* and the *Kethiv* originated in the following manner. During the first captivity, most of the canonical writings were lost, and even the few books which had been found were impaired by being thrown about; and as those who were skilled in the Scriptures were dead, Ezra and his associates restored the crown to its pristine glory; for they corrected these books, and when they found variations in the books, they decided to follow the majority [of Codd.], and wherever they could not decide properly they wrote down one reading in the text and the other in the margin, or put one down without punctuating it, &c. See *Kimchi's Introduction to Joshua*, and *Ephodi's*

וכן קשה לי בענין קרי וכתיב, חה לפי דעת רוב האחרונים שהקרי והכתיב נמצאים כן, כי בגלות ראשונה אבדו רוב הספרים ונמלמלו, והמעטים הנמצאים חשינע המלמול ויורעי המקרא מתו, ועזרא וסיעתו החזירו העטרה ליושנה, ותקנו הספרים חהם, וכאשר מצאו מחלוקת בספרים, חלכו בהם אחר הרוב לפי דעתם, ובמקום שלא חשינח דעתם על הכרוה, כתבו האחד מבפנים והאחד בחוץ או כתבו האחד ולא נקדוהו וכו', עיין בחקדמת הרד"ק ביהושע, והאפודי בפרק ז'

---

[41] An explanation of all the Massoretic phrases will be found further on, and as we cannot give the pages, not being as yet made up, we must refer to the Index, which will enable the reader easily to find the requisite information.

[42] The word זה, *this*, is omitted in the Sulzbach edition.

Treatise, cap. vii.⁴³ Abravanel, however, refutes them in his introduction to Jeremiah, and attempts in a very lengthy manner to correct their blunders; but his corrections are his blunders, for most of his arguments are untenable and shallow. I shall, therefore, not enlarge upon them.⁴⁴

Let me, therefore, simply state my own opinion upon this subject, and reply to the afore-mentioned writers. Now, I submit, if their opinions be really true,—that is to say, if the *Keri* and the *Kethiv* are owing to doubts as above mentioned,—what shall we say to the *Keri* and the *Kethiv* which are found in the books written by the captives themselves, such as Haggai, Zechariah, Malachi, Daniel, Ezra, who wrote his own book and the Chronicles; and Mordecai, who wrote the book of Esther? Were not these themselves among the Men of the Great Synagogue?⁴⁵ Take, for ex-

מספרו,⁴³ והאברבינאל השיג עליהם בהקדמתו לספר ירמי׳, והאריך לשון חשב לתקן עוותם, וחקנתו היא קלקלתו, כי רוב דבריו לא לרצון, ובמלין ומבומלין, ולכן אין לי להאריך בם:⁴⁴

אך אענה חלקי אף אני, ואשיב על דברי האנשים הנזכרים ואומר, אם כדבריהם כן הוא ר״ל שהקרי והכתיב בעבור הספקות הנ״ל, מה יאמרו על הקרי והכתיב הנמצאים בספרי הגולה שהם חני זכריה מלאכי דניאל ועזרא כתב ספרו וד״ה, ומדרכי כתב המגלה, והלא הם עצמם היו מאנשי כ״ה,⁴⁵ וחמשל בספר

---

⁴³ The Kimchi, referred to in the text, or *Redak* (רד״ק), as the Hebrew text has it, which is the acrostic of ר׳ דוד קמחי, *R. David Kimchi*, is the younger brother of M. Kimchi, to whose grammatical treatise, entitled, *the Journey on the Paths of Knowledge*, Levita wrote the commentary already alluded to, (*vide supra*, pp. 13, &c., 80, &c.) D. Kimchi, who was born in Narbonne, 1160, and died about 1235, is the author of the celebrated grammatical and lexical work, entitled *Michlol*, which Levita edited with annotations (*vide supra*, p. 79, &c.), as well as of valuable commentaries on nearly the whole Hebrew Scriptures. Comp. Kitto, *Cyclopædia of Biblical Literature*, new ed., *s. v.* KIMCHI. The passage detailing his opinion on the origin of the *Keri* and *Kethiv*, to which Levita refers, will be found together with an English translation in Jacob b. Chajim's *Introduction to the Rabbinic Bible*, p. 5 in the Hebrew, and 7 in the English.

Ephodi (אפד), is the appellation of R. Isaac b. Moses Ha-Levi, the celebrated grammarian and polemical writer, who flourished A.D. 1360-1412. It is a contraction of אמר, אני פרופיט דורי, *thus sayeth*, or *I Prophiat Duran*; and though it is the name which he especially assumed after 1391, to conceal his real person from the Christians, who, at the peril of his life, compelled him to abjure Judaism and join the benighted Christians of that day, he is also known by the name *Prophiat Duran*. His excellent grammatical treatise, entitled *the Grammar of Ephod* (מעשה אפד), to which Levita refers, has only recently been published for the first time, Vienna, 1865. The passage in question is to be found in cap. vii., p. 40, and with an English translation in Jacob b. Chajim's *Introduction to the Rabbinic Bible*, p. 4, &c., in the Hebrew, and p. 6, &c., in the English, ed. Ginsburg. For the life and writings of Ephodi, see the Introduction to his Grammar, entitled *Maase Ephod*, pp. 2-49, Vienna, 1865; and Kitto, *Cyclopædia of Biblical Literature*, new ed., *s. v.* PROPHIAT DURAN.

⁴⁴ Abravanel's view, which Levita does not even deign to state, and which he so cavalierly rejects, is given at length by Jacob b. Chajim, in his *Introduction to the Rabbinic Bible*, pp. 5, &c., in the Hebrew, and pp. 7-11 in the English. It is to be remarked, that the theory of this celebrated statesman, philosopher, theologian, and commentator, who was born in Lisbon in 1437, and died at Venice in 1508, has a greater amount of truth in it than any other hypothesis on this vexed question. Comp. Kitto's *Cyclopædia*, *s. v.* KERI AND KETHIV.

⁴⁵ The Great Synagogue (כנסת הגדולה), to which such frequent references are made in this work, denotes the council, or synod, first appointed by Nehemiah, after the return of the Jews from the Babylonish captivity, to reorganise the religious life of the people. It consisted originally of one hundred and twenty members, comprising the representa-

ample, the book of Ezra (iv. 2), where the textual reading is ולא, with *Aleph*, and they [the Men of the Great Synagogue] wrote in the margin, read ולו with *Vav*. Now if they did it because they were in doubt, not knowing whether to read לא or לו; we ask, was not Ezra there present with them? and did he himself not know whether he wrote ולא with *Aleph* or ולו with *Vav*? The same is the case with the other *Keris* and *Kethivs* found in their books. And it cannot be

עזרא כתיב ולא אנחנו זובחים (עזרא ד')
והם כתבו בהוץ ולו קרי בוי"ו, אם עשו זה
בעבור הספק, שלא ידעו אם הוא לא או לו,
יש להקשוה והלא עזרא היה שם עמהם, וכי
לא ידע הוא אם כתב ולא באל"ף או ולו
בוי"ו, וכן בשאר קרי וכתיב שבספריהם,
ואין לומר שאחרי מות המחברים ההם כתבו
שירי כנסת הגדולה הקרי מפני הספק, שהרי
לא היה להם פלפול ולא אבדו הספרים
☞ בשנים מועטות הכן, כי לא נמשך זמן
אנשי כ"ה דק קרוב למ' שנה, כדמוכח
בסדר עולם⁴⁶ ובקבלת הראב"ד⁴⁷:

answered that it was after the death of the said authors that the remaining members of the Great Synagogue wrote the *Keri* because of doubts, since there was no dispersion, nor were the books lost in ☞ those few years, for the whole period of the Men of the Great Synagogue did not last more than about forty years, as is shown in *Seder Olam*,⁴⁶ and in Ibn Daud's *Seder Ha-Kabbalah*.⁴⁷ Besides, if

tives of the following five classes of the Jewish nation. i. *The Chiefs of the Priestly Divisions* (ראשי בית אב). ii. *The Chiefs of the Levitical Families* (ראשי הלוים). iii. *The Heads of the Israelite Families* (ראשי העם). iv. *Representatives of the Cities or the Elders* (זקנים, πρεσβύτεροι), and v. *The Doctors of the Law, or the Scribes* (סופרים, γραμματείς). The number of one hundred and twenty members was, however, not adhered to after the death of Nehemiah, and ultimately it was reduced to seventy. The period of its duration extended from the latter days of Nehemiah to the death of Simon the Just, B. C. 410–300; thus embracing about one hundred and ten years. See Kitto's *Cyclopædia of Biblical Literature*, s. v. SYNAGOGUE, THE GREAT.

⁴⁶ The *Seder Olam* (סדר עולם), or the *Succession of the World's History*, is an ancient Jewish Chronicle, written by R. Jose b. Chalafta, of Sephoris, who flourished circa A.D. 100–150. It briefly chronicles the events of the world from Adam to the war under Bar-Kochba, the false Messiah. It is also called *Seder Olam Rabba* (סדר עולם רבא), = the *Major Chronicle of the World*, to distinguish it from a later Chronicle, entitled *Seder Olam Sutta* (סדר עולם זוטא), = the *Minor Chronicle of the World*. The best edition of it is that by Meyer, Amsterdam, 1699, which appeared together with the *Seder Olam Sutta*, a Latin translation, and very elaborate annotations. Levita most probably refers to chapters xxix. and xxx.

⁴⁷ The author of the *Sepher*, or *Seder Ha-Kabbalah* (ספר or סדר הקבלה), = the *Succession of Tradition*, Abraham Ibn Daud or Rabad (ראב"ד), as he is called by Levita, which is the acrostic of ר, אברהם בן דוד, *R. Abraham b. David*,—was born circa 1110, and died as a martyr 1180. The chronicle of this distinguished moral philosopher gives, in the form of annals, the history of the world from Adam to his own time (1161), showing the uninterrupted chain of tradition to his day, against the opinion of the Karaites, who denied all tradition. As supplement to this chronicle, Ibn Daud wrote a succinct history of the Roman Empire, from its foundation by Romulus till the West Gothic King Reccared, entitled, *Memoirs of the Events of Rome* (וכרון דברי רומי), and the *History of the Jewish Kings during the second Temple* (דברי מלכי ישראל בבית שני). Ibn Daud's Histories were first published, together with the *Seder Olam*, Mantua, 1513, then in Venice, 1545, Basel, 1580; the *Sepher Ha-Kabbalah*, by itself, was published with the *Seder Olam Rabba* and *Sutta*, Cracow, 1820; and with a Latin translation by Gilbert Venebrard, Paris, 1572. Levita's allusion will be found 3 a–5 a of the last mentioned edition. It must be remarked, that neither the *Seder Olam* nor the *Sepher Ha-Kabbalah* says that the Great Synagogue only continued for forty years. Graetz

the *Keri* and *the Kethiv* originated through the above-mentioned doubtful readings, we should expect these doubtful readings to occur accidentally, according to the differences of the books, and the accidents which befel them,—to be one here and one there—here a little and there a little —but not repeatedly to occur in one and the same word. Thus, for example, נערה is written in the Pentateuch twenty-two times נער, without *He*, and read נערה with *He*[48]; עפולים, *tumors*, which occurs in the text six times, and is read טחורים, *the piles*[49]; עניים, *destitutes*, found five times in the text, and read ענוים, *afflicted*, and twice *vice versa*;[50] and there are many more the like instances. Now how could the accident always happen to the expressions נערה, עפולים and עניים?

ועוד אם היה הקרי והכתיב בעבור הספקות הנ"ל, היה ראוי שיבאו הספקות על דרך המקרה, כפי מחלוקת הספרים, והחבדל שנפל בהם אחת הנה ואחת הנה, וער שם וער שם, לא על מלח אחת הרבה פעמים, כגון כ״ב פעמים נערה בתורה כתיבין נער וקריין נערה,[48] וכן ו׳ כתיבין עפולים וקריין טחורים,[49] וכן ה׳ כתיבין עניים וקריין ענוים וב׳ לחיפך,[50] ודומה לאלה רבים, איך נפל הספק על כל נערה ועל כל עפולים וענוים:

ויותר קשה לי מה שאמרו בפרק הנ״ל ח"ל, אמר רבי יצחק קריין ולא כתבן וכתבן ולא קריין הלכה למשה מסיני, קריין ולא כתבן פרת דבלכתו, איש, כאשר שאל וכו׳, כתבן ולא קריין ולא קריין נא דיסלח, אל ידרוך ידרוך הדורך, ידרוך השני כתיב ולא קרי וכו׳,[51] ומי יתן שומע לי ויבונני, איך יתכן

And my difficulty is increased by what is said in the above-mentioned section of the Talmud [*Nedarim* 37, *b*], and these are the words: "R. Isaac said, the words read from the margin but not written in the text, and the words written in the text but not read, are a Law of Moses from Sinai; the words read from the margin, but not written in the text, are פרת, *Euphrates* [2 Sam. viii. 8], and איש, *man* [*ibid.* xvi. 23]; whilst the words written in the text but not read, are נא, *now* [2 Kings v. 18], and ידרוך, *he shall tread* [Jerem. li. 3], &c."[51] Would that

has shown that its existence extended over a period of one hundred and ten years, so that Levita's argument based upon the shorter period is groundless.

[48] In the present text, we have only twenty-one instances in which the text has נער and the marginal reading נערה, viz., Gen. xxiv. 14, 16, 28, 55, 57; xxxiv. 3 (twice), 12; Deut. xxii. 15 (twice), 16, 20, 21, 23, 24, 25, 26 (twice), 27, 28, 29.

[49] The six instances in which the marginal reading substitutes טחורים for the textual עפולים are Deut. xxviii. 27; 1 Sam. v. 6, 9, 12; vi. 4, 5. Comp. *Megilla*, 25 *b*; *Sopherim* viii. 8; *Massorah magna* on 1 Sam. v. 6; *Massorah finalis*, s. v. ש״מ; *Ochla Ve-Ochla*, section 170, pp. 38, 114; Jacob b. Chajim's *Introduction to the Rabbinic Bible*, p. 9, &c. English translation.

[50] The five passages in which the *Kethiv* is עניים and the *Keri* has ענוים are as follows: Ps. ix. 13; x. 12; Prov. iii. 34; xiv. 21; xvi. 19. The instances in which the reverse is the case are Ps. ix. 19; Isa. xxxii. 7.

[51] Levita's quotation of R. Isaac's statement is abridged. Jacob b. Chajim gives it entire in his *Introduction to the Rabbinic Bible*, p. 6 in the Hebrew and p. 12 in the English translation. Of words read from the margin and not written in the text, there are ten instances, viz.—

בני, *the sons of*	Judg. xx. 13.	צבאות, *Sabaoth*	Isaiah xxxvii. 32.
פרת, *Euphrates*	2 Sam. viii. 3.	באים, *are coming*	Jerem. xxxi. 38.
איש, *man*	2 Sam. xvi. 21.	לה, *to her*	Jerem. l. 29.
כן, *thus*	2 Sam. xviii. 20.	אלי, *to me*	Ruth iii. 5.
בני, *his sons*	2 Kings xix. 37.	אלי, *to me*	Ruth iii. 17.

any one might listen to me, and explain to me how it can be said of them that they are a Law of Moses from Sinai, when, of all the instances here adduced, not a single one is to be found in the Pentateuch? And even of those marginal readings not written in the text, which the Massorites added (for R. Isaac only[52] gives five, whilst the Massorites give eight), as well as of the words written in the text, but not read (for R. Isaac only[53] gives six, whilst the Massorites give ten),—of either the one or the other, not a single[54] one is to be found in the Pentateuch. And if it be so, how can it be said that it is a Law of Moses from Sinai, which did not, as yet, exist at all?

And as if this trouble were not enough for us, some later writers must needs add that "every *Keri* and *Kethiv*, throughout the whole Bible, is a Law of Moses." But where have they been authorised to say this, since R. Isaac has only said it of the marginal readings not written in the text, and words written in the text but not read, which are the smallest of the seven classes [of *Keris* and *Kethivs*], as I shall show in the Second Part, section one? If it really is a tradition that the former alone [*i.e.* those given in the Talmud, *Nedarim*], are a Law of Moses from Sinai, I must accept it, for our sages are true, and their words are true. But for that, I should have said that the *Keris* and *Kethivs*, which occur in the Pentateuch, are a Law of Moses from Sinai; and that the men of the Great Synagogue, *i.e.* Haggai, Zachariah, Malachi, Daniel, Mishael, Azariah, Ezra, Nehemiah, Mordecai, Zerubbabel, with whom were associated other sages from the craftsmen and artizans, to the number of a

לומר בהן חל״מ, והלא כל אותם שהביא
אין 52 אחד מהן בתורה, ואפילו אותם שהוסיפו
עליהן בעלי המסורת, כי דבי יצחק לא הביא
רק 53 ח', ובעלי המסורת הביאו ח', וכן דקריין
ולא כתבן, רבי יצחק הביא ו' וזהם הביאו י',
ומכל אלה ואלה אין גם אחד מהן 54 בתורה,
וא״כ איך יאמר חש״י חל״מ מה שלא היה
ולא נברא עדיין:

ולא די לנו לצרה זאת עד שכתבו קצת
האחרונים כל קרי וכתיב שבכל המקרא
הל״מ, ומהיכן למדו לומר כן, והלא רבי
יצחק לא אמר רק על קריין ולא כתבן וכתבן
ולא קריין, שהוא המין הקטן שבכל ז' המינים,
כמו שאבאר בלוחות שניות, במאמר א', אך
אם קבלה היא שאלה הם לבדם חל״מ
אקבלהו כי הם אמת ודבריהם אמת, ולולי
זה הייתי אומר שלבד הקרי והכתיב שבתורה
הם חל״מ, ואנשי כה״ג שהם חגי זכריה מלאכי
דניאל, חנניה מישאל ועזריה, עזרא נחמיה
מרדכי זרובבל, ועוד נלוו עליהם חכמים
מחרש״ו והמסגר, עד השלמת מאה ועשרים
איש, כתבום על פי הקבלה שהיתה בידם,

Comp. *Massorah magna* on Deut. i. 1; and on Ruth iii. 17; *Sopherim* vi. 8; *Ochla Ve-Ochla*, section xcvii., pp. 28, 96. Of words written in the text but not read, there are eight instances, viz.:—

אם, *if*	. . . . .	2 Sam. xiii. 33.	אם, *if*	. . . . .	Jerem. xxxix. 12.
אם, *if*	. . . . .	2 Sam. xv. 21.	ידרך, *he shall tread*	. . .	Jerem. li. 3.
נא, *now*	. . . . .	2 Kings v 18.	חמש, *five*	. . . . .	Ezek. xlviii. 16.
את, *accusative*	. .	Jerem. xxxviii. 16.	אם, *if*	. . . . .	Ruth iii. 12.

Comp. *Massorah magna* on Ruth iii. 12; *Sopherim* vi. 9; *Ochla Ve-Ochla*, section xcviii., pp. 28, 96; Kitto's *Cyclopædia of Biblical Literature*, s. v. KERI AND KETHIV.

[52] The word גם, *even*, is omitted in the Sulzbach edition.

[53] The Sulzbach edition erroneously substitutes כי אם, *but*, for רק, *only*.

[54] מהן, *of them*, which is important to the sense, is omitted in the Sulzbach edition.

hundred and twenty persons—noted down according to a tradition which they had, informing them that our teacher Moses, peace be upon him, did not read this word as it is written in the text, because of one of the many secrets known unto them; that our teacher Moses, peace be upon him, delivered them[55] to Joshua, Joshua to the sages, the sages to the prophets, &c., &c., who put it down in the margin, as the *Keri* has it, and that Ezra was the writer thereof. This is, therefore, the very thing which he wrote in the Law of Moses.

The same thing they did with all the words in the Prophets and Hagiographa, respecting which they had a tradition from the Prophets and the sages, delivered from mouth to mouth, that they are not to be read as they are written. But as for the post-exile books, they required no tradition, for their authors were themselves present with them. Whenever, therefore, they [the men of the Great Synagogue] found a word in them which appeared to them not in harmony with the design of the context, and the simple meaning of the passage, the author gave them the reason why he had written in so abnormal a manner; hereupon they wrote the normal expression in the margin as the *Keri*. Herewith the question is fully answered, which I asked above about וְלֹא [Ezra iv. 2], since Ezra did assign a reason why he wrote in such a manner. In like manner, when they read in the book of Haggai (i. 8) וְכָבֵד, Haggai himself told them not to read וְאִכָּבֵד but וְאֶכָּבְדָה, as if the ה were written out at the end, and told them that it was owing to the five things which were in the first temple, but not in the second temple,[56] that he

שמשה רבינו ע"ח לא קרא המלה החיא ככתיבה לסוד אחד מן הסודות הידוע להם, שמשה רבינו ע"ח מסר[55] ליהושע ויהושע לזקנים וזקנים לנביאים וכו' וכתבוהו בחוץ כקריאתה ועזרא היה הסופר, וזהו מה שכהב הוא בתורת משה:

וכן עשו גם כן בנביאים וכתובים בכל המלות שחיתה קבלה בידם מפי הנביאים וחכמי הדורות איש מפי איש שלא יחיו נקראין ככתיבתן, אבל בספרי חנולה לא היו צריכין לקבלה, כי המחברים עצמם היו שם עמהם, וכשמצאו מלה אחת שנראה להם שהיא זרה כפי כוונת הענין ופשם הכתוב, אמר להן המחבר הטעם למה כתב כן בדרותה, אז כתבו המלה מחוץ כקריאתה, ובוה יהיה מיושב מה שהקשתי לעיל על ולא אנחנו זובחים, כי הוא אמר הטעם למה כתב כן, וכן כשקראו בספר חני וארצה בו ואככד (חני א'), אמר להם חני, אל תקראו ואכבד אלא וְאֶכָּבְדָה כאלו היתה ח"א כתובה בסוף, ואמר להן הטעם מפני ה' דברים שהיו במקדש ראשון ולא במקדש שני כתבתיו כן,[56] או כתבו בחוץ

---

[55] In the Sulzbach edition, הסוד, *the secret*, is inserted after מסר, *he delivered*.

[56] According to ancient tradition, the following five things, which were in the first Temple, were wanting in the second Temple: i. The Ark, with the lid and the cherubim upon it; ii. The fire from Heaven (comp. 2 Chron. vii. 1); iii. The Shechinah; iv. The Holy Ghost; and v. The Urim and Thummim. The absence of these five, the same ancient tradition declares, was indicated by the absence of the letter ה, which numerically represents *five*, from the word in question. Hence the remark in the Talmud: אמר רב שמואל בר איניא מאי דכתיב וארצה בו ואכבד וקרינן ואכבדה מאי שנא ומחוסר ה"א אלו חמשה דברים שהיו בין מקדש ראשון למקדש שני אלו הן ארון וכפורת וכרובים אש ושכינה ורוח הקודש ואורים ותומים, *R. Samuel b. Enia sayeth,* Why has the Kethiv ואכבד, *and the Keri* ואכבדה? What is meant by the absence of the ה? *It is because of the five things which made the difference between the first and second Temple. They are as follows, the Ark, &c.*

wrote so. Whereupon they wrote in the margin "Read אַכְבְּרָה." The same thing they did with all the other post-exile books.

In short, the men of the Great Synagogue made the *Keri*, in the Pentateuch, in accordance with a tradition from our teacher Moses, peace be upon him; in the Prophets and Hagiographa, in accordance with a tradition from the Prophets and sages of succeeding generations; and in the post-exile books, in accordance with the directions of the authors themselves; but never on account of any doubtful readings, as many have supposed.

☞ Now, when I gave my heart to inquire into, and examine with wisdom, all which has been done in the matter of the *Keri* and *Kethiv*, I discovered that the *Keri* and *Kethiv* are never found on *plene* and *defective*. That is to say, there is not a word to be found in the whole Bible which is written in the text *plene*, and the the marginal reading of which is *defective* or *vice versa;* and the reason is, that the sense of the word is never affected by its being *defective* or *plene*.

☞ I have also discovered this, which is important to remember, that the *Keri* and *Kethiv* are never to be found on the vowel-points and accents. That is to say, there is not a word to be found which is pointed in the text in one way, and the marginal reading of which is in another way. Nor do the *Keri* and *Kethiv* occur with respect to *Dagesh* and *Raphe*, nor in *Milel* and *Milra*, nor on *right* and *left* [*i. e.* the point on letter ש], nor on *Mapik* and *no Mapik*, nor on either of the *accents pausal* or *non-pausal*.

And the reason of it is, because there never was any difference of opinion among all Israel about the pronunciation of the words; for all alike read the Law without points, just as they had received it from Moses; and the other sacred books, as they received them from

וְאַכְבְּרָה קרי, וכן עשו בכל האחרים שבספרי הגולה:

והכלל כי אנשי כנסת הגדולה עשו הקרי שבתורה על פי הקבלה ממשה רע״ח, ושבנביאים וכתובים על פי הקבלה מנביאים וחכמי הדורורת, ושבספרי הגולה על פי המחברים עצמם, ולא בעבור הספקות כאשר חשבו רבים:

☜ והנה כאשר נתתי את לבי לדרוש ולתור בחכמה, על כל אשר נעשה בענין קרי וכתיב, עוד זה מצאתי, שלא נמצא קרי וכתיב על ענין הסר ומלא לעולם, ר״ל שלא נמצאת מלה בכל המקרא שהכתיב הוא מלא והקרי הוא חסר, או להפך, והטעם לפי שלא תשתנה הוראת המלה בעבור חסר ומלא לעולם:

☜ ועוד זה מצאת״י הכר נא ודע לך, שלא נמצא קרי וכתיב על ענין הנקודות והטעמים לעולם, ר״ל שלא נמצאת מלה שהכתיב נקוד באופן אחד והקרי באופן אחר, וכן לא יבא קרי וכתיב על דגש ודפי, ולא על מלעיל ומלרע, ולא על ימין ושמאל, ולא על מפיק או לא מפיק, וכן לא על אחד מרטעמים המספיקים או בלתי מספיקים:

והטעם לפי שלא היתה מחלוקת בכל ישראל בקריאת המלות, כי הכל היו קוראין בתורה בלי נקוד, כמו שקבלו ממשה רע״ה,

---

Comp. *Ioma,* 21 *b*. In the *Midrash Rabba*, on the Song of Songs, viii. 8, where the same thing is recorded, *the holy oil* (שמן המשחה), is substituted for the Shechinah, as one of the five things. Comp. p. 26 *a*, ed. Stettin, 1863.

the Prophets.⁵⁷ And as the points which were added in after time are simply signs and marks to indicate the pronunciation, therefore, they do not come within the province of the *Keri* and *Kethiv*. The same is the case with the variations between the Easterns and Westerns, not one of which is on the vowels and accents. By the Easterns are meant the Babylonians, and by the Westerns, the Palestinians.⁵⁸ We in all these countries are descendants of the latter, and therefore follow their readings and submit to their authority. Now the variations between these two are, respecting words and letters, *Keri* and *Kethiv*, *plene* and *defective*, but not in vowels and accents. And this is a proof that these variations were written down

ובשאר חספרים כמו שקבלו מהנביאים,⁵⁷ וחנקדות שנעשו אח״כ, חם אותות וסימנים לתכונות ולחברות חחם, על כן לא שייך בהן קרי וכתיב, וכן החילופים והפלונתוח שבין מדינחאי למערבאי, אין נם אחר מהן בנקודות ומעמים, ומדינחאי חם בני בבל, ומערבאי דם בני ארץ ישראל,⁵⁸ אשר מהם אגחנו בכל הארצות חאלו, לפיכך אנחנו סומכין על קריאתם, וחלכח כמותם, וחחילופין שביניחם הם בתיבות ואותיות, ובכתיב ובקרי, ובמלא ובחסר, ולא בנקודות ומעמים: וזח ראיח כי נכתבי החילופים חאלח קודם שהוסדו הנקודות והמעמים, אבל הפלונתות דבין בן אשר ובן נפתלי, שאינן אלא בנקודות ומעמים, אין ספק שנכתבו אחר שהוסדו הנקודות והמעמים, וזח קל לחבין:

☞ והנה שני האנשים חאלח, חיו שני ראשי ישיבות במסורת, שם האחד יעקב בן נפתלי, ושם חשני אדרון בן אשר: ⁵⁹וכתב

prior to the invention of the vowels and accents. The variations, however, between Ben-Asher and Ben-Naphtali, which simply refer to the points and accents, were unquestionably written down after the invention of the points and accents; and this is easily understood.

☞ As to these two men, they were the heads of two different Massoretic schools, and their respective names were *Jacob b. Naphtali* and *Aaron b. Asher*.⁵⁹ Maimonides, of blessed memory, writes in the *Treatise on the Love of God*, cap. viii., as follows: "The copy which

---

⁵⁷ The words ובשאר חספרים כמו שקבלו מהנביאים, *and in the other books as they received them from the Prophets*, which are essential to the argument, are omitted in the Sulzbach edition.

⁵⁸ From the Babylonian and Jerusalem Talmuds we see that, as early as the third century of the Christian era, there existed differences between the Easterns and Westerns, which affected both the reading and the exegesis of certain words (comp. Geiger, in the Hebrew Essays and Reviews, entitled, *Kerem Chemed*, vol. ix., p. 69, Berlin, 1856); and that many of the deviating renderings of the Septuagint and of the so-called Jonathan Chaldee version of the Prophets arise from their following the more ancient Eastern readings. These two schools produced in the middle of the sixth century the two systems of vocalisation which we have already described (*vide supra*, p. 61, &c.), and bequeathed to us a list of their variations (חלופים), which is given in the Rabbinic Bibles, but which is both exceedingly imperfect and incorrect. It is to this list that Levita refers in the text. The indefatigable Pinsker, who created a new era in the history of the Karaites, has greatly enriched and amended this list from two Codices, of A.D. 916 and 1010. Comp. *Einleitung in das Babylonisch-Hebräische Punktations-system*, pp. 121–132; Vienna, 1863.

⁵⁹ Aaron b. Moses b. Asher, or simply, *Ben-Asher*, as he is generally called, flourished *circa* A.D. 900, at Tiberias. He was the most accomplished scholar and representative of the Tiberian system of vocalisation and accentuation, and wrote, in the interests of the Westerns, the following works: i. *A Model Codex of the Bible*, (ספר בן אשר), furnished with the points and accents according to the Western school, which became the standard text, and which Maimonides described in such eulogistic terms;

we have followed in these matters is the famous Codex of Egypt, which contains the twenty-four books, and which had been in Jerusalem for many years, in order that other Codices might be corrected by its text; and all followed it, because Ben-Asher had minutely revised it for many years, and corrected it many times. According to this, many copies were made; and I, too, followed it in the books of the Law which I myself have written, in all its integrity."[60] And we also, throughout all these countries, follow its readings, whilst the Orientals adopt the text of Ben-Naphtali. The variations in the accents between them are confined to the smaller accents, such as *Metheg, Makiph, Munach*, one *Pashta*, or *two Pashtas*. All this will be thoroughly explained in a separate Treatise, called *Good Sense*, which, by the help of the Lord, I intend to write.[61] These variations between them, which also extend to the vowels, only refer to *Cholem, Kemetz-Chateph, Long-Kemetz, Pattach, Sheva, Chateph-Pattach*, as well as to *Dagesh, Raphe, Milel*, and *Milra*.

חרם״בם זכרנו לברכה בספר אהבה פרק ח׳ וז״ל, וספר שסמכנו עליו בדברים אלו הוא ספר הידוע במצרים שהוא כולל כ״ד ספרים שהיה בירושלם מכמה שנים לחניה ממנו הספרים, ועליו היו הכל סומכין, לפי שהניהו בן אשר, ודקדק בו שנים הרבה, וחניחו פעמים רבות כמו שהעתיקו, ועליו סמכתי בספר תורה שכתבתי כהלכתו,[60] וכן אנחנו סומכין על קריאתו בכל הארצות האלת, ואנשי מזרח סומכין על קריאת בין נפתלי, וחפלונתות שביניהן במעמים אינן אלא במעמים הקמנים, כנון מתג ומקף ומונח ובפשטא אחד וב׳ פשמין, וכל זה יחית מבואר תימב בספר טוב טעם אשר יערתי חבורו בע"ה,[61] גם חפלונתות שביניהן בנקוד זח אינן אלא בחולם ובקמץ חמוף, ובקמץ גדול ופתה, ובשוא ובחמף פתה, וכן בדנשין ורפין, ומלעיל ומלרע :

ii. *A Treatise on the Massorah*, entitled *the Massoreth of Ben-Asher* (מסורת בן אשר), stating partly the Massoretic remarks on each word in the margin of the text itself (מסרת גליונית. מסרה הסוגים), and partly at the end of the Codex (*Massorah finalis*). Comp. Pinsker, *Likute Kabmonijot*, text p. 130; iii. *A Treatise on the Accents* (ספר (בי)דקדוקי הטעמים), first printed in the Rabbinic Bible, Venice, 1517; and then again by Leopold Dukes, Tubingen, 1846; iv. *A Treatise on the Consonants and Vowels* (ספר דקדוקי האותיות והנקדות), of which fragments only have survived, which are inserted in his treatise on the accents, and against which the celebrated Saadia Gaon wrote a dissertation; and v. *A Treatise on Assonances* (שמונים וזוגי), giving eighty Hebrew words, similar in sound, but differing in sense. Moses b. David b. Naphtali, again, or simply Ben-Asher, as he is generally called, represented the Easterns, and wrote in the interests of the Babylonian school, i. A Model Codex of the Bible, and ii. A Treatise on the system of vocalisation and accentuation. Comp. Fürst, *Introduction to the Hebrew and Chaldee Lexicon*, p. xxi. A list of the variations between these two representatives of the Easterns and Westerns, is given at the end of the Rabbinic Bibles.

[60] The *Treatise on the Love of God* (ספר אהבה), which Levita quotes, is simply one of the component parts of Maimonides' gigantic work on the Biblical and traditional Laws, called *Deuteronomy; Second Law* (משנה תורה), or *Jad Ha-Chezaka* (יד החזקה) = *the Mighty Hand*, in allusion to Deut. xxxiv. 12. The part consists of the following six *Halachoth* (הלכות), or *Tractates*: i. On the reading of Shema; ii. On Prayer and the Priestly Benediction; iii. On Phylacteries, Mezzuza, and the Scroll of the Law; iv. On the Fringed Garment; v. On Benedictions, and vi. On Circumcision. The quotation in question is from Tractate iii., and the portion which treats on the Scroll of the Law, or *Hilchoth Sepher Thora*, viii. 4. The reference in the text is, to say the least, most indefinite.

[61] The treatise on the accents, entitled *Good Sense* (מוב טעם), to which Levita refers, appeared within twelve months of the publication of this statement. *Vide supra*, p. 63, &c.

☞ Now it is evident, from all I have said, that the *Keri* and *Kethiv* never occur with respect to *plene* and *defective*, nor on a single one of the vowel-points and accents. Let me, therefore, warn and caution every one who reads the folio or quarto editions of the four and twenty books published here, in Venice, in the year 278 (=1517),[62] to pay no attention to the false remarks printed in the margin, in the form of *Keri* and *Kethiv, plene* and *defective, Milel* and *Milra,* and *variations in the vowels and accents,* or to any of those things which ought not to have been done, as I have stated above. The author of them did not know how to distinguish between his right hand and his left. Not being a Jew, he knew nothing about the nature of the Massorah, and what he did put down simply arose from the fact, that he sometimes found variations in the copies which he had before him, and, as he did not know which reading was the correct one, he put down one in the margin and another in the text. Sometimes it so happened that he put the correct reading into the text, and the incorrect one into the margin, and sometimes the reverse is the case; thus, he was groping in darkness, like a blind man. Hence, they are not to be heeded, for they are confusion worse confounded.

Now, before quitting the subject of the *Keri* and *Kethiv,* let me remark, that, being anxious to know the number of all the *Keris* and *Kethivs* throughout the Scriptures, I counted them several times, and found them to be 848, and indicated this by the mnemonical sign, "*Karjan Ve-Kathban*."[63] Of these, 65 are in the Pentateuch,[64] 454 in the Prophets, and 329 in the Hagiographa.

[62] This refers to the first edition of the great Rabbinic Bible, in folio, published by Bomberg, 1516-17, and the quarto edition, also published by Bomberg, 1517. Comp. Wolf, *Bibliotheca Hebraea* ii. 367; Masch, *Bibliotheca Sacra* i. 17; Steinschneider, *Catalogus Libr. Hebr. in Bibliotheca Bodleiana,* col. 7; Kitto, *Cyclopædia of Biblical Literature, s. v.* Rabbinic Bibles.

[63] That is to say 848, which is the numerical value of קרי״ן וכ׳תבן, viz., ק 100, + ר 200, + י 10, + י 10, + ן 50, + ו 6, + כ 20, + ת 400, + ב 2, + ן 50 = 848.

[64] Levita is surely wrong in saying that there are only sixty-five *Keris* and *Kethivs* in the Pentateuch. In again going through the Massoretic notes in the Bible, we have found eighty-two. They are as follows:—Genesis viii. 17; x. 19; xiv. 2, 8; xxiv. 14, 16, 28,

It is astonishing that in the Pentateuch there should only be 65 *Keris* and *Kethivs*, 22 of whice relate to נערה, which is written in the text נער, and the marginal reading is נערה; whilst in the book of Joshua, which is only about a tenth the size of the Pentateuch, there occur 82,[65] and in the book of Samuel, which in quantity is about a fourth of the Pentateuch, there are found 133.[66] It is also to be noticed that, of the many Catalogues, Registers, and Alphabetical Lists of the *Keris* and *Kethivs* in the Great Massorah, not a single one is found in the Pentateuch. Thus, of the 62 words in which two letters are transposed;[67] the 12 words

וייש לחמוזז למה לא נמצאו בתורה רק ס״ח קרי וכתיב אשר מחן כ״ב דכתיבין נער וקרינן נערה, וספר יהושע שהוא רק כעשירית בכמות התורה ונמצאו בו ל״ב,[65] וספר שמואל שהוא כמעט חרביעית מן התורה ונמצאים בו קל״ג[66] חלא תראה כי רוב חזונין וחשימין ואלפפא ביחין מן קריין וכתבן שבמסרח הגדולה, אין גם אחד מהן בתורה, וחמשל ס״ב מלין דמוקדמין ומאוחרין,[67]

33, 55, 57; xxv. 23; xxxvii. 3, 29; xxx. 11; xxxiii. 4; xxxiv. 3 (twice), 12; xxxvi. 5, 14, 15; xxxix. 20, 22; xliii. 28; xlix. 11 (twice): Exod. iv. 2; xiii. 11; xxv. 2, 7, 13; xxi. 8; xxii. 4, 26; xxvii. 11; xxviii. 28; xxxii. 17, 19; xxxv. 11; xxxvii. 8; xxxix. 4, 21, 33: Levit. ix. 22; xi. 21; xvi. 21; xxi. 5; xxiii. 13; xxv. 30: Numb. i. 16; iii. 51; x. 36; xi. 32; xii. 3; xiv. 36; xvi. 11; xxi. 32; xxvi. 9; xxxii. 7; xxxiv. 4: Deuter. ii. 33; v. 10; vii. 9; viii. 2; xxi. 7; xxii. 15 (twice), 16, 20, 21, 23, 24, 25, 26 (twice), 27, 28, 29; xxvii. 10; xxviii. 27, 30; xxix 22; xxxiii. 9. The numbers, therefore, given in Kitto's *Cyclopædia of Biblical Literature, s. v.* KERI and KETHIV, must be corrected. The instances in which the *Keri* and *Kethiv* are on the word נער, have already been specified. *Vide supra*, p. 109, note 4ⁿ.

[65] According to our collation of the text, we find *thirty-five Keris and Kethivs* in the Book of Joshua expressly so marked, viz., Josh. iii. 18; iii. 4, 16; iv. 18: v. 1; vi. 5, 7, 9, 13, 15; viii. 11, 12, 16; ix. 7; xi. 16; xv. 4, 47, 48, 53, 63; xvi. 3; xviii. 12, 14, 19 (twice), 24; xix. 22, 29; xx. 8; xxi. 10, 27; xxii. 7; xxiv. 3, 8, 15; and at least three, though not designated *Keri*, are nevertheless such, viz., xvi. 5; xviii. 8, 9. Comp. also *ibid*. v. 15; vii. 21; ix. 7; x. 8; xii. 20; xv. 63; xxiv. 19.

[66] Equally wrong is Levita's statement about the number of *Keris* a d *Kethivs* in the books of Samuel, inasmuch as a careful perusal of the Massoretic remarks will show that there are 161, and not 133. They occur as follows:—1 Sam. ii. 3, 9, 10 (twice); iii. 2, 18; iv. 13; v. 6, 9, 12; vi. 4, 5; vii. 9; viii. 3; ix. 1, 26; x. 21; xi. 6, 9; xii. 10; xiii. 8, 19; xiv. 27, 32 (twice); xv. 16; xvii. 7, 23, 34; xviii. 1, 6, 7, 9, 14, 22; xix. 18, 19, 22, 23 (twice); xx. 1, 2 (twice), 24, 38; xxi. 12 (twice); xxii. 13, 17, 18 (twice), 22; xxiii. 5; xxiv. 9, 19; xxv. 3, 18 (twice), 34; xxvi. 5, 7 (twice), 11, 16, 22; xxvii. 4, 8; xxviii. 8; xxix. 5 (twice); xxx. 6, 24:—2 Sam. i. 8, 11; ii. 23; iii. 2, 3, 12, 15, 25; v. 2 (thrice), 8, 24; vi. 23; x. 9; xii. 9, 20, 22, 24, 31; xiii. 32, 34, 37; xiv. 7, 11, 21, 22, 30; xv. 8, 20, 28; xvi. 2, 8, 10 (twice), 12 (twice), 18; xvii. 12, 16; xviii. 3, 8, 12, 13, 17, 18; xix. 7, 19, 32, 41; xx. 5, 8, 14, 23, 25; xxi. 4, 6, 9 (twice), 12 (twice), 16, 20, 21; xxii. 8, 15, 23, 33, 34, 51; xxiii. 8 (twice), 9 (thrice), 11, 13, 15, 16, 18, 20 (thrice), 21, 37; xxiv. 14, 16, 18, 22. These, it must be remarked, do not include either the *Keri Ve-lo Kethiv* or the *Kethiv Ve-lo Keri*, which have already been enumerated (*vide supra*, p. 109, n. 51).

[67] The sixty-two words in which two letters following each other are transposed, are as follows:—

הולך	. .	Josh. vi. 13	מבואך	. .	2 Sam. iii. 25	ונורנך	. . Jerem. ii. 25
גלון	. .	Josh. xx. 8	והוזריחה	. .	2 Sam. xiv. 30	במרצותם	. . Jerem. viii. 6
גלו	. .	Josh. xxi. 27	בעברות	. .	2 Sam. xv. 28	שחטו	. . Jerem. ix. 7
וחימשני	. .	Judg. xvi. 26	נמצות	. .	2 Sam. xviii. 8	שומע	. . Jerem. xvii. 23
ותראנה	. .	1 Sam. xiv. 27	ויקלהו	. .	2 Sam. xx. 14	הידע	. . Jerem. xxvi. 14
בניה	. .	1 Sam. xix. 18	הארונה	. .	2 Sam. xxiv. 16	ובתרותך	. . Jerem. xxxii. 23
בניה	. .	1 Sam. xix. 22	האהל	. .	1 Kings vii. 45	התעתתים	. . Jerem. xlii. 20
נירה	. .	1 Sam. xix. 23	הממותים	. .	2 Kings xi. 2	אסווחיה	. . Jerem. l. 15
בניה	. .	1 Sam. xix. 23	ימות	. .	2 Kings xiv. 6	תכסלי	. . Ezek. xxxvi. 14
והגרזי	. .	1 Sam. xxvii. 8	ואכל	. .	Is. xxxvii. 30	היאהון	. . Ezek. xl. 15

which have no *Vav* conjunctive in the text, and yet are read in the margin with it, and the 11 words in which the reverse is the case;⁶⁸ the 18 words which want the suffix *Vav* in the text, and are read in the margin with it, and the 11 words in which the reverse is the case;⁶⁹ the 29 words which in the text want *He* at the end, and in the margin are read with it, and the 20 words in which the reverse is the case;⁷⁰ the alphabetical list of 75 words, every one of which is

אביות . .	Ezek. xlii. 16	הלכות .	Prov. xxxi 27	שמלי . . .	Ezra ii. 46
ומהאראל .	Ezek. xliii. 15	ובתובנתו .	Job. xxvi. 12	ומבלהים . .	Ezra iv. 4
והאריאל .	Ezek. xliii. 16	יבדר . . .	Eccl. ix. 4	ואצאה . .	Ezra viii. 17
נמר . . .	Ps. lxxiii. 2	ובמלואת . .	Esther i. 5	בצחחים . .	Nehem iv. 7
סלאיה . .	Ps. cxxxix. 6	מומכן . . .	Esther i. 16	למלוני . .	Nehem. xii. 14
ונדלותך .	Ps. cxlv. 6	ידרון . . .	Dan. iv. 9	עיות . . .	1 Chron. i. 46
כשאוה . .	Prov. i. 27	והמימנא .	Dan. v. 7	הוריחו . .	1 Chron. iii. 24
הלך . .	Prov. xiii. 20	תוכל . . .	Dan. v. 16	שטור . .	1 Chron. xxvii. 29
יומה . .	Prov. xix. 16	תוכל . . .	Dan. v. 16	ושמרימות .	2 Chron. xvii. 8
ועיף . .	Prov. xxiii. 5	והמימנא . .	Dan. v. 16	לורמה . .	2 Chron. xxix. 8
תרצנה . .	Prov. xxiii. 26	והמיובא .	Dan. v. 29		

The list of these transpositions is given in the Massorah finalis, under letter *Vav*, and in the *Och:a Ve-Ochla*, section xci., pp. 27, 93, &c.

⁶⁸ The twelve words which are in the text without the *Vav* conjunctive, but are read with it in the margin, are as follows:—

בניו . .	2 Kings iv. 7	עד . . .	Job ii. 7	אין . . .	Lamen. 5. 3
תחת . .	Isa. lv. 13	די . . .	Dan. ii. 43	וקנים . .	Lam-n. iv 16
דור . .	Prov. xxvii. 24	לא . . .	Lamen. v. 3	אינם . .	Lamen. v. 7
ילד . .	Prov. xxiii. 24	לא . . .	Lamen. v. 5	אבחנו . .	Lamen. v. 7

The eleven words which, on the contrary, have *Vav* conjunctive in the text, but not in the marginal reading, are as follows:—

וכי . .	2 Sam. xvi. 10	ויחקו . .	Jerem. iv. 5	והרשענו . .	Dan. ix. 5
ומסגרתיה	1 Kings vii. 36	ויורה . .	Jerem. v. 24	וחסד . .	Nehem. xi. 17
וראתה . .	2 Kings xi. 1	ויציאו . .	Jerem. viii. 1	ושמחה . .	Prov. xxiii. 24
ואת . .	2 Kings xvi. 12	וכל . . .	Lamen. iv. 12		

These instances are enumerated in the Massorah marginalis on Dan. ix. 5; Massorah finalis, under the letter *Vav*; and *Ochla Ve-Ochla*, sections cxvii. and cxviii., pp. 82, 101.

⁶⁹ The eighteen words, which according to the Massorah want the suffix *Vav* in the text, are as follows:—

ישתחו	Gen. xxvii. 29	וישחחו .	1 Kings ix. 9	והלוה .	Ezek. vii. 21
וישתחו	Gen. xliii. 28	וידבר .	1 Kings xii. 7	שוי .	Dan. v. 21
ויצו .	Judg. xxi. 20	יקח .	2 Kings xx. 18	וינל .	Ezra iii. 8
ויעלה .	1 Sam. vii. 9	ויתנה .	2 Kings xxii. 1	אדור .	Nehem. iii. 30
ויאמר .	1 Sam. xii. 10	ואכל .	Isaiah xxxvii. 30	אדור .	Nehem. iii. 31
אמר .	1 Sam xiii. 19	יחד .	Jerem. xlviii. 7	וקבל .	Esther ix. 27

The eleven words which on the contrary terminate with *Vav* in the textual reading, but have no *Vav* in the marginal reading, are as follows:—

ויאמרו . .	Josh. vi. 7	ויבאו .	1 Kings xii. 3	ויצהרו .	2 Kings xvi. 15
ויאמרו . .	Josh. ix. 7	ויבאו .	1 Kings xii. 21	יצאו .	Ezek. xlvi. 9
ויאמרו .	1 Sam. xv. 16	שכשהו .	2 Kings xxii. 33	ויעמדו .	Nehem. iii. 15
רגליו . .	2 Sam. xx i. 34	ויבאו .	2 Kings xiv. 13		

These instances are partly enumerated in Tract *Sopherim* vii. 1; and entirely in the Massorah marginalis on 1 Kings i. 1, xii. 3; Massorah finalis under letter *Vav*; and *Ochla Ve-Ochla*, sections cxix. and cxx., pp. 32, 102.

⁷⁰ The twenty-nine words which have no *He* in the textual reading, but have it in the marginal reading, are as follows:—

in the text written with a *Jod* in the יו״ד באמצע תיבותא וקריין וי״ו, ואלפא
middle, and in the margin read with ביתא סן ע' מלין בחפך,⁷¹ אין נם אחד מהן
Vav, and the alphabetical list of
70 words in which the reverse is the case ;⁷¹ not one of all these occurs

וארב	. .	Josh. xxiv. 3	ותעב	. .	Ezek. xxxiii. 16	נמע	. . Prov. xxxi. 16
הגנ	. .	1 Sam. ix. 26	עת	. .	Ezek. xxxiii. 48	בלל	. . Prov. xxxi. 18
ואת	. .	1 Sam. xxiv. 19	חמש	. .	Ezek. xlv. 3	את	. . . Job i. 10
וחם	. .	2 Sam. xxi. 9	ואכבד	. .	Hag. i. 8	וירא	. . Job xlii. 16
ידי	. .	1 Kings i. 37	לכן	. .	Ruth i. 12	בלל	. . Lamen. ii. 19
והית	. .	2 Kings ix. 37	וארע	. .	Ruth iv. 4	הביש	. . Lamen. v. 1
ונרא	. .	Isaiah xli. 23	ואת	. .	Ps. vi. 4	ונשוב	. . Lamen. v. 21
הן	. .	Isaiah liv. 16	רעה	. .	Ps. lxxiv. 6	את	. . Eccl. vii. 22
ירא	. .	Jerem. xvii. 8	שח	. .	Ps. xc. 8	את	. . Nehem. ix. 6
חמש	. .	Jerem. xl. 16	וארצע	. .	Prov. xxx. 18		

The twenty words which, on the contrary, terminate with *He* in the textual reading, but not in the marginal reading, are :—

ואראה	. .	Josh. vii. 21	הואתה	. .	Jerem. xxvi. 6	הרבה	. . . Ps. li. 4
ואביאה	. .	Josh. xxiv. 8	קחה	. .	Jerem. xxxi. 39	אהביה	. . . Prov. xvii. 17
הארה	. .	2 Sam. xxiii. 20	ובאה	. .	Jerem. xliii. 11	ורעה	. . Prov. xxvii. 10
וקה	. .	1 Kings vii. 23	נמצאה	. .	Jerem. xlviii. 27	מקחה	. . Dan. ix. 18
ותראה	. .	Jerem. iii. 7	רעה	. .	Micah iii. 2	אריה	. . Lament. iii. 10
באה	. .	Jerem. xv. 9	וקה	. .	Zech. i. 16	אלה	. . Ezra v. 15
הרעה	. .	Jerem. xviii. 10	ישעה	. .	Ruth i. 3		

These instances are given in the Tract *Sopherim* vii. 2 ; Massorah marginalis on Prov. xxxi. 16 ; Lament. ii. 19, v. 1 ; Eccl. vii. 23 ; Massorah finalis under letter *He*, and *Ochla Ve-Ochla*, sections cxi. and cxii., pp. 31, 99, &c.

⁷¹ The following are the words which in the textual reading have *Jod* in the middle of the word, and are with *Vav* in the marginal reading :—

אוכיר	. .	Ps. lxxvii. 12	ונשניו	. .	1 Kings xvi. 34	מידמת	. . Isaiah xii. 5
אריה	. .	2 Sam. xxiv. 18	ולשימון	. .	Isaiah x. 6	מיסירות	. . Ezek. xli. 8
בחיניו	. .	Isa. xxiii. 13	וריב	. .	Job xxxiii. 19	נסיסים	. . Ezra ii. 50
ברתיקות	. .	1 Kings vi. 21	ונצירי	. .	Isaiah xlix. 6	סימה	. . 2 Sam. xxiii. 32
בכים	. .	Prov. xxiii. 31	ונדירא	. .	Dan. ii. 22	עיניתם	. . Hos x. 10
בנים	. .	Ps. lxxix. 10	וסיסניה	. .	Dan. iii. 10	עליה	. . 1 Chron. i. 51
ניים	. .	Gen. xxv. 28	והמישד	. .	Lament. iii. 20	פסידים	. . 1 Chron. ix. 23
נדיחיו	. .	1 Chron. xii. 15	ונירה	. .	2 Kings xx.ii. 36	ציץ	. . 1 Chron. vi. 20
הדרופי	. .	1 Chron. xii. 5	הישה	. .	Ps. lxxi. 12	קריאי	. . Numb. i. 16
הסיעינים	. .	1 Chron. iv. 41	ישיב	. .	2 Sam. xv. 8	ראית	. . Isaiah xlii. 20
וישם	. .	Gen. xxiv. 33	יני	. .	Ps. lxxii. 17	ראית	. . Eccl. v. 10
ולינו	. .	Exod. xvi. 2	יצמינו	. .	Ps. lvi. 7	שים	. . Isaiah xxviii. 15
וירש	. .	Numb. xxxii. 32	ימימו	. .	Ps. ccl. 11	שיחה	. . Jerem. xviii. 22
רינים	. .	Josh. xv. 53	ירמון	. .	Ps. lxvi. 7	שביתהם	. . Jerem. xxix. 14
רינסו	. .	Judg. vii. 21	יקצרו	. .	Job xxiv. 6	שובים	. . Jerem. l. 6
ורעיתל	. .	Judg. xxi. 20	לקיש	. .	Jerem. xlviii. 7	שבייך	. . Lament. ii. 14
ויחל	. .	1 Sam. xiii. 8	לידרא	. .	Nehem. xii. 16	שילל	. . Micah i. 8
ויחר	. .	2 Sam. xx. 5	לעיזר	. .	2 Sam. xviii. 8	שעתיריה	. . Hos. vi. 10
ושיא	. .	2 Sam. xx. 25	מדין	. .	2 Sam. xxi. 20	שדין	. . Job xix. 29
ושניאל	. .	1 Chron. viii. 25	מגדיל	. .	2 Sam. xxii. 51	תחיל	. . Ezek. xxx. 16
וצמינך	. .	Ps. xvii. 14	מיסך	. .	2 Kings xvi. 18	תמיש	. . Prov. xvii. 13
וציים	. .	Ps. xlix. 15	מיצקה	. .	2 Kings iv. 5	תמריק	. . Prov. xx. 30
ונים	. .	Job vii. 5	מידו	. .	Ruth ii. 1	תרים	. . Ps. lxxix. 18
וחיתי	. .	Job vi. 2					

The following is the Alphabetical list of words, which, on the contrary, have *Vav* in the middle of the word in the textual reading, and have *Jod* in the marginal reading :—

אסורי	. .	Gen. xxxix. 20	ארוצם	. .	Jerem. l. 44	נול	. . Prov. xxiii. 24
אבוניל	. .	1 Sam. xxv. 18	בצוני	. .	2 Sam. xvi. 12	דהוא	. . Ezra iv. 9
אנוניך	. .	2 Sam. xx. 20	בור	. .	Jerem. xv. 7	הוצא	. . Gen. viii. 17
אושר	. .	Isaiah xlv. 2	בהלכיתם	. .	Nahum ii. 6	החרסות	. . Jerem. xix. 2
אולי	. .	2 Kings xxiv. 15	ברוחת	. .	1 Chron. vii. 31	הלהות	. . Jerem. xlviii. 5

in the Pentateuch.[72] There is undoubtedly a reason for all this, but I do not know it. I have now satisfied my desire in explaining that which I deemed necessary about the nature of the *Keri* and the *Kethiv*.

☞ I shall now say something about the nature of *plene* and *defective*. First of all, I say, it appears that, to the words which were found written *plene* or *defective*, nothing new whatsoever was added by the men of the Great Synagogue out of their own understanding; but that Ezra transcribed them, into his copy of the Law, just as he found them in the Codex of the Law which was made from the scroll of the Law of Moses received from Sinai, and which the prophet Jeremiah concealed,[73] according to the opinion of some, without adding anything to it or taking anything from it. The same is the case with the *defective* and *plene* of the Prophets

בתורה; [72] ועל כל פנים טעם יש בדבר, ואנכי לא ידעתי, וכאן נשלם חפצי מה שראיתי לבאר בענין קריין וכתבן:

☞ ועתה אדבר מעט מענין המלאים והחסרים, ואתחיל ואומר, כי חמלות שנכתבו חסרים או מלאים נראה כי לא חדשו אנשי כנסת הגדולה בהן דבר מדעתם, רק עזרא כתבם בתורה, כאשר מצאם במופס ס״ת אשר חותמתק מספר תורה משה אשר קבל מסיני שנגנז ירמיה הנביא לפי דעת האומרים ככה,[73] ולא חוסיף ולא גרע, וכן החסרים וחמלאים שבנביאים ובכתובים, אם נמצאו בידם נופי

הבצור	. . Zech. xi. 2	יענר	. Ezek. xlviii. 14	עשוות	. 1 Sam. xxv. 18
המבוא	. Ezek. xlii. 9	יעור	. 1 Chron. xx. 5	עטי	. Jerem. xl. 8
המבונים	2 Chron. xxxv. 3	יחאל	. 2 Chron. xxix. 14	ענוי	. Amos viii. 4
הוסר	. . Ps. v. 9	ינקטון	. Ps. lix. 16	עמרי	. 2 Chron. xiii. 19
היתוף	. Prov. xxiii. 5	יכטומו	. Ps. cxl. 10	עתורים	. Esther viii. 13
הנתונים	. Ezra viii. 17	כמטלו	. Prov. iv. 16	ציעורירהם	. Jerem. xiv. 3
הכעוסני	. Jerem. xxv. 7	לוש	. 2 Sam. iii. 15	צעוריה	. Jerem. xlviii. 4
החסטות	2 Chron. xxvi. 21	לדוגים	. Jerem. xvi. 16	צטוי	. Ezek. iv. 15
ולונו	. Numb. xiv. 36	לרוב	. Judg. xxi. 22	קראי	. Numb. xxvi. 9
ושחצוומה	. Joshua xix. 22	לשור	. 1 Sam. xviii. 6	שושק	. 1 Kings xiv. 25
רצנוף	. . Isaiah lxii. 3	לסוע	. Ezek. xli. 18	שרולק	. Jerem. xviii. 16
ואלל	. . Jerem. xiv. 3	למשוטה	. Isaiah xlii. 24	שרוהך	. Jerem. xv. 11
ותרמות	. Jerem. xiv. 14	למעוותם	. . Ps. cxix. 3	שפרורו	. Jerem. xliii. 10
וסום	. Jerem. vii. 7	מנורת	. 1 Sam. xx. 1	שמור	. 1 Chron. xxiv. 24
ואתוקידתא	. Ezek. xli. 15	מוסצה	. Jerem. xlviii. 21	שבות	. . Zeph. ii. 7
ותהלן	. 1 Chron. iv. 20	נוב	. Isaiah lvii. 19	שבות	. Ps. lxxxv. 2
יוזאל	. 1 Chron. xii. 3	נובי	. Nehem. x. 20	שלשום	. Prov. xxii. 20
הבונו	2 Chron. xxxv. 4	נשוים	. Isaiah iii. 16	תנואי	. Numb. xxxii. 7
הוקך	. . Ps. lxxiv. 11	נטשסים	. Nehem. vii. 52	תרוב	. . Prov. iii. 30
יצרע	. 1 Kings vi. 5	שום	. 2 Sam. xiv. 7	תשוה	. . Job xxx. 22

It will be seen that the Massorah finalis, under letter *Jod*, where these alphabetical lists are found, only gives seventy-two of the former, whereas of the latter it gives seventy-five. Comp. also *Sopherim* vii. 4; *Ochla Ve-Ochla*, sections lxxx. and lxxxi., pp 24, 85, &c.

[72] Levita is surely incorrect in his statement that not one of the variations specified in these lists occurs in the Pentateuch. In perusing them it will be seen, that in the list of eighteen words (No. 69), we have Gen. xxvii. 29; xliii. 28; in the list of seventy words (No. 71), we have Gen. xxiv. 33; xxv. 23; Exod. xvi. 2; Numb. i. 16; xxi. 32; and in the next list (also No. 71), Gen. viii. 17; xxxix. 20; Numb. xiv. 36; xxvi. 9; xxxii. 7.

[73] According to the traditional explanation of Deut. xxxi. 26, a copy of the entire Pentateuch was deposited by Moses in the Ark of the Covenant (Comp. *Gittin* 60 *a*; *Baba Bathra* 14-15; *Menachoth* 30 *a*; *Jerusalem Targum* on Deut. xxxi. 26). This Codex Jeremiah concealed when he concealed the Ark, together with the Tabernacle and the Altar of Incense. 2 Maccab. ii. 5.

and Hagiographa. Thus, when they [Ezra and his associates] found the very autographs of the authors themselves, as was the case with the book of Isaiah, which Isaiah himself wrote, the Psalms which David wrote, the Proverbs which Solomon wrote, and with all or part of the books which they possessed, they required no tradition to guide them, but copied exactly as they found it: *plene* wherever there was *plene*, and *defective* wherever there was *defective*. But when they did not find the autograph itself, which seems most likely to have happened, they undoubtedly followed the majority of Codices, which they had collected from different places, one here and one there, as the twenty-four books were then not joined together into one volume. Now they [Ezra and his associates] have joined them together and divided them into three parts: the Law, the Prophets, and the Hagiographa, and arranged the Prophets and Hagiographa not in the order in which they have been put by our Rabbins of blessed memory, in *Baba Bathra*, [14 a].

חספרים אשר כתבו חמחברים עצמם, בגון ישעיה שכתב הוא בעצמו, וכן תחלים שכתב דוד, ומשלי שכתב שלמה, וכן כלן או מקצתן אשר נמצאו בידם, לא חיו צדיכים לקבלח אלא הניחום כמו שמצאום, במקום מלא מלא, ובמקום חסר חסר, אבל אם לא נמצאו כמו שחוא קרוב לודאי. חלכו אחר רוב הההעתקות ונמצאות, אחת חנה ואחת חנה, כי לא חיו הכ״ד ספרים מחוברים יחד, וחם חברום ועשו מחם ג׳ חלקים, תורת נביאים וכתובים, וסדרום נביאים וכתובים זה אחר זח שלא כסדר שסדרום רז״ל בבבא בתרא:

וזחו סדרן של רז״ל סדרן של נביאים, יחושע שופטים שמואל מלבים, ירמיח ישעיח יחזקאל, חדי עשר: וסדרן של כתובין רות תחלים איוב משלי קחלת שיר חשירים קינות אסתר ד״ח, ונותנים טעמים וסברות נכונות על סדרן זח, ואין כאן מקומן:

ובעלי חמסורת סדרו נבאים בסדר חזח, רק שחקדימו ישעיח לפני ירמיח ויחזקאל, לפי שזמנו חיח קודם זמנם, וכן נמצא סדרן בכל ספרי ספרדים חמובחקים, אבל בספרי האשכנזים וחצרפתים חם כדורים בסדר של רז״ל, אכן בכתובים בעלי חמסרה סדרו של רז״ל וזחו, ד״ח תחלים איוב משלי, רות שיר חשירים קחלת קינות אסתר, דניאל עזרא, וכן בספרי חספרדים, אבל בספרי האשכנזים סדרן

The following is the order of our Rabbins, of blessed memory:—
The position of the Prophets is—Joshua, Judges, Samuel, Kings, Jeremiah, Isaiah, Ezekiel, and the twelve minor Prophets. The order of the Hagiographa is—Ruth, Psalms, Job, Proverbs, Ecclesiastes, Song of Songs, Lamentations, Esther, and Chronicles, and they [the Rabbins] gave appropriate reasons for this classification, which would be out of place here.

The Massorites too have adopted this order in the Prophets, only that they have put Isaiah before Jeremiah and Ezekiel, because he lived before them. The same order is also found in all the correct Spanish Codices; whilst the German and French Codices adopt the order of the Rabbins, of blessed memory. But in the Hagiographa, the Massorites have altered the order of the Rabbins of blessed memory as follows: Chronicles, Psalms, Job, Proverbs, Ruth, Song of Songs, Ecclesiastes, Lamentations, Esther, Daniel, Ezra, which is followed in the Spanish Codices; whereas the German Codices have the following order:—Psalms, Proverbs, Job, the Five Megilloth, Daniel, Ezra, and Chronicles. It is the custom to put the Five Megilloth in the order in which they are read in the Synagogue, according to their respective seasons, that is, Song of Songs, Ruth, Lamentations, Ecclesiastes, and Esther.[74]

☞ Having now reached the place in which I, at the beginning of this Introduction, promised to state my own opinion about the points and accents, I shall first do battle against those who say that they were given on Sinai, and then state who invented them, and when they were originated and affixed to the letters. But if anyone should prove to me, by clear evidence, that my opinion is opposed to that of our Rabbins of blessed memory, or is contrary to the genuine Kabbalah of the *Sohar*,[75] I will readily give in to him, and declare my opinion as void. Up to this time, however, I have neither found, nor seen, nor heard, any evidence, nor anything approaching to it, that is worthy to be relied upon, that the points and accents were given upon Sinai.

I shall here state what I have found written on this subject in some treatises of later writers, but not in the works[76] of the Rabbins of blessed memory. Kimchi, in his *Michlol*, after citing the statement of the Talmud that it is necessary to make a pause between the conjunctions, remarks thus: "—בְּכָל (Deut. xi. 18) is pointed with *Kametz*, because of the *Makeph*, and if it were read without the *Makeph*, it would be pointed בְּכָל with *Cholem*, and this, certainly, the Rabbins of blessed

ככה, תחלים משלי איוב, חמש מגלות, דניאל
עזרא ד״ה, וח' חמגילות נהגים לכתוב סדרן
לפי הסדר שקוראים אותן בבית הכנסת בזמנם,
דהיינו שיר רוח קינות קהלת אסתר: [74]

§ וְעַתָּה הגעתי עד המקום אשר אמרתי
בתחלת החקדמה הזאת להוות דעי אף אני
בענין הנקודות והטעמים, ואעדיוך מלחמה
נגד האומדים שנחנו מסיני, ואודיע מי יסדם,
ומתי חוסדו והושמו עם האותיות, ומי
שיוכיחני בהוכחה ברורה שדעתי זאת נגד
דעת רז״ל, וננד הקבלה האמתית שבספר
הזוהר[75] יבושל דעתי מפני דעתו, אבל עד
הנה לא מצאתי ולא ראיתי ולא שמעתי דבר
ראיה, או סמך שראוי לסמוך עליו, שהנקודות
והטעמים נתנו מסיני:

והנני אכתוב כל מה שמצאתי כתוב על
ככה בקצת דברי האחרונים אך לא בדברי[76]
רז״ל, כתב הרד״ק במכלול כאשר מביא
מאמר רז״ל צריך ליתן רוח בין חדבקים,
וח״ל, הנה בְּכָל־לְבַבְכֶם, נקוד בקמץ מפני
המקף, ואם יקרא אותו בלא מקף יהיה נקד

---

[74] The Five Megilloth are respectively read every year, on five annual festivals, as follows:—i. The Song of Songs on Passover; ii. Ruth on Pentecost; iii. Lamentations on the Ninth of *Ab*; iv. Ecclesiastes on Tabernacles; and v. Esther on Purim. These festivals occur in the succession in which they are enumerated. Hence the present order of the Five Megilloth.

[75] The important passage וננד הקבלה האמתית שבספר הזוהר, *or against the genuine Kabbalah of the Sohar*, which was first animadverted upon by Azzariah de Rossi (*Meor Enajim* 287, &c., ed. Vienna, *vide supra*, p. 52), and of which the Buxtorfs made such terrible use against Levita *(Commentarius Masoreticus,* cap. ix., p. 74, ed. Basel 1620), is entirely omitted in the Sulzbach edition. That the *Sohar* does mention the vowel-points has already been shown (*vide supra*, p. 48), and Levita's assertion to the contrary is to be accounted for on the supposition advanced by De Rossi, that it arose from his not having read the *Sohar*, which had not then been printed.

[76] The Sulzbach edition erroneously has אך בלא דברי, instead of אך לא בדברי.

memory did not say, in order that the vowel-points should in any way be changed from what they were as given to Moses on Sinai."[77] Thus far his remark. But one must hesitate to accept this statement, inasmuch as it contradicts what he has said before on the *Niphal* conjugation of the regular verb, which is ☛ as follows:[78] "The inventors of the points made a distinction between the singular third person præterite and the participle, as they are pronounced alike, and pointed the past tense with *Pattach*, under the second radical [נִפְקַד], and the participle with *Kametz* [נִפְקָד]." Thus far the substance of his remark. We therefore see, from his own words, that even he believed that there were men who invented the points, namely, ־ ־ ־ ֹ ־ , ֱ &c. Hence it is evident that when he remarks, "as they were given to Moses on Sinai," he does not mean to say the form of the points, but the five major and the five minor sounds; and this is the reason why he uses the words "to change the *vowels*," and does not say the *points*. Thus, also, when[79] he said, "*as* they were given," and not "*which* were given," his words are to be understood in the same way, and I have no need to dwell on this point any longer.

R. Levi b. Joseph, author of the book *Semadar*, says, at the beginning of his work, as follows:[80] "If any one should ask, Whence do we know that the points and accents were dictated by the mouth of the Omnipotent? the reply is, It is to be found in the Scriptures, for it is written, 'And thou shalt write upon the stones all the words of this law *very plainly*' (Deut. xxvii. 8). Now, if the points and accents, which

---

[77] Kimchi's remark, to which allusion is made in the text, is to be found on p. 25 *b* of Levita's own edition of the *Michlol*, Venice, 1545, and on p. 81 *a*, ed. Hechim Fürth, 1793.
[78] This quotation is to be found on p. 18 *b*, &c., ed. Venice, 1545, and on p. 61 *a*, ed. Fürth, 1793.
[79] The Sulzbach edition has omitted the word מה, *what*.
[80] Nothing is known of this Grammatical Treatise, entitled *Sepher Ha-Semadar* (ספר הסמדר) = *the Book of the Vine-blossom*, or of its author, beyond the fact that it is also quoted by Azzariah de Rossi (*Meor Enajim*, cap. lix.), who endorses the above-named arguments for the antiquity of the vowel-points, and by Samuel Archevolti, in his Grammatical Treatise, entitled *Arugath Ha-Bosem* (ערוגת הבושם) = *A Trellis for Aromatic Plants*, published at Venice, 1602, and Amsterdam, 1730, who also espouses its sentiments. Comp. Buxtorf, *De Punctatorum Antiquitate*, p. 42, &c., Basel, 1648.

128

make the words plain did not exist, how could one possibly understand plainly whether שלמה means *wherefore, retribution, Solomon, garment, or perfect?*" Thus far his remark. I leave it to the reader to judge whether this is reliable proof.

Again, I found another book, which seems to me to be the work called *Instruction for the Reader*, and the author of which I do not know, say as follows:[61] "There are some of the punctuators who, not knowing thoroughly the true nature of the points, ask why we do not find two *Sarkoth* on one word, seeing that there are two *Pashtin?* But had they known that there never existed more than one *Sarka*, and that no more than one *Sarka*, followed by a *Segol*, was revealed to our teacher Moses of blessed memory, they would not have asked such a question." Thus far its remark. Now all this is vain and wrong, since two *Sarkos* are frequently found, as I shall show in my book, entitled *Good Sense*, under the form *Sarka*.

Again, I found in the treatise published here, around the *Massorah finalis*, which some say is *The Book Shimshoni*, but which I say is R. Moses the Punctuator's, as I shall show in part iii., called the *Broken Tables*, as follows:[62] "It is true that the points were given on Sinai,

ואילולי חנקוד והטעמים שמבארין חתיבורת אין אדם יכול להבין ביאורם, כגון שָׁלְמָה שָׁלְמָה, שָׁלְמֹה, שַׁלְמָה, שָׁלְמָה, שָׁלְמָה, עכ"ל, ראו נא אם זאת ראיה טובה לסמוך עליה:

ועוד מצאתי בספר אחד נראה לי שהוא הספר הנקרא הוריית הקורא, ולא ידעתי מי הוא מחמברו וז"ל,[61] ויש מן הנקדנים אשר לא עלה בידם אמחת חנקוד מקשים ואומרים למה לא נעשה ב' זרקות במלה אחת כמו שנעשה ב' פשטין, ואלו ידעו שאין כעולם אלא זרקא אחת ולא חראו לו למשח רע"ה אלא זרקא אחת ואחריו סגול, לא הקשו על זה עכ"ל, והנח כל זה חבל ושקר כי נמצאו ב' זרקאות לרוב, כמו שאבאר בספר טוב טעם בתמונת הזרקא:

ועוד מצאתרי במח שנדפס פה סביב חמסרח הגדולת, ואומרים שהוא ספר השמשוני, ואני אומר שחוא של רבי משה חנקדן כמו שיתבאר בשער שברי לוחות, וזח לשונו,[62] אמת הוא שהנקוד נתן מסיני אלא

---

[61] The *Horajoth Ha-Kore* (הוריית הקורא) = *Instruction for the Reader*, by Ibn Balaam, (flourished, A.D. 1050–1090), discusses, in twenty-four chapters, the accents and vowel-points of the Hebrew language. From Dukes' publication of the Introduction and Table of Contents, it is evident that cap. i.—xvii. of this Treatise are devoted to the doctrine of the prose accents of the twenty-one sacred books; whilst cap. xviii.—xxiv. are taken up with the metrical accents of the three remaining books, viz., the Psalms, Proverbs, and Job. The seventeen chapters which discuss the prose accents were re-cast by the author himself, and designated טעמי המקרא, *A Treatise on the Accents of the Scriptures*. It was first published by the learned John Mercier, Paris, 1865, and Heidenheim inserted twelve chapters of it in his work ספר משפטי הטעמים, *On the Laws of the Accents*, Rödelheim, 1808. The second part, which assumed the name of ספר טעמי אמ"ת, *A Treatise on the Accents of Job, Proverbs, and the Psalms*, was also published first by John Mercier, Paris, 1556, and recently by G. J. Polak, Amsterdam, 1858. Comp. Fürst, *Zeitschrift der deutschen morgenländischen Gesellschaft*, vol. xx., p. 201, Leipzig, 1866; Steinschneider, *Catalogus Libr. Hebr. in Bibliotheca Bodleiana*, col. 1294, &c.

[62] The *Treatise on the Vowel-points and Accents*, by R. Moses the Punctuator, who lived in London circa A.D. 1230, is alternately designated כללי הנקוד, *the Laws of the Points* (vide infra, Part iii., sub רמ"ח; Wolf, *Bibliotheca Hebraea* i. 822); שערי הנקוד, *the Gates to the Vowel-points and Accents* (comp. *Massorah marginalis* on Amos iv. 1; Ps. cxxxvi. 3); דרכי הנצור הנגינות, *the Method of the Vowel-points and the Accents* (Wolf, *Bibliotheca Hebraea* i. 592); and הוריית הקורא, *Instruction to the Reader*

but they were forgotten again, till Ezra came and revealed them." ☞ Thus far its remark. Now the truth is that I do not understand this truth. But it is undoubtedly true that the law which Moses put before the Children of Israel was a plain Codex, without points and without accents, and even without the division of verses, as we see it to the present day.[83] According to the opinion of the Kabbalists, the whole Law is like one verse, and indeed, some of them say, like one word, from which they combine sundry Divine Names. Thus says Nachmanides of blessed memory, in the Introduction to his Commentary on the Pentateuch, which you may consult.[84]

שםםחחו עד שבא עזרא ונלחו עד כאן לש׳, ובאםח איני מבין זה האםח, אך אםח הוא שאין בו םפק שחורה אשר שם םשה לפני בני ישראל, חיה םפר פשוט בלי נקוד ובלי םעםים, ובלי םםני סופי פסוקים, כאשר אנחנו רואים חיום,[83] ולפי דעח בעלי הקבלה כל החורה היא כפסוק אחד, וי״א חיבה אחח, ויוצאין םחן שםוח של הק״בה, כםו שכחב חרם״בן ז״ל בפחיחחו לפידוש החורה ע״ש:[84]

ואני אוםר אם אםח הוא שחנקוד נחן םסני לא יםנע םהחלוקח, אם נאםר שחק״בה חראה לםשה רבנו ע״ח צורח הנקודוח וחםעםים של אש, לאםר כזה ראה חוא ָ קםץ, וכזה חוא ַ פחח, וכזה חוא ֵ צדי, וכזה חוא ֶ סגול, וכזה חוא זרקא, וכזה חוא פזֹר, וכן כלם, וםר״םה הראה חםונחם לישראל ולא שם אוחם עם החיבוח, א״כ םה חועלח חיחה

Now, I submit, if it be true that the points were given on Sinai, we cannot escape one of these two alternatives. We must either say that God revealed to Moses, our teacher of blessed memory, the forms of the points and accents in fire, saying, this ָ is the shape of *Kametz*, this ַ the shape of *Pattach*, this ֵ is the form of *Tzere*, this ֶ is the form of *Segol*, this ֯ the shape of *Zarka*, this ֯ the shape of *Pazer*, and so on; and that Moses, our teacher of blessed memory, showed these forms to Israel, and *did not* affix them

---

of the Scriptures (comp. Steinschneider, *Bibliograph. Handbuch*, p. 95, Leipzig, 1865). It was first published by Jacob b. Chajim in the margin of the Massorah finalis, Venice, 1525, to which edition Levita refers. It has since been reprinted in all the editions of the Rabbinic Bibles, and has been republished separately with a short commentary by Zebi b. Menachem, Wilna, 1822, and with corrections and German notes by the learned Frensdorff, Hanover, 1847. Levita's quotation will be found on p. 1 Hebrew text, and animadverted upon p. 1 in the German notes, of the last mentioned edition.

[83] The Synagogal Scrolls of the Law, out of which the hebdomadal lessons are read among the Rabbinic Jews, have to the present day neither the vowel-points nor the accents, nor any of the Massoretic glosses whatsoever, (*vide supra*, p. 44, &c.) It is to this fact that Levita refers.

[84] Ramban רמב״ן is the acrostic of ר׳ משה בן נחמן, *R. Moses b. Nachman* = Nachmanides, the distinguished Talmudist, Commentator, Moral Philosopher, Kabbalist, and Physician, who was born at Gerona, in Catalonia, circa A.D. 1195, and died at Acco circa 1270. The passage to which Levita refers, is as follows:— עוד יש בידינו קבלה של אםח כי כל החורה כולה שםוחיו של הק׳בה שהחיבוח םחחלקוח לשםוח בענין אחד כאלו חחשוב על דרך םשל כי םסוק בראשיח יחלק לחבוח אחרוח כגון בראש יחברא אלחים וכל החורה כן םלבד צירוסיהן וגיםסרוחיהן של שםוח, *We possess a faithful tradition that the whole Pentateuch consists of names of the Holy One, blessed be he; for the words may be re-divided into sacred names of a different import, so that it is to be taken as an allegory. Accordingly, the words* בראשיח ברא אלהים (Gen. i. 1), *for instance, may be re-divided into the words* בראש יחברא אלהים. *This is the case with the whole Law, which consists of nothing but permutations and numerals of divine names.* For a sketch of the life of Nachmanides, see Kitto's *Cyclopædia, s. v.;* and for his relation to the Kabbalah, see Ginsburg, *the Kabbalah*, p. 108, &c., Longmans, 1865.

to the words; in which case the Israelites would have derived no benefit from seeing them. Or we must say, that he *did* affix them to the words, and come to the conclusion that he wrote another Codex, besides our Pentateuch, with points and accents, and recited it with them, till they knew it, and that afterwards, each one who wished copied it. In this case the question arises, How could the points and accents be forgotten, unless we say that all these copies were afterwards lost? which is altogether incredible. Even the explanation which the sages give of Neh. viii. 8, quoted above [p. 108, &c.], does not at all mention the points. This is also the opinion of Ibn Ezra, peace be upon him, who says in his Grammar, entitled *Purity*,[85] "There are many commentators who maintain that those who divided the verses committed blunders, but this is not correct. To this class belongs R. Moses Ha-Cohen, &c., but I am perfectly astonished at it, for how could the divider commit blunders if he was Ezra the Scribe? In short, after the divider there were none so wise as he was, since we see that, throughout the whole of the Scriptures, he never made a pause which is not in its proper place." Thus far his remark. The meaning of מפסיק is the one who made the dividing accents.

Now I am astonished at his speaking here of one divider, since there is no doubt that there were many dividers, as I shall show hereafter; and since Ibn Ezra himself speaks of them in the plural, in his grammar called *The Balance*. At any rate, his words here show that he was not of opinion that the accents were given on Sinai. I

---

[85] The passage alluded to is to be found on p. 73 *a, b*, ed. Lippmann, Fürth, 1827, and in its entirety is as follows:— יש מפרשים רבים מטעים את המפסיק, ולא אמרו נכונה, מהם ר"מ הכהן שאמר כי למבזיר (איוב ל"ז ל"א) סמוך עם על כסים כסה אור (שם פסוק ל"ב), וכן ברזנו רחום תנבור (תנבקוק ג' ב') רבק עם אלוה מחתן יבוא (שם ג' ג'), ובכבר פרשתי שניהם שהם מותרחים, ומל זה אירע בעבור שמצאו בדבר היחיד שיש עשרה פסוקים במקרא שהזי ראוים להיותם רבוקים, ואני לפי רעתי · · · לא המפיק כי אם במקום ראוי. Both Buxtorf (*De Punctatorum Antiquitate*, p. 11, &c.) and Morin (*Lib.* ii., *Exercit.* xii. c. 7) have elaborated upon this passage; the one trying to prove from it that Ibn Ezra maintained the antiquity of the vowel-points, and the other to show that he regarded the Massorites as having lived after the close of the Talmud.

have also found the following words, in a book called *The Purity of the Language*:[86] "We must know that the points were given on Sinai; not that they were put on the Tables of Stone; but when the Lord spake in the holy tongue, those who heard him could distinguish between the vowel-points and syllables,[87] both short and long. Just as the vigour of the human voice utters higher or lower notes according to requirement, so ought we to distinguish from the mouth of readers between אָ with a *Kametz* and אַ with *Pattach*, between אֵ with *Tzere* and אֶ with *Segol*, between אוֹ with *Cholem* and אֳ with *Chateph-Kametz*, between אוּ with *Vav* and אֻ without the *Vav*, between אִי with *Jod* and אִ without *Jod*."[88] Thus far his remark.

ח"ל,[86] יש לנו לדעת כי הנקוד נתן בסיני ולא שקדו חלחות, אך כאשר דבר חק"בח לשון הקדש חבינו השומעים כל התנועות והקולות[87] הקמנות והגדולות כאשר נכון חדבר במוצא פה חחזק הוא חדפה, כך יש לחכיר מפי הקוראים בין אָ קמץ לאָ פתח, ובין אֵ צרי לאֶ סגול, ובין או חולם לאֳ חטוף קמץ, ובין או בויו לאֻ בלי ויו, ובין אִי ביוד לאִ בלי יוד[88] עכ"ל:

ונם כתב החכם בעל ספר הכוזר במאמר ג' מספרו וז"ל,[89] אמר החבר בלי ספק שהיח שמור בלבבות בפתחא וחקמץ והשבר והשבא והסעמים וכו', עד ושמו שבע המלכים והסעמים אותות לתכונות ההם אשר חעתיקום בקבלה ממר"עה, ומה תחשוב על אשר חקנו חמקרא בפסוקים תחלה, ואחר כן בנקוד,

The learned author of *The Khosari* also remarks, in section iii. [31,] as follows:[89] "The master replied, Doubtless the *Pattach, Kametz, Sheber, Sheva*, and the accents were committed to memory * * and they put the principal vowels and the accents as marks, to indicate what was received from Moses by tradition. What thinkest thou about it? that they have received the Bible first

---

[86] Wolf (*Bibliotheca Hebraea* i. 80, 160) conjectures that the *Purity of the Language* (צחצ שמתים), may simply be another name for the well known work of Ibn Ezra, entitled *Purity* (צחות), quoted in the preceding note. After carefully perusing, however, Ibn Ezra's work in question, and not being able to find in it Levita's quotation, we endeavoured to obtain some information on this subject. And accordingly, in addition to the information in a private communication from Dr. Steinschneider, that the *Zachoth Sephasajim* is "still extant in a MS. of De Rossi (Cod. 764)," at Parma; we have received from the learned librarian, the Abate Pietro Perreau, a description of the codex in question, of which the following is the substance. The MS. is a folio on parchment, written in Rabbinical characters, and contains four works: i. The Hebrew Lexicon of Solomon Parchon [an account of which will be found in Kitto's *Cyclopædia, s. v.* PARCHON]; ii. Several Sections (שטרים), also by Parchon, being a supplement to the Lexicon; iii. The *Zach Sephasajim*, which only extends over four folios of the MS., and is complete, as is evident from the conclusion סליק צח חמתים, here endeth the *Purity of the Languages*; and iv. The *Instruction to the Reader of the Scriptures* (ספר חורית הקורא) [a description of which has already been given. Vide *supra*, p. 123, note 81].

[87] The word וחקלות, *and the syllables*, is omitted in the Sulzbach edition, whilst וחגרולות, *the long*, is wrongly put before הקמנות, *the short*.

[88] This sentence is erroneously transposed in the Sulzbach edition.

[89] The author of *the Khosari* is R. Jehudah Ha-Levi, a very distinguished Hebraist, Poet, and Moral Philosopher, who was born in Castile *circa* 1086. For the life of this literator, as well as for an analysis of his celebrated work, entitled *Khosari*, to which Levita refers, see Kitto's *Cyclopædia, s. v.* JEHUDAH HA-LEVI. It is to be remarked that Levita's quotation is not literal. Thus the word וחנטחיה, *and pronunciation*, after וחשבר, *and Sheber*, is omitted, &c., &c.

with divisions into verses, then with vowels, then with accents, then with definitions respecting the preservation of *plene* and *defective*, and even the exact number of letters?" Thus far his remark. From this we see that he was not of opinion that Moses wrote them, but that it was only preserved in memory what Moses' pronunciation was, viz., what distinction he made between the pronunciation of *Kametz* and *Pattach*, between *Tzere* and *Segol*, &c. Would that this sage author had explained to us whom he meant by "they put"—whether the men of the Great Synagogue or the Massorites. I think that it refers to the Massorites.[90]

☞ Now this is my opinion upon the subject. The vowel-points and the accents did not exist either before Ezra or in the time of Ezra, or after Ezra till the close of the Talmud. And I shall prove this with clear and conclusive evidence.

First,—in all the writings of our Rabbins of blessed memory, whether the Talmud, or the Hagadah, or the Midrash, there is not to be found any mention whatever of, or any allusion to, the vowel-points or accents. Is it possible that, if they had the vowel-points and accents, they would not even once have mentioned the name *Kametz, Pattach, Segol,* or *Tzere?* or the *Pashta, Darga, Tebir*, &c.? Do not reply, that their existence is implied in their remarks respecting certain words: "Do not read so, but so;" *ex. gr.*, Do not read בָּנַיִךְ, but בָּנָיִךְ (Is. liv. 18); Do not read וְשָׁם, but וְשָׁם (Ps. l. 23); as well as in their declaration, "There is a solid root for the reading of the text, and there is a solid root for the traditional pronunciation:" since, according to my opinion, all this favours my conviction, that they had not the vowel-points, but that they were in the habit of reading without points, and therefore they said, "Do not read so, but so."

ואד כן בטעמים, ואד כן במסורת, על שמירת המלא והחסר, עד אשר מנו אותיותיה עכ"ל, הרי שאין דעתו שמשה כתבם רק שחיה שמור בלבבות איך קרא משה ר"ל, איך שקרא הפרש בין קמץ לפתח, ובין צרי לסגול ורומיהן, ומי יתן שפירש לנו החכם על מי שב הכנוי של ושמו אם על אנשי כנסת הגרולה, או על בעלי המסורת, ועל דעתי שחוא שב על בעלי המסורת:⁹⁰

☞ והא לך דעתי בענין הזה, אחשוב שהנקודות והטעמים לא היו קודם עזרא, ולא בזמן עזרא, ולא אחר עזרא עד חתימת התלמוד, ויש לי להוכיח זה בראיות ברורות ונכוחות:

הראיה הראשונה כי לא נמצא בכל דברי רז"ל בתלמוד ובחגדות ומדרשות לא זכר ולא רמז משום נקודה או טעם לעולם, כי איך אפשר אם היו להם הנקודות והטעמים שלא היו זוכרים פעם אחת קמץ או פתח או סגול או צרי, וכן פשטא, דרגא, תביר ורומיהן, ואל תשיבני ממה שאמרו על קצת המלות אל תקרי כך אלא כך, כמו וכל בניך למודי יהוח (ישעיה נ"ד) אל תקרי בָּנַיִךְ אלא בָּנָיִךְ, אל תקרי וְשָׁם דרך (תלים נ) אלא וְשָׁם דרך, וכן מה שאמרו יש אם למקרא ויש אם למסורת, כי לפי דעתי כל אלה לי לישועות שלא היו להם חנקוד, אלא היו רגילין לקרא כך בלי נקוד, לפיכך אמרו אל תקרי כך אלא

---

[90] Even those scholars, who like Levita regard the vowel-points as a post-Talmudic invention, most unhesitatingly affirm, that וִשָׂמוּ, *and they put*, is the predicate of אנשי כנסת הגדולה, *the men of the Great Synagogue;* comp. *Khosari* p. 249, note 8., ed. Cassel, Leipzig, 1853.

For if the vowel-points had come from Sinai, and the words in question had been pointed in a certain manner, God forbid that the Rabbins should say, "Do not read so."[91] The intelligent student will understand and admit that it is so.

Secondly,—What is still greater proof, is the following remark in the Talmud *(Baba Bathra,* 21 *b),* "Joab slew his teacher because he had performed the work of the Lord deceitfully, in reading to him זָכָר instead of זֵכֶר (Deut. xxv. 19)." Now is it credible that he would have attempted to read זָכָר with two *Kametz*, if they had had the points, and the word in question had been pointed זֵכֶר with six points. By the life of me, this could not have been done, according to my opinion.[92]

Thirdly,—In *Chagiga,* where the passage "they brought burnt offerings and killed sacrifices," &c., (Exod. xxiv. 5) is discussed, Mar

כך, כי אם היה הנקוד מסיני וחיתה המלה נקודה כך, חלילה לחם וחס לומר אל תקרי כך,[י] והמשכיל יבין וישכיל כי כן הוא :

ועוד ראיה אחרת וגדולה היא אלי, מה שאמרו רז״ל בבבא בתרא כי יואב הרג את רבו על שעשה מלאכת י״י רמיה, וחקרא לו חמתה את זכר עמלק (דברים כ״ח), היש להאמין שאם היה לחם חנקודות והיה נקוד זָכָר ב׳ו נקודות שהיה קורא זָכָר ב״ב קמצי׳, אין זאת חי אני לפי דעתי :[92]

ועוד ראיה ממח שנמצא בפרק קמא דחגינה על פסוק ויעלו עולות ויזבחו זבחים ונומר (שמות כ״ד), מר זוטרא אמר לפיסוק

[91] The Talmudic discussions on this phrase are to be found in *Sanhedrin,* 4 *a; Sebachim,* 37 *b; Pessachim,* 86 *b; Kiddushin,* 18 *b.* Levita's argument, deduced from this fact, has also been espoused and elaborated by Capellus, *Arcanum Punctat.* lib. i. cap. v., sect. 4, &c. ; and Morin, *Exercit.* lib.: *ex.* xii., cap. 3–5; *ex.* xv., cap. 3–5. Comp. also Gesenius, *Geschichte der Hebräischen Sprache,* p. 182, &c., Leipzig, 1815; Hupfeld, *Studien und Kritiken,* p. 554, Hamburg, 1830. For the attempts to refute it on the part of the vowelists, see Buxtorf, the father, *Tiberias,* cap. ix., pp. 76–86; Buxtorf, the son, *De Punctatorum Antiquitate,* p. 103, &c.; Gill, *A Dissertation concerning the Antiquity of the Hebrew Language,* p. 153, &c., London, 1767.

[92] To understand Levita's allusion, it is necessary to relate the circumstances which called forth the story quoted in the text. " R. Dime, of Nehardea, maintains that while the only is to be appointed as teacher of youths who has a good pronunciation, even if he is not so learned, since it is difficult to unlearn an acquired mistake in pronunciation." To enforce his axiom, the Rabbi narrates the following story, which relates to Joab's slaying the whole male population in Edom (1 Kings xi. 15, 16). כי אתא לקמי דדוד אמר ליה מאי מעמא עבדת הכי אמר ליה דכתיב תמחה את זכר עמלק אמר ליה והא אנן זכר קרינן אמר ליה אנא זכר אקריון אזל שיילית לרביה אמר ליה היאך אקריתן אמר ליה זכר שקל ספסירא למיקטליה אמר ליה ואמאי אמר ליה דכתיב ארור עושה מלאכת ה' רמיה אמר ליה שבקיה להחוא גברא דליקום בארור אמר ליה כתיב וארור מונע חרבו מדם אימא דאמרי קטליה ואיכא דאמרי לא קטליה *When he returned to David, he asked him, What is the reason that thou hast acted thus?* [i.e. slain the males only], *whereupon he* [Joab] *replied, Because it is written, Thou shalt blot out the males of Amalek* [Deut. xxv. 19]. *He* [David] *then said to him, We read Secher = the memory, to which he* [Joab] *replied, I have been taught to read Sachar = males, and went to inquire of his Rabbi, asking him, How dost thou teach me to read it? He* [the Rabbi] *replied, Secher = memory. Hereupon, he* [Joab] *seized his sword to slay him* [the Rabbi]. *He* [the Rabbi] *asked why? He* [Joab] *replied to him, Because it is written, "Cursed be he that doeth the work of the Lord deceitfully"* [Jerem. xlviii. 10]. *Upon which he* [the Rabbi] *said, Away with him who lays hold of a curse. He* [Joab] *said again, It is written, "And cursed be he who keepeth back his sword from blood." Some say he then killed him* [his Rabbi], *and some say he did not kill him* (Comp. Baba Bathra, 21 a-b). Levita's argument, deduced from this, that the Talmudists must have had an unpointed text—Buxtorf, the father (*Tiberias,* p. 86), Buxtorf, the son (*De Antiquitate Punctat.* p. 108, &c.), Whitfield (*A Dissertation on the Hebrew vowel-points,* p. 259, &c.), and Gill (*Dissertation,* p. 156, &c.) have tried to refute.

Sutra remarks, this discussion is necessary, in order to know where to place the dividing accent (*Chagiga* 6 *b*). From this, too, it is evident that they had no accents (see Rashi *in loco*).

Fourthly,—Almost all the names of both the vowel-points and the accents are not Hebrew, but Aramean and Babylonian; as, for instance, *Tzere, Segol, Cholem, Melaphum*; so also *Mapik, Dagesh, Darga, Tebir*, &c. Now, if it were true that they were given on Sinai, what is the meaning of Aramean names at Mount Sinai? Were not all the commandments given on Sinai in Hebrew?

I therefore submit that it is perfectly evident to me that the vowel-points neither existed nor obtained in the days of the Talmudic sages, and much less in the time of the men of the Great Synagogue. These men did not require them, for they could read without vowel-points and accents, making a pause where the sense required it, and reading on when the sense did not require a pause, just as they had heard and received it from the Prophets; as our Rabbins of blessed memory say,

פעמים וכו', גם משם ראיה שלא היו להם פעמים, עיין מה שפירש רש"י שם:

וְעוֹד אהרת כי השמות מן[98] הנקודות והטעמים רובן אינן לשון עברי רק לשון ארמי ובבלי, כגון צרי, וסגול, חולם מלא פום, וכן מפיק, דגש, דרגא, תביר, דרומיהן, ואם אמת הוא שנתנו מסיני מה ענין לשון ארמי אצל הר סיני, והלא כל המצוות נאמרו בסיני בלשון עברי:

לכן אומר אני כי ברור לי שהנקוד לא היה ולא נברא בימי חכמי התלמוד, וכ"ש בימי אנשי כנסת הגדולה, כי לא היו צריכין להם, כי היו בקיאים לקרא בלי נקד וטעמים, וקראו במקום העמדת העניין בהפסקה, ובמקום סמיכת העניין בהחמדת הדבור, כאשר שמעו וקבלו מפי הנביאים, כמו שאמרו רז"ל, ונביאים מסרוהו לאנשי כנסת הגדולה וחכמים שהיו בימיהם, כגון סנהדרי גדולה וקטנה, ונם הכהנים הנגשים אל י"י קבלו מהם דור אחר דור, עד שמכח ההרגל ידעו לקרא בלי נקוד וטעמים:

ורבים ישאלו איך היה אפשר קודם שנמצאו הנקודות ללמד לנער הקריאה הנכונה מתוך ספר שאינו נקוד, וזו אינה שאלה, כי לשון הקדש היה הלשון שדברו בו כלם, נער זקן מף ונשים, כי לא היה להם לשון אחרת, עד שגלו מעל אדמתם, וכאשר נער אחר למד עד שהכיר האותיות, היה רבו קורא עמו מתוך הספר פסוק אחד ב' או ג'

"And the Prophets transmitted it to the men of the Great Synagogue" [*Aboth* i.]; and the sages who were in their days, viz., the great and small Sanhedrim, as well as the priests who served God at the altar, received it from them, generation after generation, till by habit they knew how to read without vowel-points and accents.

Now there are some who might ask, How was it possible, before the invention of the vowel-points, to teach a child the correct reading from a book which was not pointed? But this is no question. For the sacred tongue was the language which all spoke, both young and old, children and women, since they had no other language till they were led captive from their land. When, therefore, a child was being taught to know the letters, his teacher read with him from a book each verse two or three times, till he was familiar with it, and as the child was

---

[98] The Sulzbach edition erroneously has כי השמות מן השמות עם הנקדות:

conversant with the language, he could easily remember the words which he read, and whenever he met them again he read them without difficulty. To make this more plain to you, listen to what I have seen, and I will relate it.

☛ Now when I was in Rome, I saw three Chaldeans, who arrived from the country of Prester John,[94] having been sent for by Pope Leo X. They were masters of the Syriac language and literature, though their vernacular language was Arabic.[95] The special language, however, wherein the books were written, as well as that of the gospels of the Christians which they brought with them, was Syriac, which is also called Aramean, Babylonian, Assyrian, Chaldee, Tursaea or Targum, being denominated by these ☛ seven names. Pope Leo X. had sent for them, in order to correct by their Codices his exemplar of his New Testament, which was written in Latin. I then saw in their hands the Book of Psalms, written in Syriac characters, as well as translated into Syriac; that is to say, the text was written with Syriac characters, the origin, pronunciation, and form of which greatly resemble the Hebrew. Now I saw them reading this Psalter without points, and asked them, Have you points, or any signs to indicate the vowels? and

פעמים עד שחיה שגור בפיו, ולפי שידע היה בקי בלשון ההוא חיה, נקל לו לזכור המלות שקרא, ובכל מקום שמצאם קראם בלי משנה, וכדי להבינך זה יותר אחיך שמע לי וזה חזיתי ואספרה:

☛ בהיותי ברומי ראיתי והגה שלשה אנשים כלדאים באו ממדינת פרימי יואן[94] אשר אפיס״יוד ליאון העשירי שלח אחריהם, והם היו יודעי ספר ולשון כשדים לשונם החמוני הוא לשון ערבי[95] אבל חלשון חמיוחד לחם שבו נכתבו ספריהם וכל האוונגיליון הנוצרית הוא לחם בלשון חזה, והוא לשון כשדים ☛ חנקרא גם כן ארמי, או בבלי, או אשורי, או כלדאי, או מורסאי, או תרגום, חרי שבע שמות נקראו לו, ולכך שלח האפי״סיור אחריהם, לחגית מספריהם, ספרי אווגנילין שלו חכתוב לשון לטין, ואז ראיתי בידם ספר תהלים כתוב ארמית ומתורגם ארמית, ר״ל שהיה כתוב באותיות ארמית שמוצאם ומבמאם וצודחם קרובים מאוד ללשון העברי: וראיתי שקראו באורחו תהלים בלתי נקוד, ושאלתרים לאמור חיש לכם נקורורת או אורתורת וסימנים

---

[94] Prester [= Priest] John, is celebrated, both among Latin and Oriental writers, as a Christian sovereign and priest in the far east of Asia. It is said that the information about him was first brought to Pope Eugenius III. in 1145, by two Armenian delegates who visited Rome. And a letter of Pope Alexander III., dated 1177, is still extant, which this Pontiff addressed to the said *Johannes, Rex Indorum*, and in which he is described as a Christian king of Asia, desiring union with the Catholic Church. The story about this romantic monarch was so eagerly seized by the faithful of the middle ages, because his supposed existence counteracted the unfavourable impression which the conquests of the Mohammedans and Heathens achieved in Christian countries. In the fifteenth century, he again appears in the annals of history, as *Presbyter Johannes Rex*, in Africa, and more especially in Æthiopia. Levita's reference is most probably to Nestorians or Maronites, since he describes Syriac as their ecclesiastical language. For the story about Prester John, see Ersch and Gruber's *Allgemeine Encyklopädie*, section ii., vol. xxii., pp. 219–21; Herzog, *Real-Encyklopädie für Protestantische Theologie und Kirche*, vol. v., 818; vol. vi., 765, &c.

[95] The Sulzbach edition erroneously substitutes עברי *Hebrew*, for ערבי *Arabic*. The extract of the above passage in Kitto's *Cyclopedia, s. v.* XIMENES, having been made from the Sulzbach edition, contains the same blunder, and must therefore be corrected.

they answered me, "No! but we have been conversant with that language from our youth till now, and, therefore, know how to read without points." Thus far their remark.[96]

You, therefore, see that it is possible for a man to learn by habit to read without points. The same was the case among us, prior to the invention of the points, and it continued till the time after the close of the Talmud, which took place in 3989 of the creation = 486 after the destruction of the second Temple. Since then, the sacred tongue began gradually to disappear, till the time of the Massorites, who are the men of Tiberias, which is Mouzia. They were great sages, and thoroughly conversant with the Scriptures and the structure of the language, more so than all the other Jews who lived in that generation, and none like them have existed since. This is attested by R. Jona [Ibn Ganach], the Grammarian, in his treatise on the *Quiescent Letters*, which is as follows: "The distinction between the ר with and without the *Dagesh* was well understood by the men of Tiberias, but not by us, for they knew better the purity of the language than all other Jews." Thus, also, says Abraham Ibn Ezra, who writes in the book *Purity* as follows;[97] "This is the manner of the sages of Tiberias, and they are the foundation, for from them were the Massorites, and from them we have received all our vowel-points."

☞ This, however, I observed, that the Massorites did not give names to the points, except to the *Kametz* and the *Pattach*, in which are included the *Tzere* and the *Segol;* that is, they called the *Tzere Kametz* and the *Segol Pattach*. It was not till the rise of the first grammarians that some distinction was made between these names, and that they were thus designated. Thus, for instance, they called this point ֻ the long *Kametz*, this ָ short *Kametz*, this ֹ long *Pattach*, and

המורים על התנועות, ויאמרו לי לא, אלא שאנחנו בקיאים בזה חלשון מנעורינו ועד עתח, לכן יודעים אנחנו לקרותו בלי נקוד עכ"ל:[96]

הרי שאפשר שמכח החרגיל ילמוד חאדם לקרא בלי נקוד, וכן חיה גם לנו קדם שנוסדו הנקודות, ונמשך זה עד זמן התימרת חתלמוד, שהוא שנרת נ' אלפין תתק"פט ליצירה, שחיא שנת חל"ו אחר חרבן בית שני, ומאו וחלאח חיח לשון חקדש חלוך וחסור עד זמן בעלי חמסורת, וחם אנשי מבריא חיא מעייא, וחיו חכמים גדולים ובקיאים במקרא וצחי לשון מכל שאר היחודים אשר היו ברורות חחם, ואחריהם לא קמו כמוחם, כאשר חעיד עליחם ר' יונה המדקדק בדבריו באותיות בנד"כפת ח"ל, חדיש חדנושה וחדפוניה בקיאים בה אנשי מבריא ולא אנחנו, כי הם צחי הלשון מכל חיחודים, וכן ר' אברהם א"ע כתב בספר צחות וזח לשונו[97] כן מנהג חכמי מבריא וחם חעקר כי מחם היו אנשי חמסורת, ומחם קבלנו כל הנקוד:

☞ אך זה לבד מצאתי, כי בעלי חמסורת לא קראו שמות לנקדות, רק לקמץ ולפתח, ובכללם חצרי וחסגול, דחיינו שקראו לצרי ג"כ קמץ, ולסגול ג"כ פתח, וכשבאו חמדקדקים הראשונים הבדילו מעם ביניהם בקריאת חשמות, דחיינו שקראו לנקודה הזארת ָ קמץ גדול, ולזארת ֻ קמץ קטן, ולזאת ַ פתח גדול, ולזאת ֶ פתח קטן, אבל

---

[96] The expression עכ"ל, *thus far their remark*, is omitted in the Sulzbach edition.

[97] Levita's quotation is to be found on p. 7 a of *the Zachoth* (צחות) = *Purity*, ed. Lippmann, Fürth, 1127.

this ֵ the short *Pattach*. But no mention whatever is made of the rest of the vowels throughout the whole of the Massorah, both *magna* and *parva*, wherin *Chirek* is called אִי, *Cholem* אוֹ, *Shurek* אוּ, *Kibutz* אֻ, and the *Sheva* and the three *Chataphs* are called by quite different names, as I shall explain in Part ii., section 8. For instance, the Massorites remark, "There are twenty-one words which occur twice, once with אוֹ, and once with אָו, as הָאָמֹר [Ezek. xxviii. 9], and הָאָמֹנָה [Micah i. 7]; and they have no parallel;"[98] but they do not say one with *Cholem* and one with *Shurek*. They also note, "Twenty-seven words are written with אִי, every one of which has no parallel, as לָלִין [Gen. xxiv. 23], יַפִּיל [Exod. xxi. 27];"[99] but they do not say that they are written with *Chirek*. Those Codices of the Massorah, in which the name *Cholem*, *Chirek*, or *Shurek* occurs, do not state the language of the Massorites, but display the wisdom of the transcribers, who wrote so in order to show that they understood the Massorah.

☞ I shall now[100] state to you the reason why they did not give names to the other vowels, just as they named the *Kametz* and the *Pattach*. It is this. The forms of all other vowels have signal letters appended to them. Thus, for instance, since the *Vav* and the *Jod* are the *matres lectiones* of the vowels אוֹ, אוּ, אִי; hence, the Massorites were satisfied with these designations, and did not give them any other names.[101] But the *Kametz* and the *Pattach*, which have no such

שאר הנקודות לאזכרו בשמם בכל חמסרה נדולה וקמנה, רק קראו לחידק אי, ולחולם או, ולשורק או, ולקבוץ אָו, ולשוא ולנ׳ חטפין קראו שמות אחרות, כאשר יתבאר בלוחות שניות במאמר נ׳ : וחמשל באמרם במסורת כ״א מלין חד או וחד או כמו האמור תאמר אלהים אני (יחזקאל כ״ח) לית, וחד האמור (מיכה ב׳),[98] ולא אמרו חד חולם וחד שורק, וכן כ״ז מלין דכתיבין אי וכל חד לירד דבוותיה, כגון ללין לית, יפיל לית,[99] ולא אמרו דכתיבין חירק, וחנוסחאות שנמצא בהן חולם, או חירק, או שורק, אינו מלשון בעלי המסורת, רק התחכמות הסופר שכתב כן כדי להראות שהוא הבין המסורת:

☞ ועתה[100] אודיעך הטעם למה לא קראו להן שמות כמו שקראו לקמץ ולפתח, וזה לפי צורת הנקודות האחדות יש להן סימן אותיות חמשך ר״ל הוי״ן וחיד או או אי, וחסתפקו בשמות האלו ולא קראו להן שמות אחרים,[101] אבל הקמץ והפתח שאין להן אורד

---

[98] Both in the Massorah finalis, under letter *Vav*, and in the *Ochla Ve-Ochla*, section lv., where the list in question is given, it is designated כ״א זוגין, *twenty-one pairs*. The expression מלין, *words*, in the text of Levita, must therefore be a slip of the pen. It is also to be remarked, that in the *Ochla Ve-Ochla* the names of the vowels are given (וחד בלא שום וחד קמץ שום), which, according to Levita, shows that it is a later addition, and that the title of this rubric in the Massorah finalis is the genuine old designation.

[99] The list of these twenty-seven instances is given in the Massorah finalis, under the letter *Jod*, and in the *Ochla Ve-Ochla*, section ccxiv., pp. 45, 127, &c. Neither the Massorah finalis, however, nor the *Ochla Ve-Ochla* designates the list in question, כ״ז מלין דכתיבין אי, *twenty-one words which are written with* אי. In the former it is expressly entitled דכתיב י׳ בחירק, *which are written with Jod Chirek*, thus giving the very name of the vowel-sign which Levita disputes; whilst in the latter the rubric in question is entitled כ״ז מלין דכל חד לי׳ כתי׳ י׳ במצע תיבות וכל דכות׳ כתב ו׳, *twenty-seven words, which only occur once with Jod in the middle of the word, and which in all other passages are written with Vav.*

[100] The Sulzbach edition erroneously insert והנה, *and now*, before עתה, *now*.

[101] The whole sentence והסתפקו בשמות האלו ולא קראו להן שמות אחרים, *and they were satisfied with these designations, and did not give them other names*, is omitted in the Sulzbach edition.

133

matres lectiones, had to be distinctly named. Thus, also, the short *Kametz* and the short *Pattach*, which have mostly no *matres lectiones*, as I have explained it in the "*Poetical Section*," had likewise to be specified by names, that is short *Kametz* and short *Pattach*. Afterwards came some grammarians who changed these names: they called the short *Kametz Tzere* and the short *Pattach Segol*, wherewith all others agree; but they do not agree in the names of the other vowels.

Hence there are some who call the vowel אֹ *Cholem* and others who call it *Melaphum;* thus R. Solomon b. Isaac [Rashi] calls it, in his Commentary on Exod. xv. 5 and Isa. i. 31, which you may consult. We Germans call the vowel אוּ *Melaphum;* but I do not know whence we obtained it, for in none of the works by the grammarians and the punctuators do we find it called so; they designate it *Shurek*. Again, we call the vowel אֻ *Shurek*, whilst the grammarians call it three-points, or *Kibutz;* generally, however, it is called *Kibutz of the Lips*, and some call it *Kibutz of the Mouth*. The vowel אִ is called *Chirek*: there are some who call it *Sheber;* it is so called by Ibn Ezra, in many places, and he states that this is its name in Arabic; whilst the sage author of the *Khozari* calls *Chirek* the long *Sheber* and *Tzere* short *Sheber;* but I am certain that the short *Chirek*, that is, without the *Jod*, was called *Sheber*, and the long one, with the *Jod*, was simply called *Chirek*.

Thus have I expatiated at large upon this subject, till I have made it evident that the vowel-points and the accents were neither given on Sinai, nor were they invented by the men of the Great Synagogue, but that they are the work of the Massorites, who flourished at a later period, as I have stated. In short, they are the self-same who have

---

[103] Levita's allusion is to be found in the *Khosari* ii. 8, p. 191, ed. Cassel.

הֶמְשֵׁךְ הוצרכו לקרא להן שמות מיוחדין, וכן הקמץ קטן ופתח קטן, שאין להן אתיות המשך על הדרוב כמו שבארתי בפרק שירה, לפיכך קראו להן שמות מיוחדין שהן קמץ קטן ופתח קטן, ואח"כ קמו מדקדקים אחרים ושנו את שמותן וקראו לקמץ קטן צרי ולפתח קטן סגול, ולדעת אלה הסכים דעות כלן בשוה, אבל שמות של שאר הנקודות לא הסכים עליהן דעות כלן בשוה:

יש שקורא לנקודות או חולם, ויש שקורא לו מלא פום, וכן קרא לו רבינו שלמה יצחק כמו במלת יכסימו ופעלו לניצוץ ע"ש: ואנחנו האשכנזים קוראין לנקודת או מלא פום, ולא ידעתי מאין הוציאוהו, כי אין בכל ספרי המדקדקים והנקדנים שקראו לו כן, אך קראו לו שורק, ואנחנו קוריין שורק לנקודת אֻ, והמדקדקים קורין לו שלשה נקודות או קבוץ, וחק קר שקראו לו קבוץ שפתים, ויש קורין לו קבוץ פום, ונקדת אִ קראו לו חירק, ויש שקורין לו שבר, וכן קרא לו ראב"ע בהרבה מקומות, וכתב שהוא נקרא כן בלשון ערבי, והחכם הכוזרי קרא לחירק שבר גדול, ולצרי שבר קטון,[103] וברור לי, כי החירק של תנועה קטנה, ר"ל שהיא בלי יוד הוא שקראו לו שבר, ואותו שהוא עם היוד קראו חירק סתם:

והנה האריכרתי עד הנה ביורתר, עד שבארתי ובדרתי שהנקודות והטעמים לא נתנו מסיני, וגם אנשי כנסת הגדולה לא המציאום כלל, ואינם אלא מעשי ידי בעלי המסורה שקמו אחור כך כמו שבארתי, והכלל כי הם

preserved the Law and the Prophets in their proper state; and there can be no doubt that, if they had not existed, the cake would have been entirely consumed, and the law would have become, as it were, two laws, and there would not have been found two Codices among all the copies of the Scriptures agreeing together, as is the case with the books of other authors.

Look at the many changes and variations which are to be found in the Targum of Onkelos, though a Massorah was made thereon, called[103] *The Massorah on the Targum of the Pentateuch*, because it does not follow the plan of the Massorah on the Bible in numbering the words, letters, &c., but simply enumerates some particular words, the Targum rendering of which differs from what it usually is in all other places. Thus, for instance, יְדַעְתִּי is rendered in eleven passages by יְדַעֲנָא,[104] and in all the rest by יְדַעִית; שְׁבוּ is rendered three times by אוֹרִיכוּ; עֵץ is rendered twice by אִילָן, &c., &c. See the Introduction to my Lexicon, which I wrote on all the Targums; viz.,

Onkelos on the Pentateuch, Jonathan on the Prophets, and Aquilas on the Hagiographa (some say that the latter is by R. Joseph),[105] and which I have named *Methurgeman*, before it has appeared. I hope to God to publish it soon, and to be permitted to see it before I die.[106]

In their works, however, the Massorites have toiled most diligently, and counted all the verses, words, and letters of every book, for which they are called Numberers = *Sopherim*. Hence, by their diligence, they have so far learned to know that the *Vav* in נחון

---

[103] The word הנקרא, *which is called*, is omitted in the Sulzbach edition.

[104] In the Sulzbach edition, the abbreviation י"א, *eleven*, has erroneously been resolved into יש אומרים, *some say*, which has no sense; and דמתורגם is substituted for דמתורגמין.

[105] As the discussion of the authorship of the Chaldee paraphrases is too lengthy to be entered upon here, we must refer to Kitto's *Cyclopædia*, s. v. JONATHAN B. UZZIEL, JOSEPH B. CHIJA, ONKELOS, and TARGUM, where the necessary information is given at length.

[106] Levita did live to see his Chaldee Lexicon published. For a description of it, see above, p. 69, &c.

135

[Levit, xi. 42] is the middle of all the letters in the Pentateuch; that "Moses diligently sought" [Levit. x. 16] are the middle of all the words, דָּרֹשׁ terminating the first half, and דָּרַשׁ beginning the second; and that "the breast-plate" [Levit. viii. 8] is the middle of all the verses. This they have done in all the 24 sacred books.[107] Moreover, they have counted the verses, words, and letters of each Pericope in the Pentateuch, and made marks accordingly. Thus, the Pericope *Bereshith* has 146 verses, the mnemonical sign being the name Amaziah; *Noah* has 153 verses, the mnemonical sign of which is Bezaleel;[108] thus giving a proper name as a mnemonical sign for each hebdomadal section, to indicate the number of its verses. Again, *Bereshith* has 1915 letters, and the sign is אי״ץ טי. But I must also explain to you how it is how א signifies 1000, and final ץ 900.

☞ You must observe that the Kabbalists and Massorites have taken the five final letters into the number of the alphabet, and thus made the entire letters to be 27 in number. They are divisible into

באותיות, דרש דרש משה (ויקרא ח׳) חצי התורה בתיבות, דרש מכאן ודרש מכאן, וישם עליו את החשן חצי התורה בפסוקים, וכן כל ספר וספר מן כ״ד ספרים, וכן מנו מספר לפסוקים לתיבות ולאותיות שבכל פרשה שבתורה[107] ונתנו בהן סמנים, כגון בראשית פסוקיו קמ״ו סימן אמציה, נח פכרה״יו קנ״ג סימן בצלאל,[108] וכן בכל פרשה נתנו שם אדם לסימן, האותיות בפרשת בראשית אלף ותשע מאות וחמשה עשר סימן א״ץ ט״י: והנה אף זה צריך להודיעך איך א׳ מורה על אלף, וצדי הפשוטה מורה על תת״ק:

☞ דע כי בעלי הקבלה ובעלי המסורת הכניסו ה׳ אותיות הכפולות במנין האותיות, והיו האותיות כלן כ״ז במספר, ונחלקים לג׳ חלקים, דהיינו מ׳ אותיות לכל חלק, החלק

---

[107] Levita evidently refers here to the fact recorded in the Talmud (*Kiddushin* 30 *a*), which is as follows:—לפיכך נקראו הראשונים סופרים שהיו סופרים כל האותיות שבתורה שהיו אומרים וא״ו דגחון חציין של אותיות של ספר תורה דרש דרש והתגלח של פסוקים וכרסמנה חזיר מיער עי״ן דישי חצים של תהלים והוא רחום יכפר עון חציו דפסוקים, therefore were the ancients called SOPHERIM, *because they numbered the letters of the Scriptures. Thus they say that the* VAV *in* נחון [Levit. xi. 42], *is the middle of all the letters of the Pentateuch; that* דרש דרש [*ibid.* x. 16], *are the middle of all the words; that* והתגלח [*ibid.* xiii. 33], *is the middle of the verses; that the* AIN *in* מיער [Ps. lxxx. 14], *is the middle letter of the Psalms, and that "but he, being full of compassion, forgave their iniquity"* [*ibid.* lxxviii. 38], *is the middle of the verses.* On the same page in the Talmud, we are further told as follows:—ת״ר חמשה אלפים שמונה מאות ושמונים ושמונה פסוקים הויא פסוקי ספר תורה יתר עליו תהלים שמונה חסר ממנו דברי הימים שמונה, *the Sages submit that the number of verses of the Pentateuch is* 5888, *that of the Psalms* 8 *less, and that of Chronicles* 8 *more*.

[108] From time immemorial, the Pentateuch has been divided into fifty-four sections, for the purpose of hebdomadal lessons, since some years, according to the Jewish chronology, have fifty-four Sabbaths. Each of these Pericopes, called *Parsha* (פרשה), or *Sidra* (סידרא), has a special name, which it derives from the first or second word wherewith it commences; and Jewish writers, when quoting a passage from the Pentateuch, cite the respective names of the Pericope instead of giving the chapter and verse. *Bereshith*, which Levita quotes, is the name of the first Pericope, embracing Gen. i. 1–vi. 8, and is the first hebdomadal lesson in the first Sabbath of the Jewish year. The name *Amaziah*, which is the mnemonical sign of the number of verses, indicates it by its numerical value, viz., ה 5 + י 10, + צ 90, + מ 40, + א 1 = 146. The hebdomadal lesson, *Noah*, comprises Gen. vi. 9–xi. 32, and the 153 verses of which it consists are indicated by the mnemonical sign *Bezaleel*, which is of this numerical value, viz.—ל 30 + א 1 + ל 30 and צ 90 + ב 2 = 153. A full description of the Sabbatic lessons, as well as of the manners and customs connected therewith, is given in Kitto's *Cyclopædia, s. v.* HAPHTARA.

three parts, each part consisting of 9 letters. The first part extends from א to ט, and forms the units; the second part extends from י to צ, and constitutes tens; whilst the third part constitutes the hundreds, and consists of ק ר ש ת ך ם ן ף ץ. In this manner the value of the letters rises to thousands, ת being 400, final ך 500, final ם 600, final ן 700, final ף 800, and final ץ 900. For the number 1000 we have to return to the beginning of the alphabet, and when written out fully אֶלֶף it is 1000. Some say that it is on this account called *Aleph*. When another number is added to it, it is only written א׳. This explains what I have said above, that א״ץ signifies 1900. They have also given 1534 as the number of verses in Genesis, the sign of which is א״ך ל״ד; 5842 as the number of verses in the whole Pentateuch; and 600,045 as the number of letters in the whole Pentateuch.

☞ Moreover, we find that the Massorites have also counted each separate letter of the alphabet in the whole twenty-four sacred Scriptures, and have ascertained that the letter א occurs 42,377 times, the letter ב 35,218 times, the letter ג 29,837 times, &c. Indeed a beautiful poem was written long ago on this subject, beginning "The Tent, the place of my buildings," and I have heard that Saadia Gaon is the author of it. This statement is confirmed by the fact that there are in it foreign and obscure words, which are not Biblical, such as are to be found in the work, entitled *Faith [and Philosophy]*,[109] which he wrote. I may, perhaps, append it to this treatise,

הראשון מן האלף עד המ' הוא וחלק האחדים, חשני מן היוד עד חצדי חלק עשיריות, וחלק השלישי חלק המאיות וחוא ק ר ש ת ך ם ן ף ץ, ובאופן זה יעלה מספר האוחיות לחשבון האלף, כי חתיו היא ד' מאות, וכף פשוטה ח״ק, ומ״ם סתומה ת״ד ונ׳׳ון פשוטה ת״ש, ופ״ח פשומח ח״ת, וצדי פשומה תח״ק, ולמנין אלף הוזר הדין לראש האלפא ביתא, וכוחבין אלף במלואה, ויש מי שאמר לכך נקראת אלף, וכאשר יצמרף עמח מנין אחר כותבין רק א' לכד, וזהו מה שכתבתי למעלה א״ץ, שהוא אלף ותשע מאות, וכן פסוקים של ספר בראשית אלף וחמש מאות ושלשים וארבעה סימן א׳׳ך ל״ד, וכן מספר הפסוקים של כל החורה כלו חמשת אלפים ושמונה מאות ומ״ב, ומספר אוחיות של כל התורה ששים רבוא וארבעים וחמשה:

☞ ועוד מצאנו שמנו מספר כל אות ואות של כל חעשרים וארבעה, ומצאו מספר האלפין מ״ב אלפין שע״ז, ומספר הבית ל״ח אלפין וי״ח, ומספר הגימל כ״מ אלפין וקל׳׳ז, וכן כל אות ואות, וכבד נעשה על זה חדיו יפה מתחיל אהל מכון ביני וכו', וקבלתי כי ר' סעדיה גאון חבראוחו, ונדאין הדברים, כי נמצאים בו מלות זדות וחמורות, אשר לא מלשון מקרא המה, וכמוחח נמצאים בספר אמונות[109] שחבר, ואולי אדפיסהו

---

[109] Saadia's philosophical treatise, to which Levita refers, was originally written in Arabic, *circa* A.D. 933–937, entitled כתאב אלאמאנאת ואלאעתקאדאת. It consists of ten sections, and discusses the following subjects:— Section i. The creation of the world and all things therein. ii. The Unity of the Creator. iii. Law and Revelation. iv. Obedience and Rebellion, Divine Justice and Freedom. v. Merit and Demerit. vi. The Soul and Immortality. vii. The Resurrection. viii. Redemption. ix. Reward and Punishment. And x. The Moral Law. The original Arabic, with the exception of a specimen of the Introduction, has not as yet been published. It is in Ibn Tibbon's Hebrew translation of it, made in 1186, and published in Constantinople 1562, Amsterdam 1648, Berlin 1789; and in Fürst's German translation, published at Leipzig, 1845, that this treatise is accessible to scholars.

with a short explanation, for it is difficult to understand it without a commentary.

Now I return to the former subject, and submit that, after all the work which the Massorites have done, it is impossible for any mistake or alteration whatever to happen to any of the books of the Scriptures. It is, therefore, not in vain that our Rabbins of blessed memory have said, "The Massorah is a fence to the Scriptures," and that they have also explained the words, "Every man's sword was on his thigh, because of the terrors by night" [Song of Songs iii. 8], to refer to "the Massorah, and to the signs designed to preserve the law from being forgotten in the captivity."[110] Indeed, there were hundreds and thousands of Massorites, and they continued generation after generation for many years. No one knows the time when they commenced, nor when they will end in future. For even at the present day, if any one wishes to engage in the work, and make signs and rules whereby to find out the number of words, or other Massoretic subjects, he is quite at liberty to do so; but only under this condition, that he must not add to nor diminish from anything which the men of the Great Synagogue have determined as regards *plene* and *defective*, *Keri* and *Kethiv*, the major and minor letters, the open and closed sections of the Pentateuch, &c., &c. Neither must he gainsay the statements of the Massorites respecting the vowel-points and the accents, the number of words which they have counted, and marked with mnemonical signs.

☞ Indeed I, the author of this book, have myself invented various Massoretic signs and rules, which are not to be found in the treatises of the ancients, and have embodied them in my great work, on which I have laboured more than twenty years, and which I have called *The Book of Remembrance*. I hope to God, blessed be

בסוף ההבור חזח עם קצח פידוש, כי קשה הבנתו בלי פידוש:

והנני חוזר על הראשונות, ואומר כי אחר המעשה אשר עשו בעלי המסורת אי אפשר שנפל או שיפול חילוף או שינוי בשום צד בכל ספרי המקרא, ולא להנם אמרו רז״ל מסחרת סיג לתורה, וכן דרשו על פסוק איש חרבו על ירכו מפחד בלילות (שיר ג׳), אלו המסורת והסמנים שלא תשכח תורה בגלות,[110] והאמת כי בעלי המסורות היו למאות ולאלפים דור אחר דור כמה שנים, ולא נדע לנו זמן תחלתם, גם זמן התימתם, אך עוד היום מי שיחפוץ לקרב אל המלאכה ולעשות סמנים וכללים למצא חשבון ממלות או ענינים ממסורת הרשות בידו, אך בתנאי שלא יוסיף ולא יגרע על מה שהסכימו עליהם אנשי כנסת הגדולה במלאים וחסרים, ובקרי בכתיב, ובאאחיורת גדולות וקטנות, פתוחות וסתומות בתורה וכדומה לאלה: גם לא יכחיש דברי בעלי המסורת בענין הנקדות והטעמים, וסכומי המלות שמנו חם ונתנו בהן סימנים:

☞ והלא אנכי המחבר חדשתי כמה ענינים וכללים מעניני המסורת, אשר לא נמצאו בדברי הקדמונים, וכתבתים בספרי הגדול אשר עמלתי בו עשרים שנה ומעלה, וקראתי שמו ספר הזכרונות אקוה לאל ית׳

[110] The saying that the Massorah, or the traditional pronunciation of the text, is a fence to the Scriptures, was propounded by the celebrated R. Akiba, who flourished *circa* A.D. 80–120; comp. *Aboth* iii. 13. The explanation of Song of Songs iii. 8, as referring to the Massorah, to which Levita alludes, is to be found in Rashi's Commentary *in loco*.

he, that it will soon make its appearance, as I have given it to be printed in the great city of Paris, in the kingdom of France.[111]

☞ Remark now, that the Great Massorah, which is extant, is almost endless. Indeed I believe [112] that if all the words of the Great Massorah which I have seen in the days of my life were written down and bound up in a book, it would exceed in bulk all the twenty-four books of the Bible. I have already stated in the poetical Introduction that it is not to be found collected in any book, except in the treatise *Ochla Ve-Ochla*, which is so called from its beginning words. Even the greatest part of the Massorah which has been printed here in Venice in the Great Bible is taken from this work.[113] Kimchi quotes it under the root קרב (*vide in loco*).

Now that which constitutes the Massorah marginalis is simply an abridgement of the Massorah magna; for, certainly, the Massorites would not write their remarks around the margins, since they were too small, and the space was too narrow, to contain their words. They wrote their remarks in separate treatises, and taught them publicly; hence the works were largely circulated, and the Scribes, who copied the Bible, selected from them what they pleased, each one according to his fancy, and wrote it in the margin, both above and below. Some copied large pieces, and others smaller portions, according to the size of the book into which they were writing it, as I have stated in the poetical Preface (*vide supra*, p. 94).

On the sides of the margins, however, and between the columns of the pages, the Massorites wrote down the suggestions, the mne-

---

במחרת יצא משפטו לאורה, כאשר נתתיו לחדפיסו בעיר הגדולה פאריז אשר במלכות צרפת: [111]

וְהִנֵּה דַּע לְךָ כִּי הַמַּסֹּרָה הַגְּדוֹלָה הַנִּמְצָאָה כִּמְעַט אֵין לָהּ קֵץ, וְהָאֱמֶת שֶׁשְּׁעַרְתִּי [112] אֲנִי שֶׁאִם הָיוּ כָּל דִּבְרֵי חַמַּסֹרֶת הַגְּדוֹלָה אֲשֶׁר רָאִיתִי אֲנִי בְּיָמַי כֻּלָּם כְּתוּבִים וּקְשׁוּרִים יַחַד עַל סֵפֶר, יִרְבֶּה כְמוֹתוֹ בְּכַמּוּת כָּל הָעֶשְׂרִים וְאַרְבַּע, וּכְבָר כָּתַבְתִּי בַּהַקְדָּמָה הַחֲרוּזִית כִּי לֹא נִמְצָא סֵפֶר מְחֻבָּר מִמֶּנּוּ רַק סֵפֶר אָכְלָה וְאָכְלָה חֲנֻקְרָא כֵן בַּעֲבוּר הַתְחָלָחוּ, גַּם כָּל הַמַּסֹּרָה הַנִּדְפֶּסֶת פֹּה וויני"סיה בעשרים וארבע הגדול, רובו אינו אלא מספר הוא, [113] וְהָר"דָק ז"ל הִזְכִּירוֹ בְּשֹׁרֶשׁ קרב ע"ש:

וְגַם מַה שֶּׁנִּמְצָא כָּתוּב בִּגְלָיוֹנוֹת הַסְּפָרִים אֵינוּ אֶלָּא קִצּוּר מֵהַמַּסֹּרָה הַגְּדוֹלָה, כִּי וַדַּאי בַּעֲלֵי הַמָּסוֹרֶת לֹא כָתְבוּ דִבְרֵיהֶם סָבִיב חֲנִלְיוֹנוֹת, כִּי קָצַר חֲמַצַּע מֵחַשְׁתָּרֵעַ, וְחִיָּיטָה קְטַנָּה מֵהָכִיל אֵת כָּל דִּבְרֵיהֶם, אַךְ כָּתְבוּ דִבְרֵיהֶם קוּנְטְרֵס קוּנְטְרֵס, וְלִמְּדוּם בָּרַבִּים, וְנִתְפַּשְּׁטוּ חֵחֲתָקוֹת הָחֵם חֲנָה וְחָנָה, וְהַסּוֹפְרִים כּוֹתְבֵי סִפְרֵי הַמִּקְרָא, לָקְטוּ מֵהֶם אִישׁ כָּל הַיָּשָׁר בְּעֵינָיו, וְכָתְבוּם סָבִיב חֲנִלְיוֹנוֹת לְמַעְלָה וּלְמַטָּה, יֵשׁ הֶאֱרִיךְ וְיֵשׁ קִצֵּר, לְפִי גֹּדֶל כְּרַךְ הַסֵּפֶר וְקַמְּנוֹרוֹ, כְּמוֹ שֶׁכְּרַתְבֵּרִתִי בַּהַקְדָּמָה הַחֲרוּזִית ע"ש:

אָכֵן בִּגְלָיוֹנוֹת שֶׁבְּצִדְּדֵי הַסְּפָרִים וּבֵין הָעַמּוּדִים, כָּתְבוּ הָרְמָזִים וְהַסִּימָנִים וְסִכּוּם

---

[111] For the nature and history of this work, see above, p. 28, &c.

[112] The Sulzbach edition erroneously substitutes ששמעתי, *which I have heard*, for ששערתי!

[113] This statement of Levita is contradicted by no less an authority in Massoretic lore than the learned Frensdorff. Frensdorff shows that Jacob b. Chajim, the first editor of the Massorah, which is now printed in the several Rabbinic Bibles, did not derive the greater part of his materials from the *Ochla Ve-Ochla*. Comp. Introduction to the *Ochla Ve-Ochla*, p. 10.

monical signs, the numbers of the words, and the subjects, with great brevity, indicating them by initial letters and *Notaricons;* and this is called the Massorah *parva*, as I shall explain in Part iii., called *The Broken Tables.* Moreover, on the centre of each word whereon they made any Massoretic gloss, they put a circle, referring to what the Massorah says respecting it. Thus, for instance, on וַיַּבְדֵּל, and *he divided*, which occurs three times in the Bible,[114] the circle on the top thereof refers to the נ' in the margin, or *the three times.* The same is also the case when a word only occurs once; they put a circle on it, referring to the marginal remark, לית or ל = *no other*, as I shall explain in the above-named Part. When the circle is placed between two words, the marginal remark refers to both words thus joined together. Thus, for instance, the circle between ברא°אלהים, *God created*, refers to the note in the margin, that "*thrice these words occur joined together;*"[115] the circle between פני°תהום, *the face of the abyss*, refers to "*it occurs twice conjointly;*"[116] and between רוח°אלהים, *the Spirit of God*, to "*it occurs eight times conjointly.*"[117] In the better Codices, the word *conjointly* is omitted, since the verse is understood without it, as I shall explain in the *Second Part*, section vi. When three, four, or five words are joined together for some Massoretic remark, the circle is placed between every two words. Thus, the circles between את°השמים ואת°הארץ, *the heavens and the earth*, refer to the marginal remark י"ג, "*it occurs thirteen times;*"[118] and between וידבר°יהוה אל°משה ואל°אהרן, *and Jehovah spake to Moses*

המלורה והעניינים בקצור מופלו, בראשי תבח ובנומריקון, והוא הנקרא מסרה קמנה, כאשר יתבאר בשער שברי לוחת, ועל כל מלח אשר נמסר עליה איזה דבר, עשו עגול אחד למעלח באמצע חמלח שבפנים, להורות על מח שנמסר עליח בחוץ, כגון וַיַּבְדֵּל (בראשית א') חנמצא ג' פעמים במקרא,[114] העגול מורח על ג' חנרשם בחוץ, וכן מלח חנמצאח רק פעם אחת, עשו עליה עגול להורות על מח שנרשם עליח בגיליון לית או ל', כמו שיתבאר בשער חנ"ז, וכשעגול אחד עומר בין שרתי מלורת, מה שנמסר בחוץ עומר על ב' חמלורת חסמוכות, כגון ברא°אלחים נ' דסמיכי,[115] פני°תחום ב' דסמיכי,[116] רוח°אלחים ח' דסמיכי.[117] ובנוסחאות חמדויקות לא כתיב דסמיכי, כי יספיק זולתו, כאשר יתבאר בלוחות שניות במאמר ו', וכשיסמכו ג' או ד' או ח' מלח יחד, ונמסר עליחן איזה דבר, עשו עגול בין כל ב' מלות וב' מלת, כגון את°השמים ואת°הארץ י"ג (בראשית א'),[118] וכן

[114] The three instances in which ויבדל occurs, are Gen. i. 4, 7; 1 Chron. xxv. 1.

[115] The three passages in which ברא אלהים occur conjointly, are Gen. i. 1, ii. 3; Deut. iv. 32.

[116] The two instances in which פני תהום occur, are Gen. i. 2; Job xxxviii. 30.

[117] The eight passages in which רוח אלהים occur, are as follows:—Gen. i. 2, xli. 38; Exod. xxxi. 3, xxxv. 31; Numb. xxiv. 2; Ezek. xi. 24; 2 Chron. xv. 1, xxiv. 20. They are enumerated in the Massorah magna on Exod. xxxv. 31, with the remark וכל שמואל דכר, *and every passage in Samuel is like them*, viz., 1 Sam. x. 1, xi. 6, xvi. 15, 16, 23; xviii. 10, xix. 23.

[118] The instances in which את השמים ואת הארץ occur, are Gen. i. 1; Exod. xx. 11; xxxi. 17; Deut. iv. 26; xxx. 19; xxxi. 28; 2 Kings xix. 15; Isa. xxxvii. 16; Jerem. xviii. 24; xxxii. 17; Hag. ii. 6, 21; 2 Chron. ii. 11.

and Aaron, refer to the marginal remark ב״י, "*it occurs twelve times.*"[119] Sometimes two circles are placed on one word, referring to two separate Massoretic remarks in the margin. Thus, מֵחֲטֹא, *from sinning*, one circle refers to 'ג, "*it occurs three times,*" and the other to "*it is one of the five words in the Pentateuch wherein* א *is deficient.*"[120]

☞ Notice, also, that when the total number of times that a certain word occurs in the Bible is stated, the words themselves are never quoted, but the beginning of the respective verses in which these words occur are given. Thus, on לָאוֹר [Gen. 15], the marginal remark is, "*It occurs seven times, and the sign thereof is* '*God called*' [Gen. i. 5]; '*and I will bring the blind*' [Is. xlii. 16]; '*the just Lord*' [Zeph. iii. 5]; '*therefore it is for*' [Is. lix 9]; '*the indignation of the Lord*' [Micah. vii. 9]; '*with the light He shall rise*' [Job xxiv. 14]; '*He discovereth deep things*'" [Job xii. 22]. All these are the beginnings of the verses in which the expression לאור occurs. Sometimes the Massoretic sign on the text is in Aramaic. Thus, on לאור in question, the sign is in Aramaic, "*the blind man cried, intending to go out by night, and he rose in the movning.*" On comparison, it will be found that this sign refers to each of the seven verses quoted above. When, however, the commencing words of a verse are of frequent occurrence, such as ויהי, *and it came to pass*, והיה, *and it was*, וידבר, *and he spake*, ויאמר, *and he said*, &c., two or three of the principal words in the verse are selected for the sign, and not the very word which commences the verse. But this is easily understood. Sometimes the order of the verses in the Bible is inverted, to construe an attractive mnemonical sign, by combining the

וידבר יהוה אל°משה ואל°אהרן י°ב
(שמות ו׳),[119] ולפעמים עשו על מלה אחת
ב׳ ענולים, להורות על ב׳ ענינים הנרשמים
בחוץ, כנון מחֲטֹא לי (בראשית כ׳) נ׳, והוא
חד מן ה׳ מלין דחסרי אלף בתורה, העגול
האחד מורה על הנ׳, והשני מורה על ה׳ מלין
דחסרים א׳:[120]

☞ ודע כאשר הביאו סך מנין של מלה
אחת, לחהיע כמה פעמים נמצאת במקרא,
לא כתבו חברי המלה ההיא ממש, אלא
כתבו ראשי הפסוקים אשר נמצאה בהם המלה
ההיא, וחמשל לָאוֹר ז׳, וסמנהון ויקרא אלחים
(בראשית א׳), והלכתי עורים (ישעיה מ״ב),
יהוה צדיק, על כן רחק, זעף יהוה, לאור
יקום, מגלח עמוקות, כל אלה הם ראשי
הפסוקים שנמצא בהם לאור, ולפעמים
עשו עליהן סימן בלשון ארמי, כגון על לאור
ז׳, וסימנהון בלשון ארמי צוח סומיא וסבר
למיפק בלילא וקם בצפרא, דוק ותמצא חסמן
חזה מכוון עם ז׳, הפסוקים הנ״ל, אבל
כשיש ר״ס מן מלות מורגלות, כגון ויאמר,
וידבר, וחיה, ויהי ורומיהן, לקחו ב׳ או ג׳
מלות שהן עקרי הפסוק ההוא לסימן, ולא
לקחו מלת ראש הפסוק ממש, וחזו קל להבין,
ועוד שנו לפעמים סדר הספרים של המקרא,
כדי לעשות סימן יפה בקשור דברים, דבר

---

[119] The Massorah marginalis on Numb. xix. 1, which also mentions twelve passages wherein וידבר יהוה אל משה ואל אהרן only quotes eleven, viz., Exod. vi. 13; Levit. xi. 1, xiii. 1, xiv. 33, xv. 1; Numb. ii. 1, iv. 1, 17, xiv. 26, xvi. 20, xix. 1.

[120] The three instances in which מחטא occurs, are Gen. xx. 6; 1 Sam. xii. 23; Ps. xxxix. 2. They are stated in the Massorah marginalis on Exod. xx. 6. The five instances in which *Aleph* is wanted, are Gen. xx. 6; Numb. xi. 11, xv. 24; Deut. xi. 12, xxviii. 57.

words in their proper sequence. Thus, on וָטוֹב [Gen. xviii. 7], the marginal remark is, *it occurs five times with Kametz, and the sign thereof is, in Aramaic, "an excellent youth ran and found wisdom,"* which is not according to the regular order: since *youth* is taken from *"the youth Samuel"* [1 Sam. ii. 26]; *excellent*, from *"Saul the chosen"* [1 Sam. ix. 2]; *run*, from *"unto the herd he ran"* [Gen. xviii. 7]; *and he found*, from *"and they found pasture"* [1 Chr. iv. 40]; and *wisdom*, from *"they increased wisdom"* [1 Kings x. 7].

☞ As a rule, most of the remarks of the Massorites relate to the words and things which are liable to be mistaken. Thus, on וְרוּחַ אֱלֹהִים, *and the Spirit of God*, the remark is ה׳, *it occurs eight times*,[121] for in all other passages it is רוּחַ יְהוָה, *the Spirit of Jehovah*. The same is the case with the remark on וִיהִי, *and it shall be*, *"it occurs thirty-two times*,"[122] as in all other places it is וַיְהִי, *and it came to pass;* and so in numerous other instances. Thus, also, they did not put down the word לית, *not extant*, except in the case of those words which might be mistaken, as on וְתֵרָאֶה, *and it shall be seen*, it is remarked ל׳, *no parallel;* on יֵאָכֵל, *it shall be eaten*, it is remarked, *it occurs twenty-three times;*[123] on וְיָבֹאוּ, *and they shall come*, it is noted, *it occurs seven times.*[124] But in cases of words which are not liable to be mistaken, such as מרחפת, *hovering*, or יִקָּווּ, *let them be gathered*, or וְלִמְשׁוֹל, *and to rule*, or הָרָקִיעַ, *the firmament*, &c., &c., these they have not marked with לית. Mostly, however, they noticed the words which in some places have the *Vav* prefix, and in others have

---

[121] For these eight instances, see p. 139, note 117.

[122] The thirty-two instances in which ויהי occurs with *Vav* conjunctive, in all other instances being with *Vav* conversive, are as follows:—Gen. i. 6; ix. 26, 27; Exod. ix. 22; x. 21; xviii. 19; Deut. xxxiii. 6; 1 Sam. x. 5; xx. 13; xxvii. 22; 2 Sam. v. 24; xviii. 22, 23; 1 Kings xiii. 33; xiv. 5; xxi. 2; 2 Kings ii. 9; Jerem. xiii. 10; Hos. xiv. 7; Amos v. 14; Micah i. 2; Malachi iii. 10; Ps. ix. 10; lxxxi. 16; xc. 17; civ. 20; Ruth iii. 4; iv. 12; 1 Chron. xiv. 15; xxii. 16; 2 Chron. xviii. 12; xix. 11. They are enumerated in the Massorah finalis, under the letter *He*, 23 *a*, col. 2.

[123] The remark in the Basel and Sulzbach editions, that יאכל, Niphal future, 3rd person singular, "occurs *seventeen times* (י״ז)," is surely a mistake, since the word in question occurs twenty-three times, as follows:—Gen. vi. 21; Exod. xii. 16, 46; xiii. 3, 7; xxi. 28; xxix. 34; Levit. vi. 6, 15, 16 (twice), 18, 19, xi. 34, 41; xvii. 13; xix. 6, 7, 23; xxii. 30; Numb. xxviii. 17; Deut. xii. 22; Ezek. xlv. 21. They are thus given in the Massorah finalis under the letter *Aleph*, p. 6 *b*, col. 2.

[124] The seven instances in which וְיָבֹאוּ occurs with *Sheva* under the *Vav*, called *Raphe* in the Massorah, are as follows:—Exod. xiv. 16, 17; Deut. x. 11; Josh. xviii. 4; Is. xiii. 2; Jerem. iii. 18; Ezek. xxxiii. 31. In all other passages the *Vav* has *Pattach*, which in the language of the Massorah is called *Dagesh*.

it not. Upon all this I have treated in my great work, entitled *The Book of Remembrance*, where you can see it.

Some, however, maintain that the Massorah does not notice words which are liable to be mistaken, but that it cites and counts them in order to deduce therefrom some homiletical, exegetical, or legal point. Thus, for instance, when the Massorites remark on בראשית, *in the beginning*, ג' ר"פ, "*it occurs three times at the beginning of the verse*,"[125] it is because there is a Midrash; so they also remark on ויבדל, *and he divided*, 'ג, "*it occurs three times*,"[126] in harmony with the three *separations* which are recited at the termination of the Sabbath, viz., between light and darkness, &c.; on יעופף, *shall fly*, 'ב, "*it occurs twice*";[127] and in a host of other passages. From all these words some Midrash is to be deduced, and it is for this reason that the Massorites have noted down their number. To this effect a book has been written, which is ascribed to R. Jacob Baal Ha-Turim, of blessed memory.[128]

וחברייהן אינם כן, וכל אלה הביאותים בספר הזכרונות חגדול ומשם תראם:
ויש אומרים שהביאו קצת מלות שלא יש בהן חשש, רק הביאום ומנו אותם כדי ללמוד מהן מדרשים ופשטים, ודינים ומשפטים, כגון בראשית ג' ר"פ[125] יש בזה מדרש, וכן ויבדל ג' כנגד ג' הבדלורת שאומרים בליל מוצאי שבת בין אור לחושך וכולי,[126] וכן יעופף ב',[127] וכן הרבה וחרבה מאד, ועל כלן יש לדרוש איזה דבר, לפיכך כתבו בעלי המסורת מנינם, וכן חובר על זה ספר, ויחסו אותו לר' יעקוב בעל הטורים ז"ל:[128]

[125] The three instances in which בראשית begins a verse are, Gen. i. 1; Jerem. xxvii. 1; xxviii. 1. Now the Talmud relates the following story:—בקש הקב"ה להחזיר את העולם לתהו ובהו בשביל יהודים כיון שנסתכל בדורו נתישבה דעתו בקש הקב"ה להחזיר את העולם לתוהו ובוהו מפני דורו של צדקיהו כיון שנסתכל בצדקיהו נתישבה דעתו, *God wanted to reduce the world again to void and emptiness, because of the wicked Jehojakim; but when He looked at the people of His time, His mind was appeased; God again wanted to reduce the world to void and emptiness, because of the people of Zedekiah's time, but when He looked upon Zedekiah, His mind was appeased* [Erachin, 17 a]. From this it will be seen, that the enumeration by the Massorah of these three passages in question is intimately connected with the story in the Talmud, where Jerem. xxvii. 1 and xxviii. 1 are brought together with Gen. i. 1, shewing that God wished, in those two cases where בראשית occurs, to destroy the work of the first בראשית. Comp. also *Sanhedrin*, 103 a.

[126] The three instances in which ויבדל occurs, are as follows:—Gen. i. 4; 7; 1 Chron. xxv. 7. From this the ecclesiastical legislators deduced, that "*Whoso recites the separations which God effected must not mention less than three* .... *because occurs three times*" (כל הפורת לא יפחות משלשה הבדלות), *Pessachim*, 108 b—104 a). The reference here is to the prayer which the Jews to this day offer on the Sabbath evening, at the going out of the sacred day and the coming in of the week day, and which is denominated *Havadalah* (הבדלה). In this prayer, which is as follows, are contained the three separations in question:—ברוך אתה ד' אלהינו מלך העולם המבדיל בין, *Blessed art thou, O Lord*; קדש לחל בין אור לחשך בין ישראל לעמים בין יום השביעי לששת ימי המעשה, *Our God, King of the world, who hast made a separation between the holy and the common, a separation between light and darkness, and a separation between Israel and the other nations.* Comp. also Jacob b. Chajim's *Introduction to the Rabbinic Bible*, p. 12 Hebrew and p. 32 English, ed. Ginsburg.

[127] The two instances in which יעופף occurs are, Gen. i. 20; Isa. vi. 2. From the combination of these two passages, in which alone the expression occurs, it is deduced that the angels are included in the winged creatures, created on the fifth day of the hexahemeron. Comp. *Midrasch Rabba* on Genesis. p. 3 a, ed. Stettin, 1863.

[128] Jacob b. Asheri, also called *Baal Ha-Turim*, after his celebrated Ritual Work,

148

However, I have noticed that he only explains the words which occur two, three, four, or five times, but not more. Now what is to be done with those which occur from ten, twenty, to a hundred times, &c.? As for instance, בְּעֵינֵי, *in the eyes of*, which occurs 139 times; ראש, *head*, which occurs 151 times. How is it possible to assign a reason for all these? But the words of the Law are like a hammer, which breaks the rock and divides it into many pieces, since the Law may be interpreted in seventy different ways. Herewith the Introductions are completed, by the help of Him who creates souls, and in whose name I shall commence the Treatise itself, and explain each one of the ten sections on *plene* and *defective*, their laws and regulations; and the contents thereof are as follows:—

והנה ראיתי שאינו מפרש רק המלות הנמצאות ב' או ג' או ד' או ח' פעמים, ולא יותר, ומה נעשה באותן הנמצאות י' או כ' עד מאה פעמים ויותר, כגון בְּעֵינֵי קל״מ, ראש קנ״א, איך אפשר לתת טעם על כלן, אך דברי תורה כפטיש יפוצץ סלע מתחלק לכמה נצוצות, ובשבעים פנים התורה נדרשת, ובכן נשלמו החקדמורת, בעזורת יוצר נשמורת, ובשמו אתחיל החבור, ואבאר כל דבור ודבור, מן דברות העשר, של כל מלא וחסר, ודינן ומשפטן, וזהו פרטן:

---

was born in Germany, circa A.D. 1280, and died A.D. 1340. The Commentary to which Levita refers is an exposition of the Pentateuch, and interprets the sacred text according to the hermeneutical rules called גימטריא, reducing every letter of a word to its numerical value, and explaining it by another word of the same quantity. The great value of this Commentary consists in its explanations of the Massoretic notes. The portion which treats on the Massorah has been detached from the general Commentary, and published separately in most of the Rabbinic Bibles. Comp. Kitto's *Cyclopædia*, *s. v.* JACOB B. ASHERI.

FIRST PART.

לוחות ראשונות:

SECTION I. treats on *defective* and *plene* in so far as they relate to the *matres lectiones Vav* after *Cholem* and *Shureck*, and *Jod* after *Chirek* and *Tzere*.

הדבור הראשון בביאור שעיקר חסר ומלא לא נאמר רק על וי"ו הנחה אחר החולם והשורק, והי"וד הנחה אחר החירק והצרי:

SECTION II. treats on the passages wherein the *Vav* is absent after the *Cholem* in verbs and nouns, and the difference between them.

הדבור השני בביאור המקומות שחסר בהן חוי"ו אחר החולם בפעלים ושמורת וההפרש שביניהן:

SECTION III. treats on nouns which are *Milra* and have a *Vav plene* after the *Cholem* on the top, and those which are *Milra* and have not the *Vav*; as well as of all the *Cholems* of the participle *Kal*, which are generally defective, and most of the plurals feminine which have a *Vav* at the end.

הדבור השלישי בביאור שהשמות שהם מלרע חם מלאים וי"ו אחר החולם שבראשם, ואותם שהם מלעיל חם חסרים וי"ו, וכל החולמים שבבינוני מבנין הקל חם על הרוב חסרים ורוב לשון רבות מלאים וי"ו בסוף:

SECTION IV. treats on nouns which have a small *Chirek* which is either *plene* or *defective*.

הדבור הרביעי בביאור חוי"ו השרוקה, מתי היא חסרה ובא תחתיה קבוץ שפתים:

SECTION V. (see below)

הדבור החמישי בביאור כל תיבה ששייך בה חירק גדול, ר"ל הירק עם יו"ד היא על הרוב מלאה יו"ד, וחתיבה ששייך בה חולם היא על הרוב חסרה וי"ו:

הדבור הששי בביאור היו"ד הנחה הבאה אחר הצרי והסגול, וכן יו"ד נחה חבאה אחר קמץ לכינוי הנכתר:

הדבור השביעי בביאור חמלות המלאים וחחסרים שהם של תנועה אחת, דהיינו מלות זעררות:

הדבור השמיני בביאור איך נמסר על מלה שיש בה ב' או נ' נחים קצתם מלאים וקצתן חסרים,[1] או כולן מלאים או כלן חסרים:

SECTION IV. treats on the absent *Vav* of the *Shurek*, and on the *Kibutz* being substituted in its place.

SECTION V. treats on all the words which have a long *Chirek, i. e., Chiruk* with a *Jod*, having mostly *Jod*; and on those words which have *Cholem*, being mostly defective of *Vav*.

SECTION VI. treats on the quiescent *Jod* after the *Tzere* and *Segol*, as well as on the quiescent *Jod* after the *Kametz* of the third person.

SECTION VII. treats on the *plene* and *defective* of monosyllabic words, being small words.

SECTION VIII. treats on the Massoretic marks, or words, which have two or three quiescents, some being *plene* and some *defective*,[1] or all being *plene* or all *defective*.

---

[1] The Sulzbach edition rightly inserts וקצתם חסרים, *and some being defective*, which has dropped out from the ed. Basel, 1539.

SECTION IX. treats on words which have a quiescent *Aleph*, either expressed or not, and which are called ' *with audible Alephs*,' or ' *without audible Alephs*.'

SECTION X. treats on words, the final *He* of which is either *plene* or *defective*, and are called *Maphkin He*, consisting of four kinds.

END OF THE CONTENTS OF THE FIRST PART.

SECTION I.—I, Elias Levita, the author, have already explained, in my *Poetical Dissertation*,[2] the law of the letters יהו״א, which prolong the syllables, and are quiescent; for their nature is to be quiescent in the middle and end of the word, as well as to indicate the five long vowels, respecting which I have given the mnemonical sign, " Good Elijahu."[3] Now, there ought properly to be one of the letters אהו״י after every long vowel. Thus, after *Kametz* in the middle of the word there ought to be a quiescent *Aleph*, and at the end of the word *Aleph* or *He* quiescent; after *Chirek* and *Tzere* there ought to be a quiescent *Jod*; and after *Cholem* and *Shurek* a quiescent *Vav*. But they do not generally occur so in the Scripture, and it is these which the Massorites call *defective*, and whenever they do occur they are denominated *plene*.

הדבור התשיעי בביאור חמלות שיש בהן אלף נחה כתובה או כשאינה כתובה, וקראו להן מפקין אלף או לא מפקין אלף:

הדבור העשירי בביאור המלות שתבוא בהן הה״א בסוף חסר או מלא, וקראו לה מפקין ח״א, וחן של ד' מינין:

סליקו הסימנים. מהלוחות הראשונים:

הדבור הראשון: אנכי אליהו הלוי המחבר כבר באתי בפרק שירה[2] דין אותיות יהו״א, שהם אותיות המשך והנחת, כי כן דרכם לנוח באמצע המלה ובסופה, והן מורות על חמש התנועות הגדולות, אשר נתתי סמנם אליהו טוב,[3] והנה היה מן הדאוי לחיות אחר כל תנוגה גדולה אחת מאותיות אה״וי, דהיינו אחר הקמץ שבאמצע המלה היה ראוי אל״ף נחה, ובסוף המלה אל״ף או ה״א נחה, ואחד החירק והצרי יו״ד נחה, ואחר החולם והשורק ו״ו נחה, והנה על הרוב לא יבאו במכתב, והם שקראו בעלי המסרת חסרים, וכאשר יבאו במכתב קראו להם מלאים:

☞ ודע כי העקר ורוב החסרים והמלאים שעליהם כתבו בעלי המסרת הם חוי״ו והיו״ד הנחים באמצע התיבה, הוי״ו אחר החולם והשורק, והיו״ד אחר החירק והצרי, ועל המעט כתבו מלא או חסר על האל״ף וחה״א, כאשר אבאר אח״כ, ואתחיל בחסרי הוי״ו עם החולם כי הם הרבים ואומר:

☞ Know that the import of most of the *defectives* and *plenes*, which the Massorites have marked as such, is about the quiescent *Vav* and *Jod* in the middle of the word, *Vav* after *Cholem* and *Shurek*, and the *Jod* after *Chirek* and *Tzere*; and that in only few cases did they remark *plene* and *defective* upon *Aleph* and *He*, as I shall explain hereafter. I shall begin with the absence of the *Vav* at the *Cholem*, for this occurs most frequently, and say—

---

[2] For a description of this grammatical work, see above, p. 13, &c.

[3] It will be seen that in this mnemonical sign, אֱלִי יָה הוּא טוֹב, *good Elijahu*, are contained all the five vowels, (viz., a, e, i, o, u,) both in the original Hebrew and in its English equivalent. The discussion of this subject, to which Levita refers, is to be found on p. 36 of the Poetical Dissertation, ed. Prague, 1793.

☞ Know that most of the words with *Cholem* in the Scriptures want the *mater lectionis Vav*. Still, the Massorites have not marked as *defective* every word with *Cholem* which has not the *Vav*; nor have they marked as *plene* every word with *Cholem* which has the *mater lectionis Vav*; but they have only noted those words as *defective* which generally have *Cholem* with the *Vav*, but which, in a few instances, occur without *Vav*; as I shall explain hereafter. The same is the case with the words which generally have *Cholem* without *Vav*; when these occur with *Vav* the Massorites have marked them *plene*.[4]

☞ The general rule is, that in the case of all the words which occur more as *plene* than *defective*, the Massorites enumerated the *defective*; and whenever the *defectives* are more frequent than the *plenes*, they enumerated the *plenes*, as I shall explain in the following Section. Know, moreover, that the vowel-point is never altered because of its being *defective* or *plene*, except in the case of the *Shurek* with *Vav*, which is changed into *Kibutz of the lips*, as I shall explain in Section iv.

☞ Know, also, that the meaning of the word is never changed because of *defective* and *plene*. Hence it is that there is never *Keri* and *Kethiv* with respect to *defective* and *plene*, as I have already stated in the Introduction. Know, likewise, that there is a difference between the simple word *defective*, marked on a certain word, and the Massorites saying, *and defective*, with the *Vav* conjunctive, as well as between the simple *plene* and *and plene*. This I shall explain in Part ii., Sect. viii. I shall there also explain the import of the phrases, '*entirely plene*,' '*entirely defective*,' as well as the meaning of '*partly plene and partly defective*,' and '*partly defective and partly plene*.'

SECTION II.—There is no noun to be found in the whole Bible, with *Cholem* as the last vowel, which is not written *plene*, with the *mater lectionis Vav*, except in a few instances which deviate from this rule,

---

[4] The whole of this sentence is transposed in the Sulzbach edition.

as I shall explain in the following section. Upon these *plenes* there was no necessity to remark that they are *plene* because they are the most frequent, as I have stated in the preceding Section.

☞ Know that just as nouns are generally *plene*, so verbs are generally *defective*. Thus, for example, the word פְּקֹד, *number*, whereon the Massorites remark " it occurs four times—twice *plene* and twice *defective*," viz.: "Number all the first-born" [Numb. iii. 40], and "Number the children of Levi" [*ibid.* iii. 15], both of which are *defective*, because they are verbs; whilst "Against the inhabitants of Pekod" [Jer. l. 21], and "Pekod and Shoa" [Ezek. xxiii. 23], are *plene*, because they are proper names. Thus, also, the future tense, as אֶפְקֹד, *I shall number*, and יִפְקֹד, *he shall number*, &c., which is generally *defective*, the Massorites have not noted as *defective*, because it is mostly so. And even verbs in which the second letter is quiescent, because the middle-stem letter is *Vav*, as, for instance, יָשֹׁב *he shall return*, תָּשֹׁב *thou shalt return*, אָבֹא *I shall come*, יָבֹא *he shall come*, תָּבֹא *thou shalt come*, נָבֹא *we shall come*, since these are generally *defective*, the Massorites counted the *plenes*.

Take, for example, nouns, the last vowel of which is *Cholem*, as גָּדוֹל *great*, כָּבוֹד *honour*, קָדוֹשׁ *holy*, שָׁלוֹם *peace*, רָחוֹק *far*, קָרוֹב *nigh*, צָפוֹן *north*, דָּרוֹם *south*, גִּבּוֹר *strong*, שְׁאוֹל *hades*, חֲמוֹר *an ass*, תְּהוֹם *deep*, as well as nouns which have an additional syllable, either at the beginning or end, as מִזְמוֹר *a song*, אֶשְׁכּוֹל *cluster*, זִכָּרוֹן *remembrance*, שִׁגָּעוֹן *madness*, עִוָּרוֹן *blindness*, תִּמָּהוֹן *terror*, &c., and those in which the *Vav* is the radical, as מָכוֹן *a place*, מָעוֹן *a dwelling*, מָלוֹן *an inn*: on all the above, and the like, the Massorites did not remark *plene*, because they are generally so written, but they counted the *defectives*, as קָדֹשׁ, *holy*, occurs thirteen times *defective*;[5] also when it is in the construct, as קְדֹשׁ occurs three times *defective*;[6] גִּבֹּר *strong of*, three times

מן הכלל, כאשר אבאר בדבור שאחד זה, ועל אלו המלאים אין צריך למסור מלא, כי הם המרובין, כאשר באחדי לעיל:

☞ ודע כי כמו שהשמות רובן מלאים, כן הפעלים רובן חסרים, והא לך סימן במלת פקוד שנמסר עליו ד' ב' מלאים, וב' חסרים, פקד . . כל זכר, פקד . . כל בכור שניהם חסרים, לפי שהם פעלים, אבל פקוד ושוע, יושבי פקוד (ירמיה ו'), שניהם מלאים, לפי שהם שמות, וכן העתידים אפקוד, יפקוד וכו', על הרוב חסרים, ולא נמסר עליהן חסר לפי שחן המרובין, ואפילו בפעלים נחי העי"ן שחוי"ו שרשית, כמו ישב, תשב, אבא, יבא, תבא, נבא, על הרוב חסרים, והמלאים נמנים ע"פ המסורת:

והמשל בשמות שהתנועה האחרונה חולם, כמו גדול, כבוד, קדוש, שלום, רחוק, קרוב, צפון, דרום, גבור, שאול, חמור, תהום; וכן השמות שיש להן תוספות אות בראש או בסוף, כמו מזמור, אשכול, זכרון, שגעון, עורון, ותמהון לבב; וכן כשהוי"ו שרשית כמו מכון, מעון, מלון, כל אלה ודומיהן לא נמסר עליהן מלא, כי הם המרובים, אבל נמנו החסרים, כמו קדש י"ג חסרים,[5] וכן בסמיכת קדש ג' חסרים,[6]

---

[5] The thirteen instances in which קדש, *holy*, occurs as *defective* are as follows:—Exod. xxix. 31; Levit. vi. 9, 19, 20; xxi. 7, 8; xxiv. 9; Numb. vi. 5, 8; Deut. xxvi. 19; Ezek. xlii. 13; Nehem. viii. 9, 11. They are enumerated in the Massorah marginalis on Exod. xxix. 31.

[6] The three instances in which the construct קדש is without *Vav* are, Ps. xlvi. 5; lxv. 5; Isa. xlix. 7. They are mentioned in the Massorah marginalis on Ps. lxv. 5.

defective;[7] שָׁלֹם peace of, eight times defective;[8] זָכְרֹן remembrance of, three times defective.[9] There are, again, a few words which are always defective, for which reason the Massorites did not consider it necessary to mark them as defective, as קָטֹן small, מְאֹד very, כֹּח power. About לֹא not, and כָּל all, I shall speak[10] in Section viii., if God permit.

As to the *plenes*, about which I treated above, and their like, when they occur with ה feminine, they too generally continue *plene*, as גְּדוֹלָה great, קְרוֹבָה near, רְחוֹקָה far, &c.; but the reverse is the case with plurals, both masculine and feminine, because they are generally defective, as גְּדֹלִים the great, mas., קְדֹשִׁים the holy, mas., גִּבֹּרִים the strong, mas., קְרֹבִים the near, mas., רְחֹקִים the far, mas., גְּדֹלוֹת the great, fem., קְרֹבוֹת the near, fem., רְחֹקוֹת the far, fem. This is because there are two quiescents following each other in these words, as I shall explain in its proper place, in Section viii. Thus, also, every *Cholem* which stands before ת in the feminine plural is according to rule *plene*, because it ends the word; as הַפָּרוֹת הָרַקּוֹת וְהָרָעוֹת, *the lean and ill favoured kine* [Gen. xli., 20]; לְרַקָּחוֹת וּלְטַבָּחוֹת וּלְאֹפוֹת, *to perfumers, butchers, and to bakers* [1 Sam. viii. 13]. The same rule obtains in all the plurals and participles, both active and passive; as פּוֹקְרוֹת, and פְּקֻדוֹת, as well as in the participles of all the conjugations, examples of which need not be adduced. All feminine plurals, however, which have no *Vav*, the Massorites marked as *defective*. Thus, for instance, בְּתֻלֹת *virgins*, [Esther ii. 2]; and the participles הֹלְכֹת, *they are coming down* [Exod. ii. 5]; and יֹשְׁבֹת, *they are sitting* [1 Kings iii. 17]. About the participles passive, I shall speak in its proper place, in Section vii., and I shall also discuss all this in the Section on the two quiescents, which is Section viii.

גבר נ' חסרים,[7] שלם ח' הסרים[8] זכרן נ' חסרים;[9] ויש מעמים הבאים לעולם חסרים, לכן אין צריך למסור עליהן חסר, כמו קטן, מאד, כח, ועל מלת לא וכל ארבר[10] בדבור ח' אי"ח:

והמלאים שכרתברי לעיל ורומיחם, כשבאים עם ה"א הנקבה נ"כ רובן מלאים, כמו גדולה, קרובה, רחוקה ורומהין, והרבים והרבור הם להפך, כי רובן חסרים, כמו גדלים, קדשים, גבֹרים, קרֹבים, רחֹקים, גדלות, קרבות, רחקות, וזה בעבור שיש בהן ב' נחין רצופין, כאשר אבאר במקומו, בדבור ח'; וכן כל חולם הבא לפני חי"ו לשון רבת דינו להיות מלא, בעבור שהיא בסוף המלה, כמו הפרות הרקות והרעות, לרקחות ולטבחות ולאפות, וכן דין כל לשון רבות בבינונים, ובפעולים, כמו פוקדות, פקודות, וכן בכל הבנינים מכל הגזרות, ואין צריך להביא עליחן ראיות, וכל לשון רבות שהוא בלי וי"ו נמסר עליו חסר, כמו נערות בתלאת טובות מראה (אסתר ב'), ובבינוני ונעדרותיה הולכת, ישבת בבית אחד, ובפעולים אדבר במקומו בדבור ז', ועוד ארבר בכל אלה בדבור של ב' נחים שהוא הדבור חשמיני:

---

[7] The three instances in which נבור is *defective* are, Gen. x. 8, 9; Deut. x. 17. They are given in the Massorah marginalis on Gen. x. 8.

[8] The Basel edition states that there are three instances in which שלום is *defective*; but this is evidently a mistake, for there are eight, as follows:—Gen. xxxvii. 4; 1 Sam. xvi. 4; 1 Kings ii. 5, 6; v. 26; Jerem. xv. 5; Ezek. xiii. 16 (twice). They are enumerated in the Massorah marginalis on Gen. xxxvii. 4. The Sulzbach edition omits שלום altogether, and substitutes for it ארץ.

[9] The three passages in which זכרן is *defective* are, Exod. xxviii. 12 (twice), 29.

[10] The Sulzbach edition erroneously inserts מהן *about them*, after ארבר *I shall speak*.

SECTION III.—There is no tri-literal noun to be found, the first syllable of which has *Cholem* with the *mater lectionis Vav*, except when the accent is on the ultima, since, in those which have the tone on the penultima, the *Cholem* in the first syllable is generally without the *mater lectionis Vav*. *Plenes*, for example, are עוֹלָם *eternity*, כּוֹכָב *star*, גּוֹרָל *lot*, אוֹפָן *a wheel*, אוֹצָר *a store*, תּוֹלָע *a worm*, שׁוֹשָׁן *a lily*. Also, those with *Tzere*; *ex. gr.*, יוֹבֵל *jubilee*, אוֹיֵב *an enemy*, עוֹרֵב *a raven*, שׂוֹרֵק *a vine*. These are generally *plene*; the *defectives* are but few, as לְעֹלָם *for ever*, which occurs 18 times *defective*;[11] גֹּרָל *lot*, 4 times *defective* in this form;[12] חֹתָם *seal*, 7 times *defective* in this form;[13] אֹיֵב *enemy*, three times *defective* in this form.[14] I shall acquaint thee with the meaning of בלישנא, *in this form*, in Part ii., Section ix.

Moreover, nouns derived from irregular verbs, the first radical of which is *Jod*, and which have an additional *Mem* or *Tav*, are generally *plene*; as תּוֹרָה *law*, תּוֹשָׁב *an inhabitant*, מוֹצָא *a going out*, מוֹרָא *fear*, מוֹעֵד *appointment*, מוֹפֵת *a miracle*, &c., &c. The *defectives* are exceedingly few. But the pronouns אוֹתוֹ *him*, אוֹתְךָ *thee*, אוֹתִי *me*, אוֹתָם *them*, אוֹתָהּ *her*, though they have the tone on the ultima, are generally defective. Hence, because these are the majority, therefore the *plenes* are enumerated, and not the *defectives*. Thus, on אוֹתוֹ *him*, it is remarked, "it occurs twenty-four times *plene*;"[15] on אוֹתְךָ *thee*, " it

---

[11] The eighteen instances in which לעלם occurs *defective* are as follows:—Gen. iii. 22; vi. 3; Exod. iii. 15; xv. 18; xxi. 6; xxxi. 17; xxxii. 13; Levit. xxv. 46; Deut. v. 26: xxxii. 40; 1 Kings i. 31; ii. 33; ix. 5; x. 9; Ps. xlv. 18; lxxv. 10; xcii. 9. Though the word in question is marked in each of these passages as *defective*, we could not find the entire list anywhere enumerated in the Massorah. On Exod. iii. 15, and Ps. xlv. 18, the Massorah marginalis remarks that a list of the eighteen instances is given in the Massorah on Ps. lxxv. (לעלם י״ח נמסר בתהלים סימן ע״ה). On Ps. lxxv., again the Massorah marginalis remarks that the eighteen instances are enumerated in the Massorah finalis, under the letter *Ajin Vav* (לעלם י״ח חסר וסי במס רבתא בטר ע׳); and on examining the Massorah finalis, to which we are referred again, we find that it simply states לעלם י״ד וחס׳ וסימני׳ נמסר בתלים סימן ע״ה. "*The word* לעלם *occurs eighteen times defective, and the passages are given in the Massorah marginalis on Ps. lxxv*." Comp. p. 49, col. 2.

[12] The Massorah marginalis on Levit. xvi. 8 gives the four instances in which גרל is *defective*, as follows:—Levit. xvi. 8; Numb. xxxvi. 3; Judg. i. 3; Dan. xii. 18; including, as it will be seen, the plural גרלות.

[13] The seven instances in which חותם is *defective* are as follows:—Gen. xxxviii. 18, 25; Exod. xxviii. 11, 36; xxxix. 14; 1 Kings xxi. 8 (twice). They are enumerated in the Massorah marginalis on Exod. xxviii. 11.

[14] The three passages in which איב occurs *defective* are, 1 Sam. xviii. 29; Jerem. vi. 25; xv. 11. They are given in the Massorah marginalis on 1 Sam. xviii. 29.

[15] The twenty-four instances in which אותו occurs *plene* are as follows:—Josh. xxiv. 4, 14, 22; 1 Sam. xii. 24; 2 Kings i. 15 (twice); iii. 11, 12, 26; viii. 8; ix. 27; x. 16;

occurs seventeen times *plene;*"[16] on אוֹתָךְ *thee*, fem., "sixteen times *plene;*"[17] on אוֹתִי *me*, "twenty-seven times *plene;*"[18] on אוֹתָם *them*, "thirty-nine times *plene*" in the Pentateuch, and the sign of it is "*for it is full* [= *plene*] *of dew* [טל = 39]."[19] The Massorites have also counted the *plene* of the word אוֹתָם *them*, in each book of the Bible, except Jeremiah and Ezekiel, where they have counted the *defectives*, because they are the fewer; and they likewise tell us that אוֹתָה *her*, occurs twelve times.[20] But the nouns, with the tone on the penultima, are mostly *defective;* as חֹרֶשׁ the new moon, קֹדֶשׁ *holiness*, אֹהֶל *tabernacle*, גֹּרֶן *area*, &c., &c. On קֹדֶשׁ *holiness* [Dan. xi. 31], the Massorites remark, "*there is no parallel case of plene.*" The meaning of the expression לִית, I shall explain in the Third Part, denominated *The Broken Tables*. The word שׂוֹבֶךְ *thicket* [2 Sam. xviii. 9] is also *plene;* and besides these, there are almost no *plenes* in this form of the noun.

מלאים,[16] אוֹתָךְ י"ו מלאים בלשון נקבה,[17]
אוֹתי כ"ז מלאים,[18] אוֹתם ל"ט מלאים
באוריתא, וסימן טל נמלא טל,[19] וכן בכל ספר
וספר נמנה לפי מלת אוֹתם חמלאים, חוץ
בירמיה וביחזקאל נמנין החסרים, לפי שהם
המעט אוֹתה י"ב מלאים,[20] אבל השמות שהם
בטעם מלעיל רובן דרובן חסרים, כמו חֹדֶשׁ,
קֹדֶשׁ, אֹהֶל, גֹּרֶן ודומיהן, ונמצא עוכבי ברית
קֹדֶשׁ ונמסר עליו לית מלא, ומלת לית תתבאר
בשער שברי לוחות, וכן תחת שׂוֹבֶךְ האלה
מלא, וכמעט אין עוד מלאים במשקל זה:

Jerem. xviii. 10; xxxvii. 15; Ezek. xvii. 17; xliii. 20; Hos. x. 6; Mal. i. 12, 13; iii. 22; Ps. xviii. 1; lvi. 1; lxvii. 8; ci. 5. They are confusedly enumerated in the Massorah finalis, p. 13 b, col. 2, with the remark, that throughout the books of Joshua and Judges it is likewise *plene*, with the exception of two passages.

[16] The seventeen instances in which אוֹתָךְ masculine, occurs *plene* are, Gen. xvii. 2; xx. 6; xl. 19; xli. 39; Exod. ix. 15; xxv. 9, 22; xxxii. 10; Deut. ix. 14; 2 Sam. xxiv. 24; Ezek. ii. 3, 4; iii. 27; xxix. 5; xxxviii. 4, 17; Ps. xxv. 5. They are enumerated in the Massorah finalis, p. 13 b, col. 3.

[17] The seventeen instances in which אוֹתָךְ feminine occurs *plene*, are Gen. xxxix. 9; Numb. v. 21; Judg. xiv. 15; Jerem. ii. 35; xi. 17; xxx. 14; Ezek. xvi. 4, 39, 40, 57, 59, 60; xxii. 14, 15; xxiii. 25, 29. They are enumerated in the Massorah finalis, p. 13 b, cols. 3 and 4.

[18] The twenty-seven passages in which אוֹתִי is *plene*, are Deut. xxxii. 51; Judg. x. 13; Isa. xxxvii. 6; liv. 15; lvii. 11 (twice); lviii. 2; Jerem. iv. 22; v. 22; ix. 5, 23; xiii. 5, 25; xvi. 11; xx. 11; xxv. 6; xxxi. 34; xxxvii. 18; Ezek. vi. 9; xxiii. 35 (twice); xl. 3; Ps. xxxi. 6; Esth. v. 12; Lament. iii. 2; Nehem. vi. 14. They are given in the Massorah finalis, p. 13 b, col. 3, with the remark that אוֹתִי is also *plene* throughout the books of Joshua and Judges, except in two instances.

[19] The thirty-nine passages in which אוֹתָם is *plene* in the Pentateuch are as follows: Gen. xli. 8; xlix. 28, 29; l. 21; Exod. xiv. 9; xxix. 3; Levit. x. 2; xiv. 51; xv. 10, 29; xvii. 5; xxii. 16; xxiii. 43; xxiv. 8; xxv. 55; Numb. iv. 12, 19, 23, 49; v. 4; vi. 20; vii. 3, 5, 6; xxv. 4, 17; Deut. iii. 6, 28; ix. 28; x. 15; xii. 29; xviii. 12, 13; xxvi. 16; xxvii. 26; xxxi. 7, 10. They are most confusedly enumerated in the Massorah finalis, p. 13 b, col. 4, to page 14 a, col. 1. The mnemonical sign שׂראשׁי נמלא ט"ל *for my head is filled with dew*, from *Song of Songs* v. 2, is exceedingly ingenious and beautiful. The force of it will be understood, when it is remembered that the word ראש *head*, is figuratively used for the *Law*, or the *Pentateuch*, and is so rendered by the Chaldee Paraphrasts on *Song of Songs* v. 11; that the word נמלא, *full*, is exactly the expression for *plene*; and that the numerical value of the word טל, *dew*, is 39.

[20] The twelve passages in which אוֹתה occurs *plene* are, Numb. xxii. 33; xxx. 9; 1 Sam. xiv. 27; 2 Sam. xiii. 18; Isa. xxvii. 11; xxviii. 4; xxxvii. 26; Jerem. xxxii. 31; xxxiii. 2; Hosea iv. 19; Malachi. i. 13; Ps. xxvii. 4. They are enumerated in the Massorah marginalis on Numb. xxii. 33, with the remark that וכל יהושע שופטים ויחזקאל דבר במ"ג, "*it is also plene throughout the books of Joshua, Judges, and Ezekiel, with the exception of three passages.*"

151

Moreover, all those which have Pattach before the guttural in this form are generally *defective*, as אֹרַח *way*, תֹּאַר *form*, נֹגַהּ *brightness*, נֹעַם *before*, נַעַר *sweetness*, נֹכַח *boyhood*, טֹהַר *brightness*, פֹּעַל *work*; and only a few of these are *plene*, as צֹעַר *Zoar*, which occurs three times *plene*,[21] כֹּובַע, and קֹובַע *helmet*, are sometimes *Milel*, and sometimes *Milra*; and there is a division of opinion about them. Likewise פָּרֹכֶת *copper*, כַּפֹּרֶת a *cover*, נְחֹשֶׁת *curtain*, קְטֹרֶת *incense*, שִׁבֹּלֶת *an ear*, כֻּתֹּנֶת *a tunic*, are *defective*, because they are *Milel*; תֹּולַעַת *a worm*, is an exception, for it is always written fully, except in two instances, in which it occurs *defective*.[22] The Cholems, too, of the participle *Kal*, are generally without *Vav*, whether in the singular masculine, as פֹּקֵד *remembering*, נֹצֵר *keeping*, נֹשֵׂא *forgiving* [Exod. xxxiv. 7]; or plural masculine, as אֹכְלִים וְשֹׁתִים וְחֹגְגִים, *they are eating, and drinking, and dancing* [1 Sam. xxx. 16]; or plural feminine, as עֹשְׁקֹות *oppressors*, רֹצְצֹות *crushers*, אֹמְרֹות *declarers* [Amos iv. 1].[23] It is the *plenes* of all these which are enumerated in the Massorah, as אֹוכֵל *occurs four times plene*,[24] יֹודֵעַ *ten times plene*,[25] קֹורֵא *ten times plene*.[26] The same is the case with the twenty-four instances of *plene* in the singular, which have no parallel in the whole Bible; as פֹּותֵר [Gen. xli. 8], חֹולֵם [Deut. xiii. 3], טֹוחֵן [Judges xvi. 21], &c., upon each one of which there is a Massoretic remark.[27] The word יֹושֵׁב is

[21] The three instances in which צוער is *plene* are, Gen. xix. 22, 30 (twice).
[22] The two exceptions in which תולעת is *defective* are, Exod. xxvi. 1; Deut. xxviii. 39.
[23] The whole of this passage is vitiated in the ed. Basel, 1539.
[24] The four passages in which אוכל occurs *plene* are, Gen. xxxix. 6; Isa. xxix. 8; Nahum iii. 12; Ps. xli. 10. They are enumerated in the Massorah marginalis on Gen. xxxix. 6.
[25] This is one of the passages which shows how difficult it is to understand the Massoretic language, and how easily one may mistake the meaning of Levita. In reading the above remark, one might be led to suppose that there are only ten instances in the Bible in which ידע is *plene*, whereas there are no less than twenty-three. Levita's remark, however, is explained by the Massoretic annotation on 1 Sam. xxvi. 12, where it is stated that ידע is *plene* in ten places, viz., 1 Sam. xxvi. 12: Isa. xxix. 11: Jerem. xxix. 23: Ps. i. 6; xxxvii. 18; lxxiv. 9; xc. 11: Ruth iii. 11: Esther iv. 14: Nehem. x. 29; adding וכל תריסר ד"ה קהלת ומשלי דכר, "*throughout the twelve minor Prophets, Chronicles, Ecclesiastes, and Proverbs, it is likewise* PLENE;" which is omitted by Levita.
[26] The ten instances in which קורא is *plene* are, Judges xv. 19: Isa. vi. 4; xl. 3; xlv. 3; lxiv. 6; Amos v. 8; Habak. ii. 2; Ps. xlii. 8; 1 Chron. ix. 19; 2 Chron. xxxi. 14. They are given in the Massorah finalis under the letter *Kaph*, p. 56 a, cols. 3 and 4.
[27] The twenty-four, or rather twenty-five, words written plene, which have no parallel, are as follows:—

into the streets [Ibid.], is marked as *defective*, because it is neither followed by *Dagesh* nor by a quiescent *Sheva*. Thus, also, עֲקֻדִּים *ringstraked, speckled, and* וּבְרֻדִּים *dotted* [Gen. xxxi. 10], are not marked as *defective*, because they have *Dagesh*, whilst עֲטֻפִים *the feeble*, and קְשֻׁרִים *the strong* [Gen. xxx. 42], are marked as *defective*, because they have no *Dagesh*. For the same reason שֻׁלְחָן *table*, טֻמְאָה *uncleanness*, חֻפָּה *covering*, סֻכָּה *tabernacle*, חֻקָּה *law*, &c., are not marked as *defective*, because they have a quiescent *Sheva* or *Dagesh*.

Hence every *Kibbutz* at the end of a word is marked by the Massorites as *defective*, because neither *Dagesh* nor a quiescent *Sheva* can be at the end of a word. Thus, the nouns גְּבֻל *border* [2 Sam. xxi. 5], זְבֻל *habitation* [1 Kings viii. 13], פְּרֻת *division* [Exod. viii. 19], גָּלֻת *captivity* [Obad. i. 20], &c., as well as the verbs, viz.—יַאֲרִיכֻן *ye shall prolong* [Deut. v. 16, vi. 2], תַּשְׁלִיכֻן *ye shall cast* [Exod. xxii. 30], יָקֻם *let him arise* [Gen. xxvii. 31], קֻם *arise* [Joshua vii. 10], שֻׁב *return* [Exod. iv. 19], &c.; all these, and the like, are marked as *defective*. The word נְאֻם *oracle*, however, is an exception, and the Massorites do not mark it as *defective*, because it never occurs *plene*; there is no parallel in the whole Bible of a word occurring so often, and always with *Vav defective*.

Notice, also, that most of the *Kal* participles passive singular, both masculine and femenine, are written fully. In the masculine, as כָּתוּב *it is written*, חָתוּם *sealed*, בָּרוּךְ *blessed*, עָצוּם *strong*, the *defectives* being few, as כָּמֻס *laid up* [Deut. xxxii. 34], לָבֻשׁ *dressed* [Prov. xxxi. 21], זָעֻם *despised* [Prov. xxii. 14], &c.; and feminine, as אֲרוּרָה *cursed* [Gen. iii. 17], עֲרוּכָה, שְׁמוּרָה *kept* [2 Sam. xxiii. 5], &c. The *defectives* in this case too being very few, as שְׁלֻחָה *sent* [Gen. xlix. 21], הָעֲשֻׂיָה *ordained* [Numb. xxviii. 6]. But in the construct state they are mostly *defective*, as בְּעֻלַת *wedded* [Gen. xx. iii.], שְׁכֻרַת *drunk* [Is. li. 21], אֲהֻבַת *beloved* [Hos. iii. 1], &c., there being only a few which are written fully, as עֲצוּבַת *pained* [Is. liv. 6].

(ירמיה י"ד), הנה על קבוץ של משלכים לא נמסר חסר, כי הוא ח"ק, שהרי אחריו שוא נח, ועל קבוץ של בחצורה נמסר חסר, כי אין אחריו דגש או שוא נח ; וכן עֲקֻדִּים נְקֻדִּים וּבְרֻדִּים (בראשית ל') לא נמסר עליהן חסר, כי הם דנושים, ועל הָעֲטֻפִים ללבן וְהַקְשֻׁרִים ליעקב נמסר חסר, לפי שאינם דנושים ; וכן שֻׁלְחָן, טֻמְאָה, חֻפָּה, סֻכָּה, חֻקָּה, לא נמסר עליהן חסר, כי הם בשוא נח או בדנש :

ולכן על כל קבוץ שהוא בסוף התיבה נמסר חסר, כי לא שייך דגש או שוא נח בסוף התיבה, כמו גְּבֻל יִשְׂרָאֵל, בֵּית זְבֻל לָךְ, וּשְׁמַתִּי פְדֻת, וְגָלֻת החל הזח וכו'; וכן בפעלים, למען יַאֲרִיכֻן יָמִיךְ, לכלב תַּשְׁלִיכֻן, יָקֻם נָא אָבִי, קֻם לָךְ, שֻׁב לְךָ מצרים, וישימם בעפר וָדָשׁ, על כל אלה ודומיהם נמסר חסר, ומלת נְאֻם יוצאה מן הכלל, שלא נמסר עליה חסר, לפי שלא באה לעולם מלא, ואין לח דומה בכל המקרא מלח שהיא נמצאת כל כך הרבה, וכלם חסרים וי"ו :

ודע כי רוב לשון יחיד בפעול חקל הוא מלא, כמו כָּתוּב, חָתוּם, בָּרוּךְ, עָצוּם, והחסרים חם מעטים, כמו כָּמֻס עמדי (דברים ל"ב), לָבֻשׁ שנים (משלי ל"א), וְזָעֻם ה', וכן לשון נקבה על הרוב מלא, כמו אֲרוּרָה האדמה, עֲרוּכָה בכל וּשְׁמוּרָה, וחסרים חם מעטים, כמו אֵילָה שְׁלֻחָה, הָעֲשֻׂיָה בהר סיני, אבל בסמכבות רובן חסרים, כמו בְּעֻלַת בעל, וּשְׁכֻרַת ולא מיין, אֲהֻבַת רֵעַ, ומעטים המלאים, כמו עֲצוּבַת רוח :

Thus, also, the nouns of this form are generally *plene* in the absolute state, as גְּבוּרָה *strength*, קְבוּרָה *sepulchre*, מְלוּכָה *kingdom*, &c., and *defective* in the construct, as קִבְרַת *sepulchre of* [Gen. xxxv. 20], קִבְצַת *heap of* [Ezek. xxii. 20], &c.; but *plene* are נְמוּלַת *desert* [Isa. lix. 18], &c. The plurals are very seldom *plene*, as בְּרוּכִים *the blessed* [Ps. cxv. 15], אֲרוּרִים *the cursed* [1 Sam. xxvi. 19], אֲסוּרִים *the chained* [Gen. xl. 5], &c., whilst the *defectives* are by far the most, as שְׁקֻפִים *beams*, אֲטֻמִים *closed* [1 Kings vi. 4], שְׂרֻפִים *burnt* [Numb. xvii. 4], &c. Also, כְּתֻבִים *written*, is always *defective* in the Pentateuch, though it is *plene* in the Prophets and Hagiographa; as well as the plurals feminine, which are almost all *defective*, as נְתֻנוֹת *given* [Deut. xxviii. 31], צְרֻרוֹת *bound up* [Exod. xii. 34], שְׂרֻפוֹת *burned* [Isa. i. 7], &c., the *plenes* being but few, as הַכְּתוּבוֹת *the written*, חַלּוֹנוֹת *windows*, אֲטוּמוֹת *closed*, עֲשׂוּיוֹת *the made*, רְאוּיוֹת *the seen*. The nouns, too, which are according to this form, are mostly *defective* in the masculine, as כְּרֻבִים *Cherubim*, which occurs thirteen times *defective*;[81] עַמֻּדִים *pillars*, eleven times *defective*;[82] לֵיל שִׁמֻּרִים *night of celebration* [Exod. xii. 42], and יוֹם כִּפֻּרִים *day of atonement* [Levit. xxiii. 28], are both *defective* in this form. The same is the case with the feminine plurals, as גְּבֻלוֹת *borders* [Job xxiv. 2], מַלְכֻיּוֹת *kingdoms* [Dan. viii. 22], חֲנֻיּוֹת *vaults* [Jerem. xxxvii. 16], &c. I shall again discuss this subject in Section x. which you will see.

SECTION V.—Both the prophets and other writers have paid much more attention to the quiescent *Jod* with *Chirek*, than to the quiescent

---

[81] This is another instance which shows how difficult it is to understand Levita's language without consulting the Massorah. From his remark the reader would naturally conclude that כרבים only occurs thirteen times *defective* in the whole Bible, whereas it is found so nearly thirty times. On referring, however, to the Massorah marginalis on Exod. xxv. 18, we find it remarked חסר במ״ג מלאים ונביא חסר כל אורית הכרבים, "*the word* כרובים *is defective throughout the Pentateuch, whereas it is plene throughout the Prophets and Hagiographa, with the exception of thirteen passages;*" which are as follows:—1 Sam. iv. 4: 2 Sam. vi. 2: 1 Kings vi. 25, 27; viii. 7: 2 Kings xix. 15: Ezek. x. 1, 2, 3, 6, 7, 8: Ps. lxxx. 2. There can therefore be no doubt that Levita means these thirteen instances of *defective*.

[82] The eleven instances in which עמדים is *defective* are as follows:—Exod. xxvii. 10, 11; xxxviii. 12, 17: Judges xvi. 26: 1 Kings vii. 6, 21: Jerem. xxvii. 19: Ezek. xl. 49: 2 Chron. iii. 16; iv. 12. They are enumerated in the Massorah marginalis on Exod xxxviii. 12.

Vav with *Cholem*; and this is because they have both removed and omitted the *Vav*, as I have already stated; whereas they have both left and put down the quiescent *Jod* in many places. Hence, the punctuators called the *Chirek*, followed by *Jod*, a long *Chirek*, that is, a long syllable; and *Chirek*, not followed by *Jod*, they denominated short *Chirek*, or short syllable. There are therefore two kinds of *Chireks*, one short and the other long; the short one, according to rule, is without *Jod*, and is called a short syllable; whilst the long one, according to rule, has a *Jod*, and is called a long syllable.

☞ It is for this reason that the *Chirek* of the short syllable is never marked by the Massorites as *defective*, and the *Chirek* of the long syllable is never marked as *plene*. Sometimes, however, the long syllable occurs without *Jod*, then the Massorites mark it as *defective*; as בָּנִיתִי, *I have built* [1 Kings viii. 18], רָאִתָה, *thou hast seen* [Ps. x. 14], &c.

☞ The sign whereby the *Chirek* of the short syllable may be distinguished from the *Chirek* of the long syllable, is by the absence of *Jod*. It is the same as the one I stated in the case of the *Kibbutz*. That is, whenever *Chirek* is followed by *Dagesh* or quiescent *Sheva*, it is a short syllable, and when these do not follow it, and yet *Jod* is absent, then it is a long syllable, and is *defective*, according to the Massorah. For instance, on וַהֲקִמֹתִי, *and I shall perform* [Gen. xxvi. 3], the Massorites remark, "*Jod is wanted*," because there is no *Dagesh* after the *Chirek*,[33] and, according to rule, ought therefore to be *plene*; whereas on וְהִשְׁבַּתִּי, *and I shall cause to cease* [Numb. xvii. 20], they do not remark that the *Jod* is wanting, because it is a short syllable, for there is *Dagesh* after it.

☞ According to rule, every *Chirek* which is not followed by *Dagesh*, or quiescent *Sheva*, ought to be *plene*, and is generally *plene*. That is, when it is followed by an audible letter at the end of the word, as קָצִיר

החירק יותר מחוי"ו הנחה עם החולם, וזה שעל הרוב חסירו והחסידו הוי"ו, כמו שכתבתי, אבל היו"ד הנחה השאירוה וקימוה ברוב המקומות, ובעבודה קראו מניחי הנקוד לחירק שאחריו יו"ד חירק גדול, דהיינו תנועה גדולה, והחירק שאין אחריו יו"ד קראו חירק קטן, דהיינו תנועה קטנה; והכלל כי ב' מיני חירק הם, קטן וגדול שם הוא, הקטון דינו בלי יו"ד, והוא תנועה קטנה, והגדול דינו ביו"ד, והוא תנועה גדולה:

☜ לכן כל חירק של תנועה קטנה, לא נמסר עליו חסר לעולם, ועל חירק של תנועה גדולה, לא נמסר מלא לעולם, אך לפעמים תבוא תנועה גדולה בלי יו"ד, ואז נמסר עליו חסר, כמו בנה בָנִתִי (מלכים ח'), רָאִתָה כי אתה (תהילים ט'), ודומיהן:

☜ והסימן להכיר החירק של תנועה קמצה מחירק של תנועה גדולה, כשהוא חסר יו"ד, הוא הסימן שנתתי בקבוץ, דהיינו החירק שאחריו דגש או שוא נח, הוא תנועה קמצה, וכשאינם אחריו, וחסר יו"ד, הוא תנועה גדולה, וחסר עלפי חמסורת; והמשל הנח על וַהֲקִמֹתִי את השבועה (בראשית כ"ו) נמסר חסר יו"ד, לפי שאין אחר החירק[33] דגש, והיה דינו להיות מלא, ועל וְהִשְׁבַּתִּי מעלי, לא נמסר חסר יו"ד, לפי שהוא תנועה קמנה שהרי אחריו דגש:

☜ והכלל כל חירק שאין אחריו דגש או שוא נח, דינו להיות מלא, וכן הוא מלא על הרוב, כגון כשיבא אחריו נח נראה בסוף

---

[33] Instead of שאין אחר החירק, *for there is not after Chirek*, the Sulzbach edition has שאין אחריה, *for there is not after it*.

harvest, חָסִיד pious, אֹפִיר Ophir, כַּבִּיר great, אֱוִיל a fool, כְּסִיל a fool, &c. A few of the proper names are to be found *defective*, as אֹפִר Ophir [Gen. x. 29], דְּבִר Debir [Josh. xiii. 26]; also, the name דָּוִד David is always *defective*, except in five instances in which it is *plene*.[34] The *Chirek* is never followed by a quiescent letter at the end of the word, except Aleph, as נָבִיא prophet, נָשִׂיא chief, הֵבִיא he brought, מֵבִיא bringing, אָבִיא I shall bring, יָבִיא he shall bring, תָּקִיא she shall spue out [Levit. xviii. 28]; but וַתָּקִא and she vomiteth [Levit. xviii. 25], which wants Jod, has very few parallels. But *Chirek*, before the plural termination ים, is most generally written fully, as אֲנָשִׁים חֲכָמִים וִידֻעִים *men, wise, and known* [Deut. i. 13], &c. This, however, is the case where no other *Chirek* of a long syllable precedes it, as in those instances which I have already stated, and the like cases.

☞ But when two *Chireks* do follow each other, as in כַּבִּירִים *the mighty*, אַדִּירִים *the strong*, רְבִיבִים *showers*, אַבִּירִים *the potent*, &c., the Jod of the plural is frequently omitted. Thus, הַתַּנִּינִם, *the sea monsters*, is three times *defective* in this form.[35] The same is the case with צַדִּקִים, *the righteous*, which is always *defective* in the Pentateuch, except in one place;[36] the same with נְשִׂאִים *princes*, which is so written four times in the Pentateuch; and likewise in the Prophets and Hagiographa, except in four instances where it is נְשִׂאָם.[37] The same is the case with תְּמִימִם *without blemish*; when it refers to animals it is *defective*; that is, whenever it is the predicate to sheep, rams, goats, &c. The word נְבִיאִים *prophets*, is always *defective* in the books of Samuel

---

[34] That the proper name "David is always *defective*, except in five instances, in which it is *plene*" is surely a mistake. The Massorah marginalis, both on 1 Kings xi. 4 and Ezekiel xxxiv. 23, does indeed remark that "David occurs five times *plene* (דויד ה׳ מלאים), and enumerates 1 Kings iii. 14; xi. 4, 36; Ezekiel xxxiv. 23; Song of Songs iv. 4; as the five instances; but it adds וכל תריסר ועזרא ודה״י דכו׳ מלאים, *that David is also* PLENE *throughout the twelve minor Prophets, Ezra, and Chronicles*, which is not to be gathered from Levita's statement.

[35] The three instances in which תנינים wants the *Vav* plural are, Gen. i. 21; Exod. vii. 12; Deut. xxxii. 33.

[36] The single instance in which צדיקים is *plene* in the Pentateuch is in Exod. xxiii. 8, on which the Massorah parva remarks ל׳ כל דמל, *no parallel, it is entirely* PLENE.

[37] The four instances in which נשיאם occurs are, Gen. xvii. 20; xxv. 16; Numb. vii. 10; xxvii. 2. They are enumerated in the Massorah marginalis on Gen. xvii. 20.

and Jeremiah, except in three instances in Samuel and in eight instances in Jeremiah; [38] גְּבִיעָם *goblets*, too, is always *defective*; שְׂעִירִים *goats*, is always *defective*, except in two instances; [39] צְמִידָם *bracelets* [Gen. xxiv. 80], and many others, are likewise *defective*. A few plurals, which are preceded by *Tzere* and *Chirek*, are also *defective*. Thus, אֵילָם, *rams*, has never the *Jod* plural in the Pentateuch, except in four instances; [40] the same is the case with הַיָּמִם, *the hot springs* [Gen. xxxvi. 24]. Besides the *Tzere*, we find הַיָּמִם *the days* [Numb. vi. 5], *defective*, which has no parallel in the Scripture.

Moreover, the participles *Hiphil*, because they have two *Chireks* following each other, are also wanting in most cases the *Jod* of the plural. Three instances of it are to be found in the Pentateuch, viz., מַעֲבִידָם *making labour* [Exod. vi. 5], מְקַדִּשָׁם *making holy* [Levit. xxii. 2], and מַקְצִיפָם *making angry* [Deut. ix. 22]; and some in the Prophets, as מַשְׁחִיתָם *destroying* [2 Sam. xx. 15], &c. The same occurs with *Chirek* before the termination ת, which is always *plene*, as רֵאשִׁית *beginning*, שְׁאֵרִית *residue*, אַחֲרִית *end*, תַּכְלִית *end*, &c., except in those cases where there are two *Chireks* together, as שְׁלִישִׁת *third*, רְבִיעָת *fourth*, חֲמִישִׁת *fifth*, &c., which are generally *defective*.

The rule is that all the plurals of both participles and nouns, which have not two *Chireks* following each other, are written fully, except in a few instances, as מַדֻּחָם *banished* [Lam. ii. 14], &c. Rashi's remarks on פִּילַנְשִׁים *concubines* [Gen. xxv. 6], that it is *defective*, which is taken from *Bereshith Rabba*, is contrary to the Massorah, for the Massorites mark it " *twice plene*." [41]

---

[38] Though the Massorah parva on 1 Sam. xix. 20, also remarks that נביאים occurs three times *plene* (ג' מל בליש'), yet there seem to be four instances; viz., 1 Sam. x. 11, 12; xix. 20; xxviii. 6. The eight instances of *plene* in Jeremiah to which Levita refers are, Jerem. v. 13; vii. 25; viii. 1; xxvi. 8, 11; xxviii. 8; xxix. 1; xxxv. 15. They are enumerated in the Massorah marginalis on Jerem. xvi. 2.

[39] The two passages in which שעירים is *plene* are, Isa. xiii. 21; 2 Chron. xi. 15.

[40] The four instances in which אילם is entirely *plene* are, Gen. xxxii. 15; Levit. viii. 2; Numb. xxiii. 1; Deut. xxxii. 14.

[41] The Massorah marginalis on Gen. xxv. 6 distinctly remarks that the word פילנשים occurs twice entirely *plene*, that is, with the two *Jods* after the two *Chireks*. The one

We also find the Talmud at variance with the Massorah; it takes כַּלּוֹת *finished* [Numb. vii. 1], as *defective*, and remarks on it that it is not *plene*; so also מְזוּזוֹת *doorposts* [Deut. xi. 20], according to the Talmud is *defective*, whereas according to the Massorah it is *plene*; and מַעֲבִירִים [1 Sam. ii. 24], too, is according to the Talmud *defective*, and according to the Massorah *plene*.⁴²

Notice, also, that in some of the words which have two *Chireks*, the first *Jod* is *defective*. Thus, שְׂרִגִם *branches* [Genesis xl. 10], wants the second *Jod*, whilst שָׂרִגִים *branches* [Gen. xl. 12], wants the first *Jod*; צְדִּקִים *the righteous* [Hos. xiv. 10], wants the first *Jod*, whilst צַדִּיקִם *the righteous* [Ezek. xxiii. 45], wants the second *Jod*. The same is the case with אֱוִלִים *fools*, which wants the first *Jod* five times; and there are some words wanting both *Jods*, as שָׁלִשָׁם *captains* [Exod. xiv. 7], אַדִּרִם *mighty* [Ezek. xxxii. 18].

The participles *Hiphil*, too, are found wanting the first *Jod*; as מַשְׁמִעִם, *making a noise* [1 Chron. xv. 28], מְמִתִים *killing* [Jerem. xxvi. 15], מַחְלְמִם *dreaming* [Jerem. xxix. 8], &c. All the other tenses of *Hiphil*, however, are generally *plene*, and there are but few found defective; as הִקְרִב *he offered* [Numb. vii. 19], וַיְמִצְאוּ *and they presented* [Levit. ix. 12, 18], וָאַבְדִּל, *and I have separated* [Levit. xx. 26], &c.

☞ The plurals of the passive participles *Kal*, however, sometimes occur without *Jod*, but this only takes place when the *Vav* is written fully, and it is to prevent two quiescents following each other, as I have already explained in Section ii. For example, the words נְתוּנִם נְתוּנִם *they are given, they are given* [Numb. iii. 9], are both with-

---

instance is in Gen. xxv. 6, and the other in Esther ii. 14. Now Rashi, who, in his commentary on Gen. xxv. 6, follows the traditional exposition of the Midrash, remarks, "*The textual reading is* פלגשם *defective* [that is without the plural *Jod*], *because Abraham had only one concubine, namely, Hagar, who was identical with Keturah*." But this reading, which is contrary to the Massoretic text, has evidently arisen from a pious desire to lessen the number of concubines of the father of the Hebrew nation. The *Bereshith Rabba*, from which Rashi's remark is derived, is the part of the *Midrash Rabba*, or exposition of the Pentateuch, which treats on *Bereshith* = Genesis. For an account of the *Midrash*, see Kitto's *Cyclopædia*, s. v.

⁴² For an explanation of *Mezuzah* see above, p. 95, note 18. The variations between the Talmud and the Massorah, adduced by Levita, are taken from Jacob b. Chajim's *Introduction to the Rabbinic Bible*: comp. p. 19, &c., where they are fully discussed.

out *Jod*, because they have *Vav* fully written, whilst נְתֻנִים *they are given, they are given* [Numb. viii. 16], are *defective* of *Vav*, because they have *Jod plene;* as you will see on examination.

☞ The general rule is that the *Chirek* of the long syllable has mostly the *Jod* written fully, whilst *Cholem* generally is without *Vav*. There is no necessity for me to explain to you that *Cholem* and *Chirek*, with quiescent *Vav* and *Jod* at the end of a word, are always *plene;* as יָדוֹ *his hand,* רַגְלוֹ *his foot,* יָדִי *my hand,* רַגְלִי *my foot,* &c., since it is evident that *Vav* and *Jod* can never be omitted in such cases, because a vowel-point can never be under the final letter of a word, except under *Kaph*, *Tav*, and final *Nun*. These have sometimes *Kametz* at the end of a word, as I shall explain in Section x.

SECTION VI.—A quiescent *Jod* does not follow *Tzere*, except when it belongs to the root, or when it indicates the plural. It belongs to the root, as הֵיטֵיב *doing good,* אֵיטִיב *I shall do good* [Gen. xxxii. 13], תֵּינִק *she shall nurse* [Exod. ii. 7], אֵילְכָה *I shall go* [Micah i. 1]; and it stands for the radical *He,* as צִוֵּיתִי *I commanded* [Deut. iii. 21], קִוֵּיתִי *I wait* [Isa. v. 4], and in a few more such instances. The same is the case in those nouns in which *Jod* is radical, as בֵּיתָה *house,* עַיִן *eye,* or stands for the radical *Vav*, as in צֵידָה *food,* שֵׂיבָה *old age,* the roots of which are צוּד, בּוּשׁ. I shall recur to this subject in the next Section.

The *Jod* after *Tzere*, to indicate the plural, is the same *Jod* as is used with the suffix in plural nouns of the third and second persons, both masculine and feminine, as בְּנֵיהֶם *their sons,* בְּנֵיכֶם *your sons,* בְּנֵיהֶן *their sons* (feminine), בְּנֵיכֶן *your sons* (feminine), בְּנוֹתֵיהֶם *their daughters,* בְּנוֹתֵיכֶם *your daughters,* &c., and these are never marked in the Massorah as *plene;* and a few of these are found *defective*, as נְשִׂיאֵהֶם *their princes* [Numb. xvii. 17], אֲבוֹתָם *your fathers* [Deut. i. 11]. The expressions אֲלֵהֶם *to them*, and אֲלֵכֶם *to you*, are also found *defective*

שהם מלאים וי"ו, נְתָנִים נְתָנִים הםח לי שניחן חסרים וי"ו לפי שחן מלאים יו"ד ודוק:

☜ והכלל כי חירק של תנועה גדולה על חרוב הוא מלא יו"ד, והחולם על חרוב הוא חסר וי"ו, והנח אין צריך להודיעך ולומר כי החולם והחירק שבסוף התיבה עם הוי"ו הנחה או היו"ד הנחה, הם תמיד מלאים, דהיינו שתמיד הוי"ו כתובה עם החולם, והיו"ד כתובה עם החיריק, כמו יָדוֹ, רַגְלוֹ, יָדִי, רַגְלִי ודומיחן, כי פשיטא שלא יחסרו חוי"ו והיודי"ן באלה לעולם, כי לא תבא נקדה באות שבסוף המלה לעולם, זולתי חתיו והכף והנון שהם קמוצים לפעמים בסוף התיבה, כמו שאודיעך בדבור העשירי:

הדבור הששי: לא תבא יו"ד נחה אחר הצדי רק כשהיא שרשית, או שתורה על לשון רבים, השרשירת כמו הֵיטֵיב אֵיטִיב עָמָךְ (בראשית ל"ב), וְתֵינִק לָךְ, אֵילְכָה שוֹלֵל, וכשחיא במקום ח"א שרשית, כמו יהושע צִוֵּיתִי, מדוע קַוֵּיתִי ודומיהן מעטין, ובן בשמות שהיו"ד שרשית, כמו בֵּית ח' עֵין אדם, וכן כשחיו"ד במקום וי"ו שרשית כמו צֵידָה, שֵׂיבָה, שרשם צוד, שוב, ועוד ארבר מכל אלה בדבור שאחר זה:

והיו"ד חבאח אחר הצרי להחרות על לשון רבים, היא היו"ד הבאה בכנוי חנסתרים והנסתרות, והנמצאים והנמצאות, בשמות של לשון רבים ורבות, כמו בְּנֵיהֶם, בְּנֵיכֶם, בְּנֵיהֶן, וּבְנֵיכֶן, בְּנוֹתֵיהֶם וּבְנוֹתֵיכֶם וכו', ולא נמסר עליהן מלא לעולם, ונמצאים מעטים חסרים, כמו מאת כל נְשִׂיאֵהֶם, יוסף י"י אלהי אֲבוֹתֵכֶם, ובן אֲלֵיהֶם, אֲלֵיכֶם, נמצאים חסרים, בכל ספר

in every book of the Scriptures, and they are counted according to the Massorah. Thus, also, the suffix first persons in nouns, as בִּנְעָרֵינוּ *with our youth,* בְּבָנֵינוּ *with our sons* (Exod. x. 9), are not marked by the Massorites as *plene.* But the nouns which have the pronoun, first person, pointed alike, both in the singular and plural, and in which there is no difference in the points, except that the plural has *Jod*, these are marked by the Massorites as *plene.*

Thus, for instance, יָדֵינוּ *our hands* [Deut. xxi. 7], has the Massoretic mark *plene*, whilst וְיָדֵנוּ *and our hand* (Gen. xxxvii. 27), is marked *defective*, because it is the singular, as is evident from the word תְּהִי *let it be;* so also רַגְלֵינוּ *our feet* (Ps. cxxii. 2), is marked *plene*, whilst רַגְלֵנוּ *our foot* [Ps. lxvi. 9], is marked *defective*, because it is the singular. Whereas דְּבָרֵנוּ *our word* (Josh. ii. 14), which is the singular, as is evident from the word זֶה *this;* and the expressions לִבֵּנוּ and לְבָבֵנוּ *our heart*, in which *Jod* is wanting, are never marked as *defective*, because they do not occur in the plural. But the words wherein a quiescent *Jod* is expressed after *Tzere*, which *Jod* neither belongs to the root nor indicates the plural, are always marked as *plene;* as פְּלֵיטָה *escape* [Jerem. l. 29,] הַשְׁכֵּים *early* [Prov. xxvii. 14], וְתַגֵּיד *thou shalt say* [Exod. xix. 3], and a few more like these.

Moreover, the quiescent *Jod* is also to be found after *Segol*, but this only occurs in the pronouns, second person masculine and third person feminine of plural nouns, both masculine and feminine; as בָּנֶיךָ *thy sons,* בְּנוֹתֶיךָ *thy daughters,* בָּנֶיהָ *her sons,* בְּנוֹתֶיהָ *her daughters,* and they are never marked *plene.* Many of them are found without *Jod*, especially in the case of the suffix second person masculine; as דְּבָרֶךָ *thy words* [Gen. xlvii. 30], of which there are thirteen *defectives;*[43]

---

[43] The thirteen instances in which the plural דבריך occurs *defective* are, Gen. xxx. 34; xlvii. 30: Numb. xiv. 20: Ps. cxix. 9, 16, 25, 28, 42, 65, 105, 107, 169. The Massorah marginalis, both on Gen. xxx. 34, and on xlvii. 30, mentions the three instances which occur in the Pentateuch as belonging to the thirteen *defectives*, and refers to the Massorah finalis for the whole list. But we could find no such list in the Massorah.

Y

דְּרָכֶךָ *thy ways* [Exod. xxxiii. 18], of which there are three *defective* instances; "חֲסָדֶךָ *thy mercies* [Ps. cxix. 41], which is always *defective* in the plural, and the *Segol* indicates the absence of *Jod*. And although the singular has also *Segol* when it is in pause, as יָדֶךָ *thine hand*, רַגְלֶךָ *thy foot*, אָזְנֶךָ *thy ear*, &c., the singular may be distinguished from the plural by the words with which it is connected; as יָדְךָ *thy hand* [Ps. xxxii. 4], רַגְלְךָ *thy foot* [Ps. xci. 12], אָזְנְךָ *thine ear* [Isa. xlviii. 8], שֹׁמְרֶךָ *thy keeper* [Ps. cxxi. 3], אֹיִבְךָ *thy enemy* [Deut. xxviii. 53]; all of which are singular, and it cannot be said that they are the plural with *Jod* omitted, because the verbs תִּכְבַּד *it is heavy*, תָּגוּז *it shall dash*, פָּתְחָה *it is opened*, יָנוּם *he shall sleep*, and יָצִיק *he shall oppress*, with which they are respectively connected, are singular.

Thus, also, in Jerem. xxxviii. 22, רַגְלֶךָ *thy feet*, is plural, and *Jod* is omitted, as is evident from the verb הָטְבְּעוּ *they are sunk*, the plural *Jod* is also omitted in פָּעֳלֶךָ *thy work* [Ps. lxxvii. 18], as is evident from בְּכָל *in every one*. All the feminine plurals, with the suffix second person masculine, are likewise without the *Jod* of the plural; as מִנְחֹתֶךָ *thy gifts* [Ps. xx. 4], מִצְוֹתֶךָ *thy commands* [Ps. cxix. 98], בִּקְרֹתֶךָ *thine honourable* [Ps. xlv. 10], which have always the *Cholem* before the *Segol*, as I have already explained it in the *Bachur;* and they are distinguished from nouns feminine singular in pause, with pronoun, second person, which have also ת with *Segol*, as בִּרְכָתֶךָ *thy blessing* [Gen. xxvii. 35], צִדְקָתֶךָ *thy righteousness* [Ps. lxxi. 15], by the latter having always *Kametz* before the *Segol*.

The *Jod* of the plural is likewise omitted in the suffix third person feminine, as קִבְרֹתֶהָ *her graves* [Ezek. xxxii. 25], &c. The quiescent *Jod*, indicating the plural, occurs after *Kametz*, but this only happens when it is followed by the pronominal *Vav* of third person masculine; as יָדָיו *his hands*, רַגְלָיו *his feet*, &c.; when it is never omitted, except in the

---

" The three passages in which דרכך is *defective* are, Exod. xxxiii. 18; Josh. i. 8; Ps. cxix. 37. They are enumerated in the Massorah marginalis on Exod. xxxiii. 13.

דְרָכֶךָ וחם נ' חסדים,** וכן ויבאוני חֲסָדֶךָ חסד כלם לשון רבים, וחסגול מורה על חיו"ד החסרה, ואע"פי שלשון יחיד בא נ"כ בסגול כשהוא בהפסק, כמו יָדֶךָ, רַגְלֶךָ, אָזְנֶךָ ורומיהן, תוכל להכיר היחידים מן הרבים במלות הסמוכות להם, כמו תִּכְבַּד עלי ירדך, פן תָּגוּז באבן רגלך, לא פָּתְחָה אזנך, אל יָנוּם שומרך, יָצִיק לך אויבך כלם לשון יחיד, ולא נוכל לומר שהם לשון רבים וחסרים יו"ד בעבור תִּכְבַּד, תָּגוּז, פָּתְחָה, יָנוּם, יָצִיק דסמוכים להם שהם לשון יחיד:

וכן המבעו בבוץ רַגְלֶךָ הוא לשון רבים וחסר יו"ד הרבים בראיית הָטְבְּעוּ, וכן וחניתי בכל פָּעֳלֶךָ הוא חסר יו"ד הרבים, בראיית בְּכָל, וכן לשון דבורת בכנוי הנוכח לזכר נמצאים חסרי יו"ד הרבים, כמו יזכור כל מִנְחֹתֶךָ, תחכמני מִצְוֹתֶךָ, בנות מלכים בִּקְרוֹתֶךָ, חמיד חולם לפני הסגול, כמו שבארתי בסֵפֶר הבחור: ובזה הם נבדלים מחסמות של לשון יחידה, כשיבאו בהפסק עם כנוי הנוכח שאף הם בתי"ו בסגול, כמו ויקח את בִּרְכָתֶךָ, פי יספר צִדְקָתֶךָ, תמיד קמץ לפני הסגול:

וכן בכנוי הנסתרח נמצאים חסרי יו"ד הרבים, כמו סביבותיו קִבְרֹתֶהָ, ורומחן, ונמצא יו"ד נחח המורה על לשון רבים אחר קמץ, ואין זה אלא כשיבא אחריו וי"ו כנוי הנסתר, כמו יָדָיו, רַגְלָיו ורומיהן, ולא תחסר לעולם רק

word יַחְדָּו *together*, which is always *defective*, except in Jeremiah, where it is found *plene* three times.⁴⁵ To the same category belong the expressions שְׂלָו *quails* [Ps. cv. 40], סְתָו *winter* [Song of Songs ii. 11], עָנָו *humble* [Numb. xii. 8], &c. We also find that the textual reading is *defective*, whilst the marginal reading is *plene;* as יָדָו *his hands*, in the *Kethiv*, and יָדָיו in the *Keri*, [Levit. ix. 22], צַוָּארָו *his neck*, in the *Kethiv*, and צַוָּארָיו in the *Keri* [Gen. xxxiii. 4]. But I shall discuss this subject in the Second Part, Section i.

Section VII.— Hitherto, I have treated on biliteral and triliteral words, in which all the letters are audible. I shall now discuss monosyllabic words, called little words. It is well known that the *plene* and *defective* monosyllabic words are those which have in the middle of the word either *Vav* quiescent, with *Cholem* and *Shurek*, or *Jod* quiescent, with *Chirek* and *Tzere*, and that in regard to words with other vowel-points there cannot be *plene* and *defective*, because no quiescent *Vav* or *Jod* can follow these points. On this subject I shall treat again in Section ix.

Now those pointed with *Cholem* are of two kinds. The first class consists of words, the middle letter of which is a quiescent *Vav*, as אוֹר *light*, יוֹם *day*, טוֹב *good*, מוֹר *myrrh*, קוֹל *a voice*, בּוֹס *a cup*, עוֹר *skin*, שׁוֹר *an ox*, בּוֹר *a pit*, עוֹד *again*, אוֹת *a sign*, &c. These are always *plene:* the expression לֹא *not*, is an exception, being always *defective*, except in thirty-five instances;⁴⁶ and the expression עוֹד *again*, is *defective* in fourteen instances;⁴⁷ so also דּוֹר *generation*, is *defective* when

בְּמִלַּת יַחְדָּו שֶׁהִיא חֲסֵרָה לְעוֹלָם, חוּץ בְּסֵפֶר ירמיה נמצאים ג' מלאים,⁴⁵ ובכללם שְׂלָו, סְתָו, עָנָו, ונמצאים דכתיבים חסרים וקריין מלא, כמו וישא ידו (ויקרא מ') ידיו קרי, על צוארו צואריו קרי, ועוד אדבר בם בלוחות שניות במאמר א':

הדבור השביעי: לא דברתי עד הנה רק במלות שיש בהן ב' או ג' אותיות נעות, ועתה אדבר בכלל על מלורים של תנועה אחת הנקראורת מלות זעירות; וידוע כי המלות חוזרות ששייך בהן מלא או חסר, הן אותן שיש בהן באמצע המלה וי"ו נחה עם חולם או שורק, או יו"ד נחה עם חרק או צרי; אבל אוד שאר הנקודות לא שייך מלא וחסר, כי לא שייך אחריהן וי"ו או יו"ד נחה, ועוד אדבר בם בדבור מ':

והנה הנקודות בחולם הם של ב' מינין, המין האחד הם של נחי ע"ן וי"ו, כמו אוֹר, יוֹם, טוֹב, מוֹר, קוֹל, בּוֹס, עוֹר, שׁוֹר, בּוֹר, עוֹד, אוֹת ודומיהם, הם תמיד מלאים, ומלא לא יוצאא מן הכלל שהיא תמיד חסרה, חוץ בל"ה מקומות,⁴⁶ ומלת עוד רבאא חסרה בי"ד מקומות,⁴⁷ וכן דור נמצא חסר כשיהיו שנים

---

⁴⁵ Both the Basel and the Sulzbach editions have ג' הסרים, "the word יחדיו is always *defective*, except in Jeremiah, where it is found three times defective." But this is evidently a mistake for מלאים, *plene*, since the word in question actually occurs three times in Jeremiah, viz., xlvi. 12, 21; xlix. 3.

⁴⁶ The thirty-five instances in which לוא is *plene* are, Gen. xxxi. 35: Levit. v. 1: 1 Sam. ii. 24; xix. 4: 1 Kings xviii. 5; xx. 8; xxii. 18: 2 Kings v. 17; vi. 12: Isa. xvi. 14; xxviii. 15: Jerem. ii. 25, 31; iii. 3, 12; iv. 11; v. 9, 10, 12 (thrice), 24; vi. 9; vii. 28; viii. 6, 2¹; x. 4; xv. 7, 11; xxix. 23; xlviii. 27; xlix. 20: Ezek. xvi 56; xxiv. 16: Lament. i. 12. They are enumerated, in a most confused manner, in the Massorah marginalis on Levit. v. 1.

⁴⁷ The fourteen instances in which עד is *defective* are, Gen. viii. 22; xix. 12; xl. 13: 2 Sam. xiv. 32: 1 Kings xii. 5: Jerem. ii. 9; xiii. 27; xv. 9; xxxiii. 13: Hos. xii. 1, 10: Micah i. 15: Zech. viii. 20: Ps. xxxix. 2; xxxix. 2. Comp. Massorah marginalis on Gen. viii. 22, with Jerem. xv. 9.

it is twice repeated, as לְדֹר דֹּר from generation to generation [Exod. iii. 15], לְדֹר וָדֹר from generation unto generation [Ps. x. 6], &c., as it is explained in the great Massorah.

The second class consists of those words, the second and third radicals of which are the same letters; as קֹר cold, חֹם heat, רַק but, עַל upon. All these are defective,[48] and this because of the Dagesh which they take when formative additions are made at the end, as חֹק law, with suffix is חֻקּוֹ his law; רֹק spittle, with suffix רֻקּוֹ his spittle; עֹל yoke, with suffix עֻלּוֹ his yoke. Thus, also, the word כֹּל all, from כָּלַל, has Cholem, with Vav omitted when it has the accent, except לְכֹול [Jerem. xxxiii. 8]. The Massorah remarks on it, "The Vav is not to be read, but read with Kametz-Chatuph, as is the rule with כֹּל wherever it has Makkeph," as I have explained in the Poetical Dissertation.

The infinitive and imperative of verbs ע״ע too, have always Cholem and are defective; as for instance שֹׁב return [Song of Songs ii. 17], שֹׁל תָּשֹׁלּוּ falling, ye shall let fall [Ruth ii. 16], תֹּם finished [Deut. ii. 14]. Those which have Shurek are all from roots the second radical of which is quiescent, as סוּף a reed שׁוּק a street, טוּר a wall, &c., and are always plene, because they never have Kibbutz, except the imperative of ע״ו, as קֻם arise [Josh. vii. 10], רֻץ run [1 Sam. xx. 36], שֻׁב return [Exod. iv. 19], &c. Those which have Chirek are from roots in which Jod is radical, as גִיד a nerve, סִיר a pot, סִיר a thorn, עִיר a city, שִׁיר a song, אִישׁ a man, צִיץ a flower, &c., they are generally plene; and defectives are but few, as רִב a cause [Exod. xxiii. 2], נֵר a light [Prov. xxi. 4]. In the Massorah אִישׁ a man, is noted as being three times defective, but there are differences of opinion about it among the Massorites. Thus, also, according to the Massorah, סִין Sin, is always plene, whilst צִין Zin, is always defective. There are three words which always occur defective, viz., מָן from, עָם with, and אִם if, but בִּן before Nun is simply from בֵּן of the root בָּנָה.

[48] The words כלהון חסרים, all these are defective, without which the passage has no sense, are omitted in the Sulzbach edition.

סמוכים, כמו זכרי לְדֹר דֹּר (שמות ג'), וכן לְדֹר וָדֹר ודומיהן, כמבואר במסרה גדולה:

והמין חב׳ חם מן הכפולים, כמו קֹר, חֹם, חֹק, רֹק, עֹל, כלהון חסרים,[48] וזה בעבור הדגש הבא בהן כאשר יתרבו באות שלישית, כמו מן חֹק חֻקּוֹ, ומן רֹק רֻקּוֹ, ומן עֹל עֻלּוֹ, וכן מלת כֹּל ננזרת מן כלל, כשחיא בטעם היא בחולם וחסר וי״ו לעולם, חוץ מן וסלחתי לכול עונותיכם (ירמיה ל״ג), חמסורה עליו לא קרי וי״ו, ונקרא בקמץ חטוף כדין כל כָּל המוקף, כאשר באררתי בפרק שירה:

וכן המקור והצווי מן הכפולים תמיד בחולם וחסר, כמו שֹׁב דמה לך, שֹׁל תָּשֹׁלּוּ לח (רות ב'), עד תֹּם כל הדור (דברים ב'); והשרוקים כלם מנחי העי״ן, כמו סוּף, טוּר, שׁוּק ודומיחן, וחם תמיד מלאים, דחיינו שלא יבאו לעולם בקבוץ, רק בצווי מנחי חעי״ן, כמו קֻם לך, רֻץ נא, שֻׁב לך מצרים ודומיחן; והחירוקים הם שהי״וד בחם שרשית, כמו גִיד, סִיר, סִיר, עִיר, שִׁיר, אִישׁ, צִיץ ודומיחם, על הרוב מלאים, ונמצאים פעמים חסרים, כמו לא תענה על רַב, נֵר רשעים, ובמסרה אִישׁ נ' חסרים, ויש בחן פלונתה, וכן במסרה כל סִין מלא וכל צִין חסר; ונמצאים ג' מלות שהם חסרים לעולם, והם אִם, עָם, מָן, אבל יחושע בֶּן נון חוא מן בֶּן שרשו בנה:

Those which have *Tzere* consist of four classes. The first class embraces nouns in which the second radical *Jod* is audible, as בַּיִת *house*, עַיִן *a well*, יַיִן *wine*, אַיִן *nothing*, חַיִל *strength*, אַיִל *a ram*, זַיִת *an olive*, צַיִד *hunting*, &c. When these are in the construct state, the *Jod* is quiescent with the *Tzere*, as בֵּית *the house of*, עֵין *the well of*, אֵיל *the ram of*, צֵיד *the hunting of*, אֵין *nothingness of*, חֵיל *the strength of*, &c. These are generally *plene*, and the *defectives* are very few, as חֵל *army* [Obad. 20], on which the Massorites remark it occurs five times *defective*;[49] אֵל *porch* [Ezek. xl. 48], on which the Massorites remark, "This *defective* has no parallel."[50] To this class belong those words in which the *Jod* is not audible; as אֵיךְ *how*, בֵּין *between*; some of these are *defective*, as אֵד *a mist* [Gen. ii. 6], חֵק *bosom* [Prov. v. 20], &c.; but there are very few such instances.

The second class embraces words of ע"ו, as גֵּר *stranger*, זֵד *proud*, עֵד *witness*, עֵר *Er*, צֵר *Zer*, מֵת *dead*, כֵּן *thus*, &c.; all these are invariably *defective*. The third class consists of words derived from roots ל"ה, as בֵּן *son*, גֵּו *the back*, זֵר *a crown*, עֵץ *wood*, all these are invariably *defective*. The fourth class consists of those derived from ע"ע, as חֵן *grace*, שֵׁן *a tooth*, חֵץ *an arrow*, לֵב *heart*, &c.; all these are invariably *defective*.

☞ The general rule is, that all those derived from ע"ע, whether having *Cholem* or *Tzere*, are always *defective*; whilst those with *Chirek* and *Cholem*, of ע"ו, are generally *plene*, the *defectives* being very few, as I have stated above; but when they take formative additions at the end, they are mostly *defective*. Thus, we have from טוֹב *good*, the forms טוֹבִים *the good* (mas.), טוֹבָה *good* (fem.), טוֹבַת *the good* (fem.), many of which are *defective*. The same is the case with קוֹל *voice*,

---

[49] The five passages in which חיל is *defective* are, 2 Sam. xx. 15; 1 Kings xxi. 23; Isa. xxvi. 1; Obad. 20; Lament. ii. 8. They are enumerated in the Massorah marginalis on 2 Sam. xx. 15.

[50] The reference, both in the Basel and Sulzbach editions, to וימד אל הסתח, is a mistake for וימד אל אלם. The note in the Massorah parva on the word in question is simply ל' חס' יו"ד, *no parallel with Jod defective*; so that Levita's remark that it is לית חסר באילים, *no parallel of defective, among the words* אילים, must be derived from another recension of the Massorah.

which with suffix is קֹלוֹ *his voice*, קֹלִי *my voice*, קֹלֹת *the voices*, most of them being *defective*, and which, even without any suffixal addition, occurs in this form seven times *defective*; as קֹל *voice*, הַקֹּל *the voice* [Gen. xxvii. 22]; לְקֹל *to the voice* [Exod. iv. 8 (twice)], &c.⁵¹ Thus, also, from רֹוב *contention*, we have חָרֹב [Job. xi. 2; xl. 2]. Moreover the plurals and suffixes with *Tzeres* are sometimes also *defective*; as from אַיִל *a ram*, we have אֵלִים *rams*; and a few more such instances.

SECTION VIII.—Nothing more is left for me to explain with regard to *defective* and *plene Vav* and *Jod*, except to state how the Massorites noted those words which have two or three quiescents, some of which are *plene* and some *defective*, or all of which are either *plene* or *defective*.

☞ Let me illustrate it by the example of the word הֲקִימוֹתִי *I have established*, which occurs in the Scriptures in the four following ways:—i. הֲקִימוֹתִי [Ezek. xvi. 60], which is entirely *plene*. On this the Massorites remark, "this is one of the three instances entirely *plene*.⁵² ii. On הֲקִמֹתִי [Gen. xxvi. 3], which is entirely *defective*, they wrote "one of the eleven instances entirely *defective*."⁵³ iii. On הֲקִימֹתִי [Levit. xxvi. 9], they remark, "one of six instances in which it is both *plene* and *defective*."⁵⁴ And iv. On הֲקִמוֹתִי [1 Sam. xv. 13], they remark, "it has no parallel, being *defective* and *plene*." In some recensions it is marked, "it is one of the six with the accent on the

---

⁵¹ The other three passages in which קול is *defective* are, Gen xlv. 16; Exod. xix. 16; Jerem. iii. 9. They are enumerated in the Massorah marginalis on Gen. xxvii. 22.

⁵² The other two instances in which הקימתי is entirely *plene* are, 2 Sam. vii. 12; 2 Chron. vii. 18. They are given in the Massorah marginalis on Ezek. xvi. 60, where, however, there is a mistake, inasmuch as it substitutes 1 Chron. xvii. 2 for 2 Chron. vii. 18. In the Massorah parva, on the last mentioned passage, the remark כל דמל *entirely plene*, will be found, to which Levita refers.

⁵³ The eleven passages in which הקימות is entirely *defective*, that is, has neither *Jod* after the *Chirek* nor *Vav* after the *Cholem*, are, Gen. vi. 18; ix. 11, 17; xvii. 7, 19; xxvi. 3; Exod. vi. 4: 1 Kings ix. 5: Jerem. xxiii. 4, 5; xxix. 10: Ezek. xxxiv. 29. We could not find the entire list either in the Massorah marginalis on the respective passages, or in the Massorah finalis.

⁵⁴ The other five passages in which הקימתי has *Jod plene* after the *Chirek* and *Vav defective* after the *Cholem*, are, 1 Sam. xv. 13: 2 Sam. ii. 35; vii. 12: Isa. xxix. 3: Ezek. xvi. 62. In the Massorah marginalis on Levit. xxvi. 9, where the passages are given, 2 Sam. ii. 35 is erroneously omitted, and 2 Chron. vii. 18, which is entirely *plene*, is substituted for it.

penultima," whilst in others it is marked as one of the four instances.[55] The Codices vary, as I shall explain in Section ix.

It is also to be noticed, that when a word has two quiescents, both of which are *plene*, and one of them belongs to that class of quiescents which is always plene, as I have shown in Section ii., the Massorites did not mark it *entirely plene*, but simply *plene*. And if both quiescents belong to those which are always *plene*, the Massorites did not remark upon it at all.

Thus, for example, הוֹלְכִים *they are coming* [Gen. xxxvii. 25], though *entirely plene*, the Massorites simply marked "*plene*;" that is, Vav is written fully, but the *Jod* they did not require to mark as being written fully, for it is there in accordance with the law about the *Jod* of the plural,[56] as I have explained in Section v. On לְהוֹרִיד *to go down* [ibid.], again, though *entirely plene*, the Massorites made no remark whatever, because the two quiescents therein are *plene* according to rule, as I have explained in Section iii., since *Vav*, which stands for *Jod* of the first radical, is *plene* according to law.

The same is the case with *Chirek*. When it is followed by an audible letter at the end of a word, it is generally *plene*, according to law, especially in the *Hiphil*, as I have explained in Section v. (*vide supra*, p. 156, &c.) But when both are defective, though one of them belongs to those which are generally defective, as I have explained in Section iii., the Massorites have always marked it entirely *defective;* as הֹלְכֻת *they are coming* [Exod. ii. 5], יֹשְׁבֻת *they are sitting* [1 Kings iii. 17], &c. *Vide supra*, p. 148, &c.

As to the words in which the first quiescent is *plene* and the second is *defective*, or *vice versa*, as גְּדֹלוֹת וְנוֹרָאֹת *great and wonderful*

חד מן ו' דלעיל, ולפעמים נמסר עליהן ד', ומשונין ואבארם במאמר ט':[55]

אך צריך שתדע, כשיהיו במלה ב' נחין ושניהן מלאים, ואחד מהן הוא מאותן הנחים שדרכם להיות תמיד מלאים, כמו שבארתי בדבור ב', לא נמסר עליה מלא דמלא רק מלא לבד, ואם שניהן מאותן שדרכן להיות תמיד מלאים, לא נמסר עליהן מאומה:

והמשל הוֹלְכִים להוריד מצרימה, הוֹלְכִים אעפ"י שהוא מלא דמלא, לא נמסר עליו רק מלא לבד, ר"ל מלא וי"ו, ועל חיו"ד אין צריך למסור מלא, כי כן דין יו"ד חרבים להיות מלא[56] כמו שכתבתי בדבור ה', ועל לְהוֹרִיד אעפ"י שהוא מלא דמלא, לא נמסר מאומה, כי כן דין ב' הנחים האלה להיות מלא, כמו שכתבתי בדבור ג' שהוי"ו הבא במקום יו"ד פ"א הפעל דינה להיות מלא:

וכן החירק שאחריו נח נראה בסוף המלה דינה על הרוב מלא, ובפרט בבנין הפעיל, כמו שכתבתי בדבור ח' ע"ש; אבל אם שניהם חסרים, אעפ"י שהאחד מהן מאותן שדרכן לחיות חסר, כמו שכתבתי בדבור ג', מכל מקום נמסר עליו חסר דחסר, כמו וְנֶעְדְּרוּתִיהָ הֹלְכֻת (שמות ב') יֹשְׁבֻת בבית אחד, ודומיהן ע"ש:

ובמלה שהראשון מלא והשני חסר או להפך, כמו גְּדֹלוֹת וְנוֹרָאֹת, הנה על גדולות נמסר

---

[55] In the recensions of the Massorah, printed in the Basel and Amsterdam editions of the Rabbinic Bibles, the remark is that הקמוֹתי 1 Sam. xv. 13, is one of the three instances in which it has the tone of the penultima (כ' מלעל), and the Massorah marginalis on Gen. ix. 17, gives the three instances as follows:— Gen. ix. 17; Exod. vi. 4; 1 Sam. xv. 13.

[56] The words להיות מלא *to be plene*, are erroneously omitted in the Sulzbach edition.

[1 Chron. xvii. 21], they only remarked on גְּלַת *defective*, but not *defective and plene*, because it is the law for *Cholem* of the plural to be written fully; whilst on נוֹרָאֹת *wonderful*, they simply remarked *defective*, but not *plene and defective*, because the *Vav*, which is written fully, stands for the radical *Jod*, which, according to rule, is *plene*, as I have explained all in Section iii. *Vide supra*, p. 148, &c.

There are some words with one or two quiescents, which are either *defective* or *plene*, and do not belong to those which are usually *plene* or *defective*; and yet the Massorites made no remark on them whatever. This arises from the fact that the rule has already been stated on the words in question in another place. Thus, for instance, the Massorites give the general rule, saying, that "תּוֹלְדֹת *generations*, always wants the second *Vav*, except in two instances, where it is written entirely *plene*; in one instance, where it is entirely *defective*; and in three instances, where it is *defective and plene*." [57] Hence there was no necessity for them to mark תּוֹלְדֹת *plene defective* in every passage where it occurs, since the first general rule is sufficient.

The same is the case with the word אֲבֹתֵיכֶם *your fathers*, on which they remark, "throughout the Pentateuch it is *defective of Vav*, and has *Jod* written fully, except in one instance where it is written אֲבוֹתֵיכֶם entirely fully, and in another instance where it is אֲבֹתְכֶם, with *Vav*

---

[57] There is a great difference of opinion among the Massorites as to the reading of the word in question, in the different passages of the Scriptures. The Massorah marginalis on Gen. ii. 4, remarks as follows:— תילדות ב׳ מלאים דמלאי וסי׳ אלה תולדות השמים והארץ. אלה תולדות פרץ. וחד חסר דחסי אלה תלדת יצמעאל וג׳ כה׳. תדרות עשו אבי אדר ושל אדהריו אלה תלדות יעקב ושאו אוריתא תולדות כתיב. *The word* תולדות *is twice entirely* PLENE, *viz.*, Gen. ii. 4, Ruth. iv. 8; *once entirely* DEFECTIVE, *viz.* Gen. xxv. 12; *and thrice it wants the first* VAV, *viz.*, Gen. xxxvi. 1, 9; xxxvii. 2; *whilst in all other passages throughout the Pentateuch it is written with the first* VAV, *and without the second.* Another recension of the Massorah, given in the Massorah finalis under the letter Jod, p. 35 b, col. 2, is as follows:— מן זה ספר תלדות אדם עד תולדת יצחק תכיב במ״א תלדות אדם. ומן תולדת יצחק עד סופא דסיפרא תלדות כתיב במ״ב תלדת עשו חסר דחסר תלדת ישמעאל וב׳ כתיב תולדות של דמל אלה תולדות השמים ואלה תולדות פרץ וג׳ כתבי תלדות תלדות עשו הוא אדום ושל אהרן אבי אדום אלה תלדות יעקב, *from* Gen. v. 1 *to* xxv. 19, *it is written without the second* VAV, *except in one place, viz.*, v. 1, *where it has the second* VAV *and not the first; from* Gen. xxv. 19, *to the end of the book, it is written with the second* VAV *and without the first, except in two instances, viz.*, Gen. xxxvi. 1, xxv. 12, *where it is entirely* DEFECTIVE; *in two passages, viz.*, Gen. ii. 4, Ruth iv. 18, *where it is entirely* PLENE, *and three passages, viz.* Gen. xxxvi. 1, 9, xxvi. 19. It will be seen that Gen. xxv. 19 is counted twice.

plene and *Jod* defective;"[58] hence there was no more any necessity to mark אֲבֹתֵיכֶם *defective and plene* in every single passage where it occurs in the Pentateuch. Thus, also, they counted the expression אֲבוֹתֵיכֶם *your fathers*, both in *plene* and *defective*, in all the other books of the Scriptures; and on those which do not come within this rubric they made no remark whatever. Moreover, there are some words which are classified in their *defectives* and *plenes* according to each book of the Scriptures; and some are classified according to the Law, the Prophets, and the Hagiographa.

☞ The general rule is, that, when a word occurs with two quiescents, and one of them, or both, are either *defective* or *plene*, and if there is no Massoretic remark whatever thereon, you may then take it for granted that that is because the law connected therewith had already been stated, and you will find it if you seek for it. I shall, however, recur again to this subject in the Second Part, Section ix.

וא' כתיב אֲבוֹתָם מלא וי"ו וחסר יו"ד,[58] ולכן כל חכתובים בתורה אֲבֹתֶיכָם, אין צריך למסור עליהם חסר מלא; וכן בכל ספר וספר נמנין אֲבוֹתֵיכֶם המלאים והחסרים, ועל שאר שאינו בכלל ההוא לא נמסר מאומה; וכן יש מלות אחרות שנחלקו בחסרונם ובמלואם לפי ספרי המקרא, ויש נחלקים לתורה ולנביאים ולכתובים:

☞ והכלל כשתמצא מלה שיש בה ב' נחין, ואחד מהן או שניהם חסרים או מלאים, ולא נמסר עליהן מאומה, תדע שהוא בעבור איזה כלל שנתן בהם כבר, ודוק ותמצא, ועוד אדבר מאלה בלוחות שניות במאמר ט': וכאשר יהיו במלה ג' נחים באמצע המלה, קצתן מלאים וקצתן חסרים, כמו וְהֵיטִבוֹתִי מראשותיכם (יחזקאל ל"ו) שחסר יו"ד סימן החפעיל אחר הטי"ת, והראוי וְהֵטִיבוֹתִי, והנה היה ראוי לחיות נמסר עליו מלא יו"ד קדמאה וחסר יו"ד תנינא ומלא וי"ו, ולקצר הלשון לא נמסר עליו רק לית, וכן כתיב, או וכתיב כן; וכן על ארפא מְשֻׁבֹתֵיכֶם (ירמיה ג') לא זכרו לא חסר ולא מלא אלא כן כתיב, וכן וַיְשִׁבוּם במקום חוה, נמסר עליו כן כתיב:

ודע כשיחיו בתיבה ג' נחים ושלשתן מלאים, לא נמסר עליה מלא דמלא, אלא כלו מלא, כמו וַהֲשִׁיבוֹתִיךָ בדרך אשר באת,

On a word which has three quiescents, some of which are *plene* and some *defective*—as וְהֵיטִבוֹתִי and *I shall do good* [Ezek xxxvi. 11], which wants *Jod* after *Teth*, indicating the *Hiphil*, for it ought to be הֵטִיבוֹתִי—the proper Massoretic remark should have been "the first *Jod* is *plene*, the second *Jod* is *defective*, and the *Vav* is *plene*." But for the sake of brevity the Massorites simply remark, "it has no parallel," "it is thus written," or "it is written thus."

The same is the case with the word מְשֻׁבֹתֵיכֶם *your backslidings*, [Jerem. iii. 22], on which the Massorites neither mentioned *plene* nor *defective*, but say this is the textual reading; and with וַיְשִׁבוּם *and He made them dwell* [1 Sam. xii. 8], on which they simply remark, "it is written so."

Notice, that when a word has three quiescents, and all three are *plene*, the Massorites do not remark on it *entirely plene*, but "*all plene;*" as on וַהֲשִׁיבוֹתִיךָ *and I will turn thee back* [2 Kings xix. 28], וּתְפוּצוֹתֵיכֶם

---

[58] In Exod. iii. 13, אבותיכם is entirely *plene*, and in Deut. i. 11 it has *Vav* but wants *Jod*. Comp. Massorah marginalis on Exod iii. 13.

and your dispersion [Jerem. xxv. 84], וַהֲבִיאוֹתִים and I will bring them [Isa. lvi. 7], &c.; also when all these three 'are defective, as וַיֹּרִדֻהוּ and they brought him down [1 Kings i. 53], הֲבֵאֹנֻם we have brought them [Numb. xxxii. 17], &c.; the Massorites did not remark on them *entirely defective*, but " all defective." In some Codices they are marked, " this is the textual reading," but the former is more generally used.

SECTION IX.—Hitherto I have explained the law of the *defectives* and *plenes* with regard to the letters *Vav* and *Jod*; I shall now explain the rule of the letters *Aleph* and *He*. Know, then, that *Aleph* is frequently either quiescent or wanting in the middle or at the end of some words in certain places, and that there is no parallel for these in other places. Thus, for example, שְׁלָתֵךְ *thy petition* [1 Sam. i. 17], מָלוּ *they filled* [Ezek. xxviii. 16], וַתְּזֻרֵנִי *and thou hast girded me* [2 Sam. xxii. 40], &c.; there are seventeen such instances, and they only occur in the Prophets and Hagiographa.[59] There are also five instances to be found in the Pentateuch, viz., מֵחֲטוֹ *from sinning* [Gen. xx. 6], וְנִטְמֵתֶם *and ye shall be defiled* [Levit. xi. 43], וְקָרָהוּ *and it shall befall him*, in Pericope *Va-jigash* [Gen. xliv. 29]; מָצָאתִי *I have found*, in Pericope *Behaaloscha* [Numb. xi. 11]; לְחַטָּת *for a sin offering*, in Pericope *Shelach* [Numb. xv. 24]; מֵרֵשִׁית *from the beginning*, in Pericope *Ekeb* [Deut. xi. 12].[60] Now I wonder why they did not count these with the other

[59] The Massorah only gives sixteen words, which respectively occur in one place with silent *Aleph* or altogether without *Aleph*, and have no parallel in other places. They are as follows:—

שלחך	. . . 1 Sam. i. 17	פלטר	. . 2 Kings xvi. 17	הסורים	. . Eccl. iv. 14
חטאים	. . . 1 Sam. xiv. 33	סלנסר	. . 1 Chron. v. 26	השטות	. . Nehem. iii. 13
ותזרני	. . . 2 Sam. xxii. 40	מלו	. . Ezek. xxviii. 16	קרוא	. . Esther v. 12
להשות	. . . 2 Kings xix. 25	נשו	. . Ps. cxxxix. 20	שירה	. . 1 Chron. xii. 38
וירשו	. . . 2 Kings ii. 22	ונשו	. . Ezek. xxxix. 26	קראים	. . Ps. xcix. 6
		משטו	. . Job xli. 7		

They are enumerated in the Massorah marginalis on 2 Kings xvi. 7. In the Massorah finalis, where under the letter *Aleph*, p. 1, col. 2, they are also mentioned, it is erroneously stated that there are *seventeen* instances, which has undoubtedly occasioned the error in our text. These instances are also given in the *Ochla Ve-Ochla*, section cxcix. pp. 43, 123, where one passage, viz. 1 Chron. v. 26, is wanting.

[60] For the division of the Pentateuch into fifty-four Pericopes, for hebdomadal lessons, see above, p. 135, note 138. *Vajigash* (ויגש) is the eleventh section, and comprises Gen. xliv. 18—xlvii. 27; *Behaaloscha* (בהעלותך) is the thirty-sixth section, and comprises Numb. viii. 1—xii. 16; *Shelach* (שלח), more fully *Shelach Lecha* (שלח לך), is the thirty-seventh section, and comprises Numb. xiii. 1—xv. 41; whilst *Ekeb* (עקב) is the forty-sixth section, and comprises Deut. vii. 12—xi. 25.

seventeen; thus registering them all in one list of twenty-two words with *Aleph defective* in the Bible.

Again, there are seventeen words in which the reverse is the case, wherein the *Aleph* is audible, contrary to their normal form in other passages, which the Massorites call *Maphkin Aleph;* as לְצֹנַאֲכֶם *for your sheep* [Numb. xxxii. 24], נָאוָה *comely* [Ps. xciii. 5], כְּמוֹצְאֵת *as one finding* [Song of Songs viii. 10], &c.[61] There are also forty-eight words with a silent *Aleph* in the middle of the word; as הָאסַפְסֻף *the mixed multitude* [Numb. xi. 4], וַיִּאָצֶל *and he separated* [Numb. xi. 25], &c.[62] Now on all these *Alephs* the Massorites never remark, *Aleph omitted*, or *Aleph written fully*, or *the Aleph is audible*, or *the Aleph is silent*, but simply state "*Maphkin Aleph*," or "*Non-Maphkin Aleph*."

חי"ז ויהיו כ"ב דחסרי אל"ף בקריא:

וכן י"ז מלין להפך שתנוע בהן האלף שלא כדין חברותיהן, וקורין לחן מפקין אל"ף, כנון ונדרוֹרת לְצֹנַאֲכֶם, נָאוָה קדש, כְּמוֹצְאֵת שלום; [61] וכן מ"ח מלין דכריבין אל"ף באמצע התיבה ולא קריין, כמו וְהָאסַפְסֻף, וַיִּאָצֶל מן הרות (במדבר י"א) וכו', [62] והנה על כל אלה האלפין לא נמסר חסר אל"ף, או מלא אל"ף, או קרי אלף, או לא קרי אל"ף, רק מפקין אל"ף, או לא מפקין אל"ף:

---

[61] The seventeen words which respectively occur only once with audible *Aleph*, and have no parallel in the other places, are as follows:—

ואביאסף	. . Exod. vi. 24	בלואי	. . Jerem. xxxviii. 12	נאוה	. . Ps. xciii. 5
תביאו	. Levit. xxiii. 17	באוש	. . Amos iv. 10	אזורעי	. . Job xxxi. 22
לצנאכם	. Numb. xxxii. 24	במלאכות	. . Hag. i. 13	רבאות	. . Dan. xi. 12
אדר .	. . 1 Kings xi. 17	ואשי	. . 1 Chron. ii. 13	כנאות	. Nehem. xii. 44
אסכים	. Jerem. xxv. 3	מלאכות	1 Chron. xxviii. 19	כמוצאת	Song of Songs viii.10
ובאזרוע	. Jerem. xxxii. 21	הערביאים	2 Chron. xvii. 11		

They are enumerated in the Massorah finalis under the letter *Aleph*, p. 1, col. 2, and are mentioned in the Massorah marginalis on Exodus xviii. 13, where a reference is given to the Massorah on Ps. xxx., in which place, however, nothing is to be found. They are also given in the *Ochla Ve-Ochla*, section cxcviii. pp. 43, 123.

[62] The words which respectively occur in one place with a silent *Aleph* in the middle of the word, and which have no parallel, are as follows:—

תאסון	. Exod. v. 7	רסאתי	. . 2 Kings ii. 21	ורצאתי	. . Ezek. xliii. 27
והאספסף	. Numb. xi. 4	רסאנו	. . Jerem. li. 9	ואענה	. . 1 Kings xi. 39
ויאצל	. . Numb. xi. 25	ונראו	. . Ezek. xlvii. 8	ואעשר	. . Zech. xi. 5
מטאת	. Deut. xxiv. 10	בראוך	. . 2 Kings xx. 12	קאם	. . Hos. x. 14
מראון	. Josh. xii. 20	מארת	. . Isa. x. 33	ארבאל	. . Hos. x. 14
בארומה	. Judg. ix. 41	כאביר	. . Isa. x. 13	ואמאסאך	. . Hos. iv. 6
בלאי	. Judg. iv. 21	הבאיש	. . Isa. xli. 25	מארור	. . Joel ii. 6
פלאי	. Judg. xiii. 18	ויאת	. . Jerem. ii. 13	מארור	. . Nahum ii. 11
חטאים	. 1 Sam. xiv. 33	בארות	. . Jerem. ii. 13	דאת	. . Ps. lxxxix. 11
ויאסף	. 1 Sam. xviii. 29	מאסיך	. . Jerem. xxx. 16	ותהדאונני	. . Job xix. 2
הלאמה	. 2 Sam. x. 17	השאוות	. . Ezek. xvi. 57	מאום	. . Job xxxi. 7
המלאכים	. 2 Sam. xi. 1	מאסך	. . Ezek. xxi. 6	מאום	. . Dan. i. 4
ויראו	. 2 Sam. xi. 24	השאטים	. Ezek. xxviii. 24	בודאם	. . Nehem. vi. 8
המראים	. 2 Sam. xi. 24	השאטים	. Ezek. xxviii. 26	נאשים	. . Nehem. v. 11
כבאר	. 2 Sam. xxiii. 15	באר	. . Ezek. ix. 8	למואל	. Nehem. xii. 38
סבאר	. 2 Sam. xxiii. 16	באר	. . Ezek. ix. 8	דאג	. . Nehem. xiii. 16
הבאר	. 2 Sam. xxiii. 20	ושטאתיך	. . Ezek. xxxix. 2		

They are enumerated in the Massorah marginalis on Ezekiel i. 1; Job i. 1; and in the Massorah finalis under the letter *Aleph*, p. 1 a, cols. 2 and 3. It will be seen that, instead of there being forty-eight, as mentioned in the heading of the Rubric, and by Levita, there are fifty. They are also given with some slight variation in the *Ochla Ve-Ochla*, section ciii. pp. 29, 97, &c.

The meaning of מפקין is *brought out, uttered, pronounced, audible*. So the Chaldee renders מוֹצִיא *uttering, pronouncing* [Prov. x. 18], by מפיק. I have already explained in the *Poetical Dissertations*, Sect iv., that מפיק is only applied to the letters *Vav, Jod*, and *He* when pronounced by the mouth at the end of a word, since the *Aleph* is never pronounced at the end of a word. Hence, when the Massorah uses *Maphkin Aleph*, it denotes that it has the vowel-point, as in the above-named instances. In the *Massorah Parva*, however, they are marked *defective* or *plene*, yet not marked *defective* or *plene* absolutely; but it is distinctly stated, *Aleph defective*, or *Aleph plene*. The same law obtains with regard to *He*, as I shall explain in the following Section.

There are some words in which *Aleph* is quiescent at the end of the word, as in the Register of twelve words, viz., אָבוּא *they willed* [Isa. xxviii. 12], הֲהָלְכוּא *who went* [Josh. x. 24], נָקִיא *innocent* [Jonah i. 14], &c;[63] on these the Massoretic mark is either, *Aleph redundant*, or *Aleph not to be read*. There is also another Register of seventeen words, with quiescent *Aleph* at the end of the word standing for *He*; as זָרָא *loathsome* (Numb. xi. 20), נִבְּאָה *it was erected* [Ezek. xxxi. 5], שֵׁנָא *sleep* [Ps. cxxvii. 2],[64] on every one of which the Massorites remark, "*no parallel with Aleph.*"

ופירוש מפקין מוציאין, תרגום של ומוציא דבה דמפיק סיבא, וככר בארחי בפרק שירה בשיר ד' שמפקין לא נאמר כי אם על אותיות וי"ה כשמוציאים אותם מן הפה בסוף התיבה, אבל האל"ף אין מוציאין אותה מן הפה בסוף התיבה לעולם; אבל כשנמצא במסורת מפקין אל"ף ר"ל שהיא בנקודה כדלעיל, אבל במסרה קמנה נמסר עליהן הסר או מלא, אבל לא חסר, או לא מלא סתם, רק בפירוש הסר אל"ף או מלא אל"ף; וכן דין חח"א כאשר אבאר ברבור שאחד זה:

ויש מלות שתנוח בהן האל"ף בסוף הרתיבה, כנון שימה אחרת מן י"ב מלין דכתיבין אל"ף ולא קרי, כמו ולא אָבְאָא שמוע, הֲהָלְכוּא אתון,[63] שׁוּד וּמִרְיָא, דם נָקֵא וכולי, ונמסר עליהם יתיד אל"ף, או לא קרי אל"ף; ועוד שימה אחת מן י"ז מלין שיש בהן אל"ף נחה בסוף התיבה והיא במקום ח"א, וחיח לכם לְזָרָא (במדבר י"א), נִבְּאָה קוֹמְתוֹ, לידידו שֵׁנָא וכו',[64] ונמסרן על כל אחת לית כתיב אל"ף:

[63] The twelve words which have quiescent *Aleph* at the end are as follows:—

רשׁוא	. . Numb. xiii. 9	רצוא	. . Ezek. i. 14	ננוא	. . Dan. iii. 29
והלכוא	. . Josh. x. 24	ואתוקרהא	. . Ezek. xli. 15	ושיציא	. . Ezra vi. 15
הקליא	. . 1 Sam. xvii. 17	נקיא	. . Jonah i. 14	ישׂוא	. . Ezra iii. 7
אבוא	. . Isa. xxviii. 12	נקיא	. . Joel iv. 19	ארעא	. . Dan. ii. 39

They are enumerated in the Massorah marginalis on Numb. xiii. 9; Ezekiel i. 1; Proverbs i. 1; Ezra i. 1; and in the *Ochla Ve-Ochla*, section civ., pp. 30, 98.

[64] The seventeen words which respectively have in one place a quiescent *Aleph* at the end of the word, and which have no parallel in any other place, are as follows:—

לורא	. . Numb. xi. 20	שׁנא	. . Ps. cxxvii. 2	כלא	. . Ezek. xxxvi. 5
אלמא	. . Numb. xxxii. 37	למא	. . Ezra iv. 22	יורא	. . Prov. xi. 25
ארצא	. . 1 Kings xvi. 9	בחמא	. . Dan. xi. 44	תבא	. . Prov. i. 10
אלא	. . 1 Kings iv. 18	כמסרא	. . Lament. iii. 12	הרא	. . 1 Chron. v. 26
נבהא	. . Ezek. xxxi. 5	נבטא	. . 1 Chron. ii. 49	כלא	. . Prov. xvi. 30
ושׂא	. . Job xxxviii. 11	מרא	. . Ruth i. 20		

They are enumerated in the Massorah finalis under the letter *Aleph*, p. 1 *a*, cols. 3 and 4. The heading, however, of the Rubric does not give the number, nor does the Massorah marginalis, on Ezekiel xxxi. 5; xxxvi. 5; and Ruth i. 20, where reference is made to them; nor say how many there are belonging to this class.

173

SECTION X.—The *He* is never quiescent except at the end of a word, in four different ways, which are symbolised by the expression שְׁנָתְ֒ךָ *thy sleep*, being the acrostic of, 1. שֹׁרֶשׁ *the root;* 2. נקבה *the feminine;* 3. תוספת *formative addition;* and 4. כנוי *suffix*. i. By radix is meant the radical *He* of verbs ל-ה, as עָשָׂה *to work,* בָּנָה *to build,* &c. ii. By the feminine gender, as פָּקְדָה *she visited,* שָׁמְרָה *she kept,* צְדָקָה *righteousness,* בְּרָכָה *blessing,* &c. About these two classes the Massorites say nothing. iii. By formative addition is meant the *He* added to the end of a word, which consists of two kinds, additions to verbs and additions to nouns. Additions to verbs we have in the imperative singular; as שִׁמְעָה *hear,* סְלָחָה *forgive,* הַקְשִׁיבָה *hearken* [Dan. ix. 19]; in the infinitive פְּשֹׁטָה *to strip,* עֹרָה *to make bare,* חֲגֹרָה *to gird* [Isa. xxxii. 11]; and in the future, with *Aleph* and *Nun* of אי״תן; as אֶזְכְּרָה *I shall remember,* אֶשְׁפְּכָה *I shall pour out* [Ps. xlii. 5]; נֵדְעָה *we shall know,* נִרְדְּפָה *we shall pursue* [Hosea vi. 3], &c.; and about these the Massorites say nothing. The additions to the nouns are of two kinds. Of the first are such words as מַעְלָה *upwards,* מַטָּה *downwards,* לַיְלָה *night,* נַחֲלָה *inheritance;* their distinguishing mark is that they are always *Milel;* and about these the Massorites speak but very little. The second class consists of those words which have *He* added to the end instead of *Lamed,* as our Rabbins of blessed memory remarked, "every word which should have *Lamed* at the commencement takes *He* at the end."[65]

הדבור העשירי : לא תנוח חה"א לעולם דק בסוף התיבה לבד וחן של ד' מינין, וסימן וערבת שנתך פי' שרש. נקבה. תוספת. כנוי: שרש ר"ל חה"א השרשית מפעלי נחי למ"ד חה"א, כמו עָשָׂה, בָּנָה ודומיהון; נקבה כמו פָּקְדָה, שָׁמְרָה, צְדָקָה, בְּרָכָה ודומיהן. ומן ב' חמינין האלה לא דברו דבר. תוספת ר"ל ח"א הנוספת בסוף, והיא של ב' מינין, הנוספת בפעלים, והנוספת בשמות. הנוספת בפעלים כמו בצווי יחיד י"י שִׁמְעָה, י"י הַקְשִׁיבָה, י"י סְלָחָה, וְעֹרָה חֲגֹרָה; ובעתידים עם אל״ף ונו״ן האיח״ן כמו אלה אֶזְכְּרָה וְאֶשְׁפְּכָה, נֵדְעָה נִרְדְּפָה ודומיהן, לא דברו מהן דבר; והנוספת בשמות היא של ב' מינין האחד כמו מִעְלָה, מַטָּה, לַיְלָה, נַחֲלָה, וסימנם שהם תמיד מלעיל, ומזה דברו דק מעט, והמן חשני הם החא"י'ן חנוספת בסוף החיבה במקום למ"ד, כמו שאמרו רז"ל כל תיבה הצריכה למ"ד בתחילה חמיל לה ה"א בסופה : [65]

[65] The grammatical rule to which Levita refers is recorded both in the Babylonian and the Jerusalem Talmuds as having been propounded by R. Nehemiah. In the Babylonian Talmud (*Jebamoth,* 13 *b)* it is as follows :— ר' נחמיה אומר כל תיבה שצריכה—למ"ד בתחילתה הטיל לה הכתוב ה"א בסופה, *R. Nehemiah sayeth: Every word which requires Lamed at the beginning of the Scripture gives He at the end.* In the Jerusalem Talmud, however (*Jebamoth* i. 6, p. 3 *a*, ed. Graetz), it is תני בשם רבי נחמיה כל דבר שהוא צריך למ"ד מתחילתו ולא ניתן לו, ניתן לו ה"א בסוף כגון לחוץ חוצה, לשעיר שעירה, לסוכות סוכותה, *It is propounded, in the name of R. Nehemiah, that every word which ought to have Lamed at the beginning, and has it not, takes He at the end,* as חוצה [Deut. xxv. 5] *instead of* לחוץ; שעירה [Judg. iii. 26] *instead of* לשעיר; סוכותה [Exod. xii. 37] *instead of* לסכות. It will be seen that Levita's quotation is from the Babylon Talmud; but since the Jerusalem Talmud, which contains the original rule, as is evident from the whole complexion of the passage, has not the expression תיבה, Levita's animadversions are nugatory. Equally feeble is his stricture on the word כל, since the instances which are adduced in the Talmud itself to illustrate this rule plainly show that R. Nehemiah did not mean to extend it to *every* word, but applied it to those denoting *locality*. For the use of the *local He,* see Gesenius' Grammar, section xc.

Now I have to ask two questions about this remark. The first is about their saying תיבה, which embraces nouns, particles, and verbs, whereas the *He* which stands for the *Lamed* at the beginning only occurs in nouns. The second question is about the word "*every*," the use of which is not justifiable in this place, since all nouns cannot take this *He*, except those which we find in the Bible, and these are not one in a thousand; and since they are chiefly found in names of places, and have been counted by the Massorites, as מִצְרַיְמָה to Egypt, which occurs twenty-eight times;[66] בָּבֶלָה to *Babylon*, twenty-nine times;[67] יְרוּשָׁלַיְמָה to *Jerusalem*, five times;[68] חֶבְרוֹנָה to *Hebron*, nine times.[69] There are also to be found a few others; as הָאֹהֱלָה to the tent, eight times;[70] הַבַּיְתָה to the house, eighteen times;[71] הַמִּזְבֵּחָה to the altar, five times;[72] אַרְצָה to the land, in connection with כְּנַעַן Canaan, eight times *plene*.[73] The Massorites did not count the other

והנה יש לי לחקשות על זה המאמר ב׳
קושיורת, האחרת, באמרם כל תיבה, ומלת
תיבה כוללת שם, ומלח, ופעל ; והנה הה״א
שהיא במקום למ״ד בתחלתה, לא תבא רק
על השמות ; והקושיא הב׳ באמרם כל תיבה,
ומלת כל לא חצדק במקום חוה כי לא נוכל
להמיל זאת הה״א בכל השמות, כי אם מה
שמצאנו מהן בפסוק, ואינן באחד מיני אל״ח,
ובפרט בשמות מקומות נמצאת לרוב, ובעלי
המסורה מנאום, כמו מצרימה כ״ח,[66] בבלה
כ״מ,[67] ירושלימה ה׳,[68] חברונה מ׳,[69]
ומעטים נמצאים משאר שמות, כמו האחלה
ח׳,[70] הביתה י״ח,[71] המזבחה ה׳,[72] ארצה
כנען ח׳ מלאים,[73] ולא מנו שאר ארצה

---

[66] The twenty-eight instances in which מצרימה occurs with *He* at the end are, Gen. xii. 10, 11, 14; xxvi. 2; xxxvii. 25, 28; xxxix. 1; xli. 57; xlv. 4; xlvi. 3, 4. 7, 8, 9, 26, 27; xlviii. 5; l. 14: Exod. i. 1; iv. 21; xiii. 17: Numb. xiv. 3, 4; xx. 15: Deut. x. 22; xvii. 16; xxvi. 5: 2 Chron. xxxvi. 4. They are enumerated in the Massorah marginalis on 2 Chron. xxxvi. 4.

[67] The twenty-nine instances in which בבלה occurs are, Isa. xxxix. 6: 2 Kings xxiv. 15 (twice), 16; xxv. 13: Isa. xliii. 14: Jerem. xx. 4, 5; xxvii. 16, 18, 20, 22; xxviii. 4; xxix. 1, 3, 4, 15, 20; xxxix. 7; xl. 1, 7; lii. 11, 17: Ezek. xii. 13; xvii. 12, 20: 2 Chron. xxxiii. 11; xxxvi. 6, 10. They are enumerated in the Massorah finalis, p. 16 a, cols 3, 4.

[68] The five passages in which ירושלימה occurs are, 1 Kings x. 2; 2 Kings ix. 28; Isa. xxxvi. 2; 2 Chron. xxxii. 9. They are enumerated in the Massorah marginalis on Isa. xxxvi. 2, with the remark that in four of the passages it is *defective*.

[69] The five passages in which חברונה occurs are, Joshua x. 39: 2 Sam. ii. 1; v. 1, 3; xv. 9: 1 Chron. xi. 1, 3; xii. 23, 38. They are enumerated in the Massorah marginalis on Joshua x. 39.

[70] The eight passages in which האהלה occurs are, Gen. xviii. 6; xxiv. 67: Exod. xviii. 7; xxxiii. 8, 9; Numb. xi. 26: Josh. vii. 22: Judges iv. 18. They are enumerated in the Massorah marginalis on Judges iv. 18.

[71] The eighteen instances in which הביתה occurs are, Gen. xix. 10; xxiv. 32; xxxix. 11; xliii. 16, 26 (twice): Exod. ix. 19: Josh. ii. 18: Judg. xix. 15, 18 : 1 Sam. vi. 7 : 2 Sam. xiii. 7; xiv. 31; xvii. 20: 1 Kings xiii. 7, 15; xvii. 23: 2 Kings iv. 32; ix. 6. They are enumerated in the Massorah marginalis on 1 Kings xiii. 15.

[72] This must surely be a mistake, since there are upwards of thirty instances in which המזבחה occurs, viz.— Exod. xxix. 13, 18, 25 : Levit. i. 9, 13, 15, 17 ; ii. 2, 9; iii. 5, 11, 16; iv. 19, 26, 31, 35; v. 12; vii. 5, 31; viii. 16, 21, 28; ix. 10, 14, 20; xiv. 20; xvi. 25: Numb. v. 26: 2 Chron. xxix. 22 (thrice), 24. The Massorah finalis enumerates them under the letter *Zajin*, p. 30 a, col. 1.

[73] The eight passages in which ארצה כנען occur conjointly are, Gen. xi. 31; xii. 5 (twice); xxxi. 18; xlii. 29; xlv. 17; l. 13: Numb. xxxv. 10. The entire list is nowhere given, though the Massorahs marginalis on Numbers xxxv. 10, and finalis, p. 11 a, col. 4, refer to each other for it.

instances in which אַרְצָה occurs, because this form is the most frequent. Accordingly, the Rabbins ought simply to have said, "there are some nouns which ought to begin with *Lamed*, but take *He* at the end instead." It may, perhaps, be replied, that the word כֹּל signifies *rule*, since they use it so in another place; "one cannot infer from rules." The additional *He* is also to be found after *Kametz*, under *Tav*, *Kaph*, and *Nun*, at the end of a word, as I shall explain hereafter. I have already shown, in Section v., that a vowel-point does not occur at the end of a word, except under *Tav*, *Kaph*, and *Nun*, which have sometimes *Kametz*, and are not followed by *He*.

Tav is the *Tav* with *Kametz* indicating the singular, which is to be found at the end of the preterite; as דָּרַשְׁתָּ חָקַרְתָּ שָׁאָלְתָּ, *thou hast enquired, thou hast searched, thou hast asked* [Deut. xiii. 15], &c.; by far the greater majority of them are without *He*, and those which have it are but few, as גַּרְתָּה *thou hast sojourned* [Gen. xxi. 23], נֵאַרְתָּה *thou hast made void* [Ps. lxxxix. 40], הִסְכַּנְתָּה *thou art acquainted* [Ps. xxxix. 3], &c. On these the Massorites always remark, *He plene*, but on those which have no *He* they never remark, *He defective*, except on the word נָתַתָּ *thou hast given*, on which the Massorites note "it occurs twenty-nine with *He defective*."[74]

☞ It might be asked, why they give the number of the *defectives* of this word, and not that of other words which have *He defective*, and which are very many. And since the *defectives* are the greater number, ought they not rather to have counted all the instances in which נָתַתָּ *thou hast given*, וְנָתַתָּ *and thou hast given*, occur as *plene*, which are the fewer in number? The reply is, that they have done it, because the *Tav* has *Daqesh forte*, for it is after a short vowel; and it is not normal for *Daqesh forte* to be at the end of a word, without being

מפני רבויים: והכלל שהיה להם לומר, ויש שם הצדיך למ״ד בתחילתו והמיל לו ה״א בסופו, ואולי יש לישב מלת כל כמו שאמרו במקום אחר אין למדין מן הכללות; והנה יש הה״י״ן חנוספורת אחד הקמץ שתחרי התי״ו והכ״ף והנו״ן בסוף התיבה כאשר אבאר; כבר כחבתי בדבור ה׳, כי לא תבא נקודה תחת אות בסוף התיבה, רק תחת התי״ו והכ״ף והנו״ן, הבאים לפעמים קמוצים ואין אחריהן ה״א:

התי״ו היא הרת״י הקמוצה המורה על יחיד, נמצא בסוף העוברים, כמו דָרָשְׁתָּ וְחָקַרְתָּ וְשָׁאָלְתָּ ודומיהן רובם בחסרון הה״א מפני רבויום, ויש מעטים נכתבים עם הה״א, כמו גַרְתָּה בה, נֵאַרְתָּה ברית עבדך, דרכי הִסְכַּנְתָּה ודומיחן, ותמיד נמסר עליהן מלא ה״א, אבל על חסרי הה״א לא נמסר עליהן חסרי ה״א לעולם, חוץ על מלת נָתַתָּ נמסר כ״מ חסרים ה״א:[74]

☞ ויש לשאול מה ראו על בכה למנות החחרים מזאת חמלה מכל שאר חסרי ה״א אשר רבו כמו רבו, והלא חן המדובין, והיה ילהם למנות כל נתתה ונתתה המלאים שהן המעוטים: ויש לומר לפי שהתי״ו נדגשת בדנש חזק, שהרי היא אחר תנועה קמנה, ואין דין הדנש החזק להיות בסוף התיבה בלי אות

---

[74] The twenty-nine instances in which נחת occurs without *He*, are as follows:—Gen. xl. 13; Exod. xxv. 16, 21, 26, 30; xxvi. 84; xxviii. 23, 30; xxix. 3, 6, 17; xxx. 16. 18 (twice); xl. 7 (twice), 8; Levit. ii. 15; xxiv. 7; 1 Kings viii. 34, 39; Judg. xv. 18; Ps. lxi. 6; Dan. x. 12; Nehem. ix. 15, 20, 35 (twice). They are enumerated in the Massorah marginalis on Exodus xxv. 21.

followed by either a silent or vocal letter. Hence the *He* after every *Tav* which has *Dagesh forte* at the end of a word, as you see is the case in the other instances, besides the twenty-nine in question. Thus you will also see it in וְהֲמַתָּה *and if thou shalt kill* [Numb. xiv. 15], וָמַתָּה *and thou shalt die* [Ezek. xxviii. 8], שַׁתָּה *thou hast put* [Ps. xc. 8], &c. This, however, is only the case with irregular verbs, as those mentioned above. Thus, also, in the word אַתָּה *thou*, the *He* is added because of the *Dagesh forte*, for which reason the Massorites did not require ever to make it as having *He plene*. But the regular verbs in which the *Tav* is radical, כָּרַת *to cut off*, שָׁבַת *to rest*, שָׁחַת *to destroy*, &c., these have never *He* after *Tav*, though it has *Dagesh forte*, as וְכָרַתָּ *and thou shalt cut down* [Deut. xx. 20], וְנִכְרַתָּ *and thou shalt be cut off* [Obad. 10], הִשְׁבַּתָּ *thou makest to cease* [Ps. cxix. 119], שִׁחַתָּ *thou hast destroyed* [Is. xiv. 20], and are not marked *defective*; the expression הִצְמַתָּה *thou hast destroyed* [Ps. lxxiii. 27], being an exception to this rule, is marked by the Massorites "*He* written fully."

נח או נע אחריו, ולפיכח באה ה"א אחר כל תי"ו חרנושה בדגש חזק בסוף התיבה, כמו כל שאר נָתַתָּה וְנָתַתָּה חוץ מן כ"ט: וכן וְהֵמַתָּה את העם, לשהת יורדוך וָמַתָּה, שַׁתָּה עונותינו לנגדך ורומיהן, חח דווקא בפעלים שאינו שלמים, כמו באלח שזכרתי, וכן מלת אַתָּה הה"א נוספת בעבור הדגש החזק, ואין צריך לטסור על שום אחד מאלה מלא ה"א, אבל בפעלים השלמים שהתי"ו שרשית, כמו בָּרַת, שָׁבַת, שָׁחַת, הם תמיד בלי ה"א אחריהו, אעפ"י שהדגש חזק, כמו על העיר וְכָרַתָּ, וְנִכְרַתָּה לעולם, סנים חִשְׁבַּתָּ, ארצך שִׁחַתָּ וחומיחן, ולא נמסר עליחן חסר, ומלת הִצְמַתָּה כל זונה ממך יוצאת מן הכלל, לכן נמסר עליה מלא ה"א:

והכ"ף חבא בסוף התיבה בנקודה היא חכ"ף הקמוצה לכנוי היחיד הנמצא בפעלים ובשמות ובמלות, כמו חנני מַפְרְךָ וְהִרְבִּתִיךָ נְתַתִּיךָ, ובשמות שׁוֹרְךָ וַחֲמוֹרְךָ וְעַבְדְךָ וַאֲמָתֶךָ סָמוֹךְ, ויש שנכתבו בה"א נוספת והמיד נמסר עליחן מלא ה"א, וכן במסורה כ"א מלין יחידאין. ר"ל שאין לחן דומה דכתיבין בה"א בסוף התיבה כמו וָאֲבָרְכֶכָה לפני י"י (בראשית כ"ז), לאות על יָדֶכָה, וּבְכָה ובעמך, תצבת עֹמְכָה וכו', וקראו לחן כה כ"א ודאין או ודיא, עיין במאמר ט' ונמצאים שיש לחן זוג

---

75 The whole sentence בלי אות נח או נע אחריו ולסיכך באה ה"א אחר כל תי"ו הדגושה בדגש חזק בסוף התיבה, *without being followed either by a silent or vocal letter, and hence the He after every Tav which has Dagesh forte, is entirely omitted in the Sulzbach edition.*

groups, as בּוֹאֲכָה *as thou comest*, six times; יַכֶּכָּה *he shall smite thee*, three times.[76]

The final *Nun*, with *Kametz* at the end of a word, is the *Nun* of the plural feminine, which normally is followed by *He*, as חֲגֹרְנָה *gird ye*, סְפֹדְנָה *lament ye* [Jerem. xlix. 3], צְאֶנָה *go ye out*, וּרְאֶנָה *and see ye* [Song of Songs, iii. 11], וַתָּבֹאנָה *and they came*, וַתִּדְלֶנָה *and they drew* [Exod. ii. 16], &c. There are some words which have *He* omitted; that is, they have final *Nun* with *Kametz*, as לֵכְן *go ye* [Ruth i. 12], וּמְצֶאןָ *and you may find* [Ruth i. 9]; and in the future tense, as תְּהֶיןָ *they shall be* [Deut. xxi. 15], תְּחַיֶּן *ye shall let live* [Exod. i. 19], תַּהֲרֶיןָ *they shall become pregnant* [Gen. xix. 36], תִּגַּשְׁן *they shall approach* [Gen. xxxiii. 6], &c.

☞ This only occurs in irregular verbs, and there is but one instance of it to be found in the regular verb, viz.— תִּלְבָּשְׁן *they shall clothe* [2 Sam. xiii. 18], and the Massorites have marked them all "*He* omitted." The general rule is, that *Tav* and *Kaph*, with *Kametz* at the end of a word, generally want *He*. Hence the Massorites counted the instances in which *He* is *plene*, they being the fewest; whilst in the case of *Nun* with *Kametz* at the end of a word, the *He* being mostly *plene*, they counted the *defectives*.

The *He* suffix is of two kinds. The one is suffix third person feminine, and occurs in three different ways; (*a*), when it is quiescent after *Nun*, with *Kametz* and *Dagesh*, as תַּחְתֶּנָּה *in her place* [Gen. ii. 21]; (*b*), when it has *Kametz*, and is preceded by *Segol*, as וַיִּמְצָאֶהָ *and he*

כמו בואכה ו', יככה נ' : [76]
והנה חנו"ן חקמוצה בסוף התיבה היא נו"ן הרבות שדינה לחיות אחריה ח"א, כמו קטודְנָה, חֲגֹרְנָה, צְאֶנָה וּרְאֶנָה, וַתָּבֹאנָה וַתִּדְלֶנָה וַתְּמַלֶּאנָה, ויש שיבאו בחסרון הה"א, ד"ל בנו"ן פשומח קמוצה, כמו בנותי לָכְן, (רות א') וּמְצֶאןָ, מנוחה, ובעתידים כמו כי תֶהֱיֶיןָ, לאיש שתי נשים; וַתְּחַיֶּן, את הילדים, וַתַּהֲרֶיןָ, שתי בנות לום, וַתִּגַּשְׁן, השפחות וילדיהן :

☞ וזה דווקא בפעלים שאינן שלמים, ולא נמצא רק אחד בשלמים, והוא כי כן תִּלְבָּשְׁן, בנות המלך, ועל כלן נמסר חסר ח"א : והכלל התי"ו וחכ"ף חקמוצה בסוף התיבה על הרוב הסרים ח"א לכך נמנין המלאים ח"א, והנו"ן הקמוצה בסוף התיבה, חה"א על הרוב כתובה לכך נמנין החסרים :

וה"א הכנוי היא ב' מינין, האחת היא כנוי הנקבה הפעולה הנסתרת, ובאה בג' אופנים; האחד כשהיא נחה אחר נו"ן קמוצה ורגושה, כמו ויסגור בשר תַּחְתֶּנָּה (בראשית ב'); וחב' כשהיא נקורה בקמץ וסגול לפניה, כמו וַיִּמְצָאֶהָ מלאך י"י; וחג' כשהיא במפיק אחר

---

[76] The twenty-one words, which have *He* at the end after *Kaph*, of the second person singular masculine, are as follows :—

ואברככה	. .	Gen. xxvii. 7	במה	. .	2 Sam. xxii. 30	לחלכה . . .	Ps. x. 8
ובנכה	. .	Exod. vii. 29	יצאנכה	. .	1 Kings xviii. 12	חלכה . . .	Ps. x. 14
ידכה	. .	Exod. xiii. 16	יעצרכה	. .	1 Kings xviii. 44	כסכה . .	Ps. cxxxix. 5
כמכה	. .	Exod xv. 11	הנכה	. .	2 Kings vii. 2	בכה . . .	Ps. cxli. 8
כמכה	. .	Exod. xv. 11	יענכה	. .	Jerem. vii. 27	יברוככה . .	Ps. cxlv. 10
אתכה	. .	Numb. xxii. 33	בשמכה	. .	Jerem. xxix. 25	תנצרכה . .	Prov. ii. 11
עמכה	. .	1 Sam. i. 26	הראותכה	. .	Ezek. xl. 4	כחכה . .	Prov. xxiv. 10

They are enumerated in the Massorah marginalis on Exod. vii. 29; in the Massorah finalis under the letter *He*, p. 22*a*, col. 2; and in the *Ochla Ve-Ochla*, section xcii., pp. 27, 94. The six instances in which בואכה occurs are, Gen. x. 19 (twice), 30; xiii. 10; xxv. 18; 1 Kings xviii. 46. They are given in the Massorah marginalis on Gen. x. 19. The three passages in which יככה occurs are, Isa. x. 24; Jerem. xl. 15: Ps. cxxi. 6.

found her [Gen. xvi. 7]; and (c), when it has *Mappik*, and is preceded by *Kametz*, as וַיִּסְפָּרָהּ *and he declared it*, הֱכִינָהּ *he searched it*, עֲנָתָהּ *he prepared it* [Job xxviii. 27]; כְּסוּתָהּ *her conjugal right*, כְּסוּתָהּ *her raiment*, שְׁאֵרָהּ *her food* [Exod. xxi. 10]; and רֹאשָׁהּ *her head*, יָדָהּ *her hand*, רַגְלָהּ *her foot;* on all these, and the like, the Massorites do not make any remark. But on those words which have *Mappik* in one place, and are without *Mappik* in another place, they remark, "*no Mappik*;" as בִּזָּהּ *booty* [Ezek. xxix. 19], צֵידָהּ *provision* [Ps. cxxxii. 15], &c. So there are also eleven pairs terminating with *He*, which is once *Mappik* or audible, and once *not-Mappik* or quiescent; as מִכְרָה *sell me* [Gen. xxv. 21], "no parallel, being *Raphe*," whilst the other, מִכְרָה *sell me* [Prov. xxxi. 10], has *Mappik*.[77] There are also eleven words which end with a quiescent *He*, and ought to have an audible *He*; as וַיְּטָחֻמָה *and they daubed it*, [Exod. ii. 3], הֻסָּדָהּ *the foundation thereof* [Exod. ix. 18]; עֲוֺנָה *her sin* [Numb. xv. 31], &c., on each one of these the Massorites remark, "the *He* is not audible," or, "the *He* is feeble."[78]

The second class embraces the *He* which stands for *Vav* masculine, third person, and is preceded by *Cholem;* as בְּרֵעֹה *in its shouting* [Exod. xxxii. 17], שֻׂכֹּה *its hedge* [Lament. ii. 6,] &c. On these the

[77] The eleven pairs, each one of which pair alternately occurs with an audible *He* [=*Mappik*], and with a quiescent *He* [=*Raphe*], are as follows:—

מכרה	Prov. xxxi. 10	מעונה	Deut. xxxiii. 27	לחזה	Ps. xlviii. 14
מכרה	Gen. xxv. 31	נצה	Gen. xl. 14	כבודה	Isa. xxviii. 4
שטרה	Levit. xiii. 20	נצה	Isa. xviii. 5	כבודה	Hos. ix. 10
שטרה	Levit. xiii. 4	ואתננה	Isa. xxiii. 18	חכה	Prov. v. 3
לרבעה	Levit. xviii. 23	לאתננה	Isa. xxiii. 17	חכה	Job xxxii. 4
לרבעה	Levit. xx. 16	רכבה	Nahum ii. 14	טרפה	Job xxxiii. 13
מעונה	Zeph. iii. 7	לרכבה	Ezek. xxvii. 20	טרפה	Job xxxiii. 5
		חילה	Zech. ix. 4		

They are given in the Massorah finalis under the letter *He*, p. 21 b, col. 1, and in the *Ochla Ve-Ochla*, section xliv., pp. 14, 52.

[78] This must be a mistake, since the Massorah gives eighteen words which abnormally have at the end a quiescent *He*. They are as follows:—

ותחמרה	Exod. ii. 3	בבאה	1 Kings xiv. 12	המונה	Ezek. xxxix. 16
הוסדה	Exod. ix. 18	ורחומה	Jerem. xx. 17	למינה	Ezek. xlvii. 10
עונה	Numb. xv. 31	בה	Ezek. xvi. 4	אנחתה	Isa. xxi. 2
שתה	Josh. xix. 13	כאמה	Ezek. xvi. 44	מוסדה	Isa. xxx. 32
חלבה	Judg. i. 31	הלאתנה	Ezek. xxiv. 6	הראשה	Zech. iv. 7
צדה	1 Sam. xx. 20	כלא	Ezek. xxxvi. 5	משכמה	Job xxxi. 22

Indeed Levita seems also to have mistaken the number of words contained in this rubric, in his annotations on Kimchi's Michlol (32 b, ed. Venice), where he says that there are fifteen such words. The list is given in the Massorah finalis under the letter *He*, p. 21 b, cols. 1 and 2, and *Ochla Ve-Ochla*, section xliii., pp. 14, 51.

Massorites simply remark, "this is the textual reading," or, "the textual reading is so;" *ex. gr.*, on אָהֳלֹה *his tent* [Gen. ix. 21], they remark, "four times so written;"[79] הֲמוֹנֹה *his multitude*, "four times so written."[80] In some Codices, however, we find it remarked on אָהֳלֹה, "Read אָהֳלוֹ;" so also on בְּרֵעֹה, it is remarked "Read בְּרֵעוֹ;" and in a few more. But this is a clerical blunder, for we never find that a word which has in the text *He*, with *Cholem*, has in the marginal reading *Vav*. As to the list of fourteen words which have *He* in textual reading, and *Vav* in the marginal reading, to be found in the Massorah, this refers exclusively to *Vav* with *Shurek*; as יִקְרְחָה they shall make bold [Levit. xxi. 5], where the *Keri* is יִקְרְחוּ; likewise שָׁפְכָה they have shed [Deut. xxi. 7], where the *Keri* is שָׁפְכוּ, &c.[81] I shall again refer to these in the Second Part, Section i. By the help of Him, who is the last and the first, I have thus finished Part the First; and shall commence Part the Second, by the aid of that One who has no second.

ודומיהן, לא נמסר עליהן רק כן כתיב, או כתיב כן, כמו אָהֳלֹה ד' כתיבין כן,[79] הֲמוֹנָה ד' כתיבין כן;[80] וביש נוסחאות מצאתי שנמסר על וים אָהֳלֹה אהלו קרי, וכן קול העם בְּרֵעֹה ברעו קרי וכן בקצת האחדים, וכולם מעוותי סופרים, כי לא נמצא לעולם מלח דכחיב בסופה ח"א בחולם וקרי בו"ו, ומה שנמצא במסורת י"ד מלין דכתיבין ה"א וקריין ו"ו חיינו דווקא וי"ו בשורק, כמו לא יִקְרְחָה קרחה הו קרי, ידינו לא שָׁפְכָה כו קרי ודומיהן;[81] ועוד אדבר בם בלוחות שניות במאמר ראשון, בעזרת אל אחדון וראשון, ובכן נשלם החלק הראשון, ואתחיל החלק חשני, בעזרת אחד ואין שני:

[79] The four instances in which אָהֳלֹה occurs are, Gen. ix. 21; xii. 8; xiii. 3; xxxv. 21. They are given in the Massorah marginalis on Gen. ix. 21. The Sulzbach edition has erroneously *seven*.

[80] The four passages in which המונה occurs are, Ezek. xxxi. 18; xxxii. 31, 32; xxxix. 11. The Massorah finalis, under the letter *He*, p. 24 b, col. 2, refers to Ezek. xxxix. for the enumeration of the passages, but they are not to be found in the Massorah marginalis on the chapter in question.

[81] The fourteen words with *He* at the end, which is read and considered as *Vav*, are as follows:—

יקרחה	. . Levit. xxi. 5	נושבה	. . Jerem. xxii. 6	שמכה	. . Ps. lxxiii. 2
שפכה	. . Deut. xxi. 7	היה	. . . Jerem. l. 6	המורמרה	. . Job xvi. 16
נשברה	. . 1 Kings xxii. 49	ינה	. . Ezek. xxiii. 43	עדינה	. . Lament. iv. 17
עלה	. . 2 Kings xiv. 10	שממה	. . Ezek. xxxv. 12	שלה	. . . Dan. iii. 29
נצתה	. . Jerem. ii. 15	יהיה	. . Ezek. xxxvii. 22		

They are enumerated in the Massorah marginalis on 2 Kings xxiv. 10, and on Lament. iv. 17; and in the *Ochla Ve-Ochla*, section cxiii. pp. 31, 100.

SECOND PART.
Also containing Ten Sections.

THE TABLE OF CONTENTS OF EACH SECTION IS TO BE FOUND AT THE END OF THE BOOK.

SECTION I., concerning the *Keri* and *Kethiv*.—Having stated, at the beginning of Introduction iii., the differences of opinion which obtained among modern writers about the *Keri* and the *Kethiv*, and having given at the end thereof my own opinion respecting it (*vide supra* 106, &c.), I shall now disclose to you the method which the men of the Great Synagogue have therein pursued. First of all, however, you must know that what is written in the margin is the *Keri*, that is, it is thus to be read; and what is in the text, that is, the *Kethiv*, is not to be read at all. Thus, for example, the word הוֹצֵא *bring forth* [Gen. viii. 17], as it is in the *Kethiv*, with *Vav*, and for which *Keri* is הַיְצֵא, with *Jod*. Now, the Massorites put the vowel-points of הַיְצֵא under הוֹצֵא, and it is read הַיְצֵא, being the imperative *Hiphil* of the regular verb, according to the analogy of הַפְקֵד *appoint* [Numb. i. 50]; whilst the textual הוצא, without the vowels, is the imperative of פ״י, as הוֹצֵא [Levit. xxiv. 13]. The same is the case with הוֹשֵׁר [Ps. v. 9], where the *Keri* is הַיְשֵׁר *make straight*. Hence, the punctuators pointed the textual reading with the points of the word in margin, that is, the points of the text always belong to the *Keri* in the margin; whilst the *Kethiv* is without vowel-points. The same is the case with the accents, which they have always put under the words in the text, according to what it is in the marginal reading. Thus, in 1 Chron. xxii. 7, where the textual reading is בְּנוֹ *his son*, and the marginal reading בְּנִי *my son*, the *Athnach* according to the *Kethiv* ought to be under בְּנוֹ, but because the *Keri* is בְּנִי, the *Athnach* is put under לִשְׁלֹמֹה *to Solomon*. And this is easily understood.

הא לך לוחות שניות.
בעשרה מאמרים שנויות:

לוח הסמנים של כל מאמר ומאמר, תמצא כאשר הספר נגמר:

המאמר הראשון בקריין וכתבן: הנה כתבתי בראש החקרמה השלישית המחלוקת שבין האחרונים בעניני קריין וכתבן, ובאחרונה עניתי חלקי אף אני ע״ש; ועתה באתי לחשכילך בינה בדרך אשר חלכו בה אנשי כנסת הגדולה; וקודם כל דבר צריך שתדע שכל מה שנכתב בגליון הוא הקרי, ר״ל כן קורין חמלה החיא, ומה שנכתב מבפנים לא נקרא כלל; וחמשל הוצא אתך (בראשית ח׳), כך כתיב בו״ו, והקרי הוא היצא ביו״ד, הנה שמו נקודות של היצא תחת הוצא, אבל אין קורין אותו רק היצא, שחוא צווי מבנין הפעיל על דרך חשלמים על משקל הפקד את חלוים, ונשאר בפנים הוצא בלי נקודות כדין הצווי מנחי פ״א יו״ד, כמו הוצא את המקלל; ובזה חדרך הושר לפני דרכיך, היְשֵׁר קרי, לכן מתקני הנקוד לא נקדו מלת הכתיב רק עם נקודת מלת הקרי, דחיינו הנקודות שבפנים שייכין תמיד תחת הקרי שבגליון, ונשארה מלת חכתיב בלי נקודות; וכן שמו תמיד טעם חמלה תחת הכתיב לפי משמעות הקרי; וחמשל ויאמר דוד לשלמו בנו אני היה עם לבבי וגו׳, כתיב בְּנוֹ וקרי בְּנִי, הנה לפי הכתיב היה ראוי לחיות האתנח תחת בנו, ולפי שהקרי הוא בני שמו האתנח תחת לשלמה, וזה קל לחבין:

☞ It is to be noticed, that wherever the points are more than the letters, [the punctuators] had to put two sorts of points under one letter of the *Kethiv*. Thus, in Jerem. xlii. 6, where the *Kethiv* is אנו *we*, and the *Keri* אנחנו, they had to put two points, namely, *Sheva* and *Shurek* under the *Vav* in אָנֻוּ, to correspond to the points of אֲנַחְנוּ, whilst the word אנו in the text is left without points, and is read אָנוּ, which has no parallel in the Scriptures, except in the Prayer Book, where we find מָה אָנוּ *what are we*.[1] When, however, the word in the text has more letters than are required for the points [of the marginal reading], one letter of the *Kethiv* is left without any vowel-point, as in 2 Kings xix. 23, where, the text has בְּרֶכֶב *with the chariot*, and the marginal reading is בְּרֹב *with the multitude*, the *Kaph* is left without any vowel-point; also in 2 Sam. xxiii. 21, where the *Kethiv* is אשר *which*, and the *Keri* אִישׁ *man*, the *Shin* is without a vowel-point; and in Ezra v. 15, where the *Kethiv* is אֵלֶּה *these*, and the *Keri* אֵל, the *Lamed* is left without a vowel-point.

ודע כי בכל מקום שהנקודה רבה על הכתב הוצרכו לשום במלת הכתיב ב' מיני נקודות תחת אות אחת, והמשל אשר אנו שולחים אותך (ירמיה מ"ב) אנחנו קרי הוצרכו לנקוד וי"ו של אָנֻוּ בשוא ובשורק כנקודורע מלת אֲנַחְנוּ ונשארה מלת אנו שבפנים בלי נקודות ונקראת אנו, ואן לו דומה במקרא אך בסדורי התפלות מה אנו, מה חיננו;[1] וכשהכרתיב מרובה על הנקודה השאירו בכתיב אות אחת בלי נקודה, כגון בְּרֶכֶב רכבי עליתי, ברב קרי נשארה הכ"ף בלי נקודה, וכן הכה את המצרי אשר מראת, איש קרי הרי הש"ן בלי נקודה, וכן אלה מאיא, אל קרי הלמד בלי נקודה:

וכשהכתיב מלה אחת והקרי ב' מלורע שמו תחת מלת הכתיב כל הנקדות של ב' המלח שבקרי, כנון ולשתות את שֵׁינֵיהֶם (מלכים ב' יח) מֵימֵי רַגְלֵיהֶם קרי, הרי ו' הנקודורע של מֵימֵי רַגְלֵיהֶם רחורע שֵׁינֵיהֶם; וכשהכתיב ב' מלות והקרי מלה אחת, האות שהיא בסוף התיבה הראשונה שבכתיב בלי נקודה תחסר בקרי מכל וכל; והמשל ויצא מן הַמְּעָרָה מֵהַמְּעָרָה קרי, וכן מן בַּת ציון מִבַּת קרי, הרי הנו"ן בשניהם תחסר מכל וכל; וכן ח' מלות דכתיבן תרי מלין וקריין חד

When the textual reading has one word, and the marginal reading has two words, they put under the one word of the *Kethiv* all the points of the words in the *Keri*. Thus, in 2 Kings xviii. 27, where the *Kethiv* is שֵׁינֵיהֶם *their urine*, and the *Keri* מֵימֵי רַגְלֵיהֶם *the water of their feet*, the six points of the two words מֵימֵי רַגְלֵיהֶם are put under the one word שֵׁינֵיהֶם. But if, on the contrary, the textual reading has two words, and the marginal reading one word, the last unpointed letter of the first word in the *Kethiv* is omitted altogether in the *Keri*. Thus, in 1 Sam. xxiv. 9, where the textual reading is מִן הַמְּעָרָה *from the cavern*, and the marginal reading מֵהַמְּעָרָה; and Lament. i. 6, where the textual reading is מִן בַּת *from the daughter*, and the marginal מִבַּת; the *Nun* is altogether omitted in both cases. The same is the case with the eight words, which are respectively divided into two words in the textual reading, and which are undivided in the marginal read-

---

[1] The *Prayer Books* (סדורי התפלות), to which Levita refers, are the authorised Liturgies which the Jews use to the present day.

ing. These I have given in the sixth class, for I have thus divided all the *Keris* and the *Kethivs* of the Scriptures into classes, and distributed them under seven classes, corresponding to the seven kinds of fruit for which the land of Israel was famed.[a]

I.—The first class consists of words which are read from the margin, but not written in the text, and, *vice versa*, which are written in the text but not read. This principally affects the letters *Jod*, *He*, *Vav*, *Aleph*, which thus occur in the beginning, end, or middle of a word. It must, however, be remarked that *Vav* and *Jod* do not occur in this manner when they are quiescent in the middle of a word; that is to say, *Vav* after the vowel-points *Cholem* and *Shurek*, and *Jod* after *Chirek* and *Tzere*, since such belong to the category of *defective* and *plene*, as I have explained in Part i., Section 1. But the *Vav*, which occurs in the *Kethiv* and not in *Keri*, is only after the vowel-points *Kametz* or *Chateph-Kametz*, as אֶכְרוּת *I shall covenant*, (Josh. ix. 7), אֶשְׁקוּטָה *I shall be at rest* (Isa. xviii. 4), &c. There are in all thirty-one such instances.[b] *Vav* never occurs as *Keri* in the middle of a word, not being in the textual reading; but *Jod* is found in the *Keri*, and not in the *Kethiv*, after *Kametz*. Thus, for instance, Gen. xxxiii. 4, the *Kethiv* is צַוָּארוֹ *his neck*, and the *Keri* צַוָּארָיו; and in Ps. xxiv. 6, the *Kethiv* is דֹּרְשׁוֹ *his seeker*, and the *Keri* דֹּרְשָׁיו. There

---

[a] The seven chief productions of Palestine, mentioned in Deut. viii. 8, in praise of the land, are wheat, barley, grapes, figs, pomegranates, olives, and honey. From the fact that these seven kinds are specified in the Pentateuch, Jewish legislation, long before the time of Christ, restricted the offering of the first-fruits to these alone. Comp. *Mishna Bikurim*, i. 3; *Babylon Talmud Berachoth*, 35 *a* ; Maimonides, *Jad Ha-Chezaka Hilchoth Bikurim*, ii ; Kitto's *Cyclopædia of Biblical Literature*, *s. v.* FIRST-FRUITS.

[b] The words in which *Vav* occurs after *Kametz* and *Chateph Kametz*, in the textual reading, and from which *Vav* is omitted in the marginal reading, are as follows:—

אכרות . . Joshua ix. 7	כסמו . . Ezek. xxi. 28	אשמור . . Ps. lxxxix. 29
לשאול . . 1 Sam. xxii. 15	במותי . . Deut. xxxii. 13	מלושני . . Ps. ci. 5
ולשתך . . 1 Sam. xxv. 31	במותי . . Ps. cxlviii. 4	לנאול . . Ruth iv. 6
קסומ . . 1 Sam. xxviii. 8	במותי . . Micah i. 3	ואשקוטה . . Ezra viii. 25
אשקוטה . . Isa. xviii. 4	אכתוב . . Hos. viii. 12	אשתדויות . Nehem. xiii. 23
יעבור . . Isa. xxvi. 20	עבור . . Amos vii. 8	עמוניות . Nehem. xiii. 23
אצרוך . . Jerem. i. 5	עבור . . Amos viii. 3	ורחנה . 1 Chron. vii. 34
לאכול . . Ezek. xliv. 3	וגדול . . Ps. cxlv. 8	תוקתת . 2 Chron. xxxiv. 22
חורבנים . . Ezek. xxvii. 15	וגדול . . Nahum i. 3	למעול . 2 Chron. xxxvi. 14
לכל . . Jerem. xxxiii. 8	לשאול . . 1 Chron. xviii. 10	יקצור . Prov. xxii. 8
,סגור . . . Isa. xliv. 17	תדרוש . . . Ps. x. 15	יפל . Prov. xxii. 14

They are enumerated in the Massorah finalis, under the letter *Vav*, p. 28 *a*, col. 2.

are fifty-six such instances.⁴ There are also two instances where *Jod* is after *Cholem* in the textual reading, but not in the marginal reading, as רַגְלָיו *his feet* [Ps. cviii. 18], and עֵינָיו *his eyes* [Eccl. iv. 8]; but these belong to the list of six words which have *Jod* in the *Kethiv*, and not in the *Keri*.⁵ Moreover, *Jod* is also found after *Sheva*, as in דְּבָרֶיךָ *thy words*, which occurs eight times with a redundant *Jod*,⁶ מַעֲלִילֵיכֶם *your works* [Zech. i. 4], &c. The *Vav* and *Jod* also frequently occur in the beginning and end of words in the marginal reading, and are not in the textual reading, and *vice versa;* and this is also frequently the case with *He*, which I abstain from illustrating by examples, for the sake of brevity.

קרי, וחם נ"ו במספר; ⁴ וב' יודין דכתיבין ולא קריין אחד חולם, ענו בכבל רגליו, נם עיניו לא חשבע, וחן בכלל ו' דכתיבן יו"ד ולא קרי; ⁵ ונמצאים יודין אחד שוא, כגון ח' דכתיבין דבריך יתיר ח"ד,⁶ וכן ומעלליכם חרעים ודומיהן; גם נמצאים וי"ן ויד"ין לרוב בראש התיבה ובסוף התיבה דקריין ולא כתבן או להפך; וכן חחי"ן לרוב, ולבחרי חקיצור לא אביא עליהן ראיות:

⁴ The fifty-six words which are in the textual reading without *Jod* (mostly indicating the plural) in the middle, but have *Jod* in the marginal reading, are as follows:—

צאריו . .	Gen. xxxiii. 4	אלמנתו . .	Jerem. xv. 8	גבורתו . .	. Job xxvi. 14
ועמודו .	. Exod. xxvii. 11	ימו . .	. Jerem. xvii. 11	בתחבולתו .	. Job xxxvii. 12
ענו . . .	Numb. xii. 3	מברחו . .	Ezek. xvii. 21	ואפרחיו .	. Job xxxix. 30
בינו . .	. Joshua viii. 11	שארתו . .	Ezek. xxxi. 5	מחדרו . .	. . Job xl. 17
תוצאותיו .	. Joshua xvi. 3	שלתו . .	Ezek. xl. 26	כנפו .	'. . . Job xxxix. 26
מרבו . .	1 Sam. ii. 9	חלונו . .	Ezek. xl. 22	חלצו . .	. . Job xxxi. 20
עלו . . .	1 Sam. ii. 9	ותמורו . .	Ezek. xl. 22	ילדו . .	. Job xxxviii. 41
למשפחתו .	. 1 Sam. x. 21	בצאתו . .	Ezek. xlvii. 11	ברגלו .	. . . Prov. vi. 13
אנשו . .	. 1 Sam. xxiii. 5	פרו . . .	Habak. iii. 14	בשפטו .	. . Prov. xxvi. 24
בנגדו . .	. 2 Sam. i. 11	שערו . .	. . Obad. 11	ארחתו .	. . Prov. xxii. 25
שמלתו . .	. 2 Sam. xii. 20	דרשו . .	. Ps. xxiv. 6	אדנו .	. . Prov. xxx. 10
רחמו . .	. 2 Sam. xxiv. 14	חצו . .	. Ps. lviii. 8	מרגלותו .	. Ruth iii. 14
משרתו . .	1 Kings x. 5	חסדו . .	. Ps. cvi. 45	כנותו . .	. . Ezra iv. 7
ברכו . .	1 Kings xviii. 42	דברו . .	. Ps. cxlvii. 19	חמאו . .	. Lament. iii. 39
בסוסו . .	2 Kings ix. 9	צבאו . .	Ps. cxlviii. 2	ייתרו . .	. 1 Sam. xxi. 14
כפו . . .	2 Kings iv. 34	חקו . .	. Job xiv. 5	הסתו .	Song of Songs ii. 11
מזבחתו . .	2 Kings xi. 18	בקטשו . .	. Job xv. 15	שלו .	. . . Ps. cv. 40
צפו . . .	. Isa. lvi. 10	עלומו . .	. Job xx. 11	השלו .	. . Numb. xi. 32
משלו . . .	Isa. lii. 5	ויודעו . .	. Job xxiv. 1		

They are enumerated in the Massorah finalis under the letter *Jod*, p. 34 a, cols. 2 and 3; and in the *Ochla Ve-Ochla*, section cxxviii., pp. 33 and 104. It must be remarked, that this list only registers such words as occur *once* as *defective*, and therefore excludes many other words which likewise want the *Jod* plural, but which occur more than once.

⁵ The other four which in the textual reading are without the *Jod* plural, but have it in the marginal reading, and which, with the two adduced by Levita, constitute the list of six words, are, ובהשמאיו, 1 Kings xvi. 26; דבריו, Ps. cv. 28, Dan. ix. 12; and שתריו, Prov. xvi. 27. They are given in the Massorah finalis under the letter *Jod*, p. 34 a, col. 3; and *Ochla Ve-Ochla*, section cxxix., pp. 34 and 105.

⁶ The eight passages in which the textual reading is דברך, with the plural *Jod*, and the marginal reading is without it, are, Judges xiii. 17; 1 Kings viii. 26; xviii. 36; xxii. 13; Jerem. xv. 16; Ps. cxix. 47, 161; Ezra x. 12. They are enumerated in the Massorah finalis under the letter *Daleth*, p. 19 b, col. 2; and *Ochla Ve-Ochla*, section cxxxi., pp. 34 and 105. To supplement our remark on the thirteen instances in which the reverse is the case with the word in question, that is, where the textual reading is דבר without the plural *Jod*, and the marginal reading is דברי with the plural *Jod* (*vide supra*, p. 161, note 43), we must add that the list is given in the *Ochla Ve-Ochla*, section cxxx., pp. 34, 105, and that Ps. cxix. 17 has inadvertent'y been omitted.

☞ I have, however, found this, that in all the words which have a letter in the *Keri* and not in the *Kethiv*, the points of the letter in question are put into the text without this letter, whilst the marginal reading has the letter without the point, as is usually the case. Thus, for instance, in Lam. v. 7, the text has אֵינָ֑ם *are not*, אֲנַחְנוּ *we*, and the Massoretic remark in the margin is, " Read וְאֵינָם *and are not*," " Read וַאֲנַחְנוּ *and we*." See also the similar instances, of which there are twelve in number.[7] The same method is pursued in the case of *He*. Thus, in 1 Sam. xiv. 32, the text has שָׁלָ֑ל *booty*, and the margin has, " Read הַשָּׁלָל *the booty*." See also the similar instances, of which there are thirteen in number.[8]

אַךְ זה לבד מצאתי כי כל המלות שיש בהן אות דקרי ולא כתיב, נקודת אותו האות נקוד בפנים בלי אותה האות, ובקרי נכתב אותו האות בלתי נקוד כמנהג ; וחמשל כמו אבותינו חמאו יֵ֫ינָם יְאֲנַחְנוּ עונותיהם סבלנו (איכה ח׳) נמסר בגליון ואינם קרי, ואנחנו קרי, וכן דומיחן, וחם י״ב במספר :[7] וכן עם חח״א ויעם העם אל שָׁלָל השלל קרי, ורומיחן וחן י״ג במספר :[8]

ובמלה שיש בה אות דכתיב ולא קרי, נכתב המלח בפנים עם אותו האות בלי נקוד, כגון מארץ כשרים יֵצְאוּ היו״ד כתיב ולא קרי, אך לא כתבו בגליון צאו קרי רק לא קרי יו״ד ; וכן בעל הכנפים (קהלח י׳) לא קרי ה״א ;[9] וכן באמצע המלח, כגון עם

When, on the contrary, the textual reading has a word with a letter which the marginal reading has not, the word is written in the text with the letter in question unpointed; as יֵצְאוּ *they shall go out* [Jerem. l. 8], which has *Jod* in the *Kethiv*, but not in the *Keri*. In such a case, however, the Massorites do not write in the margin, " Read צְאוּ," but simply remark, "*Jod* is not read*." The same is the case with הכנפים *the wings* [Eccl. x. 23], where the marginal remark is, " *He* is not read;"[9] and when the *He* is in the middle of the

---

[7] The twelve words which have no *Vav* conjunctive in the textual reading, and have it in the marginal reading, are as follows:—

בניכי	. . .	2 Kings iv. 7	דור	. . .	Prov. xxvii. 24	אין	. . .	Lament. v. 3
תחת	. . .	Isa. lv. 13	די	. . .	Dan. ii. 43	וזקנים	. . .	Lament. iv. 6
עד	. . .	Job ii. 7	לא	. . .	Lament. ii. 2	אינם	. . .	Lament. v. 7
ילד	. . .	Prov. xxiii. 24	לא	. . .	Lament. v. 5	אנחנו	. . .	Lament. v. 7

They are enumerated in the Massorah finalis under the letter *Vav*, p. 27 a, col. 4; and *Ochla Ve-Ochla*, section cxvii., pp. 32 and 101.

[8] The thirteen words which do not begin with *He* in the textual reading, but have *He* at the commencement in the marginal reading, are as follows:—

שלל	. . .	1 Sam. xiv. 32	כלך	. . .	1 Kings xv. 18	דבר	. . .	Jerem. xl. 3
גברים	. . .	2 Sam. xxiii. 9	מלך	. . .	2 Kings xi. 20	מלכים	. . .	Jerem. lii. 32
אחד	. . .	1 Kings iv. 8	מלך	. . .	2 Kings xv. 25	רשע	. . .	Ezek. xviii. 20
שבעה	. . .	1 Kings vii. 20	עם	. . .	Jerem. x. 10	עמים	. . .	Lament. i. 18
			ארץ	. . .	Jerem. x. 13			

They are given in the Massorah marginalis on 2 Sam. xxiii. 9; and *Ochla Ve-Ochla*, section clxv., pp. 37 and 112.

[9] There are seven such words, which, on the contrary, have in the *Kethiv He* at the beginning, but not in the *Keri*. Besides the one quoted in the text, the other six are as follows:—

החנית	. . .	1 Sam. xxvi. 22	המלח	. . .	2 Kings xiv. 7	הספרים	. . .	1 Kings xxi. 8
ההמון	. . .	2 Kings xiii. 13	הסר	. . .	Isa. xxix. 11	הסחבות	. . .	Jerem. xxxviii. 11

They are enumerated in the Massorah finalis under the letter *He*, p. 22 a, col. 2; and *Ochla Ve-Ochla*, section clxvi. pp. 37, 113.

word, as שֶׁהַתָּקִיף *who is stronger* [Eccl. vi. 10], where the marginal remark is, "*He* is not read."[10] The same, too, is the case in the forty-eight words which have *Aleph* in the middle of the word in the text, and not in the margin; on all of which it is remarked in the margin, "*Aleph* is not read;" as הָאֲסַפְסוּף *the multitude* [Numb. xi. 4], &c.[11]

☞ Now the rule is, that whenever the letters *Jod, He, Vav,* and *Aleph* are in the marginal reading, and not written in the text, the Massorites write down the entire word of the *Keri* in the margin; but, on the contrary, when these letters are written in the textual reading, and are not to be read, they simply remark in the margin, "Read not the *Aleph, He, Jod,* or *Vav.*" In one passage, however, both the remarks occur. Thus, Prov. xxiii. 23, where the textual reading is יֹלַד *he that begetteth,* without *Vav,* and the marginal reading וְיוֹלֵד *and he that begetteth,* with *Vav,* the Massorites give the whole word, remarking, "Read וְיוֹלֵד;" whilst on וְיִשְׂמַח *and he shall rejoice,* which has *Vav* in the textual reading, but not in the marginal reading, they simply remark, "Read not the *Vav.*" Notice, however, that in correct Massorahs, whenever *Vav* and *Jod* occur in the middle of a word in the textual reading, and are not read, the margin has always the remark, "The *Vav* is superfluous," or, "The *Jod* is superfluous;" and this is the proper remark.

☞ As to the other letters, besides *Jod, He, Vav,* and *Aleph,* there are only a few which are found written in the textual reading, and are not to be read; or *vice versa*. Thus, for instance: i. *Lamed* occurs four times in the middle of words in the text, and is not read; as in וּלְהָחֶם *and to the bread* [2 Sam. xvi. 2], עָלְלִין, עָלְלִין, and עָלֲלַת *they were, she was, entering* [Dan. iv. 4; v. 8, 10]. In the last three instances the second *Lamed* is not read.[12] ii. *Tzaddi,* as in מַחֲצְצְרִים *they were*

---

[10] This is but one of five instances in which the textual reading has *He* in the middle of the word, and the marginal reading has not. The other four words are בהשרה, 2 Kings vii. 12; בהחטום, 2 Kings vii. 15; כשהכל, Eccl. x. 3; שהשכם, Lament. v. 18. They are enumerated in the Massorah finalis under the letter *He*, p. 22 *a*, col. 3.

[11] For the forty-eight instances, see above, p. 171, note 62.

[12] The marginal reading is עָלִין, תִדְחָם (twice), and עֲלַת. They are also given in the Massorah marginalis on Dan. iv. 4; v. 8; and in the *Ochla Ve-Ochla,* section clii. pp. 36, 110.

B B

blowing [2 Chron. xiii. 14, xxix. 28], where the second *Tzaddi* has no vowel-point, and is not read. iii. *Shin*, as יִשָּׂשכָר *Issachar*, where the second *Shin* is not read according to Ben Asher's recension, whilst according to Ben Naphtali's it is pointed with *Sheva* as usual. iv. *Kaph*, which is found in the textual reading of בְּרֶכֶב with the chariot [2 Kings xxx. 28], whereas the *Keri* is בְרֹב *with the multitude*, and, *vice versa*, is absent in מִפְּעָרוֹת *from the caverns* [1 Sam. xvii. 23], in the textual reading, whilst the *Keri* is מִמַּעַרְכוֹת *from the armies*. v. *Ajin* occurs once in the textual reading, and not in the marginal, viz., Amos viii. 8, where the *Kethiv* is נִשְׁקָה *she shall drink*, and the *Keri* נִשְּׂקָה *it shall rise up*. vi. *Daleth* is twice not in the textual reading, viz. 1 Kings ix. 18, where the *Kethiv* is תָּמֹר *Tamor*, and the *Keri* תַּדְמֹר *Tadmor*; and Dan. ii. 9, where the *Kethiv* is the *Aphel* הִזְמִנְתּוּן *ye have agreed together*, and the *Keri* is the *Ithpael* הִזְדְּמִנְתּוּן.[13] And vii. *Cheth* is four times not in the textual reading, viz. Jerem. ii. 16, where the *Kethiv* is תַחְפְּנֵס *Tahpenes*, and the *Keri* is תַּחְפַּנְחֵס *Tehaphnehes*, and אָנוּ *we*, which occurs three times in the *Kethiv*, whilst the *Keri* has אֲנַחְנוּ, as stated above.

2.—The second class consists of letters which are interchanged in the *Keri* and the *Kethiv*. In this case, too, it principally takes place with the letters *Jod*, *He*, *Vav*, *Aleph*, as is seen: i. In the twenty-two words which are written in the text with *Jod* in the beginning of the word, and are read in the margin with *Vqv*; as יֶחְדָּל *let him cease*, in the textual reading, and in the margin וַחֲדָל *and cease thou* [Job x. 20]; יֵשִׁית *let him depart*, of the *Kethiv*, and וְשִׁית *and depart thou*, in the *Keri* [ibid.], &c.[14] ii. The ten instances in which the reverse is

[13] Comp. *Ochla Ve-Ochla*, section clxxxi., pp. 40, 117.

[14] The twenty-two words which begin with *Jod* in the text, and are read with *Vav* in the margin, are as follows:—

יבאו . . . Judg. vi. 5	יחדו . . . Jerem. xxxviii. 2	יחדל . . . Job. x. 20
יחנני . . . 2 Sam. xii. 22	ישבי . . . Jerem. xlviii. 18	ישית . . . Job. x. 20
יסצרו . . . Isa. xlix. 13	ילבשו . . . Ezek. xlii. 14	יבא . . . Prov. xviii. 17
יאבדו . . . Jerem. vi. 21	יהיה . . . Ezek. xlv. 5	ישאל . . . Prov. xx. 4
ישיח . . . Jerem. xiii. 16	יכשלו . . . Nahum iii. 3	ירום . . . Dan. xi. 12
יסורי . . . Jerem. xvii. 13	יצהר . . . 1 Chron. iv. 7	ירמות . . . Ezra x. 29
יחיה . . . Jerem. xxi. 9	יהבה . . . 1 Chron. vii. 34	יקמאון . . . Zech. xiv. 6
	יאסר . . . Ps. xli. 3	

They are enumerated in the Massorah marginalis on Hosea i. 1; 1 Chron. i. 1: in the Massorah finalis under the letter *Jod*, p. 84 a, col. 8: and in the *Ochla Ve-Ochla*, section cxxxiv., pp. 34, 106. All the editions of the *Massoreth Ha-Massoreth*, viz., Venice, 1538, Basel. 1539, and Sulzbach, 1771, erroneously state that there are fifty-two (נ״ב) such instances.

the case, as in the textual reading וְדָכָה *and he is crushed*, for which the *Keri* has יִדְכֶּה *he shall be crushed* [Ps. x. 10], &c.[15] iii. The alphabetical list of words which have *Jod* in the middle of the word in the *Kethiv*, and *Vav* in the *Keri*. These are seventy in number, the *Jod* in all these instances being pointed with *Cholem* or *Shurek*; the *Cholem* is placed upon the letter preceding the *Jod*, as the *Kethiv* אַזְכִּיר *I shall cause to remember*, and the *Keri* אֶזְכּוֹר *I shall remember* [Ps. lxxvii. 12]; גֹּיִם *princes*, the *Kethiv*, and גּוֹיִם *nations*, the *Keri* [Gen. xxv. 23], &c.; whilst the *Shurek* is put into the *Jod*, as in the *Kethiv* וַיִשֶׂם *and he placed*, וַיּוּשַׂם *and there was placed*, in the *Keri* [Gen. xxiv. 33]. The pointing in some Codices of the first *Jod* in וַיִשֶׂם with *Kibbutz* is an egregious mistake, for there is no letter to be found with the point *Kibbutz* before quiescent *Jod*; the *Kethiv* is קְרִיאֵי *the called*, where the *Jod* has *Shurek*, and the *Keri* is קְרוּאֵי [Numb. i. 16], &c.[16] The same is the case where the *Jod* is at the end of the word, as in the *Kethiv* תֵּצְאִי *thou shalt go out*, which is in the *Keri* תֵּצְאוּ *ye shall go out*; the *Kethiv* תֵּלְכִי *thou shalt go*, which is in the *Keri* תֵּלְכוּ *ye shall go* [Jerem. vi. 25]. In all these instances the *Shurek* is in the *Jod*, but no *Kibbutz* before it; and there is no *Kibbutz* before the *Jod*, viz., תֵּצְאִי תֵּלְכִי.[17] In the words, however, which have *He* at

בתפך וְדָכָה וְשׂחַ ידכה קרי, יִשּׂחַ קרי ;[15] וכן אלפא ביתא דכתיבין יו״ד באמצע חיבותא וקריין וי״ו, והן ע״ב במספר, וכל היו״דין האלח נקודון חולם או שורק החולם נקוד על חאורת שלפני היו״ד, כמו אֶזְפֹּיר מעללי יח, אזכור קרי, שני גֹיִם בבמנך גוים קרי ודומיהן; אבל חשורק נקוד בתוך היו״ד, כמו וַיִישֶׂם לפניו לאכול, וַיּוּשַׂם קרי; ויש ספרים שנקוד בפנים וַיִשֶׂם היו״ד חראשונה בקבוץ, והוא מעות גמורה, כי לא נמצא אות נקודה בקבוץ לפני יו״ד נחח; וכן קְרִיאֵי העדה היו״ד בשורק קְרוּאֵי קרי,[16] וכן בסוף החיבה, כמו אל תֵּצְאִי השדה, ובדרך תֵּלְכִי, תֵּצְאוּ קרי, תֵּלְכוּ קרי, בכולן חשורק בתוך חיו״דין ולא בקבוץ לפניהם תֵּצְאִי תֵּלְכִי :[17] אבל המלין דכה׳ ח״א בסוף וקריין

---
[15] The ten instances in which the reverse is the case, that is which begin with *Vav* in the textual reading, and have *Jod* in the marginal reading, are as fo lows:—

ושׂפּמדהו	.	Ezek. xliv. 24	ידכה	. .	Ps. x. 10	וּקֵר	. .	Prov. xvii. 27
ועשׂו	.	Ezek. xlvi. 15	רֵצוּן	. .	Prov. ii. 7	ועיף	. .	Prov. xxiii. 5
תשׂאב	. .	Isa. v. 29	וחכם	. .	Prov. xiii. 20	ורב	. .	2 Chron. xxiv. 27
			ושׂדם	. .	Prov. xi. 3			

They are enumerated in the Massorah marginalis on Hosea i. 1; 1 Chron. i. 1; Prov. xi. 3; and in the *Ochla Ve-Ochla*, section cxxxv. pp. 34. 106. Here again all the three editions of the *Massoreth Ha-Massoreth* erroneously state that there are *fifty-six* (נ״ו) such instances. It will be seen that ישׂוח, given by Levita, is not among the number.

[16] The alphabetical list of the words which have *Jod* in the middle in the textual reading, and *Vav* in the marginal reading, has already been given, *vide supra*, p. 118, note 71.

[17] The two expressions תֵּצְאִי and תֵּלְכִי, belong to the following list of twenty-four words with *Jod* at the end in the textual reading, and *Vav* in the marginal reading:

דדי	. .	2 Sam. xxiii. 9	וזעקי	. .	Jerem. xlviii. 20	ושׂמי	. .	Job xxxiii. 21
ילדתני	. .	Jerem. ii. 27	תסמחי	. .	Jerem. l. 11	נסשׂי	. .	Job xxxiii. 28
תצאי	. .	Jerem. vi. 25	תעלזי	. .	Jerem. l. 11	וחזיתי	. .	Job xxxiii. 28
תלכי	. .	Jerem. vi. 25	תפושׂי	. .	Jerem. l. 11	כלחתי	. .	Ezra x. 35
שׂאי	. .	Jerem. xiii. 20	ותצהלי	. .	. .	נשׂאי	. .	Ezra x. 44
וראי	. .	Jerem. xiii. 20	במי	. .	Isa. xxv. 10	למלוכי	. .	Nehem. xii. 14
דברי	. .	Jerem. xxiii. 18	סגבני	. .	Ps. xvii. 11	ידעי	. .	2 Chron. ix. 29
הילילי	. .	Jerem. xlviii. 20	ושׂבי	. .	Job. vi. 29	וישׂבי	. .	2 Chron. xxxiv. 9

They are enumerated in the Massorah marginalis on Jerem. i. 1.; Massorah finalis

the end in the *Kethiv*, and in the *Keri Vav* with *Shurek*, the letter which precedes the *He* is always pointed with *Kibbutz*, as יִקְרְחָה *he shall make bald* [Levit. xxi. 5], שָׁפְכָה *she has shed* [Deut. xxi. 6], &c., of which there are fourteen in number.¹⁸ There are also many other words in which the letters *Jod*, *He*, *Vav*, and *Aleph* are interchanged, but I prefer brevity.

There are also other letters which have interchanged; but this interchange only takes place in the case of those letters which resemble each other in writing, as *Beth* with *Kaph*, *Daleth* with *Resh*, *He* with *Cheth*, *Cheth* with *Tav*, *Daleth* with final *Kaph*, and *Shin* with *Teth*; or of those letters which belong to some organ of speech, as *Beth* with *Mem*, *Mem* with *Pe*, *Aleph* with *Ajin*, *Ajin* with *Cheth*, *Daleth* with *Tav*.

וי"ו שרוקה, חמיד נקוד בקבוץ באות שלפני ההי"א, כמו לא יָקְרְחָה, ידינו לא שָׁפְכָה ודומיהן, והן י"ד במספר;¹⁸ ועוד יש הרבה אחיווח יהו"א המתחלפים זו בזו ובחרתי בקצור:

וְיֵשׁ שאר אותיות המתחלפות זו בזו, אבל אין זה רק באחיות הדומח במכתב, כגון בי"ת בכ"ף, דלי"ת ברי"ש, ח"א בחי"ת חי"ת בתי"ו, ודל"ת בכ"ף פשוטה, וש"ן במי"ח; או שהם ממוצא אחד, כגון בי"ח במ"ם, מ"ם בפ"א, אל"ף בעי"ן, עי"י בחי"ת, דל"ת בתי"ו:

והמשל על כל אלו כגון י"א מלין דכריבין בי"ת וקריין כ"ף, כגון ויחי בְּאָמְרָם אליו (אסתר ג') כאמרם קרי וכו', וג' לחפך כגון מח יָבֵן דרכי יָבִין קרי, ומבני בנוי עוחת חָנָד, וְזָבוּר קרי;¹⁹ כתיב בפנים בבי"ח ודל"ת וקרי וְזָכוּר בכ"ף ורי"ש, ובזה היא אחת מב' מלין דכחיבין דל"ח וקריין

As illustrative of all these, are to be adduced : i. The eleven words which are in the *Kethiv* with *Beth*, and in the *Keri* with *Kaph*, as the *Keri* בְּאָמְרָם *is their saying*, and the *Kethiv* בְּאָמְרָם *as their saying* [Esth. iii. 4], &c.; and the three instances in which the reverse is the case, *ex. gr.* the textual reading יָבִין *he shall prepare*, and the marginal reading יָבֵן *he shall understand* [Prov. xx. 24], the *Kethiv* וְזָבוּד and *Zabbud*, and the *Keri* וְזָבּוּר and *Zaccur* [Ezra viii. 14], &c.¹⁹ ii. The textual reading being *Beth* and *Daleth*, whilst the marginal is *Beth* and *Resh*, constitutes וְזָבוּד one of the two instances which are written with *Daleth* and read *Resh*, the other instances being אֶעֱבוֹד *I shall serve*, in the *Kethiv*, and אֶעֱבוֹר *I shall pass over*, in the *Keri* [Jerem.

---

under the letter Jod, p. 84 *a*, cols. 3 and 4; and in the *Ochla Ve-Ochla*, section cxxxvii., pp. 35, 107. It is to be added, that the words תֻּצָּאִי and חֶלְקִי, after לפניהם, are omitted in the Sulzbach edition.

¹⁸ For the fourteen instances alluded to in the text, see p. 179, note 81.

¹⁹ The eleven words which have *Beth* in the textual reading, and *Kaph* in the marginal reading, are as follows :—

בשמעכם	. . Josh. vi. 5	בשמעו	. . 1 Sam. xi. 6	באמרם	. . Esther iii. 4
במלות	. . Josh. iv. 18	בשמיעך	. . 2 Sam. v. 23	חבוד	. . Ezra viii. 14
במלות	. . Judg. xix. 25	ריבו	. . 2 Kings iii. 24	זבי	. . Nehem. iii. 20
בחם	. . 1 Sam. xi. 9	יבלו	. . Job xxi. 13		

The third of the three instances in which the reverse is the case, that is, the textual words being with *Kaph*, and the marginal reading with *Beth*, is בבלי, 2 Sam. xii. 31. The first list is given in the Massorah marginalis on Hosea i. 1; 1 Chron. i. 1: in the Massorah finalis under the letter *Beth*, p. 15 *a*, col. 2: and in the *Ochla Ve-Ochla*, section cxlix., pp. 36, 109. The second list is given in the Massorah marginalis on 2 Sam. xii. 31; Hosea i. 1; 1 Chron. i. 1: in the Massorah finalis, under the letter *Beth*, p. 15 *a*, col. 2: and in the *Ochla Ve-Ochla*, section cl., pp. 36, 110.

ii. 20]; and the four instances in which the reverse is the case, as the *Kethiv* הַשְּׂרֻמוֹת *the burned cities*, and the *Keri* הַשְּׂדֵמוֹת *the fields* [Jerem. xxxi. 40], &c.[20] iii. The one instance in which the textual reading is final *Kaph* and the marginal *Daleth*, viz., the *Kethiv* יָךְ and the *Keri* יָד *side* [1 Sam. iv. 18]. iv. The four cases in which the textual reading has *Cheth* and the marginal *He*, as the *Kethiv* רְחִיטֵנוּ *our bower*, and the *Keri* רְהִיטֵנוּ [Song of Songs i. 17], &c.[21] v. The instance in which the *Kethiv* has *Shin* and the *Keri* has *Teth*, viz., וַיַּעַשׂ *and he made*, which is read וַיַּעַט *and he flew* [1 Sam. xiv. 32]. vi. The one case in which the textual reading has *Cheth* and the marginal *Tav*, viz., the *Kethiv* יֵרָחֵק *it shall snap*, and the *Keri* יֵרָתֵק *it shall be bound* [Eccl. xii. 6]. vii. The six words having *Beth* in the textual reading and *Mem* in the marginal, as the *Kethiv* בָּאָדָם *is man*, and the *Keri* מֵאָדָם *from man* [Josh. iii. 16], &c.[22] viii. The one case where the text has *Pe* and the margin *Mem*, viz., the *Kethiv* פָּרָק *broth*, and the *Keri* מָרָק *broth* [Is. lxv. 4]. ix. Where the text has *Cheth* and the margin *Ajin*, viz., the *Kethiv* חֵץ *an arrow*, and the *Keri* עֵץ *wood* [1 Sam. xvii. 7]. x. Where the text has *Ajin* and the margin *Aleph*, viz., the two instances in which the *Kethiv* has twice עַל *upon*, and the *Keri* אֶל *to*, and the *Kethiv* once עַל, whilst the *Keri* is עַל [1 Sam. xx. 24; Is. lxv. 7 Ezek. ix. 5].[23] xi. Where the text has *He* and the margin *Ajin*, viz.,

[20] The two instances of words with *Daleth* at the end in the *Kethiv*, and with *Resh* in the *Keri*, are also given in the Massorah finalis under the letter *Daleth*, p. 19 b, col. 1; and Ochla Ve-Ochla, section cxxiii., pp. 33, 103. The other three words which are written in the text with *Resh*, and are read in the margin with *Daleth*, are עמידור, 2 Sam. xiii. 37; וארמים, 2 Kings xvi. 6; and נרד, Prov. xix. 19. They are given in the Massorah marginalis on Jerem. xxxi. 40; and in the Ochla Ve-Ochla, section cxxii., pp. 33, 102.

[21] The other three words which have *Cheth* in the textual reading, and *He* in the marginal reading, are, עמיחור, 2 Sam. xiii. 37; מבחלת, Prov. xx. 21; ולחחם, Dan. ix. 24. They are given in the Massorah marginalis on Prov. xx. 21; Song of Songs i. 16; and in the Ochla Ve-Ochla, section cxxi. pp. 33, 102.

[22] The other five words which have *Beth* in the textual reading, and *Mem* in the marginal reading, are, בעבר Josh. xxiv. 15; אבנה, 2 Kings v. 12; בימין, 2 Kings xii. 10; במלך, 2 Kings xxiii. 33; וישב, Dan. xi. 18. They are given in the Massorah finalis under the letter *Beth*, p. 15 a, col. 2; and in the Ochla Ve-Ochla, section cliv. pp. 36, 110.

[23] The two instances in which the textual reading is על, and the marginal reading אל, are, 1 Sam. xx. 24; Isa. lxv. 7; and the one instance in which the textual reading is עַל with *Pattach*, and the marginal reading אל, is in Ezek. ix. 5. The *editio princeps* of the *Massoreth Ha-Massoreth*, and the Basel and Sulzbach reprints read וא' כתיב על וקרינן אל, which is manifestly a blunder. We have therefore corrected the text. The instances in question are enumerated in the Massorah finalis under the letter *Aleph*, p. 6 b, col. 3; and in the Ochla Ve-Ochla, section clxvii., pp. 37, 113.

הַפָּרָה Haupha [2 Sam. xxi. 16, 18], upon which our Rabbis of blessed memory remark, the *Kethiv* is הרפה, and the *Keri* עָרְפָה *Orpha;* but I could not find it so in all the best Codices.[24] xii. The three instances where the text has *Daleth* and the margin *Tav*, viz., the *Kethiv* אֶחָד *one* (masculine), and the *Keri* אַחַת *one* (feminine) [Is. lxvi. 17], &c.;[25] and the two in which the reverse is the case, viz., the *Kethiv* אַחַת (feminine), and the *Keri* אֶחָד (masculine) [2 Sam. xviii. 12; 1 Kings xix. 4]. xiii. The two instances in which the text has *He* and the marginal reading *Kaph*, viz., the *Kethiv* מַעַלְלֵיהֶם *their works*, and the *Keri* מַעַלְלֵיכֶם *your works* [Jerem. xxi. 13], and the *Kethiv* עֲלֵיהֶם *upon them*, whilst the *Keri* is עֲלֵיכֶם *upon you* [Jerem. xlix. 30].[26] xiv. The one instance where the text has *Resh* and the marginal reading *Beth*, viz., the *Kethiv* וָאֵשֵׁר *and where*, and the *Keri* וָאֵשֵׁב *and I sat* [Ezek. iii. 15], of which I shall speak again below, under the sixth class. And xv. The one instance in which the text has *Gimmel* and the marginal reading *Zajin*, viz., the *Kethiv* לְבַג *for food*, and the *Keri* לְבַז *for a spoil* [Ezek. xxv. 7], which is owing to the interchange of *Gimmel* and *Zajin* in the alphabet denominated *Atbach.*[27] This also accounts for the textual reading גֵּה *valley*, and the marginal reading זֶה *this* [Ezek. xlvii. 13].

מצאתי כן בכל הנוסחאות חמדויקות;[24] ודל״ח בתי״ו, כנון אחד אַחַד בתוך אחת קרי, וחם נ' במספר,[25] וב' להפך כתיב אחת וקרי אחד, כאחת המקומות (ישעיה ס'ו), באחד קרי, תחת רותם אחת אחד קרי; וב' מלין כתיבין ה״א וקריין כ״ף, כנון מפני רוע מַעַלְלֵיהֶם כם קרי, וחשב עֲלֵיהֶם מחשבה כם קרי;[26] ומלח אחת כתיב רי״ש וקרי בי׳ת, והוא וָאֵשֵׁר שם משמים וָאֵשֵׁב קרי, ועוד אזכרנו במין ו' ; ונמצאה מלה אחת כתיב נים״ל וקרי זי״ן, לְבָג לנוים (יחזק' מ״ז) לְבַז קרי, וזה לפי שתתחלף הגמ״ל והזי״ן בא״ב דאט״בא;[27] וכן גֵּה נבול כמו זה נבול :

[24] Levita must surely be mistaken, since the Rabbins do not say that the *Kethiv* is הרשה and the *Keri* ערשה, but simply try to identify the two words by way of *Midrash*, which is frequently the case. Comp. *Sota*, 42 b, and Rashi on 2 Sam. xxi. 18.

[25] The other two instances in which the textual reading has *Daleth*, and the marginal reading *Tav*, are 2 Sam. xxiii. 8, and Song of Songs iv. 2.

[26] The two instances in which the textual reading has הָם, suffix third person plural masculine, and the marginal reading כָם, suffix second person plural masculine, are also given in the Massorah finalis under the letter He, p. 22 a, col. 4, and in the *Ochla Ve-Ochla*, section cli., pp. 36, 110.

[27] In the alphabet denominated *Atbach* (אטבח), the commutation of the letters takes place according to the numerical value as represented by the respective pairs, which is effected in the following manner. The Hebrew alphabet is divided into three classes, consisting respectively of four pairs, or eight letters, and representing *ten, a hundred, and a thousand*. The first class, therefore, comprises the letters *Aleph, Beth, Gimmel, Daleth, Vav, Zajin, Cheth,* and *Teth;* the second class comprises *Jod, Kaph, Lamed, Mem, Samech, Ajin, Pe* and *Tzaddi;* whilst the third class contains *Final Mem, Final Nun, Final Pe, Final Tzaddi, Koph, Resh, Shin,* and *Tav*. When thus divided and paired, according to their numerical value, we obtain the following Table:—

1.— אט, בח, גנו, דו, every pair making 10.
2.— יצ, כפ, לע, מס,   ,,   ,,   100.
3.— קן, רם, שן, תם,   ,,   ,,   1000.

As the letters *He, Nun,* and *Final Kaph* are, from their unpairable numerical value, necessarily excluded from being coupled with any other member of the alphabet, they

8.—The third class consists of transpositions, that is, of words wherein one letter is placed in the textual reading later than it ought to be, and in the marginal reading is put earlier, as it should be. There are sixty-two such instances, and not one of them occurs in the Pentateuch, for which reason I give the mnemonical sign for them, "No transpositions in the Law, minus one."[28] Fifty-one of these affect the letters *Jod, He, Vav*, and *Aleph*; as the *Kethiv* הֹלֵךְ *going*, participle, and the *Keri* הָלוֹךְ *to go*, infinitive [Josh. vi. 13]; וְהֵימִשֵׁנִי [from ימש] *that I may feel* [Judg. xvi. 26]; and the *Keri* וַהֲמִישֵׁנִי [from מוש]; the *Kethiv* הָאֹהֶל *the tent* [1 Kings vii. 45], and the *Keri* הָאֵלֶּה *these*, &c.; whilst eleven affect the other letters, as the *Kethiv* וַתִּרְאֶנָה [from ראה] *and they saw*, and the *Keri* וַתָּאֹרְנָה [from אור] *and they became bright*, [1 Sam. xiv. 27]; the *Kethiv* תִּרְצֶנָה [from רצה] *they shall delight*, and the *Keri* תִּצֹּרְנָה [from נצר] *they shall observe* [Prov. xxiii. 26]; the *Kethiv* יָבְחַר *he shall be exempt*, and the *Keri* יָחְבַּר *he shall be joined* [Eccl. ix. 4], &c.[29] The same is the case with proper names, as the *Kethiv* שִׁמְלַי *Shamlai*, and the *Keri* שַׂלְמַי *Shalmai* [Ezra ii. 46]; the *Kethiv* שִׁטְרַי *Shitrai*, and the *Keri* שִׂרְטַי *Shirtai* [1 Chron. xxvii. 29], &c.; which obtained in consequence of each of these persons having two names.

are doubled when required, or they are coupled together among themselves, whereby they also yield 10, 100, and 1000, as follows: הה = 10, נג = 100, ך = 1000. Accordingly the commutation takes place between every pair, and the name Atbach (אט׳בח), by which this anagramic alphabet is designated, is obtained from the first two specimen pairs of the letters which indicate the interchange. Through the application of this alphabet, Prov. xxix. 21 is rendered—"*He who satisfies his desire in this world, against him it will testify at the end;*" נוסר being taken to denote *this world*, עבדו *his servant, his desire*, אחרית *the end, the last day*; whilst מנון, according to the alphabet in question, makes סהרה *witness*, the מ being exchanged with the ס, the נ with the ה, the ו with the ד, and נ again with the ה. Hence, also, we obtain לבן from לבג, the נ and ו being interchanged; and hence, too, נה from חז, to which Levita refers in the text. It must be remarked, that interpretation by the aid of this alphabet was resorted to from time immemorial, and that the exposition of Prov. xxix. 21 by its aid is already given in the Talmud. Comp. *Succa*, 52 *b*. For other anagramic alphabets, see Ginsburg, the *Kabbalah*, p. 54, &c., Longmans, 1865.

[28] To understand Levita's mnemonical sign, it is to be borne in mind that the numerical value of the word אין is sixty-one, viz., ן 50 + י 10 + א 1 = 61; that the expression *minus one* (חסר אחד), which is erroneously omitted in the Sulzbach edition, indicates that one is to be added, thus making the required number 62; and that there is also a play upon the words in the whole phrase, since it alludes to a well known hermeneutical rule denominated מוקדם ומאוחר, according to which whole sentences are transposed. Comp. Kitto's *Cyclopædia of Biblical Literature*, s. v. MIDRASH, Rules xxxi. a d xxxii.

[29] The list in question has already been given, *vide supra*, p. 116, note 67.

4.—The fourth class consists of words, the first of which took from the second, that is, of two words placed together, the first word of which took a letter from the second. This, however, only happens with the formative *He*, at the end of the first word, which belongs to the beginning of the next word. For this reason the punctuators pointed it in the textual reading with *Pattach*, whilst in the marginal reading it is made the article of the next word. There are three such instances in the textual reading, viz., the *Kethiv* הָיִיתָה מוֹצִיא *thou art leading out*, and the *Keri* הָיִית הַמּוֹצִיא [2 Sam. v. 2]; the *Kethiv* יְדַעְתָּה שָׁחַר *thou showest down*, and the *Keri* יִדַּעְתָּ הַשַּׁחַר [Job, xxxviii. 12]; and the *Kethiv* מִתַּחְתָּה לְשָׁכוֹת *from the chambers*, and the *Keri* מִתַּחַת הַלְּשָׁכוֹת [Ezek. xlii. 9].[30] There are two instances in which the reverse is the case, viz., שָׁם הַפְּלִשְׁתִּים *there the Philistines*, and the *Keri* שָׁמָּה פְלִשְׁתִּים [2 Sam. xxi. 12]; and the *Kethiv* שׁוּרַי אֲשַׁכְלִילוּ *they have finished the walls*, and the *Keri* שׁוּרַיָּא שַׁכְלִלוּ [Ezra iv. 12].[31]

5.—The fifth class embraces entire words written in the text but not read, of which there are eight instances; as יִדְרֹךְ *he shall tread* [Jerem. li. 3], which is not read; נָא *now* [2 Kings v. 18], which is in the *Kethiv* but not in the *Keri*, &c.;[32] as well as words read from the margin which are not in the text. Of these there are ten in number, viz., אֵלַי *to me*, which is in the margin but not in the text [Ruth iii. 17]; פְּרָת *Euphrates*, found in the margin but not in the text [2 Sam. viii. 3], &c.[33] I have, however, already discussed this subject, in the third Introduction [*vide supra*, p. 109, note 51].

6.—The sixth class embraces expressions which are written in the text as one word, and read in the margin as two words. Of these

---

[30] The words ומתחתה לשכות הלשכות קרי, are omitted in the Sulzbach edition.
[31] These instances are also enumerated in the Massorah marginalis on 2 Sam. v. 2; Ezra iv. 12; and in the *Ochla Ve-Ochla*, sections ci. and cii, pp. 29, 97.
[32] The Sulzbach edition wrongly substitutes נא לא קרי for נא כתיב ולא קרי.
[33] Both lists will be found on p. 109, &c., note 51. All the three editions of the *Massoreth Ha-Massoreth* erroneously state that there are *ten* (ד'י) words in the textual reading, which are not read in the marginal reading, and *eight* (ח) *vice versa*. We have corrected the text, since it is well known that the reverse is the case.

there are fifteen in number, as, the *Kethiv* בֶּנֶד in happiness, and the *Keri* בָּא נָד happiness is come [Gen. xxx. 11]; the *Kethiv* מַיָּה what is it, and the *Keri* מָה זֶּה [Exod. iv. 2], &c. Also eight words in which the reverse is the case, being in the text two words, and in the margin one; as מַבִּין יָמִין, for which the margin has מִבִּנְיָמִין from Benjamin [1 Sam. ix. 1], the textual reading לָם רַבָּה to them shall be great, and the marginal reading לְמַרְבֵּה for the increase [Isa. ix. 6], &c.[34]

☞ Now I am greatly astonished at the traditional explanation of this word, saying that there is a final *Mem* in the middle of the word; since, according to the *Kethiv*, it is not in the middle of the word, as the *Kethiv* has two words לָם רַבָּה; and since לָם may be taken for לָהֶם to them, just as אָרְאֶלָּם [Is. xxxiii. 7] stands for אֶרְאֶה לָהֶם I shall appear to them, and בְּשֵׁלָם [1 Kings xxi. 21] stands for בְּשֵׁל לָהֶם he boiled for them; so also לָם רַבָּה, as the *Kethiv* has it, is to be explained by לָהֶם רַבָּה to them is great.[35]

To this class, also, belong—i. Those words which are written in the text in one way, and for which the marginal reading has quite a different expression, as the *Kethiv* הָעִיר the city, for which the *Keri* is חָצֵר the court [2 Kings xx. 4], the *Kethiv* וְאֲשֶׁר and where, and the *Keri* וָאֵשֵׁב and I dwelled [Ezek. iii. 15], &c., which have already been mentioned under the second class, on the interchange of letters. ii. The *Kethiv* אֲשֶׁר who, for which the *Keri* is אִישׁ man [2 Sam. xxiii.

[34] The fifteen instances in which the textual reading has one word, and the marginal reading two, are as follows:—

בנד . . . . . Gen. xxx. 11	מהם . . . Ezek. viii. 6	מנהסטרה . . Job xxxviii. 1
מזה . . . . . Exod. iv. 2	מלכם . . . Isa. iii. 15	מנסטרה . . . Job xl. 6
אשדת . . Deut. xxxiii. 2	חלמאים . . Ps. x. 10	המסרוצים . . Nehem. ii. 18
מאשדם . . . Jerem vi. 29	ישימוח . . Ps. lv. 16	בנימן . . 1 Chron. ix. 4
והנחו . . . Jerem. xviii 3	לנאיונים . Ps. cxxiii. 4	לבנימיני . 1 Chron. xxvii. 12

The eight instances in which the reverse is the case, that is, the text having two words, and the margin one word, are as follows:—

כי טוב . . . Judg. xvi. 25	לם רבה . . . Isa. ix. 6	כי ענים . . Lament. iv. 3
מבין ימין . . . 1 Sam. ix. 1	מי אתי . . Isa. xliv. 24	בדר בתהם . 2 Chr. xxxiv. 6
מן המיצרה . 1 Sam. xxiv. 9	מן בת . . Lament. i. 6		

The first list is given in the Massorah marginalis on 1 Chron. xxvii. 12; *Tractate Sopherim* vii. 3; and in the *Ochla Ve-Ochla*, section xcix., pp. 29, 96, &c. The second list is given in the Massorah marginalis on 2 Chron. xxxiv. 6; *Tractate Sopherim* vii. 3; and in the *Ochla Ve-Ochla*, section c. pp. 29, 97.

[35] For the fanciful interpretations and mysterious meanings ascribed to this word, in consequence of its having a final *Mem* in the middle, see Kitto's *Cyclopædia of Biblical Literature*, *s. v.* KERI AND KETHIV.

21, with 1 Chron. xi. 28]. iii. The five groups of three words, each one of which is written in the text in one way, and is entirely different in the marginal reading. These I have already discussed, under the class of words the letters of which are more than the vowel-points. And iv. Those expressions which are written in the text as one word, and for which the marginal reading has two words entirely different to the textual reading, as the *Kethiv* כַּאֲשֶׁר *as that*, and the *Keri* כְּכֹל אֲשֶׁר *according to all that* [Ezek. ix. 11], the *Kethiv* שֵׁינֵיהֶם *their urine*, and the *Keri* מֵימֵי רַגְלֵיהֶם *the water of their feet* [2 Kings xviii. 27], &c. See above, at the beginning of this Section.

וכן ח' זונין מן נ' ג' מלים דכל חד כתיב מלה חד וקרי מלה אחדת, וככר כתבתי מהן לעיל בכלל חמלות שהכתב מרובח על הנקודה : וכן דכתיבין מלח חד וקרי כ' מלורי אחרות שאינן דומרות למלת חכתובה בפנים, כמו לאמור עשיתי כַּאֲשֶׁר צויתני, קְבֹל אֲשֶׁר קרי, וכן שֵׁינֵיהֶם מֵימֵי רַגְלֵיהֶם קרי, עיין לעיל בהתחלת חמאמר :

חמין השביעי במנונה ונאות, אמרו רז"ל כל הדברים הכתובים במקרא לגנאי קורין אותן לשבח, כמו ואיש אחר יִשְׁגָּלֶנָּה יִשְׁכָּבֶנָּה קרי, וכן בד' מקומות כתיב לשון משגל שהוא לשון מנונה וקרי לשון משכב שהוא לשון נאות,[86] וכן לאכול את חַרְאֵיהֶם ולשתות את שֵׁינֵיהֶם לפי שאיחן דברים מנונים קריין צוֹאָתָם וּמֵימֵי רַגְלֵיהֶם לשבח, וכן וּבַעֲפֹלִים שהם התחתוניות בלשון אשכנז פייגבלאטרין שהוא לשון מנונה קרי טְחוֹרִים,[87] עיין בערוך בשרש טחר :

והכלל העולה כל מה שהוא בלשון גנאי שנו אותו לשבח כדי שלא יוציא האדם דבר מגונה מפיו ; ויש מי שאומר שבשביל כך נקרא לשון העברייה[88] לשון הקדש לפי שכלה

7.—The seventh class embraces cacophonic and euphemic expressions. Our Rabbis of blessed memory say, that all the words which are written in the Scriptures cacophonically must be read euphemically, as—i. The *Kethiv* יִשְׁגָּלֶנָּה *he shall ravish her*, and the *Keri* יִשְׁכָּבֶנָּה *he shall lie with her* [Deut. xxviii. 30]. For this cacophonous term מָשְׁגָּל, which occurs four times in the textual reading, the *Keri* has always the euphemic word מִשְׁכָּב.[86] ii. חַרְאֵיהֶם *their dung*, and שֵׁינֵיהֶם *their urine*, for which, on account of their both being cacophonous terms, the *Keri* has the euphemic words צֹאָתָם *their excrement, and* מֵימֵי רַגְלֵיהֶם *the water of their feet*. And iii. עֳפָלִים, which is *a tumour near the pudenda*, denoting in German Feigblattern, and, being a cacophonous expression, is in the *Keri* טְחוֹרִים *the piles* [Deut. xxviii. 27];[87] *vide* ARUCH, s. v. טחר.

The rule which obtained is, that every cacophonous expression was changed for a euphemism, so that man might not utter anything indecent. And indeed there are some who maintain that Hebrew is for this reason called the holy language,[88] because it is all holy, and there is

---

[86] The four instances in which the *Keri* substitutes the words in question are, Deut. xxviii. 30; Jerem. iii. 2; Isa. xiii. 16; Zech. xiv. 2. Comp. Massorah marginalis on Is. xiii. 16, and *Ochla Ve-Ochla*, section clxix., pp. 38, 114.

[87] There are six instances in which the alteration in question is made in the margin, *vide supra*, p. 109, note 49. The rule of the sages, to which Levita refers, and according to which the alterations in question have been made, is given in the Talmud, *Megilla*, 25 b. Comp. also Jacob b. Chajim's *Introduction to the Rabbinic Bible*, pp. 13, 25, ed. Ginsburg.

[88] The words לשון העברייה, *the Hebrew language*, are omitted in the Sulzbach edition.

not any indecency in it, since it has neither names for the male and female generative organs, nor words for the discharge of the duties of nature, all these things being expressed by some euphemism, as I have already stated. Still, if this were the reason, it would be more appropriate to call it *the pure*, or *the decent language*, but not the holy language. R. Abraham de Balmes again remarks in his Grammar, entitled *The Possession of Abraham*, as follows: "It is called the holy language, because it was given by the Creator, blessed be his name, who is the Holiest of all holy." Thus far his remark.[39]

☞ However, I have already animadverted upon this question, among many other strictures which I made on his book, submitting that, according to his opinion, it ought more properly to be called *the language of the Holy One*, and not *the holy language*.[40] It seems, however, more appropriate to say that it is designated "the holy language," because the words of the Law, the Prophets, and all the holy statements were uttered therein, and because the Creator is therein called by His holy names, as *the Mighty One*, *the Almighty of Sabaoth*, &c., as well as His angels, *ex. gr. Michael, Gabriel*, &c., and the holy ones upon the earth, as *Abraham, Isaac, Jacob, Solomon*, &c., &c. On this account it is meet and proper to call it the holy language. Herewith the seven classes are ended, and the First Section is finished.

SECTION II., concerning *Kametz* and *Pattach*.—I have already stated, in Introduction III., that the Massorites only mention the vowel-points *Kametz* and *Pattach*, and that they include in them the minor *Kametz* and the minor *Pattach*, which are *Tzere* and *Segol*.

☞ You must, however, observe, that they have never ranged the major *Kametz* with the minor under the one number, or under the same

---

[39] For De Balmes, see above, pp. 10, 17, 21. The quotation is from section i., p. 3 a, of the Grammar.

[40] From Levita's remark, it would appear that he wrote animadversions on De Balmes' Grammar. We have, however, not been able to find any trace of this publication.

rubric. Thus, when they say that such and such a number have *Kametz*, you must know that these words are either all pointed with *Kametz* only, or with *Tzere* only; as, for instance, the alphabetical list of words, which they describe as having *Kametz* with the accent *Sakeph*; as, אֵדָע *I shall know* [1 Kings xviii. 12], בָּאֶרֶז *with cedar* [Jerem. xxii. 14].⁴¹ All the words thus alphabetically enumerated are pointed with *Kametz*, and not one of them has *Tzere*. The same designation they give to the list of words which are pointed with *Tzere*; namely, the fifteen words with *Kametz*: as תְּעַנֶּה *thou shalt afflict* [Exod. xxii. 22], הַזֵּה *sprinkle* [Numb. viii. 7], &c., all of which are pointed with *Tzere*, and not one of them with *Kametz*. The same rule obtains with *Pattach*. All the words thus described have *Pattach* only; as the six words with *Pattach*, viz., בַּמַּחֲזֶה *in the vision* [Gen. xv. 1], קָרְחָה *baldness* [Isa. iii. 24], &c.⁴² Hence you see that they made no distinction between *major* and *minor* in the naming of the vowels. Indeed, in the Massorah parva, they have not even called them by the names *Kametz* and *Pattach*, but the vowel-points are put under the letter which designates the number of instances wherein the word in question thus occurs; *ex. gr.*, the word בָּהֵן *in them*, " occurs fifteen times [ט״ו] with *Tzere* under *He*."⁴³ The same is the case with *Pattach*; as the word מַאֲכַל *eating*, " occurs

---

⁴¹ The complete alphabetical list is given in the Massorah marginalis, on Levit. i. 1. We deviate from our general practice, and do not give this alphabetical list, both because it is extremely long, and because it does not contain any material changes in the text.

⁴² The Massorah gives twenty-five such instances; they are as follows:—

תענה	. .	Exod. xxii. 22	ותקרא	. .	Jerem. xxxii. 23	העלה	. .	Habak. i. 15
מרבה	. .	Levit. xi. 42	תאבה	. .	Prov. i. 10	העברת	. .	Josh. vii. 7
לסרבה	. .	Isa. ix. 6	מלוה	. .	Prov. xix. 17	ישר	. .	Prov. iii. 6
מקרה	. .	Deut. xxiii. 11	מחסה	. .	Isa. xxviii. 17	ילד	. .	Prov. xxvii. 1
וניעשה	. .	Josh. ix. 24	מרעה	. .	Isa. xxxii. 14	כהן	. .	Ezek. xviii. 14
הראה	. .	1 Kings xviii. 1	ומצוה	. .	Isa. lv. 4	ועד	. .	Jerem. xxix. 23
תהיה	. .	Jerem xvii. 17	תראה	. .	Dan. i. 13	חבל	. .	Isa. lxvi. 7
מזרה	. .	Jerem. xxxi. 10	הזה	. .	Numb. viii. 7	פתה	. .	Ps. cxix. 130
			משה	. .	Deut. xv. 2			

They are enumerated in the Massorah finalis, under the *Koph*, p. 56 *a*, col. 1.

⁴³ The fifteen instances in which בהן occurs with *Tzere* are as follows:—Gen. xix. 29; xxx. 26, 37; Exod. xxv. 29; xxxvii. 16; Levit. x. 1; Numb. x. 3; Deut. xxviii. 52; Jerem. iv. 29; li. 43 (twice); xlviii. 9; Isa. xxvii. 16; Ezek. xlii. 14; 1 Sam. xxxi. 7. They are enumerated in the Massorah finalis, under the letter *He*, p. 24 *b*, col. 2. It is in the Massorah parva that the vowel-signs to which Levita refers are given.

197

four times with *Pattach* [רַ] under the *Kaph*,"[44] and with *Segol*, as הֶ *behold* "occurs five times [הֶ] with *Segol* under *He*."[45] Accordingly, by the vowel-point of the signal letter is to be known what the Massorah treats of; and this is easily understood.

☞ It is, however, to be remarked, that in the words with *Pattach of each Book* the Massorites have put together the *Segols* with the *Pattachs*. Let me now explain what is *Pattach of the Book*. It is known, from the laws of the vowel-points, that when *Athnach* and *Soph-pasuk* come under *Pattach* and *Segol*, they convert the latter into a long *Kametz*. Some instances, however, are left in each book of the Bible, which have not been thus converted, and these are denominated *Pattach of the Book = Pattach de Siphra*. They have been counted by the Massorah, and amount to nineteen in Genesis; as, וַיֹּאכַל *and he did eat* [Gen. iii. 6], וָמַשׁ *and Mash* [ibid. x. 23], וְכַלְנֶה *and Calneh* [ibid. x. 10], אֲבָרְכֵם *I shall bless them* [Gen. xlviii. 9]. Twelve of these have *Pattach* with *Athnach*, and seven with *Soph-pasuk*.[46] In all the other sacred books, too, they have counted those with *Athnach* separately, and those with *Soph-pasuk* separately, whilst the *Pattachs* and *Segols* they have mixed up together.

SECTION III., concerning *Dagesh, Raphe, Mappik,* and some of the laws of the *Sheva.*—It is well known that *Dagesh* is a point put in the

מאכל ד'; [44] וכן בסגול הן הֶ,[45] חרי בנקוד אות הסימן נכר במה המסורת מדברת, וזה קל להבין:

§ אכן דע כי במלות שהם בפתח דספרא ערבו הסגולים בתוך הפתוחים; ועתה אבאר מה פתח דספרא; הנה ידוע מדרך הנקוד כי לא יבא אתנח וסוף פסוק תחת פתח גדול או קמץ רק יההפכו לקמץ גדול; אבל נשארו מהן בכל ספר וספר שלא יתהפכו, והן נקראים פרחת דספרא, ונמנין על פי המסורת, והם י"ט בספר בראשית, כגון לאשה עמה וַיֹּאכַל, נתר וָמָשׁ, ואבד וְכַלְנֶה, אלי אֲבָרְכֵם, י"ב מנהון פתחין באתנח, ח' מנהון בסוף פסוק;[46] וכן בכל ספר וספר נמנים אותן שבאתנח לבד, ואותם שבס"פ לבד, והתערבו הפתחין והסגולין יחד:

המאמר השלישי בדגשין ורפין ומפקין וקצת דיני השוא: בידוע שהדגש היא

---

[44] The four passages in which מאכל occurs, with *Pattach* under the *Kaph*, are, Gen. xl. 17; 1 Kings x. 5; Job xxxiii. 20; 2 Chron. ix. 4. They are enumerated in the Massorah marginalis on Gen. xl. 17.

[45] The five passages in which הֶן occurs, with *Segol* under the *He*, are, Numb. xxiii. 9, 24; Job viii. 19; xxxiii. 12; xxxi. 35. They are enumerated in the Massorah marginalis on Numb. xxiii. 9.

[46] The list of the words which have *Pattach*, with *Athnach* and *Soph-pasuk*, is nowhere given in the Massorah. From the detached remarks in the Massorah parva, however, we gather the following twelve words, which have *Pattach* with *Athnach*:—

וחאכל	. . . Gen. iii. 6	ויגמל	. . . Gen. xxi. 8	נדר	. . . Gen. xxxi. 13
וכלנה	. . . Gen. x. 10	וקנתי	. . . Gen. xxvii. 2	מנשתי	. . . Gen. xxxiii. 8
וחדר	. . . Gen. xvi. 4	שבע	. . . Gen. xxviii. 10	במה	. . . Gen. xxxiv. 25
ויצחק	. . . Gen. xvii. 17	בת	. . . Gen. xxx. 21	עד	. . . Gen. xlix. 27

To these may be added החוזמת (Gen. xxi. 15) and משטרבם (ibid. xlii. 19). As to the seven instances in which the words have *Pattach* with *Soph-pasuk*, we could not find any more than those adduced in the text. It must, however, be remarked, that there is a great difference of opinion upon several of the passages given in the list. Comp. *the Mebin Chidoth*, on Gen. xvii. 17, p. 10 b.

bosom of a letter, whilst *Raphe* is a straight line like a *Pattach* [—] put over the letter, especially over the aspirates *Beth, Gimmel, Daleth, Kaph, Pe,* and *Tav,* as I have explained in the *Poetical Dissertation.* The Massorites speak but very little about these, and, since they have already been explained, I need not speak any more about them. You are, however, to observe, that the Massorites also call the letters *Teth, Samech, Shin, Koph, Tzaddi, Nun, Vav, Zajin, Lamed, Jod,* and *Mem* feeble letters, because they ought to have *Dagesh,* but the *Dagesh* has been dropped for the sake of ease. Most of these occur in the *Piel,* where the characteristic *Dagesh* in the middle stem letter is omitted, as in the *Nun* in וַיְקַנְאוּ and they envied [Gen. xxxvii. 11], the *Koph* in וַיְבַקְשׁוּ *and they sought* [Josh. ii. 22], the *Lamed* in שִׁלְחוּ *they sent* [Ps. lxxiv. 7], &c.

But in the letters *Beth, Gimmel, Daleth, Kaph, Pe, Tav,* the *Dagesh* is only very rarely omitted, as in מִבְּצִיר *than the vintage* [Judg. viii. 2], מִנְּבוּרָתָם *from their strength* [Ezek. xxxii. 30], and a few more; and even in the letters *Teth, Samech, Shin, Koph, Tzaddi, Nun, Vav, Zajin, Lamed, Jod, Mem,* the *Dagesh,* as I have already said, is only dropped when one of them is pointed with *Sheva,* and especially in *Mem* with *Sheva* following the article, as הַמְדַבֵּר *who speaks* [Gen. xlv. 12], הַמְלַמֵּד *who teaches* [Ps. cxliv. 1], הַמִּסְכֵּן *who is impoverished* [Is. xl. 20], &c.; all these they call feeble letters, though they have not the straight line of *Raphe* over them. Now I submit that they ought to have the *Raphe* line placed over them, to show that the *Dagesh* is dropped, *ex. gr.* יְקַנְאוּ, יְבַקְשׁוּ, שִׁלְחוּ, הַמְדַבֵּר, הַמְשַׁלֵּחַ, lest the reader should think that the Scribe has inadvertently omitted the *Dagesh* and read it with *Dagesh.* I therefore expostulated with the printers of this district for not even putting *Raphe* on the aspirates, *Beth, Gimmel, Daleth, Kaph, Pe,* and *Tav,* because they said that they did not require it, since when they had no *Dagesh* it was known that they were feeble. But this is a mistake. In

הנקודה הנתונה בנוף האות, וחרפי הוא קו ישר כמו פתח נתון על ראש האות, ובפרט באותיות בנ"ד כפ"ת, כאשר בארתי בפרק שירה; והנה בעלי המסורת לא דברו מאלה כי אם מעט וכולן מבוארים, ואין צורך לדבר בם; אך צריך שתדע כי קראו גם כן האותיות דפויות ט"ס שק"ץ נוז"לים, וזה כאשר ראויים להדגש, ונפל מהם הדגש להקל, ורובם מבנין פעל הדנוש, כגון נו"ן של וַיְקַנְאוּ בו אחיו, וקו"ף של וַיְבַקְשׁוּ הרודפים, ולמ"ד של שָׁלְחוּ באש מקדשך וכו':

אכן באותיות בנ"ד כפ"ת לא יפול הדנש מהם כי אם מעט מזער, כמו מִבְּצִיר אביעזר, מִנְּבוּרָתָם בושים, ודומיהם מעטים; ואפילו מאחירות ט"ס שק"ץ נוז"לים לא נופל הדנש לעולם רק מן תיבה הנקודה בשוא, כמו אלה שכתבתי, ועל הרוב מ"ם שואית הבאה אחר ה"א הידיעה, כמו הַמְדַבֵּר אליכם, הַמְלַמֵּד ידי, הַמִּסְכֵּן תרומה ודומיהן, לכלן קראו אותיות רפויות, אע"פי שאין עליהם קו הרפי; ואומר אני שראוי לשום עליהם קו הרפי, לחודיע שחסר הדנש, כמו יְקַנְאוּ, יְבַקְשׁוּ, שָׁלְחוּ, הַסְדַבֵּר, הַמְשַׁלֵּחַ ודומיהן, פן יחשוב הקורא שהסופר השמים הדנש ויקראם בדנש; לכן קרא אני תגר על בעלי הדפוס אשר בזה הנליל שאינן משימים דפי אפילו על בנ"ד כפ"ת, באמרם שאינם צריכים להם, מאחר שאין בהם דנש בידוע שיש בהם רפי, ומעות הוא בידם; ומ"ם במילות מרנלות

the case of well known words, as וַיִּשְׂאוּ **and they lifted up,** וַיִּסְעוּ **and they journeyed,** וַיִּקְחוּ **and they took,** וַיְהַלְלוּ **and they praised,** הַלְלוּיָהּ *praise ye the Lord,* &c., &c., from all of which *Dagesh* has been dropped, there is no necessity for placing the *Raphe* line over them, because they are the majority. The Massorites, also, call every *He* feeble which ought to have *Mappik* but has it not, as טָהֳרָה *her purity* [Levit. xii. 5], בְּאִמָּהּ *like her mother* [Ezek. xvi. 44], &c. But I have already discussed this point in Part i., Sections ix. and x., on *Mappik Aleph* and *Mappik Jod*, where I have explained which is *Mappik Aleph* and which is not.

As to *Mappik He*, it is a point in the bosom of the *He*, like *Dagesh* at the end of a word. The Germans used this point, as רָגְלָהּ *her foot,* יָדָהּ *her hand,* &c.; they would not put the point under the *He*, because they thought that it might mislead, lest the reader should read it *Chirek*. This, however, is not to be regarded, since there does not occur a point in the last letter of the word, as I have explained in Part i., Section v.

☞ It is moreover known, from the laws of grammar, that the prepositional letters, *Kaph, Lamed,* and *Beth,* are pointed according to rule with *Sheva,* except when it cannot be, as I have explained in the *Section on the Serviles*.[47] Now the Massorites call this *Sheva, Raphe,* because it can never be followed by *Dagesh*. Thus, they remark בְּבַיִת *in the house,* "occurs six times *Raphe;*"[48] בְּכֶסֶף *for money,* "occurs fifteen times *Raphe;*"[49] לְכִסֵּא *to a throne,* "occurs six times *Raphe*."[50] They are also called *Raphe* when they are not followed by the aspirates

[47] The section is the last of the four dissertations composing the *Poetical Dissertation,* and the rule here referred to is on p. 63, ed. Prague, 1793.
[48] The six instances in which בבית occurs *Raphe* are, Exod. xii. 46: 1 Kings iii. 17: 2 Sam. vii. 6: 1 Chron. xvii. 5: Isa. v. 8: Amos vi. 9. They are enumerated in the Massorah marginalis on 1 Kings iii. 17.
[49] The fifteen passages in which בכסף is *Raphe* are, Gen. xxiii. 9: Josh. xxii. 8: 2 Sam. xxiv. 24, with 1 Chron. xxi. 22, 24: 1 Kings xxi. 6, 15: Isa. xlviii. 10; lii. 3: Jerem. x. 4: Ezek. xxvii. 12: Micah iii. 11: Ps. cv. 37: Lament. v. 4: Ezra i. 4: Dan. xi. 38. They are given in the Massorah marginalis on Josh. xxii. 8.
[50] The six instances in which לכסא is *Raphe* are, Isa. xxii. 23: Jerem. lii. 32: Ps. ix. 5; cxxxii. 11, 12: Nehem. iii. 7. They are given in the Massorah marginalis on Isa. xxii. 23: Nehem. iii. 7.

Beth, Gimmel, Daleth, Kaph, Pe, and Tav; as בְּלִילָה, *in the night*, occurs three times *Raphe*;[51] and בְּחֶרֶב *with the sword*, occurs eight times *Raphe*;[52] or when they are pointed with *Chirek*, on account of the *Sheva* by which they are followed; as בִּבְהֵמָה *in cattle*, which is four times *Raphe*;[53] and בְּשָׂדַי *in the field*, five times *Raphe*,[54] &c. It is further known that the prepositional letters *Kaph*, *Lamed*, *Beth*, which are pointed with *Pattach*, indicating the contracted article

רפין[51] בְּחֶרֶב ח' רפין:[52] וכן כשהן נקודים בחיריק בסיבת חשוא הבא אחריהם, כמו בִּבְהֵמָה ד' רפין,[53] בְּשָׂדַי ח' רפין[54] ורומיהן; וידוע נ"כ כי אותיות כל"ב הפתוחים המורים על ח"א הידיעה, תמיד דנש אחריהם, לפיכך קראו לתיבות הפתחין האלה דנושין, כמו בַּכֹּל ז' דנושין,[55] לַטּוֹב ב' דנושין;[56] וכן כשהן קמוצים בעבור אח"עה מנו אותם, כמו לָאָדָם י"א קמוצים,[57] לָאִישׁ ל"ב קמוצים:[58]

והכלל כי חמיד מוני המועטים אם דנושים אם רפין, וכששניהם מועטים הם מונין את שניהן, כמו בְּטוֹב ד' רפין, בְּטוֹב

He, are always followed by *Dagesh*. The Massorites, therefore, call those letters *Dagesheḍ*, which have such a *Pattqch*; hence they remark on בַּכֹּל *in all*, "seven times *Dagesheḍ*,"[55] and לַטּוֹב *to good*, "twice *Dagesheḍ*."[56] They also counted them when they are pointed with *Kametz*, because of being followed by the gutturals *Aleph*, *Cheth*, *Ajin*, and *He*, as "לָאָדָם *to the man*, eleven times with *Kametz*;"[57] "לָאִישׁ *to the man*, thirty-two times with *Kametz*."[58]

Now the rule is, that they always counted those which are fewer in number, whether with *Dagesh* or *Raphe*, and when both happened to be few, they counted both; as בְּטוֹב *in good*; on which they remark,

[51] The three passages in which בלילה occurs *Raphe* are, Gen. xl. 5; xli. 11: Nehem. ix. 19. They are enumerated in the Massorah marginalis on Gen. xl. 5.
[52] The eight passages in which בחרב is *Raphe* are, 1 Sam. xvii. 45, 47: 2 Sam. xii. 9: Isa. xxxi. 8: Jerem. xx. 4: Ezek. xxviii. 23: Hag. ii. 22: Dan. xi. 33. They are enumerated in the Massorah marginalis on 1 Sam. xxii. 45.
[53] As בבהמה only occurs four times *Raphe*, viz., Levit. vii. 21; xx. 15; xxvii. 10, 26—we have corrected the text, which in the three editions states that the word in question is *six* ('ו) times *Raphe*. Comp. Massorah marginalis on Levit. vii. 21.
[54] The five passages in which בשדי is *Raphe* are, Numb. xx. 17; xxi. 22: Isa. v. 8: Ruth ii. 8. 22. Comp. the Massorah marginalis on Numb. xx. 17.
[55] The seven passages in which בכל occurs with *Dagesh* in the *Kaph* are, Gen. xvi. 12; xxiv. 1: 2 Sam. xxiii. 5: Ps. ciii. 19: Eccles. v. 8: Ezra x. 17: 1 Chron. xxix. 12. They are given in the Massorah finalis under the letter *Kaph*, p. 39, col. 4.
[56] The two instances in which לטוב is *Raphe*, *i. e. Pattach* under the *Lamed*, are, Numb. xxxvi. 6, and Eccles. ix. 2. They are given in the Massorah marginalis on Numb. xxxvi. 6.
[57] The eleven places in which לאדם has *Kametz* under the *Lamed* are, Exod. iv. 11: Jerem. x. 23: Zeph. i. 17: Prov. xix. 19: Job xviii. 28: Eccles. i. 2; ii. 18, 22; vi. 12 (twice); viii. 15. Both the Massorah marginalis on Jerem. x. 23, and the *Ochla Ve-Ochla*, section xv., pp. 62, 175, describe this rubric as follows:—"לאדם occurs five times with *Kametz* under the *Lamed*; it is likewise so throughout Ecclesiastes, except in one place where the *Lamed* has *Sheva*, viz., ii. 26."
[58] The thirty-two passages in which לאיש occurs with *Kametz* under the *Lamed* are, Gen. xliii. 6, 11; xlv. 22: Levit. xii. 4; xxv. 27; Numb. v. 8: Deut. xxii. 16; xxv. 9: Judg. xvi. 19: 1 Sam. ii. 15; ix. 7; xvii. 26, 27; xxvi. 23: 2 Sam. xii. 4; xviii. 11: 1 Kings viii. 39, with 2 Chron. vi. 30: Jerem. xxvi. 11, 16: 2 Kings xxii. 15, with 2 Chron. xxxiv. 23: Malachi ii. 12: Prov. xv. 23: xx. 3, 17; xxiv. 29: Job iii. 4: Ruth iii. 3: Esther vi. 9, 11. They are enumerated in the Massorah finalis under the letter *Aleph*, p. 6 a, cols. 2 and 3.

"four times *Raphe*,"[59] "nine times *Dageshed*;"[59] בְּנֶשֶׁר "like an eagle," "four times *Raphe*," כְּנֶשֶׁר "seven times *Dageshed*.[60] When they happen to be pairs, that is, two with *Raphe* and two with *Dagesh*, they call them *Milel* and *Milra*, as I shall explain in the following Section; and when both are equally numerous, as בַּדֶּרֶךְ בְּדֶרֶךְ in the way, בַּמִּדְבָּר בְּמִדְבָּר in the desert, בָּעִיר בְּעִיר in the city, they neither counted the *Raphes* nor the *Dageshes*, because they are very numerous. The exclamatory, or interrogative *He*, too, which is pointed with *Chateph-pattach*, is called *Raphe*; as הֲשֹׁמֵר the keeper? [Gen. iv. 9], is marked "not extant, *Raphe*;" הֲשֹׁפֵט the judge? [Gen. xviii. 25], is "not extant, *Raphe*"; but when it has *Pattach*, on account of being followed by the gutturals *Aleph*, *Cheth*, *He*, and *Ajin*, they do not call it *Raphe*, but *Pattached*; as הָאִישׁ a man? [Neh. vi. 11], is "not extant with *Pattach*;" הָעֶבֶד a servant? [Jerem. ii. 14], is "not extant with *Pattach*," &c.

It is also to be remarked that the Massorites likewise call *Raphe* the *Vav* conjunctive which precedes the letters *Aleph*, *Jod*, *Tav*, and *Nun*; as וְאֶשָּׂא and I shall bear, is marked "twice *Raphe*;"[61] וְיֹאמַר and he shall say, "six times *Raphe*;"[62] וְתִשְׁמַע and hear thou, "five times *Raphe*."[63] The same is the case when it is pointed with *Chirek*, because of the *Jod*, belonging to the preformatives *Aleph*, *Jod*, *Tav*, and *Nun* of the future, whereby it is followed, as I have explained in

---

[59] The four instances in which בָּטוֹב is *Raphe* are, Levit. xxvii. 10: Ps. xxv. 13: Eccl. ii. 1; vii. 14: and the nine passages in which it is בְּטוֹב with *Dagesh* in the *Teth* are, Gen. xx. 15: Deut. xxiii. 17: Isa. vii. 15, 16; Jerem. xxix. 32: Ps. ciii. 5: Job xxi. 13; xxxvi. 11: 2 Chron. vi. 41. The former are enumerated in the Massorah marginalis on Levit. xxvii. 10; and the latter, in the Massorah marginalis on Isa. vii. 15, and Job xxi. 13.

[60] The four passages in which כנשר is *Raphe*, that is has *Sheva* under the *Kaph*, are, Deut. xxxii. 11; Habak. i. 8; Prov. xxiii. 5; Job. ix. 26; and the seven passages in which the *Kaph* has *Pattach* are, Jerem. xlviii. 40; xlix. 16, 22: Hos. viii. 1; Obad. 4; Micah i. 16; Ps. ciii. 5. For the former, see the Massorah marginalis on Deut. xxxii. 11. The list of the latter we could not find any where in the Massorah.

[61] The two instances in which the *Vav* ואשא, Kal future, first person singular masculine of נשא, has *Sheva* are, Ps. lv. 13; cxix. 48.

[62] The six instances in which the *Vav* conjunctive is ויאמר Kal future, third person singular masculine, has *Sheva* are, 2 Kings ix. 17: Isa. xliv. 16, 17; lviii. 9: Habak. ii. 6: Ps. lviii. 12.

[63] This must surely be a mistake, since ותשמע only occurs twice with *Sheva* under the *Vav* conjunctive, viz., Deut. xxxii. 1: 2 Chron. xx. 9.

the Section on the Servile Letters, *ex. gr.* וִישַׁלַּח *and he will send*, on which they remarked, "fifteen times *Raphe*;"[64] וִיהִי *and it shall be*, "thirty-two times *Raphe*."[65] Or when the said *Vav* is pointed with *Shurek*, on account of *Tav* and *Nun* with *Sheva*, belonging to the preformative letters *Aleph, Jod, Tav,* and *Nun*, whereby it is followed, as וּתְדַבֵּר *and thou shalt speak*, which is marked "twice *Raphe*" [Is. xl. 27]; וְנִסְפְּרָה *and we shall declare* [Jerem. li. 10], "not extant, *Raphe*," &c.[67]

☞ The rule is, that whenever *Vav* preceding the future is pointed with *Sheva, Chirek*, or *Shurek*, they call it *Raphe*, except when it occurs in pairs, one of which has *Sheva* and the other *Pattach*. In such a case they call it *Milel* and *Milra*, as I have stated above. Mark that they always counted the instances in which it is *Raphe*, because they are the fewer, since in most cases in which *Vav* precedes the letters *Aleph, Jod, Tav*, and *Nun* it is conversive, and has *Pattach*, followed by *Dagesh*. This *Vav* conversive they did not count, because it is the most frequent; but when it has *Kametz*, because of the guttural *Aleph* belonging to the preformatives, *Aleph, Jod, Tav*, and *Nun*, they generally counted it, as וָאָשִׂים *and I shall put*, on which they remark "nine times;"[68] וָאֵדַע *and I shall know*, "three times."[69] Notice, also, that there is a kind of *Sheva*, which they call *Dagesh*, namely, *Sheva* quiescent under the gutturals *Aleph, Cheth, He*, and *Ajin*, as in יַחְפֹּץ *he shall covet*, יַחְמֹד *he shall desire*, &c., whilst they call *Raphe*, the *Chateph-pattach* and *Chateph-segol*, because *Dagesh* never follows them. I have already stated in "the Poetical Dissertation," poem viii., that in five instances the *Sheva* is called mobile, and not quiescent.

[64] Neither can we understand this remark, since וִישַׁלַּח only occurs once, viz., Exod. vi. 11.
[65] The thirty-two instances in which ויהי occurs with *Chirek* under *Vav* conjunctive have already been given. Vide supra, p. 141, note 122.
[66] The two passages in which ותדבר occurs with *Shurek* are, Isa. xl. 27: Ezek. xxiv. 27.
[67] The single instance in which ונספרה occurs, is Jerem. li. 10.
[68] The nine instances in which ואשים occurs with *Kametz* under the *Vav* are, Gen. xxiv. 47: Deut. x. 5: 1 Sam. xxviii. 21: 1 Kings viii. 21: Isa. li. 16: Jerem. xiii. 2: Malachi i. 3: Job xxxviii. 10: 2 Chron. vi. 11.
[69] The three passages in which ואדע occurs are, Isa. l. 7: Jerem. xxxii. 8: Ezek. x. 10.

☞ Let me now give you the letters *Aleph, Beth, Gimmel, Daleth,* and *He* as a new and appropriate mnemonical sign for it. *Aleph* [= first] means that whenever *Sheva* is under the first letter of a word, it is vocal, as שְׁמַע בְּנִי *hear my son* [Prov. i. 8]; *Beth* [= two] means that when two *Shevas* occur in the middle of a word, the first is silent and the second is vocal, as יִשְׁמְעוּ *they shall hear,* יִלְמְדוּ *they shall learn,* &c.; *Gimmel,* which is the initial of גדולה *long,* means that whenever *Sheva* follows a long syllable it is vocal, as שָׁמְרוּ *they kept,* וַיֵּשְׁבוּ and *they dwelled,* הוֹלְכִים *the coming,* &c.; *Daleth,* which is the initial of *Dagesh,* means that whenever *Sheva* is under a letter with *Dagesh* it is vocal, as דִּבְּרוּ *they spoke,* דִּבְּרָה a *word,* &c.; whilst the letter *He,* which is the initial of הדמות *alike* signifies that when two letters which are alike come together, and the first has *Sheva,* it is vocal, as in הַלְלוּיָהּ *Hallelujah,* where, though the first *Lamed* has no *Dagesh,* yet it is called vocal *Sheva* because of the two *Lameds,* and הִנְנִי *behold I,* in which *Sheva* is vocal because of the two *Nuns*. Remember this mnemonical sign, and treasure it up, for it is useful.

I shall return now to my first subject, and give you an example of a *Sheva,* which the Massorites call *Dagesh.* They make the following remark in the Massorah: "the expression עלמה *to conceal,* has always *Dagesh*;" that is, it is always with simple *Sheva,* as הַעְלֵם יַעְלִימוּ *hiding they shall hide* [Levit. xx. 4], &c. They also say the word חסיה *to trust,* has always *Dagesh,* as אֶחְסֶה *I shall trust* [Ps. lvii. 2], מַחְסִי *my shelter* [Ps. xci. 2], &c., except in six instances, in which it is *Raphe,* that is, with *Chateph-pattach* or *Chateph-segol,* as מַחֲסֶה *refuge* [Joel iv. 16], אֱחֱסֶה *I shall trust* [Ps. xviii. 3], &c.[70] They also remark, מעשר *tithe,* occurs three times with

---

[70] This is surely a mistake, since the Massorah marginalis on Ps. lxii. 9, enumerates nine instances in which חסיה is *Raphe,* or has *Chateph-pattach*. They are as follows:—

מחסה . . . Ps. lxii. 9	מחסי . . . Ps. lxxi. 7	לחסות . . . Ps. cxviii. 9
מחסה . . . Ps. xlvi. 2	מחסי . . . Jerem. xvii. 17	לחסות . . . Ruth ii. 12
מחסה . . . Joel iv. 16	לחסות . . . Ps. cxviii. 8	חסיה . . . Ps. lvii. 2

The Massorah, moreover, adds that וכל אחסה דכור רסי במ"א ובצל כנפיך אחסה, *the future* אחסה *is likewise Raphe, everywhere except in one instance,* viz., Ps. lvii. 2. In the Massorah finalis, under the letter *Cheth* 32 a, col. 2, where reference is made to the word in question, it is also distinctly stated that it is *nine* times *Raphe.*

☞ ועתה אחדש לך סימן יפה א, ב, ג,
ד ה: וא' ר"ל כל שוא שבראש התיבה הוא שוא נע, כמו שְׁמַע בְּנִי: ב' ר"ל כשהין ב' שואין באמצע התיבה, הראשון נח וחשני נע, כמו יִשְׁמְעוּ, יִלְמְדוּ; ג' ר"ל גדולה, פירוש כל שוא שאחר תנועה גדולה הוא נע, כמו שָׁמְרוּ, וַיֵּשְׁבוּ, הוֹלְכִים ודומיחן; ד' ר"ל דגש, כל שוא שתחת אות דגושה, כמו דִּבְּרוּ, דִּבְּרָה ודומיחן; ה' ר"ל הדמות, פירוש כשיחיו ב' אחיות דומות, והראשונה בשוא הוא נע, כמו הַלְלוּיָהּ, שחל"מד הראשונה אינה דגושה, ומ"מ נקרא חשוא נע בעבור שני הלמ"דין, וכן הִנְנִי השוא נע בעבור שני הנו"נין, וזכור זה חסימן, ותצפנהו כי טוב הוא:

והנה חוזר על הראשונות, ואתן לך משל על חשוא שקראו דנש; אמרו במסורת כל לשון העלמה בדגש, ר"ל בשוא פשוט, כמו וְאִם הַעְלֵם יַעְלִימוּ ודומיחן; וכן כל לשון חסיה דגש, כמו בצל כנפיך אֶחְסֶה, אומר לי"י מַחְסִי ודומיחן, חוץ מן ח' רפויין ר"ל בחטף פתח או בחטף סגול, כמו וי"י מַחֲסֶה לַעֲמּוֹ, צוּרִי אֶחֱסֶה בּוֹ;[70] וכן אמרו מַעְשַׂר ג' דגושים,

Dagesh, as מַעֲשַׂר the tithe of [Levit. xxvii. 30], &c.,[71] and in all other instances it is *Raphe*, that is, with *Chateph-pattach*, as מַעֲשַׂר the tithe of [Deut. xiv. 23], &c. Examine, and you will find it so.

SECTION IV., concerning *Milel*, *Milra*, and *Psik*.—Mark that there is not a single word in the whole Scripture without an accent either at the beginning, middle, or end. Now, the Massorites call the place on which the accent rests by two Aramaic names. The one is מלעיל *Milel*, which is the translation of the Hebrew מלמעלה *from above*; and the other is מלרע *Milra*, and is the translation of the Hebrew מתחת or מטה *from below*. By this is not meant that the accent is either above or below the centre of the letter, but when the accent is either on the first letter of the word, or on the middle, they call it *Milel*, and when it is on the end of the word they denominate it *Milra*. Now there are some words which, according to rule, are always *Milel*; and there are others, again, which, according to rule, are always *Milra*; whilst some, again, are at times *Milel*, and at other times *Milra*. Still there are exceptions to all these. In the book entitled *Good Sense*, which I have determined to compose, all these rules will be explained, together with all the other laws of the accents, if God permit.[72] It must be added, that the Massorites make but very few desultory remarks on this subject.

As a rule, they do not note every single word, whether it has the accent on the penultima or on the ultima, but only very occasionally mark some words which are anomalous, either in their accents or points. Thus, for instance, they give a register of thirty-eight words, which in one case only have the accent on the penultima, whilst in all other passages they have the accent on the ultima, as וְהִשְׁקִיתָ *and thou*

---

[71] The three instances in which מעשר occurs with *Dagesh* = with *Sheva* under the *Ajin* are, Levit. xxvii. 32: Numb. xviii. 24: Levit. xxvii. 30. They are given in the Massorah finalis under the letter *Ajin*, p. 51 b, col. 2.

[72] The *Dissertation on the Accents*, to which Levita refers, appeared in 1539, within twelve months of the publication of the treatise on the Massorah (*vide supra*, p. 63, &c.). The discussion on the tono accents, or *Milel* and *Milra*, is contained in the sixth chapter of the dissertation in question.

shalt water it [Deut. xi. 10], on which the Massoretic remark is, "not extant, *Milel ;"* [73] and also another register—in which the reverse is the case—of words, which in one instance only are *Milra*, whilst in all other passages they are *Milel*, as הָבָה *come now* [Gen. xxix. 21], noted "not extant as *Milra*." [74] בְּרַגְלְךָ לֵית מִלְעֵיל ; [73] וכן שימה אחת לחפף מלרע וכל חברותיה מלעיל, כמו הָבָה אֶת אשתי לית מלרע, וסימן אשתי למסח ; [74] וכן וַיּוֹסֶף נ׳, ב׳ מלעיל וא׳ מלרע, [75] וכן תֹּסֶף ח׳, ג׳ לרע וב׳ לעיל, [76] אשר הם דלעיל הם בסגול ואשר הם מלרע הם בצירי על פי הדקדוק, ובעבור השתנות כזה, הם מנו אותם ונתנו בהן סמנים, אבל מלות שאין בהן השתנות כנ"ל, כגון
They also remark on וַיֹּסֶף *and he added*, "three times, twice *Milel* and once *Milra;"* [75] as well as on תֹּסֶף *she shall add*, "five times, thrice *Milra* and twice *Milel."* [76] Those which are *Milel* have *Segol*, whilst those which are *Milra* have, according to grammar, *Tzere;* and, in consequence of this change, the Massorites counted them, and have given the marks of the passages; whilst, with regard to those in which the said change does not take place, as יִקָּרֵא *it shall be called*, which

[73] The thirty-eight words which respectively have in one instance only the accent on the penultima are as follows:—

וְהִשְׁקִית	. . Deut. xi. 10	קינה	. . Ezek. xix. 14	למה	. . Job vii. 20
לשרה	. . Deut. xvii. 12	ושבה	. . Isa. vi. 13	מנע	. . Prov. xi. 26
רבה	. . Gen. xviii. 20	שבר	. . 2 Kings vii. 6	יקרה	. . Prov. iii. 15
יצחק	. . Gen. xxi. 6	מתה	. . 1 Sam. xxx. 6	דחת	. . Prov. xvii. 10
וסר	. . Levit. xv. 13	התחתונה	. . Ezek. xl. 19	ותאמר	. . Prov. vii. 13
קצה	. . Numb. xxi. 5	החיצונה	. . 2 Kings xvi. 18	ארבעה	. . Prov. xxx. 24
חזקה	. . Judg. xviii. 28	רעה	. . Isa. xxiv. 19	חומה	. . Ezek. xlii. 20
טובה	. . Ruth iv. 15	וחגרה	. . Isa. xxxii. 11	בצע	. . Prov. i. 19
הקם	. . 2 Sam. xxiii. 1	ורדה	. . Ezek. xxiv. 11	הבו	. . Job. vi. 22
יסף	. . Judg. xiii. 21	בוקה	. . Isa. lxiii. 11	אחו	. . Job xxiii. 9
ושברתי	. . Ezek. xiv. 12	יצק	. . 2 Kings iii. 11	שמע	. . Ps. cl. 5
הרם	. . 2 Kings vi. 7	וזה	. . Job xix. 17	הרשע	. . Eccl. iii. 16
צרה	. . Isa. xxviii. 20	צרר	. . Isa. xl. 8		

They are given in the Massorah finalis, under the "variations between the Easterns and Westerns," p. 62 *a*, cols. 3 and 4. The *Ochla Ve-Ochla*, section ccclxxii., pp. 61, 171, gives seventeen additional instances, whilst it omits some which are contained in our list.

[74] The list of words which on the contrary occur only once with the accent on the ultima is as follows:—

הבה	. . Gen. xxix. 21	ואסיה	. . Levit. xxiv. 5	מרחם	. . Isa. xlix. 15
מתה	. . Gen. xxx. 1	וראיתה	. . Numb. xxvii. 13	בקר	. . Amos vii. 14
ירא	. . Gen. xli. 33	לחם	. . Judg. v. 8	חומץ	. . Ps. lxxi. 4
ויושב	. . Gen. xlvii. 11	זרע	. . Judg. vi. 8	שש	. . Prov. xxiii. 7
שתי	. . Exod. x. 1	ארצא	. . 1 Kings xvi. 9	נוכח	. . Job xxiii. 7
והעלית	. . Exod. xl. 4	השמר	. . Isa. vii. 4	סהר	. . Job xxx. 30
והביאה	. . Levit. xv. 29	שרש	. . Isa. xl. 24		

There are also two others, about which there is a difference of opinion, viz., וחצית Numb. xxxi. 27, and ומשית Zech. vi. 11. They are enumerated in the *Ochla Ve-Ochla*, section ccclxxiii., pp. 61, 172.

[75] The two instances in which וסף is *Milel* are, Prov. i. 5; ix. 2.; and the one instance of *Milra* is in 2 Sam. xxiv. 3. See the Massorah marginalis on 2 Sam. xxiv. 3.

[76] The three passages in which תסף occurs *Milra* are, Gen. iv. 2; Deut. xiii. 1; Ps. civ. 29. It will be seen that in the first two instances it is the Hiphil future of יסף *to add;* whilst in the third passage it is Kal future, second person singular masculine for תאסף from אסף *to gather.* They are enumerated in the Massorah marginalis on Exod. iv. 12, and in the *Ochla Ve-Ochla*, Section iv. of the additions, pp. 62, 173. The two passages in which it is *Milel* are, Exod. x. 28; Deut. iii. 26. Comp. Massorah marginalis on Exod. x. 28.

occurs twenty-one times,[77] and יֵדַע *he shall know*, nineteen times,[78] which according to rule ought all to be *Milra*; and though some of them are *Milel*, because of the proximity of the accents, as יִקָּרֵא *it shall be called* [Isa. xxxv. 8], יֵדַע *he shall know* [1 Sam. xx. 8], they do not say a single word inasmuch as no change of vowel has taken place in them.

יִקָּרֵא כ״א,[77] יֵדַע י״ט,[78] כלם דינם לרע. אעפ״י שיש מהם מלעיל מפני קרוב חטעמים, כמו ודרך הקרש יִקָּרֵא לח, אל יֵדַע זאת יהונתן, לא דברו מזה דבר, לפי שאין בהן השתנות חנקודה:

☞ Mark, moreover, that a kind of *Milel* and *Milra* occurs in the Massorah magna, which does not refer to the position of the accents, but to the change of the vowels. This is the case with words which occur twice, and which the Massorites denominate pairs. They are of two kinds. The first class consists of two words beginning with the serviles *Kaph, Lamed,* and *Beth,* before the preformative *Aleph, Jod, Tav,* and

☞ ודע כי נמצא במסרה גדולה ענין מלעיל ומלרע שאינו על חנחת חטעמים, רק על חשתנות חנקודות, וזה במלות שנמצאו שנים שנים שקראו להן זוגות, וחם של ב' מינין:

המין האחד הוא מן ב' מלין שראשן אותיות כל״ב, או הוי״ו שבראש האיתן, ובמלה אהת חן נקודות בשוא ובחברתה בפתח ודנש אחריה, כנון אותן שקראו לחן דנשין ורפין, כאשר כתבתי במאמר הקודם; וחכלל אין חפרש בין חדנשין והרפין, ובין אלו שקראו לחן זוגות, רק שאל חן זוגות לבד: והמשל כגון י״א זוגין חד מלעיל וחד מלרע ובי״ת בריש॒חון, כלו בְּדִמְעוֹת עיני מלעיל, בְּדִמְעוֹת שליש מלרע;[79] וכן א״ב

Nun of the future, one word of which is pointed with *Sheva*, and the other with *Pattach,* followed by *Dagesh;* as is the case with those words called *Dagesh* and *Raphe,* as I have explained in the preceding section. Normally there is no difference between those called *Dagesh* and *Raphe* and those which they call pairs, except that the latter only are arranged in pairs. Thus, for instance, the eleven pairs, one which is *Milel,* and one *Milra,* beginning with *Beth;* as בְּדִמְעוֹת *in tears, Milel* [Lament. ii. 11], and בְּדִמְעוֹת, *Milra* [Ps. lxxx. 6], &c.;[79] the alphabetical list of double pairs of words beginning with *Kaph,*

---

[77] The twenty-one instances in which יקרא occurs, are as follows: Gen. ii. 23; xvii. 5; xxxv. 10; xxi. 12; Numb. xxiii. 3; Deut. iii. 13; xxii. 6; 1 Sam. ix. 9; Isa. iv. 1; xiv. 20; xxxi. 4; xxxii. 5; lvi. 7; xxxv. 8; liv. 5; i. 26; lxii. 12; Jerem. xx. 6; Isa. lxii. 4; Prov. xvi. 21; Esther iv. 11. They are given in the Massorah marginalis on Jerem. xix. 6. It will be seen that two of the instances, viz., Numb. xxiii. 3; Deut. xxii. 6, are not from קרא, *to call.*

[78] The nineteen passages in which ידע occurs are, Josh. xxii. 22; 1 Sam. xx. 3; xxi. 8; Isa. vii. 16; viii. 4; lii. 6; Jerem. xxxvi. 19; xl. 15; xxxviii. 24; Job xiv. 21; Ps. xxxv. 8; xxxix. 7; xcii. 7; Prov. xxiv. 12; xxviii. 22; Eccl. viii. 5 (twice); ix. 12; x. 14. They are given in the Massorah marginalis on Ps. xcii. 7.

[79] The eleven pairs of words beginning with *Beth,* which respectively occur once *Milra* (i. e., with *Sheva,* or its substitutive feeble vowel) and once *Milel* (i. e., with the real vowel), are as follows:—

ברמשח	. . Ps. lxxx. 6	במצלה	. . Ps. cvii. 24	בנגע	. . Deut. xxiv. 8
ברסטוח	. . Lament. ii. 11	במצלה	. . Zech. i. 8	בנגע	. . Levit. xiii. 3
בחיין	. . Dan. vii. 12	במםלכה	. . Isa. xix. 2	בשאת	. . Exod. xxvii. 7
בחיין	. . Job xxiv. 22	במםלכה	. . Amos ix. 8	בשאת	. . Levit. xiii. 10
בחרש	. . Isa. viii. 1	בסכך	. . Ps. lxxiv. 5	בתנור	. . Levit. xxvi. 2
בחרש	. . Exod. xxxii. 4	בסכך	. . Gen. xxii. 13	בתנור	. . Levit. vii. 9
במדינות	. . Esther ix. 16	בסירות	. . Amos iv. 2		
במדינות	. . Lament. i. 1	בסירות	. . 2 Chron. xxxv. 13		

one of which is *Milel*, and the other *Milra*, as כְּאֹהֶל as the tent [Isa. xl. 22], *Milel*, and כְּאֹהֶל [Isa. xxxviii. 12], *Milra*;[80] the twenty-two pairs of two words, each beginning with *Vav*, one of which is *Milel*, and the other *Milra*, as וְיִתְאָו and he desired [1 Chron. xi. 17], *Milel*, and וְיִתְאָו and he shall desire [Ps. xlv. 12], *Milra*, &c.[81]

מן ב' ב' מלין כ"ף ברישיהן א' טלעיל וא' טלרע, כָּאֹהֶל לשברת טלעיל, כְּאֹהֶל רועי טלרע; [80] וכן כ"ב זוגין מן ב' ב' מלין וי"ו ברישיהן א' לעיל וא' לרע, וַיִּתְאָו דוד לעיל, וְיִתְאָו המלך יפיך לרע:[81]

והמין הב' הוא נאמר על שאר הנקודות. ויש מהן אלפא ביתא במסרה גדולה שקראו

The second kind comprises the other vowel-points. Of these, there is an alphabetical list in the Massorah magna giving words

They are given in the Massorah finalis under the letter *Beth*, p. 14a, cols. 3 and 4; Massorah marginalis on Isa. viii. 1; and *Ochla Ve-Ochla*, section xlix., pp. 15, 55.

[80] The alphabetical list of words beginning with *Kaph*, which only occur twice, once *Milra*, or with *Sheva* as its substitutive feeble vowel, and once *Milel*, or with the real vowel, is as follows:

כְּאֹהֶל	. . Isa. xxxviii. 12	כחום	Song of Songs iv. 3		כסוחה	. . Ps. lxxx. 17
כָּאֹהֶל	. . Isa. xl. 22	כחום	. . Judg. xvi. 12		כסוחה	. . Isa. v. 25
כארזים	. . Numb. xxiv. 6	כחתן	. . Ps. xix. 6		כסוסה	. . Prov. i. 27
כארזים	. Song of Songs v. 15	כחתן	. . Isa. lxi. 10		כסוסה	. . Isa. v. 28
כאבק	. . Isa. xxix. 5	כחלב	. . Levit. iv. 26		כסרב	. . Ps. lxxxiii. 12
כאבק	. . Isa. v. 24	כחלב	. . Ps. cxix. 70		כערב	Song of Songs v. 11
כבריח	. 2 Chron. xxxiv. 32	ככבוד	. . Isa. xvii. 13		כצר	. . Lament. ii. 4
כבריח	. Jerem. xxxi. 32	ככבוד	. . Ezek. iii. 23		כצר	. . Isa. v. 28
כגמול	. . Ps. cxxxi. 2	כמה	. . Ps. xxxi. 13		כרשע	. . Job xxvii. 7
כגמול	. . Ps. cxxxi. 2	כמה	. . Numb. xii. 12		כרשע	. Gen. xviii. 25
וכרקב	. . Prov. xii. 4	כמושת	. . Ps. lxxi. 7		כשואה	. . Prov. i. 27
וכרקב	. . Hos. v. 12	כמושת	. 1 Kings xiii. 5		כשואה	. Ezek. xxxviii. 9
וככפיר	. . Ps. xvii. 12	כמלונה	. . Isa. i. 8		כשושנה	Song of Songs ii. 2
וככפיר	. . Hos. v. 14	כמלונה	. . Isa. xxiv. 20		כשושנה	. . Hos. xiv. 6

This catalogue is given in the Massorah finalis under the letter *Kaph*, p. 38a, col. 1; and in the *Ochla Ve-Ochla*, section xi. pp. 7, 19, &c. The alphabetical order will be seen after the letter *Kaph*.

[81] The twenty-two words beginning and ending with *Vav*, each one of which occurs twice, once *Milra*, or with *Vav* conjunctive, and once *Milel*, or with *Vav* conversive, are as follows:—

ויתאו	. . Ps. xlv. 12	וישרו	. . Isa. xlv. 8		וישכנו	. . Ps. xxxvii. 29
ויתאו	. 1 Chron. xi. 17	וישרו	. . Gen. xlvii. 27		וישכנו	. . Gen. xxv. 18
ויתמהו	. . Job xxvi. 11	ויעדו	. 1 Kings xxi. 10		וירבו	. . Job xii. 15
ויתמהו	. . Gen. xliii. 33	ויעדו	. 1 Kings xxi. 13		וירבו	. . Isa. xi. 24
ויתרו	. . Numb. xiii. 2	וישבעו	. . Ps. xxii. 27		ויצקו	. 1 Kings xviii. 34
ויתרו	. . Numb. xiii. 21	וישבעו	. . Hos. xiii. 6		ויצקו	. 2 Kings iv. 40
ויהסכו	. . Job xii. 15	וינהנו	. 1 Sam. xxx. 22		ויצצו	. . Ps. lxxii. 16
ויהסכו	. 1 Sam. xxv. 12	וינהנו	. 1 Sam. xxx. 2		ויצצו	. . Ps. xcii. 8
ויחיו	. Ezek. xxxvii. 9	וינורו	. . Levit. xxii. 2		ויצאו	. . Jerem. xv. 1
ויחיו	. Ezek. xxxvii. 10	וינורו	. . Hos. ix. 10		ויצאו	. Gen. xxxiv. 26
וישנו	. . Ps. cxix. 5	וירעשו	. . Amos ix. 1		ויצברו	. . Gen. xli. 35
וישנו	. . Ps. lxxviii. 57	וירעשו	. . Isa. xxiv. 18		ויצברו	. . Exod. viii. 10
ויאסמהו	. . Habak. i. 15	וירכסו	. . Exod. xxviii. 28		ויצליחו	. . Jerem. v. 28
ויאסמהו	. 1 Sam. xiv. 52	וירכסו	. . Exod. xxxix. 21		ויצליחו	. 2 Chron. xiv. 6
וינתנו	. 2 Chron. xviii. 14	וישמיעו	. . Jerem. xxiii. 22			
וינתנו	. 1 Chron. v. 20	וישמיעו	. . Nehem. xii. 42			

They are given in the Massorah finalis under the letter *Vav*, p. 29b, cols. 1 and 2; and in the *Ochla Ve-Ochla*, section xlv., pp. 14, 52, &c. It will be seen that though the Massorah states in the heading of this rubric that there are *twenty-two* such instances, it gives *twenty-three*. This arises from the fact that the word וישבעו (Ps. xxii. 27; Hos. xiii. 6), which is an addition to this rubric, has inadvertendly been mixed up with it. In the *Ochla Ve-Ochla* it is rightly separated.

wherein those which have *Cholem,* *Shurek,* or *Kibbutz,* are called *Milel;* whilst those which have *Kametz, Kametz-chateph, Pattach, Tzere,* or *Chirek,* are called *Milra.* This, however, is only the case with groups of pairs. As, for instance, when a word occurs twice, once with *Cholem* and another time with *Kametz, Kametz-chateph,* or *Tzere;* the Massorites call the one with *Cholem, Milel,* and the rest *Milra.* Thus, אֲכָל [Gen. iii. 11] is *Milel,* אֲכֹל *eating of* [Deut. xii. 28], is *Milra;* יִדְלֹף *it shall drop* [Eccl. x. 18], is *Milel,* יִדְלַף *Jidlaph* [Gen. xxii. 22], is *Milra;* דָּעֲכוּ *they are quenched* [Ps. cxviii. 12], is *Milel,* דָּעָכוּ [Isa. xliii. 17], is *Milra;* אֹרְחוֹת, *the travellers* [Isa. xxi. 13], is *Milel,* אֹרְחַת *a company of* [Gen. xxxvii. 25], is *Milra;* הַמְשֹׁל *to rule* [Judg. ix. 2], is *Milel,* הַמְשֵׁל *to rule* [Job xxv. 2], is *Milra.*[88]

חמלורת שבחן חולם, או שורק, או קבוץ מלעיל, ואשר בחן קמץ, או קמץ חטף, או פתח, או צרי, או חירק מלרע; וזה לא נאמר רק על זוגות של שנים שנים מלין; והמשל כשיחיו ב' מלות האחת בחולם וחברתה בקמץ, או בחמף קמץ, או בצרי, קראו אותה שבחולם מלעיל והשאר מלרע; כגון לבלתי אֲכָל ממנו מלעיל, לבלתי אֲכֹל הרם מלרע, יִדְלֹף הבית מלעיל, ואת פלדש ואת יִדְלַף מלרע, דּוֹעֲכוּ כאש קוצים מלעיל, דָּעֲכוּ כפשתה מלרע, אֹרְחוֹת דודנים מלעיל, אֹרְחַת ישמעאלים מלרע, הַמְשֹׁל בכם מלעיל, הַמְשֵׁל ופחד מלרע:[88]

[88] The alphabetical list to which Levita refers, and which illustrates all his remarks on the second kind, is as follows:—

אֲכֹל	. . Deut. xii. 23	הודיענו	. . 1 Sam. vi. 2	משקלה	. . 2 Kings xxi. 13
אֲכָל	. . Gen. iii. 11	הודיענו	. . Job xxxvii. 19	למשקלת	. . Isa. xxviii. 17
אמר	. . Ezek. xxv. 8	וגעתר	. . 1 Chron. v. 20	מחלך	. . Deut. xxxii. 18
אמר	. . Prov. xxv. 7	וגעתר	. . Isa. xix. 22	מאירות	. . Ezek. xxviii. 9
ארחות	. . Isa. xxi. 13	ונחתום	. . Esther viii. 8	מאירות	. . Isa. xxvii. 11
ארחת	. . Gen. xxxvii. 25	ונחתום	. . Esther iii. 12	מאירה	. . Ps. xix. 9
אדן	. . Nehem. vii. 61	ויקם	. . Eccl. xii. 4	נתן	. . 2 Kings xxiii. 11
אדן	. . Ezra ii. 59	ויקום	. . Job xxii. 28	נתן	. . Gen. xxxvii. 9
אנס	. . Esther i. 8	ומשלו	. . Jerem. xxx. 21	נתץ	. . Judg. vi. 28
אנם	. . Dan. iv. 6	ומשלו	. . Zech. ix. 10	נתץ	. . 2 Chron. xxxiii. 3
בקרב	. . Ps. xxvii. 2	זרע	. . Ps. xcvii. 11	נחם	. . Hos. xiii. 14
בקרב	. . 2 Sam. xv. 5	וזרע	. . Levit. xi. 37	נחם	. . 1 Chron. iv. 19
במעל	. . Nehem. viii. 6	חנן	. . Gen. xxxiii. 5	נסלו	. . 1 Sam. xxix. 3
במעל	. . Josh. xxii. 22	חנן	. . Isa. xxx. 19	נסלו	. . 2 Sam. i. 10
בנער	. . Job xxxvi. 14	מדור	. . Habak. i. 13	עניתי	. . Ps. cxix. 71
בנער	. . 2 Sam. xviii. 12	מדר	. . Prov. xxii. 11	עניתי	. . Ps. xxxv. 13
גוירנו	. . Nehem. ix. 37	ידינו	. . 2 Kings vii. 4	צאת	. . Isa. iv. 4
גוירנו	. . Gen. xlvii. 18	ידינו	. . Hos. vi. 2	צאת	. . Ezek. xii. 12
דעכו	. . Ps. cxviii. 12	ידלף	. . Eccl. x. 18	קראני	. . Isa. xlix. 1
דעכו	. . Isa. xliii. 17	ידלף	. . Gen. xxii. 22	קראני	. . Job iv. 14
האמר	. . Ezek. xxviii. 9	כתם	. . Ps. lxxviii. 72	רמוני	. . Lament i. 19
האמר	. . Job xxxiv. 31	כתם	. . Isa. xviii. 5	רמני	. . 2 Sam. xix. 27
הקצור	. . Isa. lv. 2	לאמתם	. . Gen. xxv. 16	שמלתי	. . Gen. xliii. 14
הקצר	. . Micah ii. 7	לאמתם	. . Lament ii. 12	שמלתי	. . Gen. xliii. 14
המשל	. . Judg. ix. 2	לשבים	. . Isa. lxi. 1	ששמונו	. . Dan. ix. 12
המשל	. . Job xxv. 2	לשבים	. . Joel iv. 8	ושפמנו	. . 1 Sam. viii. 20
הנחת	. . Dan. v. 20	מעצור	. . 1 Sam. xiv. 6	תאומי	. . Song of Songs iv. 5
הנחת	. . Joel iv. 11	מעצר	. . Prov. xxv. 28	תאמי	. . Song of Songs vii. 4

The list is given in the Massorah finalis under the letter *Aleph,* p. 2 a, col. 4–2 b, col. 2; and in the *Ochla Ve-Ochla,* section v., pp. 5, 13, &c. The latter adds כצרוף (Zech. xiii. 9; Ps. lxvi. 10), as not being included in the Massoretic list (לבד ממסורתא), whilst it deviates in its description of הנחת and נתץ.

They call *Shurek*, *Milra*, in opposition to *Kametz*, *Pattach*, and *Tzere*; as שְׁפָטוּנוּ *they judged us* [Dan. ix. 12], is *Milel*, שְׁפָטָנוּ *he judged us* [1 Sam. viii. 20], is *Milel*; רִמּוּנִי *they deceived me* [Lam. i. 19], is *Milra*, רִמַּנִי *he deceived me* [2 Sam. xix. 27], is *Milra*; יְחַיֻּנוּ *they shall let us live* [2 Kings vii. 4], is *Milel*, יְחַיֵּנוּ *he will make us live* [Hos. vi. 2], is *Milra*. The *Kibbutz* again is *Milel*, in opposition to *Tzere* and *Chirek*; as הוֹדִיעֻנוּ *inform us* [1 Sam. vi. 2], is *Milel*, הוֹדִיעֵנוּ *teach us* [Job xxxvii. 19], is *Milra*; לְאֻמֹּתָם *according to their nations* [Gen. xxv. 16], is *Milel*, לְאִמֹּתָם *to their mothers* [Lament. ii. 12], is *Milra*. Now, though *Kametz-Chatuph* in opposition to *Cholem* is *Milra*, as I have already shown, yet in opposition to *Pattach* it is *Milel*; as הֻנְחַת *he was thrust down* [Dan. v. 20], is *Milel*, הֻנְחַת *make to come down* [Joel iv. 11], is *Milra*; נָפְלוֹ *his falling* [1 Sam. xxix. 3], is *Milel*, נִפְלוֹ *his falling* [2 Sam. i. 10], is *Milra*. Thus, also, *Kametz*, though *Milra* in opposition to *Shurek*, as I have stated, is *Milel* in opposition to *Tzere*; as זָרַע *it is sown* [Ps. xcvii. 11], is *Milel*, זָרוּעַ *sown* [Levit. xi. 37], is *Milra*. It is to be borne in mind that all which I have stated about these two kinds is only to be found in the Massorah magna; in the Massorah parva the Massorites have not remarked upon a single one of these instances, either *Milel* or *Milra*, but they simply say, "not extant."

☞ Let me now explain the meaning of *Piskin*. There is one accent called *Psak* or *Psik*, which is a straight line (|) between two words. It consists of two kinds, the one is a *Psik* not followed by the accent *Rebia*, as in וַיִּקְרָא אֱלֹהִים | לָאוֹר יוֹם *and God called the light day* [Gen. i. 4], עָשׂוּ | כָּלָה *they have done it, they have accomplished* [Gen. xviii. 21]. This is called by the Massorites *Psik of the Book*, because it occurs in every book of the Scriptures, and is enumerated in the Massorah as, in Genesis there are twenty-nine *Piskas*, in Exodus nineteen,

---

[88] The instances which illustrate all the remarks of Levita, made in this paragraph, are contained in the alphabetical list of *Milels* and *Milras* given in note 82 of the preceding page.

E E

and so forth in all the books of the Bible.[84] The second is the accent called *Le-garmiah*, which is in form like the real *Psik*, but it is always followed by the accent *Rebia*. You will find it in the treatise *Good Sense*, as well as in the Third Part called the Broken Tables, where I shall speak about it.

SECTION V., concerning Registers, Groups, Parallels, and Analogous Forms. — Our Rabbins of blessed memory frequently use the word *Shita*, saying, "a *Shita* of such and such an one," "another *Shita*," &c. To the same effect is the use of *Shita* in the Talmud, and I do not know from what language it is derived, neither does the author of *Aruch*[85] give it. I, however, find that the Chaldee of the Song of Songs paraphrases "his cheeks are like beds of balsam" [v. 13], by "the two tables of stone which He gave to his people were written in ten rows [*Shittin*], resembling the rows or beds [*Shittin*] in the garden of balsam." Thus, also, the Targum of Joseph translates, "noted it in a book" [Isa. xxx. 8], by "register it on the lines [*Shittin*] of the book." Thus, too, our Rabbins of blessed memory called the lines of a book *Shita*, when they say, "it is necessary to leave four empty lines [= *Shittin*] between each book," "the beginning of a line [= *Shita*]," "the end of a line [= *Shita*]," &c. They also remark on כְּדָרְלָעֹמֶר *Chedorlaomer* [Gen. xiv. 9], that it is to be separated into two words in one line, but it must not be separated into two lines.[86] The Massorites likewise call that *Shita* which our Rabbins of blessed memory called *Shita*, that is, a register of things

בכל הספרים; [84] וחמין חשני הוא הטעם הנקרא לגרמיה, והוא כדמות פסיק ממש, אבל תמיד אחריו רביע; ובספר טוב טעם תמצאנו, גם בשער שברי לוחות אדבר בו:

המאמר החמישי בשיטין וזוגין ודמיין ודכוותהון: הרבה שמשו רז״ל בלשון שימה באמרם שימה של פלוני, שימה אחרינה, וכן שימת התלמוד, ולא ידעתי מאיזה לשון הוא, גם בעל הערוך לא הביאו; [85] אך מצאתי בתרגום שיר השירים בפסוק לחייו כערוגת הבושם, תרין לוחי אבנין דיהב לעמיה כתיבן בעשר שיטין, דמין לשיטי גנת בוסמא, וכן ועל ספר חקה, ח״י ועל שימין דספר רשם; וכן קראו רבותינו וכרונם לברכה לשורות הספר שימה, כמו שאמרו צריך להניח ד׳ שימין בין כל ספר וספר, וכן בראש שימה, בסוף שימה; וכן כתבו על כדר לעומר פסקין ליה בתרי תיבות בשימה חדא, ולא פסקין ליה בתרי שימין; [86] וכן קראו בעלי המסורת שימה למה שקראו רז״ל שימה,

---

[84] The number of *Piskin* in each book of the Bible is as follows:—

Genesis 29	Isaiah 30	Song of Songs . . . 10
Exodus 14	Jeremiah 31	Ecclesiastes 3
Leviticus 8	Ezekiel 28	Lamentations . . . 8
Numbers 22	Minor Prophets . . . 10	Esther 5
Deuteronomy . . . 22	1 and 2 Chronicles . . 63	Daniel 8
Joshua 17	Psalms 40	Ezra-Nehemiah . . 13
Judges 7	Job 6	
1 and 2 Samuel . . 48	Proverbs 8	479
1 and 2 Kings . . 45	Ruth 4	

They are enumerated in the Massorah finalis, p. 53, &c.

[85] For the author of the *Aruch*, *i. e.*, R. Nathan b. Jechiel, see above, p. 2.

[86] The Talmudic discussion on the orthography of the proper name Chedorlaomer, to which Levita refers, is to be found in *Chulin*, 65 a.

of the same import, as a number of verses, pairs, or words which are alike either in vowel-points or in letters. Such a number they called *Shita* [= catalogue, register, list, or rubric].

The rule is, that every collection of verses or of words brought together, which is not alphabetically arranged, they called *Shita* [*i. e.*, catalogue or register]; and I have received it that such a *Shita* has not less than ten lines. These registers are of diverse import. There is a register of so many pairs of words, or of so many verses, or of so many words, or of so many letters, which it is not necessary to illustrate by examples.

☞ Let me now explain the meaning of *Sug* and *Sugin*. Mark, that the proper meaning of זוג is *a pair, two*. Thus, the Chaldee paraphrase renders a pair by זוג [2 Kings v. 17], with *Cholem*, but זֻג with *Shurek* means *a bell*, and, in the language of our Rabbins of blessed memory, a pair of phylacteries; thus, also, the phrase "to every one thou givest a pair [זוג], but me thou didst not give a pair." They call the plural, although masculine, זוּנוֹת; as, the phrase שקבל מן הזונות, which means *received from two Sages*. It is well known that the numbers are divided into two parts, namely, even and odd; the uneven are, 1, 3, 5, 7, and 9, whilst the even are, 2, 4, 6, 8, and 10. Now, the Rabbins of blessed memory call every number which is not uneven זונות, = *pairs*, *ex. gr.*, "one should not eat even [זונות], nor drink even [זונות]," always in the plural feminine; whereas the Massorites always use the plural in the masculine gender, and not only call each pair by the name *Sug*, but even things consisting of twice three, twice four, or twice five, up to ten, they denominate *Sugoth*. There are numerous instances of it to be found in the Massorah magna. There are also registers and alphabetical lists of words which have no pairs, that is, which have no parallels.

In some Codices the expression רמיין = *parallel*, is added to זונין

רוצה לומר הצעת דברים מענין אחד, כגון סכום פסוקים, או זונין, או מלות, שיש בהן חדמות מה בנקודתן, או באותיותיהן, וקראו להן שימה:

והכלל כל קבוץ של פסוקים, או מלות הרבה יחד, שאינן על סדר האלפא ביתא, קראו להן שיטין; ומקובלני שאין שיטה פחותה מעשרה שורות; ונמצאים שיטין של עניינים רבים, כגון שיטה מן כך וכך זונין, או כך וכך פסוקים, או מלות, או אותיות, ואין צורך להביאם:

☞ ועתה אבאר מה ענין זוג וזונין; דע כי סתם זוג הוא שנים, וכן תרגום של צָמֶד פרדים וג' כודנין, והוא נקוד בחולם, אבל זוג הנקוד בשורק הוא חפעמון, ובדברי רז"ל זוג תפילין, וכן לכל נתת זוג ולי לא נתת זוג; ואמרו על הריבוי אפילו על זכרים זונות, כמו שאמרו שקבל מן הזונות, פירוש מן שני תלמידי חכמים; וידוע כי המספר נחלק לב' חלקים זוג ונפרד; הנפרד א, ג, ה, ז, ט; והזוג ב, ד, ו, ח, י וכולי; ורבותינו ז"ל קראו לכל מספר שאינו נפרד זונות, באמרם לא יאכל זונות ולא ישתה זונות, כלן בלשון רבות; אבל בעלי חמסרת זכרו תמיד הרבוי בלשון זכרים, ולא לבד דברים של שנים שנים קראו זוג, כי אפילו דברים של ג' ג', או ד' ד', או ה' ה' וכולי עד עשרה, קראו זוגין, וכאלה רבות במסרה גדולה; וכן נמצאין שיטין, ואלפא ביתין מן מלין דלית לחון זוג, דוצה לומר שאין להם דומה:

וביש נוסחאות מוסיפין עם זונין רמיין,

pairs. Thus, for instance, they remark "there are five parallel pairs of words, which respectively occur twice, once the two words have the *Vav* conjunctive, and once not," as the first, וְיִשָּׂשכָר וּזְבֻלוּן and *Issachar and Zebulun*, [Gen. xxxv. 23]; and the second, יִשָּׂשכָר וּזְבוּלֻן *Issachar, Zebu'un*, [Exod. i. 3], &c.[87] Thus, also, they say that such and such verses are parallel [דמיין], as "the two parallel verses [דמיין] in which all the words terminate with the letter *Mem*," viz., Gen. xxxii. 15, and Numb. xxix. 38. The expression דמיין, however, is only used epexegetically, since it would be sufficient without it. As a rule, the Massorites never employ דמיין, except with respect to groups and verses.

☞ I shall now explain the meaning of דכוותיה. The Chaldee paraphrase renders כָּמֹהוּ *like it* [Joel ii. 2] by דכוותיה; so also כְּמוֹהֶם *like unto them* [Ps. cxxxv. 18] by דכוותהון. It, too, is simply used as an additional explanation in most places; in a few instances, however, it is really wanted, as will be seen in the Tenth Section of this Part, God helping.

SECTION VI., concerning Junctions, Severances, and Consecutives.— Mark that the expression סמיכה, which the Massorites use, denotes *approaching, belonging together, connected*, &c., as is the meaning of סָמַךְ in Ezek. xxiv. 2, which has no parallel in the Scriptures. It is, however, frequently used by our Rabbins of blessed memory, as in the phrases, *it is close* (סמוך) *upon dark, it will soon be dark; this section* (נסמכה) *is contiguous*, &c. Now, when two or more words are associated together through the addition or diminution of a letter or word, or by the interchange of words which are not in the habit of

כגון ה' זוגין דמיין, ב' מנהון נסיבין ו"ו, כגון קדמאה וְיִשָּׂשכָר וּזְבֻלוּן (בראשית ל"ה), ותנינא יִשָּׂשכָר וְזָבֻלֻן;[87] וכן כך' וכך פסוקים דמיין, כגון ב' פסוקים דמיין שכל סופי תיבחהון ממ"ן עזים מאתיים ותישים עשרים ונומר, ומנחתם ונסכיהם וגו' דיום ז', ואין דמיין אלא לתוכפת ביאור כי יספיק זולתו; והכלל כי לא כתבו דמיין רק על זוגין ועל פסוקים:

☞ ועתה אבאר ענין דכוותיה; תרגום של כָּמֹהוּ לא נהיתה דכוותיה לא הות, וכן כְּמוֹהֶם יהיו עושיהם דכוותהון יהון עובריהון; וגם הם אינן אלא לתוספת ביאור ברוב המקומות, אך בקצת מקומות הוצרכו לו, כאשר תראה במאמר י' בע"ה:

המאמר הששי בסמיכין. ויחידין ומורדפין: דע כי לשון סמיכה ששמשו בו בעלי המסרה הוא מלשון קרוב ודביקה, כמו סָמַךְ מלך בבל, ואין לו עוד דומה במקרא; אבל רז"ל שמשו בו הרבה, באמרם סמוך לחשיכה, ונסמכה פרשה זו, ורומיהן רבים; והנה כשיסמכו ב' מלות או יותר בתוספת או בחסרון אות, או מלה, אובחילוף מלה, שאין

---

[87] The five pairs of words which respectively occur once with the *Vav* conjunctive, and once without it, are,—

החסידה האנפה . . . . Levit. xi. 19	עשר נכסים . . . . . 2 Chron. i. 11
ההחסידה האנפה . . . . Deut. xiv. 18	עשר ונכסים . . . . . 2 Chron. i. 12
עין רמון . . . . . Josh. xix. 7	ששכר וזבלן . . . . . Exod. i. 3
ועין ורמון . . . . . Josh. xv. 32	וישכר זבולן . . . . . Gen. xxxv. 23
דכדין אמרין . . . . . Ezra vii. 17		
דכדין אמרין . . . . . Ezra vi. 9		

They are given in the Massorah finalis under the letter *Var*, p. 28 *b*, col. 1; and in the *Ochla Ve-Ochla*, section ccli., p. 138.

being joined in this manner, and if it only occurs so in one place, the Massorites remark thereon, "not extant so joined." Thus, on וְדָגָן וְתִירשׁ *and corn, and wine* [Gen. xxvii. 87], they remark, "not extant so joined," since, in all other places where these two words occur, the word דָּגָן *corn* has not the *Vav* conjunctive;[68] and שָׁמִיר שָׁיִת *briers, thorns* [Is. xxvii. 4], is marked "not extant so joined," since in all other places it is with *Vav* conjunctive.[69] The same is the case with words which are trans-

דרכן לחסמך באותו אופן, אם לא נמצא כזה רק במקום אחד, כתבו עליה לית דסמיך, כגון וְדָגָן וְתִירשׁ לית דסמיך, כי כל שאר דגן ותירוש בלי ו"י החיבור במלת דגן;[68] וכן שָׁמִיר שָׁיִת במלחמה לית דסמיך, כי כל שאר שמיר ושית עם ו"י החיבור;[69] וכן במלות

[68] The Massorah gives a list of sixty-two pairs, both words of which have *Vav* conjunctive, and are without parallel; viz.:—

דגן ותירוש	Gen. xxvii. 37	וזבח ומנחה	Jerem. xvii. 26
הצאן והבקר	Gen. xxxiii. 13	ובאף ובחמה	Jerem. xxi. 5
ושמשבר ולוי	Gen. xxxv. 23	והשכם ושלח	Jerem. xxvi. 5
וישׂשכר וזבלן	Gen. xxxv. 23	ועבדך ועמך	Jerem. xxii. 2
וחצרון וכרמי	Gen. xlvi. 9	ונגלה ונפרשה	Ezek. iv. 14
ואני ועמי	Exod. ix. 27	יוסף ונשים	Ezek. ix. 6
ואהרן חזור	Exod. xvii. 12	וברכב ובפרשים	Ezek. xxvi. 7
ושה וישמה	Exod. xxviii. 20	ואלמנה וגרושה	Ezek. xliv. 22
ועלה ומנחה	Exod. xxx. 9	ומשפט וצדקה	Ezek. xlv. 9
והעלה והשלמים	Levit. ix. 22	ואלמנה ויתום	Zech. vii. 10
ואלף ושבע	Exod. xxxviii. 25	והם ובניהם	1 Chron. ix. 23
ושור ושה	Levit. xiii. 23	וששים וששׁ	2 Chron. ix. 13
ועבדך ואמתך	Levit. xxv. 44	ועשר ונכסים	2 Chron. i. 12
והעמלקי והכנעני	Numb. xiv. 25	ובנינו ובנותינו	2 Chron. xxix. 9
ואתה ואהרן	Numb. xvi. 17	וארבעים ושלשה	Ezra ii. 25
וחשבון ואלעלה	Numb. xxxii. 3	ושבעים ושנים	Nehem. vii. 8
והירדן וגבל	Deut. iii. 17	ושלשים וארבעה	1 Chron. vii. 7
האתת והמפתים	Deut. vii. 19	וארבעים ושנים	Nehem. vii. 62
ובאהות ובמשתים	Deut. xxvi. 8	ועשרים ושנים	Nehem. vii. 31
ויוסף ובנימין	Deut. xxvii. 12	ועשרים ואחד	Nehem. vii. 37
ובנתיה וחצריה	Josh. xv. 45	ובני אחוד	Ezra viii. 18
ומדין ועמלק	Judg. vii. 12	ומנעלי ובריחיו	Nehem. iii. 6
וזבח וצלמנע	Judg. viii. 10	ושרתינו וכרכינו	Nehem. v. 5
וסל ומצבה	Levit. xxvi. 1	ולשמר לעשות	Nehem. x. 30
ואיש איש	1 Sam. xxvii. 11	ובניו ובנותיו	Job i. 13
וישׂראל ויהודה	2 Sam. xi. 11	ואמשאלך הודיעני	Job xxxviii. 3
וארבעים ואחת	1 Kings xv. 10	ואבהם ושרה	Gen. xxiii. 11
ושלשים ואחת	2 Kings xxii. 1	וההוד והדר	Job xl. 10
ורע וראה	1 Kings xx. 22	וחסד ואמת	Prov. xiv. 22
ודגלעד ונבל	Josh. xiii. 11	והכמל וחמן	Esther iii. 15
והכהנים והנביאים	2 Kings xxiii. 2	ולהון לאבד	Esther viii. 11
חרב ורעב	Jerem. v. 12	ועיר ועיר	Esther ix. 23
ובקר רצאן	1 Chron. xii. 40		

The list is given in the Massorah finalis under the letter *Vav*, p. 28*a*, cols. 2 and 3; and in the *Ochla Ve-Ochla*, section ccliii., pp. 50, 139, &c. The latter omits six which the Massorah enumerates, and has fifteen instances which are not given in the Massorah.

[69] This is but one out of sixteen pairs, without the *Vav* conjunctive, which have no parallel. They are as follows:—

בטוף ובנהמה	Gen. ix. 10	מלך שרים	Hos. viii. 10
יששכר זבלן	Exod. i. 3	שמש ירח	Habak. iii. 10
עין רמון	Josh. xix. 7	משה אהרן	Micah vi. 4
עיר פיר	Josh. xxi. 40	עשר נכסים	2 Chron. i. 11
שמיר שית	Isa. xxvii. 4	דגן תרוש	2 Chron. xxxi. 5
אכל שתה	Isa. xxii. 13	נשרים בנחים	Nehem. x. 20
לכהנים ללוים	Isa. lxvi. 21	השמים שמי	Nehem. ix. 6
יען ביען	Ezek. xxxvi. 3		

It will be seen that, though the Massorah states in the heading of this rubric that there

posed in a verse, as שַׁבָּת שַׁבָּתוֹן Sabbatism, Sabbath [Exod. xvi. 23], on which they remark, "not extant so joined;" since in all other passages in which these two words are joined, they are inverted.⁹⁰ חמוקדמים וחמאוחרים בפסוק, כמו שַׁבָּתוֹן שַׁבַּת קדש ליהוה לית דסמיך, כי כל שאר שבת שבתון,⁹⁰ וכן וידבר משה אל יְהֹוָה לית

are *sixteen* such instances, it only gives *fifteen*, whilst one of the passages adduced is wrong, viz., דגן חירוש 2 Chron. xxxi. 5, inasmuch as it occurs *twice* in Chron. and Deut. xxviii. 51. The *Ochla Ve-Ochla*, section cclii., pp. 50, 138, &c., which also gives this list, rightly supplies the two deficiencies, viz., שם חם Gen. x. 1; and גדולות בצורות Josh. xiv. 12. Properly speaking החסידה האנפה Levit. xi. 19; and דברי אמרץ Ezra vii. 17, belong to this rubric, and it is difficult to divine why the Massorah does not include them in it, seeing that it includes the other instances from the rubric given on p. 212, note 87.

⁹⁰ This is but one of thirty-nine instances enumerated in the Massorah, which occur in this construction, since in all other passages they are inverted. They are as follows:—

שבתון שבת	Exod. xvi. 23	everywhere else	שבת שבתון
אסתה ליהוה הוא	Exod. xxix. 18	,, ,,	אשה הוה ליהוה
חמשים לאות	Exod. xxxvi. 17	,, ,,	חמשים ללאת
אחד לעלה לחמאת ואחד	Levit. xii. 8	,, ,,	אחד לחמאת ואחד לעלה
בהכמה ובתוף	Levit. xx. 25	,, ,,	בטוף ובבהמה
לאמו ולאביו	Levit. xxi. 2	,, ,,	לאביו לאמו
אמו ואביו	Levit. xix. 3	,, ,,	אביו ואמו
הישר והטוב	Deut. vi. 18	,, ,,	הטוב והישר
משפט צדק	Deut. xvi. 18	,, ,,	צדק ומשפט
בתמים ובאמת	Josh. xxiv. 14	,, ,,	באמת ובתמים
המלך אדני	2 Sam. xiv. 15	,, ,,	אדני המלך
הקם ליהוה מזבח	2 Sam. xxiv. 18	,, ,,	הקם מזבח ליהוה
שקלים חמשים	2 Sam. xxiv. 24	,, ,,	חמשים שקלים
לזבחה לשמחה	Jerem. xliv. 6	,, ,,	לשמחה ולזבחה
קדים רוח	Hos. xiii. 15	,, ,,	רוח קדים
כירחי קדם	Job xxix. 2	,, ,,	כימי קדם
אבן ויעץ	1 Chron. xxii. 15	,, ,,	עץ ואבן
לחדות ההלל	1 Chron. xxiii. 30	,, ,,	להלל ולהדות
ראה עתה	1 Chron. xxviii. 10	,, ,,	עתה ראה
אל אל	Job xvi. 11	,, ,,	אל אל
דבש וחמאה	Job xx. 17	,, ,,	חמאה ודבש
מבהב ובחסף	Dan. xi. 38	,, ,,	בכסף ובזהב
למגן ולמחלך	Ruth iv. 9	,, ,,	מהלון וכליון
רבים פמים	Ps. lxxxix. 51	,, ,,	עמים רבים
שנים שלוש	Dan. i. 5	,, ,,	שלש שנים
והארץ נכבשה	Josh. xviii. 1	,, ,,	ונכבשה הארץ
ושה ושור	Judg. vi. 4	,, ,,	ושור ושה
וראו וידע	1 Sam. xxiii. 23	,, ,,	וידע וראו
ובני שלמה	1 Kings i. 21	,, ,,	שלמה בני
ורבו ופרו	Ezek. xxxvi. 11	,, ,,	פרו ורבו
שלוש אמות	2 Chron. xii. 13	,, ,,	שלש אמות
אחד לעלה לחמאת	Levit. xii. 8	,, ,,	אחד לחמאת ואחד לעלה
ורחץ במים את בשרו	Levit. xvi. 6	,, ,,	ורחץ בשרו במים
אך את הזהב ואת הכסף	Numb. xxxi. 22	,, ,,	את הכסף ואת הזהב
בין השמים ובין הארץ	2 Sam. xviii. 9	,, ,,	בין הארץ ובין השמים
אל ישעיהו הנביא בן אמוץ	2 Kings xix. 2	,, ,,	אל ישעיהו בן אמוץ הנביא
ביד נפויהו ובורוע חזקה	Jerem. xxi. 5	,, ,,	ביד חזקה ובזרוע נטויה
	Hos. ii. 2	,, ,,	בני ישראל ובני יהודה
כמה רחבה וכמה ארכה	Zech. ii. 6	,, ,,	ארככם וכמה רחבה
חקת שלם בכל משבתיכם	Levit. xxiii. 21	,, ,,	לדרתיכם בכל מושבתיכם

They are enumerated in that part of the Massorah finalis which is entitled *Various Readings* (חלוף קראה) p. 62 *b*, rubric 3. In the heading of this rubric, as well as in the Massorah marginalis on Job xxix. 2, where reference is made to this list, it is erroneously stated that it contains *thirty* (ל) instances, which has evidently arisen from the dropping of the letter ט [= 9]. The *Ochla Ve-Ochla*, section cclxxiii., pp. 53, 147, &c., gives

וַיְדַבֵּר מֹשֶׁה אֶל יְהֹוָה, and Moses spake to Jehovah [Numb. xxvii. 15], is marked "not extant so joined," for in all other passages it is וַיְדַבֵּר יְהֹוָה אֶל מֹשֶׁה, and Jehovah spake to Moses.

When these constructions occur more than once, the Massorites distinctly mention the number of instances, as on וַיְדַבֵּר אֱלֹהִים and the Almighty spake, they say "three times together;"[91] וַיֹּאמֶר אֱלֹהִים, and the Almighty said, "twenty-five times thus joined together,"[92] since in all other places it is וַיְדַבֵּר יְהֹוָה and Jehovah spake, וַיֹּאמֶר יְהֹוָה and Jehovah said. Indeed, when there are only two words, the correct Codices have not written down the word דסמיכי, since the circle between these two words is sufficient, as בָּרָא אֱלֹהִים the Almighty created, "occurs three times" [Gen. i. 1],[93] and there is no necessity for saying "three times thus joined together," as I have stated in the Introduction.

☞ Let me now explain the meaning of *Jechidain, Jechidin,* or *Mejuchadin,* for they are all the same. Mark, that wherever words occur joined together, and if a word, or two words, or more, with which they are thus mostly joined, are wanting either before them, or after them, or in the middle, the Massorites remark on them יחידין = *severed.* For example, i. A word wanted at the beginning viz., אֱלֹהֵי יִשְׂרָאֵל *the Almighty of Israel,* which "occurs twenty-four times alone,"[94]

---

forty instances, adding הַשָּׁבִים בַּבֹּקֶר [Prov. xxvii. 14] which otherwise is הַשָּׁבִים. Properly אֵל דִּי [Job xxvii. 2], as Dr. Frensdorff, the learned editor of the *Ochla Ve-Ochla,* rightly remarks, whereon the Massorah parva states "not extant" (לי), belongs to this rubric, since in all other passages it is אֵל דִּי.

[91] The three passages in which וידבר אלהים occur conjointly are, Gen. viii. 15: Exod. vi. 2; xx. 1. They are given in the Massorah marginalis on Gen. viii. 15.

[92] The twenty-five passages in which ויאמר אלהים occurs, are Gen. i. 3, 6, 9, 11, 14, 20, 24, 26, 29; vi. 13; ix. 8, 12, 17; xxi. 12; xvii. 15, 19, 9; xlvi. 2; xxxv. 1: Exod. iii. 14: Numb. xxii. 12: 1 Kings iii. 5, 11: Jonah iv. 9: 2 Chron. i. 11. They are given in the Massorah finalis under the letter *Aleph,* p. 8 *b,* cols. 2 and 3. All the three editions of the *Massoreth Ha-Massoreth* have *twenty-four* (כ״ד), which we have corrected, as it is a manifest blunder.

[93] For the three passages in which ברא אלהים occurs, see above. p. 139, note 115.

[94] The twenty-four (כ״ד) must be a mistake for *twenty-eight* (כ״ח), since the Massorah marginalis on Exod. xxiv. 10 distinctly enumerates twenty-eight instances in which אלהי ישראל occurs without יהוה. They are as follows: Gen. xxxiii. 20: Exod. xxiv. 10: Numb. xvi. 9: 1 Sam. v. 7, 8 (thrice), 11; vi. 5; i. 17; v. 10; vi. 3: 2 Sam. xxiii. 3: 1 Kings viii. 26: Isa. xxix. 23; xli. 17; xlv. 3, 15; xlviii. 2; lii. 12: Ezek. viii. 4; ix. 3; x. 19, 20; xi. 22; xliii. 2: 1 Chron. v. 26: Ps. lxix. 7: Ezra iii. 2; ix. 4.

for in all other instances it is preceded by יהוה *Jehovah.* ii. A word wanted in the middle, viz., כֹּה אָמַר יְהוָה אֱלֹהֵי יִשְׂרָאֵל *thus saith Jehovah, the Almighty of Israel,* which "occurs twenty-five times alone,"[95] as in all other instances it is כֹּה אָמַר יְהוָה צְבָאוֹת אֱלֹהֵי יִשְׂרָאֵל *thus saith Jehovah Sabaoth, the Almighty of Israel.* And iii. Without a word at the end, viz., יְבָרֶכְךָ יְהוָה *Jehovah bless thee,* marked "four times alone,"[96] as in all other instances it is יְבָרֶכְךָ יְהוָה אֱלֹהֶיךָ *Jehovah the Almighty bless thee,* except in the Psalms, where it is likewise so. The same is the case with עַד הַיּוֹם *till the day,* which is marked "nine times alone,"[97] since in all other instances it is עַד הַיּוֹם הַזֶּה *till this day.*

☞ Such severances are also to be found in the case of one word, as לָאֹהֶל *to the tent,* which is marked "five times alone;"[98] and עֵדוּת *law,* and מוֹעֵד *assembly,* are like it — that is, not being לְאֹהֶל הָעֵדוּת *to the tabernacle of our testimony,* and לְאֹהֶל הַמּוֹעֵד *to the tabernacle of the congregation,* which are the most in number; thus, also, יִחְיֶה *he shall live,* "occurs eighteen times alone,"[99] and חָיוֹ יִחְיֶה *living, he shall live,* is like it;" also, יְחִי *let him live,* is twice alone,[100] and יְחִי הַמֶּלֶךְ *let the*

---

[95] The twenty-five times in which כה אמר יהוה אלהי ישראל occurs without צבאות are, Exod. v. 1; xxxii. 27: Josh. xxiv. 2: Judg. vi. 8: 1 Sam. x. 18: 2 Sam. xii. 7: 1 Kings xi. 31: 2 Kings xix. 20: Isa. xxxvii. 21: 1 Kings xvii. 14: 2 Kings ix. 6: Jerem. xxi. 4; xxxvii. 7: 2 Kings xxii. 15: 2 Chron. xxxiv. 23: Jerem. xxxiv. 2, 13; xlii. 9; xlv. 2. They are given in the Massorah finalis under the letter *Aleph,* p. 4 *b,* cols. 3 and 4.

[96] The four passages in which יברכך יהוה occurs without אלהיך are, Numb. vi. 24; Deut. xv. 4: Jerem. xxxi. 23: Ruth ii. 4. They are enumerated in the Massorah marginalis on Numb. vi. 24.

[97] The nine passages in which עד היום occurs alone, without הזה, are, Gen. xix. 37, 38; xxxv. 20: 2 Sam. xix. 25: 2 Kings x. 27: 2 Chron. viii. 16: Ezek. xx. 31: 2 Chron. xx. 26: xxxv. 25. They are enumerated in the Massorah marginalis on 2 Chron. xx. 26.

[98] The five passages in which לאהל occurs by itself are. Exod. xxvi. 7, 14; xxxvi. 14, 19: 1 Chron. ix. 19. The Massorah marginalis on Exod. xxvi. 7, which treats on this rubric, is hopelessly erroneous. The only correct signal words, whereby it indicates the passages, are the first and second, viz., ועשית יריעות עזים [Exod. xxvi. 7], ובנים הקים את המשכן [Exod. xxxvi. 14]. As to the other three, they are as follows: i. ויעש שלמה, that is Numb. ix. 15, where it is לאהל העדות, which is not to the point. ii. ויעש שלמה, which is equally wrong, inasmuch as of the five verses which commence with these words, viz., 1 Kings vii. 48; viii. 65; xi. 6: 2 Chron. iv. 18, 19, not one has the word לאהל. And iii. ויקרא המלך ליהוידע, *i. e.* 2 Chron. xxiv. 6, where it is לאהל העדות, and is likewise not to the point.

[99] The eighteen passages in which יחיה, the future, occurs by itself, that is, without being preceded by חיה, the infinitive absolute, are, Gen. xvii. 18; xxxi. 32: Exod. xix. 13: Numb. xxiv. 23: Deut. viii. 3 (twice): 2 Sam. i. 10: 2 Kings x. 19: Ezek. xviii. 13, 22, 27; xlvii. 9: Ps. lxxxix. 49: Prov. xv. 27: Nehem. ii. 3: Habak. ii. 4: Eccles. vi. 3; xi. 8. They are enumerated in the Massorah finalis under the letter *Cheth,* p. 31 *a,* col. 4.

[100] The two instances in which יחי occurs by itself are, Deut. xxxiii. 6: Ps. xxii. 27. They are given in the Massorah finalis under the letter *Cheth,* p. 31 *b,* col. 1.

king live, is always like it. Moreover, when two words habitually occur in the same verse, the first without *Vav* conjunctive and the second with *Vav* conjunctive, then wherever the one with the *Vav* occurs, and its companion without the *Vav* does not precede it, the Massorites note on the word in question the number of instances in which it is to be found alone. Thus, for instance, on וּלְמַעַן *and in order that*, the Massorites remark, "it occurs nine times alone, as Exod. ix. 16, &c;[101] and when לְמַעַן is followed by וּלְמַעַן it is the same," that is, in every verse where לְמַעַן occurs, and is followed by וּלְמַעַן, it is like it, as לְמַעַן תִּירָא אֶת יְהוָֹה אֱלֹהֶיךָ וּלְמַעַן יַאֲרִכֻן יָמֶיךָ *that thou mayest fear Jehovah, thy God,—so that thy days may be prolonged* [Deut. vi. 2], &c. Thus, also, וְלִפְנֵי *and before the face of,* "is sixteen times alone," as Numb. xxvii. 21; and wherever לִפְנֵי *before,* is followed by וְלִפְנֵי *and before*, it is like it, as לִפְנֵי מֹשֶׁה וְלִפְנֵי אֶלְעָזָר *before Moses and Eliezer* [Numb. xxvii. 2].[102]

There are, moreover, some words which are called *unique*, because of the word with which they are construed, and which construction has no parallel. Thus, אַתָּה *thou* occurs eighteen times alone, as אַתָּה זֶה *thou this*, "without parallel;" אַתָּה תִהְיֶה *thou shalt be,* "has no parallel," &c.[103] Also וְאַתָּה *and thou,* "is eight times alone;" as וְאַתָּה

דכותיה; וכן כשיש ב' מלות שדרכן לבא בפסוק אחד, הראשונה בלא וי"ו החבור וחשנית עם הוי"ו, בכל מקום שנמצא אותה שעם הוי"ו, ואין לפניה חברתה בלי וי"ו, כתבו על המלח ההיא כך וכך יחידאין; והמשל כמו וּלְמַעַן פ' יחידאין, כמו וּלְמַעַן חספר באזני בנך,[101] וכל לְמַעַן וּלְמַעַן דכותיה, פירוש כל פסוק שנמצא בו למען ואח"כ ולמען דכותיה, כמו לְמַעַן תִּירָא אֶת יְהוָֹה אֱלֹהֶיךָ וּלְמַעַן יַאֲרִכֻן יָמֶיךָ ודומיהן; וכן וְלִפְנֵי י"ו יחידאין, כמו וְלִפְנֵי אֶלְעָזָר חכהן יעמד,[102] וכל לִפְנֵי וְלִפְנֵי דכותיה, כמו ותעמודנה לִפְנֵי מֹשֶׁה וְלִפְנֵי אֶלְעָזָר:

ויש מל ם הנקראים מיוחדים מצד המלה הנסמכה אליח, ואין לח דומה, כגון אַתָּה י"א יחידין, כמו אַתָּה זֶה לית דכותיה, אַתָּה תהיה לית דכותיה וכולי;[103] וכן וְאַתָּה ח' יחידין.

---

[101] The nine passages in which וּלְמַעַן occurs are, Exod. x. 2; ix. 16: Deut. ix. 5; iv. 40; xi. 9; vi. 2: Ps. xxxi. 4: 2 Kings xix. 34: Isa. xxxvii. 35. As these nine instances are distinctly given in the Massorah marginalis on Isa. xxxvii. 35, and as both the Massorah marginalis on the different passages in q estion, and the Massorah finalis under the *Lamed,* p. 43 *b*, col. 1, emphatically state that there are *nine* instances, we have corrected the text which had six (ו), and which has evidently arisen from a misprint.

[102] The sixteen passages in which וְלִפְנֵי occurs with *Vav* conjunctive, without being preceded by לִפְנֵי, are, Levit. xvi. 14, 15; xix. 14: Numb. xxvii. 21: 1 Kings vi. 20: Isa. xlviii. 7: Ps. lxxii. 5: Prov. xv. 33: Ps. cii. 1: Prov. xvii. 14; xviii. 16: Job viii. 12: Ezek. xlii. 4: Job xv. 7: Jerem. xliv. 10: Nehem. xiii. 4. They are given in the Massorah marginalis on Numb. xxvii. 21.

[103] The eleven words which are preceded by אתה, and which in this construction occur only once, are as follows:—

אתה תהיה . . Gen. xli. 40	אתה האיש . 2 Sam. xii. 7	אתה אל . . Jerem. xlvi. 28
אתה זה . . Gen. xxvii. 24	אתה קח . 2 Sam. xx. 6	אתה בן . . Ezek. xliii. 10
אתה תרבר . . Exod. vii. 2	אתה אמרת . 1 Kings i. 24	אתה מושל . . Ps. lxxxix. 10
אתה דבר . 2 Sam. xvii. 6	אתה תשמע . 1 Kings viii. 43	

They are enumerated in the Massorah finalis, under the letter *Aleph*, p. 9 *b*, cols. 1 and 2, and in the *Ochla Ve-Ochla,* section cclxi., p. 142, &c. As both the Massorah and the *Ochla Ve-Ochla* leave it beyond the shadow of a doubt that there are eleven such instances, we have corrected the text, which in all the three editions has (ד'י) *eighteen*.

כמו וְאַתָּה תהיה לית דכוחיה, וְאַתָּה תחזה תִּהְיֶה and thou shalt be, "without
ליח דכורחיה וכולי; [104] וכן הרבה ממלורה parallel," וְאַתָּה תֶחֱזֶה and thou shalt
הדבק, כמו אַל למ"ד יחידין, [105] וְאַל מ"ו see," "is without parallel," &c. [104]
יחידין; [106] וכן סְן וּמִן, אם וְאם, אַל וְאַל ודומיהן The same is the case with many of
רבים מאד: the particles, as אֶל to, occurs thirty
times alone; [105] וְאֶל and to, forty-
☞ וְעַתָּה אבאר מלת מורדפים, והיא six times alone; [106] אַל וְאַל, not and
מלת הגיונית, ופידורָה רצופים, כמו שקראו not, אם וְאם with and with, מִן וּמִן
שמות נרדפין כל חשמות שהם שוים בחדרון from and from, &c., &c.
ושונים במבטא כמו שֶׁמֶשׁ, חַמָּה, חָרֶס כמו ☞ Let me now explain the word
מורדפים, which is a logical term, denoting *connected, resembling, identical,*
just as those words are called synonyms which are identical in sense
and different in sound; *ex. gr.*, שֶׁמֶשׁ sun, חַמָּה sun, חָרֶס sun, as I
have explained in the Section on the Different Parts of Speech,

[104] The eight words which occur only once preceded by וְאַתָּה, are as follows:—

וְאַתָּה וְאַהֲרֹן . . Numb. xvi. 17	וְאַתָּה עֹשֶׂה . . Judg. xi. 27	וְאַתָּה נֹתֵן . . Ps. cxlv. 15
וְאַתָּה שָׁמַעְתָּ . . Deut. ix. 2	וְאַתָּה תַעֲשֶׂה . . 1 Kings v. 23	וְאַתָּה לְךָ . . Dan. xii. 13
וְאַתָּה עֲשִׂירָה . 1 Sam. xv. 6	וְאַתָּה אֲדֹנִי . . 1 Kings i. 20	

They are given in the Massorah finalis under the letter *Aleph*, p. 13 *b*, col. 2. The *Ochla Ve-Ochla*, section cclxii., pp. 51, 142, gives three additional instances, viz., וְאַתָּה שָׁלוֹם 1 Sam. xxv. 6; וְאַתָּה תָּבֹא 1 Kings v. 23; and וְאַתָּה נְמְשַׁךְ Ezek. xxxiii. 9. It will be seen that the two instances given by Levita in the text are not included in the Massoretic list. Indeed, though וְאַתָּה תֶחֱזֶה occurs only once, וְאַתָּה תִהְיֶה is of frequent occurrence (comp. Exod. iv. 16: Deut. xxxiii. 44: 2 Sam. v. 2: 1 Chron. xi. 2). There must therefore be a mistake in the text. The Sulzbach edition omits וְכֵן וְאַתָּה ד' יחידין כמו וְאַתָּה תִהְיֶה לית דכוחיה which renders the text of that edition perfectly unintelligible.

[105] The list of the thirty instances in which אֶל precedes words in an unparalleled manner is so hopelessly confused, that it would require more space to correct it than the limits of a note permit. We must, therefore, refer to it as it stands in the Massorah finalis under the letter *Aleph*, p. 6 *b*, cols. 3 and 4.

[106] The forty-five words which occur only once preceded by וְאַל, are as follows:—

וְאַל קַיִן . . . Gen. iv. 5	וְאַל אֲבִישַׁי . 1 Sam. xxvi. 6	וְאַל שְׁכִיזָתוֹ Jerem. xxix. 24
וְאַל אַחֹתָם . . . Gen. vi. 16	וְאַל נָבָב . 1 Sam. xxvii. 10	וְאַל יְהוּדָה . Jerem. xxx. 4
וְאַל הַדֶּבֶק . . . Gen. xviii. 7	וְאַל הָאָרוֹן . Ezek. xxxi. 13	וְאַל יִרְמְיָהוּ Jerem. xxxix. 15
וְאַל אָחִיו . . Gen. xxxvii. 10	וְאַל נַעְרוֹ . 1 Sam. x. 14	וְאַל הַנָּבֵל . Ezek. xliii. 20
וְאַל יַעֲקֹב . . . Exod. vi. 8	וְאַל צִקְלָג . 1 Sam. xx. 1	וְאַל חַשְׁלֹנוֹת Ezek. xl. 43
וְאַל מֹשֶׁה . . . Exod. xxiv. 1	וְאַל נְבִיא . 2 Kings iii. 13	וְאַל עַמִּי . Joel iv. 3
וְאַל הָאָרֶץ . . . Exod. xxv. 21	וְאַל אֲדֹנֵינוּ . Isa. lv. 7	וְאַל אֱלֹהִים . Job v. 8
וְאַל שָׂחִי . . Exod. xii. 22	וְאַל הָעַמִּים . Isa. xix. 8	וְאַל יְהוּדָה Ps. xxx. 9
וְאַל הַזְּקֵנִים Exod. xxiv. 14	וְאַל הָאָבוֹת . Isa. xix. 3	וְאַל הָאָרֶץ . Ps. l. 4
וְאַל הַלְוִיִם . Numb. xviii. 26	וְאַל שָׂרָה . Isa. li. 2	וְאַל אֲנָשִׁים Ezek. xxiii. 42
וְאַל רֵעֵהוּ . . Deut. ix. 27	וְאַל הַשַּׁמַּיִם Jerem. iv. 23	וְאַל עוֹנָם . Hos. iv. 8
וְאַל חַטֹּאתָם . Deut. ix. 27	וְאַל הַדֶּרֶךְ Jerem. xxxiii. 4	וְאַל חוּל . Jerem. xlvii. 7
וְאַל פְּרָעֹה . . Exod. vi. 13	וְאַל נְבוּכַדְרֶאצַּר Jer. xxv. 9	וְאַל לֵב . Ezek. xi. 21
וְאַל אִשְׁתּוֹ . Levit. xviii. 20	וְאַל אַרְצוֹ . Jerem. l. 18	וְאַל בִּרְכַּת . Nehem. ii. 14
וְאַל אַבְנֵר . 1 Sam. xxvi. 14	וְאַל צִדְקִיָּהוּ Jerem. xxix. 21	וְאַל מְקוֹמוֹ . Eccl. i. 5

It will be seen that the Massorah marginalis, p. 6 *b*, col. 4, gives only forty-five such instances. There must therefore be a mistake in the Massorah marginalis on Exod. xxiv. 14, where. in referring to this rubric, it is stated that there are *forty-four* (מ"ד). In the *Ochla Ve-Ochla*, section lxxxv., pp. 26, 89, &c., where this rubric is given, the heading describes it as containing forty-five (מ"ה), and the rubric only gives this number; yet it mentions two instances not contained in the Massorah finalis, viz., וְאַל עֲדַת (Numb. xxxi. 12) and וְאַל צִדְקִיָּהוּ (Jerem. xxix. 21), whilst it omits two instances, viz., וְאַל מֶאֲרָיו (Ezek. xxxi. 13) and וְאַל חוּל (Jerem. xlvii. 7), which are given in the Massorah finalis. There can, therefore, be but little doubt that the מ"ד = forty-four in the Massorah marginalis on Exod. xxiv. 14, the מ"ה = forty-five in the *Ochla Ve-Ochla*, and the מ"ו = forty-six in the text of Levita, are corruptions of the original מ"ז = forty-seven.

which see.[107] The Massorites, too, employ this expression. Thus, three verses are alike (מורדפים), each one having seventy-two letters; viz., Exod. xiv. 19–21,[108] so also the six verses which are alike, each having five biliteral words, as כִּי נָם זֶה לָךְ בֵּן [Gen. xxxv. 17], נָם לִי נָם לָךְ לֹא [1 Kings iii. 26], &c.;[109] and the six words which are alike, each having a letter repeated thrice, as בְּבָבַת in the apple [Zech. ii. 12], חָנֵּנִי pity me [Ps. ix. 14], &c.[110]

SECTION VII., concerning the *Presence and Absence of Serviles.* —Mark that נסיב denotes *taking.* Thus, in the Targum, לָקַח *he took* [Gen. ii. 22] is rendered by נסיב; likewise לֹקְחֵי *the takers of* [Gen xix. 14], is translated in the Targum נסבי. This is also the case with the word לקיחה, whenever it occurs in the preterite and participle, it is always rendered in the Targum by נסיבה *to take;* whilst the infinitive, imperative, and the future are always rendered by סיב, with the radical *Nun* omitted.

☞ Now the Massorites were in the habit of marking the prefixes with the expression *Nesiba*, and more especially the letters *Beth, Vav, Kaph, Lamed,* and *Mem.* Thus, for instance, they give a list of twenty-nine words which have the prefix *Beth,* and which in all

שבארחי בפרק המינים ע״ש;[107] ובעלי המסורה שמטו נ״כ בזאת המלח, כגון נ׳ פסוקים מורדפים דבכל חד וחד ע״ב אותיות, ויסע ויבא, ויט;[108] וכן ה׳ פסוקים בכל חד ה׳ מלין מורדפין מן ב׳ ב׳ אותיות, כמו כִּי נָם זֶה לָךְ בֵּן, נָם לִי נָם לָךְ לֹא יחיח וכו׳;[109] וכן ו׳ מלות מן ג׳ אותיות מורדפין, בְּבָבַת עינו, חָנֵּנִי יהוח וכולי:[110]

המאמר השביעי בנסיבין או משמשין וקרחין: ודע כי נסיב הוא לשון לקיחח, בתרגונום של אשר לָקַח מן האדם די נסיב מאדם; וכן לֹקְחֵי בנותיו חרנום נסבי בנתיה; וכן כל לשון לקיחה בעוברים ובבינונים מתרגמין בלשון נסיבה: אבל המקור וחציווי וחעתיד, מתורגם בלשון סיב בחסרון נו״ן חשורש:

☞ וחנה נהגו בעלי חמסורח לכתוב לשון נסיבה על אותיות השימוש שבראשי התיבות, ובפרט על אותיות בוכ״לם, כגון כ״ם מלין נסבי בי״ת בריש תיבתא וכל

---

[107] The "Section on the Different Kinds of Words" constitutes the second of the four sections, composing the work entitled "The Sections of Elias" (comp. p. 54, &c., ed. Prague, 1793), a description of which has already been given, *vide supra*, p. 18, &c.

[108] From the fact that these three verses have respectively seventy-two letters, great mysteri s have been ass gned to them from time immemorial. They have been identified with the Divine name, which consists f seventy-two words, or, according to Ibn Ezra, of the number seventy-two, viz.. י 10 + יה 15 + יהו 21 + יהוה 26 = 72; or the tetragrammaton, with each letter written out fully, viz.. הי 15 + ו״ו 22 + הי 15 + יוד 20 = 72. Comp. Rashi on *Succa*, 45 a; Nachmanides, *Introduction to his Commentary on the Pentateuch;* Ibn Ezra, *Commentary on Exodus* xiv. 19-21; xxxiii. 21; Ginsburg, *the Kabbalah,* p. 50, &c.

[109] The other three verses which respectively have five biliterals following each other are, Gen. vi. 10: 1 Sam. xx. 29: Nehem. ii. 2. They are noted in the Massorah parva on each verse, and the whole list is given in the Massorah marginalis on 1 Kings iii. 26, and Nehem. ii. 2. The text of three editions of the *Massoreth Ha-Massoreth* states that there are *six* (ו) such verses, but as this is contradicted by the explicit declarations of the Massorah, we have no doubt that it is a misprint, and have therefore corrected the text.

[110] The other four words in which the same letters follow three times are, ממזלה (Ps. cv. 13); וממזלה (1 Chron. xvi. 20); ככבי (Nehem. ix. 28); המסם (2 Chron. xv. 6). Comp. *Ochla Ve-Ochla,* section cclxvii. pp. 52, 143.

other instances have *Kaph*, as בְּמִנְחָה *in the offering* [Gen. xxxii. 21], בַּחוֹל *in the sand* [Exod. ii. 12], &c., for in all other instances it is בְּמִנְחָה *as an offering*, and בַּחוֹל *as sand*.[111] On the contrary, again, there is an alphabetical list of words which begin with *Kaph*, and which have no parallel in any other passage, as בַּבֹּקֶר *as in the morning* [Job xi. 17], and כְּיִשְׂרָאֵל *as in Israel* [2 Sam. vii. 23], being in all other instances בַּבֹּקֶר *in the morning*, and בְּיִשְׂרָאֵל *in Israel*.[112] As to the letter ו there are many alphabetical lists, rows, and registers of pairs, of words which have this prefix and which have it not. All of these are enumerated in the beginning of the work entitled *Ochla Ve-Ochla*, which I mentioned in the Poetical Introduction, which see [*supra*, p. 93]; some of them I also cited in the preceding Sections.

Let me now explain the use of the word מְשַׁמְּשִׁין, which is as follows: — When words begin with two of the servile letters, *Beth*, *Vav*, *Kaph*, *Lamed*, and *Mem*, the Massorites do not mark them נְסִיבִין *they have taken*, but מְשַׁמְּשִׁין *they employ*. Thus, for instance: i. The nineteen words which employ two *Lameds* at the beginning, and which have no parallel, as לְלוֹט *to Lot* [Gen. xiii. 5], לְלִבְנָה *to Libnah* [Josh. x. 32], &c.[113] ii. The hundred and eighteen words which

[111] The twenty-nine words which occur only once with the prefix *Beth*, and which in all other passages have *Kaph*, are as follows:—

במנחה	. . Gen. xxxii. 21	בראשנים	. . 2 Sam. xxi. 9	בעולם	. . Job xxiv. 5
בחול	. . Exod. ii. 12	בטיט	. . Zech. x. 5	בשבתו	. . Prov. xxxi. 23
בשמע	. . Exod. xvi. 8	ובדברך	. 1 Kings xviii. 36	בחם	. . Isa. xviii. 4
בשמים	. 2 Chron. xx. 29	ברצונך	. . Ps. xxx. 6	ובמנחת	. . Ezra ix. 5
בארבה	. . Exod. x. 12	ברביבים	. . Ps. lxv. 11	ובמשמשיך	. Nehem. ix. 29
בעבר	. Exod. xxxiii. 22	בעגלי	. . Ps. lxviii. 31	בכלתך	. Ezek. xliii. 23
במסלה	. . 1 Sam. vi. 12	במחלקותיהם	. 2 Chr. xxxi. 17	בברכה	. . Prov. xi. 11
בשלו	. . Isa. xvi. 14	במחלקות	. 2 Chron. xxxi. 15	בלה	. Lament. iii. 4
בקרא	. Jerem. xxxvi. 13	במחלקותם	. 2 Chron. viii. 14	בחלילים	. 1 Kings i. 40
בענקים	. . Josh. xiv. 15	ונהוציאם	. 2 Chron. xxxiv. 14		

They are given in the Massorah finalis under the letter *Beth*, p. 14 a, col. 3. The *Ochla Ve-Ochla*, section ccxv., pp. 45, 128, which also gives this list, omits בשמים (2 Chron. xx. 29), and במחלקותיהם (2 Chron. xxi. 17), whilst it adds ברמות (Gen. v. 1), and במשמרותיהם (2 Chron. xxxi. 17).

[112] As the list, of which the above are examples, contains upwards of one hundred and forty words, making it too long to be given here entire, we must refer the reader for it to the Massorah finalis under the letter *Kaph*, p. 38 a, cols. 1 and 2, and the *Ochla Ve-Ochla*, section xix., pp. 9, &c., 34, &c.

[113] The Massorah finalis, under the letter *Lamed*, p. 40 b, col. 3, gives the following list of words which have two *Lameds* at the beginning, viz.:—

begin with *Vav* and *Lamed*, as וְכֵן ; וְלִמְשֹׁל בַּיּוֹם [114] וְכֹל כְּמוֹ לְיָמִים וְשָׁנִים, וּלְיָמִים and *for days* [Gen. i. 14], שָׂמֵחַ מְשַׁמְּשִׁין וְכוּ כְּמוֹ וּמֵצִיא בְּאִתֵי ; [115] וְכֵן מְשַׁמְּשִׁין וְכוּ, וּלְמְשֹׁל and *to rule* [Gen. i. 18], מְשַׁמְּשִׁין וּכָן מְשַׁמְּשִׁין ; [116] וּכָן מְשַׁמְּשִׁין וּמַג וּמִגְבָּעוֹת אַטּוּרוֹן ; [117] וְכֵן ב' מִלִּים &c.[114] iii. The register of words which begin with *Vav*, *Mem*, and *Aleph*, as וּמֵאָז and *since then* [Exod. v. 23], &c.[115] iv. Those which begin with *Vav*, *Mem*, and *Beth*, as וּמְבָרֲכֶיךָ and *thy blessers* [Gen. xxvii. 29], &c.[116] v. Those which have *Vav*, *Mem*, *Gimmel*, as וּמִגְּבָעוֹת *and from the hills* [Numb. xxiii. 9], &c.[117] vi. The two words which have *Lamed*

לָלוּט . . . Gen. xiii. 5	לַיְלָה . . . Ps. xix. 3	לְבוּשְׁךָ . . . Isa. lxiii. 2
לְבוּנָה . . . Judg. xxi. 19	לָבִיא . . . Job xxxviii. 39	לְבוּשֶׁךָ . . . Prov. xxvii. 26
לְהָבָה . . . Isa. x. 17	לַחֹמֶץ . . . Prov. xxvii. 27	לַעֲנָה . . . Amos v. 7
לַשֶּׁכֶת . . . Jerem. xxxv. 4	לָשֵׂם . . . Josh. xix. 47	לַעֲנָה . . . Amos vi. 12
לִבְנָם . . . Hos. vii. 2	לָכִישׁ . . . Josh. x. 35	לַשׁוֹנוּ . . . Gen. x. 5

It will be seen that this list contains fifteen words, though the heading of it in the Massorah states that there are *eleven* (י"א) such instances. Why Buxtorf omits לַעֲנָה Amos v. 7, and how he came to make it fourteen (י"ד), is difficult to divine. The statement in the text of the *Massoreth Ha-Massoreth*, that there are *nineteen* (י"ט) such words, must be a misprint.

[114] For the list of the one hundred and eighteen instances in question, we must refer to the Massorah finalis under the letter *Lamed*, p. 40 *b*, col. 3; p. 41 *a*, col. 1, as it is by far too long to be inserted here.

[115] The list (שִׁטָּה) of words beginning in one instance only with *Vav* and *Mem*, is as follows:—

וּמֵאוּ . . . Exod. v. 23	וּמֵאֵל . . . Ezra iii. 7	וּכְרֵאשָׁה . . . Ruth i. 5
וּמֵאֲיָבַי . . . 2 Sam. xxii. 4	וּמֵאֱלֹהִים . . . 2 Chron. xix. 29	וּמֵאָבָל . . . Esther ix. 22
וּמֵאַחֲרֵי . . . Jerem. iii. 19	וּמַאֲצִילֶיהָ . . . Isa. xli. 9	וּמַאֲכַל . . . Ezek. iv. 10
וּמֵאֵל . . . Isa. xxix. 18	וּמֵאֲשֶׁר . . . 1 Chron. xii. 36	וּמֵאָרֶךְ . . . Eccles. viii. 12
וּמֵאַרְמָה . . . Job v. 6	וּמֵאַי . . . Isa. xi. 11	וּמֵאַהֲבַת . . . Jerem. xxii. 22
וּמֵאֲצוֹת . . . Ps. cvii. 3	וּמֵאַנְשֵׁי . . . Ps. lix. 3	וּמֵאַמֵּר . . . Esther ix. 32
וּמֵאֱלֹהַי . . . Isa. xl. 27	וּמֵאֲלוּ . . . Habak. i. 16	וּמֵאָתוֹת . . . Jerem. x. 2
וּמֵאֵלָה . . . Ps. lix. 13	וּמֵאֲלוּן . . . Prov. xxx. 14	וּמֵאָשׁוֹר . . . Zech. x. 10
וּמֵאֲסַפְכֶם . . . Isa. lii. 12	וּמֵאֲשׁוּרָיו . . . Isa. xi. 15	וּמֵאַרְצוֹ . . . Ezek. xxxvi. 20

The list is given in the Massorah finalis under the letter *Mem*, p. 44 *a*, col. 2. Of these twenty-seven, the *Ochla Ve-Ochla*, section xviii., pp. 8 and 31, &c., where this list forms the first part of a lengthy alphabetical register of words beginning with the letters *Vav* and *Mem*, only gives sixteen, and omits Nos. 2, 3, 9, 10, 11, 17, 19, 20, 22, 24, and 26, whilst it adds וּמֵאֲמַר [Dan. iv. 14].

[116] The list (שִׁטָּה) of words beginning in one instance only with *Vav*, *Mem*, and *Beth*, is as follows:—

וּמְבָרְכֶיךָ . . . Gen. xxvii. 29	וּמֵבִין . . . Dan. viii. 23	וּמִבָּמוֹת . . . Numb. xxi. 20
וּמִבָּרַךְ . . . 1 Chron. xvii. 27	וּמִבַּרְכָתַךְ . . . 2 Sam. vii. 29	וּמִבְּקָרוֹ . . . 2 Sam. xii. 4
וּמִבְּלִי . . . Job xxiv. 8	וּמַבָּא . . . Jerem. xvii. 26	וּמִבַּלְעֲדֵי . . . Isa. xliv. 6
וּמִבַּטְּנָן . . . Hos. ix. 11	וּמִבִּיאָה . . . Dan. xi. 6	וּמִבָּשָׂר . . . Isa. lviii. 7
	וּמִבְחַר . . . 2 Sam. viii. 8	

These instances are given in the Massorah finalis under the letter *Mem*, p. 44 *a*, col. 2. Of these thirteen words, the *Ochla Ve-Ochla*, section xviii., only gives five, omittting Nos. 5, 6, 7, 8, 9, 10, 11, and 12, whilst it adds וּמִבִּנְיָמִין 2 Chron. xix. 7. It must be added that וּמִבֶּטֶן is not unique, inasmuch as, besides Hos. ix. 11, quoted in the Massorah finalis, it occurs in Job xxxi. 8.

[117] The list (שִׁטָּה) of words beginning in one instance only with *Vav*, *Mem*, and *Gimmel*, is as follows:—

וּמִגְבָּעוֹת . . . Exod. xxviii. 40	וּמְגָרָשׁ . . . Numb. xxxv. 2	וּמִגְדְּפֵיהֶם . . . Isa. li. 7
וּמִגְבָּעוֹת . . . Numb. xxiii. 9	וּמְגָרָשׁ . . . Numb. xxxv. 4	וּמִגְדָּף . . . Ps. xliv. 17
וּמְגוּרָה . . . Exod. iii. 22	וּמַטְשֵׁהוּ . . . Josh. xxi. 42	וּמִגַּנֵּה . . . Malachi ii. 12
וּמְגָרָל . . . Numb. xxxvi. 3	וּמִגּוֹ . . . Job xxxi. 20	וּמִגַּעַר . . . Isa. liv. 9

Of these twelve words, which are given in the Massorah finalis under the letter *Mem*, and *He* at the end, viz., וּבַשְּׁפֵלָה and in the valley [Is. xxxii. 19] &c. vii. Those which employ *He* and *Vav* at the end of the word, as וְאַנְוֵהוּ and *I shall exalt him* [Exod. xv. 2], וַאֲרֹמְמֶנְהוּ and *I shall extol him* [ibid.] &c.[118] And viii. The expressions which terminate with *Kaph Mem*, or *He Mem*, or *Lamed Mem*,—on all these the Massorites remark, משמשין they employ, and not נסיבין they take.

☞ It is moreover to be noticed, that the Massorites not only mark the servile letters, as *Meshamshin*, but also the radical letters. Thus, for instance, the alphabetical list of words which employ *Aleph Tav*, *Beth Shin*, *Gimmel Resh*, &c., as אֹרְחַת *company of* [Gen. xxxvii. 25] is marked "not extant" where we have *Aleph* and *Tav* at the two ends; בִּיבֵשׁ *in the withering* [Isa. xxvii. 11] is marked "not extant" where we have *Beth* and *Shin* at the two ends; גְּעָר *rebuke* [Ps. lxviii. 31], is marked "not extant" where we have *Gimmel* and *Resh* at the two ends.[119] Or the alphabetical

p. 44 a, col. 3, the *Ochla Ve-Ochla*, section xviii., only gives two, viz., the fourth and eighth.

[118] The words which occur only once with *He* and *Vav* at the end are as follows:—

ואנוהו	. .	Exod. xv. 2	ועתליהו	. 2 Chron. xxii. 10	וחבואתיהו	.	Ezek. xvii. 20
וארממנהו	. .	Exod. xv. 2	והשירהו	. Jerem. xlviii. 26	ונשיהו	. .	Ezek. xxxi. 11
יבוננהו	. .	Deut. xxxii. 10	והוצאתהו	. Job xviii. 11	העירותהו	. .	Isa. xlv. 13
יצרנהו	. .	Deut. xxxii. 10	אשביעהו	. Ps. xci. 16	בקשותיהו	. Song of Songs v. 6
משיחהו	. .	Exod. ii. 10	ואראהו	. Ps. xci. 16	ונטעתיהו	. 1 Chron. xvii. 9
רעשיתיהו	. 1 Kings xvii. 12	לדרתיהו	. Numb. xi. 12	והשפילהו	. Job xl. 11
יעבדנהו	. .	Jerem. v. 22	ומעלתהו	. Ezek. xliii. 17	שנאתיהו	. 2 Chron. xviii. 7
אדהמנו	. .	Job xxix. 16	מאסתיהו	. 1 Sam. xvi. 7	ואפמינהו	. Jerem. xiii. 5
רטמסהו	. .	Ezek. xxxi. 4	שקרנוהו	. Lam. ii. 16	אכלוהו	. .	Ezek. xv. 5
מסהו	. .	Nahum i. 13	והגעתיהו	. Ezek. xiii. 14	ותזבדהו	. 1 Sam. xxviii. 24
ושמטתו	. .	Ezek. xliv. 24	והשמותיהו	. Ezek. xiv. 9			

They are given in the Massorah finalis under the letter *He*, p. 22 b, col. 3.

[119] It has already been remarked (vide supra, p. 190, &c.), that by bending the Hebrew alphabet exactly in the middle, and putting the one half over the other, a variety of anagrammatic alphabets are obtained, which derive their respective names from the first two specimen pairs of letters indicating the interchange. Here we have an alphabetical list of words which occur only once, arranged according to this anagrammatic alphabet, denominated *Athbash* (אתב"ש), that is, the first and last letter of each word in question yields this alphabet. They are as follows:—

ארחת	. .	Gen. xxxvii. 25	דוסק	. Song of Songs v. 2	זרע	. .	Ps. xcvii. 11
אתברית	. .	Dan. vii. 15	דלק	. .	Dan. vii. 9	חנם	. .	Isa. xxx. 4
ביבש	. .	Isa. xxvii. 11	דומשק	. 2 Kings xvi. 10	חרחם	. 2 Kings xxii. 14
בשלש	. .	Isa. xl. 12	הסץ	. .	Job xl. 11	מוחן	. .	Judg. xvi. 21
גור	. .	Isa. liv. 15	המץ	. .	Isa. xvi. 4	ירחם	. .	Hos. xiv. 4
גר	. .	Isa. xxvii. 9	ויך	. .	Ezek. xxxi. 7	כבל	. .	Job xxiv. 24
געד	. .	Ps. lxviii. 31	וירך	. .	Exod. iv. 26	כליל	. .	Isa. xxx. 29
			תל	. .	Esther v. 9			

This list is given in the Massorah finalis under the letter *Aleph*, p. 1 b. cols. 2 and 3; and in the *Ochla Ve-Ochla*, section xxxviii., pp. 13, 49. The latter adds the word מחון, Deut. ix. 21, whilst the learned Heidenheim remarks that ירחם, Prov. xxviii. 13. and כליל, Isa. xvi. 3, ought properly to be included in this list.

list of words which employ *Aleph* and *Beth*, *Beth* and *Gimmel*, *Gimmel* and *Daleth*, *Daleth* and *He*, &c., as אֲבִינֵר *Abiner* [1 Sam. xiv. 50], marked "not extant" where we have *Aleph* and *Beth* commencing the word; בִּגְוִיַת *in the carcase of* [Judg. xiv. 8], marked "not extant;" גָּדֵל *great* [Numb. vi. 5, Prov. xix. 19], marked "not extant;" דָּהֲרוֹת *rapid courses* [Judg. v. 22], marked "not extant," &c.[120] It is therefore evident that in most of these instances the letters are not servile, and that the Massorites mean that they are employed in the pronunciation of the particular word. Moreover, the redundance and the absence of the conjunctive particle they likewise mark as *Meshamshin*. Thus, for instance, the six words which respectively occur twice in the same section, the first time with the particle אֵת, and the second without it. The first of such a pair is אֵת אֲשֶׁר *that which*, [Gen. xli. 25], and the second אֲשֶׁר *which*, without the particle אֵת [Gen. xli. 28].[121] The four words which respectively occur twice in the same section, and which have in the first passage the negative particle לֹא, and in the second passage are without it; as the first לֹא אֲדֹנִי שְׁמָעֵנִי *not my lord, hear me* [Gen. xxiii. 11], and the second אֲדֹנִי שְׁמָעֵנִי *my lord, hear me* [Gen. xxiii. 15], &c.[122]

☞ As a rule, the difference between *Nesibin* and *Meshamshin* is, that the term *Nesibin* is only applied to a single letter of the

---

[120] This list of words, occurring only once, represents another of the anagrammatic alphabets obtained by a similar process to the foregoing, and is denominated *Abbag* (אב בג). The words ranged under the alphabet to which Levita refers are as follows:—

אבינר	. . 1 Sam. xiv. 50	חשבות	. . . Prov. vii. 16	עשרות	. . Prov. viii. 26
בגרות	. . Jerem. xli. 17	טירח	Song of Songs viii. 9	סצלות	. . Gen. xxx. 37
גדל	. . Numb. vi. 5	יברו	. . . Job xl. 30	צקון	. . Isa. xxvi. 16
דהרות	. . Judg. v. 22	כלוא	. . . Obad. 16	קראן	. . Exod. ii. 20
הומה	. . 1 Kings i. 41	למס	. . . Job vi. 40	רשם	. . Dan. vi. 10
וזהמהו	. . Job xxxiii. 20	מנע	. . . Prov. i. 15	שתי	. . Ps. lxxiii. 28
וחלתי	. . Job xxxii. 6	נסתר	. . . Gen. xxxi. 49	תתנו	. . Exod. xxii. 29
		סעפים	. . . Ps. cxix. 113		

They are given in the Massorah finalis under the letter *Aleph*, p. 1 *b*, col. 1; and in the *Ochla Ve-Ochla*, section xxxvii. pp. 13, 48, &c.

[121] The six pairs to which Levita refers we could not find either in the Massorah or in the *Ochla Ve-Ochla*.

[122] The four words which occur twice in the same sentence, once with the negative particle לֹא, and once without it, are as follows:—

לא אדני	. . . . . . Gen. xxiii. 11	לא עשיתם	. . . . . Ezek. v. 7
אדני	. . . . . . Gen. xxiii. 15	עשיתם	. . . . . Ezek. xi. 12
לא הך	. . . . . . Levit. xiii. 4	לא נחשב	. . . . . 1 Kings x. 21
הסק לבן	. . . . . . Levit. xiii. 20	נחשב	. . . . . 2 Chron. ix. 20

They are given in the Massorah finalis under the letter *Lamed*, p. 41 *b*, col. 4, and in the *Ochla Ve-Ochla*, section ccl., p. 138.

serviles at the beginning of a word, and especially to the *Vav* conjunctive, whilst the expression *Meshamshin* is employed to describe two letters at the beginning or end of a word, whether they are servile or radical, as well as to denote the absence of one of the conjunctive particles, as I have explained it. In some Codices, indeed, this order is reversed, but they are not correct.

☞ I shall now explain the expression *Karchin* = *bare*. It is the opposite to the word *Nesibin*, and is only used with regard to the letter *Vav* at the beginning of a word, and then only when there occur in one verse, or in the same section, three or four words or more, some of which have *Vav* at the beginning and some not. In such a case the Massorites mark those words which have *Vav* with *Nesibin* = *with*, whilst those which have not *Vav* are marked with *Karchin* = *bare*, *without*. Thus, for instance:—i. The six verses repeating respectively a word four times, the first two of which are *Karchin* = without *Vav*, and the second two are *Nesibin* = with *Vav*, viz., בֵּין בֵּין וּבֵין וּבֵין *between, between, and between, and between* [Deut. i. 16], &c.[123] ii. The four verses repeating respectively a word four times, the first three of which are *Karchin* = without *Vav*, and the fourth is *Nesib* = with *Vav*, viz., שָׂרֵי שָׂרֵי שָׂרֵי וְשָׂרֵי *rulers of, rulers of, rulers of, and rulers of* [Deut. i. 15], &c.[124] iii. The two verses containing respectively four words, the first of which is *Karchi* = without *Vav*, and the other three are *Nesibin* = with *Vav*, viz., בְּתוֹךְ וּבְתוֹךְ וּבְתוֹךְ וּבְתוֹךְ *in, and in, and in, and in* [Exod. xxxix. 3], &c.[125] iv. The six words in one verse, the first, second, and

[123] The six verses which respectively have the same words four times, twice with *Vav* conjunctive, and twice without it, are,—

בין בין ובין ובין	. . . . . Deut. i. 16	מפני מפני ומפני ומפני . . .	Isa. xxi. 15
אל אל ואל ואל	. . . . . Deut. xx. 3	בערי בערי ובערי ובערי . . .	Jerem. xxxiii. 13
כי כי וכי וכי	. . . . 1 Kings xviii. 27	לא לא ולא ולא	Hos. xi. 9

They are given in the Massorah marginalis on Hosea xi. 9.

[124] The four verses which respectively have the same word four times, in the first instance with the *Vav* conjunctive, and in the other three without it, are,—

שרי ושרי שרי שרי	. . . Exod. xviii. 21	אל ואל אל אל	Ps. xxvii. 9
ושרי שרי שרי שרי	. . . Exod. xviii. 25	דרך ודרך דרך דרך	Prov. xxx. 19

They are given in the Massorah marginalis on Exod. xviii. 21.

[125] The other passage in which the same word occurs four times, the first three times with *Vav* conjunctive, and the fourth without it, is פני ופני ופני פני, Ezek. i. 10.

fifth of which are without the *Vav*, whilst the third, fourth, and sixth have *Vav*, viz., רְאוּבֵן גָּד וְאָשֵׁר וּזְבוּלֻן דָּן וְנַפְתָּלִי *Reuben, Gad, and Asher, and Zebulun, Dan, and Naphtali* [Deut. xxvii. 13]. And, v. The verse שָׂדֵהוּ וְעַבְדּוֹ וַאֲמָתוֹ שׁוֹרוֹ וַחֲמֹרוֹ, *his field, and his man servant, and his maid servant, his ox, and his ass*, in Deut. v. 18, the mnemonical sign of which is שׁ״שׁ קרחי, indicating that the words beginning with the two *Shins*, viz., שָׂדֵהוּ *his field*, and שׁוֹרוֹ *his ox*, are without *Vav*, whilst the others have it.

SECTION VIII., concerning *Imaginary Readings, Misleadings, and Variations.*—Know that the expression סבירין denotes *incorrect opinion, imagination, fancy, supposition*; that is, when a man thinks or imagines in his heart that it is so and so, but it is not. In German it is *Er meint* or *wähnet*. It has the same meaning in the language of the Mishna, as סבור הייתי *I believed*, סבורים היו *they thought*; in the book of Daniel, as וְיִסְבַּר *and he thought* [vii. 25]; and in the Chaldee paraphrase, which renders the phrase, "there is a way which is right in the view of man" [Prov. xiv. 12], by "there is a way which man [דסבירין] *imagine*, &c."

Thus there are also many words in the Bible which men imagine ought to be so and so, but they are not. As, i The word מִמֶּנּוּ *from it* [Levit. xxvii. 9], on which the Massorites remark, "one of the six instances supposed to be מִמֶּנָּה *from her*," since the noun בְּהֵמָה *a beast*, is feminine. To the same effect are the other instances.[126] ii. The word וַיָּבֹא *and he came*, on which they remark, "one of the eight instances supposed to be וַיָּבֹאוּ *and they came*.[127] iii. The expression וּבְנֵי *and the sons of* [Gen. xlvi. 12], "one of the three instances supposed to be בֶּן *son of*;" and *vice versa*, the five instances in which the textual reading has בֶּן *son of*, and the conjectural reading is בְּנֵי

---

[126] The six passages in which the conjectural reading in the Massorah proposes ממנה, third person singular feminine, instead of the textual reading ממנו, third person singular masculine, because of the antecedent to which it refers, and which is feminine, are, Levit. vi. 8; xxvii. 9; Josh. i. 7; Judg. xi. 34; 2 Kings iv. 39 : 1 Kings xxii. 43. They are given in the Massorah marginalis on Levit. vi. 8; in the Massorah marginalis on Judg. xi. 34, where five instances only are given, there must therefore be a mistake.

[127] The eight places in which the conjectural reading is plural, instead of singular, are, Numb. xiii. 22 : Ezek. xiv. 1; xxiii. 44; xxxvi. 20: 2 Sam. iii. 22 : Ezek. xx. 38: Isa. xlv. 24: Jerem. li. 48. They are given in the Massorah marginalis on Numb. xiii. 22. It must be noticed that they are not all the future with *Vav* conversive.

226

sons of, as in 1 Chron. iii. 19, &c.[128] iv. The word אֲשֶׁר *which*, is in four instances supposed to be כַּאֲשֶׁר *as which*, and the ten instances in which the reverse is the case, the textual reading having כַּאֲשֶׁר and the marginal conjecture being אֲשֶׁר.[129] v. The words in which the *Vav* conjunctive is wanting, as לֹא *not* [Exod. xxiii. 13], on which it is remarked, "one of those supposed to be וְלֹא *and not*." vi. The entire absence of a word from a sentence, as the five passages which are supposed to want אִם *if*, and wherein the scribes mislead, *ex. gr.*, Gen. xxiv. 4 ; 2 Sam. xix. 8, &c.[130] vii. In the interchange of words, as the three passages in which the text has מִפְּנֵי *from the face of*, and it is supposed to be מִפִּי *from the mouth*, *ex. gr.*, Numb. xxxiii. 8, &c.[131] viii. The nine passages in which the textual reading עַל *upon*, supposed to be עַד *until*, *ex. gr.*, Gen. xlix. 18, &c. ;[132] and ix. The two passages in which the textual reading is עַל *upon*, and the conjectural reading is עִם *with*, viz., Gen. xxx. 40 ; 1 Sam. xx. 8.

Some, however, explain the word סבירין *to think it proper*, and submit that it means, "*correctly the reading ought to be so and so.*" This interpretation is strengthened by the fact that the expression occurs in the singular. Thus, in the Massorah on Gen. l. 13, it is remarked לית

וחניה ;[128] וכן ד' אֲשֶׁר דסבירין כַּאֲשֶׁר, ולהפך י' כַּאֲשֶׁר דסבירין אֲשֶׁר ;[129] וכן במלות שחסר בהן וי"ו החבור, כמו לא ישמע על פיך, חד מן דסבירין ולא ; וכן בחסרון מלה אחת ממשמעות המאמר, כמו ה' דסבירין אם ומטעין בהון, כמו כי אל ארצי ואל מולדתי תלך, כי אינך יוצא וכו' ;[130] וכן בחילוף מלה במלה, כנון ג' מִפְּנֵי דסבירין מִפִּי, כנון ויסע מִפְּנֵי החידות וכו' ;[131] וכן מ' על דסבירין עַד, כמו וידכחו על צידון ;[132] וב' על דסבירין עִם כמו ולא שחם על צאן לבן, ועשיח חסד על עבדך :

ויש מפרשין סבידין לשון סברא, ופרוש לפי הסברא היה ראוי לחיות כך ; ומה שמחזק הפירוש הזה חוא שנמצא זה חלשון בלשון יחיד, כמו מאת עפרון החתי על פני ממרא, לית דסביד אשר על פני, פירוש ליח

---

[128] The instances in which the conjectural reading substitutes ובן for the marginal reading ובני, are not *three*, as stated in the text of Levita, but *four*, viz., Gen. xlvi. 22 : Numb. xxvi. 8 : 1 Chron. ii. 8 : vii. 17. Neither is the statement that there are *five* instances in which the reverse is the case correct, since there are *six* such conjectural readings, viz., 1 Chron. iii. 19, 21, 23 ; iv. 17 ; vii. 35 ; viii. 34. They are enumerated in the Massorah marginalis on Gen. xlvi. 22.

[129] The four passages in which the conjectural reading substitutes כאשר for the textual reading אשר, are, Exod. xiv. 13 : Levit. vii. 36, 38 : Numb. iv. 49. They are given in the Massorah marginalis on Levit. vii. 36. The ten instances in which the reverse is the case are, Deut. xvi. 10 ; xxiv. 8 ; Josh. ii. 7 ; xiii. 8 ; xiv. 2 . Jerem. xxiii. 27 : Isa. li. 13 : Hos. vii. 12 : Jonah i. 14 : Hag. i. 12. They are given in the Massorah marginalis on Jonah i. 14.

[130] The passages in which the conjectural reading supplies the particle אם, are, Gen. xxiv. 4 : 1 Sam. xviii. 25 : 2 Sam. xix. 8 : Jerem. xxii. 12 : 2 Chron. vi. 9. They are given in the Massorah marginalis on Gen. xxiv. 4.

[131] The other two passages in which the conjectural reading has מפי for the textual reading מפני, are, 2 Sam. xvi. 19 : Amos v. 19. They are given in the Massorah marginalis on Numb. xxxiii. 8.

[132] The nine passages in which the conjectural reading has עד for the textual reading על, are, Gen. xlix. 13 : Josh. ii. 7 ; xiii. 16 : Judg. vii. 22 : Jerem. xxxi. 39 : Dan. ix. 27 : Nehem. xii. 22, 39 (twice). They are given in the Massorah marginalis on Gen. xlix. 13, where, however, the heading, as well as the reference to this rubric made in the Massorah finalis under the letter *Ajin*, p. 49 *b*, col. 3, states that there are eleven such instances, though it enumerates only *nine*, which agrees with the text of Levita.

במקרא עַל פְּנֵי שהסברה נותנת לחיות אֲשֶׁר
עַל פְּנֵי; וכן מפרשים כל סבירין שבמסורת
לשון סברא, אבל לא סבירא לי, כי לפי זה
היה לחם לכתוב מסתברין ודוק:

ויש נוסחאות שנמסר על קצת המלות
סבירין וממעין, או ממעין וסבירין, ואינו
אלא תוספת ביאור; אבל נמצא ממעין בלי
סבירין, הה על הדוב בפסוקים, כגון ג'
פסוקים דממעים בהן כסוף פסוק, חד יְזַרְעֲךָ
עַד עוֹלָם, וחד וּבְזַרְעֲךָ עַד עֹלָם, וחד וּבְזַרְעֲךָ
לְעוֹלָם; [183] וכן במתגורת כהונה ד' פסוקים
דממעין בהון; [184] וכן ב' סופי פסוקים
דממעין בהן בדגש ורפי, ארם נהרים לְקַלְלֶךָ
בדנש, עֹבֵדְךְ מְקַלְלֶךָ ברפי וסימן פָּכָה יעשה,
רוצה לומר, כ"ף הראשונה דגושה, והשניה
רפויה; ופסוקים דממעים בהון במעמא הן
הרבה מאוד, ואין כאן מקומם:

ויש לך לדעת כי ממעין אינו רוצה לומר
שטועין בהן בני אדם לקרותן כך, כי ממעים
היא מבנין הפעיל שהוא יוצא לשני, ופירושו
הסופרים ממעין את הקוראים; וכן מצאתי
בנוסחאות מדויקות על עֲוֹנָם והם ישאו עֲוֹנָם,
ממעין ביה ספרי למכתב אֶת עֲוֹנָם: וכן ישתו

; דּסביר אשׁר על פּני; that is, there
does not exist in the Bible the
phrase עַל פְּנֵי *upon the face of,* for
which the conjectural reading substitutes אֲשֶׁר עַל פְּנֵי *which upon the
face of.* Hence they explain all
the expressions סבירין in the Massorah as *correct opinion,* but it does
not appear correct to me, since
according to this interpretation it
ought more correctly to have been
written מסתברין.

There are Codices in which the
Massoretic remark on some words
is, "imaginary readings and misleadings," or, "misleadings and
imaginary readings;" but this is
nothing more than an additional
explanation. The word *misleadings,*
however, occurs sometimes without
the expression *imaginary reading,*
and this is mostly the case when it
refers to verses; as, for instance,
"the three verses in which the
scribes mislead with regard to

the end of the verse, one is 'and to thy seed for ever' [Gen. xiii. 15], the second 'and in thy seed for ever' [Deut. xxviii. 46], and the third 'and in thy seed for ever' [2 Kings v. 27]."[183] To the same effect, also, are the four verses which mislead in connection with the priesthoood,[184] and the two ends of verses which are misleading with regard to *Dagesh* and *Raphe*, viz., לְקַלְלֶךָ *to curse thee* [Deut. xxiii. 5], which has *Dagesh,* and מְקַלְלֶךָ *cursing thee* [Eccles. vii. 21], which is *Raphe,* and the mnemonical sign of which is פָּכָה; that is, the first *Kaph* has *Dagesh,* and the second *Kaph* is *Raphe.* As to the verses which mislead with regard to the accents, they are exceedingly numerous, but this is not the place to expatiate upon them.

You must moreover notice, that the word ממעין cannot mean that men err in these words by reading them so and so, for it is the *Hiphil* which is causative. It denotes that the scribes mislead the reader. Hence, I have found it remarked in accurate Codices on עֲוֹנָם *their iniquity* [Numb. xviii. 23], "the scribes mislead thereby in writing אֶת

---

[183] These three instances are given in the Massorah marginalis on Deut. xxviii. 46, and in the *Ochla Ve-Ochla,* section cclxviii., pp. 52, 143.
[184] The four verses in which the expression *Levites* (הלוים) precedes *Priests* (כהנים) are, Jerem. xxxiii. 21: 2 Chron. xix. 8; xxix. 26; xxx. 21. They are given in the Massorah finalis on Jerem. xxxiii. 21: 2 Chron. xxx. 21; and in the *Ochla Ve-Ochla,* section cclxxx., p. 151.

עֵונָם with the sign of the accusative before it." So also on תָּמִיד *continually* [Obad. 16], the Massorites remark, "the scribes mislead by it in writing סָבִיב *round about;*" and also on עַל יְרוּשָׁלָם *over Jerusalem* [Eccl. i. 16], "they mislead here by writing בִּירוּשָׁלָם *in Jerusalem.*" Now I have seen the remarks of those Codices, which very correctly do not write דטועין *which err.*

SECTION IX., *concerning the terms Letters, Words, Expressions, Short Letters, Accents, Certainties,* and *Transpositions.* — It is well known that each one of the twenty-two letters of the alphabet is called אוֹת *sign*, because it is a sign and mark for the utterance of the voice, and in the plural ought properly to be אוֹתוֹת. But to distinguish it from אוֹתוֹת *wonders, miracles,* it is אוֹתִיוֹת. The Massorites, however, call it אָתִין, which is the Chaldee rendering of אוֹתוֹת *signs* [Gen. i. 14]. Thus, as in the case of the names where they remark, "there are five verses in which the same names occur, differing only (בְּאָתֵיהוֹן) in their letters," viz., in the Pentateuch, *and Izhar, and Hebron, and Uzziel* [Exod. vi. 18]; in 1 Chron. *Izhar, Hebron, and Uzziel* [xxiii. 12], &c;[135] but when it is in the singular, the Massorites call it אוֹת, just as in the Hebrew. Thus they say, "there are four groups of words, each of which occurs twice in the same book, once with a word less and a letter more, and once with a word more and a letter less." The first of such a pair is, "Jehovah, thy God, thou shalt fear, and Him thou shalt serve, and by His name thou shalt swear" [Deut. vi. 13]; the second, "Jehovah, thy God, thou shalt fear, Him thou shalt

---

[135] The meaning of the Massoretic remark which Levita quotes is, that though the four names עמרם יצהר חברון עזיאל *Amram, Izhar, Hebron,* and *Uzziel,* are exactly the same in all the five passages in which they occur, as far as the words themselves are concerned, yet the letter *Vav* or the conjunctive is placed differently in each passage, as will be seen from the following enumeration of them:—

ובני קהת עמרם ויצהר וחברון ועזיאל	Exod. vi. 18.
ובני קהת עמרם ויצהר וחברון ועזיאל	1 Chron. vi. 3.
ובני קהת למשפחתם עמרם יצהר חברון ועזיאל	Numb. iii. 19.
ובני קהת עמרם יצהר וחברון ועזיאל	1 Chron. v. 28.
בני קהת עמרם יצהר חברון ועזיאל	1 Chron. xxiii. 12.

They are given in the Massorah marginalis on Exod. xvi. 18, where, however, the instance in Numb. iii. 19 is omitted, though the rubric states that there are *five* such passages. The *Ochla Ve-Ochla,* section cclxxxviii., pp. 54, 152, &c., rightly supplies this omission.

serve, *and to Him thou shalt cleave, and by His name thou shalt swear*" [*ibid.* x. 20].[136] This they do not call את, which is the Chaldee translation of אות, in order that it might not be confounded with the expression אֶת.

☞ Let me now explain the term תיבין *words.* Now it is well known that the ancients called every word תיבה, and I have instituted great search to find out the reason for it, but could not discover the meaning of it, seeing that this expression only occurs to denote the ark of Noah [Gen. vi. 14-16], and the ark in which Moses was exposed [Exod. ii. 3, 5], translated by the Chaldee תיבותא. The Massorites make the plural of תיבה to be תיבין, according to the analogy of the Hebrew מלין or מלים *words*, from מלה *word*, which is only found in Job. Many, indeed, are of opinion that there is no difference between the expressions תיבה and מלה.

☞ Now I submit that there is a difference between them, since the expression מלה denotes a word uttered by the mouth when speaking, as it is used in the writings by our Rabbins of blessed memory; *ex. gr.*, "and they repeated after him [מלה] word [במלה] for word,"

---

[136] The Massorah differs as to the number of these instances. Thus, on Isa. i. 1, the Massorah marginalis (as Levita in the text before us) remarks that there are *four* such pairs, and enumerates them as follows:—

את יהוה אלהיך תירא ואתו תעבד ובשמו תשבע	Deut. vi. 13.
את יהוה אלהיך תירא אתו תעבד ובו תדבק ובשמו תשבע	Deut. x. 20.
על פי שנים עדים או שלשה	Deut. xvii. 6.
על פי שנים עדים או על פי שלשה עדים	Deut. xix. 15.
ולא אבו שמוע	Isa. xxviii. 12.
לא אבו שמוע תרת יהוה	Isa. xxx. 9.
ואמלה על פני ואזעק ואמר	Ezek. ix. 8.
ואפל על פני ואזעק קול גדול ואמר	Ezek. xi. 13.

In the Massorah marginalis on Ezek. xi. 13, however, it is stated that there are *seven* such instances, and the following two pairs are added:—

וירשאו את שבר עמי . . . Jerem. vi. 14		והנשאו ∙ ∙ מי זה מלך הכבוד . Ps. xxiv. 7, 8
וירשאו את שבר בת עמי . . . Jerem. viii. 11		ושאו ∙ ∙ מי הוא זה מלך הכבוד . Ps. xxiv. 9

There can therefore be but little doubt that the remark in the Massorah finalis, under the letter *Vav*, p. 28 *b*, col. 4, that there are *ten* (י) such instances, has arisen from a corruption of the letter *Vav* (ו), than which nothing is more easy and common. In the *Ochla Ve-Ochla*, section ccxxxiv., p. 183, the following two pairs are added, as being found (לבד ממסורתא) apart from those stated in the Massorah:—

רק הדם לא תאכלו . . . . Deut. xii. 16		הידענים מהארץ . . . 1 Sam. xxviii. 3
רק את דמו לא תאכל . . . . Deut. xv. 23		הידעני מן הארץ . . . 1 Sam. xxviii. 9

It is also to be added that the pair which forms the fifth in the rubric given in the Massorah marginalis on Ezek. xi. 13, is, in the *Ochla Ve-Ochla*, included in those instances to be found "apart from the Massorah."

חיבה לא אמרו רק על מלה הכחובה בחוך חסםר, כמו שאמרו כל חיבה הצריכה למ״ד בתחלתה המיל לה ה״א בסופה;[187] וכן ראשי חיבות, סוםי חיבות, ולא נאמר ראשי מלוח, סוםי מלוח: אך מצאחרי קצח חמדקדקים לא הבדילו ביניהם וקראו לשניהם מלה, ולא נמצא כן בדברי הקדמונים: ופירוש קטיעין מלשון קציצה וכריתה, כמו וְקָצַץ פחילים חרגום ירושלמי וקטע יחחון, וכן יְפַלַח כליוחי יקטע כליוחי; וחנה ידוע כי נמצא א״ב מן אוחיוח גדולוח,[188]

whereas חיבה, they employ to designate what is written down in a book, as, for instance, when they say, "every word which requires *Lamed* at the beginning, takes *He* at the end,"[187] "the initials of words," "the end of words," &c.; but not מלות. Yet I have found that some grammarians make no distinction between the two expressions, and call them both מלה, but I have not found it so in the writings of the ancients.

The meaning of קטיעין is *breaking off, cutting off;* so the Jerusalem Targum renders וַיְקַצֵּץ *and he cut* [Exod. xxxix. 3] by וקטע, and יְפַלַח *he cleaveth* [Job xvi. 13] by יקטע. Now it is well known that there is an alphabetical list of words with large letters,[188] and that there is another

---

[187] The axiom of the Rabbins, to which Levita refers, has already been discussed, *vide supra,* p. 173.

[188] The alphabetical list of words in the Hebrew Scriptures, written with majuscular letters, is as follows:—

אדם	. .	1 Chron. i. 1	שבטו	. .	Job ix. 34	שמע	. .	Deut. vi. 4
בראשית	. .	Gen. i. 1	ינדל	. .	Numb. xiv. 17	בשטרפא	. .	Dan. vi. 20
והתגלח	. .	Levit. xiii. 33	וכנה	. .	Ps. lxxx. 16	ובהעמיך	. .	Gen. xxx. 42
אחד	. .	Deut. vi. 4	וישלכם	. .	Deut. xxix. 27	צמו	. .	Isa. lvi. 10
הליהוה	. .	Deut. xxxii. 6	משלי	. .	Prov. i. 1	קן	. .	Ps. lxxxiv. 4
ויתרא	. .	Esther ix. 9	נצר	. .	Exod. xxxiv. 7	אחז	. .	Exod. xxxiv. 14
זכרו	. .	Mal. iii. 22	ליני	. .	Ruth iii. 13	שיר	. .	Song of Songs i. 1
חר	. .	Esther i. 6	משפטן	. .	Numb. xxvii. 5	ותכתב	. .	Esther ix. 29
			סוף	. .	Eccles. xii. 13			

This list is given in the Massorah marginalis on Gen. i. 1; in the Massorah marginalis on 1 Chron. i. 1, however, where the list is repeated, the following alterations are made, נחון (Levit. xi. 42), is substituted for יתרא (Esther ix. 9); טוב (Eccles. vii. 1) for שבטו (Job ix. 34); both משפטן (Numb. xxvii. 5), and ובהעמיף (Gen. xxx. 42), are omitted; and תמים (Deut. xviii. 13) is substituted for ותכתב (Esther ix. 29). In the *Ochla Ve-Ochla* again, where the list is also given, section lxxxiii., p. 88, נחון (Levit. xi. 42) is substituted for יתרא (Esther ix. 9); אלמים (Dan. vii. 10), representing final *Mem*, is added; וכנה (Ps. lxxx. 16) is given instead of נצר (Exod. xxxiv. 7); and ובהעמיף (Gen. xxx. 42) is omitted. The *Ochla Ve-Ochla,* moreover, (section lxxxiii., p. 82), gives another alphabetical list of majuscular letters contained in the Pentateuch alone, which is as follows:—

אשריך	. .	Deut. xxxiii. 29	ינדל	. .	Numb. xiv. 17	שמע	. .	Deut. vi. 4
בראשית	. .	Gen. i. 1	והתמכתם	. .	Deut. xxviii. 68	ופתלתל	. .	Deut. xxxii. 5
והתגלח	. .	Levit. xiii. 33	ובך or וכך	. .	Deut. ii. 33	ובהעמיף	. .	Gen. xxx. 42
אחד	. .	Deut. vi. 4	וישלכם	. .	Deut. xxix. 27	צא	. .	Exod. xi. 8
הליהוה	. .	Deut. xxxii. 6	מה	. .	Numb. xxiv. 5	ציץ	. .	Exod. xxviii. 36
נחון	. .	Levit. xi. 42	שלשים	. .	Gen. i. 23	קן	. .	Deut. xxxii. 6
הכזונה	. .	Gen. xxxiv. 31	נצר	. .	Exod. xxxiv. 7	אחז	. .	Exod. xxxiv. 14
חכלילי	. .	Gen. xlix. 12	משפטן	. .	Numb. xxvii. 5	ערש	. .	Deut. iii. 11
טוב	. .	Exod. ii. 2	ויהם	. .	Numb. xiii. 30	תמים	. .	Deut. xviii. 13

This extended list—and be it remembered that even this list does not give *all* the

alphabetical list of words with small letters.[189] In the Massorah, every one of the large letters is called *majuscular*, and of the small letters *minuscular*, as בְּרֵאשִׁית in the beginning [Gen. i. 1] is marked *Beth majuscular*, and וַיִּקְרָא *and he called* [Levit. i. 1] is marked *Aleph minuscular*.[198] In the correct Codices the small *Vav* is not called זְעִירָא = *minuscular*, but קְטִיעָא, that is, *cut off from below*. Thus, שָׁלוֹם *peace* [Numb. xxv. 12] is marked "*Vav cut off*;" נַפְשׁוֹ *his soul* [Ps. xxiv. 4] is marked "*Vav cut off*," &c.

וא"ב מן אותיות קמנות,[189] ובמסורה קראו לכל אחת מהנדולות רבתא, והקמנות זעירא, כמו בְּרֵאשִׁית בי"ת רבתא, וַיִּקְרָא אלי"ף זעירא; חנה במסורות המדויקות לא קראו חוי"ו הקמנה וי"ו זעירא, אך וי"ו קטיעא, פירוש קצוצה מעם מלממה, כמו את בריתי שלום וי"ו קטיעא; וכן לא נשא לשוא נפשו וי"ו קטיעא:

☞ ותמהתי אני על כל המפרשים אשר ראיתי שלפי פי' כלם הוא כתיב נפשו וקרי נפשי, וכן ראיתי ברוב נוכחאות המסורה; ואין ספק כי הוא מעות סופרים, ומעו בין זה ובין פרה נפשו מעבר בשחרי, שהוא קרי נפשי; וכן הוא נמנה עם מ"א מלין דכתיבין

Now I am astonished that all the commentators whom I have consulted should take this word נַפְשׁוֹ *his soul*, as *Kethiv*, and remark that the *Keri* is נַפְשִׁי *my soul*. Indeed I have also seen some Codices of the Massorah which have the same. But there is no doubt that is a blunder committed by transcribers, who confounded the word נַפְשׁוֹ in question with נַפְשׁוֹ, in Job xxxiii. 28, which is נַפְשִׁי in the *Keri*, and which is included in the list of forty-one words, written in the text with *Vav* and read in the margin

majuscular letters.—would of itself be fatal to the ingenious theory propounded by Mr. W. H. Black, F.S.A., in a paper read before the Chronological Institute of London, (October 4, 1864), that the sum total of the majuscular letters is designed to give the date of the composition of the Pentateuch. We shall, however, show, in our forthcoming "*Manual to the Massorah*," other reasons why the majuscular letters could never have been intended as Chronograms.

[189] The alphabetical list of the minuscular letters, is as follows:—

וַיִּקְרָא	. . . Levit. i. 1	וּמֵהָרַתֶּם	. Numb. xxxi. 24	בְּסוּפָה	. . Nahum i. 3
הֵב	. . . Prov. xxx. 15	תֵּשׁ	. Deut. xxxii. 18	בְּסֻכָּה	. . Ps. xxvii. 5
וְנֻשׁ	. . . Job vii. 5	וּלְבִכְתָּה	. Gen. xxiii. 2	לְעוּת	. Lament. iii. 36
אָדָם	. . Prov. xxviii. 17	לוֹא	. Lament. i. 12	בְּשַׂרְפְּרָא	. . Dan. vi. 20
בְּהִבָּרְאָם	. . Gen. ii. 4	מְמַרִים	. Deut. ix. 24	וְצוּחַת	. Jerem. xiv. 2
וְנַפְשׁוֹ	. . Ps. xxii. 30	מוֹקְדָה	. Levit. vi. 2	פָּרֶךְ	. . Job xvi. 14
שָׁלוֹם	. . Numb. xxv. 12	וּמְטַהֲרִים	. Nehem. xiii. 30	בְּקֻמֵיהֶם	. Exod. xxxii. 25
לַשָּׁוְא	. . Ps. xxiv. 4	נְעוֹ	. . Nahum i. 3	קְצָתִי	. . Gen. xxvii. 46
וִיֻתַּר	. . Esth. ix. 9	נָרָן	. . Prov. xvi. 28	רֵאשִׁית	. Exod. xxiv. 26
חַף	. . Job xxxiii. 9	וּנְבוּשַׁזְבָּן	Jerem. xxxix. 13	פַּרְסַנְדָּתָא	. . Esth. ix. 7
מִבָּעַז	. . Lament. ii. 9	אָרָן	. . Isa. xliv. 14	פַּרְמַשְׁתָּא	. . Esth. ix. 9

The list is given in the Massorah finalis under the letter *Aleph*, p. 1 *a*, col. 1, and in the Massorah marginalis on Levit. i. 1. In the *Ochla Ve-Ochla*, section lxxxiv., pp. 25 and 89, which also gives this list, the following variations occur: יצפני (Ps. xxvii. 5) is put under the *Nun*, as having the second *Nun* smaller, whilst נעו (Nahum i. 3) is omitted. The three instances which represent the final *Nun* are also omitted; but they are, however, given under a separate rubric (comp. section clxxviii.), with the Massorah marginalis on Isa. xliv. 14: Prov. xvi. 28: Jerem. xxxix. 14). Neither does the *Ochla Ve-Ochla* give בקמיהם (Exod. xxxii. 25) under *Koph*, and ראשית (Exod. xxiv. 26) under *Resh*, which are also omitted from the list given in the Massorah marginalis on Levit. i. 1. Like the Massorah marginalis on Levit. i. 1, the *Ochla Ve-Ochla* rightly marks פרמשתא (Esther ix. 9) as having both a smaller *Resh* and *Tav*.

with *Jod*;[140] whereas נַפְשׁוֹ, in Ps. xxiv. 4, is not given in the list, because it has simply "a cut-short *Vav*." As a rule, the Massorites do not apply the term *cut-short* to any letter but *Vav*, and hence, also, they call it in one place *long*. Thus, the *Vav* in וַיְזָתָא *Vajezatha* [Esther ix. 9], is called "elongated," and not *majuscular*; since *Vav majuscular* is the one in גָּחוֹן *belly* [Levit. xi. 42], as you may see in the alphabetical list of the large letters, and the list of the twenty-two verses which have neither a short nor a long letter, that is, neither *Vav* nor *Jod*, as Ps. cv. 11, &c.[141]

The Massorites also employ the expression קטיעא = *cut short*, with regard to a word which has three quiescents, and is spelled differently in three different places, wanting the first quiescent in the first passage, the second in the second passage, and the two quiescents in

---

[140] The words written with *Vav*, prenominal suffix, third person masculine, and read with *Jod*, mostly suffix, first person, are as follows:—

מצותו	. .	Deut. v. 10	התפתחו	. .	Isa. lii. 2	ומיציאו	. .	2 Chron. xxxii. 21
תקטו	. .	Josh. vi. 9	עצמו	. .	Isa. xlvi. 11	מדו	. .	Ps. xi. 1
אזנו	. .	1 Sam. xxii. 17	ממטו	. .	Isa. lx. 21	חסדו	. .	Ps. lix. 11
כלבו	. .	1 Sam. xxv. 3	תקראו	. .	Jerem. iii. 19	רעננו	. .	Ps. cviii. 7
שנאו	. .	2 Sam. v. 8	תשובו	. .	Jerem. iii. 19	כחו	. .	Ps. cii. 24
בנפשו	. .	2 Sam. xviii. 13	אכלנו	. .	Jerem. li. 34	וידעו	. .	Ps. cxix. 79
בעינו	. .	2 Sam. xii. 9	הכמנו	. .	Jerem. li. 34	הראיתנו	. .	Ps. lxxi. 20
וישבו	. .	2 Sam. xxi. 16	הציגנו	. .	Jerem. li. 34	תחינו	. .	Ps. lxxi. 20
דרכו	. .	2 Sam. xxii. 33	בלענו	. .	Jerem. li. 34	יתרו	. .	Job xxx. 11
העצנו	. .	2 Sam. xxiii. 8	הדיחנו	. .	Jerem. li. 34	במו	. .	Job ix. 30
חצרו	. .	2 Sam. xxiii. 35	ידו	. .	Ezek. i. 8	או	. .	Prov. xxvi. 2
תלו	. .	1 Kings v. 17	חתיתו	. .	Ezek. xxxii. 32	אשתנו	. .	Dan. iii. 19
קדשו	. .	1 Kings xv. 15	רבו	. .	Hos. viii. 12	לשרשו	. .	Ezra vii. 26
נביאו	. .	2 Kings xvii. 13	ישבו	. .	1 Chron. iii. 55	וישמו	. .	Ezra x. 37
הביאו	. .	Isa. xvi. 1	בנו	. .	1 Chron. vi. 11	ידו	. .	Ezra x. 43
הברו	. .	Isa. xlvii. 13	בנו	. .	1 Chron. xxii. 7	רענו	. .	Nehem. xii. 9

From this list, which is given in the Massorah marginalis on 1 Sam. i. 1, it will be seen that there are forty-eight such instances, and not forty-one, as is stated by Levita. It is however to be remarked, that in both the Massorah marginalis on 1 Sam. i. 1, and the Massorah finalis under the letter *Vav*, p. 27 b, col. 1, where reference is made to this rubric, it is also stated that there are only forty-one such instances; whilst in the Massorah marginalis on Jerem. i. 1, where the list is repeated, it is simply headed by "these are the words" (אלין מלין), &c., without specifying the number. The *Ochla Ve-Ochla*, section cxxxvi., pp. 34, 106, &c., where the list is also given, states that there are forty-seven instances, and the whole number is duly given.

[141] The twenty-three verses which have neither *Van* nor *Jod* are as follows:— Exod. xx. 13, 15: Ps. cv. 11: 1 Chron. xvi. 18: Numb. vii. 14, 20, 26, 32, 38, 44, 50, 56, 62, 68, 74, 80: Lament. iii. 65: Josh. xii. 13, 14, 15: 1 Chron. i. 24: Ps. xix. 12: 1 Chron. xxiv. 14. They are given in the Massorah marginalis on Numb. vii. 14, where, however, the heading of the rubric, as well as the Massorah parva, states that there are only (כ״ב) twenty-two such verses; whilst the Massorah marginalis on Psalm cv. 11, which simply gives the heading, like Levita, most distinctly remarks that there are twenty-three (כ״ג) such verses. The apparent discrepancy is to be accounted for by the fact, that the four commandments, which form in our Bibles four distinct verses (viz., Exod. xx. 13–16), are alternately counted in the Massorah as one verse, and as two verses, according to the two different systems of accentuation.

the third passage. Thus on the words יַאֲרִיכוּן *they shall prolong*, which is once written יַאֲרִכֻן [Exod. xx. 11], once יַאֲרִיכֻ [Deut. v. 16], and once יַאֲרִכֻן [Deut. vi. 2]; the Massorites remark, "it has once its hand [= *Jod*] cut off, once its foot [= *Vav*] cut off, and once it has both its hand and foot cut off." I have already mentioned, in the First Part, Section viii., other phrases whereby the Massorites are in the habit of describing such anomalous words, *vide supra*, p. 166.

☞ As to the meaning of פשטין, it is well known that *Pashta* is the name of one of the accents. Now two such *Pashtas* are sometimes placed on one word, it is then called "two *Pashtin*," as I shall explain in the Treatise, entitled, "Good Sense," with the help of the Lord. Now the Massorites call *Pashtin* some words which in a few places are pointed with *Pattach*, whilst in all other instances they have *Segol*. Thus אַעֲלֶה *I shall bring up*, is marked "eight times Pashtin" [i. e. Hiphil],[142] since in all other passages it is אַעֲלֶה with *Segol* [i. e. Kal]; also וַיַּאַסְפוּ *and they gathered*, is marked "ten times Pashtin" [i. e. Kal], for in all other instances it is וַיַּאַסְפוּ [i. e. Niphal].[143]

As to the meaning of ודאין, it is well known that it is the opposite to *doubtful*, and that the German for it is gewiß. The Massorites only use it in three places; one with respect to the sacred name of the Lord, which is written אדני, and on which they remark "one hundred and thirty-four times וַדָיָא or וַדָאִין." The reason of this is, that the name יהוה, being the tetragrammaton, must not be read as it is written, for it must not be pronounced with the lips, but is to be read under the appellation אדני. This reading we have traditionally received from Moses our teacher, peace be upon him. Hence it has the vowel-points of אֲדֹנָי, as follows יְהֹוָה. The reading of it

ג' נחים, ונמצאת בג' מקומות, האחד חסר חנק הראשון, והשני חסר הנה השני, והשלישי הסרים שניהם, כמו יַאֲרִיכֻן א' כתיב יַאֲרִכֻן, וא' כרתיב יַאֲרִיכֻ, וא' כרתיב יַאֲרִכֻן, נמסר עליהן הד קמיעא ידיה, וחד קמיעא רגליה, וחד קמיעא ידיה ורגליה; וכבר כתבתי בלוחות הראשונות בדבור ח' אופנים אחרים שנוהגים לכתוב על מלות כיוצא בזאת ע"ש:

☞ ופירוש פשטין, הנה ידוע כי פשטא הוא שם אחד מן הטעמים המפסיקים, ולפעמים משימין שנים על חיבה אחת, וקורין לה ב' פשטין, כאשר יתבאר בספר טוב טעם בע"ה; והנה הם קראו פשטין לקצת מלות הנקודות בפתח וכל חברותיהן בסגול, כמו אַעֲלֶה ח' פשטין, כי כל שאר אַעֲלֶה בסגול, וכן וַיַּאַסְפוּ י' פשטין, כי כל שאר וַיַּאַסְפוּ:

ופירוש ודאין הנה ידוע כי ודאי הוא החפך מן ספק, ובלשון אשכנז גיוויס, ובמסורת שמשו בה בכ' מקומות לבד, הא' על השם הקדוש של אדנות הנכתב א' ד' נ' י', נמסר קל"ד ודאין או ודייא; וזה לפי ששם של הויה, שהוא שם של ד' אותיות אינו נקרא ככתבו כי אין לבטא אותו בפה, אך קוראין אותו בכנוי אדני, וכן קבלנו קריאתו מסר"עה, לכן הוא נקוד בנקודת אֲדֹנָי כך יְהֹוָה, אבל

---

[142] The eight passages in which אעלה is *Hiphil* future are, Exod. iii. 17: Judg. ii. 1: 1 Sam. xxviii. 11: 2 Sam. xxiv. 24: Jerem. xxx. 17; xlvi. 8: Ps. lxvi. 15; cxxxvii. 6. They are enumerated in the Massorah marginalis on Exod. iii. 17.

[143] The ten passages in which ויאספו is *Kal* are, Exod. iv. 29: Numb. xi. 32: 1 Sam. v. 8. 11; xvii. 1: 2 Sam. xxi. 13: 2 Kings xxiii. 1: 2 Chron. xxix. 15; xxiv. 11: Jerem. xl. 12. They are given in the Massorah marginalis on Exod. iv. 29, where, however, they are not designated *Pashtin*, as is stated by Levita, but (פתחין) *Psachin*.

is not certain, whilst *Adonai* is read as it is written, and its vowel-points are certain, whence it is called the *certain* name (plural וראין); and of which there are one hundred and thirty-four instances. The Massorites say that every אדני יהוה *the Lord Jehovah*, is likewise so, that is, except those to which is joined the tetragrammaton, pointed with the vowel signs of אֱלֹהִים; as אֲדֹנָי יְהֹוִה, [Gen. xv. 2; Isa. xlix. 22]. I have found two hundred and twenty-two such instances, the mnemonical sign thereof being "the *chariot of* [רכב = 222] the Lord, &c., [Ps. lxviii. 18].[144]

The second place in which the Massorites employ the expression וראין, is with respect to words ending with *He*, after *Kaph*, the suffix second person singular masculine, of which there are twenty-one in number; as וַאֲבָרְכֶכָה *and I shall bless thee* [Gen. xxvii. 7], יָדְכָה *thy hand* [Exod. xiii. 16], &c.,[145] since in all other instances the suffix second person is final *Kaph*

אינה קריאה חוודאית, אבל אדני נקרא כבתיבתו ונקודתו הוודאית, לפיכך קראו לו שם וראי, ובלשון רבים וראין, והם קל״ד, ואמרו כל אדני יהוה דכותהון, פירוש זולת אותם שסמוך אליהן שם של ד׳ אוחיות הנקוד בנקורת אלהים, כגון אֲדֹנָי יְהֹוִה מה חתן לי, כה אמר אֲדֹנָי יְהֹוִה, ומצאתים מאחים ועשרים ושנים, סמן להם רכב אלהים רבותים:[144]

והמקום חשני אשר שמשו במלת וראין הוא על מלות הגבתבות בה׳ בסוף החיבה לכנוי נוכח הזכר, וחן כ״א במספר, כמו וַאֲבָרְכֶכָה, לאות על יָדָה וכולי;[145] כי כל שאר כנוי הגובה כתיבין בכ״ף פשומה קמוצה, כמו יָדְךָ, רַגְלְךָ חפילו הה״א מפני רבויין, לפיכך אינן וראין כי תוכל להיות לקראת בשוא כמבואר בכנויי הפעלים וחשמות, אבל אלו הכ״א הם בח׳ וראין, ואין לטעות בחן; ופירוש מוקדמין ומאוחרין פרשתי במאמר ראשון במין ג׳ ע״ש:

המאמר העשירי בקריא. בספרא. בלישנא. בעניגא בפסוק: הנה קראו בעלי חמסורה לכל עשרים וארבע ספרים קריא, כמו שקראו להן בעלי החלמוד מקרא, באמרם חזרנו על כל המקרא, לעולם ישלש אדם שנוחיו שליש במקרא, וכמותם רבים;[146] ונם

with *Kametz*, as יָדְךָ, רַגְלְךָ. They dropped the *He* because of their large number, for which reason they are not certain, since they may have *Sheva*, as I have explained under the suffixes of the verbs and nouns; whilst those *Kaphs* which are followed by *He* are certain, and there can be no mistake about them. The meaning of "transpositions" I have explained in Section i., class 8, of Part ii., *vide supra*, p. 191.

Section X., concerning *Scripture, Book, Form, Connection*, and *Verse*.—The Massorites call all the twenty-four sacred books קריא, just as they are called by the Talmudists מקרא. Thus, for instance, they say, "we have run through the whole [מקרא] scripture," "a man should always divide his time into three, devoting one third to [מקרא] the Scriptures," &c.[146] They also call each separate verse *Mikra*, =

---

[144] Though the Massorah finalis, under the letter *Aleph*, p. 3 a, &c., only gives one hundred and thirty-four, yet there can be no doubt that there are many more than those enumerated under this rubric.

[145] The twenty-one words which have *He* at the end, after *Kaph*, of the second person singular masculine, have already been given (*vide supra*, p. 177).

[146] The maxim to which Levita refers was propounded by R. Tamhum b. Hanilai, and is to be found in *Aboda Sara*, 19 b. In its entirety it is as follows:—אר הנחום בר

scripture, saying, "no scripture oversteps its simple meaning,"[147] "this scripture is anteplaced," &c.

☞ I wonder how it is that most people give this name to the writings of the prophets alone; for I cannot find a reason for it in any of the works which I have seen. But my own opinion is that it arose from the fact that most of the prophets read what they had to say, as we find, "Go and *read* in the ears of the people" [Jerem. ii. 2], "and *read* unto her the *reading* which I speak to you" [Jonah iii. 2], and *read* there [Jerem. xix. 2], &c. It is for this reason that their books are called Scripture [מקרא].

It is, however, to be noticed that the Massorites do not always write the word *Scripture*, or *in Scripture*, whenever they give the import and number. Thus, for instance, on a word which occurs only once, they simply remark, "not extant," and not "not extant in the Scripture." The same is the case when it occurs twice, thrice, or more times; they do not remark on it, "twice in the Scripture," or "thrice in the Scripture," &c. In those Codices where you do find it written so, it has either been done to make it more explicit, or to ornament the writing by filling out the line, as I have already stated in the Poetical Introduction, which see.[148] In the Massorah parva it is never found, whilst the Massorah magna only uses it in a few places. Thus, when a certain word occurs many times in one book, and is only found once in the other books, they remark upon it, "not extant in the other Scriptures, but throughout such and such a book there are instances like it," as in the register of sixteen words, viz., וַיִּקַע *and he smote* [Gen. xxxii. 26], on which the Massorites remark, "it does not occur in the Scripture, but throughout Ezekiel, there are

קראו לכל פסוק לבד מקרא, באמרם אין מקרא יוצא מידי פשוטו,[147] מקרא מסורס הוא, חולחם רבים:

☜ אך חמהתי מה שההמון קוראים שם זה לספרי הנביאים ביחוד, ולא מצאתי מעם כתוב על זה בכל הספרים שראיתי, אך לבי אומר לי לפי שרוב מה שאמרו הנביאים אמרו בקריאה, כמו הלוך וקראת, וקרא אליה את הקריאה, וקראת שם ורומיהם, על כן נקראו ספריהם מקרא:

ודע כי לא על כל ענין ועל כל מנין כתבו קריא או בקריא ; והמשל על מלה הנמצאה רק פעם אחת כתבו עליה לית, ולא לית בקריא ; וכן כשנמצאה ב' או ג' פעמים וכו', לא כתבו ב' בקריא, או ג' בקריא וכו' ; ובספרים שנמצא כתוב כן, אינו אלא לתוספת ביאור, או ליפות כתיבתן כדי למלא השורה, כמו שכתבתי בהקדמה החרוזית ע״ש ;[148] ובמסרה קמנה לא נמצא לעולם, אכן בקצת מקומות הוצרכו לו במסרה גדולה, כנון כשיש מלח אחת בספר אחד הרבה פעמים ובשאר הספרים לא נמצא רק פעם אחת, כתבו עליה לית בקריא וכל ספר פלוני דכותיה, כנון שמח אחת מן י״ו מלין, וַיִּקַע כף ירך (בראשית ל״ב), לית בקריא וכל יחזקאל

חַנִילָאי לעולם ישלש אדם שנותיו שלש במקרא שלש במשנה שלש בתלמוד, *R. Tamhum b. Hanilai* propounded that man should always divide his time into three parts: one-third he should devote to the study of the Scripture, one-third to the study of the Mishna, and one-third to the study of the Talmud.

[147] The exegetical rule, that "no Scripture oversteps its simple meaning," to which Levita refers, is to be found in *Sabbath* 63 a, and in many other parts of the Talmud.

[148] For the description of the manner in which the Massoretic notes were treated, to which Levita refers, see above, p. 94.

דכותיה ; וכל הסף בִּנָּשִׁים לית בקריא וכל instances like it;" בַּנָּשִׁים *in the fe-*
שיר השרים דכותיה ;[149] *male gender* [Numb. xxxi. 18], "not
in the Scriptures, but throughout
וכן שמח אחת מן כ"א דכל חד וחד לית the Song of Songs, there are in-
בסמרא דכותיה, וכל קריא דכותיה בר מן חד, stances like it," &c., &c.[149]
כגון כל ספר בראשית וְיָלְדוּ בר מן חד   The same is the case with the
וַיָלְדוּ לו בנים אחר חמבול, וכל קריא וַיָלְדוּ register of twenty-one words which
בר מן חד וילדו לו בנים וכולי ;[150] וכן כל respectively occur only once in one
book, whilst in all the other Scriptures they are always so, except in
one instance. Thus throughout the whole Book of Genesis the word
וְיָלְדוּ *and they begat,* is used, and it is only in one instance that וַיָלְדוּ
and there were born [Gen. x. 1] is found; whilst in all the Scriptures it
is וַיָלְדוּ, and it is only in one place that וְיָלְדוּ is used [Deut. xxi. 15].[150]

[149] The sixteen words which have no parallel in the whole Scriptures, except in one
book only, where they have respectively a parallel, are as follows:—

למלאכה	. . Levit. xiii. 51	רועה	. Ezek. xxxvii. 24	מזוזות	. . . 1 Sam. i. 9
בנשים	. . Numb. xxxi. 18	ירעם	. . Ps. xlix. 15	לצבי	. . . Isa. iv. 2
ואת עשרה	. 1 Sam. xvii. 18	ויאסרהו	2 Chron. xxxiii. 11	ועדתיו	. . Deut. vi. 17
התמקדו	. 1 Kings xx. 27	לא ימות	. Prov. xiii. 13	לפני אלהים	1 Chron. xiii. 10
וצבא	. . . . Job x. 17	וחקע	. Gen. xxxii. 26	השיבנו	. Lament. v. 21
		תהלת	. . Ps. cxlv. 21		

The list is given in the Massorah marginalis on Levit. xiii. 51, where, however, nine
instances only are enumerated, as well as at the end of the Massorah finalis, in that
portion which is denominated *Various Readings* [חלוסי קראה], p. 62a, col. 4; and in
the *Ochla Ve-Ochla*, section cclxx., p. 144, where all the instances are duly specified.

[150] The twenty-one words which respectively occur only once in a particular book, whilst in all other books of the Scriptures they occur always
so, except in one instance only, are as follows:—

וַיָלְדוּ	only once in Gen. x. 1, always so in all other	וְיָלְדוּ	. Deut xxi. 15
וְרָם	,, Deut. viii. 14	Scriptures except	וְרָם	. . Isa. ii. 12
בַּסְתָר	,, Deut. xiii. 7	,, ,,	בַּסְתָר	. 2 Sam. xii. 12
וּמִגְרְשֵׁיהֶם	,, Josh. xiv. 4	,, ,,	מִגְרְשֵׁיהֶן	. Numb. xxxv. 7
אָחִיךָ	,, 2 Sam. ii. 22	,, ,,	לְאָחִיךָ	. . Gen. xxv. 16
מָשִׁיחַ	,, 2 Sam. i. 21	,, ,,	מְשִׁיחַ	. Lament. iv. 20
מִקְנֶה	,, Jerem. ix. 9	,, ,,	לְמִקְנֶה	. Gen. xxiii. 18
וּמַיִם	,, 1 Kings xxii. 27	,, ,,	וָמַיִם	. . Ezek. iv. 17
חֲדָשִׁים	,, Jerem. xxxiv. 14	ט ,,	חֳדָשִׁים	. . Isa. lviii. 6
עַל הָרָעָה	,, Jerem. xviii. 8	,, ,,	אֶל הָרָעָה	2 Sam. xxiv. 16
מַזְבְּחוֹתֵיהֶם	,, Ezek. vi. 13	,, ,,	מִזְבְּחוֹתֵיכֶם	Jerem. xvii 1
תִּקְרָאֵי	,, Zech. iii. 10	,, ,,	תִּקְרָאוּ	. Jerem. iii. 19
וַיֵצְאוּ	,, Jerem. xxxix. 11	,, ,,	וַיֹצִאֻהוּ	2 Kings xvi. 15
וְכָרֹו	,, Malachi iii. 22	,, ,,	וְכָרֹו	. Job xviii. 17
וַיִשְׂמְחוּ	,, Ps. cvii. 30	,, ,,	וְיִשְׂמְחוּ	. Job xxi. 12
תִּפְאֶרֶת	,, Ps. xxiii. 5	,, ,,	תַּעֲרֹב	. . Joel i. 20
יִצְרֹן	,, Eccles. i. 1	,, ,,	וְכָרֹון	. Levit. xxiii. 24
בְחָכְמָה	,, Eccles. ii. 21	,, ,,	בַּחָכְמָה	1 Chron. xxviii. 21
וְחוּמָא	,, Eccles. vii. 26	,, ,,	וְחוּמָא	. Isa. lxv. 20
שְׁמָרָה	,, Ps. cxix. 167	,, ,,	שָׁמְרָה	1 Chron. xxix. 18
שִׁי	,, Ps. lxxii. 20	,, ,,	שַׁי	. Isa. xviii. 7

The list is given in that part of the Massorah denominated *Various
Readings* (חלוסי קראה), p. 62 b, section i., and in the *Ochla Ve-Ochla*, section

We also find that certain words ספרא חד מלה וכל קריא חלוף לה, כנון כל
always occur in one book in the בראשית הנראה וכל קריא הנראה; ¹⁶¹ וכן כל
one form, whilst in all the other
books they occur in a different form; as, for instance, הַנִּרְאָה *who
appeared* [Gen. xii. 7], whilst in all the other Scripture it is הַנִּרְאָה.¹⁶¹

cclxxi., pp. 52, 145, &c. The text of the *Massoreth Ha-Massoreth*
describes this rubric as follows: שמה אחת מן כ״א דכל ספרא דכוותיה בר מן חד וכל
קריא לית דכוותיה בר מן חד, a register of twenty-one words, *which have parallels
throughout the book, with the exception of one instance; whilst they have
no parallel throughout the Bible, with the exception of one instance.* The
Sulzbach edition omits the second בר מן חד. But that the whole passage
is corrupted is evident, from the reference to this rubric in the Massorah
parva on Gen. x. 1, from its heading both in the Massorah finalis and in
the *Ochla Ve-Ochla*, as well as from the whole context. We have therefore
corrected the text.

¹⁶¹ The words which always occur in a certain form in one book, but
which in all other books of the Scriptures occur in a different form, are as
follows :—

הַנִּרְאָה	Gen. xii. 7	in all the other books		הַנִּרְאָה
חִירָה	Gen. xxxviii. 1	,,		חִירָם
וַאֶטְלְחָה	Exod. viii. 5	,,		וָאֶשְׁלְחָה
פֹּרֵשׂי פְּנָפַיִם	Exod. xxv. 20	,,		פֹּרְשִׂים כְּנָפַיִם
וְאִפָּה וַחֲצִי הָאַמָּה	Exod. xxvi. 16	,,		אַמָּה וַחֲצִי הָאַמָּה
סָרָאָה	Levit. xiii. 20	,,		סָרָאָה
אֶתְכֶם	Numb. xv. 14	,,		אִתְּךָ
בְּמוּגֹן	Numb. xxxiii. 42	,,		פֻּנֹן
וַנֵּסַן וַנִּסַּע	Deut. ii. 1	,,		וַיִּסָּן וַיִּסַּע
וַיִּתְקָרְבוּן וַיַּעַמְדוּן	Deut. iv. 11	,,		וַתִּקְרְבוּ וַתַּעַמְדוּ
אֵלֶּה הָעֵדוֹת	Deut. iv. 45	,:		אֵלֶּה הָעֵדֹת
כִּי הַמִּפְטָרָה	Josh. x. 23	,,		מַה מַּפְטָרָה
יָחֵל	Judg. xiii. 5	,,		יָחֵל
בִּגְשָׂה	2 Sam. xii. 3	,,		פִּשָׂה
נֹגַהּ	1 Sam. xxi. 2	,,		נֹגַהּ
בֵּית שֵׁן	2 Sam. xxi. 12	,,		בֵּית שְׁאָן
וַיְשִׁינוּם	1 Sam. xii. 8	,,		וַיּוֹשִׁיבֵם
אִתִּי	2 Sam. xv. 19	,,		אִיתַי
כִּבְחוֹר	2 Kings iii. 19	,,		מִבְחוֹר
נִבְנָה	1 Kings iii. 2	,,		נִבְנָה
פְּלִיתִי	Isa. xlix. 4	,,		פְּלִיתִי
וְקָרֵיתִי	Isa. viii. 17	,,		קָרֵיתִי
אוּרִיָּהוּ	Jerem. xxvi. 23	,,		אוּרִיָּה
הָאָה	Jerem. xxxvi. 22	.,		הֶאָח
עַל לְבִי	Jerem. vii. 31	,,		אֶל לְבִי
הַסְּרִינוֹת	Jerem. xlvi. 4	,,		הַסִּרְיוֹנוֹת
לַנְּשִׂיא	Ezekiel	,,		לִנְשִׂיא
לְחֹל	Ezek. xlv. 23	,,		לְחֹל
נְהַר כְּבָר	Ezek. i. 1	,,		נְהַר פְּרָת
יְחֶזְקִיָּה	Minor Prophets	,,		יְחִזְקִיָּהוּ
רְחָמָה	Hos. i. 6	,,		רֻחָמָה
חוּרָם	2 Chron.	,,		חִירָם
אַמְפֹּרָה	Psalms	,,		אֲמַפֵּר
בֵּית אַהֲרֹן	Ps. cxv. 10	,,		בְּנֵי אַהֲרֹן

Or they occur in a certain order in the whole Scripture, except in one book, as, for instance, in all the Scripture we have the construction שַׁבַּת שַׁבָּתוֹן *Sabbath, of Sabbatism*, except in one instance, where it is inverted שַׁבָּתוֹן שַׁבָּת *Sabbatism, Sabbath* [Exod. xvi. 23]; so, also, it is in all the Scripture, we have אָבִיו וְאִמּוֹ *his father and his mother*, except in one instance, where it is אִמּוֹ וְאָבִיו *his mother and his father* [Levit. xix. 3], and there are many instances like it.[152]

קריא שַׁבַּת שַׁבָּתוֹן בד מן חד שַׁבָּתוֹן שַׁבַּת דפרש׳ המן; וכן כל קריא אָבִיו וְאִמּוֹ בד מן חד, איש אמו ואביו חיראו וכאלה רבים: [152]

והנה כזח מבוארת גם כן מלת ספרא, ר״ל הספר שכתוב בו המלה ההיא; אך צריך שתדע כי כאשר נמסר על מלה אחת אשר בתרי עשר והם הושע, יואל, עמוס וכו׳ לית בספרא או כל ספרא דכותיה הוא משמע כל ספר תרי עשר; והמשל כנון בזכריה ואם משפחת מצרים לא תעלה, נמסר עליו ג׳

Herewith is also explained the expression ספרא, which accordingly means the particular book wherein the word in question is to be found. It must, however, be borne in mind, that when the Massorites make the remark on a word in the twelve minor Prophets, which are Hosea, Joel, Amos, &c., "it is not in the book," or "throughout the book it is to be found like it," they mean the book containing all the twelve Prophets. Thus, when it is remarked, on וְאִם *and if*, in Zech. xiv. 18, "it occurs three times at the beginning of a verse in the book," it does not

אָמֵן וְכָכֵן . . .	Ps. lxxii. 19	in all the other books .	אָמֵן אָמֵן
רֵים . . .	Job xxxix. 10	,,	רְאֵם
וְלֹא נֵדַע . . .	Job xv. 9	,,	לֹא נֵדַע
מִשְׁלֵי שְׁלֹמֹה . . .	Prov. i. 1	,,	דִּבְרֵי שְׁלֹמֹה
לַצַּדִּיק . . .	Prov. ix. 9	,,	לֶחָכָם
יְקָרָה . . .	Eccles. ix. 11	,,	יִקְרָא
חוֹלָה . . .	Eccles. v. 12	,,	חוֹלָה
עֲרָת . . .	Dan. iii. 27	,,	עֲרָת
קָל . . .	Dan. iii. 5	,,	קָל
קְבַר . . .	Dan. vii. 13	,,	קְבַר
בְּאַרְצוֹא . . .	Dan. xi. 42	,,	בְּאַרְצוֹא
יְהוֹיָקִים יְהוֹיָרִיב יוֹיָדָע יוֹצָדָק יֵשׁוּעַ .	Ezra		יְהוֹיָקִים יְהוֹיָרִיב יְהוֹיָדָע יְהוֹצָדָק יְהוֹשׁוּעַ
תִּרְבַּקִין . . .	Ruth	,,	תִּרְבַּקִן
הָרֹאִינִי הַשְּׁמִיעִנִי	Song of Songs	,,	הָרְאִינִי הַשְּׁמִיעִנִי
רַבָּתִי בַּגּוֹיִם . .	Lament. i. 1	,,	רַבַּת
וְעָשׂרִים וּמֵאָה . .	Esther	,,	מֵאָה וְעֶשְׂרִים
לַחֹדֶשׁ . . .	Esther	,,	לַחֹדֶשׁ

The list is given in that part of the Massorah finalis called *Various Readings* (חלוּפֵי קְרִיאָה), p. 62 b, col. 1, sec. ii., and in *Ochla Ve-Ochla*, sec. cclxxii., pp. 52, 146, &c. The latter adds יְלָכֵן (Ezek. i. 2), which in all other books of the Scripture is יְהוֹלָכִין, and לֵהּ (Dan. vii. 7), which is elsewhere לַהּ, whilst it omits חוּרָם (2 Chron.). It moreover rightly has לֶחָכָם (Prov. ix. 9) instead of לְצַדִּיק, in the same verse, since it is the former which is everywhere else לֶחָכָם, with *Segol* under the *Lamed*, whilst לַצַּדִּיק also occurs in Proverbs.

[152] The list which embraces thirty-nine such instances has already been given, vide supra, p. 214.

mean that it refers to Zechariah alone, but to all the minor Prophets;[153] or, when it is remarked, on חַטָּאת *sin offering*, in Micah i. 13, "it is not in the book," it means the twelve Prophets. The same is the case with the book of Ezra, which also includes the book of Nehemiah. Thus, for instance, when it is remarked, "וְאַף *and even*, occurs nine times at the beginning of a verse, and throughout Ezra it is likewise so,"[154] it also includes Nehemiah. As to the "*Pattach of the book*," I have already explained its nature in Section ii., see p. 197. The "*Piska of the book*," too, has already been explained in Section iv., see p. 209.

Let me now explain the word לשׁנא. Notice that the Massorites use it in two ways: the one when they say בלשׁנא, and the other when they remark בכל לשׁנא. If words are alike in form, having either some of the same vowel-points, or the same addition or omission of a letter, or if they belong to the same conjugation, they (the Massorites) ranged these words together under one rubric, though they differ with regard to the other letters and vowel-signs.

☞ Thus, for instance, on וַיַּנִּחֵהוּ [Gen. ii. 15], the Massorites remark, "not extant, and defective, seven times defective in this form," that is, *the future Hiphil*. One of these instances is, וַיַּנִּחֵהוּ *and he put him* [Gen. ii. 15], וַיַּנִּחֵם *and he put them* [Josh. iv. 8], תַּנִּחֵנוּ *thou shalt leave us* [Jerem. xiv. 9], &c.[155] Now, because the *Jod* in all these, which

---

[153] The other two instances in which ואף occurs at the beginning of a verse in the minor Prophets are, Amos ix. 3, 4. We could not find them specified any where in the Massorah.

[154] The nine instances in which ואף begins the verse are, Levit. xxvi. 44: Ezek. xxiii. 40: Habak. ii. 5: Ps. lxxviii. 31: Job xix. 4; xxxvi. 16: Ezra v. 10, 14; vi. 5. They are given in the Massorah marginalis on Job xix. 4; xxxvi. 16: Ezra v. 10. In the Massorah parva, on Ezek. xxiii. 40, and Ps. lxxviii. 31, where reference is made to this fact, it is erroneously stated that there are six [ו] such instances, whilst on Job xix. 4; xxxvi. 16, the Massorah parva remarks that there are ten [י] such passages: and there can be but little doubt that though this, too, is an error, the former is a corruption of the latter, since we have already seen that nothing is more easy than the corruption of *Vav* into *Jod*, and *vice versa*. The remark וכל עזרא דכותיה, is only to be found in the Massorah parva on Ezek. xxiii. 40. It has to be added that the Sulzbach edition omits נחמיה גם ספר ר"ל דכותיה עזרא וכל מ' ואת גם ואף, i. e., ואף, AND EVEN, occurs nine times at the beginning of a verse, and throughout Ezra it is likewise so, including therein the book of Nehemiah; whilst the other two editions omit [ט] nine, which we have supplied.

[155] The other instances in which the *Hiphil* is defective of the *Jod* are, Gen. xix. 16: Levit. xxiv. 12: 2 Sam. xvi. 11: 1 Kings viii. 9; xiii. 29. They are given in the

is the distinguishing mark of the Hiphil, is absent, the Massorites put them together under one rubric. When two words are written and pronounced alike, but differ in sense, they remark on them, "two of two significations." In the Third Part, entitled *The Broken Tables*, I shall again discuss this subject under the initials ת״ל, with the help of God.

Moreover, the expression בלישנא is also used for a root, with all the forms which belong to the same. Thus, it is remarked, with regard to the root רהב, "twelve instances of this root."[156]

כללו אותם בלישנא אחד; וכשיהיו ב' מלות שוות במכתב ובמבטא ושונים בפתרון, נמסר עליהן ב' מב" לישנא, ובשער. שברי לוחות אדבר בם במלת ת״ל בע״ה:

גם יש בלישנא שכולל כל מלות השרש החוא, כנון בשרש רהב י״ב בלישנא; [156] ויש בלשנא שכולל בשרש אחד רק ענין אחד שבאותו השרש, כמו בשרש עור כתבו על ויהי שדך ז' בלישנא דבבו, כי כל שאר לשוניה שבשרש זה יש להן הוראות אחרות עין בשרשו; [157] וכן בשרש שער נמסר על מאה שערים לית בלישנא, כי כל שאר לשון שער יש לו הוראה אחרת: אמנם כל לישנא לא כתבו

The term בלשנא is also used for a rubric containing those words only of a root which have the same signification. For example, in the root עור, they remark on שָׂרְךָ *thine enemy* [1 Sam. xxviii. 16], "seven times in the signification of *enemy*;" for all the other expressions of this root have another signification (vide *Lex.*, s. v.).[157] Thus, also, in the root שער, they remarked on שְׂעָרִים *measures* [Gen. xxvi. 12], "not extant in this signification;" for all the other expressions derived from שער have another meaning. The expression כל לשנא, however, the Massorites only use when a word is construed with

---

Massorah marginalis on Levit. xxiv. 12, and 1 Kings xiii. 29. In both these passages the Massorah gives ויניחהו [Levit. xxiv. 12], which is *plene* in the best Codices, as one of the seven *defectires*; whilst it omits וינחום [Josh. iv. 8], which is really *defective*, and is quoted as such by Levita. There can therefore be but little doubt that the former has been substituted for the latter, through a clerical blunder.

[156] The twelve words which belong to the same root with *He*, since in all other instances this form occurs with *Cheth*, are as follows:—

רחב . . . Ps. lxxxix. 11	ורהבם . . . Ps. xc. 10	הרהיבני . . . Song of Songs vi. 5
רחב . . . Ps. lxxxvii. 4	ירהב . . . Prov. vi. 3	ירהבו . . . Isa. iii. 5
תרהבני . . . Ps. cxxxviii. 3	רהב . . . Job. xxvi. 12	רהב . . . Isa. xxx. 7
רהבים . . . Ps. xl. 5	רהב . . . Job ix. 13	רהב . . . Isa. li. 9

They are given in the Massorah marginalis on Isa. xxx. 7; Ps. lxxxix. 11; Job ix. 13. On Isa. xxx. 7, and Ps. lxxxix. 11, Jacob b. Chajim, the editor of the Massorah, adds ואז נ״ל האחד ורהב לבנך, "and it appears to me that רהב [Isa. lx. 5], is one of these." But though this reading is to be found in Jehudah Chajug's *Treatise on the Vowelpoints and Accents* [ספר הנקוד, p. 183, ed. Dukes], yet all the best Codices, as well as most of the ancient grammarians and commentators, read the word in question with *Cheth*. Besides, the *Ochla Ve-Ochla*, section ccv. pp. 44, 124, &c., which also gives this rubric, does not include it in the list. Comp. also the remarks of Dr. Frensdorff, the learned editor of the *Ochla Ve-Ochla*, p. 44.

[157] The Massorah marginalis on Micah v. 13, gives *eight* such passages, viz., 1 Sam. xxviii. 16: Micah v. 13, 10: Isa. xiv. 21: Ps. ix. 7; cxxxix. 20: Dan. iv. 16: Jerem. v. 8. The Massorah marginalis on 1 Sam. xxviii. 16, though omitting Dan iv. 16, and Jerem. xv. 8; and the Massorah parva on Micah v. 13, and Ps. cxxxix. 20, also state most explicitly that there are [ח בליש דבבו] *eight* passages in which עור denotes enemy. It is only the Massorah parva on Isa. xiv. 21, which, like Levita, says that there are [ז] *seven* such instances. The full enumeration of them, however, by the Massorah marginalis, shows that the *seven* must be a clerical error.

another, contrary to its uniform position. Thus, for instance, they remark, "all the expressions of the root שמע *to hear*, are construed with אֶל, except twelve in this form, which take עַל;"[158] or, "all the expressions of שחיטה *to slaughter*, are construed with אֶת, except four, which are without אֶת;"[159] or, "in all phrases אָב *father* precedes אֵם *mother*, except in four instances;"[160] or, "all phrases have חֻקִּים *statutes*, before מִשְׁפָּטִים *laws*, except in eight passages;"[161] and many more like them.

☞ I shall now explain the word עִנְיָנָא. Notice that the expression עִנְיָן is only to be found in the book of Ecclesiastes, where it occurs eight times, and always in the singular. But our Rabbins of blessed memory used it very frequently, and even in the plural. It denotes *business, transaction*, in German Geschäft. Now in the Massorah it is used in the Chaldee sense of transaction, whereas in the Chaldee on Ecclesiastes it is simply rendered by גְּוָון *colour, form*. Hence when you find in the Massorah בְּעִנְיָנָא, it denotes *in this narrative of the transaction, section, chapter;* as בְּנַפּוֹ alone [Exod. xxi. 3], on which the Massorites remark, "three times, and in the section;" so, also the remarks, "not *defective* in the connection," "not *plene* in the connection."

---

[158] The twelve passages in which the verb שמע is construed with the preposition על are, Gen. xli. 15: Isa. xxxvii. 9: 2 Kings xx. 13: Jerem. iv. 16; vi. 7; xxiii. 16; xxvi. 5; xxxv. 18; li. 27: Ezek. xxvii. 30: Amos iii. 9: Nehem. ix. 9. They are given in the Massorah marginalis on 2 Kings xx. 13, and Ezekiel xxvii. 30. In both instances the Massorah gives a reference, דרשו בי״ץ ספר יהוה (*i.e.* to Isa. xxxiv. 16), which does not contain any such construction, and which must therefore have been inserted by mistake. Indeed Buxtorf, in his edition of the Rabbinic Bible, who only gives the Massoretic rubric once, viz., on Ezek. xxvii. 30, has omitted this reference.

[159] The four instances in which the verb שחט has not אֵת, the sign of the accusative, are, Levit. vi. 18 (twice): Isa. lxvi. 3: 2 Chron. xxix. 22. They are given in the Massorah finalis under the letter *Shin*, p. 58 *b*, col. 4.

[160] This must be a mistake, since both the Massorah parva and the Massorah marginalis, on Gen. xliv. 20 and Levit. xix. 3, distinctly state that there are only three instances in which אם precedes אב. viz., Gen. xliv. 20: Levit. xix. 3; xxi. 2. The last two instances are included in the Massoretic list of thirty passages, in which normal constructions are abnormally inverted, and which we have already given (*vide supra*, p. 214). Why Gen. xliv. 20 is excluded from that list we cannot divine.

[161] The eight passages in which משפטי precedes חקתי, contrary to its usual construction, are, Levit. xviii. 4; xxvi. 43: Ezek. v. 6 (twice); xviii. 17; xx. 16, 24; xxxvii. 24. The Massorah also gives Ezek. xliv. 24 as a ninth instance. But since תורתי intervenes in this passage between the two words in question, there can be little doubt that it is an addition by a later hand, and is therefore rightly excluded from this list in the *Ochla Ve-Ochla*, section cclxxviii., pp. 54, 151.

I I

☞ ועתה אפרש מלת פסוק; דע כי לשון פסוק אינו לשון עברי אך לשון ארמי, וחרבה לשונות מתורגמין כן, ר'ל בלשון הפסקה, בלשון אשכז אויףֿהורן, כמו חָדַל להיות לשרת תרגומו פסק, וכן וַיִשְׁבֹּת חמן ופסק, וַיִפְלָא העם ופסק, ולֹא יָסָף ולא פסק, מרם יְפָרַת עד לא פסק; על כן נקרא הפסוק פסוק, ומזה קראו נ"כ למקום חלוק שבין פרשה לפרשה פיסקא, כמו שאמרו ב' פרשיות בתורה דלית בהון פסקא ברישא, והם ויצא ויחי;[162] וב' פרשיות בתורה דלית בהון פסקא באמצע הפרשה, והם ויצא ומקץ;[163] וכן יש פסקא באמצע הפסוק, ד' מנחח בתורה, כנון ויאמר קין אל חבל אחיו ויהי בהיותם בשדה ודוק;[164] ויש קורין פיסקא זו פרינמא, ועוד אזכרנה בשער שברי לחות; והטעם הנקרא פסק או פסיק כבר זכרתיו במאמר ד' ע"ש:
סליק.

☞ Let me now explain the word פָּסוּק. Mark that the expression פָּסוּק is not Hebrew, but Aramaic, and many words are rendered by it, that is, by the expression פְּסָקָה, which is in German *aufhören*. Thus, חָדַל *it ceased* [Gen. xviii. 11] is rendered in the Chaldee by פָּסַק; וַיִּשְׁבֹּת *and it discontinued* [Josh. v. 12], by וּפְסַק; וַיִּכָלֵא *and he left off* [Exod. xxxvi. 6], by וּפְסַק; וְלֹא יָסָף *and he did not add* [Deut. v. 19], by פָּסַק; יִכָּרֵת *it shall be consumed* by פְסַם [Numb. xi. 33]. Hence, a verse is called פָּסוּק. Hence, also, the dividing space between the sections פִּיסְקָא, as in the remark, "there are two sections in the Pentateuch which have no *Piska* at the beginning, *i.e.*, the Pericopes *Va-Jetze* and *Va-Jechi*;[162] and other two sections in the Pentateuch which have no *Piska* in the middle of the section, *i.e.*, *Va-Jetze* and *Miketz*.[163] There is also a *Piska* in the middle of the verse; four instances of it are to be found in the Pentateuch, as Gen. iv. 8.[164] Some call this *Piska* by the name of פרינמא [= πρᾶγμα], but I shall again speak about it in the Third Part, entitled "*The Broken Tables*." About the accents called *Psak*, or *Psik*, I have already spoken in Section iv. [*vide supra* p. 209]. End.

[162] For the division of the Pentateuch into hebdomadal lessons, see above, p. 135. *Va-Jetze* (ויצא) is the seventh of the fifty-four divisions, and embraces Gen. xxviii. 10–xxxii. 3; and *Va-Jechi* (ויחי) is the twelfth Pericope, extending over Gen. xlvii. 28—l. 26.

[163] The Pericope *Miketz* (מקץ) is the tenth of the fifty-four sections or weekly lessons, and embraces Gen. xli. 1—xliv. 17.

[164] The other three instances in which there is a *Piska* or pause in the middle of a verse in the Pentateuch are, Gen. xxxv. 22: Numb. xxv. 19: Deut. ii. 8.

243

HERE IS THE TABLE OF CONTENTS OF THE TEN SECTIONS IN PART II.[165]	הא לך השמנים מהמלות המצויות, בעשרה מאמרים מלוחות השניות:[165]

SECTION I.—Concerning *Keri* and *Kethiv*, divided into seven classes.

המאמר הראשון בקריין וכתבן ונחלקין לשבעה מינים:

SECTION II.—Concerning *Kametz* and *Pattach*.

המאמר השני בקמצין ופתחין:

SECTION III.—Concerning *Dagesh, Raphe, Mapik,* and *Sheva*.

המאמר השלישי בדנשין ורפין ומפקין ובקצת דיני השוא:

SECTION IV.—Concerning *Milel, Milra,* and *Pesakim*.

המאמר הרביעי במלעיל ומלרע ובפסקים:

SECTION V.—Concerning *Registers, Groups, Resemblances,* and *Parallels*.

המאמר החמישי בשימין וזונין ודמיין ודכוותהון:

SECTION VI.—Concerning *Junctions, Severances,* and *Identical*.

המאמר הששי בסמיכים ויחידין ומורדפים:

SECTION VII.—Concerning *the Presence or Absence of Prefixes* or *Serviles*.

המאמר השביעי בנכיבין או משמשין וקרחין:

SECTION VIII.—Concerning *Conjectural Readings, Misleadings,* and *Exchanges*.

המאמר השמיני בסבירין וטפטין וחילופין:

SECTION IX.—Concerning *Letters, Words, Expressions, Short Letters, Accents, Certainties,* and *Transpositions*.

המאמר התשיעי באתין ותיבן ומלין וקטיעין ופשטין ודאין ומוקדמין ומאוחרין:

SECTION X.—Concerning *Scripture, Book, Form, Connection,* and *Verse*.

המאמר העשירי בקריא בספרא בלישנא בעינא בפסוק;

The Second Tables are now ended,
In the name of the Creator of heaven and earth;
And in the name of the Lord, the God of Spirits,
I begin the Section of the Broken Tables.

סליקו הלוחות האחרונים,
בשם בורא עליונים ותחתונים,
ובשם אל אלהי הרוחות,
אפתח שער שברי לוחות:

[165] These two lines are entirely omitted in the Sulzbach edition.

THIRD PART;
OR, THE BROKEN TABLES.

שער שברי לוחות:

אמר המחבר הנזכר, האיש אשר בכתבו נכר, ודורש לשבח ולא לגנאי, הפעם אודה את י"י, שהחייני וקיימני, ועד הנה עזרני, וכתבתי על הלוחות הראשינים, את עשרה הדברים המרוכנים, ואחריהן הלוחות האחרונות באו, ובעשרה מאמרות נבראו, וחלא במאמר אחד אשר אוסיף עתה, יוכל להכיאות כל מה שלמעלה ולמטה, בכל דברי הספר הזה עד תומם:

ועתה יעש לבי כאשר זמם, ובשם אשר שת חכמה בטוחות, ואקרא את שמו שער שברי לוחות, יען כי אבאר לו הדברים הקצרים והנשברים, והמלורת הנחתבור, בנמריקון ובראשי תבות, ובדרך רמיזה וקריצה, כמין חיבה פרוצה, וכל לשון שנשתנה, במסרה גדולה וקטנה, ובם לא רבים יחכמו, ועל לבם לא שמו, להבין מח סבה, וכבר כתבתי הסבה, בהקדמת החרוזית, כאשר שם חזית, ואעשה בהם חבור, ומפני מורה הציבור, לא אאריך הדבור, ואקיים מה שאמרו רז"ל בנמרא, לעולם ישנה אדם לתלמידיו בדרך קצרה, וככן אתחיל בשובה ונחת, למצוא חשבון אחת לאחת, בסייעתא דשמיא, יהא שמיה רבא מברך לעלם ולעלמי עלמיא:

וקודם כל קודם אתן לך כלל וסימן להכיד חמלה שחיא נדרשת בראשי תבות מן חמלה שחיא בלתי שלמה וחסר החלק האחרון ממנה; וזה כאשר חמצא ב' או ג' או ד' אותיות יחד, ועל אחת נקודה למעלה ודאי

Thus, says the author already mentioned, the man known by his writings, who works for honour and not for shame, I now render praise to the Lord, who has preserved me, and sustained me, and helped me hitherto, so that I have written the First Tables, and then the Second Tables, each consisting of ten sections. In the one Section which I now add, I shall be able to explain whatever occurs both in the First and Second Parts of this book to the end thereof.

And now my soul rejoices in the thought, and in the name of Him who ordaineth true wisdom, I call its name *The Section of the Broken Tables*, because I shall therein explain the import of the broken and abbreviated words, and of those expressions which are written in *notaricon*, and in initials, in signs, in enigmas, and in diverse phrases, both in the Massorah magna and parva. Now since there are not many who are learned in these matters, and who take it to heart to understand their utility, as I have already mentioned in the Poetical Introduction, which you may there see, I shall explain these things; and, in order to save the public trouble, I shall not lengthen my Treatise, thus acting in accordance with the following saying of our Rabbins of blessed memory in the Talmud : "one should always teach his disciples by a short method." Hence I now commence with cheerfulness to point out the reason for each thing, by the help of heaven. May the Great Name be praised, world without end.

First of all, I must give you a rule whereby to distinguish a word which is described by initials from a word which is simply abbreviated. It is as follows :—When you find two, three, or four letters together, and each one has a mark on the top, they are invariably to be taken as initials of words; but when they have not all marks, and it is only the last letter which has one mark, it is invariably an abbreviation, and the word in question wants one or two letters at the end; as you will find explained in this Section.

Now I shall begin by explaining the word לית *not extant*, since the Massorites use it more than any other expression. It is the Aramaic compound of לא *not*, and אית *is*, denoting that the word or sentence on which it is remarked has no parallel. This is also its meaning in the Targum, which renders לא יש *there is not* [Job ix. 33], by לא אית, and which frequently translates the Hebrew word אין *not, not extant*, by לית (comp. Numb. xxi. 5), and only rarely translates it לא (comp. Exod. xii. 30). In the Massorah parva, instead of לית, the Massorites write a single *Lamed* with a mark over it, as follows: לֿ. And there is no other single letter in the Massorah parva but what indicates some number, except this one. Hence, when a word occurs thirty times, the Massorites do not remark on it לֿ, lest there should be a confusion between it and לית *not*, but they note it by writing out fully the word *Lamed*. Thus, for instance, "the word וַיֹּסֶף occurs [למ"ד] thirty times;"[1] "the particle אֶל occurs [למ"ד] thirty times alone." In some Codices I have seen כ"י [= 20 and 10] instead of לֿ [= 30], but the first is more general and more correct.

היא נדרשת לראשי תבות, וכשאין עליהן נקודה, רק על אות האחדרון נקודה אחת, וראי היא מלה בלתי שלמה וחסר אות אחת, או יותר בסוף התיבה ודוק ותמצא במלורח שאכתוב לך בשער ז׃

והנה אתחיל לבאר מלת לית, כי שמשו בה בעלי המסכרת יותר מבכל שאר המלות, והיא מלה ארמית, מורכבת מן לא ומן אית פירוש לא יש, רוצה לומר אותה מלה או אותו ענין, שנמסר עליה לית, לא יש אחדת כמוהו; וכן תרגום של לא יש ביננו מוכיח (איוב ט׳), לא אית בינגא מכסין: וכן רוב אין מתורגמין לית, כמו אין לחם ואין מים לית לחמא ולית מיא; ומעטים מתורגמים לא, כמו אין בית אשר אין שם מת, לית ביתא דילא הוה חמן מיתא; ובמסכרא קמנה כתבו במקום לית למ״ד אחת בנקודה למעלה כזה לֿ, ולא נמצא אות במסכרה קמנה העומד יחידי שאינו מורח על מכפר מה רק זאת לבדה, לפיכך מלה הנמצאה שלשים פעמים אין כותבין עליה לֿ שלא לטעות בינה ובין לית, אלא כותבין למ״ד במלואה, כמו וַיֹּסֶף למ״ד,[1] אֶל למ״ד יחידאין; וכיש נוכחאות מצאתי כ״י במקום לֿ, אבל הראשון עקר, וכן עמא דבר.

---

[1] Of the thirty instances in which וסף occurs, seven are *plene* (*i.e.* ויסף), and twenty-three *defective* (*i.e.* ויסף). The *plenes* are, Numb. xxii. 26: Judg. xi. 14: 1 Sam. xx. 17; xxiii. 4: Isa. vii. 10: 2 Chron. xxviii. 22: 1 Sam. xviii. 29. They are given in the Massorah marginalis on Numb. xxii. 2, and 1 Kings xvi. 33. The twenty-three instances in which it is *defective* are, Gen. viii. 10; xviii. 29; xxv. 1 : Exod. ix. 34: Numb. xxii. 15, 25 : Judg. ix. 37: 1 Sam. iii. 6, 8, 21; ix. 8; xix. 21: 2 Sam. ii. 22; vi. 1; xviii. 22; xxiv. 1: Isa. viii. 5. Job xxvii. 1; xxix. 1; xxxvi. 1; xlii. 10: Dan. x. 18. The list of these is no where given in the Massorah. As an illustration of the various ways in which the Massorah annotates the words belonging to the same rubric, we shall specify the thirty instances before us. The Massorah parva annotates twelve passages out of the thirty. In the first instance alone, viz., Gen. xviii. 29, occurs the למ״ד = 30, to which Levita refers; on Gen. xxv. 1, it remarks כל חס במ"י "always *defective*, except seven times;" on Numb. xxii. 15, it states "it occurs twenty-nine (כ׳ט) times;" on Numb. xxii. 25, 1 Kings xvi. 33, Isa. vii. 10, 2 Chron. xxviii. 22, "it occurs (ז מל) seven times *plene*:" whilst on 2 Sam. vi. 1, it remarks, "it occurs (י״ב בסיפ) twelve times in this book." The Massorah marginalis, again, does not notice this rubric more than twice, and then only the seven instances of *plene*. which it gives on Numb. xxii. 2, 1 Kings xvi. 33, simply adding, that in all other instances it is *defective*.

אנ״ך ראשי תיבות אורייתא, נביאים,
כתובים, כן כתבו על כל מלח או לשון
הנמצא ג׳ פעמים, א׳ בתורה, א׳ בנביאים, א׳
בכתובים, כגון בָּחֲרוּ ג׳ סימן אנ״ך;[2] ויש
נוסחאות נמסר עליחן א״ב א״ב, א ב, פירוש
אחד בתורה, אחד בנביאים אחד בכתובים;
ועל מלח שלא נמצאה ו ק בנביאים וכתובים
נמסר נ״ב פירוש נביאים כתובים, כגון הָאָרֹן
כל אורייתא חסר וכל נ״ב מלא ; וכן לעולם
ח׳ חסרים בנ״כ, ר״ל בנביאים ובתובים:[3]

אפ״ס ראשי תיבות אחד פסוק סימן,
פירוש כאשר יהיו ב׳ או ג׳ דברים דומים
בפרשה אחת, או בענין אחד, או בספר אחד,
או בב׳ פרשיות, או בב׳ כפרים, ויש ביניחם
שינוי במלה אחת כתבו המפרש שביניהון,
ונתנו אליחן פסוק לסימן, כגון בפרשת אליעזר
עבד אברהם, הראשון אנכי יושב בְּקִרְבּוֹ,
והשני בְּאַרְצוֹ, וא״פס אני יהוה בקרב הארץ:
ובן קדמאה מה יעשה בָּשָׂר לִי, תנינא אָדָם לִי,

אנ״ך are the initials of אורייתא
נביאים, כתובים, the Law, the Prophets, and the Hagiographa; and
they are noted on every word which
occurs three times, once in the
Law, once in the Prophets, and
once in the Hagiographa; as בָּחֲרוּ
they chose, occurs three times, the
sign being אנ״ך.[2] In some Codices
these instances are marked א״ב א״ב
א״ב which are the initials of אחד
בתורה אחד בנביאים אחד בכתובים
once in the Law, once in the Prophets, and *once in the Hagiographa*.
When a word only occurs in the
Prophets and Hagiographa, it is
marked נביאים כתובים = נ״ב *the
Prophets, and the Hagiographa;* as
הָאָרֹן *the ark*, which is *defective*
in the Pentateuch, whilst in נ״ב =
the Prophets and Hagiographa, it
is *plene*. Thus, also, לְעוֹלָם *for
ever*, is marked "eight times *defective* בנ״כ = in the Prophets and
Hagiographa."[3]

אפ״ס are the initials of אחד פסוק סימן *one verse is the sign*, that is,
when there are two or three parallel things in one section, or in the same
narrative, or in the same book, or even in two sections, or two books,
and they only differ in one word, the Massorites note the difference
between them, and give them a verse as a mnemonical sign, as in
the Section on *Eliezer, the servant of Abraham*. Here the first statement is בְּקִרְבּוֹ *in the midst thereof* [Gen. xxiv. 3], and the second is
בְּאַרְצוֹ *in the land thereof* [*ibid.* xxiv. 37], whilst the mnemonical sign is
"*I, Jehovah, in the midst of the land*" [Exod. viii. 18].[4] Thus,
also, Ps. lvi., where in verse 5 it is בָּשָׂר לִי *flesh, to me*, whilst in verse
12 it is אָדָם לִי *man, to me*, and the mnemonical verse [א״פס] is "upon

---

[2] The three passages in which בחרו has *Kametz* under the *Cheth*, being in pause, are, Gen. vi. 2: Isa. lxvi. 4: Prov. i. 29. In all other passages it has *Chateph-pattach* under the *Cheth*. The words כן כתבו על כל מלח או לשון הנמצא ג׳ פעמים א׳ בתורה א׳ בנביאים א׳ בכתובים, are omitted in the Sulzbach edition.

[3] The instances in which לעולם is *defective* have already been given, *vide supra*, p. 149. The Massoretic remark to which Levita refers is not to be found in the printed editions of the Massorah in the Rabbinic Bibles.

[4] The meaning of the passage and the mnemonical sign is as follows :—In the first passage (Gen. xxiv. 3), giving Abraham's own words, the expression בקרבו *in the midst thereof* is used; whilst in the second passage (*ibid.* xxiv. 37), which gives Eleazer's repetitions of what his master had said, the word in question is dropped, and בארצו *in the land thereof* is substituted. To indicate this change in the words, the Massorites selected the passage in Exod. viii. 18 as a mnemonical sign, showing that just as in this sign בקרב occurs first and הארץ second, so in the two passages for which it is the mnemonical sign, and where the two words are interchanged, בקרבו occurs first and בארצו second.

the flesh of man it shall not be poured" [Exod. xxx. 32].⁵ Likewise in 1 Chron. xvi. 16, where it is וּשְׁבוּעָתוֹ לְיִצְחָק and his oath to Isaac, whilst in Psalm cv. 9 it is וּשְׁבֻעָתוֹ לְיִשְׂחָק written with a Sin, and the mnemonical sign is "and Sarah laughed" [Gen. xviii. 12]; that is, the Tzaddi is before the Sin, since Chronicles is before Psalms, as I have explained in the Third Introduction.

When the difference between two words consists in the points, they give for a sign a word which contains the two letters with the two in question. Thus, we have first לָלִין to stay over night [Gen. xxiv. 23], and then לָלוּן [ibid. ver. 25], and the mnemonical word for this difference is הֵילִילוּ howl [Isa. xxiii. 1].⁶ Compare also the first לִצְמִתֻת until extinction [Levit. xxv. 23], and the second לַצְמִיתֻת [ibid. ver. 30], where the mnemonical word is חָלִילָה far be it; and although the second Lamed in חָלִילָה has Kametz and not Pattach, they made no distinction between Kametz and Pattach; also, the first הַחַי the living [Levit. xvi. 20], and the second הַחָי [ibid. ver. 21], and the signal word הֶהָשֵׁב [Gen. xxiv. 5].⁷ Thus, also, in verses in which three or four words are alike, but in which only one word has a different servile letter, the Massorites indicate it by a mnemonical verse containing the two words in question; ex. gr., in Deut. xi. 24 it is הַמָּקוֹם the place, with the article, whilst in Josh. i. 3 it is מָקוֹם place, without the He, and the signal verse is וְהִנֵּה הַמָּקוֹם מְקוֹם מִקְנֶה and behold, the place is a place of cattle [Numb. xxxii. 1]. So, also, the first passage כִּי when [Levit. xxv. 25], the second וְכִי and when [ibid. ver. 35], and the third וְכִי and when [ibid. v. 39], are indicated by the signal verse; "and she said unto the men, I know THAT [כִּי], AND THAT [וְכִי] . . . AND THAT [וְכִי] Josh. ii. 9.

---

⁵ Here again the mnemonical sign על בשר אדם, which contains both words, בשר flesh and אדם man, shows by the position of the two words that בשר is used in the first passage and אדם in the second.

⁶ That is, since in the word חלילו, we have first לִ and then לוּ; hence the first syllable indicates לִין with Chirek, which occurs first, whilst the second syllable represents לוּן with Shurek, which occurs second in the section.

⁷ The change of the vowel-points in the word החי, having in the first place Segol under the He, and in the second place Pattach, is shown by the mnemonical expression הֶהָשֵׁב, which has twice He,—the first with Segol, corresponding to the Segol under the He in החי, in the first passage, and the second with Pattach, corresponding to the Pattach under the He in החי, in the second passage.

אם"ף consists of the initials of אתנח סוף פסוק Ethnach, and Soph Passuk. It is only put down on a word which has Kametz, on account of Zakeph, Rebii, or any other pause accent, and which has no parallel, except in the said Ethnach and Soph Passuk. Thus, הַפֶּסַח the passover [Numb. ix. 2], is marked, "not extant with Kametz, and every instance with Ethnach or Soph Passuk [אס"ף] is like it." The same is the case when the word occurs more than once, as אָבָד he perished [Isa. lvii. 1; Micah iv. 9], which is marked, "it occurs twice, and every instance with Ethnach or Soph Passuk [אס"ף] is like it." In some Codices, instead of אס"ף, they have written the form of Ethnach and Soph Passuk, as follows: ׀ ׃, and they say, "every ׀ ׃ is like it." Many have been misled thereby, thinking that it stood for Cheth and Nun, and read it חֵן peace, rest; whereas they are nothing but the forms of Ethnach and Soph Passuk.

אמ"ת is the acrostic of איוב משלי תלים Job, Proverbs, and Psalms. The Massorites assign this sign to these books, though they do not occur in this order, as I have stated in the Third Introduction, for their proper order is as follows: Psalms, Job, and Proverbs; and in accordance therewith I have also found in some Codices the sign תא"ם. But they usually write אמ"ת, because this mnemonical sign is more beautiful, since our Rabbins of blessed memory said, "always use an elevating phrase" [Pessachim, 3 a]. Now on the word עָשָׂה, with Tzere, the Massorites remark, "it occurs eight times with Kametz, and throughout אמ"ת דת"קע is like it." In this case אמ"ת does not stand for Job, Proverbs, and Psalms, but the whole of it consists of the acrostic of Deuteronomy [אלה הדברים], Proverbs [משלי], the twelve minor Prophets [תרי עשר], Chronicles [ד"ת], Psalms [תהלים], Proverbs [קהלת], and Ezra [עזרא].

שב"נ is the acrostic of שום בר נש name of the son of man, or proper name. Thus on אֲחֻזַּת Ahuzzath [Gen. xxvi. 26], "not extant, and every proper names [שב"נ] are like it."[8] It is a phrase used in the

אס"ף ראשי תיבות אתנח וסוף פסוק ולא כתבו זה רק על מלה שהיא קמוצה בעבור זקף, או רביע, או טעם אחד מפסיק, ואין דומה לח רק באתנח וסוף פסוק, כגון ויעשו בני ישראל את הַפֶּסַח וכל אס"ף דכוותיה; וכן כשיש לה דמיון, כמו אָבַד וכל אס 'ף דכוותיה, וכמו אלה רבים; וביש נוסחאות עשו במקום אס"ף חמונת האתנח וס"פ כזה ׀ ׃, ואמרו וכל ׀ ׃ דכוותיה, ורבים טועים בהם וחושבין שהם חי"ת ונו"ן וקורין חן לשון חנינה ומנוחה, ואינן אלא צורת האתנח וס"פ:

אמ"ת ראשי תיבות איוב משלי תלים, נתנו בהן זה הסימן אע"פי שאין כדורן כן, כמו שכתבתי בהקדמה השלישית, כי כדורן חלים איוב משלי; וכן מצאתי בקצת נוסחאות סימנם תא"ם, אלא נוהגין לכתוב אמ"ת לפי שהוא סימן יפה כמאמר רז"ל לשון מעלייתא נקט: והנה נמכר על מלת עָשָׂה בצירי ח' קמצין וכל אמ"ת דת"קע דכוותיה, ואיננו איוב משלי תהלים, אלא אלה הדברים, משלי תרי עשר, ד"ה, תהלים, קהלת, עזרא:

שב"נ ראשי תיבות שום בר נש, פירוש שום בן אדם, כמו שנמכר על וַאֲחֻזַּת מרעהו ליח וכל שב"נ דכוותיה, פירוש שום בן אדם לשון תרגום ירושלמי אֱנוֹשׁ המה סלה תרגום

---

[8] In the printed editions of the Massorah parva, on Gen. xxvi. 26, the remark is not ליח וכל שב"נ דכוותיה not extant, and every proper name is like it, as is stated by Levita,

Jerusalem Targum, which renders אֱנוֹשׁ *man* [Ps. ix. 21], by בַּר נָשׁ *son of man*, בֶּן אָדָם *son of man* [Job. xxxv. 8]; whilst בֶּן אָדָם, which so frequently occurs in Ezekiel, the Chaldee translates בר אדם. On אָחַז *to seize*, too, the Massorites remark, "it occurs three times with *Kametz*, and all [שׁב״ג] proper names are like it."[9] Also the four pairs, one of each pair being a proper name [שׁבן], and the other being different, as קוֹץ *a thorn* [Gen. iii. 18], and קוֹץ *Koz* [1 Chron. iv. 8], proper name; שֹׁהַם *a species of gem* [Ezek. xxviii. 13], and שֹׁהַם *proper name of a Levite* [1 Chron. xxiv. 27], &c. On a feminine proper name, however, the Massorites remark שׁוּם אִיתְּתָא *name of a woman*, as שָׂרַי the *princess of* [Judges v. 15], "not extant, and whenever it occurs as the name of a woman it is like it."

בר נש הינון לעלמי, וכן וּלְבֶן אָדָם צדקתך ובר נש דכיא; אבל בן אדם דיחזקאל מתורגנמין בר אדם, וכן אחז ג' קמצין וכל שׁב״ג רכותיה;[9] וכן ד' זוגין חד שׁב״ג וחד לשון אחד, כמו וקוץ ודרדר, וקוֹץ הוליד; וכן ושׁהם וישפה, ושׁהם חכור וכו'; אבל על שם נקבה כתבו שם איתתא, כמו ושָׂרי בישׂשכר לית, וכל שום איתתא דכוותיה:

מס״ה רוצה לומר מסרה הנדולה, כמו שנמסר על אָסוּרֵי המלך אֲסִירֵי קרי, והוא א״ב במס״ה דכתיבין וי״ו וקרי יו״ד;[10] ויש שקורין למסרה גדולה מסו״ה ולמסרה קטנה מס״ה, וכן ראית בספר עין הקורא וז״ל, ואלה הספדים אשר נתן לי אלהים בזה, מס״ה ומסו״ה ושאר מסורת מקצת כפרים טובים עכ״ל;[11] וביש נוכחאות מצאתי שקראו למסרה גדולה מס״נ ולמסרה קטנה מס״ק, כמו שיוחגין לקרא כפר מצות גדול כמ״נ וחקמן סמ״ק:[12]

but simply ליח שב״ג *not extant, proper names*. The Sulzbach edition omits the word כל before ש״ג, which renders the sentence unintelligible.

[9] The three instances in which אחז occurs with *Kametz* and *Pattach* under the first and second radicals are, Exod. xv. 14: 1 Kings i. 51: Job xxiii. 9. They are given in the Massorah marginalis on 1 Kings i. 51 and Job xxiii. 9, and in both these passages the Massoretic remark is וכל שום נבר קמץ וכולרע, *but wherever it is a proper name it has Kametz* [under the second radical], *and is Milra*, and not as Levita states in the text.

[10] The alphabetical list referred to by Levita has already been given, *vide supra*, p. 118, &c.

[11] For the work entitled *The Eye of the Reader* (עין הקורא), as well as for its author, see below, p. 257, under the initials יד״י = *Jekuthiel b. Jehudah Cohen*.

[12] The author of *The Major Book of the Commandments* (ספר מצות נדול, called סמ״נ *Semag* from its initials) is R. Moses, the celebrated Jewish preacher of the middle ages;

יָמָ"ה are the initials of יוצא מן הכלל *departing from the rule.* These initials are generally used in Treatises on the Laws of the Accents. When one of the rules of the accents is described, and there are some exceptions to it, they remark on them, " such and such are יָמָ"ה," = exceptions to the rule. Thus, for instance, before *Sarka* there ought properly to be *Munach*, but " there are thirteen [יָמָ"ה] exceptions to this rule, having *Mercha* before it;" as, with the help of the Lord, I shall explain in my book, entitled, *Good Sense.*

אָמָ"ח are the initials of אחד מלא אחד חסר *once defective, once plene.* I have already stated in Part i., Section i., that *plene* and *defective* only obtain with quiescent *Vav* and *Jod* in the middle of a word [*vide supra,* p. 145, &c]. Moreover, on words which occur *plene* or *defective* in two, three, or four places, the Massorites remark ב"מ ב"ח = "*twice plene, twice defective,*" or ג"מ ג"ח = " *thrice plene, thrice defective,*" &c., up to ten instances. But from ten and upwards they write the word *plene* or *defective* separately, and the letters denoting the number separately, as on וַיּוֹצֵא *and he brought out,* " it occurs twenty-four times, twelve times *plene* [י"ב במלאים] and twelve times *defective* [י"ב חסרים],"[13] but they never write יב"מ or יב"ח on one word.

יָמָ"ה רָאשֵׁי תֵיבוֹת יוֹצֵא מִן הַכְּלָל נוֹהֲגִים לִכְתּוֹב זֶה בְּדִינֵי הַטְּעָמִים, פֵּי' לִפְעָמִים כְּשֶׁנוֹתְנִים כְּלָל אֶחָד בַּטְּעָמִים, וְיֵשׁ הַיוֹצְאִים מִן הַכְּלָל, כּוֹרְכִין עֲלֵיהֶן כָּךְ וְכָךְ יָמָ"ה, כְּגוֹן לִפְנֵי הַזַּרְקָא דְּאָוֵי לִהְיוֹת מוּנַח, דַּק י"ג יָמָ"ה שֶׁלִּפְנֵיהֶן מֵרְכָא, כְּמוֹ שֶׁיִּתְבָּאֵר בְּסֵפֶר טוּב טַעַם בְּעֶ"ה:

אָ"ם אָ"ח רָאשֵׁי תֵיבוֹת אֶחָד מָלֵא אֶחָד חָסֵר, וּכְבָר הוֹדַעְתִּיךָ בְּדִבּוּר רִאשׁוֹן מִלֻּחוֹת הָרִאשׁוֹנוֹת, כִּי מָלֵא וְחָסֵר סְתָם לֹא נֶאֱמָר רַק עַל וי"ו וְיו"ד הַנָּחִים בְּאֶמְצָא הַמִּלָּה עַיֵּי"ש: וְכֵן עַל מִלּוֹת הַנִּמְצָאוֹת מְלֵאוֹת אוֹ חֲסֵרוֹת בְּב' אוֹ בְּג', אוֹ בְּד' מְקוֹמוֹת וְכוּ', נוֹהֲגִין לִכְתּוֹב כֵּן בָּ"מ בָּ"ח, אוֹ גָּ"מ גָּ"ח וְכוּלֵּי עַד חִיוּ"ד: אֲבָל מִן חִיוּ"ד וָאֵילָךְ כּוֹתְבוֹ מָלֵא אוֹ חָסֵר לְבַד, וְתֵיבַת הַמִּנְיָן לְבַד, וְהַמָּשָׁל וַיּוֹצֵא כָּ"ד, יָ"ב מְלֵאִים וְיָ"ב חֲסֵרִים, וְלֹא כַתְבוּ יְבָ"מ יְבָ"ח:[13]

he was born at Coucy, not far from Soissons, *circa* A.D. 1200, and died 1260. The work on the Commandments and Prohibitions consists of sermons which R. Moses de Coucy delivered on his journeys through the South of France and Spain (1235-1245), in the different Synagogues the design of which was to confirm his brethren in the ancient faith, since the orthodox religion of the Jews was at that time being undermined by the philosophy of Maimonides. The work which propounds the six hundred and thirteen precepts was first printed before 1480; then in Soncino, 1488; and in Venice, 1522, 1547, &c. Comp. Fürst, *Bibliotheca Judaica,* i. 189, &c.; Steinschneider, *Catalogus Libr. Hebr. in Bibliotheca Bodleiana,* col. 1795-1798; Graetz, *Geschichte der Juden,* vol. vii., pp. 61, 70, 72, 115, 130. Leipzig, 1863. The *Minor Book of the Commandments* (סֵפֶר מִצְווֹת קָטָן), called סמ"ק *Semay,* from the initials of its title is simply an abridgment of the greater work, made by Isaac de Corbeil, A.D. 1277, and is divided into seven parts, for the seven days of the week. It was first published at Constantinople, 1510; then at Cremona, 1556, with glosses, &c.; and at Cracow, 1596, &c. See Fürst, *Bibliotheca Judaica,* i. 186; Steinschneider, *Catalogus Libr. Hebr. in Bibliotheca Bodleiana,* col. 1103.

[13] The twelve passages in which ויצא is *plene* are, Gen. xv. 5; xxiv. 53; xliii. 23; xlviii. 12; Exod. xix. 17; Judg. vi. 19; 2 Kings xxiv. 13; 2 Chron. xxiii. 14; Ps. cxxxvi. 11; Jerem. x. 13; 1. 25; li. 16; and the thirteen instances in which it is *defective* are, Numb. xvii. 23, 24; Judg. xix. 25; 2 Sam. x. 16; xiii. 18; xxii. 20; 2 Kings xv. 20; xxiii. 6; x. 22; Jerem. xx. 3; lii. 31; 2 Chron. xvi. 2; Job xii. 22. The former are given in the Massorah marginalis on Judg. vi. 19, and the latter in the Massorah

It is, moreover, to be remarked, that they do not write this except on words which are sometimes *plene* and sometimes *defective*, as וַתּוֹרֶד *and she let down*, "occurs three times, once *plene* and twice *defective;*" פָּקוֹד "occurs four times, twice *plene* and twice *defective*," &c., &c.[14] But in those words of which either the *plenes* alone or the *defectives* alone are counted, the Massorites also only put down either the *plenes* or the *defectives*, and the respective number, as אֲבוֹתֶיךָ *thy forefathers*, "occurs three times *plene*," and do not give the initials נ"מ;[15] so also גְּדֹלָה *great*, "occurs five times *defective*," and they do not write the initials ח"ה. It is also to be noticed, that when the letters *Beth* and *Mem* occur together with two marks above, and one of the letters from *Aleph* to *Jod* is joined to them, as במ״א, or במ״ב, or במ״ג, &c., they are the initials of בר מן אחד *except one*, בר מן ב׳ *except two*, בר מן שלשה *except three*, &c. The meaning of בר is *except*; so the Chaldee renders חוּץ מִפֶּנּי, [Eccl. ii. 25], by בַּר מִנִּי *except I*. Thus the Massorites remark on בָּעוֹף *in the fowls*, "it is so in all the Scriptures except once [במ״א], where it is וּבְעוֹף AND *in the fowls;*[16] " also אֲבֹתֵיכֶם *your fathers* [Gen. xlviii. 21], on which the Massorites remark, "it is *defective* throughout the Pentateuch, except once where it is *plene*" [viz., Exod. xiii. 13], and so on up to ten instances. But, from ten upwards, the Massorites make this remark in two words, as אֲבוֹתֵיכֶם is "*plene* throughout the Hagiographa, except in sixteen instances;"[17] so also ב״מ י״א = except eleven, ב״מ י״ב = except twelve, ב״מ י״ג = except thirteen,

---

marginalis on Numb. xvii. 23. It will be seen that the Massorah gives thirteen instances of *defective*, including Judg. xix. 25, whilst Levita only mentions twelve. If the text does not contain a clerical error, Levita most probably excludes Judg. xix. 25, because the *Tzaddi* has *Chirek*, and not *Tzere*, as is the case in all the other instances.

[14] The three instances in which וְתוֹרֵד occurs are, Gen. xxiv. 18 : 1 Sam. xix. 12 (both *defective*) : Gen. xxiv. 46 *(plene)*. The Massoretic remark to which Levita refers is to be found both in the Massorah parva and the Massorah marginalis on Gen. xxiv. 18. For the instances in which פקוד occurs, see above, p. 147.

[15] The three passages in which אבותיך is *plene*, that is, has *Vav* quiescent with the *Cholem*, are, Gen. xxxi. 3 : Jerem. xxxiv. 5 : Prov. xxii. 28. They are given in the Massorah marginalis on Gen. xxxi. 3.

[16] The instances in the Bible where בעוף occurs are only three, viz., Gen. vii. 21 ; viii. 17 ; ix. 10 ; and the one passage in which it is ובעוף with *Vav* conjunctive is in Levit. xx. 25. On none of these passages, however, could we find in the printed Massorahs the remark to which Levita refers.

[17] For the orthography of אבותיכם, see above, p. 168, &c.

&c., all of which are the initials of בר מן = except, as you will find upon examination.

לק״י are the initials of לא קרי read not; they are only found in connection with one of the letters *Aleph, He, Vav,* and *Jod,* as לק״א = *Aleph, is not read,* לק״ה = *He, is not read,* לק״ו = *Vav, is not read,* לק״י = *Jod, is not read.* Comp. what I have said on this subject in Part ii., Section i., class 1 [*vide supra*, p. 182, &c.], and see also Part i., Section ix., [*vide supra*, p. 170, &c.]

כ״כ are the initials of כתיב כן *written thus,* or כן כתיב *thus written,* they are marked on those words which have two or three quiescents, some of which are *plene* and some *defective,* as I have explained in Part i., Section viii. [*vide supra*, p. 169, &c.] I have also discussed it in Part ii., Section ix. It is to be noticed that on the vowel signs and the accents the Massorites never remark כ״כ, but they write it כ״ה, which are the initials of כן הוא *it is so,* as וַתְּכַחֵשׁ *and she denied* [Gen. xviii. 15] "it is so [כ״ה] with *Kametz;*"[18] and תַּדְשֵׁא *let her sprout* [Gen. i. 11], "it is so [כ״ה] with *Marich*" [= a long line under *Tav*], &c. Moreover כ״ה stands also for the number twenty-five. Thus the Massorites remark on וַיָּשֶׁב *and he restored,* "it occurs [כ״ה] twenty-five times;"[19] on אֶחָד *one of,* "it occurs [כ״ה] twenty-five times,"[20] and it is always known from the context.

כל with a mark over the *Lamed* stands for כלהון *all,* as כל כ״כ, that is כלהון כתיבין כן *all are written so,* and כל חסרים *all are defective,* or כל מל׳ *all are plene.* But when they have two marks above, they are the initials of כל לשנא, *all the forms,* and I have already explained the

[18] That is with *Tzere* under the *Cheth,* since the *Tzere,* as has already been explained, is also called *Kametz.*

[19] The twenty-five instances in which וישב occurs are, Gen. xiv. 16; xx. 14; xl. 21: Exod. iv. 7; xv. 19; xix. 8: Judg. ix. 56; xvii. 3, 4: 1 Sam. xiv. 27; xxv. 21: 2 Sam. xv. 29; xxii. 25: 1 Kings ii. 30: 2 Kings xiii. 25; xvii. 3; xx. 11; xxii. 9: 1 Chron. xxi. 27; 2 Chron. xxxiv. 16: Job xxxiii. 26; Ps. xviii. 25; xciv. 23: Prov. xx. 26: Ezek. xliv. 1. They are given in the Massorah finalis under the letter *Jod,* p. 37 *a,* col. 1.

[20] The twenty-five instances in which אחד occurs are, Gen. xxi. 15; xxii. 2; xxvi. 10; xxxii. 23; xlviii. 22: Levit. xiii. 2: Numb. xvi. 15: Deut. i. 2; xxv. 5: Judg. xvii. 5: 1 Sam. ix. 3; xxvi. 15: 2 Sam. vi. 20; vii. 7; xvii. 22: 1 Kings xix. 2; xxii. 13: 2 Kings vi. 12; xviii. 24: 1 Chron. xvii. 6: Isa. xxxvi. 9; lxvi. 17: Ezek. xxxiii. 30; xlv. 7: Dan. x. 13. They are given in the Massorah marginalis on 2 Kings vi. 12.

וכולי, בלם ראשי תיבות בר מן, ודוק ותמצא
ל״ק ראשי תיבות לא קרי, אבל לא
נמצא זה רק עם אחת מאותיות אה״וי עמו,
כגון לק״א, לק״ה, לק״ו, לק״י, עיין במה
שכתבתי על אלה במאמר א' בסימן א', ועיין
גם כן בלוחות ראשונות בדבור מ':

כ״כ ראשי תיבות כתיב כן, או כן כתיב,
ונהגו לכתוב כן על מלה שיש בה ב' או ג'
נחים, קצתן מלאים קצתן חסרים, כאשר
בארתי בלוחות ראשונות בדבור ח'; גם
דברתי בם בלוחות שניות במאמר ט': ודע
כי על הנקודות והטעמים לא כתבו לעולם
כ״כ, כי אם כ״ה ראשי תיבות כן הוא,
כגון וַתְּכַחֵשׁ שָׂרָה כ״ה בקמ״ץ,[18] וכן תַּדְשֵׁא הָאָרֶץ
דשא כ״ה במאריך, וזולת זה רבים; ויש כ״ה
שמורה על מספר עשרים וחמש, כגון וַיָּשֶׁב
כ״ה,[19] אֶחָד כ״ה,[20] ותכידם לפי מקומן:

כל בנקודה על הלמ״ד רוצה לומר
כלהון, כגון כל' כ״כ רוצה לומר כלהון
כתיבין כן, וכן כל' חסרים, או כל' מל'; אבל
כשיש עליהן ב' נקודות, הם ראשי תיבות כל
לישנא, וכבר בארתי ענין לישנא במאמר י':

meaning of לשנא in Section x. [*vide supra*, p. 240, &c.] In some Codices, instead of כ״ל they write ת״ל, which are the initials of תרי לשנא *two forms*, as the alphabetical list of words which occur twice in the same form, but in a different sense; *ex. gr.*, אוֹרָה *I will teach* [Job xxvii. 11], and אוֹרֶה *I will shoot* [1 Sam. xx. 20], &c.; they are in alphabetical order, and number about a hundred pairs, all of them with two meanings.[21] But, forsooth, among many of them there seems to be no difference whatever, and I shall only mention the most difficult of all, כָּאֲרִי [Isa. xxxviii. 13], and כָּאֲרִי [Ps. xxii. 17]. Would that I knew the difference between them!

כ״ק are the initials of כל קריא *all the Scripture*. I have already explained, in Section x., that קריא is the designation of the twenty-four sacred books, and given the reason why they are so called. I have also explained there that the Massorites always write it out fully, that is, they write it down כל קריאה and not the initials כ״ק [*vide supra*, p. 234, &c.] But when they range many of them together, and make of them one Register, they write on each one of the words thus rubricated כ״ק, as you will see on examination.

פ״ד are the initials of פסח דספרא *Pattach of the Book*. I have already explained its import in Section ii. [*vide supra*, 197, &c]. In correct Codices it is noted in the margin against every *Pattach of the Book* פ״ד, to indicate that it is one of the number rubricated in the Massorah magna. Moreover, פ״ד are also the initials of פסקא דספרא *Piska of the Book*, the import of which I have explained in Section iv. [*vide supra*, p. 209]. This is also the case with the accent called *Legarme*, which I have likewise discussed in Section iv. [*vide supra*, p. 210];[22] and which I shall explain still further in my book called

---

[21] As this alphabetical list is by far too long to be given here, we must refer for it to the Massorah finalis under the letter *Aleph*, p. 1 *b*, col. 4—p. 2 *a*, col. 3; and the *Ochla Ve-Ochla*, section lix., p. 62, &c. Dr. Frensdorff has made some very important remarks on this rubric, p. 17, &c.

[22] The Sulzbach edition erroneously omits אשר בארתי במאמר ד, *which I have explained in Section iv.*

Good Sense. Wherever *Legarme* occurs in a verse, the Massorites write against it in the margin לנ׳, with one mark over the *Gimmel*, which signifies *Legarme*. Some have mistaken it, and thought that the word in question, on which the Massorites remarked לנ׳, occurs thirty-three times in the Bible. But, according to the rule which I have stated at the beginning of this Part, there can be no mistake about it; for, if it had referred to the number, it would have two marks, one on the *Lamed* and one on the *Gimmel*. Now, as the *Gimmel* alone has a mark, it is evident that the word is not written out fully, and that it is the abbreviation of *Legarme*.[23] I shall, however, discuss it again, in its proper place, in my book entitled *Good Sense*.

ל״ד are the initials of לית דכותיה, which I have already explained in Section v. Indeed I have not found in the Massorah ל״ד instead of לית דכותיה, but in some grammatical works which treat on the Massorah; *ex. gr.*, the *Book Semadar*, the Treatise called *The Stylus of the Scribe*,[24] and a few others.

ר״פ are the initials of ראש פסוק *the beginning of the verse*. This abbreviation, too, has been mistaken, for some have read it רפי *Raphe*, or רפין *Raphin*. But the difference between these two is, that when it has two marks over it it is the acrostic of ראש פסוק *the beginning of the verse*, as I have already stated, and when it has one point over the *Pe* it denotes רפין *Raphes*. Thus, it is remarked, the word ויאמרו *and they shall say*, "occurs nine times (רם׳) *Raphe*;"[25] ויבאו *and they shall come*, "occurs (רפ׳) seven times *Raphe*."[26] I have already explained, in Section iii. [*vide supra*, p. 198], the reason why it is called *Raphe*.

---

[23] Here the Sulzbach edition inserts the words אשר בארתי במאמר ד׳, which were omitted from the former part of the paragraph.

[24] The *Sepher He-Semadar* is as yet unknown (*vide supra*, p. 122); the *Stylus of the Scribe* will be noticed hereafter under *Kimchi*.

[25] The nine passages in which ויאמרו is *Raphe*, that is, has *Shera* under the *Vav* conjunctive, are, Deut. xxxii. 7; Jerem. xvi. 19; Joel ii. 17; Isa. xiv. 10; xliii. 9; Ps. lxx. 5; xxxv. 27; 1 Chron. xiv. 31; Job xxxviii. 35. They are given in the Massorah marginalis on Isa. xvi. 10.

[26] The seven passages in which ויבאו is *Raphe*, that is, has *Shera* under the *Vav*

טעם; בכל מקום שנמצא בפסוק לנרמיה כתבו בגליון נגדו לנ׳ בנקודה אחת על הג"מל רוצה לומד לנרמיה; ויש שטועין בזה, וחושבין כי המלה החיא אשר נמכר עליח לנ׳ היא נמצאת ל"ג פעמים במקרא, אבל לפי הכלל שנתתי בפתיחת השער הזה אין למעות בח, בי אם היה מורה על המספר היה עליח ב׳ נקודות, אחד על חלמ"ד, ואחד על חגימ"ל, עכשיו שהגימ"ל לבדה היא נקודה הוא ראיה שהמלה אינה נשלמת, ורוצה לומר לנרמיה;[23] ועוד אזכרנו במקומו בספר טוב טעם:

ל"ד ראשי תיבות לית דכותיה, וכבר בארתיו במאמר ה׳, והאמת כי במכרה לא מצאתי ל"ד במקום לית דכותיה, רק בספרי קצת המדקדקים בדברם בעניני מסורת, כגון ספר סדמדר וספר עט סופר,[24] ובזולתם מעטים:

ר"פ ראשי תיבות ראש פסוק, וגם בזה יש מקום לטעות, כי יש שקוראין אותו רפי או רפין, וההפרש שביניהם הוא באשר עליו ב׳ נקודות הוא ראשי תיבות ראש פסוק, כמו שכתבתי, וכשהוא בנקודה אחת על הפ"א רוצה לומר רפין, כגון ויאמרו ט׳ רפ׳,[25] וכן ויבאו ז׳ רפ׳,[26] וכבר בארתי במאמר ג׳ למה נקראין רפין:

255

ס״פ are the initials both of סוף פסוק *the end of the verse*, and of סופי פסוקים *ends of verses*; as אֲנִי יְהֹוָה *I, Jehovah*, "occurs twenty times at the end of verses [כ׳ ס״פ] in one book." In some Codices it is remarked on each one of these כס״ף, being the initials of כ׳ סופי פסוקים, "one of the twenty at the end of the verses." Thus, also, אֲנִי יְהֹוָה אֱלֹהֵיכֶם *I, Jehovah, your God*, which "occurs twenty-two times at the end of verses [כ״ב ס״פ];" the Massorites remark, on each of them, כבס״ף.[27]

מ״פ are the initials of מצעה פסוק, that is, "the middle of the verse."

מצע is a word by which the Jerusalem Targum renders the Hebrew תּוֹךְ and קֶרֶב. Thus, בְּתוֹךְ *in the midst of* [Job xx. 13] is translated במצע ; so also בְּקֶרֶב *in the midst of* [Ps. lxxxii. 1] is rendered by במצע. The word חוּץ *except*, in the Pentateuch and the Prophets, however, is translated מצעות or מציעותא, or מציעא; and because the language of the Massorites is mostly that of the Jerusalem Targum, they write מצע פסיק, as וְכָל יִשְׂרָאֵל *and all Israel*, " occurs thirty-five times in the middle of the verse [לה׳ מ״פ], and whenever it occurs in the beginning of a verse it is like it;"[28] so, also, וַיִּשָּׁמַע *and it was heard* "occurs three times, once at the beginning of a verse [ר״פ], once at the end of a verse [ס״פ], and once in the middle of a verse [מ״פ]."[29] In some Massorahs I have found, instead of

---

conjunctive, are, Exod. xiv. 16, 17; Deut. x. 11; Josh. xviii. 4; Isa. xiii. 2; Jerem. iii. 18; Ezek. xxxiii. 31. They are given in the Massorah marginalis on Isa. xiii. 2.

[27] The twenty passages in which אני יהוה occurs at the end of a verse are, Levit. xviii. 5, 6, 21; xix. 12, 14, 15, 18, 28, 30, 32, 37; xxi. 12; xxii. 2, 3, 8, 30, 31, 33; xxvi. 2, 45; and the twenty-one instances in which אני יהוה אלהיכם terminates the verse are, Exod. xvi. 12: Levit. xviii. 2, 4, 30; xix. 2, 3, 4, 10, 25, 31, 34; xx. 7; xxiii. 22, 43; xxiv. 22; xxv. 17, 55; xxvi. 1: Numb. x. 10; xv. 41: Deut. xxix. 5: Ezek. xx. 20. The former are given in the Massorah marginalis on Levit. xviii. 1, and the latter are enumerated in the Massorah finalis under the letter *Aleph*, p. 4a, col 4; where those which are כי אני יהוה אלהיכם, are given in one rubric, and those which are אני יהוה אלהיכם, without כי, are given in another rubric. Under the first rubric, which professes to give *ten* (י׳) instances, are mentioned Levit. xi. 44, and Joel iv. 17, neither of which is the beginning of a verse, in the present editions of the Bible. Equally erroneous is the heading of the second rubric, which professes to give *seventeen* (י״ז) instances, in which אני יהוה אלהיכם occur at the end of the verse, and only mentions fourteen.

[28] The thirty-five instances in which וכל ישראל occurs in the middle of the verse are, Deut. xxi. 21: Josh. iii. 17; vii. 24; viii. 21, 15; x. 29, 31, 34, 36, 38, 43: 1 Sam. xvii. 11: 2 Sam. iv 1; xviii. 17: 1 Kings viii. 62, 65: 1 Chron. xiii. 8; 1 Kings xi. 16; xv. 27; xvi. 17: 2 Kings ix. 14: 1 Chron. xiii. 6: 2 Chron. vii. 8; xii. 1; x. 3; xiii. 4, 15: Ezra ii. 70; Nehem. vii. 73: Ezra x. 5: 2 Chron. vii. 6: 1 Chron. xi. 4: Ezra viii. 25. They are given in the Massorah finalis under the letter *Jod*, p. 37b, cols. 1 and 2.

[29] The three passages in which ונשמע occurs with *Pattach* under the *Var*, and *Dagesh* in the *Nun* conjunctive, are, Josh ii. 11; Jerem. xxxv. 8, 10. They are given in the

מצע, the word מיסון [= μέσον], but I have not been able to discover the like of it anywhere else.

נ״א are the initials of נוסחא אחרינא *another Recension* or *Codex*. This expression is of frequent occurrence in the writings of our sages of blessed memory; as נוסח הגט *to transfer a bill of divorce*, נוסח הברכה *to transfer a blessing*, &c.; and it appears to me to denote *to transcribe, to write*, like יסחו [Prov. ii. 22], which denotes *to remove, to transfer*. Hence those words which have been transferred and copied from a book are called נוסחאות *transfers, copies, Codices*. Hence, also, the word יתנסח [Ezra vi. 11], is *to transfer, to remove*. I therefore submit that נוסחא and העתקה are almost identical.

Let me now mention the names of some of the punctuators and prælectors, which occur in some of the margins of the correct Codices of the Pentateuch. Most of these Codices are German, and I have only seldom found them in the Portuguese Pentateuchs. I shall also describe some of the titles of the books which have been written upon the subject.

רמ״ה, I have been told, is the acrostic of ר' משה חזן *Rabbi Moses Chasan*, who was one of the most correct prælectors, but I do not know who he is. It may be that this is the Moses who wrote the Treatise on the Laws of the Vowel-points, which is printed in the Great Bible round the margin of the Massorah, and begins with, "Thus saith the author, for a truth the vowel-points were given on Sinai," &c. I have already mentioned it in the Introduction to this Massoreth Ha-Massoreth [*vide supra*, p. 123]. Many think that it is the *Book of Shimshon*, but they are mistaken, for we find therein the name Moses signed in many places, as in the beginning of the Treatise, when speaking concerning the vowel-points *Tzere* and *Segol*, which commences ממכן שבתו השניח *from the place of his habitation he looketh* [Ps. xxxiii. 14]; and in another place, again, משטי החלם שמוש*

* Massorah finalis under the letter *Shin*, p. 60 *a*, col. 1. The Massoretic remark to which Levita refers is not to be found in the printed editions of the Massorah.

וביש מסורת מצאתי במקום מצע מיסון, ולא מצאתי לו חבר וריע:

נ״א ראשי תיבות נוסחא אחרינא, לשון זה נמצא הרבה בדברי חז״ל, כגון נוסח הגט, נוסח הברכה ורומיהן; ונ״ל שהוא ענין העתקה והסרה לשון יסחו ממנו שהוא כמו יוסרו ויועתקו, כן הדברים הנעתקים ונמחים מן ספר אחד נקראים נוסחאות, וכן בעזרא יתנסח עא מן ביתיה, פירוש יועתק ויוסר; לכן אני אומר שנוסחא והעתקה כמעט אחד הוא:

כאן אכתוב שמות קצת נקדנים וקוראים או חזנים, הנמצאים רשומים בקצת גליונות של החומשים המדויקים, ורובם הם אשכנים, ולא מצאתי מהם בחומשי הספרדים כי אם מעטים, גם קצת שמות הספרים אשר חובר על ככה אביא כאן:

רמ״ח נאמר לי שהוא ראשי תיבות ר' משה חזן, היה אחד מן הקוראים המהבהקים, ואנכי לא ידעתי, ויוכל להיות שהוא משה אשר חבר כללי הנקוד, הנדפסים בעשרים וארבע הגדול סביב המסרה הגדולה, שהתחלתו אמר המחבר אמת הדבר כי הנקוד נתן מסני וכו' ; וכבר זכרתיו בכפר מסורת חמסורת בהקדמה, ורבים חושבים שהוא ספר השמשוני, וטועים כי נמצא בו חתום שמו משה בהרבה מקומות, כגון בתחלת הדבור בנקודות הצירי והסגול דמתחיל ממכון שבתו השניח צור ישראל ונומר (תהלים ל״ג) ; ובמקום אחר משפט שמוש החלם שמוש ׳מטבי

the Laws respecting the use of the Cholem, &c. Whereas the book Shimshoni is nothing but the book called *Chibur Ha-Konim*, beginning with "Know that the fundamental things discussed by the Hebrews are ten," &c.[30]

מ"ש, In the above-named Codex I found a proof cited from a correct Pentateuch, saying, I found it so in the Pentateuch of R. Meier Spira, which is מ"ש = מאיר שפירע.[31]

יהב"י are the initials of יקותיאל הכהן בר יהודה *Jekuthiel Ha-Cohen b. Jehudah*, the author of the book entitled *the Eye of the Reader*, whose surname in German is Salmen Ha-Nakdan. He thus signs his name in the second poem of the book here alluded to. I have heard that he was from the the city of Prague, in the country of Bohemia; and I said, in a play upon the words, that from the walls [= lines] of the house [= in the stanzas] of his poems, he is recognised to be a Bohemian.[32] He composed a very excellent treatise, discussing the vowel-points, and the words, the accents of which are *Milel* or *Milra*,

החלם, והדומים לזה; וספר השמשוני הוא הספר הנקרא חבור חקונים מתחיל, דע כי עקרי הדברים אשר ידברו בהם העברים הם עשרה וכולי:[30]

מ"ש, מצאתי בספר הנ"ל שהוא מביא ראיה מחומש אחד מונה, ואומר כן מצאתי בחומש של מאיר שפירע, וזהו מ"ש:[31]

יהב"י ראשי היבות יקותיאל הכהן בר יהודה, והוא בעל ספר עין הקורא, וכנויו בלשון אשכנז זלמן הנקדן, וכן חתם שמו בשיר השני של ספרו ע"ש; וקבלתי שהוא היה בק"ק פראג שבמדינת פי"הם, ואני אמרתי על דרך חלצת השיר שבכותלי בתי שיריו נכר כי פהמי הוא;[32] ועשה חבור נאה מאוד בעניני הנקודות והמלות שמטעם מלעיל או מלרע, ובעניני המקפין ובלתי מקיפין,

---

[30] R. Shimshon, the grammarian (ר' שמשון הנקדן), flourished about 1240. The treatise which discusses the vowel-points and accents, and to which Levita refers, has not as yet appeared. Excerpts of it, however, have been published in Abicht's *Accentus Hebr. ex antiquissimo usu lectorio vel musico explicati*, &c.; Acced. *Porta accentuum Lat. conversa et notis illustr.*, Leipz. 1713; Delitzsch, in *Jesurun*, pp. 16, 86, 92, 192, 249, 252. Comp. Wolf, *Bibliotheca Hebræa*, vol i. 1152, iii. 1160, iv. 1003; Geiger, *Wissenschaftiche Zeitschrift für Jüdische Theologie*, vol. v., p. 423, &c., Leipzig, 1844; Fürst, *Bibliotheca Judaica*, iii. 16.

[31] All our endeavours to obtain some information about this Meier Spira have proved abortive. Wolf (*Bibliotheca Hebræa*, i. 756) simply says that Levita quotes him, whilst Fürst, the latest Hebrew bibliographer, remarks (*Bibliotheca Judaica*, ii. 372) that Spira wrote these works: i. A Treatise on Arithmetic; ii. A Commentary on Immannel b. Jacob's Astronomical Work; and iii. A Pentateuch with the Massorah. Fürst, however, omits his usual references to some works for particulars about the author.

[32] To understand this pun, which cannot be reproduced in a translation, it is to be remarked, that Levita refers to an incident in R. Gamaliel's life, recorded in the Talmud, which is as follows:—R. Gamaliel, whilst in the house of study, was asked by Jehudah, a proselyte of Ammonitish descent, whether he might come into the house of study. Gamaliel answered him in the negative, submitting that the Law [Deut. xxiii. 4] prohibited it. R. Jehoshuah was of the contrary opinion, and adduced in support of his view the declaration made in Isa. x. 13, that God had abolished the boundaries of all nations, and thus obliterated the territory of Ammon. He carried his point against Gamaliel, and the latter went to the house of his antagonist to be reconciled with him, since the altercation had assumed an angry tone. "On entering his house, R. Gamaliel perceived that the beams were black, and said to R. Jehoshuah, מכותלי ביתך אתה ניכר שחומי אתה *from the walls of thy house thou art recognised to be a blacksmith*," for which incautious remark he had again to apologise (*Berachoth*, 28 b). It will be seen that Levita refers to this remark of Gamaliel, and that the pun consists not only in the fact that בית means both *house* and *stanza*, but that שחמי *blacksmith*, with the slight alteration of the ח into ה, denotes *Bohemian*.

as well as those which have *Mappik*, and which are without *Mappik*; and he called this book *the Eye of the Reader*. Hence you find, in the margins of some Codices of the Pentateuch, עַ"ה, that is עין הקורא and sometimes it is remarked יהב"י, which is the name of the author, as I have stated.[83]

עט סופר are the initials of *Stylus of the Scribe*, which is the name of a book written by Redak,[83] and which is a compendium of the contents of the Massorah and the accents. I have found it quoted in the margins of the Spanish Codices of the Pentateuch, but not in the German Pentateuchs.[34]

רי"ן are the initials of ר' יעקב נקדן *R. Jacob, the Punctuator*. He is often quoted by the above-mentioned R. Shimshon, in his work, but I do not know who he is.[85]

מפ' is the name of a book called מַפְתֵּחַ *The Key*, as וְהַצְמִידִים *and the bracelets* [Gen. xxiv. 47], it is remarked " in *The Key* [במפ'] is without the second *Jod*;" so also בְּעֵבֶר *on the side* [Judges xi. 18], " in *The Key* is מֵעֵבֶר *beyond*." Also on *defective* and *plene*, we find it quoted in many places, and I do not know its author. I have, however, seen that Ibn Ezra makes the following remark, in his Introduction to the book called *The Balances*:—" R. Levi, the Spaniard,

וקרא שם חספר עין הקורא, וכן נמצא בקצת החומשים בגליונות ע"ה, רוצה לומר עין הקורא, ולפעמים נרשם יהב"י שהוא שם המחבר כאשר כתבתי ; [83]

ע"ם ראשי תיבות עט סופר, והוא שם ספר חברו הרד"ק, והוא קצור מעניני המסורה והטעמים, ומצאתיו רשום בגליונות של חומשי הספרדים, ולא בחומשי האשכנזים : [84]

רי"ן ראשי תיבות ר' יעקב נקדן, הביאו הרבה פעמים ר' שמשון חנ"ל בספרו, ולא ידעתי מי הוא : [85]

מפ' שם ספר נקרא מפתח, כנון וְהַצְמִידִים במפ' חסד יו"ד תנינא, וכן ויחנו בְּעֵבֶר הארמון במפ' מֵעֵבֶר ; וכן בענין חסר ומלא נמצא בכמה מקומות, ולא ידעתי מי ילדו, אך מצאתי שרא"ע כתב בהקדמתו לספר מאזנים וז"ל, ור' לוי הספרדי מעיר

---

[83] Jekuthiel b. Jehudah Cohen flourished circa A.D. 1250–1300, at Prague. The work entitled *The Eye of the Reader*, to which Levita refers, consists of Massoretic criticisms on the Pentateuch and the Book of Esther, and has been published by the learned Heidenheim, Rödelheim, 1818–1825. Jekuthiel has also written a grammatical treatise called *The Laws of the Vowel-points* (כללי הנקוד, דרכי הנקוד), the Introduction and practical part of which were also published by Heidenheim, Rödelheim, 1818–1821. Comp. Kitto's *Cyclopædia of Biblical Literature*, s. v. JEKUTHIEL.

[84] רד"ק are the initials of ר' דוד קמחי *R. David Kimchi*, the distinguished grammarian, lexicographer, and expositor, who has already been noticed (*vide supra*, p. 107). His celebrated grammatical and lexical work, entitled *Perfection* (מכלול), which was edited by Levita, has been described on p. 79, &c. To the article KIMCHI, in Kitto's *Cyclop.*, it is to be added, that Kimchi's Massoretic Treatise, entitled *The Stylus of the Scribe* (עט סופר), to which Levita refers, has recently been published for the first time, Lyck, 1864.

[85] There can be but little doubt that this R. Jacob is the celebrated Hebrew grammarian and poet called Jacob b. Eleazar, who flourished circa A.D. 1130, at Toledo. He was a distinguished writer on the vowel-points (whence he obtained the name of *Ha-Nakdan*) and on the etymology of proper names. He moreover formed a correct Recension of the text of the Hebrew Scriptures, after the model of the Codex Hilali, and it is owing to these contributions to Biblical literature that he is so often quoted by Shimshon, Kimchi, and other lexicographers and critics. Comp. Kitto's *Cyclopædia of Biblical Literature*, s. v. JACOB B. ELEAZAR.

from the city of Saragossa, is the author of the book called *The Key*." Thus far his language;[86] but I have not as yet been able to see it.[87]

סרקוסטה חבר ספר המפתח עכ"ל:[86] ואנכי לא ראתיו עד הנה:[87]

מחזורתא **Machsortha** is the name of a work, the author of which I do not know. It is quoted in the margin of the Pentateuch, as "לסבב *to compass* [Numb. xxi. 4] has *Beth* with *Dagesh*, but in the *Machsortha* it is *Raphe*."[88]

מחזורתא שם ספר ולא ידעתי מי ילדו, ונמצא בגליונות החומשים, כגון לסבב את ארץ אדום הבי"ת דנושה, ובמחזורתא לסבוב ברפי:[88]

סיני **Sinai**, is the name of a correct Pentateuch which treats on the variations of the accents; as וַיִּשְׁמַע *and he heard* [Exod. xviii. 1], has the accent *Gershaim*, but in Sinai it has *Rebia*: again, הַמִּדְבָּר *the desert* [Exod. xviii. 5], has *Sakeph*, whilst in Sinai it has *Sakeph-gadol*. But I do not know who the author of it is.[89]

סיני שם חומש מדוייק מדבר מחלוקת הטעמים, כגון וַיִּשְׁמַע יתרו בגרשים, ובסיני הוא ברביע; ועוד שם אל משה אל המדבר בזקף, ובסיני בזקף גדול, ולא ידעתי מי הוא המחבר:[89]

חומש יריחו **the Pentateuch of Jericho**, is doubtless a correct Codex

---

[86] Levita's quotation is not literal. Even in his own edition of Ibn Ezra's *Balances*, the passage is as follows:—ורבי לוי הנקרא בן אל תבאן ספרדי במדינת סרקסטה תקן ספר המפתח. and *R. Levi, who is called Ibn Al-Tabben*, &c., vide p. 197 b, ed. Levita; Venice, 1546.

[87] This R. Levi, the Spaniard, or Abulfihm Levi b. Joseph Ibn Al-Tabben, as is his full name, flourished A. D. 1120. He was a friend of R. Jehudah Ha-Levi, the celebrated poet and philosopher. Besides composing poetry himself, he wrote the Hebrew Grammar called *The Key* (מפתח), to which Lev.ta refers, but which has not as yet been published. Comp. Graetz, *Geschichte der Juden*, vol. vi., p. 131; Leipzig, 1861.

[88] *Machsortha* (מחזורתא) is the common name of the Jewish Ritual, comprising the whole annual cycle of the Daily and Festival Services. The *cycle*, as is the literal meaning of *Machsortha* (from חזר *to go round*), was generally written by the most distinguished scholars of the respective communities in the various parts of the world, embodying the local usages, and hence obtained the name of the special place where it was written, and the practice of which it depicted. The *cycle*, according to the practice of the Synagogue of Vitry, has already been mentioned (*vide supra*, p. 45), and we have to add here that these Ritnals not only contained Prayers and Hymns, but gave the text of the whole Bible, so that they became models, after which copies were made. It is owing to this fact that the Bible Codex itself was called *Machsor* (מחזור), as is the case with the Codex made after Ben-Asher.

[89] Levita's quotations are not from the Massorah marginalis on these passages, but from the outer margin. The Massoretic glosses in question are not reproduced literally by Levita, as will be seen from the following statements:—On Exod. xviii. 1, the gloss is וישמע ב' בטע' שני גרשין ר'ס בתורה סיני רביע, *the word* וישמע *occurs twice with the accent Gershain at the beginning of a verse in the Pentateuch, Sinai has Rebia;* and on Exod. xviii. 5, סיני המדבר בוקף גדול *Sinai has* המדבר *with Sakeph-gadol.* Now according to Levita's reading בסיני *in Sinai*, we are obliged to assume with him that it is the name of a Codex; but, according to the proper reading, we may adopt the opinion of Joseph Eshve, the expositor of the Massorah, which is enunciated on Exod. xviii. 1—וכזה שאמר סיני רביע דע כי בעלי מתקני הנקוד והטעמים רבים היו מגאוני חכמי טבריא ואחד מהם היה שמו סיני והוא פליג על המסורת דאמר שני מלות וישמע הנו' הכזה בטעם גרשיים ואמר הוא שהם בטעם רביע *as to the remark, Sinai has Rebia, know that the inventors of the vowel-points and accents were mostly from the spiritual heads and the sages of Tiberias. Now the name of one of these was Sinai, and he differed from the Massorah, which remarks, that* וישמע *in the two passages in question has Gershaim, and said that it has the accent Rebia.* From this it will be seen, that this great Massoretic authority does not take סיני as *Codex Sinaiticus*, but regards it as a proper name of one of the inventors of the vowel-points and accents.

of the Pentateuch, derived from Jericho. It discusses the *plenes* and *defectives*, as הַתּוֹעֵבוֹת the *abominations* [Levit. xviii. 27], is in this Pentateuch of Jericho, without the second *Jod*. So also יְלִידֵי, the *children of*, which occurs twice in the same chapter [Numb. xiii. 22, 28], the first is *plene* in the Pentateuch of Jericho, and the second is *defective*.

ספר הללי *Codex Hilali*, is quoted by Kimchi in his grammar called *Perfection*, and in his Lexicon, in the following language:—"In the *Codex Hilali*, which is at Toledo, תִּדְּרוּ *ye shall vow* [Deut. xii. 11], is found with *Daleth Raphe*." Thus far his remark. I at first thought that the Codex is so called after its author, whose name was Hillel; but I soon found that in some recensions it is spelt הלאלי, with *Aleph* between two *Lameds* (comp. the root שום in Kimchi's Lexicon). Moreover, I found that in the Constantinople edition of the *Michlol* it is pointed הֵלָּלִי, with *Tzere* under *He*, so that I do not know what it is.[40]

ירושלמי *Jerusalem Codex*, is the book on which R. Jona, the Grammarian, relied, as is attested by Kimchi. It is perhaps the Codex which Ben-Asher corrected,[41] and which remained at Jerusalem for a long time, as I stated in the third Introduction, in the name of Maimonides of blessed memory.

ספר אספמיא *Spanish Codex*, is the general name for the Spanish Codices, for they are more correct than all other exemplars, as I have already stated in the Poetical Introduction. As to אספמיא, it denotes Spain, for thus the Targum renders ספרד [Obad. 20], by ספמיא, and it is also called Hispania in Italian, and Spanien in German.

נפתלי *Naphtali*; I have already mentioned in the third Introduction the variations between Ben-Asher and Ben-Naphtali, and that we

---

[40] It is now generally acknowledged among scholars that the *Codex Hilali* derives its name from the fact, that t was written at Hilla, a town built near the ruins of ancient Babel. This Codex, which was completed *circa* A. D. 600, had not only the then newly invented vowel-points and accents, but was furnished with Massoretic glosses. It was brought to Toledo about A. D. 1100, where the grammarian Jacob b. Eleazar used it for his works, and a portion of it was purchased by the Jewish community in Africa, about A.D. 1500. Comp. Kitto's *Cyclopædia, s. v.* HILALI CODEX.

[41] For Ben-Asher, and his celebrated Codex, *vide supra*, p. 113, &c.

מונח, בא מידיחו, מרבר מענין חסר ומלא, כגון כי כל הַתּוֹעֵבוֹת האל בחומש ידיהו חסר וי"ו חסנין, וכן לְיְדֵי הענק ב' בענין, ובחומש ידיחו הראשון מלא והשני חסר:

ספר הללי מביאו הרד"ק במכלול ובשרשים ח"ל, בספר הללי אשר במולימולא נמצא אשר תִּדְּרוּ ליהוה הרל"ת רפויה עכ"ל; ואני חשבתי כי חסר נקרא כן על שם מחברו הנקרא הילל, אך מצאתי בקצת נוכחאות כתיב הלאלי באל"ף בין ב' הלמדי"ן עיין בשרש שום; גם ראיתי במכלול הנדפס בקונשטאנטינו נקרו הֵלָּלִי בצידי ההֵ"א, ולא ידעתי מה הוא:[40]

ירושלמי הוא הספר אשר סמך עליו רבי יונה המדקדק, כמו שהעיר עליו הרד"ק, ואולי הוא הספר שהגיה בן אשר שהיה בירושלים ימים רבים,[41] כמו שכתבתי בהקדמה השלישית בשם הרמב"ם ז"ל:

ספר אספמיא הוא שם כלל לספרי ספרד, כי הם מוהגים מכל שאר הספרים, כאשר כתבתי בהקדמה החרוזית; ואספמיא רוצה לומר ספרד, כי כן תרגום של נלות ירושלים אשר בִּסְפָרַד דבאספמיא, וכן נקרא בלעז אספניא, ובלשון אשכנז שפנייא:

נפתלי, כבר כתבתי בהקדמה השלישית המחלוקת שבין בן אשר ובן בן נפתלי, ואיך

follow the readings of Ben-Asher.[42] Hence we find in some Codices the opinion of Ben-Naphtali noted in the margin; as וְחָצִיתָ and thou shalt divide [Numb. xxxi. 27], which, according to the reading of Ben-Asher, is so written with two *Pashtas*, whilst, according to the reading of Ben-Naphtali, it is וְחָצִיתָ, with one *Pashta*. Hence the remark in the margin נפ׳, that is, נפתלי *Naphtali*, and in some Codices ב״נ, that is, בן נפתלי *Ben-Naphtali*. Those Codices in which the reading of Ben-Naphtali is in the text, and the reading of Ben-Asher in the margin, are incorrect, since it is a principle with us to follow Ben-Asher. Hence it is the principle which should be expressed in the text, and not in the margin.

מדינחי, that is, מדינחאי *Eastern*. I have already stated, in the above-named Introduction, the variations between the East and the West, and that we follow the Western readings [*vide supra*, p. 113]. Hence it is only necessary to note in the margin the Eastern reading, as on עַל *upon* [Judg. ix. 3], "the Eastern [מדינחאי] reading is אֶל *to.*" Those Codices which have in the margin the Western reading עַל are incorrect. Moreover, I have also stated already, in the above-named Introduction, that the variations between the Eastern and Western Codices only extend to the Prophets and Hagiographa, and that there is not a single one in the Pentateuch [*vide supra*, p. 114].

אשלמתא *completion, perfection*. The Massorites call the earlier Prophets אשלמתא קדמיתא, and the later Prophets אשלמתא תנינא. Thus "throughout the Pentateuch and the earlier Prophets [ואשלמתא קדמיתא] it is שָׁלַחְתִּי *I have sent*, and וְשָׁלַחְתִּי, with *Kametz* under the *Shin*, except in one instance, where it is וְשִׁלַּחְתִּי [Levit. xxvi. 25], with *Chirek* under the *Shin*; and throughout all the later Prophets [אשלמתא תנינא] it is the same, שִׁלַּחְתִּי and וְשִׁלַּחְתִּי with *Chirek* under the *Shin*, except in two instances, where it is שָׁלַחְתִּי [Jerem. xxiii. 21; xxix. 19]." See the Massorah magna. But I do not know why they are called אשלמתא.

אנחנו סומכים על קריאת בן אשר,[43] לפיכך נמצא בקצת הספרים נרשם בחוץ דעת בן נפתלי, כגון וְחָצִיתָ את המלקוח לפי קריאת בן אשר כן הוא בב׳ פשטין, ולקריאת בן נפתלי הוא וְחָצִיתָ בפשט אחד; וכן נרשם בגליון נפ׳ רוצה לומר נפתלי, ובנ״א ב״נ פירוש בן נפתלי; ובנוכחאות שנכתב דעת בן נפתלי בפנים, ודעת בן אשר בחוץ הוא טעות, כי העקר אצלנו דעת בן אשר, לפיכך ראוי לכתוב העקר בפנים ולא בגליון:

מדינ׳ דוצה לומד מדינחאי, כבר כתבתי בהקדמה הנ״ל החלופין שבין מדינחאי ומערבאי, ואיך אנחנו סומכין על קריאת מערבאי, לפיכך אין צריך לרשום בחוץ רק דעת מדינחאי, כמו ופשמת על העיר מדינחאי אֶל העיר, ובספרים שנרשם בחוץ למערבאי עַל הוא הטעה; וכבר הודעתיך גם כן בהקדמה הנ״ל שאין חלוף בין מדינחאי למערבאי רק בנביאים וכתובים, ואין גם אחד בתורה:

אשלמתא, כן קראו בעלי המסו׳רת נביאים ראשונים אשלמתא קדמיתא, ונביאים אחרונים אשלמתא תנינא, כגון כל אוריתא ואשלמתא קדמיתא שָׁלַחְתִּי וְשָׁלַחְתִּי בר מן אחד וְשִׁלַּחְתִּי דבר בתוככם, וכל אשלמתא תנינא דכותיה שִׁלַּחְתִּי וְשִׁלַּחְתִּי במ״ב וְשָׁלַחְתִּי, עיין במסרה גדולה; ואכי לא ידעתי למה נקראו אשלמתא:

---

[42] For Ben-Asher and Ben-Naphtali, *vide supra*, p. 113, &c.

פרינמא is the name given by the Massorites to a pause, or *hiatus*, in the middle of the verse. Thus, on "And Cain said to his brother Abel o, and it came to pass they were in the fields" [Gen. iv. 8], the Massorites remark, "one of the twenty-five *hiati* [פרינמות] in the middle of the verse:" four of these are in the Pentateuch.⁴³ I do not know from what language it is derived, and even the author of the *Aruch* does not quote it. The Italians, however, call all the *hiati* between the section, whether open or closed, פרינמא, with *Tzere* under *Pe*; and I have enquired of their sages about it, but they could not tell.⁴⁴

Now the import of open or closed sections is explained by the *Poskim*, who, however, entertain a great difference of opinion about it. Generally the open section consists of two kinds,—one is in the middle of the line, where a vacant space of about nine letters is left, and the second has a whole line left vacant, and the writing commences on the third line. In the case of a closed section, a vacant space of about three letters is left in the middle of the line, and after it the line is finished; and if the closed section terminates at the end of a line, the second line is begun in the middle. The rule is, that the open section is always at the beginning of the line, whilst the closed section is always in the middle of the line.

מיסון [= μέσον] is the *middle*. I have already discussed it under the word ס״מ [*vide supra*, p. 256].

נוסחא is *Codex, recension*. I have already described it under the word נ״א [*vide supra*, p. 256].

I shall now explain some of the mnemonical signs of the Massorah

פרינמא, כן קראו ההפסקה שבאמצע הפסוק, כנון ויאמר קין אל הבל אחיו... ויהי בהיותם בשדה, נמסר עליו כ״ה פרינמות במצע פסוק ד' מנהון בתודה,⁴³ ואיני יודע שאיזה לשון הוא, גם בעל הערוך לא הביאו, אך חלוקים קודמים כל הפסקות בין פרשה פתוחה או כתומה פרינמא בצידי חרי״ש, ושאלתי את פי חכמיהם ואין מגיד לי:⁴⁴

וענין פרשה פתוחה וסתומה מבואר בפוסקים, ויש בהן פלוגתות, והכלל שפרשה פתוחה יש לה ב' צורות, האחד בחצי השיטה ומניח חלק כשיעור מ' אותיות, וחצודה השנית מניח שיטה שלמה ומת־יל בשיטה השלישית; ופרשה סתומה מניה חלק באמצע השיטה כשיעור ג' אותיות, ואח״כ מסיים השיטה, ואם נגמר בסוף חשימה מתחיל באמצע השיטה השנית; והכלל הפתוחה תמיד בראש השיטה, והסתומה תמיד באמצע השיטה:

מיסון כמו אמצע, וכבר זכרתיו במלת ס״פ:

נוסחא פירוש העתקה, וכבר זכרתיו במלת נ״א:

ועתה אבאר קצת סימני מסורת שבתורה

---

⁴³ For the four *Piskas* in the Pentateuch, see above, p. 242. The other twenty-one are, Josh. iv. 1; viii. 24: Judg. ii. 1: 1 Sam. x. 22; xiv. 13, 19, 36; xvi. 2, 12; xix. 21; xxiii. 2, 11: 2 Sam. v. 2, 19; vii. 4; xxiv. 11: 1 Kings xiii. 20: 2 Kings i. 17: Isa. viii. 3: Ezek. iii. 16; xliv. 15. Fürst (*Hebrew Concordance*, p. 1369, cols. 1 and 2) enumerates no less than thirty-one such *Piskas*. Besides those we have given, he has 1 Sam. xvii. 37: 2 Sam. vi. 20; xii. 13; xvi. 23; xvii. 14; xv ii. 2; xxi. 1, 6; xxiv. 10, 23: Jerem. xxxviii. 28; whilst he omits Gen. iv. 8: 1 Sam. xiv. 13; xix. 21: 2 Kings i. 17: Ezek. xliv. 15. Indeed there is a great difference of opinion among critics as to the number and places of these *Piskas*.

⁴⁴ There can be but little doubt that פרינמא is the Greek πρῆγμα, πρᾶγμα.

on the Pentateuch and Prophets, since several of them are difficult to understand.

The mnemonical sign in Pericope Noah.—In Gen. x. 3, it is רִיפַת *Riphath*, with *Resh*, and in 1 Chron. i. 6 it is דִיפַת *Diphath*, with *Daleth;* and the sign thereof is "*The initials of the names of their respective books*," that is, in Genesis, which is called ראשית with *Resh*, it is written *Riphath* with *Resh*; whilst in Chronicles it is written *Diphath* with *Daleth*, according to the name of the book which is called דברי with *Daleth*.

The mnemonical sign in Pericope Va-Jerah.—In the description of Abraham, it is written "and his two young men [אִתּוֹ] *with him*" [Gen. xxii. 3], whilst in connection with Balaam it is "and his two young men [עִמּוֹ] *with him*" [Numb. xxii. 22], and the sign is, "*each man according to his language;*" that is, by Abraham, who was a Hebrew, it is written אִתּוֹ, which is Hebrew; whilst in the narrative of Balaam, who was an Aramæan, as it is said, "from Aram has Balak brought me" [Numb. xxiii. 7], it is written עִמּוֹ, which is Aramæan, as the Chaldee renders אִתּוֹ by עֲמֵיהּ. Another sign for this passage is, "*as is his name, so he is;*" that is, Abraham, which is with *Aleph*, has אִתּוֹ with *Aleph*, and Balaam, which is with *Ajin*, has it written עִמּוֹ with *Ajin*. A third sign is "*Aleph Aleph, Ajin Ajin*," i. e., Abraham with *Aleph* has *Aleph*, and Balaam with *Ajin* has *Ajin*. Another sign for it, again, is "*their letters are the signs*," that is, the different letters in their names are the signs of the respective expressions in question.

The sign in Pericope Va-Ishlach.—The sign on דִישָׁן *Dishan* with *Kametz*, and דִּשֹׁן *Dishon* with *Cholem* [Gen. xxxvi. 30], is, "every day wherein the Scroll of the Law is used it is דִישָׁן *Dishan*, with *Kametz* under the *Shin*, and it begins with the first day of the week," and the order is as follows, *Dishon, Dishan, Dishon, Dishon, Dishan, Dishon, Dishan*. This is the explanation of the Spaniards. The French differ on this subject, saying that the order is *Dishon, Dishan, Dishon, Dishan, Dishon, Dishon, Dishon, Dishan*, the sign with them being "every day on which the Scroll is read, it is דִשֹׁן *Dishon*, and beginning with Sabbath." The latter is the correct one, and the proof of it is, that what is holy is placed first, and not last.[45] Another sign is, "the rich are with *Kametz*," that is, when it is rich in letters, it has *Kametz* and is *plene*, that is it is written דִּישָׁן *Dishan*, with *Jod*; whilst דִּשֹׁן *Dishon*, with *Cholem*, is not rich, for it is *defective*.

The mnemonical sign in Pericope *Shemoth.*—On וָחָיָה *and she shall live*, with *Kametz* under the *Vav* [Exod. i. 16], the Massorites remark, "not extant, once it is וְחָיָה [Esth. iv. 11], with *Sheva* under the *Vav*, and the sign thereof is מלכת שבא, that is, by queen Esther, it is with *Sheva*."

כל יומי ספר דֹּשׁ ומתחיל ביום השבת, וזהו העקר, וסימן מעלין בקדש ולא מורידין:[45] וסימן אחד עשירים מקמצין, פירוש כל שהוא עשיר באותיות הוא בקמץ מל', רוצה לומר שנכתב ביו"ד חוא דִישָׁן, וכל דֹּשׁ בחולם אינו עשיר כי הוא חסר:

סימן בפרשת שמות, ואם בת הוא וָחָיָה ל', וא' שרבים חוחב וְחָיָה, וסימן מלכת שבא, פירוש נבי אסתר נקוד וְחָיָה בשבא:

סימן פרשת בא, ויצא מעם פרעה במכת הארבה, סימן מלך אין לארבה ויצא, פירוש ברוב שאר המכות כתיב ויצא משה מעם פרעה, אבל בארבה לא נזכר משה שהוא מלך, שנאמר ויהי בישורון מלך, וזהו סימן מלך אין לארבוז:

סימן בפרשת תזריע, דמי טָהֳרָה הה"א נחח, ימי טָהֳרָה הה"א במפיק, וסימן יהודה, פירוש הה"א שאחר יו"ד של יהודה היא נעה,

The mnemonical sign is Pericope *Boh.*—On "And he went out from Pharaoh" [Exod. x. 18], in connection with the plague of the locusts, the sign is, "*the king is not by the locusts*," that is, by most of the other plagues it is said, "and Moses went out from Pharaoh," whilst at the place of locusts the name of Moses is not mentioned, because he is king, as it is written, "and he was king in Jeshurun" [Deut. xxxiii. 5]. Hence the sign.

The mnemonical sign in Pericope *Thazriah.*—In the first טָהֳרָה *purity*, construed with בְּדְמֵי *in the blood of* [Levit. xii. 4], the *He* is *Raphe*, or quiescent; whilst the *He* of the second טָהֳרָה, connected with יְמֵי in the same verse, is with *Mappik*, and the sign thereof is יְהוּדָה *Jehudah*; that is, just as the first *He* after the *Jod* is יְהוּדָה vocal, and the

---

[45] As the above explanation of the mnemonical sign is not very clear, and as it pre-supposes a knowledge of Jewish manners and customs, it requires some further elucidation. It will be seen that the word דישן occurs *seven* times in the same paragraph (Gen. xxxvi. 20–30),—three times with *Cholem* on the *Shin* (i. e. דֹּשׁ Gen. xxxvi. 21, 25, 30), and four times with *Kametz* under the *Shin* (i. e. דִישָׁן verses 26, 28, 30). Now, as the week has seven days, corresponding to these seven instances, and, moreover, as on three of these days an appointed lesson from the Law is read (i.e. Saturday, Monday, and Thursday), and the other four days (i. e. Sunday, Tuesday, Wednesday, and Friday) are without such lessons, these corresponding again to the three instances of the *Shin* with *Cholem* and the four without it, the seven days are made the symbol of the seven times דישן; whilst the order of the three days with and the four days without the lesson from the Law is made to symbolise tho order in which דישן is read, three times with *Cholem* and four times without (i. e. with *Kametz*), beginning with the Sabbath. Accordingly, the first דישן with *Cholem* answers to Sabbath, the first day, with a lesson; the second דישן without *Cholem* answers to Sunday, which is without a lesson; the third דישן with *Cholem* answers to Monday, with a lesson; the fourth דישן without *Cholem* answers to Tuesday, without a lesson; the fifth דישן without a *Cholem* answers to Wednesday, without a lesson; the sixth דישן with a *Cholem* answers to Thursday, with a lesson; whilst the seventh דישן without a *Cholem* answers to Friday, without a lesson.

second *He* after the *Daleth* is quiescent, so the *He* in טָהֳרָהּ connected with יְמֵי is vocal [*i. e.*, beginning with *Jod*], and the one connected with דְּמֵי [beginning with *Daleth*] is quiescent. Another sign is, "*her days are revealed, her blood is concealed;*" and another, "*and we conceal her blood.*" But these are easily understood.[46]

The mnemonical sign in Pericope Phineas. — The sign here is בו"ז מי"ם, that is, in the whole of this section it is written וְנִסְכָּהּ *and his drink offering*, and כַּמִּשְׁפָּט *after the manner*, except in the order for the second day, where it is written וְנִסְכֵּיהֶם *and their drink offerings* [Numb. xxix. 19]; for the sixth day, where it is וּנְסָכֶיהָ *and her drink offerings* [ver. 31]; and for the seventh day, where it is כְּמִשְׁפָּטָם *after their manner* [ver. 33]. Hence the letters indicating the days in which these variations occur, viz., ב = second day, ו = sixth day, and ז = seventh day; together with the letters constituting the variations, viz., ם in ונסכיהם [ver. 19], י in ונסכיה [ver. 31], and ם in כמשפטם [ver. 33], yield the sign בו"ז מי"ם *pouring out water;* thus pointing out that the ceremony of pouring out the water is contained in the Law, as is propounded in the Talmud tractate *Taanith*.[47]

The sign on 2 Sam. xxi. 15–20. In this section the phrase *and there was still* [מִלְחָמָה] *war*, without the article, occurs twice [verses 15, 20]; "*and there was still* [הַמִּלְחָמָה] THE *war*," with the article, occurs twice [verses 18, 19], and the sign is "*in the centre it is* המלחמה," with the article, that is, the first and fourth, which are the outsides, are מִלְחָמָה, without the article, and the two central ones are הַמִּלְחָמָה, with the article.

The sign in 2 Kings xx. 3.—In 2 Kings xx. 3 we find "in truth and with a perfect [וּבְלֵבָב] heart," whilst in Isa. xxxviii. 3 it is "in

[46] The first and third mnemonical signs are not given in the printed editions of the Massorah.
[47] The Talmudic explanation of these variations in the words, and the law deduced therefrom, are to be found in *Taanith*, 2 *b*–3 *a*, as well as in *Sabbath*, 103 *b*. To understand the reference to the traditional enactment, it is necessary to remark, that these words also occur in connection with the other days of the Feast, but without the letters in question. As, according to the Talmudic laws of exegesis, no superfluous letter is ever used in the Bible without its having some recondite meaning (comp. Ginsburg's *Commentary on Ecclesiastes*, p. 30, &c.; Longmans, 1861), the three redundant letters have been combined into מים *water*. This exegetical rule is called נוטריקון ומסין ודרוש *letters taken from one word and joined to another, or formed into new words*. Comp. Kitto's *Cyclopædia of Biblical Literature, s. v.* MIDRASH, p. 172, rule iii. See also Jacob b. Chajim's *Introduction to the Rabbinic Bible*, p. 22, &c., ed. Ginsburg.

truth and with a perfect [וּבְלֵב] heart," and the sign thereof is "*the beginning of their respective books*," that is, the book of Kings, beginning with וְהַמֶּלֶךְ *and the King*, which has five letters, it is written וּבְלָבָב, which also contains five letters; whilst in the book of Isaiah, which begins with חָזוֹן *a vision*, consisting of four letters, it is וּבְלֵב, also of four letters.

The sign in 2 Kings xxv. 11.—In 2 Kings xxv. 11 we have "the remnant of הֶהָמוֹן *the multitude*," and in Jerem. lii. 15, "the rest of [הָאָמוֹן] *the multitude*," and the sign thereof is "*here* [הֵא] *is seed for you*," the meaning of which is well known. Moreover, in 2 Kings xxv. 12 we have וּמִדַּלַּת *and of the poor one*, whilst in Jeremiah [lii. 15] it is וּמִדַּלּוֹת *of the poor ones*, and the sign thereof is, "*poverty follows upon poverty;*" that is, Jeremiah, who speaks of the sundry desolations of the Temple, has מִדַּלּוֹת in the plural, whilst the Kings, who are rich, have מִדַּלַּת in the singular.

The sign in Isa. xxxv. 10.—In Isa. xxxv. 10 we have יַשִּׂיגוּ וְנָסוּ *they shall obtain and rejoice*, whilst in Isa. li. 11 it is יַשִּׂיגוּן נָסוּ *they shall obtain, they shall rejoice*, and the sign thereof is "*Two Vavs, two Nuns*," that is, in the first instance there are two *Vavs* together [*i.e.*, the last letter is ישינו, and the first ונסו], and in the second instance two *Nuns* meet together [*i.e.*, the last letter of ישינון, which is *Nun*, and and the first of נסו which is also *Nun*].

The sign in Ezek. xviii. 6.—In the whole of this section אָכַל *he ate*, is entirely with *Kametz* [viz., Ezek. xviii. 6, 15], except in verse 11, where it is אָכַל, half with *Kametz* and half with *Pattach*, and the sign thereof is, "*he who does not eat* [דלא אכל קמץ], *shuts his mouth;*" that is, whenever אכל is connected with לא, it is with *Kametz*.[48] In the twenty-four sacred books which have here been printed, this Massoretic remark is put into the book of Genesis on the words "in the sweat of thy brow thou shalt eat," [iii. 19], but this is an egregious blunder, and the editor did not understand it.

---

[48] It is to be remarked, that this mnemonical sign is based upon the double meaning of קמץ, which denotes both the vowel-sign *Kametz* and *to shut*, as well as upon the fact, that when אכל *to eat* is connected with לא not it has *Kametz*. Hence the play upon the words דלא אכל קמץ פומיה, when אכל and לא are together it is *Kametz*, or, *whoso does not eat, shuts his mouth*.

אלה הם הסימנים שראיתי לכתבם פה, | These are the signs which I deemed desirable to explain here, and the enquirer will doubtless discover many more; but I am tired of looking any more for them, and herewith concludes this book.
ובלי ספק המחפש ימצא יותר מאלה, ואני נלאתי לבקש עוד ; ובזה נשלם הספר מבל וכל, ישתבח אשר כל יכול :

Praised be He, above all, who is able to do all things!

והנה טרם אכלה לדבר.   שירה חדשה אחבר :

אתן לאלי יה הלל והודיה,   יען אשר היה אתי בעזרתי ;
הואל והורני דעה הבינני,   עד כי למסרת באור הכינותי ;
מה הוא בחנם לי גם כן אני חנם, אורה לכל אדם מיעוט ידיעתי ;
תרתי בכל לבי למצא דבר חפץ,   תאמין אמת כי יגעתי ומצאתי ;
מפי ספרים קבלתי ולא מפי,   סופרים ולא חבר היה בחברתי ;
חשכת אפלתה לאור הפכתיה,   נוע כככברה אותה הניעותי ;
דברי חכמיה סוד וחידותם,   מי ימצאם אם לא יחרוש בעגלתי ;

I SHALL COMPOSE A NEW SONG.   NOW BEFORE I FINISH TO SPEAK,

I give to my God praise and thanks,[49] because he was with me as my help.

He deigned to teach me knowledge; so much so, that I composed an explanation of the Massorah.

As He gave it to me freely; I also freely teach every man my scanty knowledge.

I have searched with all my heart to discover the right thing. Thou mayest believe that having laboured I found the truth.

I have received assistance from books, but not orally; nor had I any fellow labourer in my work.

I converted the obscurity [of the Massorah] into light; I have shaken it as in a sieve.

The words of the wise [in the Massorah], their secrets, and enigmas; who can find them unless he ploughs with my heifer?

---

[49] It will be seen, that the initials of the first line in the Hebrew are the acrostic of אליהו *Elias*, the author's name.

אמנם השניתי כי אין אנוש שלא,	יחטא הלא אתי תלין משוגתי;
אחלי שגיאות מי יבין וידעם,	יתקון לפי שכלו עוות שגיאותי;
האל אלהים הוא ידע וישראל,	ידע אשר לא עשיתי בגאוותי;
אף לא להראות את יקר גדולתי,	כי אם לבקשת אנשי סגולתי;
גם בעוונותי בני יצאוני,	אין מי שמי יזכור עוד אחרי מותי;
די לי אשר ספרי יחיה ולא ימות,	ידביב שפתי עת אישן בקברתי;
לכן לכה ספרי ופשוט בתוך תבל,	הראה לכל משכיל מעשה גבורתי;
ולושואלים אותך יד מי הכינתך,	תאמר ידי אליה כוננו אותי;
בן איש אשר אשר לוי שמו נקרא,	הוא אשכנזי איש חיל ואפרתי;
נגמר שנת יפר״ח תוך פרשת קרח, פה עיר ווינסיה רבתי ושרתי;	

נשלמה השירה   וכל הסםר עד גמירא׃

Forsooth I have committed errors, for there is no man who does not err, so that my error cleaves to me.

I pray, therefore, that whoever understands and knows them, may correct my errors according to his wisdom.

The Lord God knows, and also Israel may know, that I have not done this proudly;

Nor to show thereby my greatness, but simply yielded to the request of my special friends.

Moreover, on account of my sin, I lost my sons: there is none left to perpetuate my house after my death.

It is enough for me that my book will live and not die; it will speak when I sleep in the grave.

Therefore go forth, my book, circulate thyself through the world; show to every wise man the work of my strength.

To those who ask who made thee, say, The hand of Elias made me.

The son of a man who is called Asher Levi, a German, a man of valour and distinction.

It was finished in the year 298 [= 1588], in the week of the Pericope Korah, here in this city, the great and celebrated Venice.

THUS THE SONG IS BROUGHT TO AN END, AND THE BOOK TO ITS COMPLETION.

| THAT YOU MAY KNOW HOW MANY TIMES EACH LETTER OCCURS IN THE BIBLE, READ ALL THE WORDS IN THIS POEM. | לדעת מנין כל אות ואות, אשר בכל המקרא נמצאות, תקרא את כל דברי השירה הזאת: |

I have now come to fulfil my promise which I made in the Third Introduction, towards the end of it [*vide supra*, p. 186]. I there stated that, at the end of this book, I would give and explain the Poem which was written, to show the number of all the letters, as well as the number of each individual letter; that is, how many *Alephs*, how many *Beths*, how many *Gimmels*, &c., are to be found throughout the Bible. It is said that R. Saadia Gaon is the author of it; and this statement seems to be correct, since we find therein very difficult and foreign words, which are not of Hebrew origin, and the like of which are also to be found in the Treatise, entitled, *Faith and Philosophy*, which he of blessed memory wrote.[1]

Now the number of the stanzas in this Poem corresponds to the number of the letters in the alphabet. Thus, each stanza propounds the number of one letter, and is made in the form of a complete poem, each stanza being divided into four lines, but it is not written in even metres. Let me now explain it.

---

[1] Saadia's philosophical work, to which Levita refers, has already been described (*vide supra*, p. 136). That Levita most emphatically believed Saadia to have been the author of this poem, is not only evident from the above remark, but is placed beyond the shadow of a doubt, by his epilogue to it (*vide infra*, p. 278). We are, therefore, surprised at the remark of the learned Dukes, that "Elias Levita does not say expressly that R. Saadia was the author of it, but merely quotes it as a common opinion, with which he agrees" (*Berträge zur Geschichte der aeltesten Auslegung und Spracherklärung des Alten Testamentes*, vol. ii., p. 101, &c.; Stuttgart, 1844). It is now, however, almost certain that Saadia b. Joseph Bechor Shor, who flourished in France towards the end of the twelfth century, was the author of this poem, which was first published by Levita in the *editio princeps* of the *Massoreth Ha-Massoreth*, Venice, 1538. It is omitted both in the Basel (1539) and the Sulzbach (1771) editions. It was reprinted in the *Theological Decisions of the Gaonim* (שאלות ותשובות הגאונים), Prague, circa 1590; by our countryman Hugh Broughton, in his work, entitled, *Daniel, his Chaldee Vision, and his Hebrew*, &c., at the end of chap. ix., London, 1597; by Buxtorf, in his *Tiberias*, cap. xviii., p. 183, &c., Basel, 1620; in the Compilation, entitled, *Taalamoth Chochma* (תעלומות חכמה), Basel, 1629-1631; by Anshel Worms, in his *Sejag La-Thora* (סיג לתורה), Frankfort-on-the-Maine, 1766; in *Likute Ha-Shas* (לקוטי הש״ס), Koretz, 1784; by Jehudah b. Jacob, Dyherenforth, 1821; and by Fürst, in his *Hebrew Concordance*, p. 1379, Leipzig, 1840.

Mark that the number of each letter is indicated by the initials of the first two lines. Those in the first line signify thousands, and those in the second line denote the remaining numerals — that is, hundreds, tens, and units ; and in the third line he quotes one word, which indicates the verse he places under this line ; and so, also, in the fourth line he quotes one word from another verse, which he places again under this line, in such a manner, that he brings two verses under each stanza. Now in adding up the number of the two verses, you will thus obtain the number of the letter in question with which the stanza commences. You must not, however, include in this sum the numerical value of the first letter, for this simply indicates the letter under consideration, whether it be *Aleph*, *Beth*, or *Gimmel*, &c.

Thus, for example, in the first stanza commencing אהל מכון בניני *the Tabernacle, my established edifice*, the *Aleph* in אהל indicates the letter *Aleph*, whilst the initials of מכון בניני yield מ״ב = 42, which denote 42,000. In the second line, again, beginning ששם עלו זקני *whither my elders resort*, the initials are שע״ז = 377, and thus we obtain the number of the *Alephs* as 42,377. The same is the case with all the letters. As to the third line, beginning with הקהל *the congregation*, the fourth line, beginning with ולזבח *and for a sacrifice*, &c., they indicate the thirty-two verses, which are respectively placed under each stanza in smaller characters and without points, and in which the number in question occurs. Thus, the first, "all the congregation together was forty thousand," &c. [Ezra ii. 6] ; and the second, "and for a sacrifice of peace-offering, two oxen," &c. [Numb. vii. 17] ; when the number of these two verses is added up, we obtain the sum total of 42,377. The same is the case with each letter.

Moreover, it is necessary to notice, that whenever you find in a stanza two words ranged together, the initials of which denote tens, and the first of the letters is *Mem*, *Nun*, *Tzaddi*, *Pe*, or *Kaph*, it is used in

דע כי מספר כל אות ואות נרשם בראשי תיבות של ב' חלקים הראשונים, מה שבחלק הראשון נכללו האלפים, ובחלק השני נכלל שאר המספר, רוצה לומר המאיות והעשיריות והאחרים, ובחלק השלישי מביא מלה אחת המורה על הפסוק אשר הוא מביא תחת החלק ההוא, וכן בחלק הרביעי הוא מביא מלה אחת מהפסוק אשר הוא מביא תחת החלק ההוא באופן שתחת כל בית בית יביא ב' פסוקים, ובהתחבר מספר ב' הפסוקים ככה מספר האות שבתחילת הבית; אך לא רשים במספר ההוא מספר אות תיבה הראשונה, כי היא מורה על האות המבוקש, אם א', או ב', או ג', וכן כלן :

והמשל הבית הראשון מתחיל "אהל מכון "בניני, האל"ף של אהל תורה על אות האל"ף, וראשי תיבות של מכון בניני עולים מ״ב, הרי מ״ב אלפים ; והחלק השני מתחיל "ששם "עלו "זקני, ראשי תיבות שע״ז, וככה מספר האל"ף מ״ב אלפים שע״ז, וכן כל אות ואות ; והחלק השלישי המתחיל הקהל, והחלק הרביעי מתחיל ולזבח, הם סימנים ל״ב הפסוקים הנכתבים תחת כל בית ובית בכתיבה דקה בלי נקוד אשר נמצא בהם המספר הנ״ל : האחד כל הקהל כאחד ארבע רבוא וגו', והב' ולזבה השלמים בקר שנים ונומר, הנה כשיתחברו מספר שני הפסוקים יחד עולה מספרם מ״ב אלפים שע״ז, וכן נעשה כל אות ואות :

וצריך שתדע כי כאשר תמצא באיזה בית שתי תיבות מצורפות, וראשיהם עשיריות, והראשונה מאותיות מנצ״פך, אז היא תשמש

the manner in which the final *Mem, Nun, Tzaddi, Pe,* and *Kaph* are employed, and the value of which I have already explained in the above-named Introduction [*vide supra*, 136]; that is, final *Kaph* denotes 500, final *Mem* 600, final *Nun* 700, final *Pe* 800, final *Tzaddi* 900. Thus, for instance, in the fourth stanza, commencing דהר *powerful*, &c., where you find כתשועתם לעילם *like the salvation at Elam*, you must observe that the *Kaph* in כתשועתם is employed, according to the value of final *Mem, Nun, Tzaddi, Pe,* and *Kaph*, and denotes 500; whilst the *Lamed* in לעילם signified 30, as usual. The same is the case with the fifth stanza, beginning הלום *hither*, &c., where there are two *Nuns* following each other, viz., נקבנו נטעי; the first denotes 700, and the second signifies 50, as usual. This method obtains throughout. Hence, wherever one of these letters is used in this signification, you find in the middle margin one of the final letters *Mem, Nun, Tzaddi, Pe,* and *Kaph* with a circle over it, as follows :—ךֹ םֹ ןֹ ףֹ ץֹ. Examine, and you will find it so.

על דרך שישמש מנצ״פך, כמו שבארתי
מספרם בהקדמה הנ״ל, דהיינו ך מספש ת״ק,
ם ר״ד, ן ת״ש, ף ת״ת, ץ תת״ק; והמשל
בחרוז הד׳ המרחיל דהר וכולי, תמצא
״כתשועתם״לעילם תידע כי כ״פ כתשועתם
תשמש על דרך מנצ״פך, והיא ת״ק, ולמ״ד
לעילם תשמש שלשים כמשפטה; וכן בחרוז
הה׳ המתחיל הלום וכולי, יש בו ב׳ נוני״ן
רצופין, וחן ״נקבצו ״נטעי, הראשונה תשמש
ת״ש, והשניה חמשים כמשפטה, וכן כלם בזה
הדרך; לכן בכל מקום שאחת מחן תשמש
השמוש הזה, תמצא באמצע בנליון אחת
מאותיות מנצ״פך הפשומות עם עינול אחד
עליה כוח ךֹ, םֹ, ןֹ, פֹ, ץֹ, דוק ותמצא:

ובכן אתחיל החרוזה
בענינים אלה רמוזה:

And now I shall begin the Poem [2]
Which propounds these things.

[3] אֹהֶל מָכוֹן בְּנִינִי
הַקָּהָל עָשׂוּ קָרְבָּנִי

שֵׁשָּׁם עָלוּ זְקֵנִי
וּלְזֶבַח הַתּוֹדָה בָּאוּ בָּנִי

כל הקהל כאחד ארבע רבוא אלפים שלש
מאות וששים (נחמי׳ ז׳ ס״ו)

ולובח השלמים בקר שנים אילם חמשה
עתודים חמשה כבשים בני שנה חמשה
(במדבר ז׳ י״ז)

---

[2] We at first intended to give, with the Hebrew original, an English version of this poem; but, after translating half of it, we found that the peculiar construction of it, the way in which the Biblical words are therein used, and, in fact, the whole plan adopted by the writer to make it at all intelligible to the reader, would require a commentary at least three times the size of the poem itself. We have, therefore, abandoned our original intention, and simply subjoin an explanation of each stanza.

[3] א *Aleph*, occurs 42,377 times in the Hebrew Scriptures. The *Aleph* in אהל, the first word of this stanza, gives the letter the number of which is here discussed, and the letters מכבט״ש = 42,377, being the initials of the remaining words in the first and second lines, give the number of times the letter in question occurs in the Bible. The same fact is also indicated by the passages adduced from Nehem. vii. 66, and Numb. vii. 17: as in the former the number 42,360 occurs, and in the latter 17; thus yielding together 42,377.

272

⁴ בָּנַי לֹא חוֹבְרִים
בִּנְיָמִין וּסְנָנִים דּוֹבְרִים

פקודיהם למטה בנימין חמשה ושלשים
אלף וארבע מאות (במדבר א' ל"ו)

וְנִמְתָם יַאַסְפוּ חֲבֵרִים
פַּחַת הַשְּׁנֵי נְבָרִים

בני פחת מואב לבני ישוע יואב אלפים
ושמנה מאות ושמנה עשר (נחמי' ז' י"א)

⁵ גְּבָרִים בְּעֶצֶם טֹהַר
כָּל־פְּקוּדֵי הַיִּצְהָר

כל פקודי הלוים אשר פקד משה ואהרן על
פי יהוה למשפחתם כל זכר מבן חדש ומעלה
שנים ועשרים אלף (במדבר ג' ל"ט)

דְּ בֶּן לָהֶם זֹהַר
מִלְּבַד הָרִאשׁוֹן דֹּהַר

מלבד עבדיהם ואמהתיהם אלח שבעת
אלפים שלש מאות שלשים ושבע משוררים
ומשוררות מאתים (עזרא ב' ס"ח)

⁶ הָהַר לָבוֹא בְשָׁלוֹם
וּמִן הַדָּנִי בַּבָּשָׁן וַהֲלֹם

ומן הדני עורכי מלחמה עשרים ושמנה
אלף ושש מאות (דה"א י"ב, לה)

הְ בִּתְשׁוּעָתָם לְעִילּוֹם
סְנָאָה יָשׁוּב עַמּוֹ הֲלוֹם

בני סנאה שלשת אלפים תשע מאות
ושלשים (נחמי' ז' ל"ח)

⁷ הֲלוֹם מִפְּלַל־זָוִיוֹת
רְאוּבֵן יִטְרֹף אֲרָיוֹת

פקודיהם למטה ראובן ששה וארבעים
אלף ושש מאות (במדבר א' כ"א)

וְ נִקְבְּצוּ נֹטְעֵי זָלִיּוֹת
עֵילָם וְאַשּׁוּר וּמַלְכָיוֹת

בני עילם אלף ומאתים חמשים וארבעה
(נחמי' ז' ל"ד)

⁸ וּמַלְכָיוֹת עֹצֶר וָפַחַת
יְהוּדָה נָא אַל תִּשָּׁחַת

פקודיהם למטה יהודה ארבעה ושבעים
אלף ושש מאות (במדבר א' כ"ז)

זְ צוּרֵנוּ בַּעֲשׂוֹתוֹ בְּחַת
עַזְגָּד שְׁנֵי וּבֶן זוֹחַת

בני עזגר אלפים ושלש מאות עשרים
ושנים (נחמי' ז' י"ז)

⁴ בּ *Beth*, occurs 38218 times. The *Beth* in בני, the first word in the stanza, indicates the letter under discussion, and the remaining initials of the first and second lines לח'ריח = 38,218, give the number of times the letter occurs in the Bible, which is also given in the two passages quoted under this stanza, viz., Numb. i. 37, and Nehem. vii. 11; since in the former the number 35,400 occurs, and in the latter 2,818 = 38,218.

⁵ ג *Gimmel*, occurs 29,537 times. The *Gimmel* in גברים gives the letter in question, and the remaining initials of the first two lines, viz., כפד לו = 29,537, indicate the sum total, which is stated still more explicitly in the numbers to be found in the two passages adduced, viz., Numb. iii. 39, and Ezra ii. 65, in which occur the numbers 22,000 and 7,337 = 29,537. It will be seen that the *Kaph* at the beginning of the second line is used in its final value, as explained above, *vide* p. 136, 270, &c.

⁶ ד *Daleth*, occurs 32,530 times. The *Daleth* in דהר, the first word in this stanza, shows the letter under discussion, and the initials of the remaining words of the two lines, viz., לב ד'ל = 32,530, give the sum total, which is also given in the numbers found in the two passages adduced, viz., 1 Chron. xii. 35, and Nehem. vii. 38, wherein are the numbers 28,600 and 3,930 = 32,530.

⁷ ה *He*, occurs 47,754 times. The *He* under discussion is indicated in הלום, the first word in this stanza, and the number is given in the initials of the remaining words of the first two lines viz., מזן'גד = 47,754, which is also given in the numbers found in the two passages quoted, viz., Numb. i. 21, and Nehem. vii. 37, wherein are the numbers 46,500 and 1,254 = 47,754.

⁸ ו *Vav*, occurs 76922 times. The *Vav* itself is indicated in ומלכיות, the first word

273

⁹ זֹוחַת בְּגַפֶּן בָּקוּק   פֵּרִי שָׂרִיגָיו זָקוּק
וּמִן בְּנֵי אֶפְרַיִם בַּחֲבַקּוּק   בִּנְגֵי הַשֵּׁנִי חָקוּק

ומן בני אפרים עשרים אלף ושמונה מאות   בני בנוי אלפים ששים ושבעה
נבודי חיל (ר״ה א׳ י״ב, ל׳)   (נחמי׳ ז׳ י״ט)

¹⁰ חָקוּק בִּתְבוּאַת נָרָשׁ   תְּבוּסַת מְלַטֵּי זָרַשׁ
שִׁמְעוֹן שֵׁנִי יַד שׁוֹרֵשׁ   פַּשְׁחוּר לַעֲבוֹד טָרַשׁ

אלה משפחות השמעוני שנים ועשרים   בני פשחור אלף ומאתים ארבעה ושבעים
אלף ומאתים (במדבר כו׳, י״ד)   (עזרא ב׳ ל״ח)

¹¹ טָרַשׁ יְמַלְאוּ אֲסָמָיו   נְמִישׁוֹתָיו בְּתַחוּמָיו
חַיִּים לַמְסוֹךְ נְעִימָיו   אָמֵר לְהַרְבּוֹת יָמָיו:

ועשרת אלפים חיים שבּוֹ בני יהודה (דברי   בני אמר אלף חמשים ושנים (נחמי׳
הימים ב׳ כ״ח, י״ב)   ז׳ מ׳)

¹² יָמָיו שִׂמְחָה וְשָׂשׂוֹן   תּוֹלָלֵיהֶם בְּקִפְשׁוֹן
בְּלַחַם הָאָלוֹן חָסוֹן   חָרִם הָרִאשׁוֹן בְּמָסוֹן

זהב דרכמונים שש בבראות ואלף וסף   בני חרם שלש מאות ועשרים (נחמי׳
מנים חמשת אלפים וכתנות כהנים מאה   ז׳, ל״ה)
(עזרא ב׳, ס״ט)

of this stanza, and the number of times it occurs is given in the initials of the remaining words in the first two lines, viz., עץ׳כב = 76,922, which is also contained in the two passages from Numb. i. 27, and Nehem. vii. 17, viz., 47,600 and 2,322 = 76,922.

⁹ ז Zain, occurs 22867 times. The Zain itself is indicated in זוחת, the first word of this stanza, and the sum total is contained in the initials of the remaining letters of the first two lines, viz., כבס״סו = 22,867, as well as in the two passages from 1 Chron. xii. 30, and Nehem. vii. 19, viz., 20,803 and 2,067 = 22,867.

¹⁰ ח Cheth, occurs 23,447 times. The letter itself is indicated in חקוק, the first word of this stanza, whilst the number of times it occurs in the Bible is shown by the initials of the remaining letters of the first two lines, viz., כנת׳מז = 23,447. This is also stated in the two passages of Scripture adduced, viz., Numb. xxvi. 14, and Ezra ii. 38; in the first of which the number 22,200 occurs, and in the second 1247, = 23447.

¹¹ ט Teth, occurs 11,052 times. The letter itself is indicated in טרש, the first word in this stanza which begins with Teth, and the initials of the remaining letters in the first two lines, viz., יא׳נב = 11,052, give the number of times the letter in question occurs in the Bible. The number is also given in the passages of Scripture, 2 Chron. xxv. 12, and Nehem. vii. 40, adduced under this stanza, in the first of which we have 10,000, and in the second 1,052, = 11,052.

¹² י Jod, occurs 66,420 times. The Jod is indicated by the first letter of ימי, the first word in this stanza, and the number of times is given in the initials of the remaining words in the first two lines, viz., שר׳חב = 66,420. This is also given in the two passages quoted under this stanza, viz., Ezra ii. 69, which contains the number 61,000 + 5,000 + 100 = 66,100, and Nehem. vii. 35, which contains the number 320, making in all 66,420.

N N

¹³ כְּמָסוֹן לֹא זְעוּכָה
וְהַבָּקָר לְעוֹלָה לִסְמִיכָה

וחבקר ששה ושלשים אלף ומכסם ליהוה
שנים ושבעים (במדבר ל"א, ל"ח)

רָבְצוּ עֲדָרִים בְּתוֹכָהּ
כַּרְמִי נַם לָאֵל אֵין כָּמוֹכָה:

כרמי שלי לפני האלף לך שלמה ומאתים
לנטרים את פריו (שיר השירים ח' י"ב)

¹⁴ כָּמוֹךְ יָחְדָּלוּן
חַיִּים כַּמֵּתִים יִדָּלוּן

ועשרת אלפים חיים שבו בני יהודה (ד"ה
ב', כ"ה, י"ב)

עֵץ צוּגַת פֶּסֶל אוּמְלָלוּן
סוּסֵיהֶם נָטָה לָלוּן:

סוסיהם שבע מאות ושלשים וששה פרדיחם
מאתים ארבעים וחמשה (עזרא ב' ס"ו)

¹⁵ לָלוּן מָלוֹן אוֹרֵחַ
אֶפְרַיִם דּוֹר אוֹרֵחַ

פקודיהם למטה אפרים ארבעים אלף
וחמש מאות (במדבר א' ל"ג)

ךְ בַּבֹּקֶר יָאִיר זָרַח
חָרָם שֵׁנִי לוֹ לְהָסִיד מְטוֹרָח:

בני חרם אלף שבעה עשר (נחמי' ו' מ"ב)

¹⁶ מְטוֹרָח נָשְׂאוּ בֵּיתָם
גַּד נָצָבִים לַנְּחוֹתָם

פקודיהם למטה גד חמשה וארבעים אלף
ושש מאות וחמשים (במדבר א', כ"ה)

ףְ פֵּירוֹתָם הִתְמַהְמָהוּלָתָם
גְּמַלֵּיהֶם לָבוֹא מִשְׁכְּנוֹתָם:

גמליהם ארבע מאות שלשים וחמשה
חמורים ששת אלפים שבע מאות ועשרים
(עזרא ב' ס"ז)

¹³ כ Kaph, occurs 37,272 times. The Kaph in כמסון, the first word of this stanza, gives the letter in question, and the remaining initials of the first two lines, viz., ולהעב = 37,272, give the number of times the letter occurs in the Bible, which is also stated in the two passages of Scripture adduced under this stanza, viz., Numb. xxxi. 38, containing the number 36,000 + 72 = 36,072, and Song of Songs viii. 12, containing the number 1,200, = 37,272.

¹⁴ ך Final Kaph, occurs 10,981 times. This is not only indicated by the first, but more especially the last letter in כמוך, the first word in this stanza, whilst the initials of the remaining words in the first two lines, viz., יש־א = 10,981, give the number of times the letter in question occurs in the Bible. This is also shown by the numbers occurring in the two passages quoted under this stanza, viz., 2 Chron. xxv. 12, where 10,000 occur, and Ezra ii. 66, where we have 736 + 245 = 981, yielding the sum total of 10,981.

¹⁵ ל Lamed, occurs 41,517 times. The Lamed is indicated by the first letter of ללון, the first word in this stanza, whilst the number is given in the initials of the remaining words in the first two lines, viz., מאד׳ר = 41,517. This is also shown in the numbers of the two passages quoted under this stanza, viz., Numb. i. 33, where the number 40,500 occurs, and Nehem. vii. 42, where we have 1,017 = 41,517.

¹⁶ מ Mem, occurs 52,805 times. The Mem is indicated by the first letter of מטורח, the first word of this stanza, and the number of times it occurs in the Bible is shown by the initials of the remaining words of the first two lines, viz., נבנד = 52,805. This is also indicated by the numbers occurring in two passages of Scripture adduced under this stanza, viz., Numb. i. 25, and Ezra ii. 67, whe ein occur the numbers 45,650 and 435 + 6,720 = 52,805.

¹⁷ מִשְׁכְּנוֹתָם כְּמוֹ דָּשָׁאוּ   ךְ צוֹפֵיהֶם עוֹד נָאוּ
הַמֵּתִים לְפִינְחָס נִבְרָאוּ   לְבֵית יֵשׁוּעַ כִּי נִבְאָג:

ויחיו המתים במנפה ארבעה ועשרים אלף   חכמנים בני ידעיה לבית ישוע תשע מאות
(במדבר כ"ה, ט׳)   שבעים ושלשה (עזרא ב' ל"ו)

¹⁸ נִבְאוּ לִבְרָכוֹת בְּחֶשְׁבּוֹן   ךְ צְמָחֶיהָ עֲלֵי זַרְבּוֹן
מְנַשֶּׁה יָשָׁה עִצָּבוֹן   לַמֵּד בְּנִחוּמָיו נָבוֹן:

פקודיהם לממה מנשה שנים ושלשים אלף   ויחיו כל ימי למך שבע ושבעים שנה
ומאתים (במדבר א' ל"ח)   ושבע מאות שנה (בראשית ה' ל"א)

¹⁹ נָבוֹן חָכְמוֹתָיו   ן נָטוּ יוֹשֶׁר בִּירִתָיו
וַיִּהְיוּ עַל־פִּי דִבְרוֹתָיו   הַשְּׁעָרִים חָנוּ סְבִיבֹתָיו:

ויהיו פקידיהם שמנת אלפים וחמש מאות   בני השערים בני שלום בני אמר בני
ושמנים (במדבר ד' מ"ח)   מלמון בני עקוב בני חמטא בני שבי הכל
    מאה שלשים ותשעה (עזרא ב' מ"ב)

²⁰ סְבִיבֹתָיו יָבֹאוּ נְדוּדִים   ךְ בְּמֶרְכְּבוֹת פְּרוּדִים
בְּהַצּוֹתוֹ אֶת הַבּוֹנְדִים   וּמִקְצָת לְפָנָיו עוֹמְדִים:

בחצותו את ארם נהרים ואת ארם צובה   ומקצת ראשי האבות נתנו למלאכה וגו'
וישב יואב ויך את אדום בגיא מלח שנים   זהב לדרכמנים אלף מזרקות חמשים כתנות
עשר אלף (תהלים ס' ב')   כהנים שלשים וחמש מאות (נחמי' ז', ע')

¹⁷ ם *Final Mem*, occurs 24,978 times. The *Final Mem* is not only indicated by the first, but more especially by the last letter in משכנותם, the first word in this stanza which terminates in *Final Mem*. The initials of the remaining words in the first two lines, viz., כד׳עב = 24,978, state the number of times the latter occurs in the Bible, which is indicated still more explicitly in the numbers occurring in the two passages of Scripture adduced under this stanza, viz., Numb. xxv. 9, where we have the number 24,000, and Ezra ii. 36, where the number is 973 = 24,973.

¹⁸ נ *Nun*, occurs 32,977 times. The letter itself is indicated by נבאו, the first word in this stanza which begins with *Nun*, and the number of times it occurs in the Bible is shown by the initials of the remaining words of the first two lines, viz., לבץ׳עו = 32,977. This is also shown by the numbers in the two passages quoted under this stanza, viz., Numb. i. 35, where we have 32,200, and Gen. v. 31, where we have 777 = 32,977.

¹⁹ ן *Final Nun* occurs 8,719 times. The letter in question is not only indicated by the first letter in נבון, the first word in this stanza, but more especially by the last letter of the word, which is *Final Nun*. The initials of the remaining words in the first two lines, viz., חז׳ךמ = 8,719, as usual indicate the number of times the letter in question occurs in the Bible, which is also shown by the numbers to be found in the two passages of Scripture adduced under this stanza, viz., Numb. iv. 48, where the number 8,580 occurs, and Ezra ii. 42, where we have 139 = 8,719.

²⁰ ס *Samech*, occurs 13,580 times. As usual, the letter in question is indicated by the first letter in סביבותיו, the first word in this stanza, whilst the initials of the remaining words in the first two lines, viz., יבך׳ס = 13,580, show the number of times it occurs in the Bible, which is indicated still more plainly by the numbers in the two passages of Scripture cited under this stanza, viz., Ps. lx. 2, where we have 12,000, and Nehem. vii. 70, where we have 1,000 + 50 + 530 = 1580, making in all 13,580.

276

עוֹמְרִים בְּמַחְלְקוֹתֵיהֶם ²¹ קְצִינֵי עֵדָה הֵם
בְּאֹרֶךְ וְרֹחַב לָהֶם אַבְרָהָם לְזִכָּרוֹן בְּפִיהֶם:

והנותר בארך לעמת תרומת הקדש עשרת ואלה ימי שני חיי אברהם אשר חי
אלפים קדימה ועשרת אלפים ימה (יחזקאל שבעים שנה וחמש שנים מאת שנה
מ״ח, י״ח) (בראשית כ״ה, ז)

²² פִּיהֶם פָּעֳרָף פ׳ נִיבוֹ נִצְרָף
סָבִיב נִפְשָׁטָה וְנִטְרָף תַּחַת יְרִיעֹתָיו פָּרַף:

סביב שמנה עשר אלף (יחזקאל מ״ח ל״ה) ויהיו פקודיהם למשפחתם אלפים שבע
מאות וחמשים (במדבר ד׳, ל״ו)

²³ פָּרַף אֲרִינֶנּוּ ף׳ צֶדֶק עָנָה הֲגִינֶנּוּ
הָאֶלֶף וְצֶלַע נִיהֲגֶנּוּ לְעִתִּים יִדְרְכוּ צִינֶנּוּ:

ואת האלף ושבע המאות וחמשה ושבעים ומבני יששכר יודעי בינה לעתים לדעת
עשה ווים לעמודים (שמות ל״ח, כ״ח) מה יעשה ישראל ראשיהם מאתים וכל
אחיהם על פיהם (ד״ה א׳ י״ב, ל״ב)

²⁴ צִינֵנוּ יִצְנֹף וְיָצֵץ צ׳ צוֹרְרֵנוּ נְרַצֵץ
וְנֶפֶשׁ עוֹד לֹא יְקַצֵץ נַח סוֹפוֹ וְיָצֵץ צִיץ:

ונפש אדם שש עשר אלף (במדבר ויהיו כל ימי נח תשע מאות שנה וחמשים
ל״א, מ׳) שנה וימת (בראשית ט׳ כ״ט)

---

²¹ ע Ajin, occurs 20,175 times. The letter itself is indicated by the Ajin in עומרים, the first word of this stanza, whilst the initials of the remaining words in the first two lines, viz., בקע״ה = 20,175, show the number of times the letter in question occurs in the Bible. This is moreover shown by the numbers to be found in the two passages of Scripture adduced under this stanza, viz., Ezek. xlviii. 18, where we have 10,000 and 10,000, and Gen. xxv. 7, where the number is 175 = 20,175.

²² פ Pe, occurs 20,750 times. As usual, the letter in question is indicated by the Pe, the first letter in פיהם, the word with which the stanza begins, whilst the number of times the letter in question occurs is shown by the initials of the remaining words in the first two lines, viz., בכ״נ = 20,750. This number is also contained in the two passages of Scripture adduced under this stanza, viz., Ezek. xlviii. 35 and Numb. iv. 36, in the former of which the number is 18,000, and in the latter 2,750 = 20,750.

²³ ף Final Pe, occurs 1,975 times. The letter itself is not only indicated by the first letter in פורף, the word with which the stanza begins, but more especially by the last letter of this word, which is Final Pe. The initials of the remaining words in the first two lines, viz., אצי״עה = 1,975, give the number of times the letter in question occurs in the Bible, whilst the numbers in the two passages of Scripture, adduced under this stanza, show this still more explicitly, viz., Exod. xxxviii. 28, where the number 1,775 occurs, and 2 Chron. xii. 32, where the number is 200 = 1,975.

²⁴ צ Tzaddi, occurs 16,950 times. The letter itself is indicated by the Tzaddi in צינגו, the word with which the stanza begins; the initials of the remaining words in the first two lines, viz., יצי״ן = 16,950, show the number of times the word in question occurs in the Bible; and the two passages of Scripture adduced under this stanza, viz., Numb. xxxi. 40 and Gen. ix. 29, are made to state the same fact, inasmuch as the number 16,000 occurs in the first passage, and 950 occurs in the second, yielding together 16,950.

²⁵ **צִיץ** דֵּי פְרָקָיו | פָּז עָבַר בְּרַתּוּקָיו
תוֹצָאוֹת חֻקָּיו | שׁוֹפְטֶיהָ נָטָה קָו:

וְאֵלֶּה תוֹצְאֹת הָעִיר מִפְּאַת צָפוֹן חֲמֵשׁ מֵאוֹת | בְּנֵי שְׂפַטְיָה שְׁלֹשׁ מֵאוֹת שִׁבְעִים וּשְׁנָיִם
וְאַרְבַּעַת אֲלָפִים מִדָּה (יחזקאל מ״ח, ל) | (עזרא ב׳, ד׳)

²⁶ **קַו** בּוֹנֵן בְּעֶדְרֶף | צְבִי עֶדְיוֹ בְּנֶגֶף
וּמִן בְּנֵי אֶפְרַיִם צַר רוֹדֵף | פַּרְעֹשׁ בָּנָיו רוֹדֵף:

וּמִן בְּנֵי אֶפְרַיִם עֶשְׂרִים אֶלֶף וּשְׁמוֹנֶה מֵאוֹת | בְּנֵי פַרְעֹשׁ אַלְפַּיִם מֵאָה שִׁבְעִים וּשְׁנָיִם
(דברי הימים א׳, י״ב, ל) | (עזרא ב׳ ג׳)

²⁷ **רוֹדֵף** בְּרוּחַ בִּגְבוּרָה | קוֹל מַשְׁמִיעַ זִמְרָה
שִׁנְאָן הַגַּלְגַּל קָרָא | יַעֲקֹב כֵּן יֵטִיב שִׁירָה:

רֶכֶב אֱלֹהִים רִבֹּתַיִם אַלְפֵי שִׁנְאָן אֲדֹנָי בָם | וַיְחִי יַעֲקֹב בְּאֶרֶץ מִצְרַיִם שְׁבַע עֶשְׂרֵה שָׁנָה
סִינַי בַּקֹּדֶשׁ (תהלים ס״ח, י״ח) | וַיְהִי יְמֵי יַעֲקֹב שְׁנֵי חַיָּיו שֶׁבַע שָׁנִים וְאַרְבָּעִים
  | וּמְאַת שָׁנָה (בראשית מ״ז, כ״ח)

²⁸ **שִׁירָה** לְנַצֵּחַ בִּמְחוֹלוֹת | קְנוּיָה מוֹשִׁיעָה חוֹלוֹת
מִן הַנָּשִׁים נִתְעַלּוֹת | הַמְשׁוֹרְרִים עֹז תְּהִלּוֹת:

מִן הַנָּשִׁים אֲשֶׁר לֹא יָדְעוּ מִשְׁכַּב זָכָר כָּל | הַמְשׁוֹרְרִים בְּנֵי אָסָף מֵאָה אַרְבָּעִים וּשְׁמֹנָה
נֶפֶשׁ שְׁנַיִם וּשְׁלֹשִׁים אֶלֶף (במדבר ל״א, ל״ח) | (נחמי׳ ז׳ מ״ד)

²⁵ ץ *Final Tzaddi*, occurs 4,872 times. The letter is indicated both by the first, and especially by the last, letter in צִיץ, with which this stanza begins. The initials of the remaining words of the first two lines, viz.. רסף׳עב = 4,872, indicate the number of the times this letter occurs in the Bible; which is also shown by the numbers occurring in the two passages of Scripture adduced under this stanza, viz., Ezek. xlviii. 30 and Ezra ii. 4, in the former of which we have 4,500, and in the latter 372 = 4,872.

²⁶ ק *Koph*, occurs 22,972 times. The mnemonical sign for the letter in question is the *Koph* in the word קַו, with which this stanza begins, and the signs for the number of times it occurs in the Bible are both the initials of the remaining words in the first two lines, viz., כבנ׳עב = 22,972, and the sum total of the numbers contained in the two passages of Scripture adduced under this stanza, viz., 1 Chron. xii. 30, where we have 20,800, and Ezra ii. 3, where we have 2,172 = 22,972.

²⁷ ר *Resh*, occurs 22,147 times. The letter itself is indicated by the *Resh* in רודף, with which the stanza begins, and the number of times it occurs in the Bible is shown both by the initials of the remaining words of the first two lines, viz., כבק׳מז = 22,147, and by the numbers in the two passages of Scripture adduced under this stanza, viz., Ps. lxviii. 18, in which the number is 22,000, and Gen. xlvii. 28, where we find 147 = 22,147.

²⁸ ש *Shin*, occurs 32,148 times. The *Shin* itself is indicated by the first letter of שירה, which begins this stanza, and the number of times it occurs in the Bible is shown by the initials of the remaining words in the first two lines, viz., לב׳קמח = 32,148, as well as by the numbers in the two passages of Scripture adduced under this stanza, viz., Numb. xxxi. 35, where we find 32,000, and Nehem. vii. 44, where it is 148 = 32,148.

²⁹ תִּחִלָּה לְשָׂמוֹ וְתִפְאָרֶת
וּבֹקֶר פְּלִיל מְקֻטָּרֶת

קָמָה מְשׁוֹרֶרֶת
אִיּוֹב תַּמָּתוֹ תּוֹתָרֶת:

ובקר ששה ושלשים אלף (במדבר ל"א, מ"ד,)

ויחי איוב אחרי זאת מאה וארבעים שנה וירא את בניו ואת בני בניו ארבעה דורות (איוב מ"ב, ט"ז)

³⁰ תּוֹתָרַת עָבְדָהּ נָשָׁה
זָכָר הִמְלִיטָה כִּי חָשָׁה

רַעֲנָנָיו נָרְשָׁה
אָדָם הָאֶבֶן הָרֹאשָׁה:

ויהי כל כבוד וזבד במספר שמות מבן חדש ומעלה לפקדיהם שנים ועשרים אלף שלשה ושבעים ומאתים (במדבר ג' מ"נ)

ויהיו כל ימי אדם אשר חי תשע מאות שנה ושלשים שנה וימת (בראשית ח' ה')

סליק וסימנך כי זה כל האדם:

סליק

השיר נגמר אותו חבר·
אך חנהו גם ביארהו·
בה בשנה סימן לפרט·

הגאון מהר"ר סעדיה:
האיש הלוי אליה:
קטן הלוי אליה:

בנ"לך

²⁹ תּ Tav, occurs 36,140 times. The Tav itself is indicated by the first letter of תחלה, with which the stanza begins, and the number of times it occurs is shown by the initials of the remaining words in the first two lines, viz., לר׳קם = 36,140, as well as by the numbers occurring in the two passages of Scripture quoted under this stanza, viz., Numb. xxxi. 44, where we have 36,000, and Job xlii. 16, where it is 140 = 36,140.

³⁰ ת Tav without Dagesh, occurs 23,203 times. The letter in question is not only indicated by the first letter of תותרת, with which this stanza begins, but more especially by the last letter which is without Dagesh. The number of times it occurs in the Bible is shown by the initials of the remaining words in the first two lines, viz., בנ׳רץ = 23,203, as well as by the numbers contained in the two passages of Scripture adduced under this stanza, viz., Numb. iii. 43, where we have 22,277, and Gen. v. 5, where we have 930 = 23,203.

INDEX I.

MASSORETICALLY ANNOTATED PASSAGES OF SCRIPTURE REFERRED TO.

Chap.	Ver.	Page.	Chap.	Ver.	Page.	Chap.	Ver.	Page.
GENESIS.			viii.	10	245	xvii.	17	197
Chap.	Ver.	Page.	..	15	215	..	18	216
i.	1	124, 139, 142, 215, 230, 231	..	17	115, 118, 180, 251	..	19	166, 215
..	2	139	..	22	163	..	20	157
..	3	215	ix.	8	215	xviii.	6	174
..	4	139, 142, 209	..	10	213, 25	..	7	141, 218
..	5	140	..	11	166	..	11	242
..	6	141, 215	..	12	215	..	12	247
..	7	139, 142	..	17	166, 167, 215	..	15	252
..	9	215	..	21	179	..	20	205
..	11	215, 252	..	26	141	..	21	209
..	14	215, 221, 228	..	27	141	..	25	201, 207
..	15	140	..	29	276	..	29	245
..	18	221	x.	1	214, 236, 237	xix.	10	174
..	20	142, 215	..	3	263	..	12	163
..	21	157	..	8	148	..	14	219
..	24	215	..	9	148	..	16	239
..	26	215	..	10	197	..	22	151
..	29	215	..	19	115, 177	..	29	196
ii.	3	139	..	23	197	..	30	151
..	4	168, 231	..	29	157	..	36	177
..	6	165	..	30	177	..	37	216
..	15	239	xi.	31	174	..	38	216
..	21	177	xii.	5	174	xx.	3	154
..	22	219	..	7	237	..	6	140, 150, 170
..	23	206	..	8	179	..	14	252
iii.	6	197	..	10	174	..	15	201
..	11	208	..	11	174	..	16	236
..	17	154	..	14	174	xxi.	6	205
..	18	249	xiii.	3	179	..	8	197
..	22	149	..	5	220, 221	..	12	206, 215
iv.	2	205	..	10	177	..	15	197, 252
..	5	218	..	15	227	..	23	175
..	8	262	xiv.	2	115	xxii.	2	252
..	9	201	..	8	115	..	13	206
..	29	233	..	16	252	..	22	208
v.	1	168, 220	xv.	1	196	xxiii.	2	231
..	5	278	..	2	234	..	9	199
..	31	275	..	5	250	..	11	223
vi.	2	246	xvi.	4	197	..	15	223
..	3	149	..	7	178	..	18	236
..	10	219	..	12	200	xxiv.	3	246
..	13	215	xvii.	2	150	..	4	226
..	14–16	229	..	5	206	..	5	247
..	16	218	..	7	166	..	14	109, 115
..	18	166	..	9	215	..	16	109, 115
..	21	141	..	15	215	..	18	251
vii.	21	251				..	23	132, 247

Chap.	Ver.	Page.	Chap.	Ver.	Page.	Chap.	Ver.	Page.
\multicolumn{3}{l	}{GENESIS.}	xxxiii.	8	197	xliii.	11	200
xxiv.	25	247	..	13	213	..	14	208
..	28	109, 115	..	20	215	..	16	174
..	30	158	xxxiv.	8	109, 116	..	23	250
..	32	174	..	12	109, 116	..	26	174
..	33	116, 118, 187	..	25	197	..	28	116, 117
..	46	251	..	26	207	..	33	207
..	47	258	..	31	230	xliv.	17	242
..	53	250	xxxv.	1	215	..	18	170
..	55	109, 116	..	10	206	..	20	241
..	57	109, 116	..	17	219	..	29	170
..	67	174	..	20	155, 216	xlv.	4	174
xxv.	1	245	..	21	179	..	17	174
..	6	158	..	22	242	..	12	198
..	7	276	..	23	116, 212, 213	..	16	166
..	12	168	xxxvi.	1	168	..	22	200
..	16	157, 208, 209	..	5	116	xlvi.	2	215
..	18	177, 207	..	9	168	..	3	174
..	19	168	..	14	116	..	4	174
..	21	178	..	15	116	..	7	174
..	23	118, 187	..	21	264	..	8	174
..	31	178	..	24	158	..	9	174, 213
xxvi.	2	174	..	30	263	..	12	225
..	3	156, 166	xxxvii.	2	168	..	22	226
..	10	252	..	4	148	..	26	174
..	12	240	..	10	218	..	27	174
..	19	168	..	11	198	xlvii.	11	205
..	26	248	..	25	167, 174	..	18	208
xxvii.	2	197	..		208, 222	..	27	170, 207
..	3	116	..	27	161	..	28	242, 277
..	7	176, 234	..	28	174	..	30	161
..	22	166	xxxviii.	1	237	xlviii.	4	176
..	24	217	..	9	208	..	5	174
..	29	116, 117, 221	..	18	149	..	9	197
..	31	154	..	25	149	..	21	251
..	35	162	xxxix.	1	174	..	22	252
..	37	213	..	6	151	xlix.	11	116
..	46	231	..	9	150	..	12	230
xxviii.	10	197, 242	..	11	174	..	13	226
xxix.	21	205	..	20	116, 118, 249	..	21	154
xxx.	1	205	..	22	116	..	27	197
..	11	116, 193	xl.	5	200	..	28	150
..	21	197	..	10	159	..	29	150
..	26	196	..	12	159	l.	13	174, 226
..	34	161	..	13	163, 175	..	14	174
..	37	196, 223	..	14	178	..	21	150
..	40	226	..	17	197	..	23	230
..	42	154, 230	..	19	150			
xxxi.	3	251	..	21	252	\multicolumn{3}{l}{EXODUS.}		
..	10	154	xli.	1	242	i.	1	174
..	13	197	..	8	150, 151, 152	..	3	212, 213
..	18	174	..	11	200	..	16	264
..	32	216	..	15	241	..	19	177
..	35	163	..	20	148	ii.	2	230
..	49	223	..	25	223	..	3	178, 229
xxxii.	13	160	..	28	223	..	5	148, 167, 229
..	15	158, 212	..	33	205	..	7	160
..	21	220	..	35	207	..	10	222
..	23	252	..	38	139	..	12	220
..	26	235, 236	..	39	150	..	16	177
xxxiii.	4	116, 163	..	40	217	..	20	223
		182, 183	..	57	174	iii.	13	169
..	5	208	xlii.	29	174	..	14	215
..	6	177	xliii.	6	200	..	15	149, 164

Chap.	Ver.	Page.	Chap.	Ver.	Page.	Chap.	Ver.	Page.
iii.	17	233	xv.	2	222	xxviii.	12	148
..	22	221	..	11	177	..	20	213
iv.	2	116, 193	..	14	249	..	23	175
..	7	252	..	18	149	..	28	116, 207
..	8	166	..	19	252	..	29	148
..	11	200	xvi.	2	116, 118	..	30	175
..	12	205	..	7	116	..	36	149, 230
..	16	218	..	8	220	..	40	221
..	19	154, 164	..	12	255	xxix.	3	150, 175
..	21	174	..	13	116	..	6	175
..	26	222	..	23	214, 238	..	13	174
..	29	233	xvii.	12	213	..	17	175
v.	1	216	xviii.	1	259	..	18	174, 214
..	7	171	..	5	259	..	25	174
..	23	221	..	7	174	..	31	147
vi.	2	215	..	19	141	..	34	141
..	3	218	..	21	224	xxx.	9	213
..	4	166, 167	..	25	224	..	16	175
..	5	158	xix.	8	252	..	18	175
..	11	202	..	13	216	..	32	247
..	13	140, 218	..	16	166	xxxi.	3	139
..	18	228	..	17	250	..	17	139, 149
..	24	171	xx.	1	215	xxxii.	4	206
vii.	2	217	..	6	140	..	10	150
..	12	157	..	11	139, 233	..	13	149
..	29	176, 177	..	13	232	..	17	116, 178
viii.	5	237	..	15	232	..	19	116
..	10	207	..	16	232	..	25	231
..	18	246	xxi.	3	241	..	27	216
..	19	154	..	6	149	xxxiii.	8	174
ix.	15	150	..	8	116	..	9	174
..	16	217	..	10	178	..	13	162
..	18	178	..	27	132	..	22	220
..	19	174	..	28	141	xxxiv.	7	151, 230
..	22	141	xxii.	4	116	..	14	230
..	27	213	..	22	196	..	26	231
..	34	245	..	26	116	xxxv.	11	116
x.	1	205	..	29	223	..	31	139
..	2	217	..	30	154	xxxvi.	6	242
..	9	161	xxiii.	2	95, 164	..	14	216
..	12	220	..	8	157	..	17	214
..	18	264	..	13	226	..	19	216
..	21	151	xxiv.	1	218	xxxvii.	8	116
..	28	205	..	5	128	..	16	196
xi.	8	230	..	10	215	xxxviii.	12	155
xii.	16	141	..	14	218	..	17	155
..	22	218	xxv.	9	150	..	25	213
..	30	245	..	16	175	..	28	276
..	34	155	..	18	155	xxxix.	3	224, 230
..	37	173	..	20	237	..	4	116
..	42	155	..	21	175, 218	..	14	149
..	46	141	..	22	150	..	21	116, 207
..	46	199	..	26	175	..	33	116
xiii.	3	141	..	29	196	xl.	4	205
..	7	141	..	30	175	..	7	175
..	11	116	xxvi.	1	151	..	8	175
..	16	176, 177, 234	..	7	216			
..	17	174	..	14	216	Leviticus.		
xiv.	7	159	..	16	237	i.	1	196, 231
..	9	150	..	34	175	..	9	174
..	13	226	xxvii.	7	206	..	13	174
..	16	141, 255	..	10	155	..	15	174
..	17	141, 255	..	11	116, 155, 183	..	17	174
..	19–21	219	xxviii.	11	149	ii.	2	174

282

LEVITICUS.			Chap.	Ver.	Page.	Chap.	Ver.	Page.
Chap.	Ver.	Page.	xiv.	20	174	xxii.	23	218
ii.	9	174	..	33	140	..	30	141, 255
..	15	175	..	51	150	..	31	255
iii.	5	174	xv.	1	140	..	33	255
..	11	174	..	10	150	xxiii.	13	116
..	16	174	..	13	205	..	17	171
iv.	19	174	..	29	150, 205	..	21	214
..	26	174, 207	xvi.	6	214	..	22	255
..	31	174	..	8	149	..	24	236
..	35	174	..	14	217	..	28	155
v.	1	163	..	15	217	..	43	150, 255
..	12	174	..	20	247	xxiv.	5	205
vi.	2	231	..	21	116, 247	..	6	150
..	8	225	..	25	174	..	7	175
..	9	147	xvii.	4	200	..	9	147
..	18	241	..	5	150	..	12	239, 240
..	19	147	..	13	141	..	13	180
..	20	147	xviii.	1	255	xxv.	17	255
vii.	5	174	..	2	255	..	22	255
..	6	141	..	4	241, 255	..	23	247
..	9	206	..	5	255	..	25	247
..	15	141	..	6	255	..	27	200
..	16	141	..	20	218	..	30	116, 247
..	18	141	..	21	255	..	35	247
..	19	141	..	23	178	..	39	247
..	21	200	..	25	157	..	44	213
..	31	174	..	27	260	..	46	149
..	36	226	..	28	157	..	55	150, 255
..	38	226	..	30	255	xxvi.	1	213, 255
viii.	2	158	xix.	2	255	..	2	206, 255
..	8	135	..	3	214, 238	..	9	166
..	16	174			241, 255	..	25	261
..	21	174	..	4	255	..	43	241
..	28	174	..	6	141	..	44	239
ix.	10	174	..	7	141	..	45	255
..	12	159	..	10	255	xxvii.	9	225
..	14	174	..	12	255	..	10	200, 201
..	18	159	..	14	217, 255	..	26	200
..	20	174	..	15	255	..	30	204
..	22	116, 163, 213	..	18	255	..	32	204
x.	1	196	..	23	141			
..	2	150	..	25	255	NUMBERS.		
..	16	135	..	28	255	i.	16	116, 118, 187
xi.	1	140	..	30	255	..	21	272
..	19	212, 214	..	31	255	.	25	274
..	21	116	..	32	255	..	27	273
..	34	141	..	32	255	..	33	274
..	37	208, 209	..	34	255	..	37	272
..	41	141	..	37	255	..	39	272
..	42	135, 196,	xx.	4	203	..	50	180
		230, 232	..	7	255	ii.	1	140
..	43	170	..	15	200	iii.	9	159
..	44	255	..	16	178	..	15	147
xii.	4	264	..	25	214, 251	..	19	228
..	5	199	..	26	159	..	40	147
..	8	214	xxi.	2	214, 241	..	51	116
xiii.	1	140	..	5	116, 179, 188	iv.	1	140
..	2	252	..	7	147	..	12	150
..	3	206	..	8	147	..	17	140
..	4	178, 223	..	12	255	..	19	150
..	10	206	xxii.	2	158, 207, 255	..	23	150
..	20	178, 223, 237	..	3	255	..	28	275
..	33	135, 230	..	8	255	..	36	276
..	51	236	..	16	150	..	43	278

Chap.	Ver.	Page.	Chap.	Ver.	Page.	Chap.	Ver.	Page.
iv.	49	150, 226	xv.	41	. 255	xxxi.	38	. 274
v.	4	. 150	..	31	. 178	..	40	. 276
..	8	. 200	..	41	. 170	..	44	. 278
..	21	. 150	xvi.	9	. 215	xxxii.	1	. 247
..	26	. 174	..	11	. 116	..	3	. 213
vi.	5	147, 158, 223	..	15	. 252	..	7	116, 119
..	8	. 147	..	17	213, 218	..	17	. 170
..	20	. 150	..	20	. 140	..	24	. 171
..	24	. 216	xvii.	4	. 155	..	37	. 172
vii.	1	. 159	..	17	. 160	xxxiii.	8	. 226
..	3	. 150	..	20	. 156	..	42	. 237
..	5	. 150	..	23	250, 251	xxxiv.	4	. 116
..	6	. 150	..	24	. 250	xxxv.	2	. 221
..	10	. 157	xviii.	24	. 204	..	4	. 221
..	14	. 232	..	23	. 227	..	9	. 275
..	17	. 271	..	26	. 218	..	10	. 174
..	19	. 159	xix.	1	. 140	..	7	. 236
..	20	. 232	xx.	15	. 174	xxxvi.	3	149, 221
..	26	. 232	..	17	. 200	..	6	. 200
..	32	. 232	xxi.	4	. 259			
..	38	. 232	..	5	205, 245	**Deuteronomy.**		
..	44	. 232	..	20	. 221	i.	2	. 252
..	50	. 232	..	22	. 200	..	11	160, 169
..	56	. 232	..	32	116, 118	..	13	. 157
..	62	. 232	xxii.	2	. 245	..	15	. 224
..	68	. 232	..	12	. 215	..	16	. 224
..	74	. 232	..	15	. 245	ii.	1	. 237
..	80	. 232	..	22	. 263	..	8	. 242
viii.	1	. 170	..	25	. 245	..	14	. 164
..	7	. 196	..	26	. 245	..	33	116, 230
..	16	. 160	..	33	150, 177	iii.	6	. 150
ix.	2	. 248	xxiii.	1	. 158	..	11	. 230
..	15	. 216	..	3	. 206	..	13	. 206
x.	3	. 196	..	7	. 263	..	17	. 213
..	10	. 255	..	9	197, 221	..	21	. 160
..	36	. 116	..	24	. 197	..	26	. 205
xi.	4	171, 185	xxiv.	2	. 139	..	28	. 150
..	11	140, 170	..	5	. 230	iv.	11	. 237
..	12	. 222	..	6	. 207	..	26	. 139
..	20	. 172	..	23	. 216	..	32	. 139
..	25	. 171	xxv.	4	. 150	..	40	. 217
..	26	. 174	..	12	. 231	v.	45	. 237
..	32	116, 233	..	17	. 150	..	10	116, 232
..	33	. 242	..	19	. 242	..	14	. 176
xii.	3	116, 163, 183	xxvi.	8	. 226	..	16	154, 233
..	12	. 207	..	9	116, 119	..	18	. 225
..	16	. 170	..	14	. 273	..	19	. 242
xiii.	1	. 170	xxvii.	2	157, 217	..	26	. 149
..	2	. 207	..	5	. 230	vi.	2	154, 217, 233
..	9	. 172	..	13	. 205	..	4	. 230
..	21	. 207	..	15	. 215	..	9	. 95
..	22	225, 260	..	21	. 217	..	13	228, 229
..	28	. 260	xxviii.	6	. 154	..	17	. 236
..	30	. 230	..	17	. 141	..	18	. 214
xiv.	3	. 174	xxix.	19	. 265	vii.	9	. 116
..	4	. 174	..	31	. 265	..	12	. 170
..	15	. 176	..	33	212, 265	..	19	. 213
..	17	. 230	xxx.	9	. 150	viii.	2	. 116
..	20	. 161	xxxi.	12	. 218	..	3	. 216
..	25	. 213	..	18	. 236	..	8	. 182
..	26	. 140	..	22	. 214	..	14	. 236
..	36	116, 119	..	24	. 231	ix.	2	. 218
xv.	14	. 237	..	27	205, 261	..	5	. 217
..	24	140, 170	..	35	. 277	..	14	. 150

Chap.	Ver.	Page.	Chap.	Ver.	Page.	Chap.	Ver.	Page.
DEUTERONOMY.			xxiv.	10	171	iii.	16	116, 189
Chap.	Ver.	Page.	xxv.	5	173, 252	..	17	255
ix.	22	158	..	9	200	iv.	1	262
..	24	231	..	19	128	..	8	239, 240
..	27	218	xxvi.	5	174	..	18	116, 188
..	28	150	..	8	213	v.	1	116
x.	5	202	..	16	150	..	12	242
..	11	141, 255	..	19	147	..	15	116
..	15	150	xxvii.	8	122	vi.	5	188, 116
..	17	148	..	10	116	..	7	116, 117
..	20	229	..	12	213	..	9	116, 232
..	22	174	..	13	225	..	13	116, 191
xi.	9	217	..	26	150	..	15	116
..	10	205	xxviii.	27	109, 116, 194	vii.	7	196
..	12	140, 170	..	30	116, 194	..	10	154, 164
..	13	121	..	31	155	..	21	116, 118
..	13–21	95	..	39	151	..	22	174
..	20	159	..	46	227	..	24	255
..	24	247	..	51	214	viii.	11	183, 116
..	25	170	..	52	196	..	12	116
xii.	4	152	..	53	162	..	15	255
..	16	229	..	57	140	..	16	116
..	22	141	..	68	230	..	21	255
..	23	208	xxix.	5	255	..	24	262
..	29	150	..	22	116	ix.	7	116, 117, 182
xiii.	1	205	..	27	230	..	24	196
..	3	151	xxx.	19	139	x.	8	116
..	15	175	xxxi.	7	150	..	24	172
17	..	236	..	10	150	..	23	237
xiv.	18	212	..	26	119	..	29	255
..	23	204	..	28	139	..	31	255
xv.	2	196	xxxii.	1	201	..	34	255
..	4	216	..	5	230	..	32	220
..	28	229	..	6	230	..	35	221
xvi.	10	226	..	7	254	..	36	255
..	18	214	..	10	222	..	38	255
xvii.	6	229	..	11	201	..	39	174
..	12	205	..	13	182	..	43	255
..	16	174	..	14	158	xi.	16	116
xviii.	12	150	..	18	208, 231	xii.	13	232
..	13	150, 230	..	29	230	..	14	232
xix.	15	229	..	33	157	..	15	232
xx.	3	224	..	34	154	..	20	116
..	8	176	..	40	149	..	40	171
xxi.	6	188	..	51	150	xiii.	8	226
..	7	116, 161, 179	xxxiii.	2	193	..	11	213
..	15	177	..	5	264	..	16	226
..	21	255	..	6	141, 216	xiv.	2	226
xxii.	6	206, 230	..	9	116	..	4	236
..	15	109, 116	..	27	178	..	12	214
..	16	109, 116, 200	..	44	218	..	15	220
..	20	109, 116				xv.	4	116
..	21	109, 116	**JOSHUA.**			..	22	212
..	23	109, 116	i.	3	247	..	45	213
..	24	109, 116	..	7	225	..	47	116
..	25	109, 116	..	8	162	..	48	116
..	26	109, 116	ii.	7	226	..	53	116, 118
..	27	109, 116	..	9	247	..	63	116
..	28	109, 116	..	11	255	xvi.	3	116, 183
..	29	109, 116	..	18	116	..	5	116
xxiii.	4	257	..	14	161	xviii.	1	214
..	5	227	..	18	174	..	4	141, 255
..	11	196	..	22	198	..	8	116
..	17	201	iii.	4	116	..	9	116
xxiv.	8	206, 226						

Chap.	Ver.	Page.	Chap.	Ver.	Page.	Chap.	Ver.	Page.
xviii.	12	116	xiv.	15	150	iv.	13	116, 189
..	14	116	xv.	18	175	v.	6	109, 116
..	19	116	..	19	151	..	7	215
..	24	116	xvi.	12	207	..	8	215, 233
xix.	7	212, 213	..	19	200	..	9	109, 116
..	13	178	..	21	151, 152, 222	..	10	215
..	22	116, 119	..	25	193	..	11	215, 233
..	29	116	..	26	116, 155, 191	..	12	109, 116
..	47	221	xvii.	3	252	vi.	2	208, 209
xx.	8	116	..	4	252	..	3	215
xxi.	10	116	..	5	252	..	4	109, 116
..	27	116	xviii.	28	205	..	5	100, 116, 215
..	40	213	xix.	15	174	..	7	174
xxii.	7	116	..	18	174	..	12	230
..	8	199	..	25	188, 251	vii.	9	116, 117
..	22	206, 208	xx.	13	109	viii.	3	116
xxiv.	2	216	xxi.	19	221	..	13	148
..	3	116, 118	..	20	117	..	20	208, 209
..	4	149	..	22	119	ix.	1	116, 193
..	8	116, 118				..	2	141
..	14	149, 214		RUTH.		..	3	252
..	15	116, 189	i.	3	118	..	7	200
..	19	116	..	5	221	..	8	245
..	22	149	..	9	177, 236	..	9	206
			..	12	118, 177	..	26	116, 118
			..	20	172	x.	5	141
	JUDGES.		ii.	1	118	..	10	139
i.	3	149	..	4	216	..	11	158
..	31	178	..	8	200	..	12	158
ii.	1	283, 262	..	12	203	..	14	218
iii.	26	173	..	16	164	..	18	216
iv.	18	174	..	22	200	..	21	116, 118
..	21	171	iii.	3	200	..	22	262
v.	8	205	..	4	141	xi.	6	116, 139, 188
..	15	249	..	5	109	..	9	116, 188
..	22	223	..	11	151	xii.	8	169, 237
vi.	3	205	..	12	110	..	10	116, 117
..	4	214	..	13	230	..	23	140
..	5	186	..	17	109, 192	..	24	149
..	8	216	iv.	4	118	xiii.	8	116, 118
..	10	152	..	6	182	..	19	116, 117
..	19	250	..	8	168	xiv.	4	152
..	28	208	..	9	214	..	6	208
vii.	12	213	..	12	141	..	13	262
..	21	118	..	15	205	..	19	262
..	22	226	..	18	168	..	27	116, 150, 191, 252
viii.	2	198				..	32	116, 184, 189
..	10	213		1 SAMUEL.		..	33	170, 171
ix.	2	208	i.	1	232	..	36	262
..	3	261	..	9	236	..	52	207
..	37	245	..	17	170, 215	xv.	6	218
..	41	171	..	26	176, 177	..	13	166, 167
..	56	252	ii.	3	116	..	16	116, 117
x.	13	150	..	9	116, 188	xvi.	2	262
xi.	14	245	..	10	116	..	4	148
..	18	258	..	15	200	..	7	222
..	27	218	..	24	159, 163	..	12	262
..	34	225	..	26	141	..	15	139
..	37	118	iii.	2	116	..	16	139
xii.	5	287	..	6	245	..	23	139
xiii.	8	153	..	8	245	..	24	116
..	17	183	..	18	116	xvii.	1	233
..	18	171	..	21	245	..	7	116, 189
..	21	205	iv.	4	155			
xiv.	8	228						

Chap.	Ver.	Page	Chap.	Ver.	Page	Chap.	Ver.	Page
1 Samuel.			xxvi.	6	218	vii.	12	166
xvii.	17	172	..	7	216	..	23	220
..	18	236	..	11	216	..	29	221
..	23	116, 186	..	12	151	viii.	3	109, 192
..	26	200	..	14	218	..	8	221
..	27	200	..	15	216	x.	9	116
..	29	245	..	16	216	..	17	171
..	34	116	..	19	151	xi.	1	171
..	37	262	..	22	184, 216	..	13	213
..	45	200	..	23	200	..	24	171
..	47	200	xxvii.	4	116	xii.	3	237
xviii.	1	116, 233	..	8	116	..	4	200, 221
..	6	116, 119	..	10	218	..	7	216, 217
..	7	116	..	11	213	..	9	116, 200, 232
..	9	116	xxviii.	8	229	..	12	236
..	14	116	..	6	158	..	13	262
..	20	139	..	8	116, 182	..	20	116, 183
..	22	116	..	9	229	..	22	116, 186
..	25	226	..	16	240	..	24	116
..	29	149, 171, 245	..	21	202	..	31	116, 188
xix.	4	163	..	23	141	xiii.	7	174
..	12	251	..	24	222	..	18	150, 177, 250
..	18	116	xxix.	3	208, 209	..	32	116, 118
..	19	116	..	5	116	..	33	110
..	20	158	xxx.	1	218	..	34	116
..	21	245, 262	..	2	207	..	37	116, 189
..	22	116	..	6	116	xiv.	7	116, 119
..	23	116, 139	..	16	151	..	11	116
xx.	1	116, 119	..	22	207	..	15	214
..	2	116	..	24	116	..	21	116
..	3	206	xxxi.	7	196	..	22	116
..	8	226				..	30	116
..	13	141	2 Samuel.			..	31	174
..	17	245	i.	2	183	..	32	163
..	20	178, 253	..	8	116	..	50	223
..	24	116, 189	..	10	209, 216	xv.	5	208
..	29	219	..	11	116	..	8	116, 118
..	36	164	..	20	208	..	9	174
..	38	116	..	21	236	..	19	237
xxi.	2	237	ii.	1	174	..	20	116, 118
..	3	206	..	22	236, 245	..	21	119
..	12	116	..	23	116	..	28	116
..	14	183	..	35	166	..	29	252
xxii.	13	116	iii.	2	116	xvi.	2	116, 185
..	15	182	..	3	116	..	8	116
..	17	116, 232	..	12	116	..	10	116, 117
..	18	113	..	15	116, 119	..	11	239
..	22	116	..	22	225	..	12	116, 118
..	45	200	..	25	116	..	18	116
xxiii.	2	262	iv.	1	255	..	19	226
..	4	245	v.	1	174	..	21	109
..	5	116, 183	..	2	116, 192, 218	..	23	262
..	11	262	..	3	174	xvii.	6	217
..	20	118	..	8	116, 232	..	12	116
..	21	194	..	19	262	..	14	262
..	33	214	..	23	188	..	16	116
xxiv.	9	116, 181, 193	..	24	116, 141	..	20	174
..	19	116, 118	vi.	1	245	..	22	252
xxv.	3	116, 232	..	2	155	xviii.	2	212
..	6	218	..	20	255, 262	..	3	116, 118
..	12	207	..	23	116	..	8	116
..	18	116	vii.	4	262	..	9	150, 214
..	21	252	..	6	199	..	11	200
xxvi.	5	116	..	7	252	..	12	116, 190, 208

Chap.	Ver.	Page.	Chap.	Ver.	Page.	Chap.	Ver.	Page.
xviii.	13	116, 232			**1 Kings.**	xi.	36	157
	17	116, 255	Chap.	Ver.	Page.	..	39	171
..	18	116	i.	1	117	xii.	3	117
..	20	109	..	20	218	..	5	163
..	22	141, 245	..	21	214	..	7	117
..	23	141	..	24	217	..	21	117
xix.	7	116	..	31	149	xiii.	5	207
..	8	226	..	37	118	..	7	174
..	19	116	..	40	220	..	15	174
..	25	216	..	41	223	..	20	262
..	27	208, 209	..	51	249	..	29	239, 240
..	32	116	..	53	170	..	33	141
..	41	116	ii.	5	148	xiv.	5	141
xx.	5	116, 118	..	6	148	..	12	178
..	6	217	..	30	252	..	25	119
..	8	116	..	33	149	xv.	10	213
..	14	116	iii.	2	237	..	15	232
..	15	158, 165	..	5	215	..	17	255
..	23	116	..	11	215	..	18	184
..	25	116, 118	..	14	157	..	27	255
xix.	1	262	..	17	167, 169	..	33	245
..	4	116	..	26	219	xvi.	9	172, 205
..	5	154	iv.	8	184	..	26	183
..	6	116, 262	..	18	172	..	34	118
..	9	116, 118, 220	v.	17	232	xvii.	12	202
..	12	116, 192	..	23	218	..	13	232
..	16	116, 190, 232	..	26	148	..	14	216
..	18	190	vi.	4	155	..	23	117
..	20	116, 118	..	5	119	xviii.	1	196
..	21	116	..	20	217	..	5	163
xxii.	4	221	..	21	118	..	12	177, 196
..	8	116	..	25	155	..	24	207
..	15	116	..	27	155	..	27	224
..	23	116, 232	vii.	6	155	..	36	183, 220
..	25	252	..	13	156	..	42	183
..	30	177	..	21	155	..	44	177
..	33	116	..	20	184	..	46	177
..	34	116, 117	..	23	118	xix.	2	252
..	40	170	..	36	117	..	4	190
..	51	116, 118	..	45	116, 191	xx.	8	163
xxiii.	1	205	..	48	216	..	22	213
..	3	190, 215	viii.	7	155	..	27	236
..	5	154, 200	..	9	239	xxi.	2	141
..	8	116, 232	..	13	154	..	6	199
..	9	116, 184, 187	..	21	202	..	8	149, 184
..	11	116	..	26	183, 215	..	10	207
..	13	116	..	34	175	..	13	207
..	15	116, 171	..	39	175, 200	..	15	199
..	16	116, 171	..	43	217	..	21	193
..	18	116	..	62	255	..	23	165
..	20	116, 171	..	65	216, 255	xxii.	13	183, 252
..	21	116, 181	ix.	5	149, 166	..	18	163
..	35	232	..	9	117	..	37	236
..	37	116	..	18	186	..	43	225
xxiv.	1	245	x.	2	174	..	49	179
..	3	205	..	5	183, 197			
..	10	262	..	7	141		**2 Kings.**	
..	11	262	..	9	149	i.	15	149
..	14	116, 183	..	21	223	..	17	262
..	16	116	xi.	4	157	ii.	9	141
..	18	116, 118, 214	..	6	216	..	21	171
..	22	116, 262	..	15	128	..	22	170
..	23	262	..	16	128, 255	iii.	11	149, 205
..	24	199, 150, 214	..	17	171	..	12	149
			..	31	216			

288

2 Kings.			Chap.	Ver.	Page.	Chap.	Ver.	Page.
Chap.	Ver.	Page.	xix.	28	169	ix.	19	151, 216
iii.	13	218	..	34	217	..	23	213
..	19	237	..	37	109	..	33	118
..	24	188	xx.	3	265	x.	3	255
..	26	149	..	4	193	xi.	1	174
iv.	5	118	..	11	252	..	2	218
..	7	117, 184	..	12	171	..	3	174
..	32	174	..	13	241	..	17	207
..	34	183	..	18	117	..	23	194
..	39	225	xxi.	13	208	xii.	1	255
..	40	207	xxii.	1	213	..	3	119
v.	9	183	..	5	117	..	5	118
..	12	189	..	9	252	..	15	118
..	17	163, 211	..	14	222	..	23	174
..	18	109, 192	..	15	200, 216	..	30	273, 277
..	27	227	xxiii.	1	233	..	35	272
vi.	7	205	..	2	213	..	36	221
..	12	163, 252	..	6	250	..	38	170, 174
vii.	4	208	..	11	208	..	40	213
..	6	205	..	33	109	xiii.	4	255
..	12	177, 185	..	36	118	..	15	255
..	13	184	xxiv.	10	179	xiv.	15	141
..	14	209	..	13	250	xv.	28	159
..	15	185	..	15	118, 174	xvi.	2	250
viii.	8	149	..	16	174	..	18	232
ix.	4	197	xxv.	13	174	..	20	219
..	6	174, 216	xxix.	16	238	xvii.	2	266
..	14	252				..	5	199
..	17	201	1 Chronicles.			..	9	222
..	27	149	i.	1	186, 187,	..	21	168
..	28	174			188, 230	..	27	221
..	33	117	..	24	232	xviii.	10	182
..	37	118	..	46	117	xx.	5	119
x.	16	149	..	51	118	xxi.	22	199
..	19	216	ii.	8	226	..	24	199
..	22	250	..	13	117	xxii.	7	180, 232
..	27	216	..	49	127	..	15	214
xi.	1	117	..	55	232	..	16	141
..	2	116	iii.	19	226	xxiii.	12	228
..	18	183	..	21	226	..	14	250
..	20	184	..	23	226	..	30	214
xii.	10	189	..	24	117	xxiv.	11	238
xiii.	25	252	iv.	7	186	..	14	232
xiv.	6	116	..	17	226	..	24	119
..	7	184	..	19	208	xxv.	1	139
..	13	117	..	20	119	..	7	142
xv.	11	266	..	40	141	xxvii.	12	193
..	12	266	..	41	118	..	29	117, 119
..	20	250	v.	20	207, 208	xxviii.	10	214
..	25	184	..	26	170, 172, 215	..	19	171
xvi.	6	189	..	28	228	..	22	245
..	7	152	vi.	3	228	xxix.	12	200
..	10	222	..	11	232	..	15	233
..	15	117, 236	..	20	118	..	22	241
..	17	117, 170	vii.	6	255	xxxiii.	11	236
..	18	118, 205	..	7	213	xxxiv.	16	252
xvii.	3	252	..	8	255			
xviii.	24	252	..	11	226	2 Chronicles.		
..	27	181, 194	..	31	118	i.	2	213
xix.	2	214	..	34	182, 186	..	11	212, 213, 215
..	15	139, 155	..	35	226	..	12	212
..	20	216	viii.	25	118	ii.	11	239
..	23	181	..	34	226	iii.	16	155
..	25	170	ix.	4	193	iv.	6	207

Chap.	Ver.	Page.	Chap.	Ver.	Page.	Chap.	Ver.	Page.
v.	12	155	xxxiii.	11	174	ii.	3	216
..	18	216	xxxiv.	6	193	..	14	218
..	19	216	..	9	187	iii.	6	213
vi.	9	226	..	12	153	..	7	199
..	11	202	..	14	220	..	13	170
..	13	214	..	22	182	..	15	117, 152
..	30	200	..	23	200	..	20	188
..	41	201	..	33	207	..	30	117
vii.	18	166	xxxv.	4	119	..	31	117
viii.	14	220	..	13	206	iv.	17	151
..	16	216	..	25	216	v.	5	213
ix.	13	213	xxxvi.	4	174	..	11	171
..	20	223	..	14	182	vi.	8	171
..	29	187				..	11	201
xi.	15	158	EZRA.			..	14	150
xii.	30	277	i.	1	172	..	17	152
..	32	276	..	4	199	vii.	8	213
xiii.	14	186	ii.	25	213	..	11	272
..	19	119	..	36	275	..	17	272, 273
xv.	1	139	..	38	273	..	31	213
..	6	219	..	42	275	..	37	213, 272
xvi.	7	170	..	46	117, 191	..	38	272
xvii.	8	117	..	50	118	..	42	274
..	11	117	..	59	208	..	44	277
xviii.	7	222	..	65	272	..	52	119
..	12	141	..	67	274	..	61	208
..	14	207	..	69	273	..	62	213
xix.	7	221	..	70	225	..	66	271
..	8	227	iii.	2	215	..	70	275
..	11	141	..	3	117	..	73	255
xx.	9	201	..	7	172, 221	viii.	6	208
..	26	216	iv.	2	108, 111	..	9	147
..	29	220	..	4	117	..	11	147
xxi.	17	220	..	7	183	ix.	6	118
xxii.	7	221	..	9	118	..	9	213, 241
..	10	222	..	12	192	..	17	117
xxiv.	6	216	..	22	172	..	15	175
..	20	139	v.	10	239	..	19	200
..	23	216	..	14	239	..	20	175
..	27	187	..	15	118, 181	..	23	219
xxv.	3	119	vi.	5	239	..	29	220
..	12	271	..	9	212	..	35	175
..	25	273	..	11	256	..	37	108
xxvi.	6	174	..	15	172	x.	20	119
..	10	174	vii.	17	212, 214	..	29	151, 213
..	21	119	..	25	255	..	30	213
xxvii.	9	152	..	26	232	xii.	9	232
xxix.	8	117	viii.	14	188	..	14	117, 187
..	9	213	..	17	117, 119	..	16	118
..	14	119	..	18	213	..	38	152, 171
..	22	174	..	25	182	..	42	207
..	27	174	ix.	4	215	..	44	171
		17	..	5	220	xiii.	4	217
		158	x.	5	255	..	16	171
xxx.	21	227	..	12	183	..	23	182
..	25	152	..	17	200	..	30	231
xxxi.	5	213, 214	..	29	186			
..	6	152	..	35	187	ESTHER.		
..	14	151	..	37	232	i.	5	117
..	15	220	..	43	232	..	6	230
..	17	220	..	44	187	..	8	208
xxxii.	9	174				..	16	117
..	21	232	NEHEMIAH.			ii.	2	148
xxxiii.	3	208	ii.	2	219	..	14	159

LEVITICUS.

Chap.	Ver.	Page.	Chap.	Ver.	Page.	Chap.	Ver.	Page.
ii.	9	174	xiv.	20	174	xxii.	23	213
..	15	175	..	33	140	..	30	141, 255
iii.	5	174	..	51	150	..	31	255
..	11	174	xv.	1	140	..	33	255
..	16	174	..	10	150	xxiii.	13	116
iv.	19	174	..	13	205	..	17	171
..	26	174, 207	..	29	150, 205	..	21	214
..	31	174	xvi.	6	214	..	22	255
..	35	174	..	8	149	..	24	236
v.	1	163	..	14	217	..	28	155
..	12	174	..	15	217	..	43	150, 255
vi.	2	231	..	20	247	xxiv.	5	205
..	8	225	..	21	116, 247	..	6	150
..	9	147	..	25	174	..	7	175
..	18	241	xvii.	4	200	..	9	147
..	19	147	..	5	150	..	12	239, 240
..	20	147	..	13	141	..	13	180
vii.	5	174	xviii.	1	255	xxv.	17	255
..	6	141	..	2	255	..	22	255
..	9	206	..	4	241, 255	..	23	247
..	15	141	..	5	255	..	25	247
..	16	141	..	6	255	..	27	200
..	18	141	..	20	218	..	30	116, 247
..	19	141-	..	21	255	..	35	247
..	21	200	..	23	178	..	39	247
..	31	174	..	25	157	..	44	213
..	36	226	..	27	260	..	46	149
..	38	226	..	28	157	..	55	150, 255
viii.	2	158	..	30	255	xxvi.	1	213, 255
..	8	135	xix.	2	255	..	2	206, 255
..	16	174	..	3	214, 238	..	9	166
..	21	174	..		241, 255	..	25	261
..	28	174	..	4	255	..	43	241
ix.	10	174	..	6	141	..	44	239
..	12	159	..	7	141	..	45	255
..	14	174	..	10	255	xxvii.	9	225
..	18	159	..	12	255	..	10	200, 201
..	20	174	..	14	217, 255	..	26	200
..	22	116, 163, 213	..	15	255	..	30	204
x.	1	196	..	18	255	..	32	204
..	2	150	..	23	141			
..	16	135	..	25	255	**NUMBERS.**		
xi.	1	140	..	28	255	i.	16	116, 118, 187
..	19	212, 214	..	30	255	..	21	272
..	21	116	..	31	255	..	25	274
..	34	141	..	32	255	..	27	273
..	37	208, 209	..	33	255	..	33	274
..	41	141	..	34	255	..	37	272
..	42	135, 196, 230, 232	..	37	255	..	39	272
..			xx.	4	203	..	50	180
..	43	170	..	7	255	ii.	1	140
..	44	255	..	15	200	iii.	9	159
xii.	4	264	..	16	178	..	15	147
..	5	199	..	25	214, 251	..	19	228
..	8	214	..	26	159	..	40	147
xiii.	1	140	xxi.	2	214, 241	..	51	116
..	2	252	..	5	116, 179, 188	iv.	1	140
..	3	206	..	7	147	..	12	150
..	4	178, 223	..	8	147	..	17	140
..	10	206	..	12	255	..	19	150
..	20	178, 223, 237	xxii.	2	158, 207, 255	..	23	150
..	33	135, 230	..	3	255	..	28	275
..	51	236	..	8	255	..	36	276
			..	16	150	..	43	278

Chap.	Ver.	Page.	Chap.	Ver.	Page.	Chap.	Ver.	Page.
iv.	49	150, 226	xv.	41	255	xxxi.	38	274
v.	4	150	..	31	178	..	40	276
..	8	200	..	41	170	..	44	278
..	21	150	xvi.	9	215	xxxii.	1	247
..	26	174	..	11	116	..	3	213
vi.	5	147, 158, 223	..	15	252	..	7	116, 119
..	8	147	..	17	213, 218	..	17	170
..	20	150	..	20	140	..	24	171
..	24	216	xvii.	4	155	..	37	172
vii.	1	159	..	17	160	xxxiii.	8	226
..	3	150	..	20	156	..	42	237
..	5	150	..	23	250, 251	xxxiv.	4	116
..	6	150	..	24	250	xxxv.	2	221
..	10	157	xviii.	24	204	..	4	221
..	14	232	..	23	227	..	9	275
..	17	271	..	26	218	..	10	174
..	19	159	xix.	1	140	..	7	236
..	20	232	xx.	15	174	xxxvi.	3	149, 221
..	26	232	..	17	200	..	6	200
..	32	232	xxi.	4	259			
..	38	232	..	5	205, 245	**Deuteronomy.**		
..	44	232	..	20	221	i.	2	252
..	50	232	..	22	200	..	11	160, 169
..	56	232	..	32	116, 118	..	13	157
..	62	232	xxii.	2	245	..	15	224
..	68	232	..	12	215	..	16	224
..	74	232	..	15	245	ii.	1	237
..	80	232	..	22	263	..	8	242
viii.	1	170	..	25	245	..	14	164
..	7	196	..	26	245	..	33	116, 230
..	16	160	..	33	150, 177	iii.	6	150
ix.	2	248	xxiii.	1	158	..	11	230
..	15	216	..	3	206	..	13	206
x.	3	196	..	7	263	..	17	213
..	10	255	..	9	197, 221	..	21	160
..	36	116	..	24	197	..	26	205
xi.	4	171, 185	xxiv.	2	139	..	28	150
..	11	140, 170	..	5	230	iv.	11	237
..	12	222	..	6	207	..	26	139
..	20	172	..	23	216	..	32	139
..	25	171	xxv.	4	150	..	40	217
..	26	174	..	12	231	..	45	237
..	32	116, 233	..	17	150	v.	10	116, 232
..	33	242	..	19	242	..	14	176
xii.	3	116, 163, 183	xxvi.	8	226	..	16	154, 233
..	12	207	..	9	116, 119	..	18	225
..	16	170	..	14	273	..	19	242
xiii.	1	170	xxvii.	2	157, 217	..	26	149
..	2	207	..	5	230	vi.	2	154, 217, 238
..	9	172	..	13	205	..	4	230
..	21	207	..	15	215	..	9	95
..	22	225, 260	..	21	217	..	13	228, 229
..	28	260	xxviii.	6	154	..	17	236
..	30	230	..	17	141	..	18	214
xiv.	3	174	xxix.	19	265	vii.	9	116
..	4	174	..	31	265	..	12	170
..	15	176	..	33	212, 265	..	19	213
..	17	230	xxx.	9	150	viii.	2	116
..	20	161	xxxi.	12	218	..	3	216
..	25	213	..	18	236	..	8	182
..	26	140	..	22	214	..	14	236
..	36	116, 119	..	24	231	ix.	2	218
xv.	14	237	..	27	205, 261	..	5	217
..	24	140, 170	..	35	277	..	14	150

Deuteronomy			Chap.	Ver.	Page.	Chap.	Ver.	Page.
Chap.	Ver.	Page.	xxiv.	10	171	iii.	16	116, 189
ix.	22	158	xxv.	5	173, 252	..	17	255
..	24	231	..	9	200	iv.	1	262
..	27	218	..	19	128	..	8	239, 240
..	28	150	xxvi.	5	174	..	18	116, 188
x.	5	202	..	8	213	v.	1	116
..	11	141, 255	..	16	150	..	12	242
..	15	150	..	19	147	..	15	116
..	17	148	xxvii.	8	122	vi.	5	188, 116
..	20	229	..	10	116	..	7	116, 117
..	22	174	..	12	213	..	9	116, 232
xi.	9	217	..	13	225	..	13	116, 191
..	10	205	..	26	150	..	15	116
..	12	140, 170	xxviii.	27	109, 116, 194	vii.	7	196
..	13	121	..	30	116, 194	..	10	154, 164
..	13–21	95	..	31	155	..	21	116, 118
..	20	159	..	39	151	..	22	174
..	24	247	..	46	227	..	24	255
..	25	170	..	51	214	viii.	11	183, 116
xii.	4	152	..	52	196	..	12	116
..	16	229	..	53	162	..	15	255
..	22	141	..	57	140	..	16	116
..	23	208	..	68	230	..	21	255
..	29	150	xxix.	5	255	..	24	262
xiii.	1	205	..	22	116	ix.	7	116, 117, 182
..	3	151	..	27	230	..	24	196
..	15	175	xxx.	19	139	x.	8	116
17	..	236	xxxi.	7	150	..	24	172
xiv.	18	212	..	10	150	..	23	237
..	23	204	..	26	119	..	29	255
xv.	2	196	..	28	139	..	31	255
..	4	216	xxxii.	1	201	..	34	255
..	23	229	..	5	230	..	32	220
xvi.	10	226	..	6	230	..	35	221
..	18	214	..	7	254	..	36	255
xvii.	6	229	..	10	222	..	38	255
..	12	205	..	11	201	..	39	174
..	16	174	..	13	182	..	43	255
xviii.	12	150	..	14	158	xi.	16	116
..	13	150, 230	..	18	208, 231	xii.	13	232
xix.	15	229	..	29	230	..	14	232
xx.	3	224	..	33	157	..	15	232
..	8	176	..	34	154	..	20	116
xxi.	6	188	..	40	149	..	40	171
..	7	116, 161, 179	..	51	150	xiii.	8	226
..	15	177	xxxiii.	2	193	..	11	213
..	21	255	..	5	264	..	16	226
xxii.	6	206, 230	..	6	141, 216	xiv.	2	226
..	15	109, 116	..	9	116	..	4	236
..	16	109, 116, 200	..	27	178	..	12	214
..	20	109, 116	..	44	218	..	15	220
..	21	109, 116				xv.	4	116
..	23	109, 116	Joshua.			..	22	212
..	24	109, 116	i.	3	247	..	45	213
..	25	109, 116	..	7	225	..	47	116
..	26	109, 116	..	8	162	..	48	116
..	27	109, 116	ii.	7	226	..	53	116, 118
..	28	109, 116	..	9	247	..	63	116
..	29	109, 116	..	11	255	xvi.	3	116, 183
xxiii.	4	257	..	13	116	..	5	116
..	5	227	..	14	161	xviii.	1	214
..	11	196	..	18	174	..	4	141, 255
..	17	201	..	22	198	..	8	116
xxiv.	8	206, 226	iii.	4	116	..	9	116

Chap.	Ver.	Page.	Chap.	Ver.	Page.	Chap.	Ver.	Page.
xviii.	12	116	xiv.	15	150	iv.	13	116, 189
..	14	116	xv.	18	175	v.	6	109, 116
..	19	116	..	19	151	..	7	215
..	24	116	xvi.	12	207	..	8	215, 233
xix.	7	212, 213	..	19	200	..	9	109, 116
..	13	178	..	21	151, 152, 222	..	10	215
..	22	116, 119	..	25	193	..	11	215, 233
..	29	116	..	26	116, 155, 191	..	12	109, 116
..	47	221	xvii.	3	252	vi.	2	208, 209
xx.	8	116	..	4	252	..	3	215
xxi.	10	116	..	5	252	..	4	109, 116
..	27	116	xviii.	28	205	..	5	100, 116, 215
..	40	213	xix.	15	174	..	7	174
xxii.	7	116	..	18	174	..	12	230
..	8	199	..	25	188, 251	vii.	9	116, 117
..	22	206, 208	xx.	13	109	viii.	3	116
xxiv.	2	216	xxi.	19	221	..	13	148
..	3	116, 118	..	20	117	..	20	208, 209
..	4	149	..	22	119	ix.	1	116, 193
..	8	116, 118				..	2	141
..	14	149, 214	RUTH.			..	3	252
..	15	116, 189	i.	3	118	..	7	200
..	19	116	..	5	221	..	8	245
..	22	149	..	9	177, 236	..	9	206
			..	12	118, 177	..	26	116, 118
JUDGES.			..	20	172	x.	5	141
i.	3	149	ii.	1	118	..	10	139
..	31	178	..	4	216	..	11	158
ii.	1	233, 262	..	8	200	..	12	158
iii.	26	173	..	12	203	..	14	218
iv.	18	174	..	16	164	..	18	216
..	21	171	..	22	200	..	21	116, 118
v.	8	205	iii.	3	200	..	22	262
..	15	249	..	4	141	xi.	6	116, 139, 188
..	22	223	..	5	109	..	9	116, 188
vi.	3	205	..	11	151	xii.	8	169, 237
..	4	214	..	12	110	..	10	116, 117
..	5	186	..	13	230	..	23	140
..	8	216	..	17	109, 192	..	24	149
..	10	152	iv.	4	118	xiii.	8	116, 118
..	19	250	..	6	182	..	19	116, 117
..	28	208	..	8	168	xiv.	4	152
vii.	12	213	..	9	214	..	6	208
..	21	118	..	12	141	..	13	262
..	22	226	..	15	205	..	19	262
viii.	2	198	..	18	168	..	27	116, 150, 191, 252
..	10	213				..	32	116, 184, 189
ix.	2	208	1 SAMUEL.			..	33	170, 171
..	3	261	i.	1	232	..	36	262
..	37	245	..	9	236	..	52	207
..	41	171	..	17	170, 215	xv.	6	218
..	56	252	..	26	176, 177	..	13	166, 167
x.	13	150	ii.	3	116	..	16	116, 117
xi.	14	245	..	9	116, 183	xvi.	2	262
..	18	258	..	10	116	..	4	148
..	27	218	..	15	200	..	7	222
..	34	225	..	24	159, 163	..	12	262
..	37	118	..	26	141	..	15	139
xii.	5	237	iii.	2	116	..	16	139
xiii.	8	153	..	6	245	..	23	139
..	17	183	..	8	245	..	24	116
..	18	171	..	18	116	xvii.	1	233
..	21	205	..	21	245	..	7	116, 189
xiv.	8	223	iv.	4	155			

1 SAMUEL.

Chap.	Ver.	Page.
xvii.	17	172
..	18	236
..	23	116, 186
..	26	200
..	27	200
..	29	245
..	34	116
..	37	262
..	45	200
..	47	200
xviii.	1	116, 233
..	6	116, 119
..	7	116
..	9	116
..	14	116
..	20	139
..	22	116
..	25	226
..	29	149, 171, 245
xix.	4	163
..	12	251
..	18	116
..	19	116
..	20	158
..	21	245, 262
..	22	116
..	23	116, 139
xx.	1	116, 119
..	2	116
..	3	206
..	8	226
..	13	141
..	17	245
..	20	178, 253
..	24	116, 189
..	29	219
..	36	164
..	38	116
xxi.	2	237
..	3	206
..	12	116
..	14	183
xxii.	13	116
..	15	182
..	17	116, 232
..	18	113
..	22	116
..	45	200
xxiii.	2	262
..	4	245
..	5	116, 183
..	11	262
..	20	118
..	21	194
..	33	214
xxiv.	9	116, 181, 193
..	19	116, 118
xxv.	3	116, 232
..	6	218
..	12	207
..	18	116
..	21	252
xxvi.	5	116

Chap.	Ver.	Page.
xxvi.	6	218
..	7	216
..	11	216
..	12	151
..	14	218
..	15	216
..	16	216
..	19	151
..	22	184, 216
..	23	200
xxvii.	4	116
..	8	116
..	10	218
..	11	213
xxviii.	3	229
..	6	158
..	8	116, 182
..	9	229
..	16	240
..	21	202
..	22	141
..	24	222
xxix.	3	208, 209
..	5	116
xxx.	1	218
..	2	207
..	6	116
..	16	151
..	22	207
..	24	116
xxxi.	7	196

2 SAMUEL.

Chap.	Ver.	Page.
i.	2	183
..	8	116
..	10	209, 216
..	11	116
..	20	208
..	21	236
ii.	1	174
..	20	116
..	22	236, 245
..	23	116
..	35	165
iii.	2	116
..	3	116
..	12	116
..	15	116, 119
..	22	225
..	25	116
iv.	1	255
v.	1	174
..	2	116, 192, 218
..	3	174
..	8	116, 232
..	19	262
..	23	188
..	24	116, 141
vi.	1	245
..	2	155
..	20	255, 262
..	23	116
vii.	4	262
..	6	199
..	7	252

Chap.	Ver.	Page
vii.	12	166
..	23	220
..	29	221
viii.	3	109, 192
..	8	221
x.	9	116
..	17	171
xi.	1	171
..	18	213
..	24	171
xii.	3	237
..	4	200, 221
..	7	216, 217
..	9	116, 200, 232
..	12	236
..	13	262
..	20	116, 183
..	22	116, 186
..	24	116
..	31	116, 188
xiii.	7	174
..	18	150, 177, 250
..	32	116, 118
..	33	110
..	34	116
..	37	116, 189
xiv.	7	116, 119
..	11	116
..	15	214
..	21	116
..	22	116
..	30	116
..	31	174
..	32	163
..	50	223
xv.	5	208
..	8	116, 118
..	9	174
..	19	287
..	20	116, 118
..	21	119
..	28	116
..	29	252
xvi.	2	116, 185
..	8	116
..	10	116, 117
..	11	289
..	12	116, 118
..	18	116
..	19	226
..	21	109
..	23	262
xvii.	6	217
..	12	116
..	14	262
..	16	116
..	20	174
..	22	252
xviii.	2	212
..	3	116, 118
..	8	116
..	9	150, 214
..	11	200
..	12	116, 190, 208

Chap.	Ver.	Page.	Chap.	Ver.	Page.	Chap.	Ver.	Page.
xviii.	18	116, 232	\multicolumn{3}{c	}{1 Kings.}	xi.	36	. 157
..	17	116, 255	Chap.	Ver.	Page.	..	39	. 171
..	18	. 116	i.	1	. 117	xii.	3	. 117
..	20	. 109	..	20	. 218	..	5	. 163
..	22	141, 245	..	21	. 214	..	7	. 117
..	23	. 141	..	24	. 217	..	21	. 117
xix.	7	. 116	..	31	. 149	xiii.	5	. 207
..	8	. 226	..	37	. 118	..	7	. 174
..	19	. 116	..	40	. 220	..	15	. 174
..	25	. 216	..	41	. 223	..	20	. 262
..	27	208, 209	..	51	. 249	..	29	239, 240
..	32	. 116	..	53	. 170	..	33	. 141
..	41	. 116	ii.	5	. 148	xiv.	5	. 141
xx.	5	116, 118	..	6	. 148	..	12	. 178
..	6	. 217	..	30	. 252	..	25	. 119
..	8	. 116	..	33	. 149	xv.	10	. 213
..	14	. 116	iii.	2	. 237	..	15	. 232
..	15	158, 165	..	5	. 215	..	17	. 255
..	23	. 116	..	11	. 215	..	18	. 184
..	25	116, 118	..	14	. 157	..	27	. 255
xix.	1	. 262	..	17	167, 169	..	33	. 245
..	4	. 116	..	26	. 219	xvi.	9	172, 205
..	5	. 154	iv.	8	. 184	..	26	. 183
..	6	116, 262	..	18	. 172	..	34	. 118
..	9	116, 118, 220	v.	17	. 232	xvii.	12	. 202
..	12	116, 192	..	23	. 218	..	13	. 232
..	16	116, 190, 232	..	26	. 148	..	14	. 216
..	18	. 190	vi.	4	. 155	..	23	. 117
..	20	116, 118	..	5	. 119	xviii.	1	. 196
..	21	. 116	..	20	. 217	..	5	. 163
xxii.	4	. 221	..	21	. 118	..	12	177, 196
..	8	. 116	..	25	. 155	..	24	. 207
..	15	. 116	..	27	. 155	..	27	. 224
..	23	116, 232	vii.	6	. 155	..	36	183, 220
..	25	. 252	..	13	. 156	..	42	. 183
..	30	. 177	..	21	. 155	..	44	. 177
..	33	. 116	..	20	. 184	..	46	. 177
..	34	116, 117	..	23	. 118	xix.	2	. 252
..	40	. 170	..	36	. 117	..	4	. 190
..	51	116, 118	..	45	116, 191	xx.	8	. 163
xxiii.	1	. 205	..	48	. 216	..	22	. 213
..	3	190, 215	viii.	7	. 155	..	27	. 236
..	5	154, 200	..	9	. 239	xxi.	2	. 141
..	8	116, 232	..	18	. 154	..	6	. 199
..	9	116, 184, 187	..	21	. 202	..	8	149, 184
..	11	. 116	..	26	183, 215	..	10	. 207
..	13	. 116	..	34	. 175	..	13	. 207
..	15	116, 171	..	39	175, 200	..	15	. 199
..	16	116, 171	..	43	. 217	..	21	. 193
..	18	. 116	..	62	. 255	..	23	. 165
..	20	116, 171	..	65	216, 255	xxii.	13	183, 252
..	21	116, 181	ix.	5	149, 166	..	18	. 163
..	35	. 232	..	9	. 117	..	37	. 236
..	37	. 116	..	18	. 186	..	43	. 225
xxiv.	1	. 245	x.	2	. 174	..	49	. 179
..	3	. 205	..	5	183, 197	\multicolumn{3}{c	}{2 Kings.}
..	10	. 262	..	7	. 141			
..	11	. 262	..	9	. 149	i.	15	. 149
..	14	116, 188	xi.	4	. 157	..	17	. 262
..	16	. 116	..	6	. 216	ii.	9	. 141
..	18	116, 118. 214	..	15	. 128	..	21	. 171
..	22	116, 262	..	16	128, 255	..	22	. 170
..	23	. 262	..	17	. 171	iii.	11	149, 205
..	24	199, 150, 214	..	31	. 216	..	12	. 149

2 Kings.			Chap.	Ver.	Page.	Chap.	Ver.	Page.
Chap.	Ver.	Page.	xix.	28	169	ix.	19	151, 216
iii.	13	218	..	34	217	..	23	213
..	19	237	..	37	109	..	33	118
..	24	188	xx.	3	265	x.	3	255
..	26	149	..	4	193	xi.	1	174
iv.	5	118	..	11	252	..	2	218
..	7	117, 184	..	12	171	..	8	174
..	32	174	..	13	241	..	17	207
..	34	183	..	18	117	..	23	194
..	39	225	xxi.	18	208	xii.	1	255
..	40	207	xxii.	1	213	..	3	119
v.	9	183	..	5	117	..	5	118
..	12	189	..	9	252	..	15	118
..	17	163, 211	..	14	222	..	23	174
..	18	109, 192	..	15	200, 216	..	30	273, 277
..	27	227	xxiii.	1	233	..	35	272
vi.	7	205	..	2	213	..	36	221
..	12	163, 252	..	6	250	..	38	170, 174
vii.	4	208	..	11	208	..	40	213
..	6	205	..	33	109	xiii.	4	255
..	12	177, 185	..	36	118	..	15	255
..	13	184	xxiv.	10	179	xiv.	15	141
..	14	209	..	13	250	xv.	28	159
..	15	185	..	15	118, 174	xvi.	2	250
viii.	8	149	..	16	174	..	18	232
ix.	4	197	xxv.	13	174	..	20	219
..	6	174, 216	xxix.	16	238	xvii.	2	266
..	14	252				..	5	199
..	17	201	1 Chronicles.			..	9	222
..	27	149	i.	1	186, 187,	..	21	168
..	28	174			188, 230	..	27	221
..	33	117	..	24	232	xviii.	10	182
..	37	118	..	46	117	xx.	5	119
x.	16	149	..	51	118	xxi.	22	199
..	19	216	ii.	8	226	..	24	199
..	22	250	..	13	117	xxii.	7	180, 232
..	27	216	..	49	127	..	15	214
xi.	1	117	..	55	232	..	16	141
..	2	116	iii.	19	226	xxiii.	12	228
..	18	183	..	21	226	..	14	250
..	20	184	..	23	226	..	30	214
xii.	10	189	..	24	117	xxiv.	11	233
xiii.	25	252	iv.	7	186	..	14	232
xiv.	6	116	..	17	226	..	24	119
..	7	184	..	19	208	xxv.	1	139
..	13	117	..	20	119	..	7	142
xv.	11	266	..	40	141	xxvii.	12	193
..	12	266	..	41	118	..	29	117, 119
..	20	250	v.	20	207, 208	xxviii.	10	214
..	25	184	..	26	170, 172, 215	..	19	171
xvi.	6	189	..	28	228	..	22	245
..	7	152	vi.	3	228	xxix.	12	200
..	10	222	..	11	232	..	15	233
..	15	117, 236	..	20	118	..	22	241
..	17	117, 170	vii.	6	255	xxxiii.	11	236
..	18	118, 205	..	7	213	xxxiv.	16	252
xvii.	3	252	..	8	255			
xviii.	24	252	..	11	226	2 Chronicles.		
..	27	181, 194	..	31	118	i.	2	213
xix.	2	214	..	34	182, 186	..	11	212, 213, 215
..	15	139, 155	..	35	226	..	12	212
..	20	216	viii.	25	118	ii.	11	239
..	23	181	..	34	226	iii.	16	155
..	25	170	ix.	4	193	iv.	6	207

Chap.	Ver.	Page.	Chap.	Ver.	Page.	Chap.	Ver.	Page.
v.	12	155	xxxiii.	11	174	ii.	3	216
..	18	216	xxxiv.	6	193	..	14	218
..	19	216	..	9	187	iii.	6	213
vi.	9	226	..	12	153	..	7	199
..	11	202	..	14	220	..	13	170
..	13	214	..	22	182	..	15	117, 152
..	30	200	..	23	200	..	20	188
..	41	201	..	33	207	..	30	117
vii.	18	166	xxxv.	4	119	..	31	117
viii.	14	220	..	13	206	iv.	17	151
..	16	216	..	25	216	v.	5	213
ix.	13	213	xxxvi.	4	174	..	11	171
..	20	228	..	14	182	vi.	8	171
..	29	187				..	11	201
xi.	15	158	Ezra.			..	14	150
xii.	30	277	i.	1	172	..	17	152
..	32	276	..	4	199	vii.	8	213
xiii.	14	186	ii.	25	213	..	11	272
..	19	119	..	36	275	..	17	272, 273
xv.	1	139	..	38	273	..	31	213
..	6	219	..	42	275	..	37	213, 272
xvi.	7	170	..	46	117, 191	..	38	272
xvii.	8	117	..	50	118	..	42	274
..	11	117	..	59	208	..	44	277
xviii.	7	222	..	65	273	..	52	119
..	12	141	..	67	274	..	61	208
..	14	207	..	69	273	..	62	213
xix.	7	231	..	70	225	..	66	271
..	8	227	iii.	2	215	..	70	275
..	11	141	..	3	117	..	73	255
xx.	9	201	..	7	172, 221	viii.	6	208
..	26	216	iv.	2	108, 111	..	9	147
..	29	220	..	4	117	..	11	147
xxi.	17	220	..	7	183	ix.	6	118
xxii.	7	221	..	9	118	..	9	213, 241
..	10	222	..	12	192	..	17	117
xxiv.	6	216	..	22	172	..	15	175
..	20	139	v.	10	239	..	19	200
..	23	216	..	14	239	..	20	175
..	27	187	..	15	118, 131	..	23	219
xxv.	3	119	vi.	5	239	..	29	220
..	12	274	..	9	212	..	35	175
..	25	273	..	11	256	..	37	108
xxvi.	6	174	..	15	172	x.	20	119
..	10	174	vii.	17	212, 214	..	29	151, 213
..	21	119	..	25	255	..	30	213
xxvii.	9	152	..	26	232	xii.	9	232
xxix.	8	117	viii.	14	188	..	14	117, 187
..	9	213	..	17	117, 119	..	16	118
..	14	119	..	18	213	..	38	152, 171
..	22	174	..	25	182	..	42	207
..	2?	174	ix.	4	215	..	44	171
		17	..	5	220	xiii.	4	217
		18	x.	5	255	..	16	171
xxx.	21	227	..	12	183	..	23	182
..	25	152	..	17	200	..	30	231
xxxi.	5	213, 214	..	29	186			
..	6	152	..	35	187	Esther.		
..	14	151	..	37	232	i.	5	117
..	15	220	..	43	232	..	6	230
..	17	220	..	44	187	..	8	208
xxxii.	9	174				..	16	117
..	21	232	Nehemiah.			ii.	2	148
xxxiii.	3	208	ii.	2	219	..	14	159

Chap.	Ver.	Page.	Chap.	Ver.	Page.	Chap.	Ver.	Page.
ESTHER.			xviii.	28	200	xxxviii.	10	202
iii.	4	188	xix.	2	171	..	11	272
..	12	208	..	4	239	..	12	292
..	15	233	..	17	205	..	19	209
iv.	11	206, 264	..	29	118	..	30	239
..	14	151	xx.	11	183	..	35	254
v.	9	222	..	13	255	..	39	221
..	12	150, 170	..	17	214	..	41	183
vi.	9	200	xxi.	12	236	xxxix.	10	238
..	11	200	..	13	188, 201	..	26	183
viii.	8	208	..	42	221	..	30	183
..	11	213	xxii.	28	208	xl.	6	193
..	13	119	xxiii.	7	205	..	10	213
ix.	7	231	..	9	205, 249	..	11	222
..	9	230, 231, 232	xxiv.	1	183	..	17	183
..	16	206	..	2	155	..	30	223
..	22	221	..	5	220	xli.	7	170
..	27	117	..	6	118	xlii.	10	245
..	28	213	..	8	221	..	16	118, 278
..	29	230	..	14	240			
..	32	221	..	22	206	**PSALMS.**		
			..	24	222	i.	6	151
JOB.			xxv.	2	208	v.	9	119, 180
i.	1	171	xxvi.	8	205	vi.	4	118
..	10	118	..	12	117, 240	ix.	5	199
..	13	213	..	14	183	..	7	240
ii.	4	200	xxvii.	1	245	..	8	152
..	7	117, 184	..	2	215	..	10	141
iv.	14	208	..	7	207	..	13	109
v.	4	160	..	11	253	..	14	219
..	5	221	xxviii.	13	178	..	21	249
..	8	218	..	15	103	x.	6	164
vi.	2	118	..	27	178	..	8	177
..	22	205	xxix.	1	245	..	10	187, 193
..	29	187	..	2	214	..	12	109
..	13	230	..	16	222	..	14	156
..	40	223	xxx.	11	232	..	15	182
vii.	5	118, 231	..	22	119	xi.	1	232
..	20	205	..	30	205	xvii.	11	187
viii.	12	217	xxxi.	7	171	..	12	207
..	19	197	..	8	221	..	14	118
ix.	13	240	..	20	221, 283	..	25	252
..	26	201	..	22	171, 178	xviii.	1	150
..	30	232	..	35	197	..	3	203
..	33	245	xxxii.	4	178	xix.	3	221
..	34	230	..	6	223	..	6	207
x.	13	152	xxxiii.	5	178	..	9	208
..	17	236	..	9	231	..	12	232
..	20	186	..	12	197	xx.	4	162
xi.	2	166	..	19	118	xxii.	17	253
..	17	220	..	20	197, 223	..	27	207, 216
..	42	166	..	21	187	..	30	231
xii.	15	207	..	26	252	xxiii.	5	236
..	22	140, 250	..	28	187, 231	xxiv.	4	231, 232
xiv.	5	183	xxxiv.	31	208	..	6	182, 183
..	21	206	xxxv.	8	249	..	7	229
xv.	9	238	xxxvi.	1	245	..	8	229
..	15	183	..	11	201	..	9	229
..	27	217	..	14	208	xxv.	5	150
xvi.	11	207, 214	..	16	239	..	13	203
..	14	163, 231	xxxvii.	12	183	xxvii.	2	208
..	16	179	..	19	208	..	4	150
xviii.	11	222	xxxviii.	1	193	..	5	231
..	17	226	..	3	213	xxx.	6	220

Chap.	Ver.	Page.	Chap.	Ver.	Page.	Chap.	Ver.	Page.
xxx.	9	. 218	lxxii.	16	. 207	cvi.	45	. 183
xxxi.	4	. 217	..	17	. 118	cvii.	3	. 221
..	6	. 150	..	19	. 238	..	20	. 236
..	13	. 207	..	20	. 236	..	24	. 206
xxxii.	4	. 162	lxxiii.	2	117, 179	cviii.	7	. 232
xxxiii.	14	. 256	..	27	. 175	..	15	. 183
xxxiv.	8	. 206	..	28	. 223	cxv.	10	. 287
..	13	. 208	lxxiv.	5	. 206	..	15	. 155
..	27	. 254	..	6	. 118	cxviii.	8	. 203
xxxvii.	18	. 151	..	7	. 198	..	9	. 203
..	29	. 207	..	9	. 151	..	12	. 208
xxxix.	2	140, 163	..	11	. 119	cxix.	9	. 161
..	7	. 206	lxxv.	10	. 149	..	16	. 161
xl.	5	. 240	lxxvii.	12	118, 187	..	17	161, 183
..	17	. 252	..	13	. 162	..	28	. 161
xli.	3	. 186	lxxviii.	31	. 239	..	37	. 162
..	10	. 151	..	38	. 135	..	41	. 162
xlii.	5	152, 173	..	57	. 207	..	42	. 161
..	8	. 151	..	72	. 208	..	47	. 183
xliv.	17	. 221	lxxix.	10	. 118	..	48	. 201
xlv.	10	. 162	lxxx.	2	. 155	..	65	. 161
..	12	. 207	..	6	. 207	..	70	. 207
..	18	. 149	..	14	. 135	..	71	. 208
xlvi.	2	. 203	..	16	. 230	..	79	. 232
..	5	. 147	..	17	. 207	..	98	. 162
xlviii.	14	. 178	lxxxi.	16	. 141	..	105	. 161
xlix.	15	118, 236	lxxxiii.	12	. 207	..	107	. 161
l.	4	. 218	lxxxiv.	4	. 230	..	113	. 223
..	23	. 127	lxxxv.	2	. 119	..	119	. 175
li.	2	. 223	lxxxvii.	4	. 240	..	130	. 196
..	4	. 118	lxxxix.	10	. 217	..	161	. 183
lv.	13	. 201	..	11	171, 240	..	167	. 236
..	16	. 193	..	18	. 118	..	169	. 161
lvi.	1	. 150	..	29	. 152	cxxi.	3	. 162
..	5	. 246	..	40	. 175	..	6	. 177
..	7	. 118	..	49	. 216	cxxii.	2	. 161
..	12	. 246	..	51	. 214	cxxiii.	2	. 172
lvii.	2	. 203	xc.	8	118, 176	..	4	. 193
lviii.	6	. 152	..	10	. 240	cxxix.	3	. 119
..	8	. 183	..	11	. 151	..	5	. 207
..	12	. 201	..	17	. 141	cxxxi.	2	. 207
..	18	. 277	xci.	2	. 203	cxxxii.	11	. 199
lix.	3	. 221	..	12	. 162	..	12	. 199
..	13	. 221	..	16	. 222	..	15	. 178
..	16	. 119	xcii.	1	. 217	cxxxv.	18	. 212
lxi.	6	. 175	..	7	. 206	cxxxvi.	6	. 233
lxii.	9	. 203	..	8	. 207	..	11	. 250
lxv.	5	. 147	..	9	. 149	..	20	170, 240
..	11	. 220	..	20	. 232	cxxxviii.	3	. 240
lxvi.	7	. 118	xciii.	5	. 170	cxxxix.	5	. 177
..	9	. 116	xciv.	25	. 252	..	6	. 117
..	10	. 208	xcvii.	11	. 208	cxl.	10	. 119
..	15	233, 234	xcix.	6	. 170	cxli.	8	. 177
lxvii.	8	. 150	ci.	5	150, 182	..	11	. 118
lxviii.	31	220, 222	cii.	5	. 153	cxliv.	1	. 198
lxix.	7	. 215	ciii.	5	. 201	cxlv.	6	. 117
lxx.	5	. 254	..	19	. 200	..	8	. 182
lxxi.	4	. 205	civ.	29	. 205	..	10	. 177
..	7	203, 207	cv.	9	. 247	..	15	. 218
..	12	. 118	..	11	. 232	..	21	. 236
..	15	. 162	..	13	. 219	cxlvii.	19	. 183
..	20	. 232	..	28	. 183	cxlviii.	2	. 183
lxxii.	1	. 255	..	37	. 199	..	4	. 182
..	5	. 217	..	40	163, 183	cl.	5	. 205

PROVERBS.			Chap.	Ver.	Page.	Chap.	Ver.	Page.
Chap.	Ver.	Page.	xxii.	14	154, 183	vii.	23	118
i.	1	172, 230, 238	..	20	119	..	37	236
..	5	205	..	25	183	viii.	5	206
..	8	203	xxiii.	5	117, 119,	..	12	221
..	10	196			187, 201	..	15	200
..	15	223	..	7	205	ix.	2	200
..	19	205	..	13	236	..	4	117, 191
..	20	172	..	23	185	..	11	238
..	27	117, 207	..	24	117, 118, 184	..	12	206
..	29	246	..	26	117, 191	x.	3	185
ii.	7	187	xxiv.	10	177	..	14	206
..	11	177	..	12	206	..	18	208
..	22	256	..	29	200	..	23	184
iii.	6	196	xxv.	7	208	xi.	8	216
..	15	205	..	28	208	xii.	4	208
..	30	119	xxvi.	24	183	..	6	189
..	34	109	xxvii.	1	196	..	13	230
iv.	16	119	..	9	224			
v.	3	178	..	10	118	SONG OF SONGS.		
..	20	165	..	14	161, 214	i.	1	230
vi.	3	240	..	19	200	..	17	189
..	13	183	..	24	117, 184	ii.	2	207
vii.	13	205	..	26	221	..	11	163, 183
..	16	223	..	27	221	..	17	164
viii.	17	118	xxviii.	13	222	iii.	8	137
..	26	223	..	17	231	..	11	177
ix.	2	205	..	22	206	iv.	2	190
..	9	238	xxix.	21	191	..	3	207
x.	18	172	xxx.	10	183	..	4	157
xi.	3	187	..	14	221	..	5	208
..	11	220	..	15	231	v.	2	150, 222
..	25	172	..	18	118	..	6	222
..	26	205	..	24	205	..	11	150, 207
xiii.	20	117, 187	xxxi.	2	232	..	13	210
xiv.	12	225	..	10	178	..	15	207
..	21	102	..	16	118	vi.	5	240
..	22	218	..	18	118	vii.	4	208
xv.	23	206	..	21	154	viii.	9	232
..	27	216	..	23	220	..	10	171
..	33	217	..	27	117	..	12	274
xvi.	19	109						
..	21	206	ECCLESIASTES.			ISAIAH.		
..	27	183	i.	1	200, 236	i.	7	155
..	28	231	..	2	200	..	8	207
..	30	172	..	5	218	ii.	12	236
xvii.	10	205	..	16	228	iii.	5	240
..	13	118	ii.	1	201	..	15	193
..	14	217	..	18	200	..	16	119
..	27	187	..	22	200	..	24	196
xviii.	16	217	..	25	251	iv.	1	206
..	17	186	..	26	236	..	2	236
xix.	16	117	iii.	16	205	..	4	208
..	17	196	iv.	8	183	v.	8	199, 200
..	19	189, 223	..	14	170	..	24	207
xx.	3	200	v.	8	200	..	25	209
..	4	186	..	10	118	..	28	209
..	17	200	..	12	238	..	29	187
..	21	189	vi.	3	216	vi.	2	142
..	24	188	..	10	185	..	4	151
..	26	252	..	12	200	..	13	205
..	30	118	vii.	1	230	vii.	4	205
xxi.	4	164	..	19	201	..	10	245
xxii.	8	182, 251	..	21	227	..	15	201
..	11	208	..	22	118	..	16	201, 206

Chap.	Ver.	Page.	Chap.	Ver.	Page.	Chap.	Ver.	Page.
viii.	1	207	xxx.	5	171	xlix.	4	237
..	3	262	..	7	240, 241	..	6	118
..	4	206	..	9	229, 241	..	7	147
..	5	245	..	18	152	..	9	149
..	17	237	..	19	208	..	13	186
ix.	6	193, 196	..	29	222	..	15	205
..	15	221	..	32	178	..	22	234
x.	6	118	xxxi.	8	200	l.	7	202
..	13	171, 257	xxxii.	11	173, 205	li.	2	218
..	17	221	..	14	196	..	7	221
..	24	177	..	19	222	..	9	240
..	38	171	xxxiii.	7	193	..	13	226
xi.	11	221	..	12	172	..	16	202
xii.	5	118	xxxiv.	16	231	..	21	154
xiii.	2	141, 255	xxxv.	8	206	lii.	2	232
..	16	194	..	10	266	..	3	199
..	21	158	xxxvi.	9	252	..	5	183
xiv.	10	254	xxxvii.	6	150	..	6	206
..	12	152	..	16	139	..	12	215, 221
..	20	175	..	21	216	liv.	6	154
..	21	240	..	26	150	..	9	221
xvi.	3	222, 232	..	30	116, 117	..	13	227
..	4	222	..	32	109	..	15	150, 222
..	14	220	..	35	217	lv.	2	208
xvii.	13	207	xxxviii.	12	207	..	4	196
xviii.	1	206	..	16	196	..	7	218
..	4	182, 220	..	13	258	..	13	117, 184
..	5	178, 208	xxxix.	6	174	..	20	236
xix.	2	205	xl.	3	151	lvi.	10	230
..	3	218	..	12	222	lvii.	1	248
..	22	208	..	20	198	..	11	150
xxi.	2	178	..	22	207	..	19	119
..	5	213	..	24	205, 207	lviii.	2	150
..	13	208	..	27	202, 221	..	6	236
..	15	224	xli.	7	152	..	7	221
xxii.	23	199	..	9	221	..	9	201
xxiii.	1	247	..	17	215	lix.	18	154
..	13	118	..	23	118	lx.	5	240
..	17	178	..	25	171	..	21	232
..	11	178	xlii.	16	140	lxi.	1	208
xxiv.	2	152	20	20	118	..	10	207
..	10	207	24	24	119	lxii.	3	119
..	18	207	xliii.	9	254	..	4	206
..	19	205	..	14	174	lxiii.	2	221
xxv.	10	187	..	17	208	..	12	205
xxvi.	1	165	xliv.	6	221	lxiv.	6	151
..	2	174	..	14	231	lxv.	4	189
..	16	223	..	16	118, 201	..	7	189
..	20	182	..	17	182, 201	lxvi.	3	152, 241
xxvii.	4	213	..	24	193	..	4	246
..	9	222	xlv.	2	118	..	7	170, 196
..	11	150, 208, 222	..	3	151, 215	..	10	183
xxviii.	4	150, 178	..	8	207	..	17	190
..	12	172, 229	..	13	222	..	21	213
..	15	118	..	15	215			
..	17	196, 208	..	24	225	JEREMIAH.		
..	20	205	xlvi.	11	232	i.	1	187
xxix.	3	166	..	17	252	..	5	182
..	5	207	xlvii.	13	232	ii.	2	235
..	8	151	xlviii.	2	215	..	9	163
..	11	151, 184	..	7	217	..	13	171
..	18	221	..	8	162	..	14	201
..	23	215	..	10	199	..	15	197
xxx.	4	222	xlix.	1	208	..	16	186

R R

Chap.	Ver.	Page.	Chap.	Ver.	Page.	Chap.	Ver.	Page.
Jeremiah.			xiv.	9	239	xxvii.	1	142
ii.	20	189	..	10	141	..	16	174
..	21	152	..	14	119	..	18	174
..	25	116, 163	..	16	158	..	19	155
..	27	187	xv.	1	207	..	20	174
..	31	163	..	5	148	..	22	174
..	35	150	..	7	163	xxviii.	4	174
..	62	261	..	8	183	..	8	158
iii.	2	194	..	9	118, 163	xxix.	1	158, 174
..	3	163	..	11	119, 149, 163	..	3	174
..	7	118	..	16	183	..	4	174
..	9	166	xvi.	2	158	..	8	159
..	12	163	..	9	254	..	10	166
..	18	141, 255	..	11	150	..	14	118
..	19	221, 236	..	16	119	..	15	174
..	22	169	xvii.	1	236	..	20	174
iv.	5	117	..	7	196, 203	..	21	218
..	11	163	..	8	118	..	23	116, 151, 163, 196
..	14	152	..	11	183			
..	16	241	..	13	186	..	24	218
..	22	150	..	19	184	..	25	177
..	23	218	..	23	116	..	32	201
..	29	169	..	26	213, 221	xxx.	4	218
v.	8	240	xviii.	3	193	..	14	150
..	9	163	..	8	236	..	16	171, 283
..	10	163	..	10	118, 150	..	21	208
..	12	213	..	16	119	xxxi.	10	196
..	18	158	..	22	118	..	23	216
..	22	150, 222	xix.	2	118, 235	..	32	207
..	24	117	xx.	3	250	..	34	150
..	28	207	..	4	174, 200	..	38	109
vi.	7	118, 241	..	5	174	..	39	226, 118
..	9	152, 163	..	11	150	..	40	189
..	14	229	..	17	178	xxxii.	8	202
..	21	186	xxi.	3	214	..	17	139
..	25	147, 187	..	4	216	..	21	171
..	29	193	..	5	213	..	23	116, 196
vii.	25	158	..	9	186	..	31	150
..	27	177	..	13	190	xxxiii.	2	150
..	28	163	xxii.	2	213	..	4	218
..	31	237	..	6	179	..	8	164, 182
viii.	1	117, 158	..	12	226	..	13	163, 222
..	6	116, 163	..	14	196	..	21	227
..	7	119	..	22	221	xxxiv.	2	216
..	11	229	xxiii.	4	116	..	5	251
..	20	163	..	5	116	..	13	216
ix.	5	150	..	16	241	..	14	236
..	7	116	..	18	187	xxxv.	4	221
..	9	236	..	21	216	..	8	255
..	23	150	..	22	207	..	10	255
x.	2	163, 199, 221	..	24	139	xxxv.	15	158
..	13	184, 250	..	27	226	..	18	241
..	18	152	xxv.	8	171	xxxvi.	10	206
..	23	200	..	6	150	..	12	152
xi.	17	150	..	7	119	..	18	220
xiii.	2	202	..	9	218	..	22	287
..	5	150, 222	..	34	213	xxxvii.	7	216
..	16	186	xxvi.	5	241	..	15	150
..	20	187	..	6	118	..	16	155
..	25	150	..	8	158	..	18	150
..	27	163	..	11	158, 200	xxxviii.	2	186
xiv.	2	221	..	15	159	..	11	184
..	3	119	..	16	200	..	12	171
..	8	240	..	23	237	..	16	110

Chap.	Ver.	Page.	Chap.	Ver.	Page.	Chap.	Ver.	Page.
xxxviii.	24	206	li.	48	255	v.	7	223
..	28	262	lii.	11	174	vi.	9	150
..	52	162	..	17	174	..	13	236
xxxix.	7	174	..	31	250	vii.	21	117
..	11	236	..	32	184, 199	viii.	1	152
..	12	110				..	4	215
..	13	231	LAMENTATIONS.			..	6	193
..	14	231	i.	1	193, 206, 238	ix.	3	215
..	15	218	..	6	181, 193	..	5	189
..	19	261	..	12	163, 231	..	6	213
xl.	1	174	..	16	152	..	8	171, 229
..	3	184	..	18	184	..	11	194
..	7	174	..	19	208, 209	x.	1	155
..	8	119	ii.	2	117, 184	..	2	155
..	12	233	..	4	207	..	3	155
..	15	177, 206	..	6	178	..	6	155
..	16	118	..	8	165	..	7	155
xli.	17	223	..	9	231	..	8	155
xlii.	9	216	..	11	206	..	10	202
..	20	116	..	12	208, 209	..	19	215
xliii.	10	119	..	14	118, 158	..	20	215
..	11	118	..	16	222	xi.	12	223
xliv.	6	214	..	19	118	..	13	229
..	10	217	iii.	2	150	..	22	215
..	13	152	..	4	220	..	24	139
xlv.	2	216	..	10	118	xii.	13	274
xlvi.	4	237	..	12	172	xiii.	14	222
..	8	233	..	20	118	..	16	148
..	12	163	..	36	231	xiv.	1	222
..	21	163	..	39	183	..	4	178
..	25	152	..	65	232	..	8	222
..	28	217	iv.	3	193	..	12	205
xlvii.	7	218	..	6	184	..	22	152
xlviii.	4	119	..	12	117	xv.	5	222
..	5	118	..	16	117	xvi.	4	150
..	7	117	..	17	197	..	39	150
..	9	196	..	20	236	..	40	150
..	18	186	v.	1	118	..	44	178
..	20	187	..	3	117, 184	..	56	163
..	21	119	..	4	199	..	57	150, 171
..	26	222	..	5	117, 184	..	59	150
..	27	118	..	7	117, 184	..	60	150, 166
..	40	201	..	18	185	..	62	166
xlix.	3	163, 177	..	21	118, 236	xvii.	12	174
..	16	201				..	17	150
..	20	163	EZEKIEL.			..	20	174, 222
..	22	201	i.	1	171, 172, 237	..	21	184
..	30	190	..	2	238	xviii.	6	266
l.	1	118	..	8	232	..	13	216
..	6	118, 179	..	10	224	..	14	196
..	8	184	..	14	172	..	17	241
..	11	187	ii.	3	150	..	20	184
..	15	116	..	4	150	..	22	216
..	18	218	iii.	15	152, 190, 193	..	27	216
..	21	147	..	16	262	xix.	14	205
..	25	250	..	23	207	xx.	16	241
..	29	109, 161	..	27	150	..	20	255
li.	3	110, 192	iv.	9	152	..	24	241
..	9	171	..	10	221	..	31	216
..	10	202	..	12	208	..	38	225
..	16	250	..	14	213	xxi.	16	152
..	27	241	..	15	119	..	28	182
..	34	232	..	17	236	xxii.	14	150
..	43	196	v.	6	241	..	15	150

Chap.	Ver.	Page.	Chap.	Ver.	Page.	Chap.	Ver.	Page.
xxii.	18	. 119	xxxix.	11	. 179	iv.	4	185, 221
..	20	. 155	..	16	. 178	..	6	. 208
xxiii.	16	. 118	..	26	. 170	..	9	. 117
..	23	. 147	xl.	3	. 150	..	16	. 240
..	25	. 150	..	4	. 177	v.	7	. 117
..	29	. 150	..	15	. 116	..	8	. 185
..	35	. 150	..	19	. 205	..	10	. 185
..	40	. 239	..	22	. 183	..	20	. 209
..	42	. 218	..	26	. 183	..	21	. 117
..	43	118, 179	..	43	. 218	..	29	. 117
..	44	. 225	..	48	. 165	vi.	10	. 223
xxiv.	2	. 212	..	49	. 155	..	20	. 230
..	6	. 178	xli.	8	. 118	..	21	. 231
..	11	. 205	..	15	119, 172	vii.	7	. 238
..	16	. 168	xlii.	4	. 217	..	9	. 222
..	27	. 202	..	9	119, 192	..	10	. 230
xxv.	6	. 171	..	13	. 147	..	12	. 206
..	7	. 190	..	14	186, 196	..	13	. 238
..	8	. 208	..	16	. 117	viii.	22	. 155
xxvi.	7	. 213	..	20	. 205	..	23	. 221
xxvii.	12	. 199	..	24	. 222	ix.	5	. 117
..	15	. 182	xliii.	2	. 215	..	12	183, 208, 209
..	20	. 178	..	10	. 217	..	18	. 118
..	30	. 241	..	15	. 117	..	19	. 178
xxviii.	8	. 176	..	16	. 117	..	21	. 222
..	9	132, 208	..	17	. 222	..	24	. 189
..	13	. 249	..	20	150, 218	x.	12	. 175
..	16	. 170	..	23	. 220	..	13	. 252
..	23	. 200	..	27	. 171	..	18	. 245
..	24	. 171	xliv.	1	. 252	xi.	6	. 221
..	26	. 171	..	3	. 182	..	12	171, 189
xxix.	5	. 150	..	5	. 186	..	18	. 189
..	19	. 178	..	15	. 262	..	31	. 150
xxx.	16	. 118	..	22	. 213	..	33	. 200
xxxi.	4	. 222	..	24	187, 222, 241	..	38	. 214
..	5	172, 183	xlv.	3	. 118	..	44	172, 238
..	7	. 223	..	7	. 252	xii.	13	149, 218
..	11	. 222	..	21	. 141			
..	13	. 218	..	23	. 237	Hosea.		
..	18	. 179	xlvi.	9	. 117	i.	1	186, 187, 188
xxxii.	13	. 159	..	15	. 187	..	6	. 237
..	25	. 162	xlvii.	8	. 152	ii.	2	. 214
..	30	. 198	..	9	. 216	iii.	1	. 154
..	31	. 179	..	10	. 178	iv.	6	. 171
..	32	179, 232	..	11	. 183	..	8	. 218
xxxiii.	9	. 218	..	12	. 152	..	19	. 150
..	30	. 252	..	13	. 190	v.	12	. 207
..	31	141, 255	..	14	. 118	..	14	. 207
xxxiv.	23	. 157	xlviii.	16	. 110	vi.	2	208, 209
..	29	. 166	..	35	. 276	..	3	. 173
xxxvi.	3	. 213				..	10	. 118
..	5	172, 178	Daniel.			vii.	2	. 221
..	11	169, 214	i.	4	. 171	..	12	. 226
..	12	. 179	..	5	. 214	viii.	1	. 201
..	14	. 116	..	13	. 196	..	10	. 213
..	20	222, 225	ii.	9	. 186	..	12	182, 232
xxxvii.	9	. 207	..	22	. 118	ix.	10	178, 207
..	10	. 207	..	39	. 172	..	11	. 221
..	22	. 179	..	43	117, 179	..	15	. 152
..	24	236, 241	iii.	5	. 238	x.	6	. 150
xxxviii.	4	. 150	..	10	. 118	..	10	. 118
..	9	. 207	..	19	. 232	..	14	. 171
..	17	. 150	..	27	. 238	xi.	9	. 224
xxxix.	2	. 171	..	29	172, 179	xii.	1	. 163

Chap.	Ver.	Page.		Chap.	Ver.	Page.		Chap.	Ver.	Page.
HOSEA.				i.	16	223, 228		**ZEPHANIAH.**		
xii.	10	163		..	20	154, 165, 260		i.	9	152
xiii.	6	207						..	17	200
..	14	208		**JONAH.**				ii.	7	119
..	15	214		i.	14	172, 226		iii.	5	140
xiv.	4	222		iii.	2	235		..	7	178
..	6	207		iv.	9	215				
..	7	141		vi.	13	236		**HAGGAI.**		
..	10	159						i.	8	111, 118
				MICAH.				..	12	226
JOEL.				i.	2	141, 160		..	13	171
i.	20	236		..	3	182		ii.	6	139
ii.	2	212		..	7	182		..	21	139
..	6	171		..	8	118		..	22	200
..	17	254		..	13	239				
iv.	3	218		..	15	163		**ZECHARIAH.**		
..	8	208		..	16	201		i.	4	183
..	11	208, 209		ii.	7	208		..	8	206
..	16	203		iii.	2	118		..	16	118
..	17	255		..	11	199		ii.	6	212
..	19	172		iv.	9	248		..	12	219
				v.	10	240		iii.	10	236
AMOS.				..	13	240		iv.	7	178
iii.	9	241		vi.	4	213		vi.	8	152
iv.	1	151		vii.	9	140		..	11	205
..	2	206						vii.	10	213
..	10	171		**NAHUM.**				viii.	20	163
v.	7	221		i.	2	152		ix.	4	178
..	8	151		..	3	182, 231		..	10	208
..	14	141		..	4	152		x.	5	220
..	19	226		..	13	222		..	10	221
vi.	9	199		ii.	6	118		xi.	2	119
..	12	221		..	11	171		..	5	171
vii.	8	182		..	14	178		xiii.	9	208
..	14	152, 205		iii.	3	186		xiv.	2	194
viii.	3	182		..	12	151		..	6	186
..	4	119						..	18	237
..	8	186		**HABAKKUK.**						
ix.	1	207		i.	8	201		**MALACHI.**		
..	3	239		..	13	208		i.	3	202
..	4	239		..	15	196, 207		..	12	150
..	8	206		..	16	221		..	13	150
..	13	152		ii.	2	151		..	14	152
				..	4	216		ii.	12	206, 221
OBADIAH.				..	6	201		iii.	10	141
i.	4	201		iii.	10	213		..	22	150, 230, 236
..	10	176		..	14	183				
..	11	183						2 **MACCABEES.**		
								ii.	5	119

INDEX II.

MASSORETIC LISTS QUOTED ENTIRE.

א

א how many times found in the Bible, 271.
Sixteen words with silent Aleph, or altogether without Aleph, 170.
Seventeen words which occur only once with audible Aleph, 171.
Fifty words which have only once silent Aleph in the middle, 171, 185.
Twelve words which have only once quiescent Aleph at the end, 172.
Seventeen words with quiescent Aleph at the end, which have no parallel, 172.
אבנב, Alphabetical list, according to, 223.
אבותך three times, 251.
אהלה occurs four times, 179.
אויב three times definite, 149.
אותה twelve times plene, 150.
אותו twenty-four times plene, 149, 150.
אותי twenty-seven times plene, 150.
אותיות גדולות, Alphabetical lists of, 230.
אותיות קטנות, Alphabetical lists of, 231.
אותך masculine, seventeen times plene, 150.
אותך feminine, seventeen times plene, 150.
אותם thirty-nine times plene, 150.
אחד twenty-five times, 252.
אחו three times with Kametz and Pattach, 249.
אל thirty times construed with other words in an unparallelled manner, 218.
אלהי ישראל twenty-eight times, 215.
אם five times, supposed to be wanting in the text, 226.
אם three times before אב, 241.
אני יהוה twenty times at the end of a verse, 255.
אני יהוה אלהיכם twenty-one times at the end of a verse, 255.
אעלה Hiphil future eight times, 233.
ארצה כנען eight times, 174.
אשר in four times, supposed to be כאשר, 226.
את השמים ואת הארץ occurs thirteen times, 139.
אתבש, Alphabetical list of words, according to, 222.
אחה eleven times in an unique construction, 217.

ב

ב how many times found in the Bible, 272.
Twenty-six words which occur only once with Beth, and which in all other instances have Kaph, 220.

Eleven words with Beth in the textual reading, and Kaph in the marginal reading, 188.
Six words with Beth in the textual reading, and Mem in the marginal reading, 189.
בבית six times Raphe, 199.
בבלה twenty-nine times, 174.
בבדמה four times Raphe, 200.
בהן fifteen times with Tzere, 195.
באמה six times, 177.
בחרב eight times Raphe, 200.
בחרו three times with Kametz under the Cheth, 246.
במוב four times Raphe and nine times with Dagesh in the Teth, 201.
בכל seven times with Dagesh in the Kaph, 200.
בכסף fifteen times Raphe, 200.
בלילה three times Raphe, 200.
בן in four instances, supposed to be בני, 225, 226.
בעוף three times, 251.
ברא אלהים three times, 139, 215.
בראשית begins a verse three times, 142.
בשדה five times Raphe, 200.

ג

ג how many times found in the Bible, 272.
גבור three times defective, 148.
גורל four times defective, 149.

ד

ד how many times found in the Bible, 272.
Two words with Daleth at the end in the textual reading, and Resh in the marginal reading, 189.
Two words with Daleth in the marginal reading, and with Tav in the textual reading, 196.
דבריך plural, thirteen times defective, 161.
דבריך eight times with Jod plural in the textual reading, but without it in the marginal reading, 183.
דרכיך three times defective, 162.

ה

ה how many times it occurs in the Bible, 274.
ה in twenty-nine instances, is wanted in the textual reading, but is supplied in the marginal reading, 117, 118.

ה in twenty instances is in the textual reading, but not in the marginal reading, 118.

Thirteen words without He at the beginning in the textual reading, but with it in the marginal reading, 184.

Seven words with He at the beginning in the textual reading, but not in the marginal reading, 184.

Five words with He in the middle in the textual reading, and without it in the marginal reading, 185.

Twelve words with He second radical, whilst in all other instances it is Cheth, 240.

Thirty-two words ending in He and Vav, 222.

Fourteen words terminating with He in the textual reading, and with Vav in the marginal reading.

Twenty-one words with He at the end after Kaph, second person singular masculine, 177.

Eleven words which respectively occur twice, once with audible, and once with quiescent He, 178.

Eighteen words which abnormally terminate with quiescent He, 178.

Two instances in which the textual reading has הם suffix, third person plural masculine, and the marginal reading כם suffix, second person plural masculine, 190.

האהלה eight times, 174.

הביחה eighteen times, 174.

המונה four times, 179.

המובחה thirty times, 174.

הקימותי twice entirely plene, eleven times entirely defective, and six times Jod plene, and Vav defective, 166.

ה׳ five times with Segol, 197.

ו

ו how many times it occurs in the Bible, 272, 273.

Twenty-three verses which have neither Vav nor Jod, 282.

ו conjunctive in eleven instances in the Kethiv, but not in the Keri, 117.

ו suffix, not in the Kethiv in eighteen instances, but in the Keri, 117.

ו suffix in eleven instances in the textual reading, but not in the marginal, 117.

ו in seventy-five instances, to be found in the middle of, or in, the textual reading for which the marginal reading has Vav.

Ten words beginning with Vav in the marginal reading, and with Jod in the textual reading, 187.

Twenty-five words with Vav plene, without parallel, 151, 152.

List of thirty-three words with Vav after Kametz and Chateph-Kametz in the textual reading, and without Vav in the marginal reading, 182.

Forty-eight words terminating in Vav in the textual reading, and in Jod in the marginal reading, 232.

Twenty-two words beginning and ending with Vav, which occurs twice, once Milel, and once Milra, 207.

Five pairs of words which respectively occur twice, once with Vav conjunctive, and once without, 212.

Sixty-two pairs of words in which both numbers have Vav conjunctive, 218.

Sixteen pairs without Vav conjunctive, 213, 214.

Twenty-seven words beginning with Vav and Mem, 221.

Thirteen words beginning with Vav, Mem, and Beth, 221.

Twelve words beginning with Vav, Mem, and Gimmel, 221, 222.

Four proper names occurring five times in the same order, but with the Vav conjunctive differently placed in each passage, 228.

Six verses having the same words four times, twice with Vav conjunctive, and twice without it, 224.

Four verses having respectively the same word four times, the first with Vav, and the other three without it, 215.

Forty-eight words in the textual reading with Vav at the end, and in the margin with Jod, 282.

ואדע three times, 202.

ואל forty-five times in an unparalleled construction, 218.

ואם three times at the beginning of a verse, 288, 239.

ואת nine times at the beginning of a verse, tion, 239.

ואמא twice with Sheva under the Vav, 201.

ואטים nine times with Kametz under the Vav, 202.

ואתה eight times in an unique construction, 218.

ויאמר six times with Sheva under the Vav, 201.

ויאמר אלהים twenty-five times. 215.

ויאמרו nine times with Sheva under the Vav, 254.

ויאמרו Kal ten times, 233.

ויבא in eight instances, supposed to be ויבאו, 225.

ויבא with Sheva under the Vav, occurs seven times, 141, 254, 255.

ויבדל occurs three times, 139, 142.

וידבר אלהים three times, 215.

וידבר יהוה אל משה ואל אהרן occurs twelve times, 139, 140.

וידו occurs thirty-two times, 141, 202

ויוסף thirty times, 245.

וַיִּסְחוּ twice Milel, 205.
וַיֵּרְצוּא twelve times plene, 250.
וַיְנַחֲדוּ Hiphil defective, seven times defective, 239, 240.
וַיֵּשֶׁב twenty-five times, 252.
וכל ישראל thirty-five times in the middle of the verse, 255.
לְמַעַן nine times, 217.
וּלְשֵׁנִי sixteen times, 217.
וַנִּשְׁמַע three times with Pattach under the Vav, and Dagesh in the Mem, 255, 256.
וַתְּדַבֵּר twice with Shurek, 202.
וַתּוֹרֵד three times, 251.
וְהִשְׁתַּחוּ twice with Sheva under the Vav, 201.

ז
ז how many times found in the Bible, 273.
זכרון three times definite, 148.

ח
ח how many times found in the Bible, 273.
Four words with Cheth in the textual reading, and with He in the marginal reading, 189.
חברונה five times, 174.
חותם seven times definite, 149.
חיל five times definite, 165.
חלושין, 113.
חסידה nine times with Chateph-pattach, 203.

ט
ט how many times found in the Bible, 273.
טמולים see טהורים.

י
י how many times it occurs in the Bible, 273.
Twenty-two words with Jod at the beginning in the textual reading, and with Vav in the marginal reading, 186.
Fifty-five words with Jod in the middle in the textual reading, and without Jod in the marginal reading, 183.
Twenty-four words with Jod at the end in the textual reading, and Vav in the marginal reading, 187.
י in seventy instances in the middle of a word in the textual reading, for which Vav is to be found in its marginal reading.
יאכל occurs seventy-three times, 141.
יברך יהוה four times, 216.
ידי nineteen times, 206.
ידע twenty-three times plene, 151.
יהיה eighteen times, 216.
יהי twice, 216.
יוצאים four times plene, 152.
יושבים ten times plene, 152.
יוסף occurs twice, 142.
ירא twenty-one times, 206.
ירושלימה five times, 174.
ישנלנה four times, altered into ישכבנה, 194.

כ
כ how many times found in the Bible, 274.
Those words beginning with Kaph in the textual reading, and Beth in the marginal reading, 188.
Twenty-one words beginning with Kaph, which occur twice, once Milel and once Milra.
כה אמר יהוה אלהי ישראל twenty-five times, 216.
כנשר four times Raphe, 201.
כרובים thirteen times defective, 155.
כתיב in fifteen instances one word, and the Keri two words; and in eight instances two words, and the Keri one word, 198.
כתיב ולא קרי eight instances, 110, 192.

ל
ל how many times found in the Bible, 274.
Fifteen words beginning with two Lameds, 220, 221.
לא once in four phrases, and once not, 223.
לאדם eleven times with Kametz under the Lamed, 200.
לאהל five times, 216.
לאור occurs seven times, 140.
לוא thirty-five times plene, 163.
למוב twice Raphe, 200.
לאיש thirty-two times with Kametz under the Lamed, 200.
לכסא six times Raphe, 199.
לעולם eighteen times defective, 149.

מ
מ how many times found in the Bible, 275.
מאכל four times with Pattach, 197.
מוקדמין ומאוחרין sixty-two instances of, 116, 117, 191.
מורדין six verses, 219.
מורדסין six words, 219.
מחמאה occurs three times, 140.
מלין, sixteen words without parallel, 236.
מלין, twenty-one, which respectively occur only once in a particul. r book, 236, 237.
מלין, fifty-one, which always occur in a certain form in one book, but which in all other books of the Scriptures occur in a different form, 237, 238.
מלעיל thirty-eight words only once Milel, 205.
מלרע twenty-two words only once so, 205.
מלעיל ומלרע an alphabetical list of words, 208.
ממנו in six instances supposed to be ממנה, 225.
מעשר three times with Sheva under the Ajin, 204.
מסני three times supposed to be מסי, 226.
מצרימה twenty-eight times, 174.
משפטי precedes חקתי eight times, 241.

301

נ
נ how many times found in the Bible, 275.
נער written so twenty-one times in the text, and in the marginal reading נערה, 109.
נשיאם four times, 157.
נחה twenty-nine times, 175.

ס
ס how many times found in the Bible, 275.
סמך thirty-nine instances in which the construction is inverted, 214, 215.

ע
ע how many times found in the Bible, 276.
עד זום nine times, 216.
עור fourteen times defective, 163.
עור eight times in the sense of enemy, 240.
על nine times, supposed to be עד, 226.
על twice in the textual reading, but אל in the marginal reading, 189.
עמדים eleven times defective, 155.
ענים five times in the Kethiv, and in the Keri ענוים, 109.
עטולים six times in the Kethiv, and in the Keri מחורים, 109, 194.

פ
פ how many times found in the Bible, 276.
Pattach with Athnach, list of instances, 197.
פני תהום occurs twice, 139.

צ
צ how many times found in the Bible, 276, 277.
צוער three times plene, 151.

ק
ק how many times found in the Bible, 277.
קדוש thirteen times defective, 147.
קדוש the construct, three times defective, 147.
קורא ten times plene, 151.
קרי ולא כתיב ten instances, 109.

ר
ר how many times found in the Bible, 277.
רוח אלהים occurs eight times, 139, 141.

ש
ש how many times found in the Bible, 277.
Four words with Resh in the textual reading, and Daleth in the marginal reading, 189.
שחט four times without את, 241.
שלום eight times defective, 148.
שמע twelve times construed with על, 241.

ת
ת how many times found in the Bible, 278.
תולעת twice defective, 151.
תנינים three times withe Jod plural, 157.
תסף three times Milra, 205.

INDEX III.

MASSORETIC TERMS AND ABBREVIATIONS EXPLAINED.

	Page.		Page.		Page.
אבנב	. 223	ירושלמי	. 260	סמיכין	. 212-214
אותיות גדלות	. 230	כ״ב	. 252	ס״ם	. 255
אותיות קטנות	. 231	כל־	. 252	סתרא	. 236-239
אמבה	190, 191	כ״ק	. 254	ספר הללי	. 260
א׳מ א׳ח	. 250	כתיב ולא קרי	110, 192	פתח	195, 196
אמ׳ת	. 248	ל	. 245	ענינא	. 241
אנ־ך	. 246	לית	. 245	ע״ס	. 258
אס׳ח	. 248	ל׳ד	. 254	פ״ד	. 253
אסממיא	. 260	ל׳ק	. 252	פסוק	. 242
אס׳ס	. 246	לשנא	239-241	פסקא	209, 210
אשלמתא	. 261	מדינחו	. 261	פסקא דסתרא	209, 210
אתבש	. 222	מוקדמין ומואחרין	. 191	פרינמא	. 262
אתין	228, 229	מורדסין	218, 219	פשטין	. 233
ב״ח	. 250	מחזורתא	. 259	פתח דסתרא	. 197
ב״ם	. 250	מטעין	227, 228	קמיצא	232, 233
במ׳א	. 250	מיסון	. 262	קמיצין	. 230
במ׳ב	. 250	מלא	145-148	קמץ	195, 196
נ׳ח	. 250	מלא דמלא	. 167	קרחי	224, 225
נ״ם	. 250	מס׳ה	. 249	קרי	180, &c.
דגש	197, 198	מ״ס	. 255	קריא	234-238
דכותיה	. 212	מלעיל	204, &c.	קרי ולא כתיב	109, 198
דמין	211, 212	מלרע	204, &c.	רבתא	. 231
דואן	232-234	מסיק	. 199	ר״ן	. 258
זוגין	. 211	מ״ש	. 257	רמ׳ח	. 256
ועירא	. 231	משמשין	220-224	ר״ם	. 254
חומש יוחדו	259, 260	נ״א	. 256	רפה	197, &c.
חסר	145-148	נוסחא	. 262	שב׳ג	. 248
חסר דחסר	. 116	נסבין	219, 220	שוא	202, &c.
יהב׳י	. 257	נפתלי	. 260	שימא	210, 211
יחידאין	215-218	סבירין	225-227	תא׳ם	. 248
ימ׳ה	. 250	סיני	. 259	תיבין	. 229

INDEX IV.

MASSORETIC LISTS QUOTED IN THIS BOOK, WHICH ARE ALSO FOUND IN THE OCHLA VE-OCHLA.

OCHLA VE-OCHLA. Section.	LEVITA. Page.	OCHLA VE-OCHLE. Section.	LEVITA. Page.	OCHLA VE-OCHLA. Section.	LEVITA. Page.
v.	208	cxi.	118	clii.	185
xi.	207	cxii.	118	cliv.	189
xv.	200	cxiii.	179	clxvii.	189
xviii.	221, 222	cxvii.	117	clxix.	194
xxxvii.	228	cxviii.	117	clxx.	109
xxxviii.	222	cxix.	117	clxxxi.	186
xliii.	178	cxx.	117	ccv.	240
xliv.	178	cxxi.	189	ccxv.	220
xlv.	207	cxxii.	189	ccxxi.	236, 237
lxxx.	118	cxxiii.	189	ccxxii.	238
lxxxi.	119	cxxviii.	183	ccxxxiv.	229
lxxxii.	230	cxxx.	161, 183	ccl.	223
lxxxiii.	230	cxxxi.	183	ccli.	212
lxxxiv.	231	cxxxiv.	186	cclii.	214
lxxxv.	218	cxxxv.	187	ccliii.	213
xci.	117	cxxxvi.	232	cclxi.	217
xcii.	177	cxxxvii.	188	cclxii.	218
xcvii.	110	cxliv.	109	cclxx.	236
xcviii	110	cxlv.	184	cclxxiii.	214, 215
xcix.	193	cxlvi.	184	cclxxviii.	241
c.	193	cxlviii.	171	cclxxxviii.	228
cii.	192	cxlix.	170, 188	ccclxxii.	205
ciii.	171	cl.	188	ccclxxiii.	205
civ.	172	cli.	190	iv. additions	205

INDEX V.

TOPICS AND NAMES.

A

ABBAG, alphabet denominated, 223.
ABRAVANEL, Isaac, 9, 10; his view of the Keri and Kethiv, 107.
——— Samuel, 12.
ACHA of Irak, his system of vowel-points, 61, 63.
ADRIAN, Matthew, 66.
ALCALA, Alphonso de, his contributions to the Complutensian Polyglott, 9.
ALLEMANO, Jochanan, 11, 12.
ALMANZI, Guespo, 45.
ARAMA, Isaac, 10.
——— Moses, 10.
ATHBACH, alphabet denominated, 190, 191.
ATHBASH, alphabet denominated, 222.

B

BABA Buch, see LEVITA.
BACHUR, see LEVITA.
BAEHR, on the Poetical Accents, 65.
BALMES, Abraham de, 10; his Hebrew Grammar, 17, 21, 195.
BARUCH of Benevent, 12.
BEN-ASHER, 45, 65, 113, 114.
BENJAMIN of Rome, 81.
BEN-NAPHTALI, 45, 114.
BERAB, Jacob, 10.
BIBLE, the, by whom arranged and divided, 120.
BIBLES, Rabbinic, 9.
BLACK, W. H., his opinion about the design of the majuscular letters, 231.
BLAYNEY, 60.
BOMBERG, Daniel, his Hebrew publications, 21; his connection with Levita, 22.
BOOTHROYD, Dr., 60.
BROUGHTON, Hugh, his opinion of the vowel-points, 51.
BUBER, Life of Levita, 3, 78.
BUXTORF, the father, his defence of the antiquity of the vowel-points, 53, 54, 55–57.

C

CALVIN, 48, 49.
CAPITO, W. F., his date, contributions to Hebrew literature, &c., 66.
CAPPELLUS, Lewis, his controversy with the Buxtorfs about the antiquity of the vowel-points, 54–57.

CARO, Isaac b. Joseph, 10.
CHAJATH, Jehudah b. Jacob, 12.
CHAJUG Jehudah, 20.
CHRONOLOGY, Jewish, 3.
CLARK, Samuel, on the antiquity of the vowel-points, 59.
COMPOUNDS, book on the, see LEVITA.
CONJECTURAL Readings, 225–227.
COOPER, Joseph, on the antiquity of the vowel-points, 59.
CORBEIL, Isaac de, the author of the Compendium of R. Moses' work on the Commandments and Prohibitions, 250.
CORONEL, Paul, his connection with the Complutensian Polyglott, 9.
COUTHIN, Ferdinand, Bishop of Algarve, his description of the heart-rending scenes at the compulsory baptisms of Jewish children, 8.
CRETENSIS, see MEGIDO.

D

DAVIDSON, A. B., Outlines of Hebrew Accentuation, 65.
DAVILA, 9.
DEFECTIVES, 145–148.
DUREN, Isaac, 2.

E

EGIDIO, Cardinal, his interview with Levita, 14, 15; instigates Levita to write the Hebrew Grammar, 16; his connection with Levita, 96, &c.
EPHODI, his view of the origin of the Keri and Kethiv, 206; Grammatical work, 107.
EWALD, Jahrbücher, 62.
EZEKIEL, the Vision of, 98.

F

FAGIUS, Paul, his date, 66; connection with Levita, 67; printing establishment and contributions to Hebrew literature, 68–78.
FARISSOL, Abraham, his account of the labours of converted Jews to demonstrate the truth of Christianity from Kabbalistic works, 9; his cosmography, 10.
FRENSDORFF, Dr., 4, 23, 35, 39, 94.
FULKE, William, 51.

FUNST, Dr. Julius, Geschichte des Karäerthums, 62.

G

GALATINUS, Petrus, his work entitled On the Mysteries of the Catholic Truth, 15.
GANS, David, his historical work called *Seder Olam*, 3; his date, and opinion about the edition of Levita's Grammatical work, 75.
GEIGER, Dr. Urschrift, 62.
GILL, Dr. John, on the antiquity of the vowel-points, 59.
GOOD Sense, book of, see LEVITA.
GRAETZ, his critique on Isaac Zarphati's Epistle, 7.

H

HARDING, Dr. Thomas, his controversy with Bishop Jewel, 50.
HEBREW, called Sacred, language, 195.
HEIDENHEIM, the Laws of the Accents, 65.
HEILPRIN, Jechiel, his historical work called *Seder Ha-Doroth*, 3; opinion about the date of Levita's publications, 75, 76.
HEREDIA, Paul de, Kabbalist, 9.
HERMES, the worship of, 98.
HEXAHEMERON, the work of, 98.
HILALI, Codex, 260.
HOLMES, Dr., his article, *Levita*, in Kitto's Cyclopædia, 2, 3, 79.
HUTCHINSON, John, his view of the Hebrew verity and the vowel-points, 60; his school, *ibid*.

I

IBN Akmin, 20.
IBN Al-Tabben, his date, and Grammar, called the Key, 259.
IBN Baalam, his date, and works, 123; his opinion about the antiquity of the accents, 123.
IBN Danan, Saadia, 10.
IBN Daud, Abraham, called Rabad, author of the Chronicle Seder Ha-Kabbalah, 108.
IBN Ezra, his date, and Grammar, 45, 125.
IBN Ganach, Jonah, 20, 131.
IBN Jachja, David, his contributions to Biblical literature, 81, 82.
IBN Jachja, Joseph, 10.
IBN Verga, Jehudah, 12.
ISAAC b. Meier, 2.

J

JACOB b. Asheri, called Baal Ha-Turim, his Massoretic commentary, 142, 143.
JACOB b. Chajim, editor of the Massorah, 9, 21; his date and works, 38, 39; his connection with the Ochla Ve-Ochla, 94; his Introduction to the Rabbinic Bible, 107, 109, 194.

JACOB b. Eleazar, his date, and Recension of the Bible, 258.
JEHOVAH, the mysteries connected with the name, 219.
JEHUDAH Ha-Levi, his work entitled Khozari, 126, 133; opinion about the antiquity of the vowel-points, 126, 127.
JEKUTHIEL Ha-Cohen, his date and Massoretic work, 257, 258.
JEREMIAH the prophet conceals a copy of the Law, 119.
JELLINEK, Dr. Adolph, his contributions to the History of the Crusades, 7.
JEROME, St., quoted in support of the antiquity of the vowel-points, 52, 53.
JETZIRA, the book, 98.
JERUSALEM, Codex, 260.
JEWEL, John, Bishop of Salisbury, his controversy with Dr. Harding, 50.
JEWISH CONVERTS diffuse Biblical knowledge, 9.
JOSE, b. Chalaphta, reputed author of the Chronicle *Seder Olam*, 108.
JEWS, persecuted at Mayence, 6; at Trent, *ibid*. Earnestly solicited by Isaac Zarphati to quit Germany, and seek shelter under the Crescent, 6, 7; expelled from Spain, 7; from Portugal, 8; their children forcibly baptised, *ibid*.
JUSTINIANI, translator of the More Nebuchim, 36.

K

KABBALAH, the, studied by Christians, 10, 12, 15, 39.
KALISCH, Dr., his notice of Levita in the Hebrew Grammar, 3; of Luther's and Calvin's opinions about the antiquity of the vowel-points, 49.
KERI and Kethiv, various opinions about the origin thereof, 103–112; numbers of in the Bibles, 115, 116.
KHOSARI, see Jehudah Ha-Levi.
KIMCHI, David, his Grammatical and Lexical works, 79, 107, 258; his opinion about the antiquity of the vowel-points, 121, 122.
KIMCHI, Moses, the time he flourished, 13; his Hebrew Grammar, 13, 36.

L

LAW, Synagogal Scrolls of the, 124; division of, for hebdomadal lessons, 135, 170.
LEVITA, surnamed Bachur, its signification, 2; the date of his birth, *ibid*; his removal from Germany to Padua, 7; his contributions to the revival of Hebrew learning, 10; his flight to Rome and interview with Cardinal Egidio, 14, 15; his journey to Fagius, 66; works, in chronological order:—

Commentary on M. Kimchi's Hebrew Grammar, 13, 14, 36, 80-83, 92.
Baba Buch, 14.
Bachur, 16, 73-76, 92.
Tables of Paradigms, 17.
A Treatise on Compounds, 17, 18, 80, 92.
Poetical Dissertations, 18, 19, 80, 92, 145, 199, 202, 219.
Concordance to the Massorah, 20, 23-35, 137.
Aramaic Grammar, 20.
Massoreth Ha-Massoreth, 40-44.
Treatise on the Accents, called *Good Sense*, 63-65, 114, 123, 204.
Tishbi, 68.
Methurgeman, 69-72.
Nomenclature, 73.
German translation of the Pentateuch, Five Megilloth, and Haphtaroth, 78.
German version of the Psalms, 79.
Annotations on Kimchi's Grammatical and Lexical works, 79.
LANDAU, 2.
LEVI, b. Chabib, 10.
LEVI, b. Joseph, his Grammar entitled the Vine-blossom, 122.
LIGHTFOOT, Dr., his view of the antiquity and authority of the vowel-points, 57, 58.
LETTERS, majuscular and minuscular, alphabetical lists of, 230, 231.
LOANZ, Jacob b. Jechiel, 10; teaches Reuchlin Hebrew, 12.
LOWTH, Bishop, his view about the vowel-points, 59.
LULLY, Raymond, his connection with the Kabbalah, 11.
LUZZATTO, Treatise on the vowel-points in Halichoth Kedem, 62.
LUTHER, Martin, his sentiments about the Jews, 38, 39; his view of the origin and antiquity of the vowel-points, 49.
LYRA, Nicolas de, his date, forerunner of the Reformation, his opinion about the vowel-points, 16, 17.

M

MAIMONIDES, his date and great philosophical work, 36; work on Biblical and Traditional Law, called Jad Ha-Chezaka, 114, 182.
MANTINO, Jacob, 10, 36.
MARTIN, Gregory, his opinion about the Hebrew vowel-points, controversy with William Fulke, &c., 51.
MASSORAH, how treated by copyists, 94; signification of the word, 102, 104; its order of the Bible, 120, 121; magna, and marginalis, 138, 139.
MEDIGO, Elias del, or Elias Cretensis, teacher of Mirandola, 11.
MESSER, Lion, his works, 10.
METHURGEMAN, see LEVITA.
MEZUZAH, the, 95.

MICHAELIS, J. D., Anfangs-Gründe der Hebräischen Accentuation, 65.
MIRANDOLA, John Pico della, his connection with the Kabbalah, 11.
MORINUS, John, his opinion about the Hebrew verity and the vowel-points, 50.
MOSES, Ha-Darshan, his date, and work on the Commandments and Prohibitions, 249, 250.
MOSES, the Punctuator, his date and works, 123, 124; his opinion about the antiquity of the accents, *ibid.*

N

NACHMANIDES, Moses, his date, opinion about the mystic import of the Law, 124.
NATHAN, Isaac, author of the first Hebrew Concordance, 21.
NATHAN b. Jechiel, 2.
NAPHTALI, see Ben Naphtali.
NATRONI II., b. Hilai, his opinion about the antiquity and authority of the Hebrew vowel-points, 44.
NOAH, the seven commandments of, 99.
NOMENCLATURE, see LEVITA.
NUMERALS, how expressed, 135, 136.

O

OCHLA Ve-Ochla, described by Levita, 93, 94, 138.
OWEN, Dr. John, his controversy with Bishop Walton about the antiquity and authority of the vowel-points, 58, 59.

P

PRATENSIS, Felix, editor of the first Rabbinic Bible, 9, 21.
PRESTER JOHN, 130.
PALESTINE, the seven productions of, 182.
PENTATEUCH, the, a copy of deposited by Moses in the Ark of the Covenant, 119.
PERREAU, Abate Pietro, 126.
PFEFFERKORN, his malignity against the Jews, 12; his date and works, 37, 38.
PINSKER, Einleitung in das Babylonisch-Hebräische Punktationssystem, 62.
PINNER, Dr., Prospectus, 62.
PISCATOR, John, his opinion of the vowel-points, 51.
PLENE, 145-148.
PROPHIAT Duran, see EPHODI.
PURITY of Language, an anonymous grammatical treatise, 126.

R

RASHI, 105.
RAYMOND Martin, his opinion about the Hebrew verity and vowel-points, 45, 46.
RICIO, Paul, his Kabbalistic labours, 9.
REMEMBRANCE, book of, see LEVITA.

REUCHLIN, his connection with the Kabbalah, 11, 12.
ROSSI, Azariah de, his date, refutation of Levita's arguments for the novelty of the vowel-points, &c., 52, 53; his Meor Enajim quoted, 122.

S

SABA, Abraham, 12.
SAADIA, Gaon, 20; his date, and philosophical treatise, 136, 269.
SACCUTO, Abraham, 10.
SCRIBES, their name and connection with the Massorah, 135.
SEDER Ha-Kabbalah, 108.
SEDER Olam, the Chronicle, 108.
SEMLER, J. S., his connection with the German translation of the *Massoreth Ha-Massoreth*, 42, 44.
SEFORNO, Obadiah, 10.
SELVE, George de, Bishop of Lavour, his literary connection with Levita, 22; encourages him to undertake the Massoretic Concordance, 23–25, 37.
SHRAJA, Joseph, 12.
SIMON b. Jochai, reputed author of the Sohar, 48.
SIXTUS IV., patronises the Kabbalah, 11.
SHIMSHON, the Grammarian, his date, and treatise on the vowel-points and accents, 257.
SOHAR, the, its view of the antiquity and authority of the vowel-points, 48, 121.
SPIRA, Meier, 257.

STEINSCHNEIDER, Dr., 2, 14, 17, 126.
STERN, Leseauge, 65.
SYNAGOGUE, the Great, its constitution, 107, 108.

T

TEMPLE, the Second, five articles wanted in it which were in the first Temple, 111.
TRANSPOSITION of letters, sixty-two instances of, 116.

V

VALENCIA, Jacob Perez de, his date, opinion about the vowel-points, &c., 47.
VOWEL-POINTS, the, controversy about their antiquity and authority, 44–63; becomes a dogma in Switzerland, 64; superlineary system of, 61; interlineary system of, 61, 62; Levita's opinion about their antiquity, 121, &c.

W

WALTON, Brian, his view of the antiquity of the vowel-points, 57.
WHITFIELD, P., on the antiquity of the vowel-points, 59.
WRIGHT, Dr. William, 100.

Z

ZAMORA, Alphonso de, his contributions to the Complutensian Polyglott, 9.